The Origins of Drama
in Scandinavia

For
MY FATHER
and
in memory of
JÓN GUNNAR ÁRNASON

The Origins of Drama in Scandinavia

TERRY GUNNELL

D. S. BREWER

© Terry Gunnell 1995

All Rights Reserved. Except as permitted under current legislation no part of this work may be photocopied, stored in a retrieval system, published, performed in public, adapted, broadcast, transmitted, recorded or reproduced in any form or by any means, without the prior permission of the copyright owner

First published 1995
D. S. Brewer, Cambridge

ISBN 0 85991 458 5

D. S. Brewer is an imprint of Boydell & Brewer Ltd
PO Box 9, Woodbridge, Suffolk IP12 3DF, UK
and of Boydell & Brewer Inc.
PO Box 41026, Rochester, NY 14604–4126, USA

British Library Cataloguing-in-Publication Data
Gunnell, Terry
  Origins of Drama in Scandinavia
  I. Title
  839.52009
  ISBN 0–85991–458–5

Library of Congress Cataloging-in-Publication Data
Gunnell, Terry, 1955–
  The origins of drama in Scandinavia / Terry Gunnell.
      p.   cm.
  Includes bibliographical references and index.
  ISBN 0–85991–458–5 (alk. paper)
    1. Scandinavian drama – History and criticism.   2. Drama, Medieval – History and criticism.   3. Eddas – History and criticism.   4. Folklore – Scandinavia.   5. Scandinavia – Antiquities.   I. Title.
  PT7082.G86   1995
  839'.5–dc20   94–32586

The paper used in this publication meets the minimum requirements of American National Standard for Information Sciences – Permanence of Paper for Printed Library Materials, ANSI Z39.48–1984

Printed in Great Britain by
St Edmundsbury Press Ltd, Bury St Edmunds, Suffolk

Contents

List of tables	x
List of figures	xi
Preface	xvii
Acknowledgements	xix
Illustrative material: Acknowledgements	xxii
List of abbreviations	xxiv

INTRODUCTION		1
A.	Ancient Scandinavian drama and the scholars	1
B.	Drama: A definition	10
C.	Drama, myth and ritual	15
D.	Conclusion	21

CHAPTER I

Dramatic Activities in Early Medieval Scandinavia   23
I: The Evidence of Archaeology and Literature

A.	The conditions for the development of drama	23
B.	Ritual *leikar* and drama	24
	1. The concept of *leikr* in early Scandinavia	24
	2. The evidence of placenames	30
	3. *Leikar* and ritual	32
C.	The archaeological evidence	36
	1. The information provided by archaeology	36
	2. The Bronze Age petroglyphs of Scandinavia (1500–500 B.C.)	37
	3. The Kivik stones (c.1200 B.C.)	47
	4. The Gallehus horns (c.A.D.400)	49
	5. Cult wagons, and the worship of Nerthus and Freyr (c.A.D.100)	53
	6. The Oseberg tapestry (c.835–850)	60
	7. The Torslunda, Valsgärde and Vendel plates (sixth-seventh century) and the '*gothikon*'	66

		8. The archaeological evidence: Conclusion, and relationship to later accounts of cult ritual at Uppsala	76
	D.	Literary evidence for ritual dramatic activities	80
		1. The literary evidence for masks and ritual disguise	80
		2. The *leikgoði* and the *Syrpuþingslög*	87
	E.	Conclusion	92

CHAPTER II

Dramatic Activities in Early Medieval Scandinavia II: The Folkloristic Evidence   93

A.	The application of folkloristic material	93
B.	Mainland Scandinavian costumed processions, house-visits and performances related to the Christmas period	95
	1. Christian origins for Yuletide costumed traditions: The *Stjärnspel*, Knut and Lucia	95
	2. *Halm-Staffan*	100
	3. The *julebukk/julegeit*	107
	4. The 'killing' of the *julebukk*	117
	5. The origin and role of the *julebukk*	122
C.	Costumed combat traditions in Scandinavia	128
	1. The battle between Winter and Summer	128
	2. The sword and hoop dances	130
D.	The seasonal 'mock-marriage' in Scandinavian folk tradition	133
	1. The winter marriage	133
	2. The spring/summer marriage	135
E.	The continuation of pagan ritual in Scandinavia?	140
F.	The transportation of dramatic folk traditions	141
G.	The evidence for a shared tradition of 'folk drama' in the North Atlantic Scandinavian settlements	142
	1. England and Ireland	142
	2. Iceland: The *vikivaki* games	144
	3. Possible origins of the *vikivaki* games	154
	4. *Grýla* in Icelandic, Faroese and Shetland seasonal custom	160
	5. The dating of the North Atlantic seasonal customs	178
H.	Conclusion	179

CHAPTER III

The Eddic Poems and Drama   182

A. The Eddic poems as oral poetry   182
B. The dating of the extant texts of the Eddic poems   184
C. The forms of Eddic poetry   185
    1. General grouping   185
    2. The use of direct speech in different forms of Eddic poetry   186
D. The prose in the Eddic poems   194
E. The dialogic poems in *ljóðaháttr*   203
    1. *Skírnismál, Hárbarðsljóð, Vafþrúðnismál, Lokasenna* and *Fáfnismál*: General relationships   203
    2. The marginal speaker indications in the Edda manuscripts   206
    3. The question of the blended prose-and-verse form   212
    4. Snorri Sturluson, the dialogic poems and the *Prose Edda*   218
F. The prose in the mythological dialogic poems   223
    1. *Fáfnismál*   223
    2. *Lokasenna*   225
    3. *Skírnismál*   229
    4. *Vafþrúðnismál* and *Hárbarðsljóð*   232
    5. Conclusion   233
G. The difficulties involved in a one-man performance of the dialogic poems   236
    1. Introduction. Rules for the performance of dialogue by a single performer   236
    2. *Lokasenna*: The difficulties of performance   238
    3. *Skírnismál*: The difficulties of performance   247
    4. *Fáfnismál*: The difficulties of performance   256
        a. The text   256
        b. Difficulties in speaker identification in an oral performance of the *ljóðaháttr* strophes of *Fáfnismál*   260
        c. Setting, movement and other dramatic elements in *Fáfnismál*   265
        d. Conclusion   268
    5. *Hárbarðsljóð*: The difficulties of performance   269
    6. *Vafþrúðnismál*: The difficulties of performance   275
H. Conclusion   281

CHAPTER IV

Marginal Speaker Notation in the Edda   282
and Early Manuscripts of Drama

A. The marginal notation in the Edda manuscripts   282
B. Other early medieval Scandinavian manuscripts containing dialogues   283
C. European manuscripts of dramatic works, 1000–1300   290
    1. The problem   290
    2. Terence and his imitators   291
    3. The drama of the church   296
    4. The travelling entertainers   298
D. The use of the margin to indicate speakers in dramatic manuscripts   300
    1. General   300
    2. *Babio*   308
    3. *La seinte resurreccion*   313
    4. *The harrowing of Hell*   314
    5. *Le mystère d'Adam*   316
    6. The origins and provenance of the system of marginal speaker notation   320
    7. Differences from the Edda manuscripts   322
E. Scandinavian contact with European dramatic manuscripts   324
    1. Literary contacts with England and France   324
    2. Scandinavian knowledge of the concepts of drama   325
    3. Scandinavian knowledge of European liturgical drama   326
F. Conclusion   329

CHAPTER V

Performances of Poetry and Song Involving More than   330
One Participant in Early Medieval Scandinavia

A. The evidence regarding solo performance   330
B. Oral performance involving more than one participant outside the Germanic world   331
C. Oral performance involving more than one participant among the Germanic peoples   334
D. Oral performances involving more than one participant in Scandinavia   335
    1. *Seiðr*   335
    2. Alternate singing?   338

	3. The *senna* and *mannjafnaðr*	341
	4. *Að ljóða á*	343
	5. *Mansöngsvísur*	346
E.	Conclusion	348

CONCLUSION	351
APPENDIX: The *leikarar* in Scandinavia	358
Bibliography	365
Index	399

Tables

I	The proportion of speech, 'blended strophes' and prose in the Eddic poems	188
II	The Eddic poems: Verse forms, dating, the proportion of speech/ narrative, transitions in speaker, and number of speaking roles	191
III	The 'blended strophes': Narrative/ speech proportions	195

Figures

CHAPTER I

1	Procession of figures in bird masks. Stone Age petroglyph from Gåshopen, Finnmark (from Simonsen, *Arktiske helleristninger i Nord-Norge*, II)	38
2	Horned god based on the costume of a medicine man? Stone Age petroglyph from Amtmannsnes, Finnmark (from Helskog, *Helleristningene i Alta*)	38
3–5	Acrobats and ships in petroglyphs from Skebbervall, Kville; and Bro and Sortorp, Tanum, Bohuslän (from Almgren, *Hällristningar och kultbruk*)	38
6	Horn-playing dancers on a ship. Petroglyph from Lycke, Tanum, Bohuslän (from Almgren, *Hällristningar och kultbruk*)	38
7	Ship drawn by horses. Petroglyph from Ekenberg, Norrköping, Östergötland (from Almgren, *Hällristningar och kultbruk*)	40
8	Ship held aloft by horned figure. Petroglyph from Öster-Röd, Kville, Bohuslän (from Almgren, *Hällristningar och kultbruk*)	40
9	Ship being held by a god? Petroglyph from Brandskogen, Boglösa, Uppland (from Almgren, *Hällristningar och kultbruk*)	40
10	Sun symbol held by a worshipper. Petroglyph from Stora Backa, Brastad, Bohuslän (from Almgren, *Hällristningar och kultbruk*)	40
11	Giant figure in a procession. Petroglyph from Hvitlycke, Tanum, Bohuslän (from Almgren, *Hällristningar och kultbruk*)	40
12	Giant figure in a procession. Petroglyph from Ekenberg, near Norrköping, Östergötland (from Gelling and Davidson, *The chariot of the sun*)	40
13	Horned figures blowing *lurer*: Bronze Age petroglyph from Kalleby, Tanum, Bohuslän (from Almgren, *Hällristningar och kultbruk*)	42
14	'The Dancer': Petroglyph from Vilhelmsberg, Simris, Skåne (from Gelling and Davidson, *The chariot of the sun*)	42
15	Horned, masked figure with hammer: Bronze Age petroglyph from Lövåsen, Tanum (from Gelling and Davidson, *The chariot of the sun*)	42
16	Model figure with horned helmet: Grevensvænge (photo: Nationalmuseet, Copenhagen)	44

17	Horned helmet from Viksø (photo: Nationalmuseet, Copenhagen)	44
18	Bronze Age horned head-dress from Hagendrup, near Kalundborg, Sjælland (photo: Nationalmuseet, Copenhagen)	44
19	Men in animal masks and costumes: Bronze Age petroglyph from Yellen, Kville, Bohuslän (from Gelling and Davidson, *The chariot of the sun*)	44
20	Horned figures engaged in mating and battle. Petroglyph from Tuvene, Tanum, Bohuslän (from Almgren, *Hällristningar och kultbruk*)	46
21	The *hieros gamos* and the archer god? Petroglyph from Varlös, Tanum, Bohuslän (from Almgren, *Hällristningar och kultbruk*)	46
22	Scenes from a ritual drama? Petroglyph from Fossum, Tanum, Bohuslän (from Almgren, *Hällristningar och kultbruk*)	46
23	The *hieros gamos*? Petroglyph from Hvitlycke, Tanum, Bohuslän (from Almgren, *Hällristningar och kultbruk*)	46
24–25	Kivik: Stones 8 and 7 (from Almgren, *Hällristningar och kultbruk*)	48
26	Figures in bird costumes: Petroglyph from Kallsängen, Bottna, Kville, Bohuslän (from Gelling and Davidson, *The chariot of the sun*)	50
27	Figure in bird costume: Petroglyph from Kallsängen, Bottna, Kville, Bohuslän (from Gelling and Davidson, *The chariot of the sun*)	50
28–30	Masked figures and others: The Gallehus horns (from Oxenstierne, *Järnålder, guldålder*)	52
31	Dancing figure on the Gummersmark brooch (photo: Nationalmuseet, Copenhagen)	58
32	Dancing figure on the Ålleberg collar (photo: Antikvarisk-topografiska arkivet, Stockholm)	58
33	Gold foil from Hauge, Kleppe, Rogaland, Norway (photo: Historisk Museum, Bergen; photographer, Ann-Mari Olsen)	58
34	Horned man and wagon in procession: The Oseberg tapestry (Oldsaksamlingen, Universitet i Oslo; drawing by Sofie Krafft)	58
35	Dancing women: The Oseberg tapestry (Oldsaksamlingen, Universitet i Oslo; drawing by Sofie Krafft)	62
36	Celebrants: The Oseberg tapestry (Oldsaksamlingen, Universitet i Oslo; drawing by Sofie Krafft)	62
37	Horned man and '*berserkr*' in animal skin: The Oseberg tapestry (Oldsaksamlingen, Universitet i Oslo; drawing by Sofie Krafft)	62
38	Masked and costumed female '*valkyrja*'? The Oseberg tapestry (Oldsaksamlingen, Universitet i Oslo; drawing by Mary Storm)	62

39	Woman in bird costume and mask? The Oseberg tapestry (Oldsaksamlingen, Universitet i Oslo; drawing by Sofie Krafft)	64
40	Amulet from Ekhammar, Uppland (photo: Antikvarisk-topografiska arkivet, Stockholm)	65
41	Pendant from Birka, Uppland (photo: Antikvarisk-topografiska arkivet, Stockholm)	65
42	The Finglesham buckle (photo: The Institute of Archæology, Oxford)	65
43	The Sutton Hoo helmet plate (by courtesy of the Trustees of the British Museum)	65
44	Horned dancer and 'berserkr' in animal costume: Torslunda matrix (photo: Antikvarisk-topografiska arkivet, Stockholm; photographer: Iwar Anderson)	68
45	Bound monster and man: Torslunda matrix (photo: Antikvarisk-topografiska arkivet, Stockholm; photographer: Iwar Anderson)	68
46	Monsters and man: Torslunda matrix (photo: Antikvarisk-topografiska arkivet, Stockholm; photographer: Iwar Anderson)	69
47	The 'snake charmer': Smiss III stone, När, Gotland (photo: Gotlands Fornsal; photographer: Raymond Hejdström)	69
48	Fresco of masked fighters from the cathedral of Hagia Sophia in Kiev (photo: Hagia Sophia cathedral, Kiev)	73
49	Animal masks found in Hedeby harbour (photos and drawing: Archäologische Landesmuseum der Christian-Albrechts-Universität, Schleswig)	73
50	*Rangle* (iron rattle) found on the Oseberg ship (Oldsaksamlingen, Universitet i Oslo; drawing by Sofie Krafft)	77

CHAPTER II

51	*Lussia* and *jolesvein* (drawing: Norsk Etnologisk Gransking, NEG 5830)	99
52	*Halm-Staffan* (Björkö) (Nordiska Museet; drawing by Gunnar Hallström in 'Halmstaffan')	103
53	Man-sized straw *Julgubbe* (Värmland) (photo: Göteborgs Stadsmuseum)	103
54	Distribution map: The *julebukk* in Norway (from Eike, 'Oskoreia og ekstaseriter')	106
55	Distribution map: The *julegeit* in Norway (from Eike, 'Oskoreia og ekstaseriter')	108
56	*Julegeita* mask with clacking jaws (Fredrikstad) (photo: Frederikstad Museum)	111
57	*Julegeita* mask (Vest Agder) (photo: Flekkefjord Museum)	111

58	Sheep skin *julebukk* mask (Buskerud) (photo: Norsk folkemuseum: NF L48338)	111
59	*Julebukk* mask (Setesdal) (Setesdalsmuseet; photo: Norsk folkemuseum)	111
60	*Julbock* and *Julget* (Vemdalen, Härjedalen) (photo: Nordiska Museet)	113
61	*Julbock* (Sko, Uppland) (photo: Nordiska Museet)	113
62	*Julbock* (Mangskog, Värmland) (photo: Nordiska Museet)	115
63	*Julbock* and *Staffan* singers (Nås, Dalarna) (photo: Nordiska Museet)	115
64	The battle between Summer and Winter (from Olaus Magnus, *Historia de gentibus septentrionalibus*)	129
65	The sword and hoop dance (from Olaus Magnus, *Historia de gentibus septentrionalibus*)	129
66	A Jonsok wedding (Balestrand, Sogn) (photo: Fylkesarkivet i Sogn og Fjordane)	131
67	Wooden mask found at Stóraborg, by Eyjafjöll, Iceland (Þjóðminjasafn Islands; photo: Guðmundur Ólafsson)	146
68	Scale drawing of the Stóraborg mask (drawing: Mjöll Snæsdóttir)	147
69	A modern reconstruction of Háa-Þóra (photo: Sveinn Einarsson)	152
70	Shetland *skeklers* (Fetlar) (photo: Shetland Museum)	169

CHAPTER III

71	*Codex Regius* of the Elder Edda, MS Gl.kgl.sml.2365, 4to, p.26 (photo: Stofnun Árna Magnússonar, Reykjavik)	209
72	MS AM 748 I, 4to, fol.3r (photo: Det Arnamagnæanske Institut, København)	211
73	*Codex Regius* of the Elder Edda, MS Gl.kgl.sml.2367, 4to, p.25 (photo: Stofnun Árna Magnússonar, Reykjavik)	213
74	MS AM 748 I, 4to, fol.1v (photo: Det Arnamagnæanske Institut, København)	215
75	MS AM 748 I, 4to, fol.2v (photo: Det Arnamagnæanske Institut, København)	217

CHAPTER IV

76	*Konungs skuggsjá*. AM 243 b α fol., p.66 (photo: Det Arnamagnæanske Institut, København)	285
77	*The dialogues of Gregory the Great*. AM 677, 4to, fol.36v (photo: Det Arnamagnæanske Institut, København)	287
78	*Elucidarius*. AM 674, 4to, fragment, fol.21r (photo: Det Arnamagnæanske Institut, København)	289

79	Terence, *Andria*, 775–803; 854–861. *Codex Vaticanus* (Vatican Library, MS 3868), fol.15v (photo: Biblioteca Vaticana)	293
80	Hrotsvitha, end of *Dulcitius* and start of *Calimachus* Cologne, Historisches Archiv MS W* 101, fol.8r (photo: Historisches Archiv, Köln)	294
81	Terence, *Phormio*, ll.606–628. *Codex Bembinus*, Vatican Library, MS 3226, fol.66v (photo: Biblioteca Vaticana)	295
82	*The Play of the conversion of St Paul. The Fleury Play-book*, Orléans, Bibliothèque de la Ville, MS 202 (178), p.230 (photo: Bibliothèque Municipale, Orléans)	297
83	Rutebeuf, *Le miracle de Theophile*. Paris, BN, f.fr.837, fol.300v (photo: Bibliothèque Nationale, Paris)	299
84	*Planctus Mariæ* (Cividale). Cividale, Reale Museo Archeologico MS CI, fol.74r (photographer: Elio Ciol)	301
85	*Semiramis*. Paris, BN, f.lat. 8121A, fol.31r (photo: Bibliothèque Nationale, Paris)	303
86	*De nuntio sagaci*. British Museum, Additional MS 49368, fol.47v (photo: by permission of The British Library)	305
87	*Dame Sirith*. Oxford, Bodleian, MS Digby 86, fol.165r (photocopy provided by courtesy of the Bodleian Library, Oxford)	307
88	*Gilote et Johane*. British Museum, MS Harley 2253, fol.67*r (photo: by permission of The British Library)	309
89	*Babio. Codex Lincolniensis*, MS Lincoln Capit.105, fol.90v (photo: Lincoln Cathedral Library and Nottingham University Library)	311
90	*Babio*. Oxford, Bodleian, MS Digby 53, fols 39v–40r (photo: The Bodleian Library, Oxford)	312
91	*La seinte resureccion*. Paris, BN, f.fr.902, fol.98r (photo: Bibliothèque Nationale, Paris)	315
92	*The harrowing of Hell*. British Museum, MS Harley 2253, fol.56r (photo: by permission of The British Library)	317
93	*Le mystère d'Adam*. Bibliothèque Municipale de Tours, MS 927, fol.23v (photo: Bibliothèque Municipale de Tours)	319
94	*Le mystère d'Adam*. Bibliothèque Municipale de Tours, MS 927, fol.33v (photo: Bibliothèque Municipale de Tours)	321

Preface

The following work is essentially a revised and extended edition of my doctoral thesis, 'The concept of ancient Scandinavian drama: a re-evaluation', which was submitted and successfully defended at the University of Leeds in the autumn of 1991. Some of the material in Chapters III and IV has previously been published in Icelandic in the articles 'Skírnisleikur og Freysmál', in *Skírnir*, 167 (1993), 421–459, and 'Spássíukrot? Mælendamerkingar í handritum eddukvæða og miðaldaleikrita', in *Skáldskaparmál*, 3 (1994), 7–29.

Where possible, all references to the Eddic poems in the following are drawn from the (incomplete) editions of the poems published by Jón Helgason in *Eddadigte*, I–III. Where this is not possible (as in the case of the second part of the heroic poems), then references are drawn from Neckel and Kuhn's *Edda: Die lieder des codex regius nebst verwandten denkmälern*, I: Text (4th ed.). All use of italics in passages taken from the Eddic poems and the *Prose Edda* is that of the present author.

Unless otherwise stated, all translations into English have been made by the present author. It should be stressed that in the case of poetry, no attempt has been made to recreate the metre or alliteration of the verse. The sole intention is to offer a literal translation to aid those readers who do not understand Icelandic or the other Scandinavian languages. Where there is a possibility of two different translations, or a double meaning is implied, as in words like *ægishiálmr* ('helmet/mask of terror') or *kveða* ('sing/chant'), then both meanings have been given in the translation, as shown above.

For the most part, references to other works given in the footnotes include the name of the author and a shortened title. Dates are only added where they are important for chronological purposes, or are needed to distinguish between different editions of a particular work. Icelandic authors are always referred to by their Christian names unless they use a family name.

Publication of this work has been aided by
a grant from the Dorothea Coke Memorial Fund

Acknowledgements

I should like to express my gratitude in particular to my supervisor, Dr Rory McTurk of the University of Leeds, for his help and learned advice throughout my work on the thesis that forms the basis for this book, and for his friendship, optimism, endless patience, and work far beyond the demands of duty in reading through the early versions of this work. I am also especially grateful to Dr Andrew Wawn of the University of Leeds for having the patience to read over not only the thesis but also the book, and in particular for his friendship, hospitality, continued useful advice, humour, and sense of reality which, I dare to hope, has prevented this work from moving too far into the realms of theory; and to Professor Jón Hnefill Aðalsteinsson of the University of Iceland, Reykjavík, for placing his knowledge on questions of pagan Scandinavian belief and folkloristics at my disposal, and for the time and trouble he took in reading through and commenting on the original thesis. Without the encouragement of these three friends and scholars, neither the thesis nor the book would ever have been completed.

I am also grateful to all of the following people: to Peter Meredith of the University of Leeds for reading through and commenting on the material contained in the Introduction and Chapter IV of this book, and for his advice regarding questions of medieval drama; to Professor Peter Dronke of the University of Cambridge for his advice and comments on questions to do with marginal notation in medieval manuscripts; to Mjöll Snæsdóttir of the National Museum of Iceland for reading over the original version of Chapter I, and her practical advice on questions of archaeological evidence; to Árni Björnsson of the National Museum of Iceland for reading through the draft version of Chapter II, and for his comments and advice on certain aspects of Icelandic folklore; to Dr Jón Samsonarson of the Arnamagnean Institute in Reykjavík for reading through the draft of Chapter II, and for his useful comments with regard to the *vikivaki* games and the Grýla verses; to Dr Sverrir Tómasson, Dr Jónas Kristjánsson and Dr Stefán Karlsson, also of the Arnamagnean Institute in Reykjavík for their advice regarding the material contained in Chapter IV, and for examining the marginal notation of the *Codex Regius* and other Icelandic MSS with me; to Dr Jonna Louis-Jensen of the Arnamagnean Institute, Copenhagen, for offering her time to examine the notation of the *AM 748* MS with me; to Dr M. Bateson of the Hallward Library in the University of Nottingham for providing me with information about the Lincoln Cathedral MS of *Babio*; to Dr Oliver Pickering of the Brotherton Collection in the University of Leeds for giving up time to discuss the question of marginal notation in early English manuscripts; to Dr Lynette Muir for her help and advice regarding French MSS of drama in the early Middle Ages; to Kees Samplonius of the University of Amsterdam for a number of

Acknowledgements

valuable pieces of advice concerning both archaeology and the sagas; to Ögmundur Helgason of the Manuscript Department of National Library of Iceland for his patience in helping me to decipher the MS of Þorsteinn Péturson's *Manducus*; to Peter Vosicky, and Dr Sigurður Pétursson of the University of Iceland for examining the original Greek text and translations of the account of the *gothikon* for me; to Dr Ólafur Halldórsson of the Arnamagnean Institute in Reykjavík for his advice with regard to the different versions of *Gunnars þáttr helmings*; to Niamh Doran for help with reading through certain French texts; to Teitur Benediktsson of Hamrahlíð College in Reykjavík for advice on certain Latin expressions; to Maria-Claudia Hess, and Nick Hannigan of the University of Iceland for translating certain German texts; to Dr Þorvarður Helgason of Hamrahlíð College for help in reading through other German texts, and continued encouragement as regards this project; to Professor Jóan Pauli Joensen and Turid Sigurðardóttir of the Faroese Academy, and Guðrún Matthíasdóttir of Hamrahlíð College for their help with my research into the Faroese *grýlur*, to the Faroese television service for providing me with a copy of the television programme, *Manna millum*; to Brian Smith, the Shetland Archivist for reading over the section on the *skeklers*, and for his advice concerning these traditions; to Irma Totskaya, in charge of scientific research at the Cathedral of Hagia Sophia in Kiev, for her help with regard to the frescos in the cathedral, and to Larissa Pigareva of the Russian Embassy in Reykjavík for her help in translating Russian texts; to Mrs Shute of the Inter-Library loans department of the Brotherton Library in Leeds for endless patience in the face of constant demands, and for her continued readiness to help at all times; to the Inter-Library department of the Library of the University of Iceland for similar services in Iceland; to the Royal Irish Academy for generously providing me with photocopies of the lithograph facsimile of the *Lebor na Huidre* MS; to the students of the Department of Folkloristics at the University of Iceland, and to the Ásatrúarfélagið for their interest in this subject and their desire to work with me in staging an experimental outdoor performance of *Skírnismál* in the late winter of 1992; to Stanislaw and Barbara Szczycinski for supplying me with information regarding Polish folk customs and the performance of *Ludus Danielis*; to Professor Dr Kurt Schietzel of the Archeological Museum of Christian-Albrechts-University in Schleswig for graciously providing me with a copy of Inga Hägg's *Die Textilfunde*; to Dr J. D'Arcy and Robert Berman of the University of Iceland for their readiness to read over certain early proofs of this work in spite of the limited amount of time available to them; to Professor Vésteinn Ólasson and Gísli Sigurðsson of the University of Iceland, and to the theatre historian and director Sveinn Einarsson for their interest and encouragement; and in particular to Agnette Kristjánsdóttir of Hamrahlíð College for rescuing Chapters I and II from destruction. Any errors that remain after all of this help are naturally my own.

Finally, I am deeply grateful to my colleagues in the English department of Hamrahlíð College for putting up with my frequent absences during the

Acknowledgements

work on this project; to the Icelandic Science Foundation for providing me with the two grants that made the writing of this book possible; and to Tobba, Liv Anna and Helga Sólveig for their love, help and encouragement, and generally for putting up with me throughout the long period that I have been involved in this work.

Terry Gunnell
Reykjavík, March 1994

Illustrative Material: Acknowledgements

I would like express my gratitude to the following institutions, individuals and companies for their kind assistance and cooperation in providing me with pictures and photographs, and kindly granting me the permission to use this material in the present book: Instituttet for sammenlignende kulturforskning, Oslo (fig.1, copied from Simonsen, *Arktiske helleristninger i Nord-Norge*, II, pl.LX); Professor Knut Helskog (fig.2, copied from Helskog, *Helleristningene i Alta*, p.112); Kungl. Vitterhets Historie och Antikvitets Akadamien, Stockholm (figs 3–11, 13, and 20–25, copied from Almgren, *Hällristningar och kultbruk*, figs 82, 18, 17, 15, 41c, 45a, 156, 1, 87, 7, 81, 79, 80, 75, 117 and 118); The Orion Publishing Group Ltd (figs 12, 14 15, 19 and 26 27, copied from Gelling and Davidson, *The chariot of the sun*, figs 24f, 51, 52a, 45c, 52c and 31); Nationalmuseet, København (figs 16–18 and fig. 31); Bokförlaget Natur och Kultur, Stockholm (figs 28–30, copied from Oxenstierne, *Järnålder, guldålder*, pls 44–45); Antikvarisk-topografiska arkivet, Stockholm (fig.32, figs 40–41, and figs 44–46); Historisk Museum, Universitet i Bergen (fig.33); Oldsaksamlingen, Universitet i Oslo (figs 34–39, and fig.50); the Institute of Archæology, Oxford (fig.42); the British Museum, London (fig.43); Gotlands Fornsal (fig.47); Hagia Sophia cathedral, Kiev (fig.48); Archäologische Landesmuseum der Christian-Albrechts-Universität, Schleswig (fig.49); Norsk Etnologisk Gransking (fig.51); Nordiska Museet, Stockholm (fig.52 and figs 60–63); Göteborgs stadsmuseum (fig.53); *Norveg: Tidsskrift for etnologi og folkloristikk* (figs 54–55, copied from Eike, 'Oskoreia', 267–267); Frederikstad Museum (fig.56); Flekkefjord Museum (fig.57); Norsk folkemuseum, Oslo (figs 58–59); Fylkesarkivet i Sogn og Fjordane (special thanks to Gunnar Urtegaard) (fig.66); Guðmundur Ólafsson (fig.67); Mjöll Snæsdóttir (fig.68); Sveinn Einarsson (fig.69); the Shetland Museum (fig.70); Stofnun Árna Magnússonar, Háskóli Íslands, Reykjavík (fig.71 and fig.73); Det Arnamagnæanske Institut, Københavns Universitet, København (fig.72 and figs 74–78); La Biblioteca Apostolica Vaticana, Città del Vaticano (fig.79 and fig.81); Historisches Archiv, Köln (fig.80); Bibliothèque Municipale, Orléans (fig.82); Bibliothèque Nationale, Paris (fig.83, fig.85 and fig.91); Museo Archeologico Nazionale de Cividale, and Elio Ciol (fig.84); The British Library (fig.86, fig.88 and fig.92); The Bodleian Library, Oxford (fig.87 and fig.90); Lincoln Cathedral Library and Nottingham University Library (fig.89); and Bibliothèque Municipale de Tours (figs 93–94).

I would also like to thank the Bibliothèque Nationale, Paris, for providing me with photocopies of the MSS of *Querolus*, and *Le jeu de saint Nicolas*); Trinity College Library, Dublin for providing me with photocopies of the relevent folios from the *Book of Leinster*; the Deutsche

Illustrative Material: Acknowledgements

Staatsbibliothek in Berlin for providing me with slides of the German MS of *Babio*; Setesdalsmuseet for sending me another photo of the Setesdal *julebukk* mask; Gerhard Milstreu of Tanums Hällsristningsmuseum for sending me more recent pictures of the rapidly deteriorating Tanum petroglyphs; and especially Guðmundur Ingólfsson of Ímynd, Reykjavík for generously processing other photographs for me.

Abbreviations

A	AM 748 MS of the Elder Edda
A.D.	anno domini
Aarbøger	*Aarbøger for nordisk oldkyndighed og historie*
Act.arch.	*Acta archaeologica*
Akv.	*Atlakviða in grænlenska*
Alv.	*Alvíssmál*
AM	Arnamagnæan(sk,-us)
Am.	*Atlamál in grænlensku*
ANF	*Arkiv för nordisk filologi*
B.C.	Before Christ
Bdr.	*Baldrs draumar*
BN	Bibliothèque Nationale
Br.	*Brot af Sigurðarkviðu*
c.	circa
cf.	compare
Ch./ch.	Chapter
cm.	centimetres
CR	The *Codex Regius* of the Poetic Edda
DMC	Karl Young, *The drama of the medieval church*
DS	*Danske studier*
e.g.	exempli gratia
ed(s).	editor(s), edited by
et al.	and others
etc.	et cetera
ff.	following
f.fr.	fonds francais
fig(s).	figure(s)
f.lat.	fonds latines
Fm.	*Fáfnismál*
FN	*Fornaldarsögur Norðurlanda*, 3 vols, ed. Guðni Jónsson and Bjarni Vilhjálmsson (Reykjavík, 1943–1944)
fol.	folio
fols	folios
Ghv.	*Guðrúnarhvöt*
Gl.kgl.saml.	Gammel kongelig samling
Gðr.I	*Guðrúnarkviða I (in fyrsta)*
Gðr.II	*Guðrúnarkviða II (önnur)*
Gðr.III	*Guðrúnarkviða III (in þriðja)*
Grm.	*Grímnismál*

Abbreviations

Grp.	*Grípispá*
Grt.	*Grottasöngr*
Háv.	*Hávamál*
Hdl.	*Hyndluljóð*
HH.I	*Helgakviða Hundingsbana I (in fyrri)*
HH.II	*Helgakviða Hundingsbana II*
HHj.	*Helgakviða Hjörvarðssonar*
Hlð.	*Hlöðskviða*
Hlr.	*Helreið Brynhildar*
Hm.	*Hamðismál*
Hrbl.	*Hárbarðsljóð*
Hym.	*Hymiskviða*
i.e.	id est
ÍF	*Íslenzk fornrit* (Reykjavík, 1933–); in progress
JS	Jón Sigurðsson
KLNM	*Kulturhistorisk leksikon for nordisk middelalder*, ed. Magnus Már Lárusson, Jakob Benediktsson et al., 22 vols (Reykjavík, 1956–1978)
lit.	literally
l(l).	lines
Ls.	*Lokasenna*
MM	*Maal og minne*
MS(S)	manuscript(s)
no.	number
NAR	*Norwegian archeological review*
NM	*Neuphilologische Mitteilungen*
NRA	Norsk Riksarkivet
Ny kgl.saml.	Ny kongelig samling
Od.	*Oddrúnargrátr*
p(p).	page(s)
PE	Snorri Sturluson, The *Prose Edda*
r.	recto
rev.	revised, revised by
Rm.	*Reginsmál*
Rþ.	*Rígsþula*
Saga-Book	*The Saga-Book of the Viking Society*
Sd.	*Sigrdrífumál*
Sgk.	*Sigurðarkviða in skamma*
Skm.	*Skírnismál*
SRA	Svenska Riksarkivet
SS	*Scandinavian studies*
st(s).	strophe
sv.	sub voce
TCD	Trinity College, Dublin

Abbreviations

TMM	*Tímarit Máls og menningar*
trans(s).	translator(s), translated by
v.	verso
Vkv.	*Völundarkviða*
Vm.	*Vafþrúðnismál*
vol.	volume
vols	volumes
Vsp.	*Völuspá*
Þrk.	*Þrymskviða*
4o/4to/4:o	quarto
8vo	octavo

Introduction

A. Ancient Scandinavian Drama and the Scholars

There can be few first-time readers of the thirteenth-century corpus of Old Icelandic poems known as the Elder or Poetic Edda who are not struck by the wide variety of poetic material gathered together here under one heading.[1] The poems in question, which in broad terms deal with Nordic gods and fabled Germanic heroes, are composed in several different metres and a diversity of styles. They also vary in age and provenance. Not without reason, one is drawn to think of the Edda not as a collection of homogeneous poems, but rather as a miscellany of 'ancient' popular material, similar in concept to the other large collections of miscellaneous popular and religious poetic material put together elsewhere in Europe.

One of the most striking features of the Edda, however, is the dramatic quality of many of the 'poems' included in the collection. Indeed, works such as *Skírnismál* and *Lokasenna* stand out from the body of contemporary poetry in the early Germanic world by virtue of the fact that they are composed entirely of dialogue, interspersed with occasional terse comments in prose. It is only natural that certain scholars in the past should have considered that these works might be dramas of some kind. It was such an idea that inspired the writing of Bertha Phillpotts' *The Elder Edda and ancient Scandinavian drama* in 1920. Phillpotts' somewhat daring conclusion was that many of the Eddic poems represented the 'actual shattered remains of ancient religious drama', that is to say, the remnants of pagan ritual dramas which had existed in Scandinavia prior to the settlement of Iceland in the late ninth century.[2] The essential problem with such an argument, however, has always been that there is nothing in the Icelandic sagas which states conclusively that 'dramas' were ever performed in early medieval Scandinavia, least of all Eddic dramas. This reason, among others which will be discussed below, has resulted in the idea of 'ancient Scandinavian drama' never receiving much serious attention from scholars

---

[1] For the texts of the Edda, see the editions of Neckel and Kuhn (*Edda*), and Jón Helgason (*Eddadigte*, I–III [incomplete]). Several translations of these poems are available in English: for example, Hollander, trans., *The poetic Edda*, and Auden and Taylor, trans., *Norse poems*. For recent general examinations of the poems and their genre, see Vésteinn Ólason, 'Eddukvæði', and Jónas Kristjánsson, *Eddas and sagas*, pp.25–82. The most detailed examination of the poems is still Einar Ólafur Sveinsson's *Íslenzkar bókmenntir*.
[2] Phillpotts, *The Elder Edda*, p.114.

of Old Icelandic during the more than seventy years since Phillpotts' book was written.

During the last twenty years or so, however, in the wake of works like Lord's *The singer of tales*, attention has begun to focus again on the oral *performance* of works in the early medieval world.³ In the case of Eddic poetry, such discussion is both relevant and important since many of the poems may have been (in essential form) several hundreds of years old when they eventually came to be recorded in the thirteenth century. This new interest in the performance of the Eddic poems has understandably resulted in a number of scholars starting to reconsider Phillpotts' ideas about dramatic performance, albeit in slightly tentative, general terms.⁴ Furthermore, the last few years have also seen several exciting experiments by actors, teachers and directors in presenting some of the Eddic poems in a dramatic fashion,⁵ something that will hopefully be extended in the future under the stimulus of Peter Brook's recent production of the *Mahabharata*.⁶ As these performances have demonstrated, works like *Skírnismál*, *Lokasenna* and *Hárbarðsljóð* can be highly effective in dramatic performance. What is now needed, however, is a detailed re-evaluation of the evidence for drama having existed in early Scandinavia, on the basis of modern research and modern research techniques. The aim of the present book is to undertake such a re-evaluation.

As was pointed out above, the idea that some of the Eddic poems such as *Skírnismál*, *Hárbarðsljóð*, *Vafþrúðnismál*, *Fáfnismál* and *Lokasenna* might be dramas, or the remnants of such, is not original. Indeed, Phillpotts herself was hardly the first scholar to make this suggestion. Her work represents rather the high-water mark of a conviction that had begun to

---

3 See further the references to the work of Dronke, Axton, Brennan, Opland, and others in *Chapter IV, D*, and *Chapter V, C*.
4 See, for example, Martin, *Ragnarök* (1972), passim (on Phillpotts in particular, see p.2 and pp.26–31); Holm-Olsen, ed., *Edda-dikt* (1975), p.320; Lönnroth, 'Skírnismál' (1977), pp.170–171 and p.178; Haugen, 'The Edda as ritual' (1983), pp.3–5 in particular; Davidson, 'Insults and riddles' (1983), pp.25–46, p.86; Bibire, 'Freyr and Gerðr' (1986), pp.21–22; McKinnell, 'Motivation in Lokasenna' (1987–1988), 251–252; Jón Hnefill Aðalsteinsson, 'Norræn trú', (1988), pp.51–53; Machan, ed., *Vafþrúðnismál* (1988), pp.16–17, p.21, and p.34; Gísli Sigurðsson, 'Eddukvæði' (1989), p.302, and most recently, Sveinn Einarsson, *Íslensk leiklist*, I (1991), pp.41–62.
5 For example, the performances of *Lokasenna* by members of the Icelandic department at Hamrahlíð College in Reykjavík (1979 and 1986), students at Durham University (see McKinnell, 'Motivation in Lokasenna', 252), and Rúnar Guðbrandsson with Leiksmiðjan for the Ásatrúarfélag in Reykjavík (1993); that of *Ragnarök* in York Minster (1988), a presentation which involved sections of several poems including *Baldrs draumar* and *Völuspá*; and Greger Hansen's one-man performances of *Baldrs draumar*, *Völuspá*, *Völuspá in skamma*, *Þrymskviða*, *Skírnismál* and *Lokasenna* in German: *Recken, runen, reisenweiber*, Galdraloftið, Reykjavík, 21 March, 1991. Recently, a group of enterprising students of Folkloristics at the University of Iceland, in cooperation with the Ásatrúarfélag, staged an experimental outdoor performance of *Skírnismál* on the evening of 21 December, 1992, under the direction of the present author.
6 *The Mahabharata*, adapted from the Sanskrit original by Peter Brook and Jean-Claude Carrière, was first presented in Avignon in 1985.

A. Ancient Scandinavian Drama and the Scholars

appear in scholarly works as early as the late eighteenth century when F. D. Gräter (1789) chose to publish *Lokasenna* in play form with a list of *dramatis personæ* and scene divisions.[7] Gräter's implication that *Lokasenna* should be seen as a play was followed up in 1822 by the influencial Icelandic scholar Finnur Magnússon in the commentary on his Danish translations of the Edda.[8] Like Gräter before him, Finnur compared the creator of *Lokasenna* to Aristophanes and Lucian,[9] but he extended the argument by suggesting that *Skírnismál* and *Hárbarðsljóð* might have been presented dramatically at pagan religious festivals or as part of seasonal folk celebrations.[10] This particular idea should be seen in the context of an earlier argument made by Finnur (1813) on the basis of the description of the *gothikon* (see below, Chapter I, C.7), that 'the Goths or the Norse warriors in the service of the Greek Emperor celebrated Yule with songs and theatrical dance.'[11]

During the years that followed, similar statements about the dramatic qualities of the dialogic poems were made by a number of European scholars. J. E. Rydquist (1836) was the first scholar to give any reasoned argument for why some of the Eddic poems should be seen as dramas, underlining the obvious predominance of dialogue in works like *Skírnismál*, and predating Phillpotts in his suggestion that the internal prose in the dialogic poems replaces dramatic action.[12] According to Rydquist, the rest of the prose in these poems might have been based on prologues and epilogues that originally accompanied the dramatic works.[13] This argument for the existence of drama in early Scandinavia is then provided with a context through references to Scandinavian dramatic folk traditions such as that of the *julebukk* (see below Chapter II, B.3–5), and to Finnur Magnússon's ideas regarding the *gothikon* in Constantinople (see above). Rydquist's argument later received weighty support from Müllenhoff's

---

[7] Gräter, *Nordische Blumen*, pp.209–233. It might be noted that in spite of Gräter's suggestion, the Danish playwright Oehlenschläger still felt compelled to write in 1807 that 'there is no sign of dramatic poetry anywhere in Old Norse literature, unless one wishes to regard the lyrical dialogic fragments of the poetic Edda as being such' ('hele den gamle nordiske Litteratur viser intet Spoer af noget dramatisk Digt, men mindre man vil regne de lyriske Dialog-Fragmenter i Sæmunds Edda derhen'): Oehlenschläger, Introduction to *Nordiske Digte*, p.13.

[8] The close connections between Gräter and Finnur Magnússon are illustrated by the collection of letters Finnur wrote to Gräter between 1815 and 1823. See Petersen, ed., *Breve fra Finn Magnusen til F. D. Gräter*. These letters contain no discussion on the subject of drama, but show a shared interest in the *gothikon* (p.3).

[9] Finnur Magnússon (as Finn Magnusen), *Den Ældre Edda*, II, p.134, pp.269–270 and pp.279–280; and Gräter, *Nordische Blumen*, p.220, note, and p.222, note.

[10] Finnur Magnússon, *Den Ældre Edda*, II, p.173, note **, and pp.135–136.

[11] 'Götherna, eller de nordiska Krigare, som stodo i Grekiska Kejsarnes Krigstjenst, firade Julen med Sanger och theatralske Danse': Finnur Magnússon (as Finn Magnusen), 'Forsög til forklaring', 315 and 307.

[12] Rydquist, 'Nordens äldsta skådespel', 170–171.

[13] Finnur Magnússon had earlier made a similar suggestion, that 'the prose interpolations announce scene changes' ('de indskudte prosaiske Stykker . . . tilkjendegive Scenernes Forandring'): Finnur Magnússon, *Den Ældre Edda*, II, p.173, note **.

independent conclusion (1879) that the dialogic and monologic poems of the Edda were an ancient form which might have had an origin in folk drama.[14]

Müllenhoff's statement was essentially a counter to F. G. Bergmann's earlier affirmation (1838) that dialogic poetry was a comparatively recent development that had grown out of the older epic.[15] Bergmann, however, had been struck in his own time by the dramatic qualities of the poems, and the commentary accompanying his French translations of the Eddic poems (1838 and 1871) is worth notice because of its objective examination of the form of the poems and their demands of performance.[16] Bergmann, for example, is unique in making the same suggestion as that made in this book that the names of the speakers in manuscripts of the dialogue poems should be seen as a later editorial emendation, rather than an essential part of the poems.[17] Similarly, while believing that dialogue was a later development, Bergmann also emphasises that 'the moment the narration is replaced by the dialogue and the poet conceals himself . . . behind the character that speaks, the transition from epic to drama has commenced; indeed, drama is already in operation.'[18] Bergmann even goes as far as echoing Finnur Magnússon's suggestion that *Skírnismál* might have been composed for a fertility ritual connected to the worship of Freyr.[19] Nonetheless, he refrains from making the definite statement that 'les Islandais' had reached the stage of 'drame proprement', largely because he feels they did not have the means of establishing 'un théâtre'.[20]

Bergmann's observations and reservations were echoed in 1849 by Wieselgren, who dubbed *Lokasenna* 'en Eddisk Tartuffe',[21] and by Ljunggren (1864) who was more wary than his predecessors about drawing conclusions owing to the apparent lack of solid evidence, but still felt bound to include the Eddic poems in his history of early Swedish drama.[22] In 1883, however, following Müllenhoff's statements about the dialogic form and its possible relationship to folk drama, Guðbrandur Vigfússon and F. York Powell evidently felt confident enough to credit *Lokasenna*, *Hárbarðsljóð* and *Skírnismál* to the 'Western Islands' Aristophanes' in

---

[14] Müllenhoff, 'De alte Dichtung von den Nibelungen', 152.
[15] Bergmann, *Poëmes Islandais*, pp.21–22. This argument was later to be taken up by scholars such as Heusler and Davíð Erlingsson: see below, *Chapter III, section D* and note 113.
[16] Bergmann, *Poëmes Islandais*, pp.20–24, and *Le message de Skirnir*, pp.43–51 and pp.67–71.
[17] Bergmann, *Poëmes Islandais*, p.23.
[18] '. . . du moment que la narration est remplacée par le dialogue, et que le poëte se dérobe, pour ainsi dire, derrière le personnage qu'il fait parler, la transition de l'épopée au drame commence, ou plutôt elle s'est déjà opérée': Bergmann, *Poëmes Islandais*, p.22. Translation by Niamh Doran.
[19] Bergmann, *Le message de Skirnir*, pp.70–71.
[20] Bergmann, *Poëmes Islandais*, p.24.
[21] Wieselgren, *Sveriges sköne litteratur*, II, p.59.
[22] Ljunggren, *Svenska dramat*, pp.3–9.

A. Ancient Scandinavian Drama and the Scholars

their influential *Corpvs Poeticvm Boreale*, on the basis that the text of all three poems is 'purely dramatic'.[23] In line with this conclusion, these two scholars adopted the same approach as Gräter in their translations of the 'Aristophanic' poems which are broken up into scenes, and accompanied by stage directions written in the present tense.[24] In the same book, *Reginsmál*, *Fáfnismál* and *Sigrdrífumál* are also classified together under the heading of 'The old play of the Wolsungs',[25] the authors envisaging the dramatic form as 'a natural development of those earlier Didactic Dialogues between Teacher and Pupil' such as *Loddfáfnismál* (*Hávamál*, sts 111–137).[26] Further stimulus was added to the movement by the appearance of Mannhardt's *Wald- und Feldkulte* (1874–1876), Frazer's *The golden bough* (first published in 1890) which gave rise to the works of the Cambridge school,[27] and somewhat later, Nilsson's collection of Swedish folk material, *Årets folkliga fester* (1915). These works made popularly available a mass of folk tradition (much of it semi-dramatic). The first two works, in particular, placed stress on the apparent links between these later dramatic folk traditions and early pagan ritual in the Germanic world. A typical conclusion of Frazer's work, for example, was the argument that 'the myth of Balder's death was not merely a myth . . . but . . . formed, so to say, the text of the sacred drama which was acted year by year as a magical rite to cause the sun to shine, trees to grow, crops to thrive, and to guard man and beast from the baleful arts of fairies and trolls, of witches and warlocks.'[28] Mannhardt's and Frazer's works were to be highly influential on the work of Old Norse scholars such as Henrik Schück and Magnus Olsen, both of whom, during the same period, produced important

---

[23] Guðbrandur Vigfússon and Powell, ed. and trans., *Corpus Poeticvm Boreale*, I, p.lviii, p.lxvii, and pp.100–127. In this work, *Hárbarðsljóð* is directly called a 'little drama' (I, p.117).
[24] The translation of *Lokasenna*, for example, begins as follows: 'FIRST SCENE, in Eager's hall (Okeanos); all the Gods and Goddesses, save Thor, present at a banquet. Loki appears at the door.
Loki at the door to Eldi the Cook. "Tell me, Eldi . . ." ' See Guðbrandur Vigfússon and Powell, *Corpvs Poeticvm Boreale*, I, pp.100–123. A similar use of scene divisions and present tense stage directions is found in these scholars' translations of *Grímnismál*, *Vafþrúðnismál*, *Alvíssmál*, *Grógaldr*, *Fjölsvinnsmál*, *Eiríksmál* and *Hákonarmál*.
[25] Guðbrandur Vigfússon and Powell, *Corpus Poeticvm Boreale*, I, pp.30–44.
[26] Guðbrandur Vigfússon and Powell, *Corpvs Poeticvm Boreale*, I, p.31. Indeed, in this work, *ljóðaháttr* (the poetic metre used for many of the dialogic poems) is translated simply, if wrongly, as 'the Dialogue metre' (I, pp.439–441).
[27] The 'Cambridge school' of Classical Anthropology centred in particular around the works of scholars such as Jane Harrison, Gilbert Murray and Francis Cornford dealing with the origins of Greek drama, and the postulated close connection between myth and ritual in the development of drama: see in particular Murray, 'Excurus' (1912); Harrison, *Themis* (1912) and *Ancient art* (1913); and Cornford, *The origins of Attic comedy* (1914). See also Hooke, ed., *Myth and ritual* (1933), and Gaster, *Thespis* (1950), two other important works heavily influenced by the same ideas. For a sensible modern critique on this school of thought, see Friedrich, 'Drama and ritual', passim.
[28] Frazer, *The golden bough*, VII.2, p.88.

arguments linking the Eddic poems (in particular *Skírnismál*) to assumed ancient Scandinavian ritual and later folk traditions.[29]

The influence of the works mentioned above, combined with the influence of the Cambridge school, soon led to the appearance of four other apparently independent works dealing with various aspects of ancient Scandinavian ritual drama, all of which were published within a short space of time between the two world wars. Vestlund's article, 'Åskgudens hammare förlorad' (1919), envisaged a dramatic ritual as forming a background for the myth of the loss of Þórr's hammer, most clearly depicted in the Eddic poem, *Þrymskviða*. Seven years later, Almgren's influential *Hällristningar och kultbruk* (1926) argued that many of the Bronze Age petroglyphs of Bohuslän depicted elements of ancient ritual fertility drama (see further below, Chapter I, C.2–3.). Grönbech's 'Essay on ritual drama' (1932), appended to the English translation of his *Vor folkeæt i oldtiden*, attempted to recreate a dramatic ritual out of *Völuspá* on the basis of the ritualistic language and imagery used in the poem.[30] The most important work on the subject, however, was without doubt Phillpotts' *The Elder Edda and ancient Scandinavian drama*.

Phillpotts, who was directly influenced by Schück, Olsen and the Cambridge school,[31] stands apart from her predecessors predominantly because of the detailed examination of the form and content of the dialogic *ljóðaháttr* poems contained in the first part of her book.[32] Her conclusion that the poems represent the remnants of ancient ritual dramas originally performed in Norway is based on several valid observations. Apart from noting the fact that these poems are largely composed of speech occasionally interspersed with short passages of prose, Phillpotts also draws attention to particular features of the oral tradition that regularly occur in the dialogic poems, such as the unusual frequency of incremental repetition. This, Phillpotts feels, 'must ultimately go back to a tradition of improvisation', and 'a tradition of two or more speakers uttering alternate strophes'.[33] Another dramatic feature Phillpotts notes is the occurrence of supernumerary figures in the poems, such as the slave-woman, the horse and the herdsman in *Skírnismál*. Like certain comparable characters in medieval drama, these figures serve little real purpose

---

[29] See Olsen, 'Fra gammelnorsk myte og kultus' (1909), passim; and Schück, *Studier i nordisk litteratur* (1904), II, pp.181–199 and pp.263–282; *Studier i Ynglingatal*, II (1906), pp.60–62 and pp.80–83; and *Svenska folkets historie*, I,i (1914), p.266. It is revealing to trace the development of Schück's ideas over time through his often large-scale revisions of the first volumes of *Illustrerad svensk litteraturhistoria*: see second edition, I (1911), pp.23–26 and pp.85–90; and the third edition, I (1926), pp. 38–40, pp.107–111, pp.148–149 and pp.154–155; in comparison to the first edition, I (1895–1896), pp.33–34 and pp.116–117, where no attempt is made to link dramatic folk tradition with ritual or the Eddic poems.

[30] See Grönbech, *The culture of the Teutons*, II, pp.260–341.

[31] It is interesting to note, in terms of comparison, that Jessie Weston's *From ritual to romance* (1920), one of the most famous products of this school, was written at the same time as Phillpotts' book under very similar influences.

[32] Regarding the *ljóðaháttr* metre, see below, Chapter III, C.2.

[33] Phillpotts, *The Elder Edda*, p.98.

A. Ancient Scandinavian Drama and the Scholars

apart from helping to set the scene in spoken terms.[34] Possibly most important of all, however, is Phillpotts' examination of the prose contained within the dialogic poems, and her argument that it must have been a later addition which possibly replaced earlier physical action.[35] This suggestion was placed alongside the noteworthy observation that the extant poetic text of the dialogic works (and often the prose too) lacks description of central actions which must have always been essential features of the narratives that lay behind the poems. Good examples of such are the implied meeting of Freyr and Gerðr in *Skírnismál*, and the actual slaying of important figures such as Fáfnir and Reginn in *Fáfnismál*, and Vafþrúðnir in *Vafþrúðnismál*. None of these actions are described in poetry, yet all of them are arguably essential to the works in question.[36] Phillpotts concludes that 'we have only to suppose that these dialogues were *acted* in heathen Norway, even in the rudest pantomimic style, to understand why prose 'asides' would be superfluous for the Norwegians' and thus necessary for the Icelanders who, she argues, could never have seen the poems acted.[37]

The weakness of Phillpotts' work is that she goes too far, bases too much on general assumption, and tries too hard to fit the Eddic poems within the myth-ritual framework suggested by Murray and the Cambridge school. These scholars envisaged Greek drama as having evolved out of a complex seasonal vegetation ritual based on the death and resurrection of nature as personified by the year *daimon*, or divine king. According to Murray, this ritual involved the common pattern of the *Agon* (or contest), and *Pathos* (or ritual death as announced by a *Messenger*), followed by the *Threnos* (lamentation), *Anagnorisis* (discovery) and comfort-bringing *Theophany*.[38] Phillpotts accordingly went out of her way to find all of these features in the Eddic poems, believing that the 'Northern drama' was closer to its ritual roots than that of Greece. Here, she felt, it was possible to witness 'the Fertility-ritual almost in the act of developing from magical into commemorative drama' (i.e. tragedy).[39]

For Phillpotts, the body of 'dramatic' *ljóðaháttr* poems, which are all assumed to have originated in pagan Norway, is replenished with other 'lost' works that are either based on fragments or on the assumption that certain 'later' *fornyrðislag* poems (such as *Þrymskviða*, *Hyndluljóð* and the *Helgakviður*) must have been based on earlier dramatic works in

---

[34] Phillpotts, *The Elder Edda*, pp.109–110.
[35] This argument had been advanced previously by Rydquist: see note 12.
[36] Phillpotts, *The Elder Edda*, pp.100–110. The same applies to the death of Geirroðr in *Grímnismál*.
[37] Phillpotts, *The Elder Edda*, p.107.
[38] Murray, 'Excursus', pp.342–344. Similar ideas are reflected in the pattern suggested in Hooke, ed., *Myth and ritual*, p.8; and in Gaster's concept of *Kenosis* ('emptying') and *Plerosis* ('filling'), which involved the key ritual elements of *Mortification*, *Purgation*, *Invigoration*, and *Jubilation*: see Gaster, *Thespis*, pp.4–33.
[39] Phillpotts, *The Elder Edda*, pp.194–195.
[40] Phillpotts, *The Elder Edda*, pp.47–57.

ljóðaháttr.⁴⁰ This incremented body of material allows Phillpotts to assume the existence of recurring 'stock scenes', such as the culmination of the poems in a killing and/ or a love or wooing scene, and the central element of the flyting,⁴¹ all of which fit into the aforementioned ritual pattern of the marriage, death and resurrection of the seasonal god which Phillpotts sees as lying behind the *Helgakviður* in particular.⁴² To support this idea of a ritual dramatic tradition parallel to that encountered in ancient Greek drama, she points haphazardly to the common use of disguise in the poems and sagas,⁴³ and to individual dramatic folk traditions from both Scandinavia and England, apparently assuming that English folk traditions must have had roots in Scandinavian ritual.⁴⁴

The immediate reaction to Phillpotts' work was, in John Lindow's words, 'admiring, but non-committal'.⁴⁵ The most influential review, however, was that of Andreas Heusler who reiterated his earlier criticism of Müllenhoff's argument concerning the relationship between the dialogic Eddic poems and folk drama⁴⁶ by posing three questions: 'Is there any evidence of ritual plays having existed in pagan Scandinavia? Is it possible to say that the myths behind the poems dealing with the gods and heroes were based on such plays? Could such plays help to explain the artistic form of the poems?'⁴⁷ Heusler himself answered all of these questions in the negative, and received general support for this opinion from Noreen in the following year.⁴⁸

During the fifty years that followed, the question of early Scandinavian

---

41 Phillpotts, *The Elder Edda*, pp.111–114.
42 Phillpotts, *The Elder Edda*, pp.129–159 and pp.191–198.
43 Phillpotts, *The Elder Edda*, pp.115–117.
44 See, for example, Phillpotts, *The Elder Edda*, p.119, pp.122–127, pp.132–133, p.136 and pp.138–139. Phillpotts' view of English folklore was not unique. See the references given in *Chapter II*, note 193 for other examples of the same approach during this period.
45 Lindow, *Scandinavian mythology*, p.355. See further the following reviews: *TLS* (Thursday, 16 December, 1920), 857; Einar Ólafur Sveinsson, in *Skírnir*, 45 (1921), 157–159; Schröder, in *Anglia Beiblatt*, 32 (1921), 148–155; Ker, in *The modern language review*, 17 (1922), 201–202; Heusler, in *ANF*, 38 (1922), 347–353; Major, in the *Yearbook of the Viking Society*, 6–16 (1914–1924), 70–72; and Hollander, 'Recent studies in the Helgi poems' (1924), 119–125. All the above make relevant criticisms, but probably the most useful, objective review is that of Schröder which contains similar comments to those given above.
46 For Müllenhoff, see above, note 14. For Heusler's reaction, see Heusler, 'Der Dialog', in *Kleine Schriften*, II, pp.632–633 (originally published in 1902).
47 'Hat es im heidnischen Norden rituale Schauspiele gegeben? Können wir Fabeln unsrer Götter-und Heldendichtung aus solchen Schauspielen herleiten? Erklären sich Kunstformen unsrer Dichtung aus solchen Schauspielen?': Heusler, Review of Phillpotts, 350.
48 See Noreen, 'Studier, III' (1923), 3–5, and *Den norsk-isländska poesien* (1926), p.65. Noreen is less convinced of the non-existence of drama than Heusler, but remains highly sceptical. Nonetheless, after examining the dynamics of *Lokasenna* ('Studier, III', 22–23), even he feels compelled to state, like Bergmann before him (in *Poëmes Islandais*, pp.23–24), that the composers must have been on the verge of creating what he terms 'en verklig dramatisk litteratur' ('real dramatic literature'): 'Studier, III', 23, echoed in *Den norsk-isländska poesien*, p.69.

A. Ancient Scandinavian Drama and the Scholars

drama became almost taboo amongst Old Norse scholars.[49] For example, in spite of his positive, but somewhat condescending review of Phillpotts' book in 1921 (see note 45), Einar Ólafur Sveinsson seems to carefully avoid making any statements on the subject of drama in his *Íslenzkar bókmenntir í fornöld* (1962). In discussing *Skírnismál*, for example, he admits the possible link with early ritual poetry involving more than one speaker, but echoes de Vries in concluding that 'the path from one to the other is long, and there is a enormous difference between such ancient poetry, if it ever existed, and *Skírnismál*, similar to the difference between a root and a flower.'[50] Such cautious approaches are typical of this period,[51] and culminate in Hallvard Magerøy's unconditional statement in 1981 that 'the Icelanders had no theatre'.[52] The general attitude of the time to Phillpotts' work is well summed up by Ohlmarks' statement in 1948: 'Antiquated but interesting'.[53]

This attitude was probably brought about by several factors, not least of them being Heusler's review. In addition to noting the obvious weaknesses of Phillpotts' book, one must also consider the influence of the wave of disfavour that swept over the Cambridge school's over-theoretical myth-and-ritual arguments during the years after the Second World War. Furthermore, Old Icelandic scholars during this period had become more interested in the safer territories of philology and the written text than in the more questionable area of oral performance. Thus, while Phillpotts' book continued to have a certain influence in other fields such as theatre studies,[54] the concept of ancient Scandinavian drama received very little

---

[49] According to Árni Björnsson in conversation (1990), Einar Ólafur Sveinsson actually used the word 'tabú' (perhaps ambiguously) when invited to discuss Phillpotts' theories in university classes.

[50] 'Ferillinn þar á milli virðist vera ógn langur og munurinn mikill á þeim forna kveðskap, ef til hefur verið, og *Skírnismálum*, eins og munur á rót og blómi': Einar Ólafur Sveinsson, *Íslenzkar bókmenntir*, p.278. (See also p.377 on the *Helgakviður*.) See also de Vries in *Altnordische Literaturgeschichte* (first edition, 1941–1942), I, p.164 (second edition [1964–1967], II, p.105). In later years, however, de Vries went slightly farther in his revision of *Altgermanische Religionsgeschichte* (1956–1957), I, pp.39–40 and pp.444–445, where he suggested that poems like *Skírnismál* should be seen as a development from older cult drama. No statement, however, is made about whether these more recent re-workings should be seen as dramatic or not.

[51] See, for example, Jón Helgason, *Norrøn litteraturhistorie* (1934), pp.31–32, and 'Norges og Islands digtning', p.32 and p.38; Ström, *Nordisk hedendom* (second edition, 1967), p.180; and Turville-Petre, *Myth and religion of the North* (London, 1964), pp.174–175. A similar conclusion is made in Sveinn Einarsson's recent *Íslensk leiklist*, I (1991), p.61.

[52] Magerøy, ed., *Bandamanna saga* (1981), p.xvii. It is noteworthy that no mention at all is made of the dramatic aspects of the *ljóðaháttr* poems in Jónas Kristjánsson's recent *Eddas and sagas* (1988).

[53] 'Föråldrad men intressant': Ohlmarks, *Eddans gudesånger*, p.34

[54] Raglan, in *The hero* (1936), p.232, goes as far as suggesting that even the sagas have their roots in ritual drama, thus extending a less extreme suggestion made by Phillpotts in *The Elder Edda*, p.206, that 'the theory of the dramatic origin of the Edda poems explains ... the technique of the sagas'. See also Stumpfl, *Kultspiele* (1936), pp.41–43, and pp.194–196; Hunningher, *The origin of the theatre* (1955), p.27 in particular; and Spiers, *Medieval English poetry* (1957), pp.270–271 and pp.307–319 in particular. Most recently,

attention in the area of Old Norse studies, except in the work of Holtsmark, Höfler, and Strömbäck. None of these scholars, however, seems to have had much lasting impact in terms of reviving the question of ritual drama.[55] The only idea to receive somewhat grudging acceptance was the suggestion made by Jón Helgason that *Hárbarðsljóð* might have been performed by two men improvising the text as they went along. However, it is noteworthy that even here no mention is ever made of the word 'drama'.[56] As noted above, it was not until the last few years that scholars at last began to reconsider Phillpotts' ideas from a new practical viewpoint, free of the former prejudice that had become attached to the myth-ritual theory.

B. Drama: A Definition

The above review of past scholarship on the question of the relationship between the Edda and 'ancient Scandinavian drama' reveals several interesting features, not least being the fact that the emphasis has tended to be on the ritualistic aspects of the poems on one hand, and the lack of literary evidence on the other. Very little, if anything, has been said about the demands of performance or the way in which the poems were recorded in the manuscripts themselves. Furthermore, none of the above scholars ever really defines what he or she means by 'drama', thus providing great scope for wide-ranging theory, petty criticism, and general misunderstanding.

There is naturally little likelihood that drama existed in early Scandinavia if 'drama' is to be seen in the terms offered by the *Oxford English dictionary*. In fact, the dictionary supplies no real definition of drama as a genre, but *a* drama is described as 'a composition in prose or verse, adapted to be acted upon *a stage*, in which *a story* is related by means of *dialogue and action*, and is represented *with accompanying gesture, costume and scenery, as in real life*; a play' (my emphases).[57] Complex defini-

---

Phillpotts' hypothesis is referred to positively, yet objectively, in Axton's *European drama* (1974), p.34, note 5.

[55] See Holtsmark, 'Myten om Idun og Tjatse' (1949) (on the possibility that Þjóðólfr úr Hvini's poem *Haustlöng* from the late ninth century is a description of a ritual drama); 'Leik og skjemt' (1950); and 'Drama' (1958). See also Strömbäck, 'Cult remnants' (1948); and Höfler, (among other articles) 'Das Opfer im Semnonenhain' (1952). Of similar importance is Ursula Dronke's attempt to revive the ritualistic approach to *Skírnismál* in 'Art and tradition in *Skírnismál*' (1962). Dronke's ideas are echoed most recently in Talbot's article, 'The withdrawal of the fertility god' (1982).

[56] Jón Helgason, 'Norges og Islands digtning', p.35. Jón's ideas are based partly on an observation by de Vries in *Literaturgeschichte* (1941–1942), I, p.170, and are supported tentatively by Einar Ólafur Sveinsson, in *Íslenzkar bókmenntir*, p.292, and more readily by Holm-Olsen, who, in *Edda-dikt* (1985), p.321, suggests that the poem might have been "spilt" som en liten komedie' ('acted as a little comedy'). See also Sveinn Einarsson, *Íslensk leiklist*, I, 49–50, and most recently, Vesteinn Ólason, 'Eddukvæði', p.102.

[57] *OED*, second edition, sv. Drama, 1.a.

B. Drama: A Definition

tions of this kind are all too commonly encountered outside the immediate field of theatre studies.[58] Yet, as any modern theatre practitioner will agree, such a definition must be regarded as not only highly clumsy and misleading but also 'downright incorrect'.[59] Indeed, it implicitly rules out the inclusion of improvised drama, mime, the cinema and television, radio drama (which involves nothing beyond sound effects and voices), street theatre (which may entirely lack a stage), and numerous other kinds of blatantly non-realistic theatre. Similarly misleading is the idea held by some that 'drama requires the cooperation of several people for its being',[60] a belief that would appear to ignore the dramatic one-man performance.

In simple terms, while full-scale *theatre* in the sense of a performed spectacle often tends to avail itself of many of the features listed above, *drama* is capable of existing without the need of any of them, as will be explained below: it can manifest itself without costume, scenery or stage. Even the element of 'plot' need be nothing more than 'something that requires one or more human anthropomorphic subjects, a temporal dimension indicating the passing of time, and a spatial dimension giving a sense of space.'[61] While Aristotle's unities may be relevant for the best of classical tragedies, they are no longer considered to be the necessary model for all drama.[62]

Reducing drama to its fundamentals, one comes down essentially to the performer and his audience.[63] Strictly speaking, though, even the audience is only necessary if the term 'audience' is stretched to accommodate the actor's being aware of his outer appearance or the effect his acting is likely to have. It is unnecessary to go any further. While an audience may be implicit in the actual 'function' of drama, that is to say in the creation of 'theatre' as spectacle, it is hardly necessary for the 'act' of drama itself.[64] Even when an actor rehearses in private, he will still regard himself as being engaged in 'drama'. The same lack of a formal audience is evident in, for example, drama therapy, role-play in teaching, or dramatic experiment of the kind Brook was involved in during the work on the 'Theatre of Cruelty' season with the Royal Shakespeare Company.[65] In all of these

---

[58] See, for example, Holtsmark, 'Drama', p.294.
[59] Esslin, *The anatomy of drama*, p.9, on the Oxford definition.
[60] Williams, *The drama of medieval England*, p.1. See also Holtsmark, 'Drama', p.294; and Nicoll, *The theory of drama*, p.30.
[61] Pfister, *Theory and analysis*, p.196.
[62] See Esslin, *The field of drama*, p.15, and Pfister, *Theory and analysis*, pp.1–2 and p.198.
[63] See, for example, Bentley, *The life of the drama*, p.150: 'The theatrical situation, reduced to a minimum, is that A impersonates B while C looks on.' See also Southern, *The seven ages*, p.21; Esslin, *The anatomy of drama*, p.23; and Nicoll, *The theory of drama*, p.31.
[64] On the difference between 'theatre' and 'drama', see also Southern, *The seven ages*, p.22 and p.42.
[65] On this range of non-theatrical drama, see also Devlin, *Mask and scene*, p.3. On Brook's experiments, see Marowitz, 'Notes', pp.46–48.

Introduction

cases, *everyone* present is involved in the act itself, similar to the participants in a religious ritual.[66]

'Drama', in the sense in which the word will be used in this book, has very few restrictions or limitations in its scope. It is a wide-ranging phenomenon that overlaps on one side with solo recitation and story-telling,[67] and on several other sides with the areas of ritual, spectacle, children's games of make-believe and the living art 'performances' of modern artists. The common denominator is the actual *performer* of drama, for 'there is no drama without *actors*, whether they are present in flesh and blood, or projected shadows up on a screen, or puppets.'[68] In essence, the performer is engaged in the momentary living creation of an alternative world (or a section of it) *within* this one, to the extent that what he is acting is not himself but someone or something else that 'belongs' to a different time and/or place. This 'illusion' of double reality creates its own costume and setting in the minds of both the performer and beholder. It is in these features, the imposition of 'make-believe', the creation of the living double reality, and in the 'act' itself that the essence of drama is to be found.[69]

The 'act' naturally involves live 'performance' in some manner. Therefore, when allied to a written text, drama transforms the text into something wider than a simple work of literature since it involves the addition of a system of semiotics extending beyond the arguably limited dimensions of the merely spoken or written word. As Esslin comments, 'what makes drama drama is precisely the element which lies outside and beyond the words and which has to be seen as action – or *acted* – to give the author's concept its full value.'[70]

This statement raises the question of whether *all* textual performance should be regarded as 'drama'. In answer to this, it can be said that the key feature which differentiates drama from other forms of active oral presentation like recitation or oratory is that of 'representation' or 'mimicry', and it is this particular element, rather than full-scale drama of the kind suggested by the dictionary definition, which researchers like Young, Axton and Southern have tried to find evidence of when conducting their own important investigations into the early manifestations of drama in early medieval Europe.

---

[66] See also Pfister, *Theory and analysis*, p.12.
[67] See below, *Chapter I*, note 3.
[68] Esslin, *The anatomy of drama*, p.11.
[69] A similar emphasis is placed on the aspect of make-believe by Williams, in *The drama of medieval England*, p.2; Esslin, in *The anatomy of drama*, p.19; and most recently by Beckerman, in *Theatrical performance*, pp.14–16. The idea of the creation of an alternative reality is also stressed in Berthold, *A history of world theatre*, p.1, and Abrahams, 'Folk drama', p.352.
[70] Esslin, *The anatomy of drama*, p.14. Esslin goes further in his later work, *The field of drama*, pp.103–104, where he lists twenty-two 'sign systems' involved in drama alone. Only four of them, i.e. 'the basic lexical, syntactic, referential meaning of the words', the style, the 'individualisation of characters' and the overall structure, refer to the literal text. The rest involve elements of performance. See also, more recently, on the same subject, Pfister, *Theory and analysis*, pp.7–11.

B. Drama: A Definition

Karl Young, for example, when trying to discern the moment at which church ritual becomes 'drama', reached the conclusion that the essential element of 'genuine drama' was 'not forms of speech and movement' (such as a dialogue conducted by moving priests) 'but *impersonation*. A play . . . is, above all else, a story presented in action, in which the speakers or actors *impersonate* the characters concerned' (my emphases).[71] For Young, 'impersonation' meant that 'in some external and recognizable manner the actor must pretend to be the person whose words he is speaking, and whose actions he is imitating. The performer must do more than merely *represent* the chosen personage; he must also *resemble* him, or at least show his intention of doing so.'[72] This is an important feature to bear in mind when considering the relationship between ritual and drama. In this sense, the pure Catholic Mass, for example, *cannot* be regarded as drama in spite of its verbal exchanges and symbolic actions. The same rule naturally applies to any purely ritual actions that involve no attempt at personification, imitation, or more precisely 'mimicry', the term used by Axton to define the art of drama 'at its simplest'.[73]

Similar definitions are offered by Richard Southern in his analysis of what he terms the 'seven ages of the theatre', that is to say, the seven stages through which dramatic activity passes before it becomes the fully fledged 'theatre' everyone knows today. In the present context, Southern's classification of the initial stages of this development is of most interest.

Southern envisages three central necessities for 'theatre': the performer, the audience and 'the mask'.[74] The 'mask' (which can also be interpreted in terms of facial changes, or voice alteration) represents the borderline between oratory and drama since it signifies visually the move into mimicry, the performer's taking on of another character. This is the point at which Southern envisages the 'first stage' of drama, something that involves in essence nothing more than 'the costumed player; or the player's presentation of his costumed self – costumed so as to act as some other self', using little more to carry off the act than voice, gesture, appearance and, where necessary, basic properties.[75] As has been mentioned above, 'costume' is unnecessary in literal terms, but like the mask, it represents, in one form or another, a common feature in most primitive forms of drama, and, symbolically, represents little more than the external assumption of character, something that can be accomplished in numerous other ways.[76]

Within this preliminary phase, Southern places such basic traditional

---

[71] Young, *DMC*, I, p.80.
[72] Young, *DMC*, I, p.80.
[73] Axton, *European drama*, p.17. Axton's term of 'mimicry' has to be considered more appropriate than 'impersonation' in the light of the freedom and scope of presentation that it suggests.
[74] Southern, *The seven ages*, pp.28–29.
[75] Southern, *The seven ages*, p.32.
[76] As Berthold illustrates in *A history of world theatre*, pp.1–2, the actor of mime and primitive theatre, for example, often needs little more than his own body to 'evoke whole worlds'.

folk performances as those of the leaf-clad Bavarian Wildman, the Padstowe Hobby Horse, and the English Mummers' plays, all of which for him represent various sub-stages in the early development of drama, ranging from the mere seasonal appearance of the costumed figure, through procession, to a simplistic play using words to accompany the various movements. The movements themselves may represent little more than a simple ritual pattern involving, in the case of the Mummers' plays, a basic combat scene and a death followed by restoration to life. Yet even in the Mummers' plays, all the aspects of latter-day 'theatre' are apparent in the elements of the special occasion, the use of a rudimentary playing area (a cleared space), costume, action, and words which here 'are not introduced fundamentally for the sake of the meaning they might impart'; 'it remains a thing *done* not said'.[77] The way, however, is opened for development into the composition of 'plays', something which in religious activity often occurs with the dramatic application of the living, spoken myth to the ritual movement (if the myth was not present from the start).[78]

Such simple performances lead on to Southern's 'second stage' in which the performers graduate 'from a masked religious rite to a rhythmic act given by a specialised mask; they add words; then at a religious revolution they expand the show, put aside "superstitions", reduce the masks, bring in human characters, begin to add secondary resources to the players, and suffer the incursion of poetry.'[79] This stage, for Southern, is exemplified by the large-scale drama of Tibetan religious festivals. As is already apparent, none of Southern's aforementioned examples approaches the complexity of the detailed *Oxford dictionary* definition. All the cited forms, however, represent types of drama capable of development in a wide variety of directions.

Seen essentially in terms of 'mimicry', and the sense of '*acting out* any event or description whatever', drama has to be regarded as a common element of human activity,[80] and there is no reason to assume that early Scandinavian society should have formed an exception to this rule. As will be illustrated in the following chapters, activities that come under the heading of 'drama' as defined above must have existed in Scandinavia during the period in question, as part of sacrificial activities (the *blót*) and/or games (*leikar*), just as they have existed in more recent times. The question remains as to whether there is any reason for assuming that such activities developed beyond mere mimicked improvisation as a form of storytelling or light entertainment. The evidence for such must be drawn in part from mythological material. However, as in the case of 'drama', it is necessary to define the limits within which mythological material can be used as evidence for ritual drama.

---

[77] See Southern, *The seven ages*, pp.49–50 and p.52.
[78] See further below, *section C*.
[79] Southern, *The seven ages*, p.98.
[80] Kirk, *Myth*, pp.24–25. See also Havemeyer, *Drama of savage peoples*, pp.6–13, and p.241.

C. Drama, Myth and Ritual[81]

The essential difficulty when looking for the evidence of dramatic activity in the early Scandinavian world is, as ever, the absence of any objective contemporary account of such activities. To what extent, therefore, is it possible to presuppose the existence of 'ritual drama' on the basis of myths, or the evidence of ritual? A central weakness of the arguments made by the scholars of the Cambridge school and others of their time like Phillpotts and Grönbech was the assumption that it was possible to isolate ritualistic motifs within myths, and thereby assume the existence of rituals connected to these myths.[82] This connection of the mythical storyline to a supposed acted ritual obviously implied the existence of drama. Such an approach is well illustrated by Gaster's suggestion in later years that:

> wherever we find in ancient literature a mythological text which is either expressly or implicitly associated with a seasonal occasion, which contains appreciable portions of dialogue, and the plot of which conforms ... to ... the Ritual Pattern, what we have before us, in however attenuated or developed a form, is a specimen of Drama.[83]

The premises for such an argument are based on ideas like those of Leach who argued that 'myth, in my terminology, is the counterpart of ritual; myth implies ritual, ritual implies myth, they are one and the same,'[84] with myth being 'not so much a justification for ritual as a description of it'.[85] Yet such suggestions must be considered highly suspect unless the term 'myth' is to be limited to such a degree that it is possible to state like Fontenrose that 'if a story has not been associated with cult or ritual, explicitly or implicitly, it is better not to call it myth, but legend or folktale.'[86]

People have always told stories, and as Kirk among others has shown, myth can exist without ritual and ritual can exist without myth.[87] A good example of the former are the Trickster stories of the Plains Indians, many of which were created for the purpose of entertainment, moral education,

---

[81] The material covered in the following section is dealt with in more detail in the thesis that forms the basis for the present book. See Gunnell, 'The concept of ancient Scandinavian drama', 23–63.

[82] See Friedrich, 'Drama and ritual', passim, and Kirby, Ur-drama, pp.vii–xvi, for modern assessments of the myth-ritual school.

[83] Gaster, Thespis, p.56.

[84] Leach, Political systems, p.13.

[85] Leach, Political systems, p.172. See also Harrison, Themis, p.328; Propp, Theory and history of folklore, p.117; Hocart, The progress of man, pp.223–224; de Vries, Heroic song, p.228; and Martin, Ragnarök, p.11, where similar assertions are made.

[86] Fontenrose, Python, p.434.

[87] Kirk, Myth, pp.9–31. See also Burkert, Structure and history, pp.56–57, and the information given in Kluckhohn, 'Myths and rituals', pp.93–105 (see in particular, pp.94–95).

or as explanations of natural phenomena rather than for ritual purposes.[88] There is nothing to suggest that a poem like *Þrymskviða*, telling of Þórr's amusing quest to regain his stolen hammer, should not have developed in the same way. It is evident, however, that sometimes, elsewhere in the world, longer myths have become attached to rituals as a development of the original spontaneous and later institutionalised words attached to the ritual ('authentic' myths[89]), or as an explanation of the ritual act ('aetiological' myths[90]), or simply because the ritual act has become complex enough to resemble the existing myth.[91] The resulting conjunction between myth and ritual almost certainly, in the initial stages, will have more effect on the form of the myth than on that of the ritual which naturally tends to be more conservative.[92]

The combination of ritual and myth by necessity implies the fundamental elements of drama, since at that point the performers of the rite are seen as actually *representing* the mythical bodies, however abstract the performance may be. Yet the most obvious problem with applying a definition of the kind suggested by Leach and Gaster is that in many cultures like that under discussion in this book a wealth of mythical material exists, but there is little or no evidence about the form of the rituals that were supposedly attached to them. How then is one supposed to differentiate between the practical sacred myths and those others that were told for entertainment or for the purpose of explanation?

Further problems exist with Gaster's hypothesis. Myth in most cases has been passed down orally, separate from any supposed rituals that may have been suppressed or died out, and while some predominantly sacred myths told in poetic form may well have retained their basic characteristics,[93] most others would be open to all forms of transformation and external influence, as can be seen merely from the evidence of folktale transmission all over the world. Motifs can be borrowed, lost and transferred, and over the passage of time, ancient motifs might suddenly appear in other tales that are essentially new creations. The same can be said about Gaster's 'portions of dialogue'. For this reason, unless it is certain that a given text was definitely in religious use as part of a given ritual at a given time, it is hard to argue anything concrete about its ritual purpose or original content. The ritual elements may well be accidental or borrowed. Similarly, as

---

[88] See, for example, Thompson, *The folktale*, pp.319–328, and Wiget, *Native American literature*, pp.15–21.
[89] Harrison, *Themis*, p.16 and pp.329–330.
[90] Harrison, *Themis*, p.16.
[91] See Burkert, *Homo necans*, pp.29–34.
[92] See Fontenrose, *Python*, pp.461–462.
[93] In spite of the general theories of oral tradition, there is good reason to believe that, in some cultures, sacred texts (usually maintained in poetic form for the purposes of retention) may have remained intact for many centuries. This seems to have been the case, for example, amongst the Zuñi and Navajo nations of the south-western states of America and Mexico. Amongst the Zuñi, certain officials guarded the sacred chants, ensuring that they were accurately transmitted: see Day, *The sky clears*, p.70, and Wiget, *Native American literature*, p.32.

C. Drama, Myth and Ritual

Fontenrose shows, even if the text *was* used in a ritual, it need not necessarily reflect the ritual or be directly attached to it. The recitation of the poem, like those from the Near East mentioned by Gaster, may merely form one element of the ritual. In such a case, the poem would not be a dramatic text in itself, even though it might offer an interpretation of later ritual actions. A recitation of this kind need be no more dramatic than, for example, the reading of a lesson on the Last Supper as part of the Mass: only if the Holy Communion and the reading occur at the same time, thus allowing the congregation to 'see' the priest 'as' Jesus, will the ceremony become anything approaching drama.[94]

A myth with ritual elements and passages of dialogue like that mentioned by Gaster therefore need have nothing to do with ritual or drama. For this reason alone, it is impossible to argue, like Phillpotts and her contemporaries, that works such as *Vǫluspá*, the *Helgakviður* or *Þrymskviða* should necessarily have arisen from drama, on the grounds that such works echo aspects of the seasonal ritual and/ or have large passages of dialogue.

The key feature in the discussion has to be that of evidence of performance. In other words, rather than starting with the myth, and proceeding to assume the existence of ritual and drama, it is more logical to start from the evidence for ritual or dramatic performance. The relationship of ritual to drama is obviously much closer than that of myth to drama, and there are much firmer grounds for assuming that if a sacred ritual existed in a society, this ritual probably also included some element of representation. Similarly, if a deeply-rooted dramatic folk tradition with strong ritualistic elements is encountered, or evidence is found pointing to the early dramatic performance of a myth, then there must be good reason to consider the possible relationship between the tradition or the myth and earlier ritual.

Nonetheless, the aforementioned close relationship between ritual and drama also needs defining. In essence, both drama and ritual are 'play' activities in Huizinga's sense of 'play':

> a free activity standing quite consciously outside 'ordinary' life as being 'not serious', but at the same time absorbing the player intensely and utterly. It is an activity connected with no material interest, and no profit can be gained by it. It proceeds within its own proper boundaries of time and space according to fixed rules and in an orderly manner. It promotes the formation of social groupings which tend to surround themselves with secrecy and to stress their difference from the common world by disguise or other means.[95]

As Huizinga shows, theatre and many forms of primitive ritual, like all aspects of public 'play', share the common feature of tending to be

---

[94] See further Glynne Wickham's discussion of the *Quem Quaeritis* tropes in 'The beginnings of English drama', pp.12–16.
[95] Huizinga, *Homo ludens*, p.13. See also Pfister, *Theory and analysis*, pp.11–12, on the relationship between drama, play and ritual.

Introduction

performed in a particular marked-out area, recognised by both audience and participants, which separates the participants from the ordinary world outside.[96] Furthermore, drama and ritual share numerous other characteristics ranging from the special atmosphere created by the live performance, to the sense of occasion and the artificial recreation of actions that are supposed to have taken place in a different time, events that are 'believed in' and treated as actually taking place in the present by all the participants of the event.[97]

In short, as Esslin writes, 'one can look at ritual as a dramatic, a theatrical event – and one can look at drama as ritual. The dramatic side of ritual manifests itself in the fact that all ritual has a mimetic aspect; it contains an action of a highly symbolic, metaphorical nature.'[98] The emphasis here, however, must be placed on the word 'dramatic'. While symbolic ritualistic acts like 'speaking in tongues' and the symbolic breaking of bread and drinking of wine in the Catholic Mass can be regarded as 'dramatic' and 'theatrical', they cannot be regarded as 'drama'.[99] The same applies to the simple oblation reflected in, for example, the Norwegian folk traditions of leaving out ale, bread or sour cream porridge on an ancient grave mound for spirits like the *huldre folk* or *gardvord* at Christmas time; or to folk dancing like the northern English sword dance whenever it is presented without any clear spoken or implied semi-narrative context. Such acts can be regarded as forms of ritual, yet hardly as performances of drama.[100]

In spite of this, it is clear that the distinction between ritual and drama is a fine one, and there is little difficulty in seeing how the dramatic art can evolve out of ritual. Indeed, there is good reason to argue that a 'ritual' can be seen as 'drama' so long as it displays the prime requisites in that the participants of the ritual must be clearly seen by the audience, or other participants, as representing someone or something other than their own persons in the ritual action. The model for such a representation in the case of a ritual will logically tend to be found in mythical material, be it in the form of the tribal totems, gods, or some mythical ancestral hero. As Friedrich summarises this development, 'with the entrance of myth, the amorphous demonic forces and the terrifying theriomorphic gods of older ritual gave way to human-shaped gods; as a consequence, rituals came to

---

[96] Regarding this element of 'separation', note also Eliade's notion of the recreation of 'sacred time' in ritual: see Eliade, *Patterns*, pp.388–408, and *Myth and reality*, pp.18–19.
[97] See further, La Fontaine, *Initiation*, pp.181–182; Esslin, *The anatomy of drama*, pp.27–28; Kirby, *Ur-drama*, pp.2–32 (on shamanist performance); Burkert, *Structure and history*, pp.45–48, and 'Greek tragedy', passim; and Friedrich, 'Drama and ritual', p.181.
[98] Esslin, *The anatomy of drama*, p.27.
[99] It is therefore hard to agree with Hardison's argument summed up in *Christian rite*, pp.77–79, that the Mass should be regarded as drama on the basis that the priest becomes the role that he plays: see also Tydeman, *The theatre in the Middle Ages*, pp.37–39.
[100] For references to the Norwegian traditions, see *Chapter II*, note 244. Similar distinctions are made by Durkheim (*Elementary forms*, pp.359–360), who shows that amongst the aborigines in Australia, while one tribe may not have a single rite that does not involve imitative action, others keep to simple non-dramatic oblations like those mentioned above for the same ends.

C. Drama, Myth and Ritual

crystallize around a new core: gods, who, once endowed with an individuality of their own, can be conceived as experiencing everything that concerns and moves man.'[101] Myth, then, serves to 'restate' ritual, in the sense that it provides a relevant narrative relating the actions and sufferings of an individual god in human form. 'In literary terms, the union of myth and ritual means that ritual has attained to a narrative plot. The simple mimesis of older ritual has been transformed into the complexity of *mimesis praxeos*, the representation of an action in the Aristotelian sense.'[102]

As was stressed above, however, drama does not need a complex 'seasonal pattern' or an Aristotelian storyline to exist. And when looking for evidence of drama, as in the present study, it is not necessary to search solely for the 'high art' form of drama encountered in Greece. Drama is capable of existing in a much more rudimentary form.[103] It can be found in ritual. It can also exist within elementary games activities outside ritual.[104]

There is reason therefore to question Gaster's statement that 'Drama is everywhere more than mere mimesis . . . it consists essentially not in a single mimetic act but in a series of acts, arranged in a specific pattern and manifesting a specific plot,'[105] the plot in question being one that predominantly involves recognisable elements of the full seasonal ritual described above.[106] Certainly, Gaster's key features of *mortification, purgation, invigoration* and *jubilation* can often be found in a ritual, and certainly, all of these elements occur in the high-art tragic drama of the Greeks. Yet a solid mythological plot of this kind is not necessary for drama which, as Southern has demonstrated, can easily be based around a single action or event. There is much sense in Grönbech's comment that 'ritual drama is made up largely of symbolic acts, in no way realistically representing the act implied, but these conventional gestures shade off by degrees into imitative movements and attitudes, more or less suggestive of acting in our theatres.'[107] As Burkert emphasises, 'continuous stories appear in ritual only exceptionally.'[108]

As the ritual songs of the North American Indians illustrate, the element of speech accompanying ritual dance occurs at a very early stage (if not

---

[101] Friedrich, 'Drama and ritual', p.184.
[102] Friedrich, 'Drama and ritual', p.184. See also Gaster, *Thespis*, pp.5–6 and p.49; Brody, *The English mummers*, p.121; and Harrison, *Themis*, p.126, on this development from simple ritual to drama.
[103] See, for instance, the examples of primitive theatre in other cultures provided in Havemeyer, *Drama of savage peoples*, pp.31–325; Kirby, *Ur-drama*, passim; and Bertholt, *A history of world theatre*, pp.1–8.
[104] See references given above in note 77.
[105] Gaster, *Thespis*, p.3.
[106] See note 38 above.
[107] Grönbech, *The culture of the Teutons*, II, p.265, echoed by Raglan, in *The hero*, pp.282–283. See also Martin, who, in *Ragnarök*, p.10, sensibly states regarding the themes of the seasonal ritual that 'sometimes these themes appear separately, sometimes together'.
[108] Burkert, *Homo necans*, p.32,

from the beginning), the words serving either to describe the ritual movements of the dance or the character being portrayed. A full-scale narrative myth may be implied by the presence of the 'masked' character, symbols and movement, but it is not necessary. Indeed, to this extent, there is a certain validity to Harrison's definition of myth as *legomen*, 'the thing said', 'the spoken correlative of the acted rite, the thing done',[109] an expression of accompanying emotions and sensations which in the ritual context can be seen as 'a re-utterance or pre-utterance . . . a focus of emotion and uttered collectively or at least with collective function'.[110] Even at this stage, however, it is possible to talk of 'drama' being performed.

As was mentioned above, drama comes into existence the moment a performer mimics or imitates another being or creature, or even something more abstract, thus simultaneously creating an illusory living world in the midst of the external real surroundings in the sight or hearing of others, however momentarily this may be. All of this occurs even in the earliest stages of ritual at the level of Durkheim's 'imitative rites' which need little more storyline than that the performer moves, and acts.[111] Indeed, as Devlin points out, 'Whenever an account of archaic ritual implies the taking on of roles, or the acting-out of a situation, we know we are in the field of theatre.'[112] A good example of such is the North American Plains Indian 'Buffalo dance' where the ritual dance is accompanied by words describing the movements and actions of the buffalo, thus linking the present act to an original ritual act which took place in 'sacred time' (the time at which the gods created the world[113]), but little more than that.[114] The myth is more implicit than explicit, and the words may be no more than an outpouring related to the act and context.[115] Yet, as was mentioned above, drama in essence is already present.

In short, drama can be involved in the simplest of imitative rituals, as long as those watching or participating are aware of the element of representation. If these actions then take on a narrative form, however, there is little doubt that the narrative will be a myth and the performance a recognisable 'ritual drama'.

This brings one back to the question of the degree to which it is possible to assume that a ritual once lay behind a myth, and that the myth represents a ritual drama. As was mentioned above, in many cases this is impossible. However, the examination of mythological texts like those of the Near East, the *Rig Veda* or the Elder Edda can still be highly revealing, and especially if they are examined first and foremost in the context of their

---

109 Harrison, *Themis*, p.328.
110 Harrison, *Themis*, p.330. Similar ideas are given by Hooke in *Myth and ritual*, p.3.
111 See Durkheim, *Elementary forms*, pp.351–359.
112 Devlin, *Mask and scene*, p.4.
113 On 'sacred time', see the references in note 96 above.
114 See, for example, 'The rising of the Buffalo Men', or 'The black bear song', in Day, *The sky clears*, pp.108–109.
115 See Harrison, *Themis*, pp.328–329.

D. Conclusion

original oral performance. If such a performance of the extant mythological text *demands* dramatic presentation in order for the text to be understood by the audience, then there is certainly good reason to re-examine the relationship of this text to religious ritual on the basis of what has been said above. If the performed text seems to centre upon ritualistic action, and has links with popular tradition and seasonal festival then there is even further reason to believe that the acted performance involves elements, or reflections of the original acted ritual. This will be reinforced still further if direct implications of accompanying physical action appear within the mythical text, similar to those commonly found, for example, in the ritual songs of the North American Indians.[116] It is this practical criterion, rather than any search for a seasonal pattern, that will form the basis for the examination of the Eddic poems and their possible context in this book.

D. Conclusion

When searching for evidence of drama having existed in Scandinavia between 700 and 1300, it is not enough simply to point to the ritual elements in myth and poetry. Nor is it necessary to find full-scale dramatic works or the complete *year drama*. All that needs to be found is evidence of public displays of mimicry or representation having taken place, and as has been indicated above, if such evidence is to be found anywhere, it will be found in the extant material concerning ritual, folk games and other forms of public entertainment; in seasonal dramatic folk traditions that can be reasonably assumed to have roots in earlier ritual; and, most valuable of all, in the form of certain mythological narratives contained in early manuscripts.

During more than the seventy years that have passed since Phillpotts wrote *The Elder Edda and ancient Scandinavian drama*, a large amount of new material has been assembled, especially in the area of archaeology and folkloristics. Similarly, there are several important aspects of the dialogic poems that have not received enough attention, especially the questions of the present structure of the poems, and their extant written form in the *Codex Regius* and AM 748 manuscripts. There is good reason, therefore, for re-opening the question of 'Eddic drama' at the point where Heusler left off, by examining the three questions that Heusler posed with regard to Phillpotts' theory about the form and likely context of the dialogic poems. The examination that follows commences with a review of the archaeological, literary, and folkloristic material that might provide a context for dramatic presentation of the Eddic poems. Essentially, however, it is based

---

[116] See, for example, the 'Black bear song' of the Osage Indians: 'Sacred is *the act* by which my hands *are browned*/ It is *the act* by which I offer my prayer./ Sacred is *the act* by which my hands *are blackened*/ It is *the act* by which I offer my prayer . . .' (My emphases): published in Day, *The sky clears*, p.108.

Introduction

on the evidence of the dialogic poems themselves and the manuscripts that contain them. Emphasis is placed on the demands that these poems would have made on the oral performer, and the way in which the scribes themselves viewed these works in the thirteenth century. To the best of my knowledge, neither of these important aspects of the question has ever been discussed in any detail in the past. The aim here is to present an objective examination of all the relevant material available, free of any previous assumptions about the form and demands of 'seasonal drama' such as those that pervade Phillpotts' work. As the following chapters should demonstrate, the facts speak for themselves without any need for such a theory.

CHAPTER I

Dramatic Activities in Early Medieval Scandinavia
I. The Evidence of Archaeology and Literature

A The Conditions for the Development of Drama

There can be little dispute that compared with elsewhere in Europe, the solid evidence for dramatic activities having taken place in Scandinavia during the late Iron Age and early Middle Ages is very limited. The evidence that *does* exist, however, is sufficent to demonstrate that while 'drama' in the Oxford dictionary sense of the word was almost certainly non-existent in Scandinavia, just as it was throughout most of Europe in c.1000, more elementary dramatic activities definitely *were* taking place.

At least three fundamental elements appear to have made a significant contribution to the development of drama as an established art form in other western countries. According to David Mills, for example, a 'large-scale sense of community' is essential for the existence of drama, which is the 'most socially dependent of art forms'. Mills therefore argues that medieval drama in England derived primarily from the development of village communities and 'the awareness of the community as an economic, social, and "religious" unit'.[1] Another key element, well illustrated by the development of drama in Ancient Greece and in the medieval church, is the role of religious activities, which often provide an outlet for imitative tendencies. Indeed, as has been shown in the previous chapter, many rituals are essentially imitative. Organised religion also adds a sense of occasion, highlights the importance of the event, and provides the elements of mythical storyline, character, costume and spectacular effects. Furthermore, it can encourage the development of a fixed or semi-fixed text designed to accompany dramatic action. The most important features for the development of drama, however, have to be the influence and potential of the individual artistic performer found in all societies. Such figures are capable of inspiring the development of the purely religious performance into the realms of art. Yet solo performers are also active outside the sphere of

---

[1] Mills, 'Drama and folk-ritual', p.122.

organised religion, and when we examine the evolution of drama in the medieval world, it is impossible to ignore the role played by individual professional entertainers such as the *ioculatores*, travelling the roads of Europe with their fixed dramatic 'turns' and properties. Improvised secular performances, such as those presented by the *ioculatores* or local storytellers, always contain within themselves the capacity to develop into regularly performed semi-concrete tales, sketches, or small 'plays', which can then live on independently within the oral tradition.[2]

All of the conditions mentioned above were fulfilled in the society of early medieval Scandinavia, and were probably in existence in most of southern and south-western Scandinavia from a much earlier period. For example, there is little question that a sense of community must have existed from an early point in time: the fact that human dwellings in Scandinavia were often isolated was adequately compensated for by regular seasonal religious and/ or judicial gatherings in each area, and by the strength of the familial society in mainland Scandinavia. Within this society, formal religious activity clearly possessed the propensity to develop into public spectacle and drama, as will be illustrated in the following chapters. Concerning the role of the individual performer, evidence suggests that foreign professional entertainers like the *ioculatores*, known for their dramatic skills, may have been traversing Scandinavia as far back as the ninth century (see the *Appendix*). Yet Scandinavia can hardly have been a vacuum in dramatic terms before that time. It also had its own native performers in the shape of poets and storytellers, and some of these, like their equivalents in more recent times, must have presented their poems and tales in a semi-dramatic style that was easily capable of developing into a wholly dramatic one-man performance.[3]

B. Ritual 'Leikar' and Drama

1. The Concept of 'Leikr' in Early Scandinavia

In general terms, the conditions in Scandinavia prior to the time that the Eddic poems were recorded in the early thirteenth century were hardly adverse to the development of drama as a 'genre'. Yet the fact remains that Icelandic and Norwegian manuscripts of the twelfth and thirteenth centuries never make any mention of staged 'drama' taking place. Amongst other things, this lack of evidence raises the questions of terminology and

---

[2] Similar conditions are mentioned in Berthold, *A history of world theatre*, p.3, i.e. the need for 'creative forces', and the necessity of 'urbane self-assertion on the part of the individual' and a 'metaphysical superstructure'.

[3] Several Norwegian and Swedish story-tellers from the last two centuries gained reputations for the skills of mimicry or imitation they exhibited when telling stories. See, for example, Bø, Grambo et al., *Norske segner*, p.43 and pp.46–47; Hodne, *Jørgen Moe*, p.117; and, in particular, the work and description of the gypsy storyteller, Johan Dimitri-Taikon, presented in Tillhagen, *Taikon berättar*; see especially pp.11–18.

B. Ritual 'Leikar' and Drama

1. The concept of 'leikr' in early Scandinavia

conceptual classification. Europe during the period in question lacked any agreed term to describe the dramatic act as an independent genre. This is largely because drama at that time seems not to have been regarded as a separate art form, but rather as one aspect of other activities. In medieval records in Europe, therefore, dramatic performance is not referred to as 'drama', but instead tends to come under the all-embracing heading of 'games', or simply 'play'.

As Glynne Wickham sums up the situation:

> If we are to approach the drama of the Middle Ages intelligently . . . we must first dismiss all our contemporary notions of what a theatre should be, and how a play should be written, and then go on to substitute the idea of community games in which the actors are the contestants (mimetic or athletic or both) and the theatre is any place appropriate and convenient both to them as performers and to the rest of the community as spectators. If the contemporary catch phrase 'total theatre' has any meaning, it finds a truer expression in medieval than in modern terms of reference; for song, dance, wrestling, sword play, contests between animals, disguise, spectacle, jokes, disputation and ritual all figure, separately or compounded, in the drama of the Middle Ages, which was devised in celebration of leisure and for a local community.[4]

Wickham probably stretches the argument a little too far. Nonetheless, if drama was to be found anywhere in early medieval Europe (outside the formal environments of the court, church and monastery[5]), it was amidst the ceremonies, seasonal fairs, public gatherings and folk traditions of the common people, many of which were built around the essential remnants of older folk rituals and provided a venue for all forms of public entertainment.[6]

Elsewhere in Europe, the recreative activities mentioned above were all classed simply as 'games' or *ludi*, drama included. This is testified to by the various applications of words like *play*, *jeu* and *Spiel* which were used to classify all of these activities in the Middle Ages and continue to be used in this sense even in our own time.[7] In Scandinavia, the equivalent terms for 'play' from a very early period, were the words *leikr* and *íþróttir*. As will be shown below, these words had an equally broad meaning to those mentioned above.[8] The first word, however, is of particular interest, not only

---

[4] Wickham, *The medieval theatre*, p.4. Similar comments are made about religious and folk drama by Abrahams, in 'Folk drama', p.355.
[5] Dramatic readings of texts were possibly taking place in monasteries and at courts from the tenth century onwards. In the same period, drama was beginning to develop as part of the monastic liturgy. See Dronke, *Women writers*, pp.57–59, and Tydeman, *The theatre in the Middle Ages*, p.35.
[6] See also Abrahams, 'Folk drama', p.357; Mills, 'Drama and folk ritual', passim (on the development from ritual to folk tradition and drama); and the detailed information provided in Baskerville, 'Dramatic aspects of medieval folk festivals', 19–87.
[7] See Huizinga, *Homo ludens*, pp.28–45.
[8] The word *íþróttir* is used almost interchangably with *leikr* in *Gylfaginning*, in *Edda* (1926), p.49, and *Þiðriks saga af Bern*, I, p.266. If there was any difference in meaning

1. The concept of 'leikr' in early Scandinavia

because of its existence in certain intriguing words and expressions found in the sagas and early poetry, like 'leikgoði' ('play-priest') and 'Freys leikr' (Frey's 'play' or 'game'),[9] but also because of its appearance in early Scandinavian placenames like Leikvangr and Leikvöllr (both meaning 'play field'). On the basis of the European evidence, if dramatic activities existed at all, they would also be expected to come under the heading of *leikar*. Yet what exactly *was* the Scandinavian concept of *leikr* in the early Middle Ages (and before)? What evidence exists to suggest that this word might have been applied for dramatic activities like its counterparts in other languages?

In the Gothic translation of the Greek version of the Bible, *laikan* is used as a translation for 'to leap with joy' or 'exult', and *laiks* is used for 'dance'.[10] Similarly, in Old Norse, *leikr* is used to translate the Latin words *ludens* and *jocum*, both of which were commonly applied to 'play' activities: In *Stjórn* (thirteenth – fourteenth century), for example, 'Et visus est eis quasi ludens loqui' (*Vulgata, Genesis* 19,14) is translated as 'Enn þeir hugdu. at hann taladi medr leik ok skalkeið' ('It seemed to them he spoke in jest and mockery'). 'Forte joco dictum est' (from Petrus Comestor's *Historia scholastica*, ch.45) is translated as 'hann taladi þetta med leik ok kallzi' (lit. 'he said this playfully and jokingly').[11]

Of particular interest, however, is that fact that the word *leikr* also was clearly seen as having certain religious connotations even in the Middle Ages. Certainly, in extant literature from the twelfth to the fourteenth centuries, *leikr* is predominantly applied to forms of 'skemmtun' ('entertainment'), and used for the whole range of sports from sword play and combat[12] to ball games like *knattleikr* and *torfleikr*;[13]

---

between the two words, *íþróttir* might be said to apply to the physical or mental activity in itself, while the *leikr* is the demonstration of these abilities in public performance. For examples displaying the range of the use of the word *íþróttir*, see also *Morkinskinna*, p.15; *Orkneyinga saga*, p.130; *Króka-Refs saga*, p.127; *Göngu-Hrólfs saga*, p.387; *Rauðúlfs þáttr* in *Flateyjarbok* (1860–1868), II, pp.294–296; *Jóns saga helga hin elzta* in *Biskupa sögur* (1858–1878), I, p.155 and p.163; *Nitida saga* (AM 226 8to), quoted in Ólafur Davíðsson, *Íslenzkar gátur*, II, p.37; *Alexanders saga*, p.3; and most interesting of all, *Ynglinga saga*, p.17 and p.19, where the word is applied to ritualistic activities.

[9] See below in this section, and *sections B.2 and D.2*.
[10] *Die Gotische Bibel*, p.89 (Luke 1,41; 1,44); p.111 (Luke 6,23); and p.143 (Luke 15,25: 'laiks').
[11] See *Stjórn*, p.122 and p.218; *Bibliorum Sacrorum*; p.13; and Petrus Comestor, *Historia scholastica*, p.1132.
[12] As in kennings for battle such as 'hildileikr' or 'Hildar leikr': See *Fafnismál*, st.31, and *Bjarkamál*, st.3 in *Eddica minora*, p.31. For examples of *leikr* or *leika* being used alone in the sense of battle or fighting, see, for example, *Fóstbræðra saga*, p.149; *Gunnlaugs saga*, p.54; and *Grettis saga*, p.231. Also worth noting is the direct application of the word *leikr* to a tournament in *Sögubrot af fornkonungum*, p.117. See also *Tristrams saga og Ísoddar*, p.93.
[13] See, for example, *Egils saga*, pp.98–100; *Eyrbyggja saga*, pp.112–113 (*torfleikr*) and pp.115–117; and *Gísla saga*, pp.49–50 and pp.57–59. *Knattleikr* seems to have been a form of hockey. *Torfleikr* was probably similar but apparently also involved the throwing of lumps of turf.

B. Ritual 'Leikar' and Drama

1. The concept of 'leikr' in early Scandinavia

swimming;[14] various acrobatic tricks like the juggling of knives;[15] and other displays like those performed in water by Örvar-Oddr in *Örvar-Odds saga*.[16] *Leikr*, however, is not limited to physical activity. It is also used for board games like chess,[17] as well as for music;[18] children's games;[19] dalliance;[20] and even magical tricks.[21]

Nonetheless, there are strong suggestions that the word must originally have had an even wider meaning extending beyond mere leisure activities. In *Fóstbrœðra saga*, *leikr* is used to describe the ritual of 'brotherhood' undertaken by Þorgeirr Hávarsson and Þórmóðr Bersason: 'This ritual (*leikr*) was as follows: three strips of turf should be cut loose from the ground. The ends of the turf should remain attached to the earth, but the loops should be raised so that men could walk beneath them. They carried out this *leikr* . . .'[22] A similar reference in found in *Laxdœla saga* where *leikr* is applied to an act of witchcraft (*seiðr*) that had a number of dramatic overtones including singing, action, a raised platform, and often some form of costume: 'Kári could hardly sleep because the ritual (*leikr*) was directed against him.'[23] In a later manuscript of the saga, the word

---

[14] See, for example, *Rígsþula*, st.41. For the use of *leikr* for wrestling competitions in water, see, for example, *Laxdœla saga*, p.117.

[15] I.e. Ólafur Tryggvason's *handsaxaleikr* in *Heimskringla*, I, p.333. Note also the reference to the man met by King Gylfi when entering Valhöll, who 'played with knives, and had seven in the air at one time' ('lék at handsǫxum ok hafði vii. senn á lopti'), in *Gylfaginning: Edda* (1926), p.9. The nature of the other indoor 'leikar' mentioned in *Edda*, p.10, is totally open to discussion.

[16] *Örvar-Odds saga*, p.369.

[17] See *Rígsþula*, st.41. In *Hálfdanar saga Eysteinssonar*, pp.293–294, *tafl* is listed alongside other sports like *knattleikr* and archery, all of which come under the heading of *leikar*. See also *Örvar-Odds saga* (1888), p.6.

[18] See, for example, the use of the word 'strengleikar' in the description of musical entertainment in *Víglundar saga*, pp.66–67. Other examples of the verb *leika* being used for the playing of instruments are found, for instance, in *Rémundar saga*, p.16 and p.340.

[19] See *Heimskringla*, II, p.108, and *Laxdœla saga*, p.231. See also notes 30 and 31 below.

[20] *Brot úr miðsögu Guðmundar biskups Arasonar*, in *Biskupa sögur* (1858–1878), I, p.605: '. . . þau vóru vön til slíkra leika' ('. . . they were used to such amorous games'). See also *Ljósvetninga saga*, p.64: 'Veisusynir . . . sóttu þangat leika.' The meaning of the word *leikar* here would appear to be slightly ambiguous. Andersson and Miller's recent translation of the saga in *Law and literature* retains this ambiguity by simply stating that the foster brothers in question here participated in 'games' (p.204).

[21] See *Þorsteins þáttr bœjarmagns*, pp.412–413.

[22] 'Sá leikr var á þá lund, at rísta skyldi þrjár torfur ór jǫrðu langar; þeira endar skyldu allir fastir í jǫrðu ok heimta upp lykkjurnar, svá at menn mætti ganga undir. Þann leik fromdu þeir . . .': *Fóstbrœðra saga*, p.125.

[23] 'Kári sofnaði nær ekki, því at til hans var leikr gǫrr': *Laxdœla saga*, p.106. The various forms of magic and divination, including *seiðr*, that Óðinn is reported to have practised and taught mankind are also classed as 'íþróttir' in *Ynglinga saga*, p.17 and p.19. Runeworking is placed under the same heading in *Orkneyinga saga*, p.130. (See note 8 above on *íþróttir* and its similarity to *leikr*.) On the relationship between *seiðr* and shamanistic activities elsewhere, see Strömbäck, *Sejd*, passim. Concerning the close links between shamanistic ritual and dramatic performance, see especially Kirby, *Ur-drama*, pp.1–32. Regarding the Scandinavian accounts of *seiðr*, see further Chapter V, D.1 below.

1. The concept of 'leikr' in early Scandinavia

'leikr' is directly substituted with 'seiðrinn', suggesting that the two words, in at least one sense, were regarded as being almost synonymous.[24]

This particular use of the word *leikr* has encouraged many scholars to believe that the expression 'Freys leikr', found in Þorbjörn hornklofi's poem *Haraldskvæði*, st.3 (c.900?), must have referred originally to some form of Yuletide ritual dedicated to the god, Freyr:

He wants to drink (to?) *jól* (Yule) outside –	Uti vill jól drekka,
if he can decide alone,	ef skal einn ráða,
the fame-seeking ruler –	fylkir enn framlyndi,
and to perform Frey's *leikr*;	ok Freys leik heyja;
the young man was tired of the fireside	ungr leiddisk eldvelli
and sitting indoors,	ok inni (at) sitja,
(in) the warm women's room	varma dyngju
or (on) down filled cushions.	eða vǫttu dúns fulla.[25]

Admittedly, in a later verse attributed to Björn jarnsiða in *Ragnars saga loðbrókar*, the same expression reappears as an obvious kenning for battle. However, as several scholars have pointed out, this particular application is probably based on a misunderstanding, since Freyr's role appears to have been related consistently to fertility rather than war.[26]

The possibility that leikr could be applied not only to ritual, but also to dramatic activities is strengthened by the use of the term *paðreimsleikr* to cover the whole range of spectacular activities (including drama) that were presented in the Hippodrome in Constantinople when Sigurðr Jórsalafari visited that city in the early twelfth century.[27] Also interesting is the

---

[24] See *Laxdæla saga* (1889–1891), p.131.
[25] See *Heimskringla*, I, p.112, and *Fagrskinna*, p.61. See Grundtvig, *Nordens mythologi*, p.430; Olsen, 'Hild Rolvsdatters vise', 29–30; Celander, *Förkristen jul*, p.11; Briem, *Heiðinn siður*, p.179; Árni Björnsson, *Jól*, p.36; Kuhn, 'Philologisches', pp.277–279; and Bjarni Aðalbjarnarson, in *Heimskringla*, I, p.112, note.
[26] See *Ragnars saga loðbrókar*, p.136: 'Þat var fyrst, er fórum,/ Freys leika tókk heyja,/ þars andvíga áttum/ öld, í Rómaveldi' ('The first thing that happened when we travelled,/ 'Frey's *leikar*' were performed/ where we met opposition/ in the Roman Empire'). While there are several different interpretations of some of these lines, scholars are agreed that 'Frey's *leikar*' here must mean 'battle'. From the context provided for Þorbjörn hornklofi's verse in *Heimskringla*, it would appear that Snorri Sturluson suffered from the same supposed misunderstanding.
[27] See *Fagrskinna*, pp.319–320, and *Morkinskinna*, p.164, where the account is more complete. A word that appears to be 'paþreimr' is given as a direct translation of the Latin word *Jpodromum* (class. *hippodromus* and *hypodromus*) in MS Gl.kgl.saml. 1812: see Scardigli and Raschellà, 'A Latin-Icelandic glossary', p.304. As Davidson points out in *The Viking road*, p.197, the Hippodrome was 'used not only for chariot races but also for animal shows, fights, games and boxing, fireworks and various acrobatic and musical entertainments,' including performances by mimes and clowns. All these activities are reflected in the wall and ceiling frescos in the Cathedral of Hagia Sophia in Kiev: see further below, *section C.7*. Regarding the dramatic activities going on in Constantinople

B. Ritual 'Leikar' and Drama

1. The concept of 'leikr' in early Scandinavia

application of the word *leikari* as a translation of the Latin words *histriones* and *mimus*, both of which were commonly used for performers known to include dramatic skills among their many talents.²⁸ The same understanding of the word is found in *Þiðriks saga af Bern* where the verb *leika* is applied to the idea of both dance and *performance*.²⁹

As might be expected, *leikr* is also used in connection with children's games of make-believe. Bishop Guðmundr Arason, for example, is said to have always played the bishop in his costumed *barnaleikar* ('children's games') with Ögmundr Þorvarðson.³⁰ A similar reference is found in *Njáls saga*, where Höskuldr Dalla-Kollsson and Hrútr Herjólfsson observe two boys playing ('léku') with a young girl in the roles of Mörðr gígja, his daughter Unnr, and Hrútr himself.³¹ In both of these references, the words *leikr* and *leika* are probably used in their modern senses of 'games' and 'play'. The references, however, emphasise that Scandinavian children like children everywhere else must have also indulged in role-playing games during the Middle Ages. Such activities obviously also came under the heading of *leikr*. Did the interest in such activities abruptly come to a halt in Scandinavia with the onset of adulthood?

Considering the above, there is little doubt that the public 'háð' ('mockery') described in *Gunnlaugs saga* must have also involved role-play, and that it would have been considered a *leikr*. The performance in question, which Gunnlaugr ormstunga observes somewhere outside Trondheim in Norway, takes place in a field or marked-out area ('á vǫllum'), in the centre of a ring of people ('mannhringr'), and involves the combat of two men who are apparently pretending to be Gunnlaugr himself and his

---

before and after this time, see Nicoll, *Masks*, p.148 and pp.209–212; and La Piana, 'The Byzantine theatre', 171–211.

²⁸ See for example, *Thomassaga erkibiskops*, p.76, where 'loddara ok læikara' is used to translate 'histrionum' in William Fitzstephen's *Vitæ Sancti Thomæ*. See also *Rómverjasögur*, p.53 (Palæstra, LXXXVIII), where 'lækari' is a translation of 'histrionem' in Sallust, *Bella Iugurthinum* (LXXXV, 39), pp.318–319. For further references concerning the dramatic skills of the *mimi*, see the Appendix.

²⁹ *Þiðriks saga af Bern*, I, pp.264–266, on the performance of the *leikari* Ísungr's pretend bear at the court of king Osantrix: 'His bear *leikr/* performs and leaps about . . .' ('Þa leicr hans biorn oc hoppar þar eptir . . .'). The king asks, 'Is there anything else he can perform (*leika*) other than what you have told us about and we have witnessed?' ('Kann hann noccot at leika fleira en nv er sagt oc ver havum sett').

³⁰ *Guðmundar saga góða*, in *Sturlunga saga* (1878), I, p.94: '. . . áttu þeir Guðmundr ok Ögmundr barnleika saman, ok mörg önnur ungmenni með þeim. En til ins sama kom jafnan um atferli þeirra ok leika at nest-lokum, hvat sem fyrst var upp [tekit], at Guðmundi var gört mítr ok bagall ok messu-föt, kirkja ok altari; ok skyldi hann vera biskup í leiknum; en Ögmundi öx ok skjöldr ok vápn; ok skyldi hann vera hermaðr' ('. . . Guðmundr and Ögmundr played games together with many other young people. All of their games, however, tended to end in the same way: Guðmundr was equipped with a mitre, cope and crosier, since he was supposed to be the bishop in the game, while Ögmundr had an axe, shield and other weapons. He was supposed to be the warrior'). See also *Guðmundar saga biskups*, in *Guðmundar sögur biskups*, p.35.

³¹ *Brennu-Njáls saga*, pp.28–29.

adversary, Hrafn Önundarson.³² The dramatic features of this game are obvious.

The concept of *leikr* therefore had a wide framework of meaning, and should always be considered in the broad sense suggested by Huizinga in *Homo ludens* (see *Introduction, section C*). When it is encountered as an element in placenames like Leikvangr; an unexplained name like that of Þórólfr leikgoði;³³ an expression like 'Freys leikr' associated with Christmas;³⁴ or even the mention of the renowned 'danzleikar' at the Reykhólar wedding described in *Þorgils saga ok Hafliða*,³⁵ the range of possible interpretations is enormous. Even though the emphasis in the examples given above has clearly been on the sporting elements of 'play', connections with dramatic games, or other more ritualistic activities like those described in *Fóstbræðra saga* and *Laxdæla saga* can by no means be ruled out. Indeed, there is a strong suggestion that *all* forms of games might have originally had some general relationship to religious activity.

2. The Evidence of Placenames

As Alexander Bugge has shown, Norwegian placenames taking the form of *Leikvin, Leikvangr*, and *Leikvöllr* (found behind modern placenames such as Løken, Leikanger and Lekvoll) often occur in centralised positions in settlements, in close proximity to churches, older pagan places of worship and *þing* sites.³⁶ Some scholars have attempted to argue that names of this kind are related to fish or bird breeding grounds.³⁷ However, it seems clear that the words *leikvangr* and *leikvöllr* were both understood as meaning 'games site' or 'games field' in the early Middle Ages,³⁸ and such an interpretation cannot have been new. Many of these placenames are extremely old and their positioning points to the fact that large-scale

---

³² See *Gunnlaugs saga*, pp.99–100. See also further below, *section D,1*.
³³ See *section D.2* below.
³⁴ See references given in note 25 above.
³⁵ See *Sturlunga saga* (1878), I, p.19. The actual form of these dances and the other 'margs-konar leikar' has to remain unclear. For further references to dance 'games' at this time, and discussion of the possible content of such games, see Jón Samsonarson, *Kvæði*, I, pp.ix–xxvi.
³⁶ Regarding these placenames, their dating, later variants, and proximity to religious sites, see Rygh, *Norske gaardnavne*, especially Rygh's *Forord og inledning* to this work, pp.64–65. See also Olsen, *Hedenske kultminder*, p.217; Bugge, 'Tingsteder', 195–212, and most recently, Holm, *De nordiska anger-namnen*, pp.539–545, and pp.725–726.
³⁷ See, for example, Sahlgren, 'Hednisk gudalära', 10–12, and most recently, Bergfors, 'Sockennamnet Leksand', 93–99.
³⁸ In other words, places where tournaments, wrestling competitions, horsefights or *knattleikr* matches are held. See *Bærings saga*, p.96; *Tristrams saga og Ísoddar*, p.90 and p.92; *Þorsteins saga Víkingssonar*, pp.203–204; *Göngu-Hrólfs saga*, p.379; and *Gunnars saga keldugnúpsfífls*, pp.366–367. As Holm points out in *De nordiska anger-namnen*, p.726, a man named 'Thyrikr af Leikvangum' from Sogn in Norway is called 'Terrius de Campis Ludi' in a Latin letter from 1289, and 'Terri des Champs de Jeu' in a later letter in French.

B. Ritual 'Leikar' and Drama

organised 'games' gatherings must have played a central role in social life from a very early period.³⁹ Indeed, fixed sites were still being used for 'games' gatherings during the Viking period, as is revealed by the existence of similar placenames in both Iceland (Leikskáli, Leikskálar, Leikskálavellir, Leikskálaholt and Leikvellir⁴⁰) and Shetland (Levna [*Leikvin*] Meadow⁴¹).

2. The evidence of placenames

As mentioned above, the mainland Scandinavian 'games' sites tend to be found close to centres of pagan worship and later church sites, which suggests that the 'games' in question had both social and cult significance.⁴² Indeed, as several scholars have pointed out, many of the 'games' sites are also found in close proximity to other placenames which originally might have designated as horse-racing courses (*skeið*).⁴³ Of all sports, it seems that both horse-racing and horse-fighting must have had particular significance within the pagan religion of Scandinavia.⁴⁴

---

³⁹ See Bugge, 'Tingsteder', 201–207. Bugge echoes Rygh and Olsen (see note 36 above) in seeing Leikvin as the oldest name (possibly dating back as far as 500 B.C.). This seems to have been replaced first by the name Leikvangr in prehistoric times, and then by Leikvöllr during the final years of pagan religion.

⁴⁰ According to an account in *Eyrbyggja saga*, pp.115–117, Leikskálavellir in Breiðavík seems to have been related to a temporary building in which people could stay during games meetings. See also *Hrafnkels saga*, p.100; *Eiríks saga rauða*, p.198 and p.405; *Landnámabók*, p.130; and Björn Bjarnason, *Íþróttir fornmanna*, p.63.

⁴¹ This site was apparently used for games of football in earlier times. Another Shetland placename possibly related to horse-racing is Ske (*Skeið*): see Jakobsen, 'Shetlandsøernes stedsnavne', 147 and 167.

⁴² Nonetheless, it is important to bear in mind Sahlgren's warning against overhastiness in drawing conclusions from placenames, and especially with regard to what he calls the 'kilometermetoden' (i.e. the relating of placenames that occur within a limited radius): see Sahlgren, 'Hednisk gudalära', 2–22. Similarly, one cannot trust that the cultic placename elements *vin* and *vangr* necessarily mean that the *leikvin* and *leikvangar* themselves had a cult significance, or that early Christian churches were always placed on pagan sites as seems to have occurred in Mære in Norway. See Olsen, *Hedenske kultminder*, p.130, note 1; O. Olsen, *Hørg, hov og kirke*, pp.236–275; Lidén, 'From pagan sanctuary', 3–32; and O. Olsen, 'Comments', 25–27.

⁴³ See Wessén, 'Hästskede och lekslätt'; and Solheim, *Horse-fight*, pp.161–162. Examples given by Solheim include Skeiðflóti and Leikvodden in Setesdal where horsefighting and horse races used to take place, and Leikskálar and Skeiðsbrekkur in Haukadalur, mentioned in *Eiríks saga rauða*, p.198 and p.405, and *Landnámabók*, p.130: Solheim, *Horse-fight*, pp.76–77 and pp.163–173. Considering the cultic importance of the horse Freyfaxi in *Hrafnkels saga*, it is possible that similar associations at one time lay behind the Leikskálar in Hrafnkelsdalur where Sámr Bjarnason is supposed to have lived: see *Hrafnkels saga*, p.100. However, as Sahlgren points out in 'Hednisk gudalära', 2–22, many *skeið* placenames would seem to be related to roads, paths or boundaries rather than to horse racing.

⁴⁴ See further the references in notes 56, 70, and 71 below.

3. 'Leikar' and Ritual

As Elias Wessén has emphasised, in primitive societies it is extremely difficult to draw a clear line between 'games' and ritual.[45] This would seem to be supported by the literary evidence concerning play activities in Scandinavia during the pagan and early medieval period which suggests that the various *leikar* in Scandinavia were often closely connected to religious festivals and ritual activities. For example, accounts of the large pagan festival in Uppsala mention apparently mimetic dances that were performed by worshippers, and 'sveinaleikar' ('boys' games') played by children.[46] The latter activity is directly paralleled by the picture depicting ball players sitting amidst figures obviously engaged in semi-dramatic ritual activities on one of the now lost Gallehus horns (c.400).[47]

Games, then, seem to have taken place at religious festivals. Yet, as has been suggested above, the *leikr* itself could also become a form of ritual activity. In this context, it is interesting to note the highly ritualistic atmosphere surrounding the *hólmganga* (duel) described in both *Egils saga* and *Kormáks saga*. *Kormáks saga* even provides some precise details about the so-called 'duelling law' ('hólmgöngulög') which contained specifications about the 'ring' in which the duel was to be fought. According to the law in question, the area had to be sanctified prior to the combat by the use of a sacrificial ritual known as the 'tjösnublót'.[48] Evidence also suggests that traditionally the victor of the contest was expected to sacrifice a bull, or *blótnaut*, immediately after the contest.[49] Interestingly enough, the *hólmganga* was one of the first traditions to be banned after the acceptance of Christianity in Iceland.[50] There is good reason to wonder whether this ban was set merely on the basis of humanitarian concern.

It might be noted that the postulated close connection between games, ritual and religious belief was not limited to Scandinavia. The same phenomenon commonly occurs in other cultures, and is typified in the *paðreimsleikr* performed in Constantinople (see *section B.1* above). According to *Morkinskinna*, these games were regarded as having prophetic value since a 'games' victory for the Emperor apparently presaged victory for him in warfare.[51] Even closer relationships between games and

---

[45] Wessén, 'Hästskede', 120.

[46] See *Ynglinga saga*, p.63. The 'sveinaleikr' appears to be a form of ball game, like *knattleikr*, but played by children. See also *Egils saga*, p.100, and *Flóamanna saga*, p.250. Regarding Saxo's description of the mimes' 'effeminate' dance at Uppsala, see below, *section C.8* and the *Appendix*.

[47] See *section C.4* below; *figs 28–29*; and, for the ball players, the photographs of modern reproductions of the horns in Davidson, *Scandinavian mythology*, p.78.

[48] See *Kormáks saga*, pp.237–238. Regarding this particular ritual, the nature of which is far from certain, see Olsen, 'Tjösnur', 342–346.

[49] See *Kormáks saga*, p.290, and *Egils saga*, pp.209–210.

[50] See *Gunnlaugs saga*, pp.95–96. Indeed, almost all of the games mentioned above came to be banned by the church in Iceland in later times. The actual reason in each case, however, has to remain uncertain. See Ólafur Davíðsson, *Íslenzkar gátur*, II, pp.11–17.

[51] See *Morkinskinna*, p.164.

B. Ritual 'Leikar' and Drama

seasonal religious festivals are demonstrated by the enormous 'ball play' games of the Aztecs, Incas, and the Indians of the North American Plains.[52] Such games, of course, find loose parallels closer to home in the Shrovetide and Christmas ball games played in many central and northern areas of the British Isles.[53] Of particular interest are the traditional games of football and tug-of-war that used to take place at Christmas and on New Year's Day in Orkney and Shetland. Both places, of course, had deep-rooted associations with Scandinavian culture.[54]

3. 'Leikar' and ritual

In Scandinavia, 'play' activities and sports seem to have often been linked to religious holidays or natural feast days from an early period. In more recent years, for example, it is noticeable that the majority of Scandinavian costumed traditions, like those of the *julebukk*, *Halm-Staffan*, and the *stjärngossar*, are restricted to the Christmas period.[55] This connection is not new. Olaus Magnus (1555) mentions an early Swedish tradition involving horse-races on ice which were supposed to have taken place in Öster- and Västergötland on the second day of Christmas.[56] Olaus' account may be slightly untrustworthy, but the tradition he describes has obvious parallels in certain customs known in Scandinavia in more recent times, such as the *Staffans reid* ('Staffan's ride') or *annandagsskeid* ('Second day ride').[57]

On several occasions, the sagas mention large-scale day-long *leikmót*, or 'games meetings',[58] and it appears that many of these gatherings were also

---

[52] Concerning the Aztecs and Incas, amongst whom the relationship between sports, dramatic activities, music, dance and ritual would seem to have been particularly evident, see von Hagen, *The ancient sun kings*, p.61, and p.263. Descriptions of the ball games of the Plains Indians are given in McCracken, *George Caitlin*, pp.139–142, and Hocart, *The progress of man*, pp.241–242. See also Hocart, p.292, for another example from Ceylon.

[53] See Hole, *A dictionary of British folk customs*, pp.272–275, and pp.139–143. Concerning the possible ritual origin of these games, see Bord, *Earth rites*, pp.222–223; Eliade, *Patterns*, p.320; and Hole, *A dictionary of British folk customs*, pp.142–143.

[54] See, for example, Hole, *A dictionary of British folk customs*, pp.272–273; Saxby, *Shetland traditional lore*, p.84; and Marwick, *The folklore of Orkney*, pp.103–104, p.120, and pp.126–127.

[55] See *Chapter II, B.1* below.

[56] Olaus Magnus, *Historia de gentibus septentrionalibus* (Book I, ch.24), pp.40–41; translated into Swedish in *Historia om de nordiska folken*, I, p.54. See also Strömbäck, 'St Stephen', 133–147, where reservations are expressed about the authenticity of this account and its application to genuine pagan practice.

[57] See further Lid, *Jolesveinar*, pp.9–42, and pp.126–129; Wessén, 'Hästskede', 107–109; and Celander, *Nordisk jul*, pp.262–268. Concerning the connection between the Christmas races and semi-dramatic Scandinavian folk customs, see further *Chapter II, B.2* below.

[58] See *Laxdæla saga*, p.136; *Egils saga*, pp.98–100; *Eyrbyggja saga*, p.115; and *Kjalnesinga saga*, pp.16–22. Interestingly enough, in the last example, the games, which are also classified as 'gleði' ('entertainments'; p.16), seem to take place indoors. Kolfiðr Þorgerðarson, for example, appears to watch them from a loose chair 'on the floor' ('á golfinu') in front of the bench ('pallr') where Búi Andríðsson and others are sitting (p.18). That the bench in question is indoors is emphasised by a later comment that on another visit to these 'games', 'Kolfiðr went back to *the house*, and over to the bench where Búi sat' ('Kolfiðr sneri *til stofu* ok gekk at pallinum, þar sem Búi sat . . .'): *Kjalnesinga saga*, p.22.

3. *'Leikar'* and *ritual*

closely associated with pagan festivals such as that of the *vetrnætur*, or 'winter nights', which were celebrated in the middle of October.[59] *Eyrbyggja saga*, for example, states directly that 'the Breiðvík men had an autumn tradition of playing *knattleikr* at Leikskálavellir 'at the time of the *vetrnætur*'.[60] Similarly, the 'many kinds of entertainment and games' ('margs konar skemmtan ok leika') said to have been held by Vigfúss hersi at Vǫrs (Voss) in Norway in *Víga-Glúms saga* might well have been associated with the 'feast' ('veizla') mentioned shortly afterwards which is clearly linked to the *vetrnætur* and the *dísablót* ('sacrifice to the *dísir*').[61] Furthermore, in *Gísla saga Súrssonar*, Þorgrímr Freysgoði is said to have planned 'to hold an autumn gathering at the time of the *vetrnætur* to celebrate the coming of winter and sacrifice to Freyr',[62] and it can be assumed that the *knattleikr* games described in the saga must take place at around the same time.[63] The general implication seems to be that at one time a tradition existed of 'games' being performed as part of the *vetrnætur* festival which was dedicated in some parts to the fertility god, Freyr.[64] Indeed, the link with Freyr is supported by the fact that weddings are often recorded as taking place at this time of the year.[65]

Another pagan festival also possibly associated in places with Freyr was that of the winter solstice,[66] and once again, it is noteworthy that on several occasions 'games' gatherings are specified as having taken place during *jól*, the Yuletide period. Good examples are the outdoor games played by Haraldr hárfagri's men in Gudbrandsdal as part of the king's 'jóla-veizla' in *Hauks þáttr hábrókar*; the two days of games held at Ásbjarnarnes for Kjartan Ólafsson in *Laxdæla saga*; the *glíma* (wrestling) competition in *Króka-Refs saga*; the *knattleikr* in *Hálfdanar saga Eysteinssonar*; and the *glíma* and tug-of-war competitions in *Hjálmþés saga ok Ölvís*.[67]

---

[59] Regarding the evidence concerning the festivals and sacrifices held during the *vetrnætur* (at the start of winter) and at the winter solstice, see, for example, Briem, *Heiðinn siður*, pp.176–179; Jón Hnefill Aðalsteinsson, 'Blót and þing', 27; and Ström, *Nordisk hedendom*, p.91.

[60] *Eyrbyggja saga*, p.115: 'Þat var siðr Breiðvíkinga um haustum, at þeir hǫfðu knattleika um vetrnáttaskeið.'

[61] *Víga-Glúms saga*, pp.16–17. The *dísablót* in western Scandinavia was usually celebrated at the time of the *vetrnætur*, at the start of winter. The *dísir* were female fertility spirits often seen as guardians of the family and farmstead. See, for example, Ström, *Nordisk hedendom*, pp.192–195.

[62] '. . . at hafa haustboð at vetrnóttum ok fagna vetri ok blóta Frey': *Gísla saga*, p.50.

[63] See *Gísla saga*, pp.49–50 and pp.57–61. Note also that the site of the games seems to be in close proximity to the grave mound of Þorgrímr Freysgoði, which, it can be assumed, must have been a holy site, or placed near one.

[64] Both *Gísla saga* and *Víga-Glúms saga* display particular interest in the worship of Freyr.

[65] See, for example, *Vatnsdæla saga*, p.86 and p.116.

[66] Ström, *Nordisk hedendom*, pp.89–91.

[67] See *Hauks þáttr hábrókar*, in Flateyjarbok (1860–1868), I, p.579; *Laxdæla saga*, p.136; *Króka-Refs saga*, p.129; *Hálfdanar saga Eysteinssonar*, p.294; and *Hjálmþés saga ok Ölvís*, pp.266–272. See also the information given above regarding Christmas sports in Orkney and Shetland (note 54).

B. Ritual 'Leikar' and Drama

However, none of the games in these examples is ever placed in direct relation to any religious activity, and, as with the games activities performed at harvest time and at *þing* meetings (see below), it must be remembered that any gathering of people would have been an occasion for sports. Furthermore, the tendency seems to have been to play *knattleikr* on ice, and thus, whatever the context, it would have been a sport confined to winter. Nonetheless, the information provided above gives further reason for believing that the 'Freys leikr' associated with *jól* should be seen in terms of games or religious ritual rather than warfare.

3. 'Leikar' and ritual

As mentioned above, *jól* and the *vetrnætur* were not the only periods set aside for 'games' gatherings. The same possibly applied to the original autumn harvest celebrations. The Norwegian folklorist, Svale Solheim, believed that the remnants of these seasonal celebrations could be detected in certain Norwegian festival traditions still current in the nineteenth century, and in the less recent activities associated with the autumn *þing* or *leið* (local judicial meetings) and *hestaþing* ('horse gatherings') in Iceland.[68] This is a complicated question. It seems probable, however, that the communal gatherings centred around the autumn horse-races, horse-fights, and *hestaþing* in Iceland were seen in later years as having implicit pagan connotations. This is implied, for example, in Bishop Oddur Einarsson's prohibition in Iceland (1592) against priests attending 'horse-fights, vigils, gatherings of common people and shepherds, and *other* relics of pagan ceremony'.[69] The strong superstition surrounding horse-fights is demonstrated still further by an old Telemark belief that if horses fought well in a horse-fight, the year would be prosperous. Other Telemark superstitions included specific instructions for the burial of any horse that died in such a combat, namely that the horse should not be moved, but instead be buried at the spot where it died, accompanied by its harness, bit and saddle, since none of these could ever be used on another animal.[70] Such superstitions provide interesting parallels to the earlier mentioned belief concerning the *paðreimsleikr*, and Olaus Magnus' comment that in the early Swedish horse-races, the horses that won were often sacrificed to the gods.[71] It

---

[68] See Solheim, *Horse-fight*, passim. For references to the *hestaþing* and *hestavíg*, see *Víga-Glúms saga*, p.43 and p.61; *Flóamanna saga*, p.272; *Svarfdæla saga*, pp.193–194; *Ljósvetninga saga*, p.17; *Sturlunga saga* (1878), I, p.147; and *Brennu-Njáls saga*, pp.150–151 (*hestavíg*).
[69] '... sacerdotes eqvorum concertationes, vigilias, opilionum & infimæ plebis conventicula talesqve Papismi aut Gentilismi reliqvias, non modo graviter prohibeant, sed multo magis iisdem ipsi abstineant': Finnur Jónsson, *Historia ecclesiastica Islandiæ*, III, p.337 (Ch.IV, 6, article 8). Regarding these autumn gatherings in Iceland, see further Árni Björnsson, 'Smalabúsreið', 69–82. Regarding the 'vigilias' or *vökunætur*, see below, Chapter II, note 275. In answer to Solheim's argument (pp.79–109) that the above might have parallels in a Hebridean Michaelmas custom known as *oda*, see also Whitaker, 'Traditional horse races', 83–93.
[70] Solheim, *Horse-fight*, pp.49–50.
[71] Olaus Magnus, *Historia de gentibus septentrionalibus* (Book I, ch.24), pp.40–41; translated into Swedish in *Historia om de nordiska folken*, I, p.54. Strömbäck, in 'St Stephen', 145, again sees this comment as being influenced by Roman accounts.

1. The Information Provided by Archaeology

would seem that the view of horse-fights as a form of religious sacrifice must have lived on in popular belief for a long time.

The problem is that, in spite of the superstition, there is even less evidence directly linking horse-races and horse-fights to a particular pagan autumn festival than there is for connecting other games to the *jól* or *vetrnætur* festivals. Nonetheless, the suggestion that games of some kind must have formed an intrinsic part of an early autumn festival in Sweden in the late thirteenth century might find some support in a fragment of Sturla Þórðarson's *Magnúss saga Hákonarsonar*, which states how on one occasion the Swedish King Valdimarr was unable to meet the Norwegian king because he had to be present at the *leikr* which took place in his country on 'Matheus-messo' (21 September).[72] The games in question must be assumed to have had some national importance. Furthermore, it is unlikely that they had a Christian origin.

All in all, the predominantly literary evidence concerning 'games' activities given above contains little proof of drama having taken place. It does, however, suggest that *leikar* were associated with religious festivals, and thus strengthens the possibility that the *leikar* which were originally performed at the various *leikvin* and *leikvangar* in Scandinavia had cult significance. This in turn provides a valid context for the examination of the evidence for dramatic activity in early Scandinavia which follows. As will become apparent, dramatic *leikar* must also have originally taken place at these seasonal festive gatherings in Scandinavia alongside sporting competitions, just as they did in the rest of Europe during the Middle Ages.

C. The Archaeological Evidence

1. The Information Provided by Archaeology

Prior to the advent of writing, the only documentary material available from Scandinavia regarding games, ritual and drama is that provided by archaeological finds. The problem with such evidence, however, is that it is *static* and *visual*. It provides individual items and images that often lack any detailed context, and when images that seem to pertain to cult activities are encountered, there is rarely any suggestion of the words or sounds that originally might have accompanied or been associated with these images. Regarding drama, therefore, all that the researcher can do is sift through the available material in search of obvious *visual* proof of roleplay. This can only be provided by the appearance of unnatural costumes in a context that points to human enaction rather than mythological narrative. In short, one is looking for evidence depicting the use of animal disguise and/ or masks, which might result in an unreal emphasis being placed on this form of activity as against any other form of more natural

---

[72] 'Valdimarr konungr ... fór ... at leik sínum upp í Svía(ve)lldi': Sturla Þórðarson, *Magnús saga Hákonar sonar*, p.365.

dramatic presentation. Nonetheless, it becomes immediately clear that costumes and representation of animal figures must have played a role in pagan Scandinavian religion from a very early point in time.

2. The Bronze Age petroglyphs of Scandinavia

2. *The Bronze Age Petroglyphs of Scandinavia (1500–500 B.C.)*

The earliest evidence of animal disguise in Scandinavia appears in several Stone Age petroglyphs from Finnmark and Nordland in northern Norway. These carvings, which are by no means common, depict people wearing what seem to be bird masks or animal horns (see *figs 1–2*). Other contemporary petroglyphs from the same area (Atla) also contain images of dancers, processions, and figures holding aloft poles with bird- or elk-heads on them. It has been argued that these particular petroglyphs represent religious activities, and the likelihood is that the masked figures must have appeared in a similar context, that is to say, as part of ceremonial or shamanistic ritual.[73]

Proof that such elementary dramatic activities continued in later times on a much larger cult scale is provided by the petroglyphs of the late Bronze Age. Bronze Age rock carvings are found in a number of areas scattered throughout Scandinavia. Those of most interest in the present context, however, occur along a broad belt of land running across Scandinavia from Östergötland in the east of Sweden, through Bohuslän and Østfold to Rogaland on the west coast of Norway. Of particular importance are the petroglyphs from the area around Bohuslän in south-west Sweden.[74]

Numerous interpretations have been given for the symbols and images found in the Scandinavian petroglyphs. In some cases, as with the Stone and Bronze Age petroglyphs from the north of Norway and Sweden where the symbols tend to be confined to animals and hunting scenes, it seems probable that the rock carvings usually had a directly magical purpose, and were designed to give luck in hunting, or to improve the fertility of depleted animal stocks.[75] The southern Swedish petroglyphs, however, are more complex. They were created within an agrarian society, and while many of them are limited to simple symbols of ships, trees, suns, serpents,

---

[73] Regarding the bird-headed figures from Alta and Gåshopen, see further Simonsen, 'The magic picture', p.208. Concerning the 'dancing shaman' from Amtmannsnes, and the horned figure on skis from Rødøy, see Helskog, *Helleristningene i Alta*, p.15, pp.53–55, and p.112; and Davidson, *Pagan Scandinavia*, p.25 and plate 5.
[74] The central work on these petroglyphs is still Almgren's *Hällristningar och kultbruk*. More recently, see Gelling and Davidson, *The chariot of the sun*, which contains further illustrations, and is strongly influenced by Almgren's ideas. See also Janson, Lundberg and Bertilsson, eds., *Hällristningar och hällmålningar i Sverige*, a detailed and up-to-date review of scholarship on the subject, which provides a detailed regional analysis of the Swedish petroglyphs. A list of the main sites in Denmark, Norway and Sweden is also given in Gudnitz, *Broncealderens monumentalkunst*, pp.121–127.
[75] See Simonsen, 'The magic picture', p.197, and Hultkrantz, 'Hällristningsreligion', pp.46–49.

Fig. 1. Procession of figures in bird masks. Petroglyph from Gåshopen, Finnmark: Stone Age.

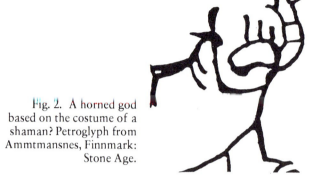

Fig. 2. A horned god based on the costume of a shaman? Petroglyph from Ammtmansnes, Finnmark: Stone Age.

Figs. 3–5. Acrobats on ships.
Petroglyphs from Skebbervall, Kville, Bohuslän (fig.3); Bro, Tanum, Bohuslän (fig.4); and Sortorp, Tanum, Bohuslän (fig.5).

Fig. 6. Musicians and dancers on a ship. Petroglyph from Lycke, Tanum, Bohuslän.

C. The Archaeological Evidence

axes, ploughs, animals and so on, others depict numerous human figures engaged in 'play' activities such as fighting, dancing or mating.

Sometimes, several layers of images appear to have been placed on top of each other, all carved at the same site over a long period of time. Sometimes this makes it difficult to assess whether particular figures were meant to form part of one and the same picture or not. Furthermore, interpretations of these pictures have ranged widely. Certain scholars in the past suggested that the petroglyphs depict historical events, while others in more recent times have assumed that the images are mythological or wholly symbolic.[76] Most, however, concur that the carvings have religious significance, although the question of whether such significance is related to a cult of the dead or to one concerned with fertility is still under discussion.[77]

The intention here is not to engage in the discussion of interpretation. Nor will any attempt be made to suggest that the images should be linked directly to the mythology of the Eddic poems: the temporal distance between the two art forms is far too great. Indeed, since so little is known about the culture that created the petroglyphs, it is impossible to draw any firm conclusions about the beliefs and religion of the artists. All that can be stated is that the roots of this religion were probably Indo-European.[78] What is of importance for the present examination, however, is that these petroglyphs contain images that represent elements of certain cult rituals as they must have been performed at this time.[79] This is emphasised primarily by the presence of figures blowing horns (or *lurer*) alongside other images of dancers, acrobats or celebrants, all of which are placed around the central images of the ship or the sun (see *figs 3–6*).[80] Other petroglyphs depict these ships being dragged by animals or men, and sometimes being carried, perhaps in the form of a model (see *figs 7–9*).[81] There is also

2. The Bronze Age petroglyphs of Scandinavia

---

[76] On the idea of the petroglyphs being a form of historical record, see, for example, Eckhoff, 'Hällristningar på Kinnekulle', 123, echoed in Schück, *Forntiden*, pp.56–61 and pp.64–66. For the mythological argument, see Bing, 'Helleristningsstudier', 77–116, and 'Rock carvings', 275–300; and most recently, Hultkrantz, 'Hällristningsreligion', pp.50–57. For the suggestion that the carvings are essentially artistic creations, see Müller, 'Billed- og fremstillingskunst', 157–161.

[77] See Ekholm, 'De skandinaviska hällristningarna', 275–308, and Nordén, 'Hällristningarnas kronologi', 57–83, on the idea that the petroglyphs are related to a cult of the dead. The main spokesman for the suggestion of a fertility cult was Almgren, in *Hällristningar*. Most scholars today are inclined to support the latter argument. Furthermore, Hultkrantz has recently argued that the fertility and death cults should be seen as parts of one and the same phenomenon: see Hultkrantz, 'Hällristningsreligion', p.51.

[78] See Schjødt, 'The 'meaning' of the rock carvings', pp.180–196; Gelling and Davidson, *The chariot of the sun*, pp.34–39; and Hultkrantz, 'Hällristningsreligion', pp.50–51.

[79] See Almgren, *Hällristningar*, passim, and B. Almgren, 'Hällristningarnas tro', 73–85.

[80] See also the following illustrations contained in Almgren, *Hällristningar*: Dancers and acrobats: figs 16a and b, p.21; and fig.77, p.113. Celebrants: fig.19b, p.22; figs 55 a–g, p.90; fig.72, p.108; and fig.87, p.120. See also Gudnitz, *Broncealderens monumentalkunst*, p.110; Ström, *Nordisk hedendom*, plates 4a and b; and B. Almgren, 'Hällristningarnas tro', 82–83.

[81] See also Almgren, *Hällristningar*, fig.5, p.12; and figs 45 b–d, p.80; and Gelling and Davidson, *The chariot of the sun*, p.64. Almgren (pp.76–83) suggests that most of the

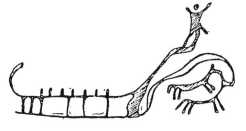

Fig. 7. Ship being dragged by horses. Petroglyph from Ekenberg, near Norrköping, Östergötland.

Fig. 8. Horned figure holding a ship. Petroglyph from Öster-Röd, Kville, Bohuslän.

Fig. 9. Figure holding a boat with oarsmen. Petroglyph from Brandskogen, Boglösa, Uppland.

Fig. 10. Figure holding a sun symbol. Petroglyph from Stora Backa, Brastad, Bohuslän.

Fig. 11. Giant figure being followed in a procession. Petroglyph from Hvitlycke, Tanum, Bohuslän.

Fig. 12. Giant figure being drawn in a procession. Petroglyph from Ekenberg, near Norrköping, Östergötland.

C. The Archaeological Evidence

evidence of people bearing aloft what seem to be cult axes, spears, swords and sun symbols (see *fig.10*).[82] Less commonly, giant figures also appear, apparently being drawn by men in processions (see *figs 11–12*).[83]

These active cult images from southern Sweden find three-dimensional parallels in Danish archaeological discoveries dated to the same period like the Trundholm sun chariot from north Sjælland, and the three small backward-bending female figurines from Grevensvænge, south Sjælland, which were originally accompanied by two horn-helmeted figures, and attached to a model cult ship. Indeed, the petroglyph images of cult processions and symbols suggests that the Trundholm chariot might be a model of a full-size sun symbol that was originally drawn through the fields as one central feature in such ceremonies.[84]

While it is possible that the petroglyphs are merely depictions of actions that men believed to be happening on the spiritual plane, it is also obvious that the form of the depictions must in all events be based on contemporary religious activities that people knew from their own experience. This is especially evident from the pictures of the *lurer*, since many such instruments have been discovered in Norway and Denmark.[85] Even more interesting is the fact that, in the present context, these instruments are sometimes depicted as being played by horned (and possibly tailed)[86] figures, thus implying that such figures must also have actively taken part in the ceremonies (see *fig.13*).[87] Horned figures of this kind are portayed in a variety of contexts (*figs 14–15*), including mating and battle scenes (see *fig.20*).[88] In one carving a horned man even seems to be carrying a ship (see *fig.8*). Considering its proportions, the latter figure was probably meant to

2. The Bronze Age petroglyphs of Scandinavia

---

large ships on the petroglyphs were drawn up onto land, and bases this idea largely on the fact that ships are sometimes shown being pulled: see for example Almgren, fig.41, p.76. Gelling, however (*The chariot of the sun*, pp.63–65), assumes that most of the celebrations depicted as taking place on board the ships must have taken place on water. He, like Bertil Almgren in 'Hällristningarnas tro', 81, sees the carried ships as small votive offerings.

[82] See, for example, Almgren, *Hällristningar*, fig.9, p.15; and fig.49, p.88.

[83] See also Almgren, *Hällristningar*, fig.5, p.12.

[84] See Glob, *The mound people*, pp.99–103, p.106, p.143, p.160, and pp.164–166; and Shetelig and Falk, *Scandinavian archaeology*, pp.156–157.

[85] At least one hundred Bronze Age horns exactly like those depicted have been found in Denmark and Norway alone. Many of them have been found in pairs like those shown in the petroglyphs: Davidson, *Pagan Scandinavia*, p.59, and Hagen, 'Gjenklang fra en fjern fortid'.

[86] The 'tail' may well also be 'a hammer-shaped sword sheath' as Bing suggests ('Rock carvings', 281). However, it seems surprising that that the artists should have depicted such items and no other clothing on the figures who appear to be otherwise naked. The suggestion that the the rear appendages must be tails in most cases is also made by Gelling, who also argues that the exaggerated calves on figures like those depicted in *figs 14–15* might even be a representation of skins tied to the legs: Gelling and Davidson, *The chariot of the sun*, pp.112–114.

[87] See also Almgren, *Hällristningar*, fig.38, p.71.

[88] See also Gelling and Davidson, *The chariot of the sun*, p.32.

Fig. 13. Horned men playing horns. Petroglyph from Kalleby, Tanum, Bohuslän.

Fig. 14. "The Dancer". Petroglyph from Vilhelmsberg, Simris, Skåne.

Fig. 15. Horned, masked figure bearing a hammer. Petroglyph from Lövåsen, Tanum, Bohuslän.

C. The Archaeological Evidence

2. The Bronze Age petroglyphs of Scandinavia

represent a protecting god.[89] However, as has been pointed out above, the image of the god must reflect that of the priest or worshipper. There can be little doubt that these horned figures depict men who, on cult occasions, originally dressed in animal skins, and wore animal headdresses (if not masks) like the Stone Age skin-clad 'sorcerer' of Trois Frères.[90]

The Bronze Age twin figurines found in Grevensvænge, however, are obviously wearing horned *helmets*, rather than animal skins (see *fig.16*). These helmets bear a close resemblance to those full-sized helmets found at Viksø in north Sjælland which were apparently imported from Italy (800–400 B.C.) (see *fig.17*).[91] Logically, this might suggest that the Swedish petroglyph figures are also meant to be wearing helmets of the same kind. Furthermore, the fact that the Viksø helmets were imported might point to their having an everyday significance related to social rank rather than to cult activity.

Nonetheless, it should also be remembered that the Grevensvænge figures, along with the dancing figurines mentioned above, were originally attached to a model cult ship. Furthermore, as will be shown below, almost a thousand years later horned helmets of the same kind are still depicted as being worn by what seem to be priest figures on one of the Torslunda matrices and in other Iron Age motifs like those depicted on the Oseberg tapestry. The idea that horned headwear in the Bronze Age was directly associated with a *deity* of some kind is supported still further by the bronze and gold horned headdress found in a bog near Hagendrup in north-west Sjælland. As Jensen points out, this headdress is too small to have been worn by an adult, but may have been placed on a wooden idol (see *fig.18*).[92] Finally, the nature of certain of the petroglyphs would seem to remove any doubt that horned animals and birds *were* definitely impersonated as part of ceremonies (see *fig.19* and *figs 26–27* below).[93] The evidence of the imported helmets, therefore, should not detract from the idea that the horned and horn-helmeted figures were meant to be representing something.[94] It might be suggested, though, that the helmets represent a development away from the original shamanistic context of animal skins like those depicted in the petroglyphs. In short, the holy figure represented by the helmeted man has become more personalised.[95]

---

[89] Hultkrantz, 'Hällristningsreligion', p.55.

[90] See, for example, Campbell, *The way of animal powers*, pp.75–76 and pp.156–157.

[91] See Schutz, *The prehistory of Germanic Europe*, pp.164–165; and Jensen, *I begyndelsen*, p.334.

[92] See Jensen, *I begyndelsen*, p.284.

[93] The former picture shows a man wearing stag horns and moving on all fours. See Gelling and Davidson, *The chariot of the sun*, p.96. Regarding bird costumes, see the following section on the Kivik stones.

[94] Various discussions of the nature and associations of the horns, which belong variously to stags, goats, and bulls, are given in Glob, *Mound people*, pp.141–142; Bing, 'Rock carvings', 277, 280–283, and 290–291; and in particular, Gelling and Davidson, *The chariot of the sun*, p.112.

[95] See further B. Almgren, 'Hällristningarnas tro', 97–107, on the appearance of personalised gods in the petroglyphs. On the links between the animal figures and shamanism,

Fig. 16. Model figure with a horned helmet from Grevensvænge, south Sjælland: late Bronze Age.

Fig. 17. Horned helmet from Viksø (800–400 B.C.).

Fig. 18. Horned head-dress from Hagendrup, near Kalundborg, Sjælland: Bronze Age.

Fig. 19. A man acting a horned animal accompanied by others wearing bird masks. Petroglyph from Yellen, Kville, Bohuslän.

C. The Archaeological Evidence

2. *The Bronze Age petroglyphs of Scandinavia*

It is natural to conclude that the actions performed by the figures in the petroglyphs were probably linked to a myth or basic scenario. The idea that the scenes depicted in the petroglyphs reflect the existence of some form of 'sacred drama' was emphasised particularly by the Swedish archaeologist, Oscar Almgren, who, like many scholars of his time, was strongly influenced by the works of Frazer, Mannhardt, Nilsson and others. Almgren therefore saw the ship ceremonies on the petroglyphs in the context of other Indo-European cultures, ranging from Greece and Rome to Egypt and Babylon, all of which appear to have known a fertility ritual related to the passage of the fertility god on a ship, and a seasonal drama involving the motif of the *hieros gamos* (or 'sacred marriage') accompanied by the elements of death and resurrection. For Almgren, the actions of the costumed figures, the horn players, and the adorants and dancers around the ship and the sun symbols, had to belong to a ritual drama, the ship providing a form of stage for what were 'more or less, dramatic games'.[96] As examples, Almgren points to certain petroglyphs from Tanum in Bohuslän which arguably involve the elements of the *hieros gamos* and violent death in close proximity to one another (see *figs 20–23*). Almgren sees the combatants in these depictions as the fertility god and his rival, the scene being 'one component in the drama enacted on the cult ship . . . one scene in the seasonal drama'.[97]

Considering the many-layered nature and the complexity of the petroglyphs, Almgren's argument concerning 'seasonal drama' can be regarded as little more than theory.[98] Nonetheless, the carvings *do* argue for the existence of abstract dramatic representations forming part of cult practice at this time, representations that were equivalent in the very least to the

---

see Glosecki, *Shamanism*, pp.24–27. On the elements of shamanism in early Scandinavian literature, see further Eliade, *Shamanism*, pp.379–387, and in particular, Buchholtz, 'Shamanism', 7–20. See also Fleck, 'The 'knowledge criterion'', 50–58, about warnings against placing too much faith in Eliade's suggestions. On the question of shamanist performance, see Gunnell, 'The concept of ancient Scandinavian drama', 47–51, regarding the vague difference between the performer 'becoming' or 'representing' a character or entity. Certainly, the shaman is said to 'become the beast himself', rather than represent it (Glosecki, *Shamanism*, p.26). However, he must also be seen as an extremely proficient 'performing artist', who utilises many of the best techniques of theatre. See Glosecki, *Shamanism*, pp.45–46.

[96] '. . .mer eller mindre dramatiska upptåg': Almgren, *Hällristningar*, p.69.

[97] '. . . ett led i det spelade dramat på kultskeppet . . . en scen i årtidsdramat': Almgren, *Hällristningar*, p.119. See also Almgren *Hällristningar*, figs 47 a–c, pp.82–83, which depict embracing couples standing on the ships themselves. Almgren sees the same rival figures in another image of an axeman apparently killing an archer: see *fig.22* above. See further, Gelling and Davidson, *The chariot of the sun*, pp.68–78.

[98] A similar argument is made by Malmer in 'Principles', pp.91–93. For the most part, however, Almgren's general argument that the petroglyphs should be seen in terms of cultic ritual is still accepted by archaeologists. See, for example, the comments in Shetelig and Falk, *Scandinavian archeology*, pp.166–169; Ström, *Nordisk hedendom*, pp.22–30; Davidson, *Pagan Scandinavia*, p.54; Nordbladh, 'Interpretation of south Scandinavian petroglyphs', p.143; and Schjødt, 'The 'meaning' of the rock carvings', p.188.

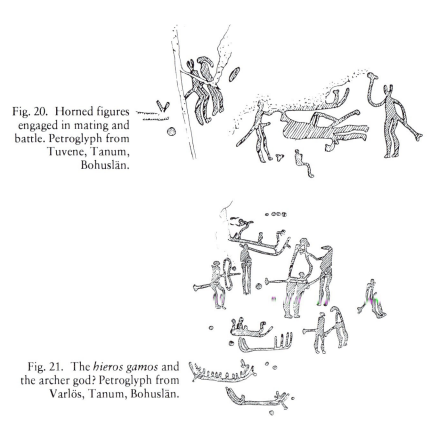

Fig. 20. Horned figures engaged in mating and battle. Petroglyph from Tuvene, Tanum, Bohuslän.

Fig. 21. The *hieros gamos* and the archer god? Petroglyph from Varlös, Tanum, Bohuslän.

Fig. 22. Scenes from a ritual drama? Petroglyph from Fossum, Tanum, Bohuslän.

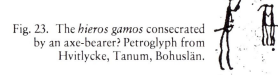

Fig. 23. The *hieros gamos* consecrated by an axe-bearer? Petroglyph from Hvitlycke, Tanum, Bohuslän.

C. The Archaeological Evidence

elementary stages of drama (see *Introduction, section B*). Clearly, too, the early Scandinavians already had an eye for public performance, music and spectacle.

3. The Kivik Stones (c.1200 B.C.)

The existence of theriomorphic, or simple costumed representation as a central feature of religious activities during the Swedish Bronze Age is indicated still further by images depicted on the Kivik grave tablets from south-east Skåne which belong to a similar period (see *figs 24–25*).[99] Here there is little doubt that the figures all belong together in a particular context, and the presence of *lurer*-players once again implies that the carvings must represent religious activities rather than wholly symbolic or mythological material. Amongst other actions depicted on the tablets is a costumed procession in which a line of eight curved 'female' figures in long dresses follow a male figure who may well be dancing. Elsewhere, another eight 'female' figures stand on either side of what is perhaps a cauldron of some kind. Of particular interest is the fact that the 'female' figures are not depicted in the usual way with long hair, but instead seem to have pointed bird heads like the figures in the Norwegian Stone Age petroglyphs mentioned in the previous section.[100]

Firm conclusions are again impossible here. Yet the evidence of a number of winged and masked human bird figures found in several Bohuslän petroglyphs suggests that the bird disguise cannot have been a rare phenomenon in the religious rituals of southern Sweden at this time (see *figs 26–27*).[101] Furthermore, the idea of female bird figures playing a role in a funeral procession raises logical associations with the image of the *valkyrjur* who in later times were said to collect spirits of dead warriors and wear swan-skins ('álptarhamir') which could be removed at will.[102] However, whether any connection exists between such a later motif and

---

[99] See also Glob, *The mound people*, pp.108–113. For a recent review of material concerning the Kivik stones, see Verlaeckt, 'The Kivik petroglyphs'.
[100] See Glob, *The mound people*, pp.110–114; Davidson *Pagan Scandinavia*, pp.48–49; Gelling and Davidson, *The chariot of the sun*, p.101; B. Almgren, 'Hällristningarnas tro', 74–75; and Verlaeckt, 'The Kivik petroglyphs', 8–9 and 17–18. Almgren, it might be noted, sees the pointed headgear in terms of a veil rather than anything to do with birds. His doubt about the costume is shared by Verlaeckt, who nonetheless talks of the women as 'disguised'. Ström, in *Nordisk hedendom*, p.31, sees the rite depicted as a 'funerära skådespel' ('a funereal play').
[101] See also Gelling and Davidson, *The chariot of the sun*, pp.114–116, and B. Almgren, 'Hallristningarnas tro', 75, 82–84 and 86, on the winged bird figures from Kallsängen in Bohuslän. For further examples of figures which seem to have beaks, see Bertilsson, 'Bohuslän', p.84, p.105, p.111 (on Kallsängen), and pp.117–120. Bertilsson, p.94, argues that some of these 'beaks' may represent helmets. B. Almgren, however, relates the winged figures to cranes which return to western Sweden annually on a particular week which, in folk tradition, signified the arrival of the spring and the time for ploughing to commence: see B. Almgren, 'Hällristningarnas tro', 84.
[102] See, for example, the prose introduction to *Völundarkviða*.

Fig. 24. The Kivik grave, Stone 8: Skåne.

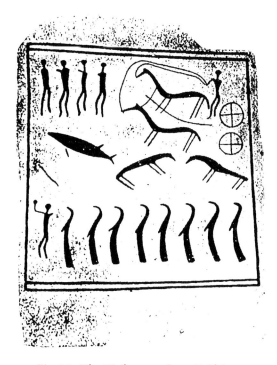

Fig. 25. The Kivik grave, Stone 7: Skåne.

C. The Archaeological Evidence

these ancient Bronze Age rituals can be little more than a matter of tempting conjecture.

As was mentioned above, the existence of dancers and musical instruments in the Bohuslän carvings suggests that the other actions taking place in the petroglyphs are not merely imaginative representations of the activities of the gods, but reflect genuine cult activities. In other words, it seems likely that ships, model or otherwise, formed the centre of the ritual, that certain figures clad themselves in animal skins or horned helmets of some kind in order to represent or 'become' a god or particular animal, and that some form of *hieros gamos* was performed involving costumed representatives of the various powers. The dramatic tradition would appear to have been established. This raises the possibility that when such images reappear in archaeological finds from later times, they too might reflect similar enacted ritual activities rather than purely mythological events.

Such conjecture is particularly interesting in the case of the image depicted on the sandstone lid of the Maltegården cremation urn (c.600 B.C.), which has many similarities to Swedish petroglyphs of the *hieros gamos*. The Maltegården urn lid, however, contains an additional motif of a tree, plant, or ear of corn which is placed directly behind the female figure.[103] This motif later reappears accompanying the images of embracing and perhaps dancing couples on certain minute Viking Age gold foils like those found in Hauge, Rogaland, in Norway, where the female figure is depicted holding a plant (see *fig.33* below).[104] The recurrence of these images naturally points to the longevity and conservatism of pagan religious practices related to fertility in Scandinavia.

4. *The Gallehus Horns (c.A.D.400)*

The end of the Bronze Age appears to have witnessed a deterioration in the social and religious organisation of the area in question, and the horned figures in the petroglyphs of southern Sweden seem to die out.[105] Yet almost one thousand years later, they are encountered again on the shorter of the two golden horns found at Gallehus in Schleswig.[106] These horns, which are now lost, but of which detailed drawings were made, contained several depictions of apparently costumed figures, some of whom seem to

---

[103] A colour photograph of the Maltegården carving is provided in Magnusson, *Hammer of the North*, pp.76–77. For interpretations of the Maltegården carving, see further Glob, *The bog people*, p.166, and Davidson, *Pagan Scandinavia*, pp.61–62.
[104] Regarding the gold foils, see further below, note 140. The idea of an enacted *hieros gamos* encourages the drawing of parallels between these scenes and the account of the Nerthus cult given in *Germania*, and that of the god Freyr given in *Gunnars þáttr helmings*. See further below, section C.5.
[105] See Almgren, *Hällristningar*, pp.153–154, and Gelling and Davidson, *The chariot of the sun*, pp.87–88.
[106] As Ström points out in *Nordisk hedendom*, p.64, the horns probably had some sacral significance and were in all likelihood buried in the earth as an offering.

Fig. 26. Figures in bird costumes. Petroglyph from Kallsängen, Bottna, Kville, Bohuslän.

Fig. 27. Figure in bird costume. Petroglyph from Kallsängen, Bottna, Kville, Bohuslän.

C. The Archaeological Evidence

4. *The Gallehus horns*

be engaged in sacrificial activities (see *figs 28–30*).[107] The shorter horn shows two horned men, one carrying what seems to be a horn, ring or shield and an inverted spear, the other bearing a sickle and a sharp object that might be a spear, sword, or rod of some kind.[108] Below these is a three-headed figure bearing an axe in one hand and drawing a goat with the other.[109] The goat, it might be noted, has horns of a similar shape to those on the horned figures, thus adding weight to what was stated above (in *section C.2*) about the link between the horned men and animals.

The element of drama is emphasised still further by the presence of several other intriguing costumed figures on the longer Gallehus horn. The first of these is a bearded, horn-bearing figure dressed in a long robe, with long, flowing hair (see *fig.29*), and thus opposed to the other figures on the horns who are beardless, have short hair, and are either naked or wearing short tunics. Long hair, in the Bronze Age petroglyphs and other images from the early Iron Age such as the picture stones from Gotland, is always used as a means of identifying female figures. The conclusion therefore must be that the bearded figure on the Gallehus horn is meant to be a male in female disguise. Such a figure should be viewed in the context of Tacitus' reference in *Germania*, ch.43, to the priests of the Naharvali, who were dressed as women ('sacredos muliebri ornato').[110]

More interesting still is that below this bearded figure, there are two opposed armed figures with human bodies and what would appear to be animal masks, one resembling a wolf head, the other that of a bird (see *fig.30*).[111] Considered alongside the horned, combating figures depicted on the earlier Swedish petroglyphs, these two masked figures add support for the argument that costumed ritual combat originally formed part of pagan ritual ceremony, and continued to do so in the early Iron Age.[112]

The central problem with interpreting these images is that the figures on the horns occur in an almost random fashion within the general context of what appear to be sacrificial and festal activities. Yet caution is necessary

---

[107] Illustrations of these horns based on the original drawings are also provided in Olrik, 'Gudefremstillinger', 1–35, plate II; Oxenstierna, *Järnålder*, plate 44; and Davidson, *Scandinavian mythology*, p.78 (a colour photograph of a reconstruction).
[108] Olrik, in 'Gudefremstillinger', 3–5, associates these two horned figures with Óðinn and Freyr, but this can be nothing more than loose conjecture.
[109] Some scholars have over-hastily associated these figures with Þórr and/ or the later figure of Scandinavian folk tradition, the *julebukk*. See, for example, Olrik, in 'Gudefremstillinger', 4–5; Ellekilde, *Vor danske jul*, pp.83–84; Oxenstierna, *Järnålder*, p.64; and, more tentatively, Davidson, *Pagan Scandinavia*, pp.87–88. Regarding the *julebukk*, see further *Chapter II, B.3–5*.
[110] See Tacitus, *Germania*, pp.202–203. On this subject, see further Schück, *Studier*, II, 83–84, and most recently, McTurk, *Studies in Ragnars saga*, pp.25–27. See also *Chapter V*, note 31, below for further references to the possible continuation of such practices in the Viking period.
[111] See Davidson, *Pagan Scandinavia*, p.87. The form of the heads varies in different illustrations. Oxenstierna's illustration in *Järnålder* takes the form described above.
[112] It might be noted that sword dancers are also depicted on the Hochdorf funeral couch from Switzerland (c.530 B.C.): see Schutz, *Prehistory*, pp.267–268.

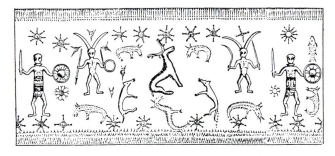

Fig. 28. A section of the shorter Gallehus horn.

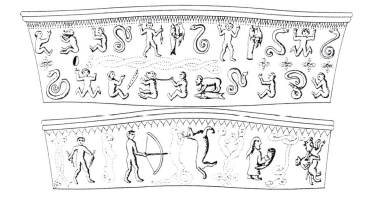

Fig. 29. A section of the longer Gallehus horn.

Fig. 30. Masked figures from the longer Gallehus horn enlarged.

C. The Archaeological Evidence

before immediately assuming such a ritual context because several of the other images depicted on the horns clearly originate in foreign mythology, such as the figure of a classical centaur, a two-headed horse, and the three-headed 'man' who has close Celtic parallels.[113] In spite of this, the reappearance of the horned figure and the goat, and the early instance of the horn-bearing 'female' figure so often encountered in later Scandinavian motifs,[114] emphasise that the Gallehus horns should not be ignored as a source concerning ancient Scandinavian beliefs.[115] Furthermore, since the horned and masked figures have close parallels in the earlier, cultic Bronze Age carvings, and reoccur later in the more obviously active context of the Torslunda matrices, there is reason for tentatively accepting Oxenstierna's argument that some of the Gallehus images reflect cultic activities.[116] Indeed, further support for such a hypothesis is provided by the evidence of Tacitus' *Germania*, which implies that semi-dramatic rituals involving human representation of the gods had already been taking place in the same area of Denmark at a slightly earlier period as part of the Nerthus cult.

5. Cult wagons, and the worship of Nerthus and Freyr

5. Cult Wagons, and the Worship of Nerthus and Freyr (c.A.D.100)

Tacitus' much-quoted account in *Germania*, ch.40, of the ceremonies related to the goddess Nerthus in the area around Schleswig-Holstein or Jylland[117] is of particular interest here for several reasons. First of all, it suggests that the images of the Bronze Age petroglyphs depicting the *hieros gamos* and processions related to a fertility deity had parallels in southern Scandinavia as late as A.D.100, when Tacitus wrote his account. Secondly, it provides the first reliable evidence that the ceremonies were now associated with a *named* goddess, who must therefore have had her own mythological background.[118] This in turn implies that enacted rituals to do with the goddess probably had a mythological parallel, and that the same must have applied to the ritualistic images depicted on the Gallehus horns more than three hundred years later. As has been pointed out in the *Introduction* (section C), the difference between such a mythologically based, enacted ritual and a ritual 'play' is minimal.

In brief, Tacitus states that the goddess Nerthus, attended by a priest, periodically processed amongst the peoples of the area in a cart or chariot

---

[113] See Oxenstierna, *Järnålder*, p.63; and Bay, 'Nogle bemærkninger', 1–20. Bay suggests that all the motifs are foreign.
[114] See Lindqvist, *Gotlands bildsteine*, I, figs 85, 137, 124 and 134; and Nylén and Lamm, *Stones, ships and symbols*, pp.72–73.
[115] See Shetelig and Falk, *Scandinavian archeology* p.208, and Oxenstierna, *Järnålder*, p.63.
[116] See Oxenstierna, *Järnålder*, pp.63–64, and Davidson, *Pagan Scandinavia*, p.88.
[117] See Ström, *Nordisk hedendom*, p.40.
[118] Nerthus has close associations with the other Scandinavian Vanir gods related to fertility in later sources, such as Njörðr, Freyr and Freyja. See, for example, Turville-Petre, *Myth and religion*, pp.171–172.

5. Cult wagons, and the worship of Nerthus and Freyr

usually kept in a sacred grove on an island.[119] The probability has to remain that the 'goddess' in these processions took the form of an idol. Nonetheless, as Turville-Petre points out, 'it is likely that the fertility goddess with her male companion and the god with his female were thought of as husband and wife,'[120] especially if Tacitus' account is viewed in the light of, for example, *Gunnars þáttr helmings* which implies that the goddess or god might also on occasion be impersonated or represented by a human being. Whether this was so or not in 100, Tacitus' account seems to give a clear example of the elementary dramatic ritual described in the Introduction (*section B*). As Almgren pointed out, an interesting parallel to this account and the religious activities centred around the ships in the Bronze Age petroglyphs is found in a much later description in *Gestorum Abbatum Trudonensium* of a protracted ship procession that travelled by land and water from Aachen to Loos and further in 1133.[121] Other later literary parallels to Tacitus' account, closer to home, are found in the description given in *Rögnvalds þáttr ok Rauðs* of a walking, talking image of Þórr that was kept in a temple on an island in the north of Norway; in the description of Þórr's chariot or wagon in *Ólafs saga Tryggvasonar hin mesta*; and in the account given in *Hauks þáttr hábrókar* of how the god 'Lýtir' travelled in person to the sacrifice in Uppsala in a special wagon that awaited his arrival for three nights.[122] Most interesting of all, however, is the account concerning the image of Freyr in *Gunnars þáttr helmings*.

As suggested above, *Gunnars þáttr helmings* represents one of the strongest pieces of evidence for processions of the kind described in *Germania* also having taken place in Sweden, perhaps as late as the Viking period itself. At the very least, it provides evidence that people in the early fourteenth century accepted the idea that pagan religious processions and human representation of the gods were still taking place during the reign of Ólafr Tryggvason (c.995–1000).[123] Some scholars have pointed to possible foreign models for this story, but as Turville-Petre has pointed out, it seems more probable that the account was based essentially on native Scandinavian tradition.[124]

The *þáttr*, which often comes under the heading of *Ögmundar þáttr dytts*, forms part of *Ólafs saga Tryggvasonar hin mesta* and can be found

---

[119] Tacitus, *Germania*, pp.196–197.
[120] Turville-Petre, *Myth and religion*, p.172. See further Ström, *Nordisk hedendom*, p.41; de Vries, *Religionsgeschichte*, II, pp.191–193; and Lid, 'Gudar og gudedyrking', p.112. Lid goes further and relates Tacitus' account to the later folk traditions of the 'May wedding': see further *Chapter II, D.2*.
[121] *Gestorum Abbatum Trudonensium*, Book XII, chs 10–14, pp.309–311. On this account and its parallels, see further Almgren, *Hällristningar*, pp.28–30, and Rudwin, *The origin of the German carnival comedy*, pp.10–12.
[122] See *Flateyjarbók* (1860–1868) I, p.292, p.320, and III, pp.579–580. Regarding Þórr's 'kjerra', see further below. On the Lýtir account, see further Strömbäck, 'Lytir', pp.283–293.
[123] See, for example, Davidson, *Gods and myths*, p.94.
[124] See Turville-Petre, 'Fertility of beast and soil', pp.249–252. For a wider bibliography and background for the *þáttr*, see Jónas Kristjánsson, ed., *ÍF* IX, pp.LV–LXIV.

C. The Archaeological Evidence

eight manuscripts, including that of *Flateyjarbók*.¹²⁵ The *Flateyjarbók* version of the *þáttr* (c.1390) is of particular interest because it contains some small but revealing differences in wording to the slightly earlier AM 61 manuscript of *Ólafs saga* which was probably written in the second half of the fourteenth century.

In short, the *þáttr* describes how Gunnarr helmingr, on the run from Ólafr Tryggvason's Norway, takes refuge in Sweden with the 'kona' ('woman'/ 'wife') of the god Freyr. Freyr, himself, takes the form of an idol, but 'the image of Freyr was so very powerful that the devil spoke with people from inside the idol'.¹²⁶ Moreover, 'the people of the country believed that Freyr was alive, as he seemed to be in some ways, and they expected that he would need to have sexual relations with his wife.'¹²⁷ Like the priest of Nerthus, Freyr's wife 'was supposed to . . . have control over the temple, and everything that belonged to it'.¹²⁸

After a three-day stay with them, Gunnarr accompanies the god and his wife on their winter procession across the mountains to another site in order to take part in certain 'feasts' ('ueitzslur'), the purpose of which is to bring fertility to the crops ('gera monnum arbot'). The god and his wife travel in a sacred wagon, and are accompanied by a number of other servants, including Gunnarr who is expected to lead the horse. During the journey, the party is beset by a blizzard, and Gunnarr, impatient of walking, attempts to take a seat in the wagon, whereupon he is physically attacked by the god. They wrestle, and when Gunnarr eventually wins, 'the devil that had concealed itself within the image rushed out of it, leaving nothing but the empty body/ a log of wood behind.'¹²⁹

5. Cult wagons, and the worship of Nerthus and Freyr

---

¹²⁵ See *Óláfs saga Tryggvasonar en mesta*, II, pp.9–18, which contains all the variants of the *þáttr*. The quotations that follow are taken from the text given in Flateyjarbok (1860–1868), I, pp.335–339. See also *Ögmundar þáttr dytts*, pp.109–115. It might be noted that a section of *Ögmundar þáttr dytts* (not including *Gunnars þáttr*) is also found attached to a fragmentary version of *Víga-Glúms saga* in the *Vatnshyrna* MS from c.1400. This emphasises the fact that *Ögmundar þáttr* probably once existed separately from *Ólafs saga*: see *Víga-Glúms saga*, ed. Turville-Petre, pp.96–98. As Jónas Kristjánsson suggests in the introduction to *ÍF* IX, p.LVI, there is good reason to believe that *Ögmundar þáttr* and *Gunnars þáttr* both lived independently in the oral tradition. See, however, more recently Harris, 'Ögmundar þáttr dytts', 156–182, on the apparent *literary* unity of these accounts.

¹²⁶ '. . . suo miogh (var) magnat likneski Freys at fiandinn talade vid menn ór skurgodinu.' As Turville-Petre points out in 'Fertility of beast and soil', p.249, the image of a talking idol was in itself not uncommon during this period in Europe. See, for example, *Rögnvalds þáttr*, in *Flateyjarbok* (1860–1868), I, p.292, and p.296, which uses almost identical words to *Gunnars þáttr*: 'feandinn mællti vid hann or skurgodinu' ('the devil spoke with him from inside the idol'). Another suggestion of a talking idol which is apparently possessed by the devil occurs in *Flateyjarbok* (1860–1868), I, pp.400–403 (*Olafs saga Tryggvasonar hin mesta*): see Strömbäck, 'Lytir', pp.287–288. For comparable examples from Danish folk tradition related to a figure named 'Bovi' or 'Bovmand', see *Chapter II, note 53*.

¹²⁷ '. . . uar þat atrunadr landzmanna at Freyr uære lifande sem syndizst j sumu lagi ok ætludu at hann munde þurfa at æiga hiuskarparfar vid konu sina.'

¹²⁸ '. . . skyllde hon ok mest rada firir hofstadnum ok ǫllu þui er þar la til godahussins.'

¹²⁹ 'hleypr þa ór likneskinu sa feande sem þar hafde leynzst ok uar þa skrokkrinn æinn

5. Cult wagons, and the worship of Nerthus and Freyr

Gunnarr proceeds to smash the idol into pieces ('braut hann þat allt j sundr'). However, the degree of destruction must be open to question because *Flateyjarbók* states that following this, Gunnarr takes the god's place, and dresses himself in the 'umbuning' ('covering'/ 'framework') of the idol.[130] He and Freyr's wife then eventually arrive at the site of the celebrations. Gunnarr wins esteem not only because of his arrival in such weather and the fact that 'he now walked with other people, and ate and drank like everyone else',[131] but especially because Freyr's wife is found to be pregnant.

Apart from its interest as evidence for holy processions probably having taken place in Sweden during the Viking period,[132] the above account is important here because it seems to point to some dramatic representation not only of the god's wife (Gerðr or Freyja?[133]) but also of the god himself who is not only able to talk but is also a capable wrestler. This element, of course, may have been drawn from Christian sources, but the idea of acting is supported by the fact that the people both *like* and *accept* the idea of the living god as impersonated by Gunnarr who dresses in the god's costume, and presumably wears a mask of some kind since he is recognised *as* the god rather than an ordinary man.[134]

Concerning the costume itself, the word 'umbúningr' (*Flateyjarbók*) suggests that the guise in question was seen as being something more substantial than clothes, and lays open the possibility that it might have been made of straw or bark. Parallels for such a guise are found in the costumes of certain statuesque figures from later Scandinavian and Shetland folk tradition, and in Örvar-Oddr's guise of the 'Næframaðr' or 'Bark-man' in *Örvar-Odds saga*.[135] It might be noted that the other manuscripts of

---

tomr eftir.' Other MSS use the more logical words 'tré stokkr' ('log') rather than 'skrokkrinn' which may be a scribal error.

[130] Most other MSS of *Gunnars þáttr helmings* use the word 'búnað' ('clothing') instead of 'umbúning' which only appears in *Flateyjarbók*. As Ólafur Halldórsson has pointed out to me in conversation, this is not a normal scribal error, and thus raises the question of which version was the original. All logic would suggest that 'búnað' is a correction of the more obscure 'umbúning' rather than the other way around. For another interesting example of the use of the word 'umbúningr', again related to pagan ritual, but now probably applied to a platform for *seiðr*, see *Eiríks saga rauða*, p.207: 'var henni veittr sá úmbúningr, sem hon þurfti at hafa til að fremja seiðinn' ('she was given the *umbúningr* [equipment?] that she needed to perform the *seiðr*'). Regarding *seiðr*, see below, *Chapter V, D.1*.

[131] '. . . hann gekk nu med monnum ok at ok drak sem adrir menn.'

[132] It must be considered questionable, however, whether wagons or carts would have been taken over the mountains of Sweden at this time, especially during the winter. A sledge would have been more likely. See, for example, Lund, 'Paa rangel', 103, and Christensen et al., *Oseberg-dronningens grav*, pp.119–122.

[133] Lid, in *Jolesveinar*, p.116, sees Freyr's wife here as probably representing Freyja.

[134] Turville-Petre, in 'Fertility', p.252, feels that the story 'may preserve memories of a similar ritual procession or drama in which a man impersonated the god and a woman the goddess'. Similar ideas are reflected in, for example, Phillpotts, *The Elder Edda*, p.119; Krappe, 'Le legende de Gunnar Half', 231; Ström, *Nordisk hedendom* (first edition, 1961), pp.38–39; and Lid, *Jolesveinar*, p.116.

[135] Regarding these figures see below *section D.2*, and *Chapter II, B.2 and G.4*. Lid, in

C. The Archaeological Evidence

5. Cult wagons, and the worship of Nerthus and Freyr

Gunnars þáttr state that all that remained after the 'devil' had left the idol was a 'tréstokkr einn tómr', in other words, 'a hollow log' rather than an 'empty body'. Furthermore, as mentioned above, the statement that Gunnarr totally destroyed the idol must be drawn into question in the light of his reception by the people. Indeed, the overall visual image that is given of Gunnarr as Freyr is that of a living statue of some kind. In the very least, Gunnarr must be visualised as wearing a large, stylised 'human' mask of some kind like those that seem to be worn by the dancing figures depicted on the earlier Gummersmark brooch from Sjælland in Denmark, and Ålleberg collar from Sweden (c.600–300 B.C.) (see *figs 31–32*).[136]

The above evidence encourages further consideration of whether the description of the winter procession contained in *Gunnars þáttr helmings* might be related in some way to the expression 'Freys leikr', discussed above, which is placed in particular relation to the period of the winter solstice (*jól*).[137] In this context, it might also be noted that the *hieros gamos* of Freyr and Gerðr implied by the events in the Eddic poem *Skírnismál* is also given a winter setting.[138] Furthermore, as will be shown below, numerous Yuletide mock-marriage traditions used to exist all over Scandinavia.[139] The possibility that such also existed in pagan times cannot be ignored. Indeed, many scholars have suggested associations between such a *hieros gamos* ritual and the numerous tiny gold foils from the Viking period discovered in many parts of mainland Scandinavia which commonly depict a couple embracing each other and/ or kissing (see *fig.33*). Whatever their significance, there seems little doubt that these foils were connected in one way or another with pagan worship.[140]

Jolesveinar, p.151, suggests, less convincingly, that the 'umbúningr' points to Gunnarr being equipped with a phallus, 'something that was necessary if one was to represent Frey' ('dette høyrde med når mann skulde representera Frøy'). Nonetheless, considering what is known of Freyr idols, it is likely that the outer form of the *idol* would have been equipped with a phallus. The phallus alone would hardly have been enough to disguise Gunnarr's identity from the other Swedes.

[136] See further Holmqvist, 'The dancing gods', 101–103.
[137] See the references given in note 25 above.
[138] *Skírnismál*, sts 10 and 42: 'Myrkt er úti' ('It is dark outside') and 'Lǫng er nótt' ('One night is long'). These words are hardly relevant to the summer months in northern Scandinavia, when 'night' hardly exists. Regarding *Skírnismál*, see also below, *Chapter III, G.3*.
[139] See *Chapter II, D.1* below.
[140] See Olsen, 'Fra gammelnorsk myte og kultus', 30–31. The most recent discussion of these gold foils in the context of *Skírnismál* is given by Steinsland in *Det hellige bryllup*, p.77 and pp.155–160. See also Holmqvist, 'The dancing gods', 101–127, and Watt, 'Guldgubberne', pp.373–386, for a practical examination of the figures in the light of other archaeological finds. Regarding the possibility that these foils might represent votive offerings, see O. Olsen, 'Comments', 26. For photographs and drawings of some of the numerous foils found at Helgö, Hauge (Kleppe), Mære, Ektorp, Bodaviken, Borg, Sorte Muld, and Slöinge, see also Holmqvist, 'Die Eisenzeitlichen Funde', 269; Gelling and Davidson, *The chariot of the sun*, plate 8; Lidén, 'From pagan sanctuary', 18; Stenberger, 'Ektorp's borg', 213; Oxenstierna, *Järnålder*, plate 69; Munch, 'Hus og hall', p.327; Hedeager, *Danernes land*, p.330; and, most recently, Lundqvist, Rosengren and Callmar, 'En fyndplats'.

Fig. 31. Dancing figure from the Gummersmark brooch (600–300 B.C.).

Fig. 32. Dancing figure from the Ålleberg collar: Karleby, Västergötland (600–300 B.C.).

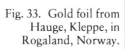

Fig. 33. Gold foil from Hauge, Kleppe, in Rogaland, Norway.

Fig. 34. Oseberg tapestry fragment: Horned man and wagon in procession.

C. The Archaeological Evidence

The extant text of *Gunnars þáttr helmings* was not recorded until the fourteenth century, which means that many of the suggestions made above must remain purely conjectural. Nonetheless, the account *does* offer several close parallels to that given in *Germania* not only in terms of the processing god who brings fertility,[141] but also as regards the sacred marriage, and the idea of the sacrosanct holy wagon that must not be touched. That such wagons existed in real life is supported by archaeological evidence in the form of the two early Iron Age wagons that were deposited in the bogs at Dejbjerg, in Jylland, at a time close to that of Tacitus' account. It is highly tempting to draw direct parallels between these wagons and those of Nerthus and Freyr described above.[142]

5. *Cult wagons, and the worship of Nerthus and Freyr*

Of even more interest is the elaborate Viking Age wagon found on the Oseberg ship. This vehicle seems to have been incapable of turning corners, and was thus probably only used for very short distances like that between a farm or temple and a meeting place. There is therefore an even greater likelihood that this particular wagon was used for sacred purposes rather than for daily travel.[143] Furthermore, the decoration on the Oseberg wagon is highly reminiscent of the description in *Ólafs saga Tryggvasonar hin mesta* of the god Þórr's cart or chariot which was supposedly kept in the temple at Mære in Trøndelag, Norway, and could be moved forward with ease:

> (In the temple) there was no lack of holy images. Þórr sat in the middle. He was the most honoured. He was enormous, and worked all over in gold and silver. Þórr was equipped in such a way that he was sitting in a cart, or chariot. This was very splendid: in front of it, two wooden goats had been harnessed, both very finely carved. Both the cart and the goats ran on wheels. The horns of the goats were roped with twisted silver. Everything was made with expert craftmanship.[144]

---

[141] Another interesting parallel to the above account is found in the Telemark folk legend, 'Thor og Urebø-Urden', which describes a personal visit made by Thor to two country weddings. See the two versions of this legend contained in Bø et al., eds., *Norske segner*, pp.89–90, and Liestøl, *Norsk folkdikting*, III, pp.116–117 (translation in Craigie, ed., *Scandinavian folk-lore*, pp.14–16). This idea of Þórr also moving and visiting farms 'in person' is supported by the description of the image of Þórr given in *Rögnvalds þáttr* (see note 126 above), mentioned above, and that of Þórr's 'kjerra' (wagon or chariot) given in *Ólafs saga Tryggvasonar hin mesta*: see note 144 below.

[142] See Shetelig and Falk, *Scandinavian archeology*, pp.187–188; Ström, *Nordisk hedendom*, p.42; Turville-Petre, *Myth and religion*, p.173; and Glob, *The bog people*, pp.167–171. Davidson, in *Pagan Scandinavia*, p.74 is less certain. Indeed, certain scholars have pointed out that parts of the Dejbjerg wagon are Celtic, and that the two wagons may even have originated in central Europe: see Schutz, *Prehistory*, p.292.

[143] For a description of the wagon, see Brøgger and Schetelig, *Oseberg-fundet*, II, pp.3–33, and Christensen et al., *Oseberg-dronningens grav*, pp.119–123 and pp.248–249. All the above authors believe that the wagon must have been a 'kultvogn'.

[144] '. . . er þeir kuomu j hofit skorti þar æigi skurgoð. Þor sat j midiu hann var mest tignadr. hann var mikill ok allr buinn gulli ok silfre. sa var umbunadr Þors at hann sat j kerru. hon var miog glæsilig. firir henni voru beittir trehafrar .ij. hardla uel geruir. a huelum lek huortueggia kerran ok hafrarnir. hornnatog hafranna uar slungit af silfri. allt var þetta smidat med undarliga myklum haglæik': *Flateyjarbok* (1860–1868), I, p.320.

I. Dramatic Activities, I: Archaeology and Literature

6. *The Oseberg tapestry*

In the light of the archaeological evidence, such a literary description is not so far fetched. In general, it would seem that the Dejbjerg and Oseberg wagons lend credence to the later literary descriptions of ritual processions.

6. The Oseberg Tapestry (c.835–850[145])

More informative still is the tapestry that was buried with the Oseberg wagon which offers further insight into such holy processions as those mentioned above. Among other things, the tapestry contains a depiction of what must be interpreted as a religious procession involving one wagon with two figures in it, at least one of whom is a woman (see *fig.34*), and two or more covered wagons, which, as Anne Stine Ingstad has recently argued, are probably meant to contain holy images of some kind.[146]

The tapestry, however, also depicts a number of obviously costumed figures that are strongly reminiscent of many of the earlier images discussed above. Among other things, one notes again the element of female figures in animal and bird disguise, the wearing of horns by priest figures, and the suggestion of disguised combat involving figures in animal costume. The two last features occurred on the Gallehus horns four hundred years prior to the time of the Oseberg burial and they are also found on the Torslunda matrices which will be discussed below. Once again, these features point to the continuation of an almost homogeneous religious tradition with very ancient roots.

The images contained in the Oseberg tapestry are often extremely unclear and enigmatic, but nonetheless clear enough to suggest that what is being portrayed in the pictures should be viewed in a ritual context. This is evident not only from the wagon processions,[147] but also from the row of dancing female figures (see *fig.35*),[148] and the line of celebrants who have a stance similar to that often depicted on the Bronze Age petroglyphs (see *fig.36*).[149] Finally, and perhaps most telling, is the image of the sacrificial

---

[145] Christensen et al., *Oseberg-dronningens grav*, pp.227–229.
[146] See the illustrations of the relevant fragments in Krafft, *Pictorial weavings*, pp.30–31 (fragments 1 and 2), and also Mary Storm's recreation of part of the tapestry published in Hougen, 'Osebergfunnets billedvev'. See also Ingstad's revealing analysis of these pictures and their accompanying symbols (accompanied by the same pictures) in Christensen et al., *Oseberg-dronningens grav*, pp.231–256. Ingstad gives good reason for believing that the woman in the wagon should be the Oseberg queen herself who appears to have been a powerful priestess figure, possibly even regarded as the earthly incarnation of Freyja. Ingstad's argument that the covered wagons should hold the images of Freyja, Óðinn and Njörðr rather than any other gods, however, must remain purely theoretical.
[147] See Krafft, *Pictorial weavings*, p.30 (fragment 1), p.31 (fragment 2), and p.32 (fragment 3).
[148] See Krafft, *Pictorial weavings*, p.36 (fragment 7). The fact that several magical swastika symbols appear between the dancers lends credence to the idea of the dance having religious connotations to do with fertility: see Christensen et al., *Oseberg-dronningens grav*, p.235.
[149] See Krafft, *Pictorial weavings*, p.33 (fragment 4), and Christensen et al., *Oseberg-dronningens grav*, p.220 and pp.242–243.

C. The Archaeological Evidence

tree bedecked with a number of human corpses,[150] thus supporting Adam of Bremen's later description of the sacrificial grove near the heathen temple at Uppsala.[151]

Bearing this ritual background in mind, a more detailed examination can now be made of the costumed figures which occur both on those tapestry fragments depicting the procession itself, and on other fragments of less certain context. One of the latter fragments, for example, contains the image of an armed male figure, clad in what appears to be a complete animal skin (except for a hole for the nose and mouth), approaching another larger figure who is wearing what seems to be a bull-horned helmet, and carrying a pair of crossed spears (or perhaps twigs) in his left hand (see *fig.37*).[152] The horned figure reappears, more clearly, in one of the procession fragments, again holding a pair of crossed spears in one hand, but now grasping a sword by the blade or sheath with the other (see *fig.34*).[153]

Another fragment, which might originally have been attached to the section containing the skin-clad man,[154] depicts a group of women bearing shields. Some, however, seem to be wearing boar-like animal masks and skins, causing Hougen to class them as 'shield-maidens (*valkyrjur*) with boar-heads' (see *fig.38*).[155] On yet another fragment, another female figure clad as a bird of prey with wings and a bird head appears standing in front of what might be interpreted as a temple building (see *fig.39*).[156] Regarding the boar-headed figures, it is worth noting that Tacitus writes of the Aestii (from the area around the coast of Lithuania) as wearing 'boar figures', or according to Mattingly, 'boar masks', ('insigne superstitionis formas aprorum gestant') as an emblem of the Mother of the gods whom they worshipped.[157] The boar was also a recognised symbol on Scandinavian helmets like that found at Sutton Hoo, and as Davidson suggests, the *formæ* mentioned by Tacitus 'may have been masks or helmets which

6. *The Oseberg tapestry*

---

[150] See Krafft, *Pictorial weavings*, p.35 (fragment 6), Hougen, 'Osebergfunnets billedvev', 114; and Christensen et al., *Oseberg-dronningens grav*, pp.242–244.
[151] See Adam of Bremen, *Gesta Hammaburgensis Ecclesiæ Pontificum*, Book IV, ch.27, pp.259–260; translated in *The history of the Archbishops of Hamburg-Bremen*, p.208. This description bears certain resemblances to that given by Tacitus in *Germania*, ch.39, pp.194–195, regarding the Semnones' practice of sacrificing victims in a sacred grove or forest.
[152] See, for example, Krafft, *Pictorial weavings*, p.32 (fragment 3), and Hougen, 'Osebergfunnets billedvev' 101 and 115 (figs 7a, and 9).
[153] See Krafft, *Pictorial weavings*, p.30 (fragment 1), Hougen, 'Osebergfunnets billedvev', 93 (fig.1), and Storm's recreation published with Hougen's article.
[154] Hougen, 'Osebergfunnets billedvev', 114.
[155] See Hougen, 'Osebergfunnets billedvev', 104, fig.7b, and Davidson, *Pagan Scandinavia*, p.122.
[156] See Christensen et al., *Oseberg-dronningens grav*, pp.245–246.
[157] See Tacitus, *Germania*, ch.45, pp.206–207; and Tacitus, *On Britain and Germany*, p.138.

Fig. 35. Oseberg tapestry fragment: Dancing women.

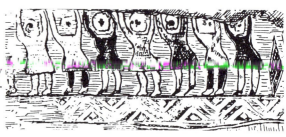

Fig. 36. Oseberg tapestry fragment: Celebrants.

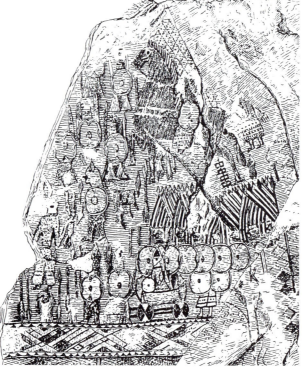

Fig. 37. Oseberg tapestry fragment: A horned man, and a figure in animal costume.

Fig. 38. Oseberg tapestry fragment: A *valkyrja* in a boar's head?

C. The Archaeological Evidence

covered the face'.[158] In this connection, one might note the motif of the goddess Freyja disguising Óttarr heimski as a boar in *Hyndluljóð* (see sts 7, 45 and 49).[159]

6. *The Oseberg tapestry*

On the Oseberg tapestry, however, the boar-heads are worn by women. It is therefore logical to see them as worshippers or *valkyrjur* of Freyja who, apart from being related to fertility,[160] also had the role of a goddess of Death, sharing the choice of those who die in battle with Óðinn.[161] The same interpretation would be applicable to the winged and bird-headed figures on the tapestry. As was mentioned above in *section C.3*, some accounts of the *valkyrjur* describe them as shedding their 'swan-skins'. The Oseberg bird figure, however, is nothing like a swan. It has closer parallels with Freyja's falcon 'feathered skin' ('fiaðrhamr') that bestows the gift of flight in *Þrymskviða* (sts 3, 5 and 9).[162] It also brings to mind Óðinn's name 'Arnhöfði' ('Eagle-head'), which is listed in a twelfth-century *þula* contained in some manuscripts of the *Prose Edda*.[163]

It is probable that some of what is depicted in the tapestry has a mythological context.[164] Nonetheless, as with the Bronze Age petroglyphs, it seems clear from the obvious *costumes* of the 'valkyrjur' that the depiction of such mythological figures would seem to be based on their representation in cultic activities.[165] In this sense, the costumes of the 'valkyrjur' are of particular interest since they raise the question of whether the costumes were merely a form of insignia for priestesses or whether they were used for actual dramatic representation. The bird wings and face-covering bird and boar masks must add weight to the latter suggestion.

It can also be assumed that the horned figures (if they are not idols) probably reflect priest figures of some kind, who, in wearing the helmets, visibly took the role of gods.[166] Indeed, their posture, helmets, and the objects they carry are all encountered elsewhere in other near contemporary

---

[158] See Davidson, *Gods and myths*, p.99; and Bruce-Mitford, *Aspects*, p.200, p.206 (Sutton Hoo), plate 67a (Benty Grange), and plate 59b (Torslunda).
[159] See also Glosecki, *Shamanism*, pp.53–58.
[160] The boar was a symbol for both Freyr and Freyja. See, for example, Turville-Petre, *Myth and religion*, p.166 and p.176.
[161] See *Grímnismal*, st.14.
[162] The suggestion that this 'fiaðrham' is that of a falcon ('valr') is given in *Edda* (1926), p.70, p.90 and p.188. It is noteworthy that Freyja is not the only goddess to be associated with the falcon. In the same work (p.90), Frigg is also described as 'drótning . . . vals-hams' ('the queen of the falcon form').
[163] The *þula* only appears in the AM 748 and AM 757 MSS of *Snorra Edda*. See *Den norsk-islandske skjaldedigtning*, B.I, p.672, A.I, p.681. It is obviously related to the tales of Óðinn changing himself into eagle shape, as in *Edda* (1926), p.73. Further evidence for bird costumes having been worn in the early Viking period might be provided by a small gold figure from Trønninge, Holbæk, Denmark, which Mackeprang argues seems to be wearing a cloak of feathers: see Mackeprang, 'Menschendarstellungen, 242–243.
[164] See, for example, Turville-Petre, *Myth and religion*, p.57.
[165] Similar ideas are expressed by Davidson, in *Pagan Scandinavia*, p.121; and Ingstad, in Christensen et al., *Oseberg-dronningens grav*, p.243.
[166] Davidson, in *Pagan Scandinavia*, p.122, and Bruce-Mitford, in *Aspects*, p.208, suggest

1. Dramatic Activities, 1: Archaeology and Literature

6. The Oseberg tapestry

Fig. 39. Oseberg tapestry fragment: A woman in a bird costume?

material such as the two amulets found at Ekhammar in Uppland, and in Birka in Sweden; the fragmentary designs found in Uppsala in Sweden and Caenby in Lincolnshire; the Finglesham buckle; and certain helmet plates found at Sutton Hoo and Valsgärde (see *figs 40–43*).[167] Yet while the amulets and the figures on the helmet plates might be said to represent the gods themselves, this is less likely in the case of the figures on the Oseberg tapestry. Since they are standing amidst the other human figures in the procession, it is more probable that they, like the bird- and boar-costumed figures, represent human beings *in the roles* of the gods. Whether such representations at the time went further than that of a Catholic priest officiating in a Mass is, of course, open to question. Unfortunately, the all-important 'sound-track' of the performance is missing.

The question of the male figures in animal costume is perhaps simpler. They may well belong to the special class of *berserkir* warriors as Hougen and Ingstad suggest.[168] Such an idea is supported by references in the *fornaldarsögur* to warriors taking the shape of wolves or bears.[169] Both the costumed figures on the tapestry and the shape-changing figures in these accounts might logically be explained by the verse comments in Saxo

that the figure might have been associated with Óðinn. Ingstad, in Christensen et al., *Oseberg-dronningens grav*, p.235, sees the figure as possibly representing a shaman.
[167] Photographs and drawings of the related Uppsala fragment and the Sutton Hoo motifs are provided in Arent, 'The heroic pattern', plates 19–21. Regarding Sutton Hoo, the Caenby fragment, and the Valsgärde 7 motif, see also Bruce-Mitford, *Aspects*, pp.39–40, p.208, and plates 14 a–d, 53b, and 54 a–c. Close similarities to the head gear of these figures are also found on the Viking Age horned-head buckle-mould, and the winged-bird/ horned helmet depicted on another buckle from Ribe in Denmark: see Jensen, *Ribes vikinger*, p.34 and p.50.
[168] Hougen, 'Osebergfunnets billedvev', 104 and 114, and Christensen et al., *Oseberg-dronningens grav*, p.245.
[169] See the references given below in note 239.

Fig. 40. Amulet from Ekhammar, Lungsängen, Stockholms-Näs, Uppland.

Fig. 41. Pendant from Birka (Björkö), Adelsö, Uppland.

Fig. 42. The Finglesham buckle.

Fig. 43. Dancing warriors in horned helmets: The Sutton Hoo helmet plate.

Grammaticus's *Gesta Danorum*, Book I (c.1200), that 'bold warriors have frequently concealed/ themselves beneath the pelts of beasts';[170] and Þorbjörn hornklofi's statement in *Haraldskvæði*, st.21 (c.900?) that 'ulfheðnar ('wolfskins') are those who bear blood-splattered shield-rims in battle' ('Ulfheðnar heita/ þeirs í orrostum/ blóðgar randir bera').[171] Indeed, many scholars have argued that dressing in bear or wolf skins was an intrinsic part of the *berserkr* tradition.[172]

The proximity of the skin-clad figure to the horned priest in the Oseberg tapestry, however, suggests other connotations than that of a normal battle, especially because it forms a close parallel to an earlier motif found on one of the matrices for helmet plates found in Torslunda. The matrix in question depicts yet another angle of dramatic ritual.

7. The Torslunda, Valsgärde and Vendel Plates (sixth-seventh century) and the 'Gothikon'

The idea that combat scenes must have formed part of early Scandinavian ritual is supported by the evidence of a number of Bronze Age petroglyphs[173] and also by the motif of the animal-masked warriors on one of the Gallehus horns. That mock-combats and weapon dances were also taking place in the Iron Age would appear to be confirmed by the motifs depicted on certain sixth- and seventh-century helmet plates and matrices discovered in Vendel, Torslunda and Valsgärde in Sweden, and at Sutton Hoo in England, and on bracteates from Pleizhausen, Gutenstein and Obrigheim in Germany.[174] Many of these images would appear to be based on the idea of a recognised ritual combat between a man and a mock-monster of the kind described by Eliade and de Vries.[175]

Recurrent motifs include a man in a horned helmet dancing alongside an

---

[170] Saxo Grammaticus, *Gesta Danorum*, p.14; trans. in *The history of the Danes*, p.16.
[171] See *Den norsk-islandske skjaldedigtning*, B.I, p.25; A.I, p.28.
[172] Concerning the *berserkir* in this regard, see de Vries, *Religionsgeschichte*, I, p.223, and pp.454–455, and II, pp.97–99; and Davidson, *Gods and myths*, pp.66–69. Bjarni Aðalbjarnarson, however, in a note on *Ynglinga saga*, pp.17–18, note 8, argues that the first element of the word *berserkr* means 'bare' rather than 'bear'.
[173] See Almgren, *Hällristningar*, pp.107–114.
[174] See Arent, 'The heroic pattern', pp.130–145, and Bruce-Mitford, *Aspects*, pp.39–40, pp.43–45, pp.199–200, pp.207–208 and pp.214–222. Arent (p.134 and p.145), associates these motifs with cult practice and initiation rituals. See also de Vries, *Religionsgeschichte*, I, p.363, pp.492–493, p.498, and p.503; and Davidson, *Pagan Scandinavia*, p.99.
[175] See Eliade, *Rites and symbols*, pp.35–36, and de Vries, *Heroic song*, pp.222–224. Concerning Scandinavian warrior initiation ceremonies of the kind discussed above, note also Eliade, *Rites and symbols*, pp.81–83, and Danielli, 'Initiation ceremonial', passim. On the basis of accounts given in *Víga-Glúms saga*, and *Grettis saga*, and the story of Höttr contained in *Hrólfs saga kraka*, pp.56–62, Danielli envisages a Yuletide ritual in which young men were initiated by *berserkir* figures, and had to fight some form of 'monster' to gain acceptance in male society. Danielli's argument is slightly tenuous, but, in the light of the above, worth serious consideration.

C. The Archaeological Evidence

armed monster figure (see *fig.44*);[176] an armed warrior facing a bound horned monster (see *fig.45*);[177] and a warrior being devoured by two such creatures (see *fig.46*),[178] an image that offers an intriguing parallel to the enigmatic carving of the female 'snake charmer' in the ram-horned helmet on the Smiss stone from Gotland (dated 500–700; see *fig.47*).[179] In the present context, however, the most valuable motif is that of the dancing horned man and the 'armed monster'.

7. *The Torslunda, Valsgärde and Vendel plates and the 'gothikon'*

It is probable that this image of the dancing man in the horned helmet found on a Torslunda matrix and the Obrigheim and Gutenstein bracteates would have been recognisable all over the Scandinavian world in the late Iron Age. For example, the horns on the helmets of these figures end in birds' heads, like those on the helmets worn by the Sutton Hoo, Caenby, Birka, Ekhammar and Finglesham figures.[180] Like the Finglesham figure, the Torslunda and Gutenstein horned men have spears in each hand.[181] In the case of the Ekhammar and Obrigheim images, and probably also those from Caenby and Valsgärde and Sutton Hoo, the same figure is found in another position, now often accompanied by a twin, carrying a sword in one hand and crossed spears or twigs in the other, in other words, in exactly the same pose as the horned figures on the Oseberg tapestry.[182]

---

[176] A matrix from Torslunda, and the Gutenstein and Obrigheim bracteates: see Arent, 'The heroic pattern', plates 15, 17 and 18. A colour photograph of the former is given in Magnusson, *Hammer of the North*, p.109.

[177] The Torslunda motif is echoed in that on the Vendel I helmet plate: see Arent, 'The heroic pattern', plates 1 and 5. A colour photograph of the former is given in Magnusson, *Hammer of the North*, p.59. While it is possible to accept Olrik's suggestion in 'Gudefremstillinger', 8, that the bound Torslunda monster seems to be horned, his proposal that the picture depicts Þórr and his goat (9) must be regarded as much more doubtful. Nonetheless, the image does offer an interesting parallel to that of the three-headed giant and the goat depicted on the shorter Gallehus horn: see above, *section C.4*.

[178] A matrix from Torslunda, a design from Valsgärde 8, and the purse-lid from Sutton Hoo: see Arent, 'The heroic pattern', plates 2–4, and 9. The actual nature of the animals depicted here must remain open to speculation. On this question, see further Glosecki, *Shamanism*, p.182 and p.209; Bay, 'Nogle bemærkninger', 11; and Bruce-Mitford, *Aspects*, pp.43–45, and plates 15 a–f.

[179] See Nylén and Lamm, *Stones, ships and symbols*, pp.40–41.

[180] These horned helmets bear a certain resemblance to the helmets found at Viksø, and those worn by the Grevensvænge figurines one thousand years previously (see above, *figs 16–17*). Once again, this would seem to testify to some degree of religious stability and conservatism over all of this time.

[181] The spears are inverted in the case of the Torslunda and Gutenstein figures, but the Finglesham man holds his weapon the correct way up. This, however, should not detract from their similarities. The Finglesham man also has bent knees, suggesting movement like the dance of the other two. This dancing horn-helmeted figure also appears in a different situation on the Valsgärde 8 helmet, where he seems to be leaping over the back of a horse: see Arent, 'The heroic pattern', plate 25.

[182] The Sutton Hoo and less obvious Valsgärde figures come in pairs, the crossed spears being held in the outer hands. The figure on the Uppsala fragment, with crossed spears in the right hand would seem to have belonged to a similar pair formation. In all of these cases, the spears are inverted: see Bruce-Mitford, *Aspects*, pp.39–40, p.208, and plates 14 a–c and 54 a–c. In the case of the individual Ekhammar figure, however, the crossed rods seem too small to be spears. Nonetheless, like the figure in the Caenby fragment, the

Fig. 44. A dancing figure in a horned helmet, leading a man in animal costume: Helmet-plate matrix from Torslunda, Öland.

Fig. 45. A bound monster and a man: Helmet-plate matrix from Torslunda, Öland.

Fig. 46. Monsters and a man: Helmet-plate matrix from Torslunda, Öland.

Fig. 47. The "snake charmer": Smiss III stone, När, Gotland.

7. The Torslunda, Valsgärde and Vendel plates and the 'gothikon'

There can be little doubt that the horn-helmeted man in all of these cases was meant to represent one and the same figure. The probability, considering the two birds on the helmets, is that the figure was related to Óðinn who, according to *Grímnismál*, st.20, and the *Prose Edda*, possessed two ravens named Huginn (Thought) and Muninn (Memory), which sat on his shoulder and informed him about everything that was going on in the world.[183]

The Torslunda matrix, however, was obviously not meant to depict a mythological occurrence. Indeed, in both the Torslunda and Gutenstein designs it is clear that the armed 'monster' facing the horned man is no abstract, imaginative creation, but a deliberate picture of a human being wearing a mask and costume. The head in the Gutenstein design is more monster-like, but that on the Torslunda matrix is closer to that of a wolf. As Arent suggests, there is good reason to believe that this figure should be seen as some form of *ulfheðinn* or *berserkr*.[184]

The fact that the Torslunda matrix seems to depict an actual event adds further weight to the argument that the same applies to the actions depicted on the Oseberg tapestry, and encourages further examination of the events depicted on the other Torslunda matrices. Considering that the two-legged figure facing the horned man on the Gutenstein bracteate is wearing a dragon-head, rather than that of a wolf, there is good reason to wonder whether the 'monsters' on the other motifs from Torslunda and on the Vendel I helmet should not also be seen as costumed and masked humans taking the role of 'monsters'. These other monsters also stand upright, are man-sized, and one of them (*fig.45*) has plaited designs on its body which resemble those on the clothes of one of the human figures (*fig.46*).[185]

Arent has argued convincingly that, in general terms, the image of the 'wolf-warrior' and the helmeted figure on the Torslunda, Gutenstein and

---

Ekhammar man is holding a sheathed sword below the hilt in his right hand. This offers a direct parallel to one of the Oseberg horned men who has the sheathed(?) sword in what appears to be his left hand – unless, for some intriguing reason, he has been depicted with his back turned. It might be noted that the Torslunda figure, like the Sutton Hoo, Valsgärde and Uppsala figures, also seems to be dancing. Furthermore, he has a sword hanging from his shoulder and thus possesses the same number of implements as the crossed-spear figures. The probability must be that both scenes belong to a related ritual.

[183] See *Edda* (1926), p.39. The suggestion that this figure should be Óðinn has been made by several other scholars. See, for example, Olrik, 'Gudefremstillinger', 9, and Oxenstierna, *Järnålder*, p.237. Oxenstierne argues that the figure is a 'priest of Oðinn playing the role of the one-eyed war god in a cult drama' ('Odenspräst, som spelar de enögde krigsgudens roll i ett kultdrama'). There must be some question, however, about whether any of the horned figures have only one eye.

[184] See Arent, 'The heroic pattern', p.137. Similar ideas are suggested by Ström, in *Nordisk hedendom*, pp.110–111; Dumézil in *The stakes of the warrior*, p.43; Davidson in *Pagan Scandinavia*, pp.99–100; and Oxenstierna, in *Järnålder*, p.237.

[185] The idea of plaited material brings to mind the plaited straw used to make the costumes of the Shetland *grøleks* and *skeklers* in later folk tradition. See further below, Chapter II, G.4.

C. The Archaeological Evidence

Obrigheim designs does not point to a real battle, but rather to a form of 'weapon dance', such as that suggested by Bruce-Mitford in connection with the horned figures on the Sutton Hoo helmet.[186] According to Arent, such a dance might have had similarities to the dances of certain German tribes described earlier by Tacitus,[187] but appears to have been related more to 'ritualistic mock deaths and initiation rites'.[188] Arent associates the Torslunda motifs with initiation rites rather than any seasonal ceremony, but as she herself points out, in primitive religion both initiation ceremonies and seasonal rituals related to the New Year commonly involve similar elements associated with renewal, such as a combat with a chthonic being, followed by the motifs of death and reawakening.[189]

7. *The Torslunda, Valsgärde and Vendel plates and the 'gothikon'*

As part of her argument for such performances having taken place in Germanic cult ritual, Arent refers to the evidence of sword dancers wearing wolf attire at Zürich in 1568.[190] However, much closer parallels with stronger direct Scandinavian associations can perhaps be found in an eleventh-century ceiling fresco from Kiev, in the tenth century account of a 'Gothic' dance held in Constantinople, and in the two animal masks recently found in the harbour at Hedeby.

The ceiling fresco, commonly called 'The fight of the guisers' ('Borba ryazenyh'), is found above the stairway of the cathedral of Hagia Sophia in Kiev built by Jaroslav the Wise in 1037.[191] The other stairway walls are decorated with a series of illustrations of theatrical entertainers in the Hippodrome of Constantinople, ranging from acrobats to dancers and mimes, all of whom are performing in front of an audience. This is therefore the context in which the ceiling pictures above the staircase should be viewed.[192] In the fresco in question, a figure wearing a bird-like mask[193] and

---

[186] Bruce-Mitford, *Aspects*, p.200 and p.208.
[187] Tacitus, *Germania*, ch.24, pp.166–167. See also note 112 above on the Hochdorf sword dancers.
[188] See Arent, 'The heroic pattern', p.138. See also Glosecki, *Shamanism*, pp.182–183, on possible parallels in shamanistic initiation.
[189] See Arent, 'The heroic pattern', p.139 and p.141. Regarding the shared aspect of renewal or rebirth in these two rituals, see further Eliade, *Patterns*, pp.398–408 and p.412; *Rites and symbols*, pp.xii–xiv; and *Cosmos and history*, p.69. The notion of links between creation myths and initiation rituals is echoed by de Vries in *Heroic song*, p.222.
[190] Arent, 'The heroic pattern', pp.138–139.
[191] See Berthold, *A history of world theatre*, pp.225–226. According to Davidson, in *The Viking road*, p.210, the frescoes were probably painted c.1054. According to a letter from Irma Totskaya, director of scientific research in the cathedral, the other name for the fresco is 'The fight between a man and a beast'.
[192] See Dalton, *Byzantine art*, pp.301–302; Hamilton, *The art and architecture of Russia*, p.71; and A. V. Grabar, quoted in Vysotsky, *Svetskie freski Sofijskogo sobora v Kieve*, p.127.
[193] Some scholars write of there being more than one figure wearing masks, but according to Irma Totskaya (see note 191), this is the only picture of its kind. There has been some discussion amongst Russian scholars about the nature of the mask. Some, such as A. V. Grabar (1962), have regarded it as a wolf mask, while others have suggested that the lower part of the mask was possibly moveable, and that the mask was meant to represent a goat's head of the kind known in European folk tradition. V. P. Darkevich (1975),

7. *The Torslunda, Valsgärde and Vendel plates and the 'gothikon'*

carrying a spear, is opposed by another moustached figure bearing a shield and an axe, the weapon most typically associated with the Scandinavian Varangian Guard which served the Emperor of the Eastern Roman Empire in Constantinople (see *fig.48*).[194] This image bears a striking similarity not only to the warrior/monster motifs from Torslunda and Vendel I, but also to the combating monsters depicted on the earlier Gallehus horn. Again, both the form of the picture and its context suggest that the fresco is based on actual events. The main difference here is that the figures occur within the context of entertainment rather than ritual, although, as certain scholars have argued, the performance in question may have taken place during the Christmas festival.[195] Whatever the purpose of the performance was, the shape of the bird mask detracts from it being regarded as any practical form of helmet.[196] There is little doubt that it should be seen as a mask of some kind used for some dramatic purpose, rather than for effective personal protection.

With some persuasiveness, several scholars have suggested that the Hagia Sophia fresco should also be seen in the context of the 'gothikon' performed by 'Gothic' warriors for the Emperor of the Eastern Roman Empire in Constantinople on the ninth day of Christmas in the mid-tenth century.[197] This performance is described in some detail in Constantine VII

---

however, suggests the figure is a 'dog's head' of the kind associated with the earlier pagan religion of the area, and depicted in certain Byzantine manuscripts from the eleventh – twelfth centuries. A summary of scholarly comment is given in Vysotsky, *Svetskie freski Sofijskogo sobora v Kieve*, p.127.

[194] A colour photograph of the fresco is contained in Vysotsky, *Svetskie freski Sofijskogo sobora v Kieve*. Regarding the nature of the Varangian axes, see Blöndal, *Væringjasaga*, pp.293–294, and Davidson, *The Viking road*, p.180, p.186 and p.191. It might also be noted that one of the figures on the wall painting below is Jaroslav's daughter Ellisif, who at about this time married Haraldr Sigurðarson harðráði. Haraldr, who later died at Stamford Bridge in 1066, seems to have served Jaroslav in Kiev c.1031–1034, and between 1034 and 1042 was a commander in the Varangian Guard in Constantinople. See Davidson, *The Viking road*, pp.207–227.

[195] Dalton, *Byzantine art*, pp.301–302. This suggestion would add weight to the argument being made above concerning the possible relationship between the figures and a seasonal ritual. It also strengthens the possibility that the image is related to the *gothikon* discussed below. See also Hamilton, *The art and architecture of Russia*, p.71. As Vysotsky shows in *Svetskie freski Sofijskogo sobora v Kieve*, p.127, a number of Russian scholars (N. P. Kondakov [1888]; D. V. Ainalov and E. K. Redin; and V. P. Darkevich [1975]), have associated this picture with the pre-Christmas festival of 'Svyatki' which is takes place on 3 January, which is also considered by some to have been the date of the *gothikon* performance discussed below.

[196] The suggestion that the figures should be associated with gladiators is made by Davidson, in *The Viking road*, p.198. To the best of my knowledge, no other illustrations of gladiators from this time depict them wearing masks of this kind, and no such association is made by any of the scholars mentioned in Vysotsky's *Svetskie freski Sofijskogo sobora v Kieve*.

[197] N. P. Kondakov, *Ofreskah lestnits Kievo-Sofijskogo sobora* (1888), p.353, quoted in Vysotsky, *Svetskie freski Sofijskogo sobora v Kieve*, p.127; echoed in Berthold, *A history of world theatre*, pp.225–226. Regarding the dating, Vogt, in *Commentaire*, II, p.186, suggests that the performance took place on 2 January. See, however, note 195 above.

Fig. 48. The fresco of the masked warrior in the cathedral of Hagia Sophia, Kiev.

Fig. 49. Animal masks from Hedeby.

7. The Torslunda, Valsgärde and Vendel plates and the 'gothikon'

Porphyrogenitus' *Book of ceremonies* (c.953).[198] According to the account, the 'dance' or battle representation was performed by two groups of men (possibly representing the two ruling Hippodrome factions, the 'Blues' and the 'Greens'[199]) accompanied by two pairs of skin-clad warriors[200] who wore 'various masks'. The performance itself involved two kinds of circle dance. The first involved one group dancing in a ring within a circle made by the other, while in the second, two separate circle dances were conducted around the individual leaders of the two groups. Both dances were accompanied not only by the clashing of staves on shields, and rhythmic shouts involving the word 'Toúl!'[201] but also by chants of praise in a conglomeration of languages, including Gothic, Latin, Hebrew and Greek.[202] These chants seem to have used a central voice and chorus. The dramatic element, however, is stressed by the fact that the action seems to have been related to battle.

From the nature of the accompanying spoken text, it seems evident that the reporter did not understand all of the words he/ she heard. It can therefore be assumed that the performers must have been of foreign origin rather than local actors.[203] Furthermore, since there is no evidence of any

---

[198] The original text, with a French translation is given in Constantin VII Porphyrogénète, *Le livre des cérémonies*, II, pp.182–185; see also Vogt's *Commentaire* on this edition, II, pp.186–191. The text is also published with a Latin translation in Kraus, 'Das gotische Weihnachtsspiel', pp.224–227. The earliest translation into German is found in von Massmann, *Gothica minora*, 366–373. Various summaries and translations of the account are given in Phillpotts, *The Elder Edda*, pp.186–188; Axton, *European drama*, pp.33–34; Blöndal, *Væringjasaga*, pp.290–291; Sjöberg, 'En germansk julfest', 31–35; and de Vries, *Religionsgeschichte*, I, pp.452–453. All of these, unfortunately, display a variety of interpretations and misunderstandings. I am grateful to both Peter Vosicky and Dr Sigurður Pétursson for re-examining the text and the translations of this account for me.

[199] The text says nothing about the performers' relationship to the Hippodrome. They are merely called the 'Blues' and the 'Greens'. This suggests that they either represented the two factions, or, just as likely, since they were performing a conflict, they were simply dubbed with these names as a form of contemporary joke, in the same way that children often name their own football teams after national football clubs.

[200] The type of animal skin is not mentioned. The skins, however, were worn with the fur turned outwards.

[201] The meaning of the word *Toúl* is still vague, but most scholars associate the word with the Old Norse *jól* (Gothic: *jiúleis*), meaning 'Yule': see, for example, Blöndal, *Væringjasaga*, p.291, and Sjöberg, 'En germansk julfest', 32.

[202] See Constantin VII Porphyrogénète, *Le livre des cérémonies*, II, p.186; Phillpotts, *The Elder Edda*, p.186; Blöndal, *Væringjasaga*, p.291; Axton, *European drama*, p.34; and Berthold, *A history of world theatre*, p.224. As Blöndal points out, the text itself is extremely unclear, but more recent investigations have shown that although the main part of the text is in Latin with Greco-Christian additions, there is evidence that it was perhaps of Gothic origin: Berthold, *A history of world theatre*, p.224. As Axton stresses, all that is recorded of the Gothic verses are the closing fragments, but this Gothic text might go back to the sixth century.

[203] For the suggestion that the performers were Greek, see Vogt, *Commentaire*, II, p.186, note 2; de Vries, *Religionsgeschichte*, II, p.452; Blöndal, *Væringjasaga*, pp.290–291; and most recently Vésteinn Ólason in *The traditional ballads*, p.37, note 7. The idea that the *gothikon* was presented by Scandinavians of the Varangian Guard was made as early as 1813 by Finnur Magnússon: see *Introduction*, note 11, and *Veterum borealium*

C. The Archaeological Evidence

body of Gothic warriors having been in the Varangian Guard after the time of Justinian (c.500),[204] it is natural to consider the possibility of an association between the *gothikon* and the Scandinavians who, along with Russian mercenaries, dominated the Guard during the period in question.[205] Many of these Scandinavians must have had close links with the island of Gotland or the areas of Västergötland and Östergötland in Sweden, the inhabitants of which, it might be assumed, were also entitled to call themselves 'Goths'.[206]

There are obvious similarities in costume between the performers of the *gothikon* and the skin-clad figures depicted on the Torslunda matrices and the Oseberg tapestry.[207] The use of masks is also reflected in the Kiev fresco and on the Gallehus horns. Finally, the appropriate link with the Christmas season should be noted.[208] Indeed, shield-rapping like that mentioned in the account of the *gothikon* is later described as having been a particularly Varangian tradition, usually carried out on Christian religious festivals whenever the Guard used to wish the Emperor luck in their own language.[209] In spite of the reservations of some scholars,[210] there is still good reason for placing the account of the *gothikon* alongside the previously listed evidence for early ritualistic dramatic activities having taken place in Scandinavia.[211]

Up until very recently such arguments were regarded as being little more

7. *The Torslunda, Valsgärde and Vendel plates and the 'gothikon'*

---

mythologiæ lexicon, p.481, note **. This idea was supported by Cronholm, in *Wäringarna*, p.212, and Sjöberg, in 'En germansk julfest', 34–35. More tentative arguments that the dancers must have been at least Germanic are made in Berthold, *A history of world theatre*, p.224; Phillpotts, *The Elder Edda*, p.186; Axton, *European drama*, p.33; and Tydeman, *The theatre in the Middle Ages*, p.7.

[204] See Sjöberg, 'En germansk julfest', 34, and Phillpotts, *The Elder Edda*, p.186.

[205] See Blöndal, *Væringjasaga*, pp.217–222, and Jones, *A history of the Vikings*, p.266. Blöndal states that this composition continued until 1066, after which time the Scandinavians and Russians were joined by a number of English warriors of Scandinavian descent.

[206] Regarding the key position of Gotland on the route to Constantinople, see Davidson, *The Viking road*, p.17, p.63, and p.300.

[207] The possible link with the Torslunda figures is also noted by Davidson, in *Pagan Scandinavia*, p.100.

[208] See also *section B.3* above on the performance of *leikar* during the winter-solstice period.

[209] See Blöndal, *Væringjasaga*, p.287. This fact is echoed in the later fourteenth-century *Book of offices*, wrongly attributed to Codinus Curopalata (c.1400): see also Blöndal, *Væringjasaga*, p.282 and p.290. According to Blöndal, since the *Book of offices* makes no direct mention of the *gothikon*, the custom must have soon gone out of practice, if it was ever regular at all. However, as Sjöberg points out in 'En germansk julfest', 35, there must be a link between the *gothikon* and this later practice of axe-clashing carried out by the (now English-speaking) Varangians before the Emperor at Christmas time.

[210] See above, note 203.

[211] Phillpotts, *The Elder Edda*, p.187, concludes that the element of the circle dance might 'give us some idea of the part played by the chorus in ancient Scandinavian ritual drama'. Axton similarly sees this performance as 'the earliest example of medieval battle-play', but like Phillpotts feels that the account should not be regarded as a description of an original folk or even ritual dramatic dance, but rather of 'a traditional performance firmly enclosed by a courtly and Christian framework': Axton, *European drama*, p.34.

8. Conclusion

than conjecture. However, in 1979–1980 conclusive evidence that such masks and animal costumes must have been used occasionally by the Scandinavians was provided by the discovery of two tenth-century felt animal masks (possibly of a sheep and bull) in the harbour at Hedeby (see *fig.49*). The smaller sheep's head mask measures 19 x 14 cm, and would thus have fitted a young adult. The larger, snouted bull or calf's head mask, of which only half was found, would have measured in a complete state 40 x 26 cm.[212] Whatever their purpose, these items remove any doubt that animal masks must have been used in *leikar* and/ or rituals during the Viking period.[213]

8. The Archaeological Evidence: Conclusion, and Relationship to Later Accounts of Cult Ritual at Uppsala

On the basis of the above, it can be concluded that dramatic activities similar to those depicted on the Bronze Age carvings were still taking place as part of religious ceremonies in Scandinavia during the early Viking Age. Many of these enactments seem to have taken the form of totemistic, costumed, ritualistic activities associated with initiation ceremonies and/ or larger religious festivals such as that connected with the winter solstice. Especially apparent are the recurring motifs of the mock fight involving costumed figures, those of costumed processions and dance,[214] and perhaps also that an enacted *hieros gamos* associated with the mid-winter period, all of which are illustrated by the various archaeological finds described above. Central to all of the above are the horned figure, and the animal disguise which is often associated with a goat, wolf, bear, bull or bird figure. In general, such activities fit well under the heading of *leikar* as defined at the start of this chapter, and it is not difficult to imagine such costumed rituals taking place alongside sports as part of outdoor religious festivity on various recognised local *leikvangar* or *leikvellir* situated close to cult centres. Indeed, as has been shown, the Swedish petroglyphs and the Gallehus horns effectively demonstrate the combination of sports and dramatic ritual activity.

The evidence presented above adds not only weight but also a visual dimension to Saxo Grammaticus' much-quoted account (c.1200) of the hero Starcatherus' disgust with the 'womanish body movements, the clatter of actors on the stage ('scænicosque mimorum') and the soft tinkling of

---

[212] See Hägg, *Die Textilfunde*, pp.69–72 and pp.185–188, and Sawyer, *Da Denmark blev Danmark*, p.129.
[213] See also Weiser-Aall's argument in *Julenissen*, pp.33–48, that the later *julebukk* and *julegeit* traditions (see below, Chapter II, B.3–5), which involve masks of a similar kind, may have been originally related in part to initiation rituals carried out during the Yuletide period.
[214] See Holmqvist, 'The dancing gods', passim, which gives a convincing argument for a ritual dance tradition running throughout the period under discussion.

C. The Archaeological Evidence

8. Conclusion

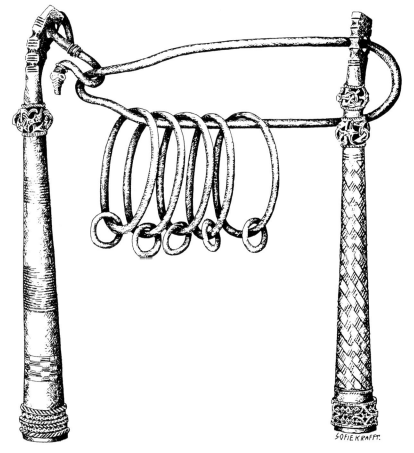

Fig. 50. A rattle (*rangle*) from the Oseberg grave.

bells' at the large-scale outdoor pagan festival that apparently took place in Uppsala every nine years.[215]

There may be some question about the authenticity of this description which was written some forty years after the acceptance of Christianity in Sweden.[216] Nonetheless, it is clear that when Saxo used the word *mimi* he was not limiting the word to jugglers, but was implying performers who commonly included skills of mimicry and imitation among their many

---

[215] Saxo Grammaticus, *Gesta Danorum*, Book VI, p.154; translated in *The history of the Danes*, p.172. See also Holmqvist, 'The dancing gods', p.102: Holmqvist suggests that the use of bells in dance might be supported by the dancing figures on the Ålleberg collar (c.600–400 B.C.) which appear to have bells around their ankles (see *fig.32*).
[216] Olrik, in *Kilderne til Sakses oldhistorie*, I, p.118, was particularly dubious about the terminology of this account. Nonetheless, he later argued that this section of Saxo's work might have originated in a lost poem concerning Starkaðr's youth: see Olrik, *Danmarks heltedigtning*, II, pp.89–90. More recently, a slightly more ambivalent position is taken by Olaf Olsen, who comments in *Hørg, hov og kirke*, p.63, that the account 'kan rumme en historisk kærne' ('might have some historical basis').

8. Conclusion talents.²¹⁷ Considering the evidence given above and the religious context of the Uppsala festival, which was probably dominated by the worship of Freyr,²¹⁸ there is reason to believe that Saxo's account must have some historical basis. For example, Saxo's mention of 'bells' might find support in the shape of the iron *rangler* ('rattles') of the kind found in the grave of the Oseberg queen (see *fig.50*).²¹⁹ More than two hundred of these mysterious Viking Age implements have been found, usually individually and commonly in richly equipped graves. Most come from south-eastern Norway, although they are also known as far north as northern Trøndelag.²²⁰

Various explanations have been given for the purpose of the *rangler* which were obviously designed to create noise. Some scholars have tried to see them as part of a trace for a cart or sledge.²²¹ Others, however, considering the seemingly ritualistic context in which the *rangler* were found on the Oseberg ship,²²² have associated them primarily with religious activity, suggesting that they were perhaps a means of calling up good spirits or warding off bad ones, or simply a mark of religious authority.²²³ Whatever their purpose, rattles are often related to fertility practices and an association with the cult of Freyr or Freyja would make good sense.²²⁴

Saxo's account becomes even more interesting when placed alongside the earlier, more trustworthy, yet independent description of the Uppsala festival given by Adam of Bremen (c.1070), an account which seems to have been based largely on eye-witness reports.²²⁵ Among other things, Adam

---

²¹⁷ For references regarding the role of the *mimi* at this time, see the *Appendix*. In general, most scholars in the early years of this century accepted the pantomimic implications of this description. See, for example, Phillpotts, *The Elder Edda*, p.120; Hammarstedt, 'Kvarlevor', p.512, and Läffler, 'Det evigt grönskande trädet', p.640. More recently, and almost certainly taking this description in combination with that given by Adam of Bremen (see below), Holtsmark has concluded that the festival must have involved cult-drama. See, for example, Holtsmark, 'Drama', p.293. Davidson, in *Gods and myths*, pp.96–97, is less assured about the authenticity of the account but agrees that it 'implies some kind of performance, possibly ritual drama', which may well also have involved some kind of ritual marriage.
²¹⁸ Saxo writes that during his time in Sweden, Starcatherus had been staying with the 'sons of Frø' ('filiis Frø'): Saxo Grammaticus, *Gesta Danorum*, Book VI, p.154; trans. in *The history of the Danes*, p.172. The same idea is supported by *Ynglinga saga*, p.16 and pp.23–24. In Adam of Bremen's account, however, the central god appears to have been Þórr: see Adam of Bremen, *Gesta Hammaburgensis ecclesiæ pontificum*, Book IV, chs.26–27, pp.258–259; trans. in *The history of the Archbishops of Hamburg-Bremen*, pp.207–208.
²¹⁹ See, for example, Christensen et al., *Oseberg-dronningens grav*, pp.93–94 and p.249; and in particular, Lund, 'Paa rangel', passim.
²²⁰ Only three such *rangler* have been found in Sweden. None have been found in Denmark. See, for example, Lund, 'Paa rangel', 51–54.
²²¹ See, for example, Petersen, *Vikingetidens redskaper*, pp.42–56; and Lund, 'Paa rangel', 76–85, and 90–103.
²²² See Lund, 'Paa rangel', 48 and 76.
²²³ See, for example, Lund, 'Paa rangel', 71–76.
²²⁴ Lund, 'Paa rangel', 86–88.
²²⁵ See Holtsmark, 'Drama', p.293, and O. Olsen, *Hørg, hov og kirke*, p.119.

C. The Archaeological Evidence

8. Conclusion

provides a further element of the soundtrack accompanying ritual activity by noting that 'the incantations customarily chanted in the ritual of a sacrifice of this kind' (that is, the hanging of victims in trees) 'are manifold and unseemly' ('multiplices et inhonestae').[226] It is possible that these songs might have been associated with the mimetic activities mentioned by Saxo, and perhaps also with poems such as those of the Edda, but once again, firm conclusions are impossible. Neither of these accounts provides any detailed information about the 'texts' accompanying the ceremonies in question. Furthermore, nothing is said about whether the actions of the '*mimi*' were ever placed within a mythological context, something that would imply that they were actually representing something rather than merely dancing.[227] If they *were* acting, then the performance in question would obviously be something much more developed than a simple dramatic ritual. Indeed, it would point to ritual plays being performed on a large scale.

One further minor piece of evidence might be considered in support of the idea of large-scale 'dramatic' presentation taking place at Uppsala. This is a scholium which exists in an early twelfth-century manuscript of Adam's work.[228] Here, the Uppsala temple is described as standing 'on level ground with mountains all about it *like a theatre*'.[229] This statement does not necessarily mean that theatrical activities definitely took place at Uppsala, and cannot have been based on any visual similarity between the mounds at Uppsala and any old Roman theatre buildings the writer may have known.[230] The word *theatrum*, which was chosen deliberately, was evidently being used in a practical sense. The implication must be that a distinction existed between the audience and the active participants in the festival; in other words, that people used the grave mounds at Uppsala to watch the actions taking place below.[231] If dramatic or costumed actions like those depicted on the Oseberg tapestry, the Torslunda matrices or the

---

[226] Adam of Bremen, *Gesta Hammaburgensis ecclesiæ pontificum*, Book IV, ch.27, p.260; trans. in *The history of the Archbishops of Hamburg-Bremen*, p.208.

[227] The only exception to this rule is the account of the *gothikon* discussed above in section C.7 in which the actions of the dancers appear to have been loosely placed within the context of a specific battle.

[228] Scholium 139 (135). There is some disagreement about the dating and authenticity of the scholium. Lindquist, in 'Hednatemplet', 91, feels sure that Adam himself wrote the note. However, Turville-Petre, in *Myth and religion*, p.245, is uncertain about the authenticity of this particular account, feeling that the descriptions are not those of an eyewitness.

[229] '... in planitie situm montes in circuitu habet positos ad instar theatri': Adam of Bremen, *Gesta Hammaburgensis ecclesiæ pontificum*, Book IV, p.258; trans. in *The history of the Archbishops of Hamburg-Bremen*, p.207.

[230] The mounds appear to stand in a row rather than in a circle like the old Roman theatre buildings: see Lindquist, 'Hednatemplet', 113 and 115–117). On the use of the word *theatrum* at this time, see further Marshall, 'Theatre in the Middle Ages', passim.

[231] See, for example, Lindqvist, 'Hednatemplet', 118, and Davidson, *Pagan Scandinavia*, p.142. There has been some dispute about the likelihood of the audience ever having been permitted to sit on the holy mounds. See, for example, Birkeli in Sundquist, *Östra Aros*, pp.147–148; and O. Olsen, in *Hørg, hov og kirke*, p.139.

1. The literary evidence for masks

I. Dramatic Activities, I. Archaeology and Literature

Gallehus horns were taking place in front of this audience, performed by 'actors' as Saxo suggests, this small piece of evidence would bring the performance even further into the field of drama. All three main elements of the actor, songs and audience would be now present.

D. Literary Evidence for Ritual Activities

1. The Literary Evidence for Masks and Ritual Disguise

The archaeological and 'historical' evidence examined above provides a context within which the dialogic poems of the Elder Edda might conceivably have originated, and, with good reason, scholars in the past have examined both *Skírnismál* and parts of *Hávamál* in relation to the *hieros gamos* ritual.[232] Furthermore, the context of an initiation ceremony would be well suited to catachetic poems such as *Vafþrúðnismál*, *Alvíssmál*, and *Fáfnismál* which commences with the killing of a possibly masked human monster figure like that depicted on one of the Torslunda matrices.[233] Yet, once again, this is mere conjecture, and the conjecture is hardly aided by the other Old Norse literary evidence which, in comparison to the archaeological evidence, would seem to be extremely scant.

Old Norse literature, of course, contains numerous examples of characters adopting unexplained disguises that do not seem to have been assumed for the sole purpose of escaping public attention.[234] An obvious example of such is Örvar-Oddr's appearance in the shape of the anonymous 'Barkman' ('Næframaðr') in *Örvar-Odds saga*.[235] The majority of such disguises, however, are directly related to animals, and might be said to stem from faint memories of the ritualistic use of animal costumes described in the previous section. Interestingly enough, goats seem play a central role in these disguises, as in the cases of Gram's use of a goat-skin costume to impersonate a giant in *Gesta Danorum*, Book I;[236] Hrómundr Gripsson's

---

[232] Regarding *Skírnismál*, see, for example, Olsen, 'Fra gammel norsk myte', 17–36; Phillpotts, *The Elder Edda*, p.137; Dronke, 'Art and tradition', pp.250–268; and Talbot, 'The withdrawal of the fertility god', 31–46. On *Hávamál*, see Svava Jakobsdóttir, 'Gunnlöð', 215–245.

[233] Regarding *Vafþrúðnismál* and *Fáfnismál*, see further *Chapter III*, G.4 and 6 below.

[234] See further the many useful examples given by Phillpotts, in *The Elder Edda*, pp.115–117, pp.141–143, and pp.152–153, and van Sweringen, in 'The disguise motif', 220–239. Both scholars, however, go too far in that they often fail to discriminate between unexplained costumes and those used solely for the purpose of spying or avoiding a difficult situation.

[235] *Örvar-Odds saga*, pp.359–360: 'Hann spennir þá at sér um bol ok fætr næfrum. Síðan gerir hann sér næfrahött mikinn á höfuð sér. Er hann ekki öðrum mönnum líkr, meiri miklu en allir menn aðrir, er hann er allr þakinn næfrum.' ('He attaches bark to his legs and torso. He next makes a huge bark hat for his head. He is then totally different to other men; when completely covered in bark he is much bigger than everyone else.')

[236] Saxo Grammaticus, *Gesta Danorum*, Book I, pp.13–14; trans. in *The history of the Danes*, p.16.

D. Literary Evidence

1. The literary evidence for masks

donning of a goat-beard before going into battle in *Hrómundar saga Gripssonar*;[237] and Þorleifr jarlsskáld's use of a goat-beard and two sharpened sticks as part of his Yuletide disguise in *Þorleifs þáttr jarlsskálds*.[238] Closely related to these descriptions of animal related disguises are the accounts of shape-changing from the legendary *fornaldarsögur*, such as Sigmundr and Sinfjötli's use of wolf-skins ('úlfahamir') in *Völsunga saga*, and Böðvarr Bjarki's transformation into a bear during battle in *Hrólfs saga kraka*.[239] These accounts have often been placed in the context of shamanistic practices or warrior societies such as the *berserkir* and the *ulfheðnar*.[240] As has been mentioned above, obvious parallels to the last two accounts mentioned above can be seen in the skin-clad figures on the Oseberg tapestry and Torslunda matrix, and in the account of the *gothikon* examined above in *section C.7*.

Especially interesting in this context is the more contemporary account from *Kormáks saga* concerning Steinarr Önundarson's appearance at the spring Þórsnessþing in Iceland, dressed in a 'bear-skin coat with a mask ('gríma') in front of his face'.[241] Steinarr intends to challenge Hólmganga-Bersi to combat. Nonetheless, the purpose of the disguise is totally unclear, since while Steinarr may have been classed as a 'trouble-maker' ('óeirumaðr'),[242] there is nothing in either *Kormáks saga* or *Egils saga* to suggest that he was ever regarded as a *berserkr* or needed to hide his identity.[243] Indeed, even though Steinarr conceals his name from Bersi in the scene in question, his adversary promptly recognises who he is.[244] As with many of the other accounts of animal costumes, it would seem that only part of the story is being told.

The above account is the only example of animal disguise (if indeed that

---

[237] *Hrómundar saga Gripssonar*, p.274: 'Hann tekr sér kylfu í hönd, bindr sér grátt ok sítt geitarskegg ok setr síðan hatt á höfuð sér.' ('He takes a club in his hand, attaches a long, grey goat beard to himself, and then places a hat on his head.') This unexplained costume is reminiscent of Óðinn's disguises when visiting Miðgarðr, and particularly his guise in *Hárbarðsljóð*.

[238] *Þorleifs þáttr jarlsskáld*, p.220. Regarding Þorleifr's costume see also below *Chapter II, B.5*. The same motif occurs elsewhere in *Eymundar þáttr Hringssonar*, in *Flateyjarbok* (1860–1868), II, p.128.

[239] *Völsunga saga*, p.15 and *Hrólfs saga kraka*, pp.87–89. See also the suggestions of shape-changing in *Egils saga*, p.4, and *Landnámabók*, p.347 and pp.355–356. For more recent parallels in Scandinavia, see for example, Bø et al., *Norske segner*, p.62, pp.64–66 and pp.248–252; Klintberg, *Svenska folksägner*, pp.246–250; and Kvideland and Sehmsdorf, *Scandinavian folk belief*, pp.74–80.

[240] Böðvar Bjarki's behaviour is closely paralleled by that of Óðinn in *Ynglinga saga*, p.18. Both accounts have been compared to shamanistic practices. See Eliade, *Shamanism*, pp.380–381. Regarding the *berserkir* and *ulfheðnar*, see above, notes 170–172.

[241] *Kormáks saga*, pp.247: 'Þar sat maðr mikill ok sterkligr í bjarnskinnsólpu ok gríma fyrir andliti.' Regarding the meaning of the word *gríma*, see below, *section D.1*.

[242] *Kormáks saga*, p.239.

[243] See also *Egils saga*, pp.277–283.

[244] Considering the context, it is tempting to compare the element of disguise here with that of Sigurðr Fáfnisbani, who in *Fáfnismál*, st.2, names himself 'Gǫfugt dýr' ('noble animal'): see further *Chapter III*, note 283.

1. *The literary evidence for masks*

is what was meant) in the Icelandic family sagas. Direct evidence of such activities from the contemporary world of thirteenth- and fourteenth-century Scandinavia is even more scant. In *Íslendinga saga*, a man named Steingrímr *Skinngrýlu*son is mentioned as taking part in the battle at Breiðabólstaðr (1221),[245] and, as Finnur Jónsson has pointed out, the female name 'Skinngrýla' probably means 'skin-monster'.[246] Meanwhile, in records from Bergen dated 1307, one finds the name 'Arnaldus Jolahest' ('Arnald Christmas horse').[247] Considering their date, neither of these references can be directly related to pagan ritual. As will be shown below, however, they fit well into the pattern of later dramatic folk tradition in Scandinavia.

The number of references to animal disguise in the legendary and everyday world of the sagas is clearly limited. On the other hand, it is evident that in the world of Old Norse *mythology*, shape-changing is almost second nature. A recurring motif is that of the magical bird costume, exemplified by the *valkyrjur* who commonly take on the shape of swans,[248] and Freyja's falcon 'fiaðrhamr' ('feather-skin') or 'hauks bjalli' ('hawk's skin') in which Loki flies to and from Jötunheimar in both *Þrymskviða*, sts 3, 5 and 9, and Þjóðólfr úr Hvini's *Haustlöng*, st.12.[249] Also worth consideration is Óðinn's use of the name 'Arnhöfði' which is possibly a reference to his own flight from Jötunheimar in the shape of an eagle, followed by the giant Suttungr in a similar guise.[250] As was mentioned above (*sections B.2* and *B.6*), it is tempting to place such references alongside the archaeological evidence depicting bird costumes from Bohuslän, Kivik and the Oseberg tapestry. Indeed, the question must be raised as to whether the appearance of omniscient talking birds in a purely dialogic section of *Helgakviða Hjörvarðssonar*, sts 1–4, and in *Fáfnismál*, sts 32–44, might not also stem from the same idea of ritualistic 'shape-changing'.

The gods and their adversaries, however, do not limit themselves to

---

[245] *Sturlunga saga*, (1878), I, pp.244–247. A character with a related name, Grýlu-Brandr, is also mentioned elsewhere in *Íslendinga saga*: see *Sturlunga saga* (1878), II, p.171.
[246] 'Skind-uhyre' or 'skind-skræmsel': see Finnur Jónsson, 'Tilnavne', 328, and 347. On the possible links between this figure and later dramatic folk traditions in the North Atlantic islands, see below, *Chapter II, G.4*.
[247] See *Diplomatarium Norvegicum*, VIII, p.29. See also Strömbäck, 'Cult remnants', 114, and Almqvist, 'Midfjordingamärren', 11, on the possibility that this figure may have been related to an early Norwegian Christmas tradition that has since died out. However, see also *Chapter II, G.4* on the more recently recorded Faroese tradition involving a figure known as the *jólhestur*.
[248] As in the prose introduction to *Völundarkviða*, and the description of Lára in *Hrómundar saga Gripssonar*, p.280: 'Ein fjölkynngiskona var þar komin í álptar ham. Hún gólaði með svá miklum galdralátum, at engi gáði at verja sik Ólafs manna.' ('A sorceress in the shape of a swan had arrived there. She sang such powerful magic that none of Ólafr's men took care to protect themselves.') The nature of the singing and the costume worn here encourages comparisons between this account and that of Þorbjörg lítil-völva in *Eiríks saga rauða*, pp.206–207. See further below, *Chapter V, D.1*.
[249] See *Edda* (1926), p.70, p.90, and p.188.
[250] See *Skáldskaparmál*, in *Edda* (1926), p.73. See also de Vries' discussion of a possible ritual origin to these names in *Religionsgeschichte*, II, p.64.

D. Literary Evidence

bird-disguises. In *Þrymskviða*, sts 19–32, Þórr, accompanied by Loki, dons bridal garb. At the start of *Reginsmál* (prose introduction and sts 1–4), Otr appears as an otter and Andvari transforms himself into a pike. Loki, meanwhile, makes appearances in the shape of a seal, a salmon, a fly and a mare.[251] The god most associated with disguise, however, is Óðinn, who is known for appearing under any one of a wide variety of names.[252] Two of Óðinn's names, Grímnir and Grímr (*Grímnismál*, sts 46–47[253]) literally mean 'the "man" in the helmet or mask'.[254] Interestingly enough, some suggestion as to the nature of the helmet or mask in question is provided by the fact that the same two names also appear in a *þula* (name list) for *goats*.[255] This double use of the names accordingly raises the possibility of a direct link between Óðinn and the horned figures so often encountered in archaeological material. It also adds weight to the idea that the horned figures on the Torslunda matrix and Oseberg tapestry were not merely wearing regalia but were meant to be *representing* somebody, a figure that even in the thirteenth century was still associated with a particular animal.

1. The literary evidence for masks

The above review of literary references concerning unusual forms of costumed disguise would seem, on the surface, to support the idea that if costumed representation ever existed then it must have been predominantly related to pagan religion, and must have died out with the advent of Christianity. Certainly, as has been pointed out above, with the exception of the semi-legendary *Gunnars þáttr helmings* and the accounts of the Uppsala festival written by Saxo Grammaticus and Adam of Bremen, literary support for ritual dramatic performance having taken place in Scandinavia would seem to be minimal and fragmentary.[256] It is

---

[251] See the prose conclusion to *Lokasenna*, and *Edda* (1926), pp.42–43, 60–61, 83 and 98.
[252] See, for example, the list of names given in *Grímnismál*, sts 46–50, and Óðinn's disguised appearances in *Hárbarðsljóð*, *Vafþrúðnismál* and *Reginsmál*.
[253] See also the name *þula* of Óðinn's names contained in the AM 748 and AM 757 MSS of *Snorra Edda*, given in *Den norsk-islandske skjaldedigtning*, A.I, p.681, B.I, p.672.
[254] 'Den með hjælm eller maske': Sveinbjörn Egilsson and Finnur Jónsson, *Lexicon poeticum*, p.205.
[255] *Edda* (1926), p.210. The name Grímr is also applied to a goat in *Droplaugasona saga*, p.177. In an occasional verse composed by Ólafr Tryggvason, two drinking horns are named Grímar: *Den norsk-islandske skjaldedigtning*, A.I, p.152, B.I, p.145. The name Grímr also appears in two name *þulur* of dwarf and serpent names in the AM 748 and AM 757 MSS of the *Prose Edda*: *Den norsk-islandske skjaldedigtning*, A.I, p.680 and p.685, B.I, p.672 and p.675. The name Grímnir also appears amongst the names of the jötnar: *Edda* (1926), p.196 and p.198. See also note 273 below. Concerning the link between goats and Óðinn as the god of magic, see *Brennu-Njáls saga*, pp.37–38; *Eyrbyggja saga*, pp.51–52; *Vatnsdæla saga*, p.96 and pp.127–128; *Grettis saga*, p.209; and *Reykdæla saga*, pp.192–193, for examples of the working of magic (especially casting illusions or changing the weather) by waving or wrapping a goat-skin around the head: 'Að veifa heðni/ gizka' or 'að vefja heðin'.
[256] One other semi-legendary account that may reflect 'dramatic' ritual (and give a visual aspect to Óðinn's account of his self-sacrifice in *Hávamál*, st.138) is that of Starkaðr's sacrifice of King Víkarr in *Gautreks saga*, pp.26–27. See also Saxo Grammaticus, *Gesta Danorum*, Book VI, p.153; trans. in *The history of the Danes*, pp.171–172. If nothing else, this account of a 'mock-sacrifice' which goes fatally wrong implies that mock-sacrifices of this kind must have been understood in the oral tradition.

1. *The literary evidence for masks*

noteworthy that only one tentative example of an animal 'costume' (that worn by Steinarr Önundarson) is found in the Icelandic family sagas. On dramatic games, folk plays, and large-scale pagan ritual, the sagas would appear to be almost as silent as they are on the actual performances of the Eddis poems.[257] It is perhaps not unnatural that scholars such as Hallvard Magerøy should have arrived at the conclusion that 'the Icelanders had no theatre'.[258]

Such a statement, however, is over-hasty. That the Scandinavians of the early Middle Ages, like their Bronze and Iron Age ancestors, still enjoyed semi-dramatic performances can be assumed from the growing popularity of the foreign *leikarar* or mimes in Scandinavia, possibly from the time of Haraldr hárfagri onwards.[259] The *leikarar*, however, were not the only people to 'act' for public entertainment. It is clear from the sagas that the Scandinavians also had a healthy interest in home-grown public shows of imitation, particularly in the field of satire. This is evident from the 'háð' or 'mockery' performed in imitation of Gunnlaugr Ormstunga and Hrafn Önundarson in *Gunnlaugs saga Ormstungu*, and the references in *Íslendinga saga* to the 'new dance-songs' ('danza-görðir') performed by Kolbeinn Arnórsson's men, and the 'many dance-songs and many other kinds of joke' ('danza marga ok margs-konar spott annat') directed at Loftr Pálsson by the men of Breiðabólstaðr.[260] Elsewhere, in *Gísla saga*, it is suggested that Gísli Súrsson had a reputation as 'the best of mimics' ('in mesta hermikráka').[261] Admittedly, the expression *hermikráka*, used at the time when Gísli has just escaped capture by convincingly impersonating a half-wit, occurs solely in a fourteenth-century manuscript of *Gísla saga*. Yet whether the statement about Gísli's skills of impersonation has any historical basis or not, the term *hermikráka* must have been understood and applied to people where relevant during the thirteenth and fourteenth centuries. As in all other societies, there must have been a demand for such an expression.

In short, the medieval Scandinavians, the Icelanders included, were hardly as 'undramatic' as Magerøy would imagine. Even after the acceptance of Christianity, when public sacrificial meetings no longer took place, opportunities for larger-scale performances of satire and other material would have been provided by social events such as the seasonal *þing* meetings, weddings and religious festivals; in fact, by any occasion when people had reason to gather together. As was pointed out at the start of this chapter, while the Scandinavians lacked a word for 'drama', they would

---

[257] See *Chapter V, A*.
[258] Magerøy, ed., *Bandamanna saga*, p.xvii.
[259] See the references given in the *Appendix*.
[260] See *Gunnlaugs saga*, pp.99–100 (see above, note 32) and *Sturlunga saga* (1878), I, p.245 and II, p.68. For other saga references to dances, see *Chapter II*, note 255.
[261] *Gísla saga*, p.85. Considering the mention of satire above, note that Aasen, in his *Norsk ordbog*, p.287, classes a *hermar* or *hermekraake* as 'a mimic; especially someone who mimics other people to make fun of them': 'Efteraber; især En som efteraber Andre til Spot.'

D. Literary Evidence

1. The literary evidence for masks

have classified such activities as a form of *leikr*. On the basis of both the archaeological and literary evidence, there is good reason to assume that the various seasonal *leikmót* did not only involve sporting activities but also other forms of games and performances, including satirical drama.[262]

It should be remembered, however, that the sagas can hardly be regarded as presenting a comprehensive overview of social behaviour, be it that of the Age of Settlement in Iceland (c.870–1000) or that which existed during the period in which the sagas were written and the Eddic poems recorded (the twelfth to fourteenth centuries). For the main part, objects and actions are only mentioned in the sagas if they have importance for the narrative itself.[263] Another characteristic of saga writing that must be considered is the tendency to identify characters on the basis of their external appearance. In other words, disguised characters seem to *become* the role that they have taken on for the duration of the disguise being worn. In *Þorleifs þáttr jarlsskálds*, for example, the moment that Þorleifr dons his goat-beard and takes up his sticks, he 'becomes' the 'stafkarl' ('tramp') he is representing. He is not named again until his disguise is removed. It is the 'stafkarl' who utters the magical poetic curse 'Jarlsníð' against Jarl Hákon, not Þorleifr.[264] The same technique is applied, for example, when Gunnarr Hámundarsson takes on the guise of Kaupa-Heðinn in *Njáls saga*, when Ǫrvar-Oddr becomes the 'Bark-man' in *Ǫrvar-Odds saga*, and when Gunnarr helmingr becomes Freyr in *Gunnars þáttr helmings*.[265] This naturally raises the question of how Icelandic writers would have described a 'play' if they had seen one. Indeed, how would tales of such ritual-dramatic performances have been preserved in the oral tradition? In short, the apparent lack of evidence for drama in the sagas cannot be totally trusted or taken at face-value.

Regarding the question of whether all pagan activities promptly died out in Iceland with the adoption of Christianity in 1000, more than two hundred years before the sagas came to be written, it is worth considering a short statement contained in Gunnlaugr Leifsson's *Jóns saga helga* which was written in the early twelfth century. Concerning the central figure of the saga, Bishop Jón Ögmundarson, Gunnlaugr writes:

> With the rough and bitter rasp of punishment (he) filed down all unnatural behaviour, wizardry and monstrosity, black magic and alchemy, and all

---

[262] See above, *section B*.
[263] In this context, it is interesting to compare the sagas to English literature from the nineteenth century, at a time when folk drama is known to have been a widespread phenomenon in rural communities throughout the British Isles. In spite of this, references to Mummers' plays in the classic novels of the period would seem to be few and far between. Furthermore, those few references which *do* occur can hardly be regarded as accurate social records. See, for example, Hardy, *The return of the native*, pp.121–139, and Scott, *The pirate*, pp.465–468. Regarding the Mummers' plays of the nineteenth century, see, for example, Helm, *The English Mummers' play*, passim.
[264] See *Þorleifs þáttr jarlsskálds*, pp.220–223.
[265] *Brennu-Njáls saga*, pp.59–60 and 63–65; *Ǫrvar-Odds saga*, pp.359–369; and *Flateyjarbok* (1860–1868), I, pp.338–339.

1. The literary evidence for masks

illusory hocus-pocus, and stood up against all ancient arts with all might and main, because great and evil remnants of pagan traditions remained in the Christian world that had not been uprooted from the Holy fields when Christianity was in its infancy.[266]

This account, written almost a century after the death of the slightly fanatical Bishop Jón, contains many echoes of similar hagiographic accounts written about churchmen abroad, and should be treated with caution.[267] Nonetheless, the audience of the saga, knowing Icelandic conditions, were obviously ready to believe what was stated in the saga about the continuation of older pagan practices, including various forms of 'illusory hocus pocus'.

Bearing this in mind, it is worth looking at the saga material from another angle. Certainly, there are no direct accounts of ritual-dramatic performances in the sagas. Yet is it possible that these literary works contain other kinds of evidence that point to pagan dramatic *leikar* having taken place, or even simple dramatic cameos? It seems clear, for example, that the concept of facial masks (*grímur*) bearing the features of either an animal or man must have been recognised by Icelanders at the time of the sagas. In certain cases, the word *gríma* implies simply a facial covering of some kind to disguise identity,[268] and the same idea of concealment probably lies behind the use of the word *gríma* for 'night' in *Alvíssmál*, st.30, *Hervararkviða*, st.5, and a name *þula* contained in the AM 748 and AM 757 manuscripts of the *Prose Edda*.[269]

On other occasions, however, the implication is related more to external expression or appearance.[270] This would seem to apply in the case of the expression, 'það renna tvær grímur á einhvern' (meaning someone is 'in two minds') of which the earliest use is found in *Grettis saga*.[271] Similarly, the phrases 'gyltar grímor' ('gilded heads') mentioned in *Guðrúnarkviða II*,

---

[266] 'Svarf hann ok af snarpri og bitrligri hirtíngar þél alla óháttu, fjölkýngi ok fordæðuskap, galdra ok gerníngar, ok allan sjónhverfiligan kuklaraskap, ok stóð í mót allri illri forneskju með öllum mátt ok megni, þvíat áðr var eptir í kristninni miklar ok illar afleifar heiðins siðar, er eigi var upp rætt or guðligum akri meðan kristnin var úng': *Jóns saga hins helga*, in *Biskupa sögur* (1858–1878), I, p.237.

[267] See Jón Samsonarson, *Kvæði*, I, x–xi.

[268] See *Halldórs þáttr Snorrasonar inn fyrri*, pp.256–260; the elder *Frostaþingslög* (Frostaþing law), art.62, in *Norges gamle lov*, I, p.175; and the elder *Gulaþingslög* (Gulaþing law), art.134, in *Norges gamle lov*, I, p.56. See further, Robberstad, ed., *Gulatingslovi*, p.363.

[269] See *Hervarar saga*, p.200; and *Den norsk-islandske skjaldedigtning*, A.I, p.683, B.I, p.674.

[270] See Sveinbjörn Egilsson and Finnur Jónsson, *Lexicon Poeticum*, p.203.

[271] *Grettis saga*, p.234: 'Dulizk hefir margr í morgin/ menja runnr við kunnan; rinna víst á runna/ ranns ímu tvær grímur', meaning in literal terms, 'Many a person has failed to recognise me this morning even though I am known to them. A person would seem to have two faces.' The last line, in modern terms, means 'a person seems to be in two minds' or to 'be unsure'. Various inconclusive attempts have been made to explain the origin of this expression: see Halldór Halldórsson, *Íslensk orðtök*, pp.205–207; Einar Ólafur Sveinsson, 'Ágrip', 213; and Halldór Halldórsson, *Íslenzkt orðtakasafn*, I, p.199.

D. Literary Evidence

st.16, and 'búnar grímur' ('decorated heads') in Arnórr Þórðarson's *Hrynhenda*, st.4,[272] appear to refer to decorative items such as facial 'masks' or dragon heads, rather than any form of concealment. The same thing probably applies when the word *gríma* is used for a helmet in various poetic kennings.[273] Here, the idea is almost certainly related to the visual image of a 'helmet-mask', similar to the helmets found at Vendel and Sutton Hoo,[274] rather than to the elements of protection or concealment.[275]

It must be considered unlikely that the concept of facial masks originated in later satirical performances. Bearing in mind this probability that the word *gríma* has roots in ritual, it is worth re-examining two particular saga references that appear to link the wholly pagan religious concept of the *goði* or priest-chief with that of games or *leikar* known from later times.[276] One of these references involves a popular game related to something known as the 'Syrpuþingslög' or 'Syrpuþing law'. The latter concerns the word *leikgoði* ('play-priest'). Both references seem obscure when examined independently, but considered in the light of the archaeological evidence that has been discussed above, and later Scandinavian folklore, they offer a faint bridge between earlier ritual practice and later dramatic folk custom.

2. The 'Leikgoði' and the 'Syrpuþingslög'

Þórólfr leikgoði is mentioned in *Vatnsdæla saga* and one version of *Landnámabók*.[277] Neither work explains the origin of his by-name or its purpose; certainly Þórólfr does not seem to have belonged to any family that would have granted him the right to be a *goði*.[278] All that is known about him is that he was involved in a killing and then later disappeared into a

---

[272] *Den norsk-islandske skjaldedigtning*, A.I, p.333, B.I, p.307.

[273] See *Skáldskaparmál*, in *Edda* (1926), p.205 (a *þula* of names for helmets); *Egils saga*, p.145 ('grímu grund', i.e. head or face); *Gísla saga*, p.58 ('grímu Þróttr', i.e. warrior); *Háttatal*, st.15, in *Edda* (1926), p.156 ('grundar grímu gjaldseiðs', i.e. Ægishjálmr); and *Ólafs drápa Tryggvasonar*, st.15, ('gunnar grímu', i.e. helmet): see *Den norsk-islandske skjaldedigtning*, A.I, p.576, B.I, p.571. Like the names Grímnir, and Grímr, the word *gríma* is also used as a name of a 'monster' figure, and is found in the name list of female trolls in *Edda* (1926), p.197.

[274] See Bruce-Mitford, *Aspects*, plates 47 a–b, 48, 49b, and 55.

[275] Davidson, in *Gods and myths*, p.99, suggests that boar masks like those mentioned by Tacitus might have been a forerunner to the boar helmets. See the reference given above in note 157.

[276] See Phillpotts, *The Elder Edda*, pp.120–122.

[277] See *Vatnsdæla saga*, pp.127–129, and *Landnámabók: Melabók*, p.98. Þórðarbók is the only extant version of *Landnámabók* to contain the name of Þórólfr. Written in the seventeenth century, it contains material drawn from both *Skarðsárbók* and the now fragmentary *Melabók*. Þórólfr leikgoði was almost certainly mentioned in *Melabók*, which probably in turn used *Vatnsdæla saga* as a source: see O. Olsen, *Hørg, hov og kirke*, pp.63–64, note 44.

[278] See Phillpotts, *The Elder Edda*, p.121, and more recently Jón Hnefill Aðalsteinsson, 'Norræn trú', p.53.

2. The 'leikgoði' and the 'Syrpuþingslög'

river in the middle of the Icelandic wilderness. Everything else must be conjecture based on the form of Þórólfr's by-name.

In 1907, Finnur Jónsson made the suggestion that *leikgoði* meant 'a chieftain in a game, or the leader/ director of the game'.[279] Phillpotts, however, went further, and attempted to explain the role of the *leikgoði* by reference to the tale of Vöðu-Brandr Þorkelsson, who, according to *Vöðu-Brands þáttr*, was the person who established the so-called 'Syrpuþingslög'.[280] Even though it is not referred to elsewhere, this activity must have been recognised by the thirteenth-century audience since the above statement does not seem to warrant further explanation from the author. On the basis of the evidence given in the *þáttr*, the *Syrpuþingslög* appears to have been a form of nocturnal mock-court run by Brandr, which gained great popularity during Brandr's stay with Þorkell Geitison. Interestingly enough, the most common sufferers at the hands of the court seem to have been women.[281]

In general terms, it seems logical to compare this tradition with other 'folk' courts known elsewhere in Europe in which members of the community were punished for moral rather than criminal offences by young, masked men who used to appear regularly at certain times of the year when they would light-heartedly enact ancient judicial practices.[282] Reflections of such a system of folk justice in Scandinavia are perhaps found in later traditions like that of the *Knutsgubbe*.[283]

In general, there is little to support Phillpotts' far-reaching idea that the *Syrpuþing* meeting went as far as being 'a dramatised burlesque of the ceremonies and speeches of an ordinary "Thing" '.[284] The statement that 'women found the judgements of the court rather hard, since they could not present a defence' ('konum þykkja ríkt bornir kviðirnir, er þær kómu eigi fram vǫrn nýtri'[285]) suggests that the emphasis was on the court, rather than government. It is probable that Björn Sigfússon is closer to the point when he writes that 'the Syrpuþing was a light-hearted mockery of *þing* proceedings in which sentences were passed and defences made. The actual judicial proceedings, however, were probably somewhat immoral'.[286] On

---

279 'Hövding i en leg, el.leges styrer, anfører': Finnur Jónsson, 'Tilnavne', 277.
280 *Vöðu-Brands þáttr*, p.129. The *þáttr* forms part of one of the two major redactions of *Ljósvetninga saga*.
281 *Vöðu-Brands þáttr*, pp.129–130.
282 See Weiser-Aall, *Julenissen*, p.42. Weiser-Aall refers here in part to K. Meuli's article 'Charivari', in *Festschrift Franz Dorniseiff zum 65. Geburstag*, ed. Hans Kusch (Leipzig, 1953), pp.231–243.
283 See below, *Chapter II, B.2*, note 46.
284 Phillpotts, *The Elder Edda*, p.120.
285 *Vöðu-Brands þáttr*, p.129.
286 'Syrpuþing hefur verið gamansöm stæling á þinghaldi, þar sem kviðir voru bornir og varnir fram færðar, en málaferlin líklega miður siðleg': Björn Sigfússon, ed., *Vöðu-Brands þáttr*, p.129. Nonetheless, considering the complaints of the women, Andersson and Miller, in *Law and literature*, p.150, probably go too far in their suggestion that this 'mock court . . . would have served the social function of teaching people about legal procedure and how to negotiate its mazes.'

D. Literary Evidence

2. The 'leikgoði' and the 'Syrpuþingslög'

the basis of the *þáttr* alone, it is questionable whether the *Syrpuþing* can be classed as a form of dramatic activity in itself.[287] Nonetheless, as several scholars have pointed out, it is impossible to ignore completely the possible connection between the *Syrpuþing* and the magical 'Syrpuvers' mentioned at the conclusion of the 'Buslabæn' in *Bósa saga ok Herrauðs*.[288]

Phillpotts went on to argue that as the 'chairman' ('formaðr') of the *þing*, Brandr took on the role of a *goði*, something that Þorkell seems to imply in his statement that 'it looks like a new chieftain has arrived in the district, and men seem to be deserting his predecessor.'[289] Phillpotts suggests therefore that Brandr has assumed the role of a 'leikgoði', or 'play-priest', with all the implications of the name.[290]

Phillpotts' suggestion, however, did not go unchallenged. In more recent years, Einar Ólafur Sveinsson attempted to interpret the *leikgoði* in more mundane terms in relation to certain Icelandic children's games involving king or farmer figures, such as the 'King's game' (*Kóngsleikur*), the 'Giantess game' (*Skessuleikur*) and the 'Giant game' (*Risuleikur*).[291] Einar Ólafur's suggestion, however, has to be dropped, if only because all these games involve people taking the central role on an alternating basis. It is unlikely that the games would lead to anybody ever becoming 'king' or 'goði' for life. Furthermore, it is important to note the witch-hunting theme that seems to dominate that part of *Vatnsdæla saga* in which Þórólfr disappears in the river. The implication is that the *leikgoði*, like the *hofgoði* ('temple-priest'), must have had strong associations with pagan religion.[292]

Considering the wide range of meaning applied to the word *leikr*, as discussed in *section B.1* above, Wessén initiated a slightly different and broader approach to the figure of the *leikgoði*. His argument was that the *leikgoði* was probably involved in the organisation of such cult 'games' as those that seem to have been performed at the autumn and winter festivals.[293] Wessén's approach was accepted by Lid, who went even further towards drama by relating the *leikgoði* to the cult performances at Uppsala.[294] The same definition of the 'organiser of cult games' has since

---

[287] See the arguments for drama given in Phillpotts, *The Elder Edda*, pp.121–122, and Holtsmark, 'Drama', p.294. See also the discussion of this idea in Sveinn Einarsson, *Íslensk leiklist*, I, pp.16–17.

[288] *Bósa saga ok Herrauðs*, p.474. Both the Syrpuvers and the Syrpuþing proceedings take place during the night hours. The meaning of the word *syrpa*, however, is unclear. See the discussion in Phillpotts, *The Elder Edda*, p.121, and Andersson and Miller, *Law and literature*, p.150.

[289] 'Er hér því líkast sem nýr hǫfðingi sé kominn í sveit ok gangi menn af hendi þeim, sem áðr er fyrir': *Vöðu-Brands þáttr*, p.130.

[290] See Phillpotts, *The Elder Edda*, p.121; and Vogt's supporting suggestion in Vogt, ed., *Vatnsdæla saga*, p.128, that *leikgoði* means 'spielkönig'.

[291] See Einar Ólafur Sveinsson, ed., *Vatnsdæla saga*, p.127, note 2, and Ólafur Davíðsson, *Íslenzkar gátur*, II, p.99, p.107, p.112 and p.115.

[292] Regarding the *hofgoði*, i.e. the *goði* who took care of the temple, see *Eyrbyggja saga*, pp.8–9.

[293] Wessén, 'Hästskede', 111. See also further above, *section B.3*.

[294] See Lid, 'Gudar og gudedyrking', p.105.

2. The *'leikgoði'* and the *'Syrpuþingslög'*

been accepted with minor variations by a number of scholars, such as Sigfús Blöndal who saw the figure as being the 'leader of the cult dance'.[295] Yet what evidence is there to suggest that such a role ever existed in Icelandic society?

A close, and so far unnoted parallel from later times is found in the shape of a figure known as the *gadebasse* that used to exist in Danish folk tradition, predominantly in Jylland. The earliest reference to a character of this name appears in an account from Ribe, dated 1596. This account describes how 'several *gadebasser* run up to the farm yelling, shouting and screaming',[296] a description that has many interesting similarities to other Scandinavian Christmas traditions that will be examined in more detail in the following chapter. According to Møller, even though the tradition later adopted foreign elements, the role and name of the *gadebasse* seem to be old and to have native roots.[297] The actual meaning of the word, *gadebasse*, is unclear, but *gade* means 'street', 'path' or 'common land', and the *basse* usually means either an animal such as a boar or bear, or simply a stout person.[298] More interesting in the present context, however, is Feilberg's definition of the *gadebasse*'s *role* in more modern times as 'the man who is chosen by the other men of the group or society to be the leader on the road, and the organiser of the annual games sessions.'[299] Such elected games-leader figures seem to have been far from rare in Scandinavia. Lid, for example, points to what might be the remains of a similar tradition from Setesdal in Norway, where a group of costumed figures known as *drykkjebassann'* used to visit farms regularly at Christmas under the leadership of a figure known as the *guddursbasse*.[300] Other close

---

[295] See Blöndal, 'Dans i Island', p.165; de Vries, *Religionsgeschichte*, I, p.442, note 5; and Jón Hnefill Aðalsteinsson, 'Norræn trú', p.52.

[296] 'Dersom nogen gaadebasser løber att gaden och buger, rober oc skriger': see Kalkar, *Ordbog*, II, p.1.

[297] Møller, 'Sommer i by', 125. See also Troels-Lund, *Dagligt liv*, VII, p.104, and Lid, *Joleband*, p.109.

[298] See Feilberg, *Bidrag*, I, p.53; Kalkar, *Ordbog*, I, p.110; Aasen, *Norsk ordbog*, p.43; Lid, *Joleband*, pp.243–246; and the examination of the use of the word *Totabassi* in Davíð Erlingsson, 'Eyjólfr has the last laugh', pp.85–88. For slightly different interpretations, see Troels-Lund, *Dagligt liv*, VII, p.103; and Skar, *Gamalt or Sætesdal*, III, p.358, where alongside the other interpretations, a 'basse' is defined as a *julebukk*, and to 'basseklæ seg' ('dress up in *basse* clothes') is to dress up as a *julebukk*. Regarding the figure of the *julebukk* ('Yule-goat'), see further *Chapter II, B.3–5*.

[299] 'Den karl, som af lagets andre karle vælges til at være fører (på gaden) og at forestå årets legestuer': Feilberg, *Bidrag*, I, p.412. See also Kalkar, *Ordbog*, II, pp.1–2, and Møller, 'Sommer i by', 123. Much of Feilberg's account is based on a Latin account written c.1684 by Jens Mundelstrup from Århus: see Kalkar, *Ordbog*, II, p.2. Regarding the figures of the *gadebasse* and *gadelamme* in general, see Troels-Lund, *Dagligt liv*, VII, pp.103–105, p.189 and p.200; Nilsson, *Årets folkliga fester*, p.86; Lid, *Joleband*, p.109; Møller, 'Sommer i by', 123–125; and Olrik and Ellekilde, *Nordens gudeverden*, II, pp.621–623.

[300] See Lid, *Joleband*, pp.42–43, and pp.108–109, based on Skar, *Gamalt or Sætesdal*, II, 42–43. According to Skar, this group were called 'jolebassann'' in more recent times. The figures are also closely linked to the *julebukk* tradition which is examined more fully in *Chapter II, B.3–5*.

D. Literary Evidence

2. The 'leikgoði' and the 'Syrpuþingslög'

Scandinavian parallels are found in figures such as the later *majgreve*, the *julebisp*, and the Shetland *skudler*.[301] Like many of these figures, the *gaddebasse* was usually chosen at one of the main folk festivals of the year,[302] the choice either being made by lot, or as the result of a horse-race, or a competition involving the throwing of a brand high into the air.[303] Following this, the *gadebasse* usually chose a female partner named the *gadinde* or *gadelamme*, and the two of them later paired off the males and females of the area for the other festivities of the year.[304]

As Olaf Olsen warns with good reason, it is important not to read too much into the word *leikgoði*.[305] However, the word exists, and in the light of what has been said above about the word *leikr*, it is not too far-fetched to consider associations with a figure like the *gadebasse* who ruled and organised the Shrovetide, May and Midsummer festivities and the 'games' traditionally connected to them, and in earlier times might have acted as a folk-judge for social and moral offences. Considering the nature of the later folk traditions which will be discussed below, it would not be unnatural to assume that a certain amount of dramatic activity was associated with this role, particularly in earlier times when the various seasonal processions and games were more closely related to cult activities and ritual.[306] A role like that played by the *gadebasse* would embrace all the suggestions mentioned above by scholars ranging from Finnur Jónsson to Nils Lid. It would hardly have been out of place in the Icelandic society described in *Vatnsdæla saga*. Furthermore, if such pairing activities as those associated with the *gadebasse* tradition (and the later *julestuer* and *vökunætur* in Denmark and Iceland[307]) also occurred as part of the *Syrpuþingslög*, it would explain even further the comment made by the Christian author of

---

[301] Regarding the *majgreve* and *majinde*, see below, Chapter II, D.2. On the *skudler*, see references in Chapter II, G.4. Regarding the *julebisp* and *kongeleg*, see Chapter II, D.1. For direct comparisons in the offerings given to the *gadebasse* and *julebisp*, see Møller, 'Sommer i by', 123, and Troels-Lund, *Dagligt liv*, VII, p.74.

[302] See Lid, *Joleband*, p.109; Troels-Lund, *Dagligt liv*, VII, p.103; and Møller, 'Sommer i by', 123–125.

[303] See Feilberg, *Bidrag*, I, p.412; Troels-Lund, *Dagligt liv*, VII, p.103; and Møller, 'Sommer i by', 123–124. Other Scandinavian traditions involving the choosing of a 'king' by way of a horse-race are the Shrovetide horse-races from Skåne in Sweden and Vestfyn in Denmark. The Skåne tradition has a further comparable element to that of the *gadebasse* in that the winner of the race not only becomes king, but is then allowed to choose himself a wife: see Olrik and Ellekilde, *Nordens gudeverden*, II, p.1073. Olrik and Ellekilde suggest logically that the tradition originated in the Christmas horse-races held in Scandinavia (see Chapter II, B.2), but like other customs, was later transferred to Shrovetide. For German parallels to this custom, see Eliade, *Patterns*, pp.313–314.

[304] See, for example, Møller, 'Sommer i by', 124.

[305] O. Olsen, *Hørg, hov og kirke*, pp.63–64, note 44.

[306] It is only in this context (i.e. when the games are still associated with cult) that one might consider accepting Holtsmark's suggestion that the *leikgoði* was Óðinn's 'representative in the cult play' ('representant i kultspillet'): Holtsmark, 'Myten om Idun og Tjatse', 45–46.

[307] See Chapter II, G.2.

I. Dramatic Activities, 1. Archaeology and Literature

Vöðu-Brands þáttr about the stress under which women in particular were placed at the *Syrpuþing* gatherings.

E. Conclusion

In conclusion, the archaeological evidence argues that costumed disguises must have been used in ritual activity prior to the advent of Christianity in Scandinavia. The direct literary evidence suggests that some faint memories of such ritual 'games' activities may have continued into the thirteenth century. However the evidence of the sagas might also be seen as pointing to a development from ritual into folk games. Stronger support for remnants of the older 'dramatic' rituals having still been in existence during the Middle Ages in Scandinavia in the form of seasonal processions and costumed 'games' is provided by the evidence of such folk traditions from the sixteenth century onwards. As will be demonstrated in the following chapter, the fundamental core of these traditions is significantly similar to the shape of the pre-Christian rituals described above. Indeed, the central traditions seem to have been so deeply rooted in the folk culture of the Scandinavian countries that they must have originated in native superstition and belief.

CHAPTER II

Dramatic Activities in Early Medieval Scandinavia
II The Folkloristic Evidence

A. *The Application of Folkloristic Material*

Any general examination of the Yuletide, Shrovetide, May and Midsummer festivities of Scandinavia over the previous few centuries will reveal that the Nordic countries have hardly been lacking in semi-dramatic folk customs comparable to those found elsewhere in Europe. The urge to take part in costumed procession and performance evidently is, and has always been, as natural to the Scandinavians as it is to the other inhabitants of any other part of the world.

It also becomes apparent that these costumed Scandinavian traditions, predominantly related to the Yuletide period, have a fundamental core. In simple terms, this core involves the common features of a loose 'procession' which often takes the form of basic house visits carried out by a disguised figure or group of figures (the most common of which are a horned animal figure, a woman and/or a figure dressed in straw); and then the element of a mock-marriage, often represented simply by the pairing of males and females in games. In a very general sense, these key elements provide parallels to the much older ritualistic costumed traditions that were proposed in the previous chapter on the basis of the extant archaeological and literary evidence.

The essential difficulty with the application of such material is that information concerning popular dramatic custom in Scandinavia is extremely scant prior to 1500. For the most part, we are forced to rely on accounts from the eighteenth and nineteenth century. Folk traditions come into being in a variety of ways, and it is, of course, impossible to assume, as many scholars appear to have done in the previous century, that all extant customs must be the remnants or descendants of ancient rituals. On the contrary, it is necessary to consider the possibility of transformation over time, the influence of the church and foreign traditions, and the likelihood that a tradition may even have evolved comparatively recently.

These considerations, however, need not rule out the possibilities that certain traditions may be of great age, even if the earliest accounts concerning them are comparatively recent. As Bringéus notes, 'Even if we avoid all speculation about the form of pre-Christian seasonal festivals . . . it is important to remember that the men of the church did not commence their activities in a land totally lacking in seasonal custom.'[1] Indeed, it seems clear that many church traditions were deliberately designed to replace or transform already existing seasonal customs, an approach that is exemplified by Pope Gregory the Great's message to St Augustine in 601 about methods of dealing with pagan religious customs. Among other things, Gregory makes the suggestion that 'if the shrines are well built, it is essential that they should be changed from the worship of devils to the service of the true God . . . And because they are in the habit of slaughtering much cattle as sacrifices to devils, some solemnity ought to be given them in exchange for this.'[2] There is good reason to believe that the same approach was often adopted in the conversion of Scandinavia, a perfect example being King Óláfr Tryggvason's effective Christian renaming of the old pagan festivals in Norway.[3]

If an early origin to a custom is to be surmised, it is important that clear analogies to this custom can be found in earlier documentary material. Yet even then, it is necessary to distinguish between related material and material that is merely comparative. Early Icelandic literary references, for example, are not necessarily applicable to later customs from Sweden; the cultural and linguistic backgrounds of these countries are similar, but this does not mean that the actual cultures and traditions of the two countries have ever been identical or spring from common roots. The material involved in such a comparison is not only separated by enormous distances but also by many hundreds of years. While comparative material of this kind should never be ignored, it can never be conclusive. In the long run, all that can be achieved in many cases is a logical hypothesis based on the available material.[4]

The following examination will be concentrated primarily on those dramatic folk traditions from Scandinavia that cannot be easily explained by arrival of Christianity or other foreign influences, traditions which on the basis of the extant evidence appear to be native and deeply rooted in the societies that practise them. For practical reasons the examination will be divided into two main parts, the discussion and classification of the mainland customs being followed by an analysis of the popular dramatic traditions found in the original Viking North Atlantic colonies. As will be seen, this approach is particularly useful in helping to establish some dating for

---

[1] 'Även om vi avstår från spekulationer om hur de förkristna årsfesterna mera konkret utformats på svensk botten är det viktigt att komma ihåg at kykans män inte började sin verksamhet i ett land utan seder förknippade med årets växlingar': Bringéus, Årets festseder, p.235. See further Bringéus' useful discussion on the development in approach to the dating of folk traditions, in Årets festseder, pp.230–256.
[2] The translation and original text are given in Bede's Ecclesiastical history, I.30, pp.106–109.
[3] See reference in note 216 below.
[4] See Bringéus, Årets festseder, p.234.

B. Related to the Christmas Period

the customs in question. For the most part, however, all of the customs in question have close enough parallels in the archaeological and literary evidence presented above for a pre-Christian origin to be postulated.

B. Mainland Scandinavian Costumed Processions, House-visits and Performances Related to the Christmas Period

1. Christian Origins for Yuletide Costumed Traditions: The 'Stjärnspel', Knut and Lucia

1. Christian origins for Yuletide costumed traditions: The 'Stjärnspel', Knut and Lucia

In general terms, there are five central Scandinavian Christmas traditions which always seem to have contained a strong element of dramatic activity:

a. The festival of Lucia in Sweden and Norway on 12–13 December.[5]
b. The *Staffansreid* or *Staffans skeid* ('Staffan's ride' or 'Staffan's race'),[6] which used to take place in a variety of forms in Norway, Sweden and Swedish-speaking Finland usually on 25 or 26 December.
c. The *Stjärnspel* ('Star play') or *Trettondagsspel* ('Thirteenth-day play') most commonly encountered in Sweden, but also performed in various forms in both Norway and Denmark (where it is also known as the *Helligtrekongerspill*). The *Trettondagsspel* is usually performed on 6 or 13 January, the *Stjärnspel* at any time during the later part of the Christmas period.[7]
d. The visits of the *julebukk* ('Yule-goat'; male) or *julegeit* ('Yule-goat'; female) throughout Scandinavia, usually commencing after Christmas Day (see further below in *section B.3*).
e. The 'sweeping' or 'knocking out' of Yule by *Knut* on 7 or 13 January in many parts of Scandinavia.[8]

At least four of these traditions in their present form would appear to have a strongly Christian flavour, reflected by their associations with the figures of St Lucia, St Stephen (Staffan),[9] the martyred Danish St Knut (Knut Lavard), and the nativity, the last of which is represented as part of the *Stjärnspel* and *Trettondagsspel* usually enacted during house-visits by the figures of the 'Three Kings' bearing a star. Indeed, there is reason to

---

[5] On the general features of this tradition, see Celander, *Nordisk jul*, pp. 40–48; Nilsson, 'Julen', pp. 21–23; Eskeröd, *Årets fester*, pp. 170–175; Bringéus, *Årets festseder*, pp. 23–30; and Bø, *Vår norske jul*, pp. 24–28.

[6] For general information on this practice, see Olrik and Ellekilde, *Nordens gudeverden*, II, pp. 1068–1075.

[7] For general information regarding this custom, see Celander, *Nordisk jul*, pp. 334–337, and *Stjärngossarna*, passim; and more recently, Bringéus, *Årets festseder*, pp. 101–107. For a summary of Danish customs, see Schmidt, 'Helligtrekongersangere'.

[8] Regarding this tradition in general and the dating in different areas, see Celander, *Nordisk jul*, pp. 338–340. Concerning the tradition of acting the role of Knut, see, for example, Bø, *Vår norske jul*, pp. 177–178; and Keyland, *Julbröd*, pp. 41–43 and p. 93.

[9] Regarding the religious background to the popular figure of *Staffan*, see, for example, Feilberg, *Jul*, I, pp. 213–222; Djurklou, 'Hvem var 'Staffan Stalledräng'?'; Celander, 'Til Stefanslegendens og Staffansvisornas utveklingshistoria'; and Strömbäck, 'St Stephen', and 'Staffan'.

II. Dramatic Activities, II: Folkloristic Evidence

1. Christian origins for Yuletide costumed traditions: The 'Stjärnspel', Knut and Lucia

believe that the *Stjärnspel* folk plays, which have often blended with the more locally rooted *Staffan* processions,[10] originally evolved out of medieval nativity dramas known in mainland Europe.[11] Nonetheless, the *Stjärnspel* tradition, like the modern Lucia customs, probably gained impetus in Scandinavia through performances carried out by the Latin schools during the sixteenth and seventeenth centuries.[12]

It is easy to point out the general Christian associations of these traditions. It is not so simple, however, to offer Christian explanations for all the local variations of these customs. Indeed, many of these variations support the suggestion mentioned above that the Christian festival activities often replaced earlier seasonal customs, or attracted and adopted other customs that were originally associated with other dates. A good example of the latter development is the hybrid Scandinavian Shrovetide (*fastelavn*/ *fastlagen*) tradition which had a Christian origin, and reached its height among the ruling classes in the larger towns and cities of Scandinavia, where it seems to have attracted all kinds of folk customs more typically associated with older seasonal festivals in the surrounding countryside.[13]

The superficial nature of some of the Christian festivals is especially clear in the case of the figure of *Knut*, since the saint obviously never had anything to do with 'sweeping' or 'knocking out' Christmas. Magnus

---

[10] Both the followers of *Staffan* who perform the 'Staffansvisan', and the Three Kings tend to be dressed in white and carry stars. On occasion, the figure of *Staffan* also leads the *stjärngossar* ('star-boy') processions. See, for example, Celander, *Stjärngossar*, pp.428–432.

[11] There is no evidence for any liturgical Christmas plays having taken place in Scandinavia itself during the Middle Ages. Regarding the connection between the *Stjärnspel* and medieval drama, see Djurklou, 'Hvem var "Staffan Stalledräng"?', 337; Blom, *Ballader*, pp.76–82, and especially, Celander, *Stjärngossarna*. See also Lid, *Jolesveinar*, p.24, on the somewhat unlikely possibility that the Dynnasteinn (c.1050) from Nordre Dynna in Hadeland, Norway, might depict an early version of a Three Kings play. Regarding the possible link between liturgical drama and the star carried by both the kings and the *Staffansgossar*, see, for example, Tydeman, *The theatre in the Middle Ages*, p.42, and Nilsson, 'Julen', p.54. For descriptions of performances and texts of Three Kings plays from Norway, Denmark and Sweden from the seventeenth century onwards, see Celander, *Stjärngossarna*, pp.32–39; and pp.49–228, and Schmidt, 'Helligtrekongersangere', passim. For an examination of the development of these plays and their texts, see also Norlind, *Studier*, pp.285–326.

[12] On the *Lucia* tradition in this respect, see Nilsson, 'Julen', p.22, and Bringéus, *Årets festseder*, pp.24–26. Regarding the *Stjärnspel*, see Celander, *Stjärngossarna*, pp.17–22, and pp.44–48.

[13] Regarding Swedish Shrovetide activities, see Nilsson, *Årets folkliga fester*, pp.281–294, and Bringéus, *Årets festseder*, pp.117–129. On Danish activities, see Troels-Lund, *Dagligt liv*, VII, pp.94–126. Descriptions of Shrovetide traditions often mention elements more closely associated with other times of the year, like horse-races (see *section B.2 below*), plough processions (see Nilsson, *Årets folkliga fester*, pp.292–293; Olrik and Ellekilde, *Nordens gudeverden*, II, pp.1018–1020), the choosing of the *gadebasse* (see Troels-Lund, *Dagligt liv*, VII, pp.103–104), and the reappearance of the *julebukk* amongst the other masked figures (see *section B.3 below*). Regarding other Shrovetide costumes, see Troels-Lund, *Dagligt liv*, VII, pp.118–126.

B. Related to the Christmas Period

1. Christian origins for Yuletide costumed traditions: The 'Stjärnspel', Knut and Lucia

Olsen has thus sought to establish an early relationship between the traditional figure of *Knut* and other figures like the legendary King Orre, and the spirit of Þorri, a personification of the early Scandinavian fourth winter month beginning c.13 January.[14] Considering the fact that *Knut* is often acted in folk tradition, it might be noted that both *Knut* and *Þorri* are identified in the rhymes sung about them by the same sole visual characteristic of a beard.[15] A faint possibility exists that this shared feature has roots in a visual tradition of disguise which originally applied to both figures at this time of the year. The vestiges of such a tradition might possibly be found in the unique account given by Jón Árnason of how Icelandic farmers used to 'welcome Þorri onto the farm' ('að bjóða Þorra í garð') by hopping around their farms half-dressed on the first morning of Þorri, their wives following suit on the first morning of Góa, the following month.[16]

An even more intriguing blend of features is encountered in the case of the Swedish festival of Lucia, typified in many people's minds by the image of the innocent white-clad girl in the candle-crown, singing 'Santa Lucia'. This Christian image, however, is countered by the continuing use of the name *Lusse långnatt* ('Lusse long-night') in both Swedish and Norwegian folk belief, which suggests that at one time the festival must have been more intrinsically related to the old winter solstice.[17] In all probability, this association reaches as far back as the fourteenth century when, as a result of the Julian Calendar, 13 December had actually become the date of the solstice.[18] Such seasonal associations imply that what was being celebrated on this day in many parts of Sweden must have often been something other than the figure of the Christian saint. This view is strengthened still further by the evidence of other, lesser-known folk traditions involving the figure of *Lucia*, *Lussi* or *Lusse* in the Swedish and Norwegian countryside.

In south Västergötland and Småland, for example, 'Lusse' traditions often centred around men dressing up as old women, and women dressing up as old men, in the roles of *Lussegubbar* and *Lussegummar*.[19] This element of male *and* female characters appearing together might have some distant relationship to another revealing (and most definitely un-Christian)

---

[14] See Olsen, 'Kung Orre'; and Lid, *Joleband*, pp.226–227, and pp.241–242.
[15] For example, 'Torren med sitt Skjegg/ lokkar Borni under Sole-Vegg' ('Þorri with his beard/ tempts children out below the sun-lit wall'): Olsen, 'Kung Orre', 11. For other variants from Sweden and Denmark, where the main character sometimes becomes Þórr or Staffan, see Olsen, 'Kung Orre', 12; Lid, *Joleband*, pp.189–192; and Troels-Lund, *Dagligt liv*, VII, p.62.
[16] See Jón Árnason, *Íslenzkar þjóðsögur*, II, pp.572–573; and Árni Björnsson's comments on this account in *Þorrablót*, pp.29–42.
[17] For a distribution map of the use of this name in Sweden and a discussion of its origin, see Campbell and Nyman, *Atlas*, 1, p.52, and 2, pp.111–112. Regarding Norwegian talk of 'Lussinått den lange', see Alver, 'Lussi', pp.108–112.
[18] See, for example, Celander, *Nordisk jul*, p.36; Nilsson, 'Julen', p.23; Alver, 'Lussi', 108–109; Bø, *Årshøytidene*, p.17; and Bringéus, *Årets festseder*, p.12.
[19] Celander, *Nordisk jul*, p.46. In Eda, Värmland, the *Lussegubbar* wore white shirts, with straw belts, straw shoes, and straw leggings.

II. Dramatic Activities, II: Folkloristic Evidence

1. Christian origins for Yuletide costumed traditions: The 'Stjärnspel', Knut and Lucia

aspect of the *Lucia* festival as it occurred elsewhere in parts of Småland, Östergötland and Dalsland. Here, the usual white-clad *Lucia* figure, now sometimes known as the *Lussebrud* ('Lusse-bride'), was occasionally accompanied by a *Lussegubben* or *Lusse-brudgummen* ('Lusse-bridegroom'), and/or bridesmaids and torchbearers.[20] As several scholars have noted, this bridal figure can have nothing to do with the virginal St Lucia described in the *Legenda aurea*.[21] Indeed, the difference between the two figures is emphasised by traditions from Bohuslän in which the *Lussebrud* was acted by the mother of an illegitimate child, and followed by a procession of other costumed figures including not only a *Lussegubbe*, but also a *Lussebock* ('Lusse-goat'), and a straw-clad *Halm-Staffan* figure.[22] As Celander suggests, these *Lucia*-brides, or brides and bridegrooms, should probably be classified alongside other Scandinavian mock-marriages rather than as part of any Christian festival.[23] Possible links with the pagan winter *hieros gamos* mentioned in connection with Freyr in the previous chapter cannot be completely ruled out.[24]

The appearance of *Lussi* figures in the shape of old women or old men reflects yet another intriguing aspect of the *Lucia* tradition in Scandinavia. In the countryside of western Norway and in some parts of Sweden, 'Lusse'/ 'Lussi'/ 'Lussia' was rarely envisaged in the form of a maiden in white. On the contrary, she was regarded as a dangerous female troll who was supposed to visit farms at night on or about 13 December, sometimes accompanied by a group of other terrifying spirits (the *Lussiferd*, or 'Lussiride').[25] Just as *Lucia* was enacted in Sweden, this 'evil' character was sometimes brought to life by members of the community in a shape that on occasion appears to have resembled that of another central Scandinavian figure, the *julebukk* ('Yule-goat'). This relationship is not only visible in the drawing of *Lussia* from Forsand in Rogaland, Norway (see *fig.51*),[26]

---

[20] See Celander, *Nordisk jul*, p.45. Nonetheless, as Celander shows here, the *Lussebrud* usually appears alone. See also the case of the Dalarna *Lussiner* below.
[21] See for example, Boberg, 'Lussegubben', 65, and Celander, *Nordisk jul*, p.45.
[22] Boberg, 'Lussegubben', 65. On the *Lussebock* and *Halm-Staffan*, see below, *sections B.2 and 3*. The link with straw figures is emphasised by the often-quoted example of the straw *Lussebrud* doll: see references in note 47 below. For a distribution map of the various Swedish traditions involving the *Lussebrud*, see Campbell and Nyman, *Atlas*, 2, p.56, karta XXIX.
[23] Celander, *Nordisk jul*, p.45. On the 'mock-marriage' traditions, see further *section D*.
[24] These Yuletide folk-marriages and bridal figures are particularly interesting in view of the fact that in Norway, at least, as far back as the twelfth century a ban was placed on all marriages not only during the three weeks preceding Christmas, but also during the Christmas period itself: see *Norges gamle love*, I, pp.16–17 (*Elder Gulaþingslög*, art.27); p.150 (*Frostaþingslög*, III, 9); p.343 (*Borgarþingslög*); p.381 (*Heiðsævislög*); and *Diplomatarium Islandicum*, II, p.15, p.418, and p.812, which demonstrates that similar laws were in force in Iceland as far back as the late thirteenth century.
[25] See Lid, *Joleband*, pp.60–62; Celander, *Nordisk jul*, pp.30–33; Bø, *Vår norske jul*, pp.24–28; and most recently Alver, 'Lussi', pp.112–118. In Norway, the *Lussi* tradition is largely restricted to the area between Setesdal and Hardanger, occurring especially along the coast: see the distribution map provided in Eike, 'Oskoreia', 266.
[26] See further Eike, 'Oskoreia', 265–266 and 269, on these Norwegian traditions, and the

B. Related to the Christmas Period

1. Christian origins for Yuletide costumed traditions: The 'Stjärnspel', Knut and Lucia

Fig. 51. *Lussia* and a *jolesvein* (Forsand, Rogaland).

but also in the descriptions of the *lussebockar* ('Lusse-goats') from Västergötland and Värende, and the *Lussiner* from Malung in west Dalarna, Sweden.[27] The *Lussiner*, for example, are reported as having gone around in pairs in the early morning, wearing red hoods, with goat skins on their backs and straw about their necks, demanding meat and bread. According to the informant, people used to follow the *Lussiner* and ask them whether they were supposed to be male or female goats.[28]

In their extant form, the customs connected with *Lussi* were obviously not Christian, but they can hardly be regarded as the concrete remnants of any ancient tradition to do with the old winter solstice. As the figures of the *Lussiner* demonstrate most effectively, these traditions should rather be seen as a hotch-potch of various early customs and beliefs associated with the Yuletide period in general that have become mixed up with other more superficial beliefs connected with the Christian saint's day.[29] Here they were in turn linked to the image of Lucifer (attracted by the name *Lucia*

---

description of the Norwegian *Lussia* depicted above in *fig.51*, in Weiser-Aall, *Julenissen*, pp.32–33.
[27] See Celander, *Nordisk jul*, p.45,
[28] Celander, *Nordisk jul*, p.45.
[29] See Alver, 'Lussi', pp.117–118, and Bø, *Vår norske jul*, pp.25–28.

2. 'Halm-Staffan' and the appearance of the horned *julebukk*),³⁰ and the more widespread phenomenon of the 'Wild Ride' of spirits which, in Norway, went under various other names such as the *Oskoreia* and *Juleskreia*, and was more commonly associated with Christmas night itself.³¹ The nucleus of the Norwegian *Lussi* tradition, however, would seem to be a supernatural female or animal figure that used to appear 'in person' in certain communities during the period leading up to Christmas. As will be shown below (*section G*), such a hypothesis is supported by the evidence of closely related traditions found in the Faroe Islands, Shetland, and probably also Iceland, which may go back as far as the thirteenth century.

The precise nature of this female Yuletide figure is uncertain, and it must be questionable whether all the traditions related to her were ever homogeneous. Considering the nature of the Scandinavian landscape, it would be unwise to imagine that any agreed pattern of ritual or mythology ever existed throughout Scandinavia prior to or during the Viking period, and the same applies to folk traditions in later times. Nonetheless, there are two semi-dramatic Nordic traditions related to Yuletide that warrant particular attention if only because they seem to occur, in one form or another, over an extraordinarily wide area of territory, ranging from eastern Sweden to the North Atlantic islands. The figures in question are the straw man and the goat, the latter of which, as has been shown above, seems to be intimately connected in some areas with the Norwegian image of *Lussi*. No convincing explanation for the origin of these two figures outside Scandinavia or within Christian tradition has yet been given.

2. Halm-Staffan

The widespread, and deep-rooted tradition of 'Staffan's ride' or the 'Second-day ride' (*Staffansritt, Staffans reid, Staffans skeid, annandagsskeid*), which may have originated in the more ancient Yuletide races noted in the previous chapter,³² also gained strong Christian associations through its links with St Stephen. Indeed, in parts of Sweden, these rides on the second day of Christmas became intimately connected with the performances of the white-clad *Staffansdrängar* ('Staffan's lads') who used to visit farms bearing the image of 'the shining star' ('den ljusa stjärnan') mentioned in the *Staffansvisa* ('Ballad of Staffan') they commonly sang on their arrival.³³

As was mentioned above, however, the horse-races themselves appear to

---

³⁰ Boberg's suggestion in 'Lussegubben', 66–69, that the acted troll-like image of *Lussi* might have an origin in a supposed imported tradition involving the figures of Lucifer and St Nicholas must be considered unlikely. On the evidence for such St Nicholas traditions in Scandinavia, see further *section B.5* below.
³¹ Regarding these supernatural Scandinavian 'Wild Rides', and their connection with *Lussi*, see especially Celander, 'Oskoreien', and Eik, 'Oskoreia', passim.
³² See *Chapter I, B.3*.
³³ See references in notes 6 and 10 above.

B. Related to the Christmas Period

2. 'Halm-Staffan'

represent a much older sub-strata of tradition than that involving the star or the *Staffansdrängar*. It is also clear that in many local traditions the figure of *Staffan*, who led the costumed rides between farms, had little to do with the image of the Christian saint. He often seems to have been closer to the image of the *julebukk* or a Santa Claus figure, dressed, for example, in an old sheepskin or simply disguised as an old man with grey hair and a beard.[34] Of particular interest is the fact that in certain eastern areas of Sweden (northern Östergötland, Södermanland and Uppland) and southern Finland, the *Staffansdrängar* were led by a figure completely wrapped in straw or corn, and was sometimes known as *Halm-Staffan* ('Straw-Staffan'). According to an account from Uppland, the performer himself 'was tall and well-built, but dressed in the straw costume he became so large that he could hardly squeeze through the doors of the buildings where the singing was supposed to take place' (see *fig.52*).[35] Another account of a *Staffan* figure from western Nyland, a Swedish-speaking part of Finland, describes him as being dressed in plaited straw, with boots and headwear made of the same material. This figure was carried into farm living-rooms by two assistants, and there used to hold a form of sermon which concluded with his followers singing the *Staffansvisan*.[36]

This appearance of the straw man under the same name in Finland is of special interest, because, as Nils Lid pointed out, certain intriguing parallels exist between the *Halm-Staffan* traditions and Finnish horse-races in which the image of the Finnish god Peko was drawn on a sledge at Candlemas (2 February). Lid proceeded to draw logical comparisons between both of these customs and the account of Freyr's winter journey described in *Gunnars þáttr helmings*.[37] Indeed, Magnus Olsen had earlier suggested that some close relationship might have existed between the figures of Peko and Freyr who was associated with both horses and fertility.[38] Whether or not any basis exists for these proposed relationships, the use of such straw- or bark-clad figures in pagan times would certainly help explain how a living image of Freyr could suddenly be transformed into a seemingly inanimate 'log' in *Gunnars þáttr*.[39] Early links between Freyr and such large straw figures such as *Halm-Staffan* might also

---

[34] See Lid, *Jolesveinar*, p.31. Naturally, the skins might also be related to a realistic representation based on Staffan's supposed profession as a stableboy (*stalledräng*).
[35] 'Stor og lång var han i sig selv, men i halmdräkten blev hann så stor, at han knappt kunde tränge sig in genom dörrarna till de stugor, där man skulle sjunga' (Björkö, Uppland): Halmström, 'Halmstaffan', p.228, also quoted in Olrik and Ellekilde, *Nordens gudeverden*, II, pp.1079–1080. See also Celander, *Nordisk jul*, p.274.
[36] See Celander, *Nordisk jul*, p.277. For further examples from Uppland, see Celander, *Stjärngossarna*, pp.430–433, and Hallström, 'Halmstaffan', 228–231. For other examples from Finland, see Lid, *Jolesveinar*, p.33 and p.36. See also the references given in note 46 below on the Danish *Staffensmanden*.
[37] See Lid, *Joleband*, p.150 and p.156. On *Gunnars þáttr*, see Chapter I, C.5.
[38] Olsen, *Hedenske kultminder*, pp.111–115.
[39] See also Schager, *Julbocken*, pp.84–86, on the use of birch-bark for costumes or masks in Sweden.

2. *'Halm-Staffan'* conceivably lie behind Loki's strange description of Freyr's servant Byggvir in *Lokasenna*, st.44 and st.46, as 'the little one/ that I spy wagging his tail/ with a begging look' who 'in the bench straw/ could not be found,/ when men were fighting'.[40] Read with a tone of sarcasm, these words would be well-suited to a large straw-clad figure like those described above which were known for collecting gifts from farmhouses during Yuletide.

Staffan, however, was not the only figure to appear dressed in straw in later centuries. In another Uppland area, *Staffan* himself used to be clad in white, but appeared accompanied by several variously costumed figures including a *staffansbock* ('Staffan's goat') and three or four *staffansgossar* ('Staffan's lads') who were so completely wrapped in straw that their faces were rendered indistinguishable.[41] In parts of Dalsland, the same costume was worn by a figure known as the the *julegoppa*.[42] In general, the straw man seems to have been a relatively common figure at one time in Scandinavia, particularly in Sweden. Such costumes are also reflected in the guises used by the earlier mentioned Värmland *Lussegubbar* and, to a lesser degree, also the *Lussiner*,[43] the Värmland *halmgubbar* ('strawmen')[44] and the *julbock* from parts of Östergötland, Dalsland and Bohuslän in Sweden.[45]

These disguised straw figures cannot be examined without some reference to the even more numerous inanimate man-sized straw figures that used to be well-known in Denmark and Sweden. Some of these figures, such as the Danish *Staffensmanden* and the Swedish *Knutsgubben* (from Skåne and western Sweden) evidently had an effective social role: on particular nights during the Christmas period they would be placed outside or thrown into the houses of those deserving public rebuke with vilifying or mocking notes attached to them. In central Sweden, in the area centring around Uppland, these defamatory 'human' figures were replaced by straw goats. Like the figures made in human shape, these goats could end up

---

[40] 'Þat it litla/ er ek þat lǫggra sék,/ ok snapvíst snapir' . . . 'í fletz strá/ finna ne máttu,/ þá er vágo verar.'
[41] See Celander, *Nordisk jul*, p.274. On other names for *Staffan*'s followers, see Celander, *Nordisk jul*, p.276.
[42] See Järlgren, 'Julegoppan', 26, 31–32, and 38–39, and Gjötterberg, 'Näbberfru', 19–21, on straw costumes from Småland and Lithuania. As is shown in the references cited in note 139 below, the name *julegoppa* was also applied to a bird-like disguise found in Dalsland.
[43] See references given above in note 28.
[44] See Celander, *Nordisk jul*, p.343.
[45] See Lid, *Joleband*, p.45; Celander, *Nordisk jul*, pp.308–309; and Olrik and Ellekilde, *Nordens gudeverden*, II, p.1080. Mannhardt, in *Wald- und Feldkulte*, II, p.193, also refers to a 'julbuck' from Bergslagshärad which took the form of a straw man with goat's horns. See also Keyland, *Julbröd*, p.56, for a description of a similar straw *julbock* from Skedevi in Östergötland. Another link between the straw figures and the *julebukk* is found in the *julbockar* or *skråbuker* from Värmland, who wore belts of straw or pig hair about their waists and carried bells between their legs: see, for example, Celander, *Nordisk jul*, p.345. Parallels to the straw belts are found in the costumes of the Papa Westray *gyros* in Orkney. See further below, *section G.4*.

B. *Related to the Christmas Period*

2. '*Halm-Staffan*'

Fig. 52. *Halm-Staffan* (Björkö).

Fig. 53. A man-sized straw *julgubbe* (Järnskog, Värmland).

being passed around the entire community overnight since people rarely wished to keep such tokens of ill-will beneath their roofs.⁴⁶

Other straw figures, however, seem to have had more private, superstitious importance. Unlike the *Staffensmanden* and the *Knutsgubben*, these figures held a position of reverence in farmhouses over the Christmas period (see *fig.53*). This is well demonstrated by the account of the *Lussebrud* doll from Eda in Värmland which was clad in a dress, pullover, hat and bright ribbon, and placed in the centre of the dance-floor where the ensuing Lusse dance took place around it.⁴⁷ Similar traditions have been

---

⁴⁶ Regarding these types of straw figure, see, for example, Bringéus, *Årets festseder*, pp.109–115; Celander, 'Julbocken', 94–95, and *Nordisk jul*, pp.103–106; Keyland, *Julbröd*, p.80; and more recently, Schager, *Julbocken*, pp.93–98. On the *Staffensmanden*, from north Jylland, see further Celander, *Nordisk jul*, pp.278–279.

⁴⁷ See Celander, *Nordisk jul*, p.39. Note also the description of the Dalsland *Jul(e)goppa(n)* doll, given in the same book, pp.307–308. As Celander points out, *goppa* in local dialect might be taken to mean 'feeble old woman', and thus there is reason for grouping both this figure and the bird-like *julegoppa* disguise from the same area (Celander, p.308) with the *Lusse/ Lussi* figures mentioned above. See also note 43 above for references to the *julegoppa* as a straw man.

2. 'Halm-Staffan' recorded from Dalsland and Värmland in Sweden, Nyland in Swedish-speaking Finland, and Trøndelag in Norway where straw figures were known to be set up in a special place in the farmhouse over the Christmas festival, and given beer and schnapps to drink.[48] It is noteworthy that the treatment of these figures closely parallels the respect bestowed on certain wooden domestic 'idols' from Telemark and Setesdal that are described in Norwegian accounts from the eighteenth century.[49] Indeed, there can be little doubt that the revered straw men and straw goats were also regarded as household idols of a kind. The question remains whether they are the descendants of pagan idols or Catholic saints. Whatever the answer, straw figures, both inanimate and enacted, seem to have carried considerable weight as objects of superstitious belief.[50]

The enacted straw figures, however, remain unexplained in terms of Christian or foreign influence, and the probability is that they have very early roots, possibly related to seasonal fertility customs of some kind.[51] Indeed, early Scandinavian associations between straw effigies and fertility are supported by the account (c.1300) of a Danish Franciscan monk in Dublin named Petrus concerning certain Danish women who constructed a straw figure named Bovi as part of an entertainment for a friend who was pregnant. The straw-man was said to have come to life while the women were carrying it in a chain-dance, apparently possessed by the Devil who spoke from inside Bovi.[52] While the name of Bovi and the motif of the Devil's arrival are probably derived from earlier medieval legends concerning the cursed ring dance at Kölbigk,[53] the same cannot be said about the

---

[48] See, for example, Celander, *Nordisk jul*, pp.193–194, and 'Julbocken', 94; and Olrik and Ellekilde, *Nordens gudeverden*, II, p.935.

[49] See Lid, *Joleband*, pp.158–166. The same kind of reverence is reflected in a Swedish tradition in which a straw *julbock*, often made from the last harvested sheaf, was sometimes carried around by the *stjärngossar*: see Lid, *Joleband*, pp.46–47. On similar harvest traditions from the Western Hebrides and Orkney, involving images known as the *gobhar-bacach / gobhar bhacach* ('lame goat': Skye), the *Cailleach* ('Old woman': Islay, Kintyre and Lewis) and the *bikko* ('bitch': Orkney), see Maclagan, 'Notes', 148–151; and Macleod Banks, *British calendar customs: Scotland*, I, pp.79–80, and *British calendar customs: Orkney and Shetland*, pp.9–10. On the occurrence of straw figures in general, see Nilsson, 'Julen', pp.39–40; Lid, *Joleband*, pp.43–47; and Olrik and Ellekilde, *Nordens gudeverden*, II, pp.931–938. On German parallels, see Mannhardt, *Wald- und Feldkult*, II, p.183; Frazer, *The golden bough*, V,ii, pp.325–327; and Rudwin, *The origin of German carnival comedy*, p.16.

[50] As is shown below in *section G.4*, some very interesting close parallels to the figure of *Halm-Staffan* also appear in Shetland.

[51] See Lid, *Jolesveinar*, passim. Olrik and Ellekilde, in *Nordens gudeverden*, II, p.937, similarly relate these customs to early pagan belief. However, see also the comments made in Nilsson, 'Julen', p.40, and Celander, *Nordisk jul*, pp.308–309.

[52] For the original account in Latin and a Danish translation, see Olrik and Olrik, 'Kvindegilde i Middelalderen'. The mid-fourteenth-century MS containing this account is kept in the library of Durham Cathedral.

[53] This motif later reappears in several folk legends concerning the spiritual dangers of dancing. A typical example is the legend from eastern Jylland of the farm girl that danced with a possessed straw image of the *julebukk* ('Bovmand'): see Olrik and Ellekilde, *Nordens gudeverden*, II, pp.932–933, and Simpson, ed., *Scandinavian folktales*, pp.80–81.

B. Related to the Christmas Period

2. 'Halm-Staffan'

straw figure and its connections with dancing and childbirth. Such a motif would seem to be separate in origin, and it is partially echoed in the description of the Värmland *Lussebrud* doll given above. The most important feature of this account, though, is that it proves straw figures must have been known in southern Scandinavia before 1300. Indeed, as Montelius has pointed out, similar customs of making straw men 'every new year' were also recorded in nearby Estonia as early as in the late fourteenth century.[54]

Returning to the figure of *Staffan* and the possibility of links with pagan religion, it is interesting to note further parallels to the *Staffan* tradition found in northern Scandinavia in the shape of a disguised Lapp figure named *Stallo*. Like Peko, *Stallo* bore several close similarities and relationships to the figure of *Staffan*. However, he had the distinguishing feature of being equipped with some form of phallus, which poses even closer associations with the god Freyr.[55] Furthermore, *Stallo*, like both *Staffan* and Freyr, used to be accompanied by an escort when undertaking Yuletide journeys between farms. In this case, however, the escort often came in the shape of two or more *hamenn* ('tall men'), reminiscent of the two men who bore in *Halm-Staffan* in Nyland, and the other pairs of costumed attendants found accompanying disguised figures in similar dramatic traditions from Norway, Estonia and Iceland.[56] These *hámenn* usually preceded their leader into the farmhouses, and as in most other costumed Scandinavian traditions, a 'tax' had to be paid before they could be got to leave.[57] In general, all the information provided above gives good reason to believe that the figure of the straw-man/ *Halm-Staffan* probably goes back to pagan times.

See also Lid, *Joleband*, p.47, and Feilberg, *Jul*, II, p.229. As mentioned above, the devilish leader of the Kölbigk dance is said to have been named 'Bovo' in an earlier twelfth-century MS: see Strömbäck, 'Kölbigk I', 9; Stumpfl, *Kultspiele*, p.173 and pp.179–180; and note 335 below. Some scholars have suggested that Bovi might be related to 'Bous' (Búi), the son of Rinda, who avenges the death of Baldr in Saxo Grammaticus, *Gesta Danorum*, Book III, p.73. Bous, however, has nothing to do with either straw or dance.

[54] Montelius, 'Solguden', 96–97.

[55] The costume itself varied, but was usually made as ugly as possible, involving ragged clothes and other items such as seaweed. All accounts, however, talk of the stick ('en stor kullbrand', 'en stav', 'en phallos', 'en stor stokk') which *Stallo* used to poke the girls with, before demanding payment of a 'tax'. This item was usually held. However, in Storfjord, Lyngen, in the early eighteenth century, it would seem that the stick was worn as a phallus. See the various descriptions of the *Stallo* tradition given in Lid, *Jolesveinar*, pp.43–44.

[56] Regarding *Stallo's hámenn*, see Lid, *Jolesveinar*, pp.43–44. Concerning *Halm-Staffan*, see the references given in note 37 above. On the two tall (now female) figures that accompany a phallic buck figure in certain Estonian Shrove Tuesday activities, see Lid, *Jolesveinar*, p.89. See also below, *section G.2* on the Icelandic *julebukk*-like figure of the *þingálp* which appeared at wake gatherings accompanied by two men dressed as *skjald-meyjar* ('shield-maidens').

[57] Regarding *Stallo* and his links with other Scandinavian folk traditions, see Lid, *Jolesveinar*, pp.43–70.

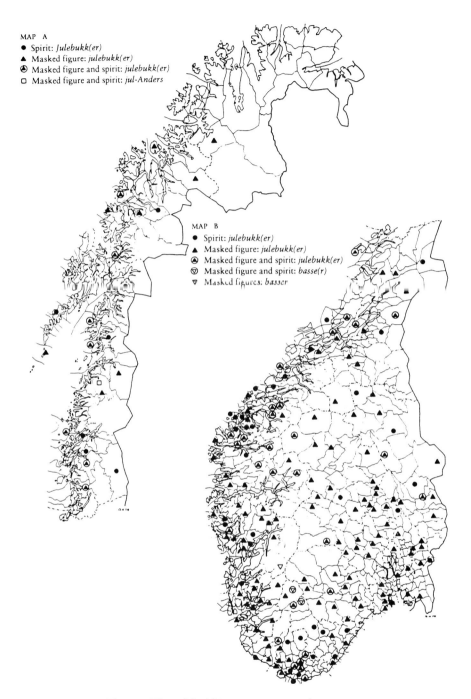

Fig. 54. The *julebukk* in Norway: Distribution map.

B. Related to the Christmas Period

3. The 'Julebukk'/ 'Julegeit'[58]

Of all the mainland Scandinavian figures that used to appear at Christmas, the most recurrent and widespread was that of the *julebukk* or *julegeit*. In the last century, this figure was still known throughout Norway (see *figs 54–55*) and in large parts of Sweden.[59] Farther back in time, the *julebukk* was probably also a common figure in Denmark, but there it seems to have disappeared during the early nineteenth century (if not earlier), most likely as a result of vehement opposition from the clergy.[60]

The popularity of the goat figure, and its deep-rootedness in mainland Scandinavian culture is attested to by the way that it became attached to all of the traditions that have been mentioned above, in the form of, for example, the *lussebock*,[61] the *staffansbock*,[62] the *Nyårsbokk, nyårsgeit* ('New Year's goat') and *trettenbekren* 'Twelfth-night goat'),[63] and the Värmland *julbockar* or *skråbuker* (linked in particular with 13 January, a date which was more commonly associated with *Knut*).[64] The goat even came to take a central role in many of the aforementioned *Stjärnopol*.[65] Here, it seems to have blended on occasion with the figure of Judas who is also often dressed in skins with a blackened face,[66] but on occasion gives himself away by talking of having 'come from the forest' ('kommen från skogen'), a habitat more commonly reserved for supernatural beings like the *julebukk* in its spiritual form.[67] As has been noted above, the figures of 'Lussia' and the accompanying 'jolesvein' in *fig.51* are also both equipped with goat horns.[68] Furthermore, in parts of Sweden, the name 'julbock'

---

[58] Regarding the general character of the *julebukk*, see Lid, *Joleband*, pp.51–58; Celander, *Nordisk jul*, pp.305–308, and 'Julbocken', passim; Olrik and Ellekilde, *Nordens gudeverden*, II, pp.932–933, p.937, pp.951–952, and pp.1080–1082; Weiser-Aall, *Julenissen*, pp.23–55; and Schager, *Julbocken*, passim.

[59] These figures were less common in southern Sweden and in Swedish-speaking Finland: see Celander, *Nordisk jul*, p.305.

[60] See further below, notes 92 and 102–103.

[61] See above, section B.1.

[62] See above, section B.2.

[63] See Weiser-Aall, *Julenissen*, p.30, and Celander, *Nordisk jul*, p.306.

[64] See above, note 45. On further links between the goat figure and this date, see Celander, *Nordisk jul*, p.306. See also Weiser-Aall, *Julenissen*, p.49, on the suggestion that the *julebukker* originally had the role of both ushering in and 'sweeping out' the Yuletide festival.

[65] See Lid, *Jolesveinar*, pp.22–23; Celander, *Stjärngossarna*, pp.423–428; and Feilberg, *Jul*, I, p.206, and II, pp.247–248 (on a play from Bergen).

[66] See Feilberg, *Jul*, I, p.206, and II, pp.248–249; Norlind, *Studier*, p.311; and Celander, *Stjärngossarna*, p.458 on the interchangeability of Judas and the *julebukk*.

[67] See Feilberg, *Jul*, I, p.209, and II, p.249; Celander, *Stjärngossarna*, p.419–420; and Norlind, *Studier*, p.319. In many areas, the spirit of the *julebukk* is also supposed to spend most of the year in the woods which it leaves at Christmas time to approach farms: see Bø, *Vår norske jul*, p.146.

[68] The *Lussia* figure here had one goat's horn, and one ram's horn, while the *jolesvein* ('Christmas man') wore two goat's horns. In both cases, the horns were attached to a piece of wood which was tied to the performer's head, something that offers an interesting parallel to the Bronze Age horns shown in *fig.18* above. See further Weiser-Aall, *Julenissen*, p.33. On other links between the *julebukk* and *julesveiner*, who, like the

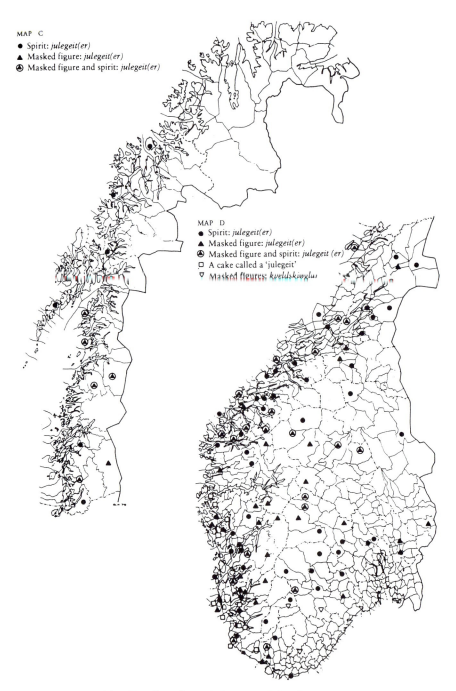

Fig. 55. The *julegeit* in Norway: Distribution map.

B. Related to the Christmas Period

was applied to the living Yuletide figure wrapped in straw,[69] an association echoed by the smaller straw *julbockar* that even nowadays serve as traditional Swedish Christmas decorations.[70]

3. *The 'Julebukk'/ 'Julegeit'*

In very general terms, the *julebukk* shares many features with not only traditional German and Austrian figures like the *Habergeis*, but also with certain English Hobby Horses.[71] A typical *julebukk* costume might involve a horned and bearded goat-head with clacking jaws, attached to a long pole held by the performer who would be bent over and covered with a large sheep- or goatskin, or simply a sheet of some kind (see *figs 56–63*).[72] Another recurrent feature of the costume seems to have been the use of bells, an element that invites comparisons with the Iron Age *rangler* discussed in the previous chapter (*section C.8*).[73] Otherwise, numerous variations in costume existed, especially as regards the nature of the mask which ranged from being made from the actual skin of the recently slaughtered animal,[74] to masks of wood with iron teeth[75] or simple blackened

---

julebukk, were regarded as dangerous figures that moved in on farms at Christmas, see Weiser-Aall, *Julenissen*, pp.33–34 and p.38; and Lid, *Joleband*, p.42 and pp.51–63.

[69] Celander, in 'Julbocken', 97–98, gives examples of such figures from Bohuslän, Dalsland, Bergslagen and north Östergötland. Only in the last two cases, however, is the figure made up to look like a goat. See also above, note 45, for further examples from Värmland, and Schager, *Julbocken*, p.51, on a 'julgubbe' from Kristdala in Småland which moved around on its knees wearing a sheaf of long straw over its head.

[70] See Celander, 'Julbocken', 94. In eastern Jylland, Denmark, however, the straw *julebuk* often took the form of a man, perhaps because of local prohibitions: Lid, *Joleband*, p.47. Regarding these prohibitions, see further notes 92 and 102–103 below.

[71] See illustrations in Bø, *Vår norske jul*, p.145, and Nilsson, *Årets folkliga fester*, plate 46. See further, Mannhardt, *Wald- und Feldkult*, II, pp.183–186. On English traditions, see further note 110, and *section G.1* below.

[72] See the descriptions in Lid, *Joleband*, pp.39–42, most of which come from the southern and western areas of Norway. See also Weiser-Aall, *Julenissen*, pp.23–32; Celander, *Nordisk jul*, pp.305–309; and the illustration in Celander, 'Julbocken', 99. See also the many descriptions and illustrations of Swedish costumes given in Keyland, *Julbröd*, passim, and Schager, *Julbocken*, pp.82–92.

[73] See, Olrik and Ellekilde, *Nordens gudeverden*, II, p.956; Eike, 'Oskoreia', 256–257, and 271; Schager, *Julbocken*, p.89; Lid, *Joleband*, p.39; Keyland, *Julbröd*, passim; and Celander, *Stjärngossarna*, pp.425–428 (see also p.431 on the use of bells with the Uppland *Halm-Staffan*). See, *section G.2* (for example, the references given in notes 263 and 289), concerning Icelandic games and traditions that involve the use of rattling implements such as keys.

[74] As in the account from Valdres given in note 81 below. See further the accounts from Bø, Telemark, and Forsand, Rogaland, quoted in Weiser-Aall, *Julenissen*, pp.25–26, and p.78, note 87, which both mention the use of the head-skin or skull of a calf's or cow's head for the mask. As Weiser-Aall suggests, this form of mask, which is used annually and implies connections with the Christmas slaughtering of animals, is probably closer to the original form of the mask and costume. On this idea, see also Celander, 'Julbocken', 102–103.

[75] See, for example, Lid, *Joleband*, p.40. In some cases birch bark was also used, thus providing parallels with the costume worn by Örvar-Oddr as the 'Næframaðr': see Keyland, *Julbröd*, p.99 and p.110; Schager, *Julbocken*, p.86; Weiser-Aall, *Julenissen*, p.24; and *Chapter I, D.1*.

3. The 'Julebukk'/ 'Julegeit'

faces (see *figs* 58–63).[76] The number of horns occasionally varied,[77] as did the physical appearance of the goat which was usually enacted by one man, but in several cases is reported to have been performed by two.[78] Probably the most famous *julebukk* is the simple variety depicted in Ludvig Holberg's short play, *Julestue* ('The Christmas Party'; 1724), scene 9, 'wrapped in a white sheet with two horns on its forehead'.[79]

As Weiser-Aall suggests, it is possible that the element of the clacking jaws was borrowed from the German and Austrian goat costumes.[80] This, however, should not be taken to mean that the goat figure itself was originally a foreign import. Indeed, it might be noted that even the pole does not seem to have been a necessity in Scandinavia where, in many cases, the costume seems to have borne a close resemblance to those of the monsters and 'berserkr' depicted on the Torslunda matrices. In Valdres, for example, 'they used to make a mask from the skin of a male goat's head. The mask had to have horns and a long beard. And then he wore a pair of disgusting skin trousers, and an old skin jacket, had a bell hung around his neck, and generally did himself up the best he could.'[81] Furthermore, certain scholars have recently argued that many legends concerning seasonal visiting spirits like the 'Wild Ride' or the spiritual *julebukk* and *julesveinar* might have been based originally on visits by people in such disguises as those described above, since for both children and more primitive people, the dividing line between the masked performer and the actual spirit seems very unclear.[82] As has been pointed out in the previous chapter, the same vagueness about identity occurs in saga accounts involving

---

[76] Weiser-Aall, *Julenissen*, p.24 and Schager, *Julbocken*, p.86.

[77] In a description of the *kveldsgjøgla* from Nissedal, the goat figure had only one horn: Lid, *Joleband*, p.40. Generally, however, two horns were used. Note, for example, the comment from Møre og Romsdal quoted in Weiser-Aall, *Julenissen*, p.78, note 85: 'To horn måtte det alltid være' ('It must always have two horns').

[78] See Lid, *Joleband*, p.39 and p.42, on examples from Hallingdal and Voss in Hordaland; and Keyland, *Julbröd*, pp.98–101, for two other examples from Värmland.

[79] 'Svøbt udi et hvidt Lagen med to Horn in Panden': Holberg, *Comoedierne*, p.391. This figure, called a 'Julebuk' in the play, should not be confused with another disguised figure that later appears in scene 13 (p.399), with 'a blackened face, and a stick in his mouth holding two candles, and riding on two men with their backsides to each other' ('kullet i Ansigtet, med en Pind i Munden, hvorpaa staaer to Lys, ridende paa to Karle, som vende Rumpene til enanden'). Nothing in the play states that this second figure should also be regarded as a 'Julebuk'. The two figures are probably meant to be different, the latter representing something similar to the *Hvegehors* (see notes 92–93). Nonetheless, on comparable Danish traditions in which the *julebukk* and *julebisp* bore candles on sticks in their mouths, see Feilberg, *Jul*, II, pp.228–229, and Ellekilde, *Vor danske jul*, p.300. See also the references for descriptions of two-man goat figures from Värmland in the previous note, and the references concerning the candle-bearing Icelandic 'stag' and *þingálp* figures that appeared in the Icelandic *vikivaki* games, given in notes 260 and 284 below.

[80] Weiser-Aall, *Julenissen*, p.32.

[81] 'Dei hadde på hann ei maske av hovudskinnet på ein geitebukk. Maska måtte ha horn og langt skjegg. So hadde han på seg ei fæl skinnbrok og ei gamal skinntrøye, hengde ei bjølle um halsen, og stase seg elles ut de beste han kunde:' quoted in Lid, *Joleband*, p.39.

[82] See in particular, Eike, 'Oskoreia', 232–234 and 264–273. Eike's ideas are largely based on those of Höfler, expressed in *Verwandlungskulte*, pp.44–68.

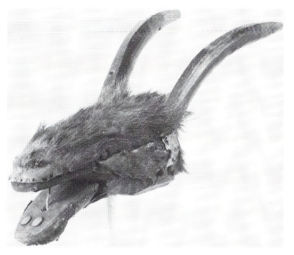

Fig. 56. A *julegeita* mask with clacking jaws (Frederikstad).

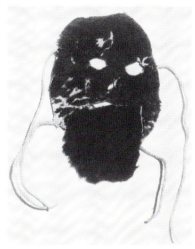

Fig. 58. A copy of a sheep-skin *julebukk* mask made by Anna Samuelsen (Ulvdal, Buskerud).

Fig. 57. A *julegeita* mask (Vest-Agder).

Fig. 59. A *julebukk* mask made of black-painted wood, a horse tail, cow-skin and cloth (Setesdal).

3. The 'Julebukk'/ 'Julegeit'

role-play and disguise.[83] Bearing all of the above in mind, Weiser-Aall has argued that distant memories of two-legged figures in goat costume might be reflected in a description of the *julebukk* spirit from Vest-Agder, which was supposed to have been 'like a man below the waist and a goat above' ('nedentil som en mann og oventil som en bukk'), totally opposite to the classical image of the satyr, but exactly like the costumed *berserkr* figures depicted on the Torslunda matrix and the Oseberg tapestry.[84]

In this shape, and occasionally accompanied or replaced by another being, the female *julegeit*,[85] and/ or a large following of other characters,[86] the *julebukk* used to pay visits on farms, stopping to receive a near compulsory offering of food and drink, and sometimes to dance. On occasion, however, the behaviour of this creature seems to have become particularly ribald: one account from south Trøndelag, for example, tells of how the *julebukker* 'were usually furious so they butted people, and the first one each goat butted (lit.'stabbed') was supposed to become his wife.'[87] Another similar description was given by E. M. Arndt, a German traveller to Sweden in the early nineteenth century, who commented on how the young people who dressed up in goat costumes 'acted so freely with the young men and women, started kissing them at the same time as stabbing at them with their enormous horns; they even whipped them with brushwood.'[88] In some cases, as with a goat figure from Estonia, the disguise seems to have been more obviously phallic,[89] thus emphasising the similarities with the equivalently ribald figure of *Stallo* described above.[90]

Nowadays, the tradition of dressing up as *julebukker* tends to be carried out by children rather than by adults, and in most places, the Santa Claus figures of the *julenisse* and *jultomte* have replaced that of the goat.[91] There would seem to be little doubt, however, that the custom has early roots.

---

[83] See *Chapter I, D.1*.
[84] Weiser-Aall, *Julenissen*, p.53. A comparable description of the spiritual 'Jolereidi' comes from Haus in Norway where the being is described as 'eitt lodden utyske i menneske skapnad' ('a hairy monster in the shape of a man'): Quoted in Eike, 'Oskereia', 265.
[85] See, for example, the account from V. Slidre in Valdres in Lid, *Joleband*, p.39, and the account from south Trøndelag given below, which also mentions both types. Usually, however, the *julebukk* and *julegeit* are interchangeable. Weiser-Aall, in *Julenissen*, p.27, on the basis of more recent research, suggests that the name *julegeit* is more common. Nonetheless, see the distribution maps of the names given in *figs 54–55*.
[86] See, for example, the descriptions of the Norwegian and Swedish processions given in Lid, *Joleband*, p.41, and Celander, *Nordisk jul*, p.308.
[87] 'De var oftest sinte saa de stanget noen, og den første bukkene stanget, skulde være bruden hans og omvendt': quoted in Lid, *Joleband*, p.42.
[88] '. . . unge folk iførte sig bukkeham med horn og tilbehør og fo'r så løs på de unge piger og karle for at kyse dem, idet de stak efter dem med deres vældige horn og kunde vel også piske dem med ris': Feilberg, *Jul*, II, p.230.
[89] See Lid, *Jolesveinar*, p.89.
[90] See note 55 above. See also the descriptions of the comparable behaviour of *Háa-Þóra*, the *þingálp* and *hjörtur* in the Icelandic *vikivaki* games in Jón Samsonarson, *Kvæði*, I, p.lix, p.lxiii and p.lxxiii, and that of the Faroese *grýla* in Heinesen's short story of the same name, 'Grylen', pp.39–43. Regarding these figures, see further below, *sections G.2–4*.
[91] Lid, *Joleband*, p.41, and Weiser-Aall, *Julenissen*, p.24.

Fig. 60. *Julbock* and *Julget* (Vemdalen, Härjedalen).

Fig. 61. *Julbock* (Sko, Uppland).

II. Dramatic Activities, II: Folkloristic Evidence

3. The 'Julebukk'/ 'Julegeit'

The earliest known direct reference to the *julebukk* occurs in Denmark, in Bishop Peder Palladius' *Visitatsbog* (1543) which contains a prohibition to Sjælland farmers against 'all night drinking and unsuitable night-time entertainments such as *Hvegehors* ('Rocking-horse'), *Hvidebjørn* ('Polar bear'), *Julebuk*, *Huggetønde* ('Barrel-hacking'), *Daaretønde* ('Fool's barrel') at weddings and so forth.'[92] The *Hvegehors* was probably similar to the English Hobby Horse.[93] It was probably disguises such as this, the *Hvidebjørn* and the *Julebuk* that Christiern Pedersen was refering to in his *Jærtegnspostil* (1515) when he wrote of the 'terrifying masks and other devilish guises' ('Rædegrimer eller anden Djævleham') worn by people in parts of Denmark at Christmas time. These figures probably also formed part of the 'Christmas games and other ungodly forms of behaviour' ('Juleleg og andet ugudeligt Væsen') complained about by Bishop Niels Jespersen with regard to the inhabitants of an area of Laaland in 1563.[94] In 1672, the *Julebuk* is also mentioned in P. I. Colding's Danish *Dictionarium Herlovianum*, alongside other Christmas games such as the choosing of the *Julebisp* ('Christmas bishop') and 'Legens konge' ('the game king') [95]

In Sweden, the *julbock* is referred to as early as 1555 in Olaus Magnus' description of Shrovetide masking which mentions people wearing horned bulls' or goats' heads, and making the appropriate sounds for the particular animal being depicted.[96] Nonetheless, it would be reasonable to assume that the connection with Shrovetide must represent a later stage in the development of the custom. As Peder Palladius' prohibition suggests, the goat was already strongly associated with Christmas in Denmark at this time, and the same probably applied to Sweden where a prohibition of the 'so called *julebock* game' ('julebocksleken') was later published in Malmö in 1695.[97]

The first real description of the *julebukk* figure appears in Norway in C.

---

[92] 'Forvar eder at i iche sidde natthen offuer oc slemme, alle natdriche oc utilbørlig nathvecht, som er huægehors, huidebørn, iullebuch, huggetønde, daartønd i brøllup oc andet sadant er altsammen afflagt, til landtzting under kongenss sværdtt, huo der findes met': Palladius, *Visitatsbog*, p.144; see also the commentary on this passage given on pp.220–225 of the same book. Ellekilde, in *Vor danske jul*, pp.280–281, gives another description of the *Hvegehors* from 1850, and explains the *Daaretønde* as some form of guessing game. Nonetheless, neither the *Huggetønde* or the *Daaretønde* have ever been satisfactorily explained.
[93] Jacobsen, in Palladius, *Visitatsbog*, pp.222–223.
[94] Pedersen's and Jespersen's statements are both quoted in Ellekilde, *Vor danske jul*, pp.277–279.
[95] See Ellekilde, *Vor danske jul*, p.281. Regarding the *julebisp*, see further below, *section D.1*.
[96] Olaus Magnus, *Historia de gentibus septentionalibus* (Book XIII, ch.42), p.463; translated into Swedish in *Historia om de nordiska folken*, III, p.80. Regarding other Shrovetide costumes and dramatic traditions in Sweden, see Svensson, 'Årsfester', p.66. Regarding Denmark, see Troels-Lund, *Dagligt liv*, VII, pp.118–120, and Møller, 'Aarsfester', pp.116-124. In Norway, the tradition seems to have been limited to the Hansa centre of Bergen: see Bondevik, 'Høgtider', p.90.
[97] See Eskeröd, *Årets fester*, p.200. On this question, see further Bregenhøj, *Helligtrekongersløb*, pp.124–126.

Fig. 62. Kneeling *Julbock* (Mangskog, Värmland).

Fig. 63. *Julbock* and *Staffan* singers arriving (Nås, Dalarna).

3. The 'Julebukk'/'Julegeit'

Jensøn's *Norske dictionarium* (1646) where a *rågeit* ('pole-goat') from Sunnfjord is described as 'a person disguised with a sheet or blanket placed over a piece of wood shaped like a pair of tongs, who frightens small children.'[98] The first mention of the 'clacking jaws' appears in Jørgen Sorterup's detailed description (1722) of the costume worn by the Danish *Julebuk*, an 'ugly monster' ('hæsligt uhyre') that visited farmhouses near Slagelse in 1678.[99]

The range of the references given above suggests that in the early seventeenth century, the *julebukk* must have been an extremely widespread Scandinavian phenomenon involving a number of local names and variants. Indeed, as early as the late sixteenth century, the same figure is found in Iceland under the different name of the 'Fingálpn'.[100] The Yule-goat, however, was destined to disappear from Danish soil during the eighteenth century largely as a result of church pressure and state laws that were less easily enforced in Norway and Iceland.[101] Local bans like that of Peder Palladius were followed up by a national Danish law against the *julebukk* custom in 1668.[102] Yet another law, the so-called Norwegian Law, or *Norsk-lov*, relating to Norway (and thus relevant also to Iceland), was then passed in 1687, and stated, in usefully general terms, that 'All frivolous and contemptible games at Christmas or other times, and the Lenten races, are strictly prohibited, and offenders must be seriously punished.'[103] Such laws reflect the mood of the time. However, they also emphasise the fact that the traditions must have been widespread enough to warrant royal attention. As has been pointed out above, similar bans were attempted in Sweden: the Malmö order of 1695 was followed by further prohibitions against both the *julbock* and the 'star' (associated mainly with the *Stjärnspel*) in Stockholm (1721), Karlskrona (only the goat; 1754), Örebro (1777) and Kungälv, near Göteborg (1786).[104] That these prohibitions failed to have any long term effect is suggested by the fact that a further prohibition had to be made in Karlskrona in 1808.[105]

---

[98] 'Et formummet Menniske med et Sengeklæde paa et Træ giort som en Tang ofver sig oc skremmer smaa Børn': quoted in Lid, *Joleband*, p.42.
[99] See Olrik and Ellekilde, *Nordens gudeverden*, II, p.956.
[100] See further below, *section G.2-3*.
[101] Troels-Lund argues, a little unconvincingly, that the disappearance of the *julebukk* in Denmark came about largely as a result of a ban on the ownership of goats that was instituted in Denmark in the mid-sixteenth century: Troels-Lund, *Dagligt liv*, VII, p.64, and V, p.91.
[102] See Feilberg, *Jul*, II, p.228; and Olrik and Ellekilde, *Nordens gudeverden*, II, p.956.
[103] 'Al lætfærdig og forargelig Legen om Jul, eller andre Tider, og Fastlavens Løben forbydis strengeligen, og bør alvorligen at straffis': *Kong Christian den femtes Norske Lov*, p.753: NL 663, lib.6, cap.3, art.11.
[104] For the text of these prohibitions, see Celander, *Stjärngossarna*, pp.50-51; and Schager, *Julbocken*, pp.38-40.
[105] See Celander, *Stjärngossarna*, p.51.

B. Related to the Christmas Period

4. The 'Killing' of the 'Julebukk'

Unlike the *Stjärngossar* or *Staffan*, the visit of the *julebukk* was not traditionally associated with any given song or 'play'. Quite the opposite: more often the *bukk* was known for the way it 'bleated in an ugly, rough voice' ('brækte med grovt, fælt mæle').[106] Elsewhere, as today, the masked members of the *julebukk* groups visiting farms and houses tended to disguise their voices in other ways, for example by using 'reverse speech' (that is, speaking while inhaling), the object of the game being to escape recognition as long as possible.[107]

Nonetheless, as has been pointed out above, the *julebukk* had a tendency to ally itself with other more dramatic presentations like the *Stjärnspel*,[108] and several scholars have drawn particular attention to a semi-dramatic song performed by the figures of a 'father' and 'son' who led the *julebukk* in Bergen at some time during the mid-nineteenth century.[109] At least seven extant versions of this song have been recorded in various places that range across the width of Scandinavia from Bergen to Öland. One such version from Bergen describes how the father and son build a boat before proceeding to shoot a goat which is then apparently sold piecemeal (the skin, wool, beard, legs and so on) in a series of offers and replies.[110] Once this business has been completed, the goat suddenly returns to life and gallops off accompanied by the words, 'Op stander den bokken aa rister sit skjæg/ Han haapte og sprang paa femte vægg,/ paa femte vægg' ('Up gets the goat

---

[106] See, for example, Lid, *Joleband*, pp.39–40, and p.42 for three such references from Gudbrandsdal, Hallingdal and Vestnes; Keyland, *Julbröd*, pp.39–40, for another example from Västergötland; and Schager, *Julbocken*, p.43.

[107] My information here is based on conversations with a number of older people in Balestrand, in western Norway, where the figure of the buck itself has disappeared and been replaced by a group of heavily disguised children who 'gå julebukk'. On the element of disguise and the guessing of identity, see Bø, *Vår norske jul*, p.139. For parallels in Danish traditions, see Bregenhøj, *Helligtrekongersløb* pp.28–35. For parallels in Faroese and Shetland traditions, see the references given in notes 353 and 374 below. On other parallels from Newfoundland, involving a comparable type of utterance, linked with what are often similar disguises and guessing games, see Halpert, 'A typology', pp.37–40; Szwed, 'The mask of friendship', p.110; Faris, 'Mumming', p.131; and Widdowson and Halpert, 'The disguises', pp.152–160. For similarities in Ireland, see Gailey, *Irish folk drama*, pp.48–49 and p.93.

[108] See also Jón lærði Guðmundsson's seventeenth-century account of the games involving the goat-like 'Fingálpn' in Iceland, quoted in note 257 below. This account also seems to imply the existence of a basic storyline.

[109] See Troels-Lund, *Dagligt liv*, VII, pp.66–67, and Lid, *Joleband*, pp.47–48, for two variants of this song from Bergen. The former (dated 1860) is also contained in Feilberg, *Jul*, II, pp.231–232, and Norlind, *Studier*, pp.329–331. The latter originates in Nicolaysen, 'De norske bukkevise', 212–214, where it is accompanied by a description of the performance by the three 'actors'.

[110] An interesting analogy to the piecemeal selling of the *bukk* is found in the song accompanying the 'slaying' of the Derbyshire 'Old Tup', a figure with many close similarities to the *julebukk*. See Cawte, *Ritual animal disguise*, pp.110–117, and Abrahams, 'Folk drama', pp.355–356. Regarding the close parallels in guise between many of the English animal figures and the *julebukk*, and the difficulties of drawing conclusions from these parallels, see further below, *section G.1*.

4. The 'Killing' of the 'Julebukk'

and he shakes his beard,/ he leapt and ran along the roof,/ along the roof').[111]

This song was 'performed' dramatically as part of a normal house-visit by the *julebukk* and there is every implication that all the other variants of the song must have been acted out in a similar fashion.[112] Considering this aspect of performance, certain variants of the song awake particular interest. For example, one version from Gudbrandsdal, Voss and Sunnfjord relates, albeit in a slightly more confused and fragmented form, how the goat is placed *on board* the boat, a motif also found in Swedish variants of the song from Blekinge, Värmland, Öland, Skåne and elsewhere.[113] Even more intriguing is an unexplained feature of the 1860 variant from Bergen, and of those from Blekinge, Öland and Bohuslän, where after the death of the goat[114] the creature is systematically covered by a series of coloured cloaks before it returns to life.[115] In yet another variant from Bohuslän, this particular version of the 'play' seems to have blended with the *Stjärnspel*, and the text even contains stage directions. In this case, the bearded, horned 'bock', after dancing with the figure of Josef, is killed by his partner. The 'bock' then lies down, as if dead ('som om han varit död') and, to the accompaniment of a song describing the actions, is covered with the series of coloured cloaks (red, white and black in this case). After this, the goat suddenly returns to life, gets up on its knees, and pounds the floor with its club ('Bocken gick då på knä och slog sin klubba i golvet').[116]

Before leaping to Frazerian conclusions regarding the death and resurrection element of the *julebukk* tradition, it should be noted that not all the songs state that the *julebukk* is killed by someone else;[117] and in certain variants from Gudbrandsdal, Voss and Sunnfjord, the goat never returns to life.[118] Arguably, therefore, the importance of this feature should not be overrated. Furthermore, as Norlind has suggested, the final verse concerning the miraculous resurrection of the goat might have been added for

---

[111] Nicolaysen, 'De norske bukkevise', p.214. Also quoted in Lid, *Joleband*, p.48.
[112] See, for example, Troels-Lund, *Dagligt liv*, VII, pp.66–67, and the account from Öland given in Feilberg, *Jul*, II, pp.231–232.
[113] For the Gudbrandsdal variant, see Lid, *Joleband*, p.48. For the texts of the versions from Sunnfjord, Voss, Öland, and Blekinge and a discussion of the likely chronological derivation of these texts, see Norlind, *Studier*, pp.326–332. Norlind's conclusion (p.328) is that the Norwegian texts are closer to the original than the Swedish. For further comments on the variants, see also Celander, *Stjärngossarna*, pp.400–404. Most of the Norwegian texts mentioned here were first published in Støylen, *Norske barnerim*, pp.60–61.
[114] In Blekinge, the killing is done by hand, rather than by gun.
[115] See the references given above for details concerning the colour of the cloaks which, at one stage, must have all had some symbolic meaning. For example, in most cases, a red cloak is placed on the goat the moment it dies.
[116] See Lindquist, 'Äringsriter', 20, and Lid, *Jolesveinar*, pp.30–31.
[117] For example, the 1860 variant from Bergen tells how the goat falls from a mountain: see Nicolaysen, 'Den norske bukkevise', 214.
[118] See Norlind, *Studier*, p.329.

B. Related to the Christmas Period

practical reasons to allow the performer to leave the room on two (or four) legs.[119]

Nonetheless, some support for the idea that the killing (and resurrection) of the goat *was* a recognised dramatic motif is provided by the evidence of Norwegian and Swedish children's games like 'Slaughtering the goat', 'Slaughtering the Christmas bull' and 'Resuscitating the dead goat',[120] and two versions of Norwegian folk plays involving the Three Kings and *Staffan*. The first play, in a verse on 'St Stephen', contains stage directions stating that 'The skin-clad figure lies down' ('De skindklædte lægger sig ned') and 'The skin-clad figure gets up' ('Den skindklædte reiser sig'), this second action being echoed in the words "Stand up,' says Simeon' ('Stander op, siger Simeon').[121] In the second play, *Staffan* himself boasts of how 'I have been out in the snow and slush, and fought with the great *julbock*',[122] a statement which offers a tempting parallel to the sixteenth-century accounts of the seasonal battle between Winter and Summer known in Denmark and Sweden.[123]

As one of the examples given above implies, the concept of falling and rising at Christmas was evidently not limited to the *julebukk*. Interestingly enough, a few *Staffan* songs contain the same motif, which occurs in a particularly original fashion in an early sixteenth-century Icelandic translation of a Norwegian poem dealing with the nativity, 'Fyrirlát mér jungfrúin hreina'.[124] This work (st.11 [10]) contains a very odd description of how 'Stephanus' allows himself to be hacked into three pieces before returning to life, an image that totally contradicts the traditional account of the saint's unquestioned martyrdom by stoning: 'Stephanus let sig neyda/ ok höggva í hlutina þrja/ hann reis upp af deyda/ sa þar Herodes á.'[125] Faint

4. The 'Killing' of the 'Julebukk'

---

[119] Norlind, *Studier*, p.332. Norlind also suggests here that the motif of covering the goat might have been originally related to the hunters' need to hide their catch.
[120] On these games, 'Slakta bocken', 'Slakta juloxen' and 'Blåsa liv in den daude bukken', see Celander, *Nordisk jul*, p.302 and p.304, and 'Slakta julbocken', p.35; and Støylen, *Norske barnerim*, p.91.
[121] A song from Mandal (1850), quoted in Lid, *Jolesveinar*, p.22. No explanation of the identity of 'Den skindklædte' is given. A similar idea may be echoed in another description of a nativity play from Bergen which included the figure of 'a goat with large horns which, at a particular point in the song, fell to the ground, whereupon all the others hit it freely with their sticks' ('en buk med vældig horn, som på ett bestemt sted i sangen faldt til jorden, hvorpå alle de andre slog løs på han med deres stokke'): Feilberg, *Jul*, II, pp.247–248. See also Nilsson, *Årets folkliga fester*, p.270, on a similar Swedish tradition in which an acted animal entered a room in the middle of a dance of young people with blackened faces. The disguised performers then performed the 'slaughter' of the animal to the accompaniment of a song. Nothing here is stated about the resurrection of the animal (whatever it was supposed to be).
[122] 'Jag har varit ute i snö och slask, i köld og frost, och stridit med den stora julbocken': Feilberg, *Jul*, I, p.208.
[123] See below, *section C.1*.
[124] For an example of a *Staffan* song with this motif, see, for example, Strömbäck, 'St Stephen', p.140. Regarding the Icelandic translation, see Jørgensen and Vésteinn Ólason, 'Fyrirlát mér jungfrúin hreina'.
[125] For further references to the legend of St Stephen (*Staffan*) in Scandinavia, see note 9

4. The 'Killing' of the 'Julebukk'

memories of this same action would also seem to lie behind certain Danish 'Three Kings plays', in which one of the kings with a blackened face ('The King of Morians land') is struck by another who has a staff, and has to ask for mercy.[126] This element is not common in Denmark, but is clearly related to the popular scene in many Swedish 'star plays' in which Herod forces the blackened-faced 'King of Morieland' to fall to his knees in homage.[127] As Celander points out, this 'falling and rising' feature of the *Stjärnspel* appears to be limited to Scandinavian 'Three Kings plays', and is thus probably based on some other local tradition, perhaps to do with an execution scene, like that found in the *julebukk*-songs.[128]

Bearing this in mind, it is worth noting several other analogies to the 'death of the goat' found in Scandinavia, such as the Dalarna Shrovetide tradition of 'Shooting the bear' ('Å skjuta björnen').[129] This activity seems to have grown out of certain spring customs in which a bear, enacted by one or two boys, was led in a procession by two masked children wearing bells, and a mock bride and bridegroom. A related tradition in certain northern Swedish wedding ceremonies involved the 'bear' being chased, 'killed' and then borne on a sledge to the place of the wedding, at which point the animal was 'stabbed', thus opening the cask of alcohol he carried and allowing his 'blood' to be drunk.[130] A further analogy is encountered in

---

above. Possibly this image of Stephanus' resurrection was influenced by the early medieval motif of the roasted capon which returned to life to confirm Stephen's (or the Three Kings') announcement of Jesus' birth. On use of the capon motif in Scandinavia, see Strömbäck, 'Staffan', 191–195. The other possibility is that Stephanus' resurrection was originally added for practical reasons to allow the performer to 'get off the stage', as Norlind suggests with regard to the semi-dramatic 'goat songs' discussed above. It might be added that it is doubtful whether 'Fyrirlát mér jungfrúin hreina' was performed dramatically in Nidaros Cathedral as Jørgensen and Vésteinn Ólason suggest (see above, note 11). To the best of my knowledge, no liturgical drama covers such a large amount of action (running from the Annunciation to the Crucifixion) in such a short space of time (24 strophes). Nonetheless, the image of Stephanus' resurrection remains very puzzling. It might well be related to some fifteenth-century popular Norwegian Christmas tradition involving *Staffan* which included an enacted death (like that of the divided *julebukk*; see above, notes 110–111) and resurrection.

126 See Celander, *Stjärngossarna*, pp.37–38; and Schmidt, 'Helligtrekongersangere', 60–63.

127 See Celander, *Stjärngossarna*, pp.37–38, p.167 (photograph), and pp.308–312; and Schmidt, 'Helligtrekongersangere', 60–63.

128 See Celander, *Stjärngossarna*, pp.311–312, and pp.462–463, for examples of this scene in which the black king is symbolically beheaded or has his heart removed by Herod or his servant. The fact that it is the 'blackened faced' king that is executed raises the possibility that his character attracted elements previously attached to other strongly disguised figures like the *julebukk*, which was often enacted with a blackened face. See the references given in note 77 above.

129 See Lid, *Joleband*, pp.48–49.

130 Regarding these traditions, see Lindquist, 'Äringsriter', 20–24. For similar Norwegian and Swedish traditions involving the drinking of the 'blood' of the *julegrisen* (the 'Christmas pig') and the *julebukk*, see further Lid, *Joleband*, p.49, and Celander, 'Slakta julbocken', pp.25–36. A rural Jylland tradition related to St Stephen's Day involved the drinking of warm red wine as a reminder of Stefan's blood ('det röde öl skulde minde om Stefans blod': Celander, 'Til Stefanslegendens och Staffansvisornas utvecklingshistoria', 150).

B. Related to the Christmas Period

4. The 'Killing' of the 'Julebukk'

a Danish Lent tradition from southern Sjælland called 'Shooting the stag' ('At skyde hjorten'). Here, a young man was 'dressed in a sheepskin coat with the wool facing out . . . He had a pair of grey homespun trousers on, and a pair of old white woollen socks outside his shoes. On his head he wore a hat made of the same material as the coat, and to the front of this were attached two small deer horns. On his hands he was wearing white mittens.'[131] Like the 'bear', the 'stag' was 'hunted', 'shot' and carried home on a stone sledge to a celebration of food and dance.[132]

Whether or not the above customs are directly related to each other is perhaps beside the point. Their main value is that they underline the possibility that in some areas of Norway, a similar enacted 'sacrifice' of the goat was presented in connection with the Christmas festival. Indeed, as several scholars have pointed out, further support for this may be found in an old Setesdal custom in which the animal slaughtered for Christmas (which had previously been fed on the final sheaf of corn from the last harvest) was known as the *julebjukke*.[133] Similar names (the *julegeit* or *julebukk*) were also given to a particular form of bread or cake baked specially for Christmas in some areas of Norway.[134] Scholars in the past have linked both of the above traditions with beliefs related to a fertility spirit,[135] and generally the idea that the folk plays centring on the goat might have roots in some earlier folk ritual cannot be ruled out. Nonetheless, the importance of the boat in the *julebukk* songs and the puzzling, almost ritualistic custom of covering the body of the 'dead' goat with coloured cloaks remain an intriguing enigma.[136]

The Swedish and Danish traditions related to the 'bear' and 'stag' emphasise that the *julebukk* was not the only animal disguise to feature in Scandinavian folk tradition. Bear disguises were also known in Norway,[137] and both horse and bulls' heads are reported to have been used as masks in certain areas of Bohuslän, in Sweden.[138] Even more interesting is the fact that in some other parts of Sweden the *julebukk* was replaced or abetted by

---

[131] 'En arbejdsmand . . . var iklædt en fåreskinds kofte med ulden udad . . . Han havde et par grå vadmelsbukser på og et par gamle hvide uldstrømper udenpå skoene. På hovedet bar han en hue af samme slags som koften, og foran på huen var fastgjort et par mindre hjortehorn. På hænderne havde han hvide bælgvanter': J. Olsen, 'En Fastelavnsskik', 127.
[132] A very close parallel to this custom is found, Cawte, *Ritual animal disguise*, p.192.
[133] Skar, *Gamalt or Sætesdal*, II, p.34. This connection is also stressed in Lid, *Joleband*, p.33 and p.51; in Celander, *Nordisk jul*, p.188, and 'Slakta julbocken', p.31; and in Nilsson, 'Julen', p.51.
[134] See, for example, Lid, *Joleband*, pp.72–73; Weiser-Aall, *Julenissen*, pp.51–52; Keyland, *Julbröd*, p.82; and Schager, *Julbocken*, pp.55–56.
[135] See further below, note 168.
[136] See further Lindquist, 'Äringsriter', 16–24, and Almgren, *Hällristningar*, pp.75–76 and p.123, on the question of whether the descriptions of the bear and stag being borne on sledges, and the buck being carried on the boat (as in the Bohuslän songs about the *julebock*) could be related to certain Bronze Age petroglyphs from Bohuslän, especially one from Sandåker depicting a stag on a boat.
[137] See Lid, *Joleband*, pp.105–107. The bear, or bear spirit, that offerings are made to here is sometimes known as *basse/ bassi*. See above Chapter I, D.2 on the *gadebasse*.
[138] Gjötterberg, 'Näbberfru', 25. See also Keyland, *Julbröd*, pp.100–101, on a pig disguise

5. The origin and role of the 'Julebukk'

a birdlike being with a long beak, known as the *julegoppa* ('Christmas bobber' or 'Christmas hag'; Dalsland), *julkyppa* ('Christmas chicken'; Bohuslän), *julkråka* ('Christmas crow'; Värmland), *julgås* ('Christmas goose') or *nyårsgås* ('New Year's goose'). Such figures are all powerfully reminiscent of the bird figures depicted in archaeological finds and Old Norse mythology which were discussed in the previous chapter.[139]

5. The Origin and Role of the 'Julebukk'

The origin of the *julebukk* has long been a question of much dispute. Several scholars, noting that the majority of early references to animal disguise in Europe originate in the Celtic countries, have proposed that the Scandinavians must therefore have imported these traditions from elsewhere at an early date.[140] Others, such as Feilberg, suggest that the *julebukk* was a later borrowing from Germany, a descendant of figures like the north German *Klapperbock*, *Habergeiss*, and *Erbsenbär*, which Feilberg imagines had pagan origins, but which did not arrive in Scandinavia until the time of the Hansa merchants.[141]

The suggestion of a German origin has been developed in recent years by other scholars who argue that the *julebukk* possibly entered Scandinavia as part of a European St Nicholas custom, since in later German folk custom, for example, St Nicholas often appeared in the company of a devil figure that seems to have blended with the *Habergeiss* and its counterparts.[142] Most recently, Guðmundur Ólafsson has even argued that such a custom might have come to Iceland as far back as the late twelfth century.[143]

---

from Värmland, and Järlgren, 'Julegoppan', 32, on a game from Töftedal in Dalsland involving the flaying of a straw-covered figure called a 'buse' which walked on all fours.

[139] Regarding these bird figures, see Celander, *Nordisk jul*, pp.307–308; Keyland, *Julbröd*, pp.100–101; and Järlgren, 'Julegoppan', 30–31. See also note 329 on the *Kveldsjøgl* from Vest-Agder, Norway. As Celander notes in *Nordisk jul*, p.307, the *jultyppa* bird costume from Dalsland was also used on Lady Day (25 March) and at Easter to represent a *trana* (crane). See also above, Chapter I, C.3 (especially note 101) for references on the Swedish petroglyphs depicting bird costumes.

[140] Regarding these early reports, see, for example, Feilberg, *Jul*, II, pp.221–226, and Alford, 'The Hobby Horse', 122–125. On the basis of this written evidence, Ellekilde, in *Vor danske jul*, pp.82–83, suggests that the practice of dressing up in women's clothes and as animals was originally adopted from the Celts by the Germans, and later spread to Scandinavia. Ellekilde argues that the predominance of the goat guise in Scandinavia might be related to these Celtic animal costumes becoming associated with the worship of Þórr.

[141] See Feilberg, *Jul*, II, pp.234–238. Regarding the German traditions, see further Nilsson, *Årets folkliga fester*, pp.172–178, and, for an overall picture, Mannhardt, *Wald- und Feldkult*, II, pp.155–198.

[142] See Boberg, 'Lussegubben', passim; Eskeröd, *Årets fester*, pp.200–201; Bø, *Vår norske jul*, pp.146–148; Schager, *Julbocken*, pp.21–34, and slightly more tentatively, Bringéus, *Årets festseder*, p.60. Regarding the link between the German figures and the St Nicholas tradition, see further Nilsson, *Årets folkliga fester*, pp.171–178.

[143] See Guðmundur Ólafsson, 'Jólakötturinn'.

B. Related to the Christmas Period

Although the faint chance that the *julebukk* originated in this way can never be ruled out entirely, these associations with St Nicholas must be viewed in the light of several important considerations. Certainly, St Nicholas became a popular protective saint in Scandinavia during the Middle Ages,[144] and there is evidence that after the Reformation the German *Christkindlein* was known in certain limited areas of southern Scandinavia in the shape of the *Kink Nissen* (Kvie in Vall, and Gotland), and *Kinken* (Runö in Estonia).[145] There is, however, little or no evidence of the Scandinavians ever adopting any costumed traditions involving St Nicholas himself prior to very recent times. Indeed, whenever a present-bearing figure is recorded as having visited Scandinavian houses in the early years of this century, it usually seems to have taken the shape of a locally known figure such as *Staffan* or the *julebukk* rather than Nicholas.[146] Concerning Guðmundur Ólafsson's hypothesis of an early medieval costumed Nicholas tradition that has now almost completely disappeared, it should be borne in mind that folk traditions involving the appearance of a Nicholas figure do not seem to have gained popularity in France and north-west Germany until the thirteenth century. It is thus highly unlikely that they appeared in Iceland in the twelfth century.[147] Furthermore, in the liturgical and vernacular Nicholas plays from the period in question, the figure of the Devil is noticeably absent.[148] The same would seem to apply to the medieval pictures of Nicholas found in the churches of Gotland, and in Vigersted in Denmark.[149] The Devil and Nicholas evidently did not become inseparable in folk tradition until a much later date.

In general, there is strong reason to question whether the Devil and the *julebukk* were ever intrinsically related in popular Scandinavian folk tradition where, as often as not, the Devil was depicted as having a horse-hoof rather than that of a goat.[150] With regard to religiously based folk dramas in Scandinavia, like the *Stjärnspel*, it might be noted that even when the *julebukk does* appear, hardly any reference is ever made to the name of the Devil who might be expected to have found a good home in such

5. The origin and role of the 'Julebukk'

---

144 See, for example, Schager, *Julbocken*, pp.24–26, on the early Nicholas cult in Gotland.
145 The *Christkindlein* replaced the figure of Nicholas after the Reformation. Regarding these figures, see Eskeröd, *Årets fester*, p.201, and Nilsson, *Årets folkliga fester*, p.173.
146 See Celander, *Nordisk jul*, p.107, and Schager, *Julbocken*, pp.30–33, where reference is also made to a 'Niklas' figure from south Gotland who distributed gifts to children (and also received them). The description of this figure, however, provides little to differentiate 'Niklas' from other Scandinavian folk figures such as *Staffan* or the *julebukk*.
147 See, for example, Eskeröd, *Årets fester*, p.200.
148 See the two plays from Hildesheim (eleventh-twelfth century), the three plays from the monastery of St Benoit-sur-Loire (twelfth century), and Hilarius' *Ludus super iconia Sancti Nicolai* (c.1130), published in Young, *DMC*, II, pp.311–314, pp.325–327, pp.330–332, pp.338–341, pp.343–348 and pp.351–357. See also Jean Bodel's *Le jeu de Saint-Nicolas* (c.1199–1201).
149 Schager, *Julbocken*, p.25, and Pio, *Bogen om julen*, pp.98–99.
150 See, for example, Klintberg, *Svenska folksägner*, p.203 and p.206. Even when Satan is said to have horns, there is rarely any suggestion of their being goat-horns.

5. The origin and role of the 'Julebukk'

performances on the German model.[151] The figures of the goat and the Devil were clearly not always synonymous in the public mind.

Arguably, it was the clergy of the seventeenth and eighteenth century who first proposed a relationship between the *julebukk* and the Devil, under influence from mainland Europe.[152] For the clergy, however, *any* horned figure would have attracted such comparisons; furthermore, during this period of clerical animosity, it also seems apparent that any *costumed* figure was viewed as having Satanic associations. Such attitudes are expressed particularly vividly in the booklet *Manducus eður leikafæla* ('Manducus or game-monster'), written c.1760 by the Icelandic priest, séra Þorsteinn Pétursson, in response to certain dramatic games in his own country which will be examined in more detail below.[153] Séra Þorsteinn's belief was that 'those who make themselves costumes of tatters for dance-games and private parties are the Devil's apes and a laughing-stock, hateful to the angels, God, and all good people,'[154] especially since, according to the Bible, the Devil was the first being to ever make use of disguise. As pointed out above, séra Þorsteinn's short book reflects the spirit of his times: between the years 1738 and 1746, the theatre in Denmark and Norway was completely prohibited for comparable religious reasons.[155]

Nonetheless, the deciding feature in the question of whether the *julebukk* evolved out of a Devil figure in an imported Nicholas tradition must be the relationship of the *julebukker* to gifts. In Norway in particular, the *julebukker* possessed the recognised trait that 'they don't give anything; they demand things and they are given them' ('Julebukkene gir ikke noe, de krever og får noe').[156] Such a tradition is completely opposed to the typical

---

[151] See Norlind, *Studier*, p.311. For the few examples of the Devil having a role in a *Stjärnspel*, see Celander, *Stjärngossarna*, p.416.

[152] See the accounts given in Olrik and Ellekilde, *Nordens gudeverden*, II, pp.956–957; Troels-Lund, *Dagligt liv*, VII, pp.64–65; Celander, *Stjärngossarna*, p.425; and Feilberg, *Jul*, II, pp.229–230 (see also note 53 above), all of which reflect the attitude of the seventeenth- and eighteenth-century Danish and Swedish clergy, which must have led to the prohibitions mentioned above in *section B.3*, and the eventual disappearance of the *julebukk* in Denmark before the nineteenth century. A similar attitude is echoed in a story from Malmö in 1728 which probably stems from the same tradition: see Bringéus, *Årets festseder*, p.60.

[153] Parts of séra Þorsteinn's work are published in Ólafur Davíðsson, *Íslenzkar gátur*, III, pp.20–25, and in Jón Samsonarson, *Kvæði*, I, pp.xl–xlvi. See further, *sections G.2–4* below. A key influence on séra Þorsteinn's work, and another mirror of the times, was Erik Pontoppidan's *Everriculum fermenti veteris, seu Residuæ in Danico orbe cum paganismi tum papismi reliquiæ* (1736) which made a powerful attack on Danish folk customs and beliefs associated with May Day, Midsummer, Christmas, and Shrovetide: see Pontoppidan, *Fejekost*, pp.15–16 and pp.23–33.

[154] 'Þeir sem smíða sér tötrabúning í gleðileikjum og gestaboðsveizlum, þeir eru réttir djöfulsins apar og athlægi, en andstygð einglunum, guði og góðum mönnum': quoted in Ólafur Davíðsson, *Íslenzkar gátur*, III, p.23.

[155] See Marker and Marker, *The Scandinavian theatre*, pp.69–71.

[156] Weiser-Aall, *Julenissen*, p.24. A similar characteristic is found in the Shetland and Faroese traditions discussed below in *section G.4*.

approach of Nicholas who, when he does eventually appear in Swedish folk tradition, is usually conceived of as a bringer of gifts.[157]

5. *The origin and role of the 'Julebukk'*

As Nilsson concludes, even though the majority of *reports* of animal disguise come from the Celtic countries and Germany, there is every reason to believe that parallel traditions must have also existed in Scandinavia at a very early stage.[158] Such an argument makes good sense considering the archaeological evidence of animal disguise and horned figures in Scandinavia presented in the previous chapter. Indeed, the early existence of a mainland Scandinavian *julebukk* tradition with similar characteristics to those found in more recent years might provide a logical context for the central event of *Þorleifs þáttr jarlsskáld* which was recorded in *Flateyjarbók* in the late fourteenth century. The scene in question depicts Þorleifr's performance of the magical poetic curse 'Jarlsníð' for Jarl Hákon Sigurðarson, one Christmas Eve in Hlaðir. The disguise adopted by Þorleifr to enable him to enter Hákon's hall and perform the poem is supposed to be that of a 'stafkarl', an itinerant old beggar. Yet this rather odd guise also bears a striking resemblance to that associated with the *julebukk* in more recent times:

> Þorleifr now puts together a beggar's costume, and attaches a goat beard to himself. He then took a large leather bag, placed it under the beggar's costume, and arranged it so that everybody would imagine that he was eating the food which he threw into the bag, because the bag's opening was placed by his mouth behind the goat beard. He then took two crutches with points on the bottom of each . . .[159]

Þorleifr stumbles into the hall, and uses his crutches to bring about a disturbance with the other beggars, and this in turn results in his being brought before Jarl Hákon. He states that his name is Níðungr Gjallandason (lit. 'Young Insult, the son of Screeching') and that he has come from the east. In his past, he says, he was welcomed by all the great, but nowadays he is forced to endure abject poverty in the forests and open countryside. He asks for food, and on being granted this, proceeds to work his way through at least two table servings. Eventually he stops in order to chant the curse which ends in Þorleifr's disappearance from the locked hall, and Jarl Hákon's loss of his beard and the hair on one side of his head.

What is of interest here is the context that has been provided for Þorleifr's revenge on Jarl Hákon. He arrives at Christmas 'from the forest' wearing a goat's beard with a bag behind it to receive food, walking on 'four' legs, and expects to be allowed to receive the best of food and to have the right to insult the other guests and even his host. Indeed, the name he

---

[157] See Bringéus, *Årets festseder*, p.69.
[158] Nilsson, *Årets folkliga fester*, p.177.
[159] 'Þorleifr byr ser nu stafkallz georui ok bindr ser gæitarskegg ok tok ser æina stora hit ok let koma undir stafkallz georuina ok bio suo vm at ǫllu(m) skyllde synazst sem hann æti þann kost er hann kastade j hijtina. þuiat giman hennar var uppi vid munn honum vndir gæitarskegginu. sidan tekr hann hækiur tuær ok uar broddr nid(r) or huorri': *Flateyjarbok* (1860–1868), I, p.210. See also *Þorleifs þáttr jarlsskálds*, p.220.

5. The origin and role of the 'Julebukk'

announces and his general demeanour both imply that he is likely to cause trouble. None of these features, however, is necessary for the central motif of the story, that is to say, the performance of the poem which could be carried out anywhere, at any time, and in any form of disguise. Certainly the motif of the bag and the feat of eating are later found in Scandinavia in folktale type AT 1088 ('The eating contest with the dumb troll'),[160] but *Þorleifs þáttr* involves no such contest, and has no obvious 'dumb troll' either. The motif here must come from another source.

A different explanation is necessary, and would definitely be provided if the story was viewed in the context of a fourteenth-century tradition involving the Christmas visit of a goat-like figure that, like so many other figures of the same type in other countries, not only disguised its personality, but also had the right to demand food and to insult its hosts if it were not received well enough.[161] All that Þorleifr lacks are the horns. Such an argument is bound to be inconclusive, but it is worth bearing in mind that the name 'Arnaldus Jolahest', mentioned in the previous chapter, comes from Bergen during the same period (the early fourteenth century).

Further proof of the *julebukk*'s age and intimate relationship with Scandinavia is found in the fact that, in many areas, it is closely associated with a nature spirit of the same name to which offerings were given in order to ensure its passivity during the Christmas period (see *figs 54–55* above).[162] An echo of such a belief is found in the 'worship' of the straw *julbock* as a form of Yuletide household 'idol'.[163] In general, as Nilsson concluded, it seems 'unbelievable that the *julbock* should have been borrowed from the south' when 'it is intimately connected with the Scandinavian Christmas' in so many different ways.[164] Attempts to explain the figure of the goat and its 'resurrection' with the worship of Þórr, however, are probably too simple and largely inadequate as a general explanation for the entire *julebukk* phenomenon.[165] Beliefs, associations and traditions vary by

---

160 See Aarne and Thompson, *The types of the folktale*, p.357, and Hodne, *The types of the Norwegian folktale*, p.217.

161 Regarding the traditions involving insults when in costume, see, for example, Davidson, 'Insults and riddles', pp.40–41. Regarding the use of two sticks and the food bag in the *julebukk* tradition, see, for example, Schager, *Julbocken*, p.37; Weiser-Aall, *Julenissen*, p.23 and pp.28–30; Lid, *Joleband*, p.42; and Pio, *Bogen om julen*, p.18 (illustration). See also below, note 283 for references concerning descriptions of the 'stag' known in the Icelandic *vikivaki* games. This figure was constructed in a similar way.

162 See Lid, *Joleband*, pp.51–58, and Eike, 'Oskoreia', 255 and 264–265, for examples from Norway. For Swedish examples, see Celander, 'Julbocken', 99–100. Regarding the parallel figure of the Icelandic *finngálkn*, see below, note 258. Several scholars have suggested in recent years that many of the accounts mentioned above may be based on faint reminiscences of actual figures rather than echoes of past belief. See, for example, Weiser-Aall, *Julenissen*, pp.52–53, and Eike, 'Oskoreia', passim.

163 See above, *section B.2*.

164 'Å andre sidan förefaller det otroligt, att julbocken skulle vara ett lån söderifrån ... julbocken är äfven på annat sätt intimt förbunden med den nordiska julen': Nilsson, *Årets folkliga fester*, p.269.

165 The relationship with Þórr is suggested by, amongst others, Ljunggren, in *Svenska dramat*, p.126; Troels-Lund, in *Dagligt liv*, VII, p.64; Olrik and Ellekilde, in *Nordens*

B. Related to the Christmas Period

area, and, as was suggested in the previous chapter, there is equal reason to assume that in many areas the Scandinavian goat-horned figure, in its original form, was linked with Óðinn in his guise of Grímr or Grímnir.¹⁶⁶

5. The origin and role of the 'Julebukk'

All in all, the *julebukk* is a highly complex figure, and it would be foolish to suggest that the traditions associated with it were ever homogeneous throughout Scandinavia.¹⁶⁷ Whether the *julebukk* originated as a Scandinavian nature spirit related to a fertility cult,¹⁶⁸ or as a key figure in the 'Wild Ride',¹⁶⁹ or as a semi-official figure related to initiation rites and social control¹⁷⁰ is almost impossible to say.¹⁷¹ The probability is that all of these elements played some part in the development of the recorded custom with varying local emphases, the tradition possibly having been strengthened and altered in tone under the influence of foreign parallels more directly related to the Catholic church. Most important for the present argument, however, is the suggestion that the dramatic *julebukk* custom was known in some form or other as far back as the early Middle Ages, whence there is only a short step in time to the older pagan traditions involving animal costume examined in the previous chapter. The close connections with a spiritual figure, and the relationship with household worship and social organisation all suggest that the *julebukk* formed part of a continuing

---

gudeverden, II, p.937 and p.1081; and most recently, Schager, in *Julbocken*, pp.57–63. All of these scholars relate the killing and resurrection of the *julebukk* to Þórr's self-reconstituting goats described in *Gylfaginning*, in *Edda* (1926), pp.44–45. Certain other scholars, however, see this particular motif in the *Prose Edda* as having a Celtic origin: See, for example, Chesnutt, 'The beguiling of Þórr', pp.36–41.

[166] See *Chapter I, D.1*. Regarding Óðinn's possible relationship to Yuletide tradition, fertility customs and the Wild Ride of the dead, see de Vries, *Contributions*.

[167] See Bø, *Vår norske jul*, p.146.

[168] See Mannhardt, *Wald- und Feldkult*, II, pp.155–200 (especially pp.183–198); Frazer, *The golden bough*, V, ii, pp.327–328 and pp.281–288; Nilsson, *Årets folkliga fester*, p.270; Lid, *Joleband*, p.51; and Celander, *Nordisk jul*, p.118, and 'Julbocken', 96–104, where, logically enough, emphasis is placed on a possible origin in the wearing of the skin of the sacrificial victim, and links with the Christmas festival and *dísablót*. See also above, notes 74 and 81, and Burkert, 'Greek tragedy' for parallels in ancient Greece. With regard to the idea of sacrifice, see also Simpson, 'Some Scandinavian sacrifices', 195 and 199–202, where a possible relation between such sacrificial traditions and the pagan Scandinavian *níðstöng* is suggested.

[169] Celander, 'Oskoreien', p.85. See also Eike, 'Oskoreia', passim; and de Vries, *Contributions*, pp.22–24, regarding the intermingling of elements from fertility and death cults in the Yuletide festival.

[170] See further *Chapter I*, notes 213 and 282; Eike, 'Oskoreia', 283–284; and Weiser-Aall, *Julenissen*, pp.33–53. Like Lid, Nilsson, and Celander, Weiser-Aall argues (p.32) that the figure is very old and native to Norway. A similar argument is made by Bregenhøj whose conclusion that the *julebukk* was a figure related to social control and organisation in many ways follows on from that made by Weiser-Aall: see Bregenhøj, *Helligtrekongersløb*, pp.126–132. In this sense, the masked figure would have similarities with the role of the *leikgoði* and *gadebasse* discussed in *Chapter I, D.2*.

[171] Bø, in *Vår norske jul*, p.146, finds none of these arguments convincing as an origin for the *julebukk*, although he accepts that elements of all of the above can be found in the related traditions. Clearly all of the above aspects find enough parallels in the archaeological evidence given in the previous chapter to support their possible links with earlier pagan custom.

II. Dramatic Activities, II: Folkloristic Evidence

1. The battle between Winter and Summer

tradition that was related in some way to much more ancient pagan figures. As will be demonstrated below in *sections G.2 and 4*, such a hypothesis is supported still further by the appearance of the same figure under different names in the North Atlantic islands.

C. Costumed Combat Traditions in Scandinavia

1. The Battle between Winter and Summer

Olaus Magnus' description in 1555 of the Swedish combat between the skin-clad figure of Winter ('dux hyemalis') and the leaf and flower-clad Summer, or Lord of Flowers ('comes florialis') on the first of May[172] is regularly quoted by scholars wishing to prove the existence of ritual drama in Scandinavia, largely because it fits so neatly into the Frazerian mould of the life-cycle drama (see *fig.64*).[173] However, there are obvious difficulties involved in placing too much weight on this account alone because, as with so many of Magnus' traditions, the custom in question appears to have involved members of the higher social classes rather than the common people. Furthermore, the name *comes florialis* would seem to point to a possible origin in, or relationship to, German customs of a similar nature.[174] The same argument probably applies to a closely related contemporary Danish Shrovetide tradition which is described in very similar terms to those used by Magnus,[175] and seems to have existed in Aalborg as far back as the mid-fifteenth century.[176] All of the above accounts therefore have to be examined first and foremost in the context of the German customs associated primarily with Shrove Tuesday and the start of Lent.[177]

In spite of this, as Granlund has pointed out, there is a faint possibility that the roots of the tradition described by Olaus Magnus might be native, and that the tradition represents a 'poeticising of an old game' ('poetisering av ett gammalt upptåg') based on a form of weather prophecy performed only during those years when the winter was exceptionally long, as seems to have been the case in Magnus' account where icicles are described

---

[172] See Olaus Magnus, *Historia de gentibus septentionalibus* (Book XV, ch.8–9), p.503; translated into Swedish in *Historia om de nordiska folken*, III, pp.135–136. Magnus relates this tradition in a wider sense to the southern Swedes and Goths.
[173] See Phillpotts, *The Elder Edda*, p.120, p.156 and p.163; Schück, *Studier i Ynglingatal*, II, pp.60–62, and *Litteraturhistoria*, in particular the third edition (1926), I, pp.107–108; Lid, *Joleband*, pp.132–134, and *Jolesveinar*, pp.104–105; and Stumpfl, *Kultspiele*, pp.200–211.
[174] See Liungman, *Der Kampf*, p.160, and Nilsson, *Årets folkliga fester*, p.95.
[175] See Møller, 'Aarsfester', p.120 and p.133, on traditions from Holbæk Amt, Falster, Lolland and Himmerland. For other early Danish accounts, see Troels-Lund, *Dagligt liv*, VII, pp.106–107, and Olrik and Ellekilde, *Nordens gudeverden*, II, pp.635–636.
[176] See Liungman, *Der Kampf*, pp.71–72; and Granlund, 'Vinterns och Sommargrevens strid', 65.
[177] A comprehensive collection and classification of these traditions and their related songs is given in Liungman's *Der Kampf*.

C. Costumed Combat Traditions

Fig. 64. The fight between Winter and Summer.

Fig. 65. Sword and hoop dancers.

as still being in evidence in early May.[178] In very general terms, it is tempting to draw comparisons between this idea of seasonal conflict and the brief mention in certain Scandinavian folk plays of *Staffan* or Josef fighting and defeating the skin-clad *julebukk*.[179] Furthermore, a very similar tradition is known to have existed in the Isle of Man until the end of the eighteenth century, involving a battle between the troops of the Queen of May and the Queen of Winter, the latter being acted by a man dressed in furs and woollens. In the light of what Granlund suggests regarding

---

[178] See Granlund, 'Vinterns och Sommargrevens strid', 70–74. See Olaus Magnus, *Historia de gentibus septentionalibus* (Book XV, ch.8) p.503; translated into Swedish in *Historia om de nordiska folken*, III, p.135. According to Granlund in 'Vinterns och Sommargrevens strid', 74, the tradition probably disappeared with the arrival of Lutheranism which would possibly have associated such a custom with Catholic weather processions.

[179] See references given in notes 116 and 122 above.

2. The sword and hoop dances

weather prophecy, it is interesting to note that here the success of the Queen of May's forces was evidently not guaranteed.[180]

The possibility thus exists that in some parts of Scandinavia, dramatised or at least costumed seasonal combat might have been performed during the early Middle Ages.[181] In this regard, it is worth noting that many of these these physical battles in Europe had counterparts in verbal poetic duels between 'Summer' and 'Winter' such as those that seem to have taken place in both Germany and Anglo-Saxon England.[182] This invites consideration of whether such an oral tradition in an earlier phase might not have provided the context for a poem like *Hárbarðsljóð*, which involves a verbal poetic boasting contest, or *mannjafnaðr*, between the bearded Hárbarðr, who brags about his successes with women (a winter activity), and the younger Þórr, who is prouder of his battle exploits (a summer activity), and is hindered from coming home.[183]

2. The Sword and Hoop Dances

The concept of seasonal symbolic combat has sometimes also been applied to the semi-dramatic Shrovetide sword and hoop dances that Olaus Magnus describes as taking place in Sweden in the sixteenth century (see *fig.65*),[184] especially because there is some reason for assuming that native costumed weapon dances were still being practiced by the Scandinavians as late as the eleventh century.[185] These Swedish sword and hoop dances in a

---

[180] See Hole, *A dictionary*, p.203; Bord, *Earth rites*, p.187; and Liungman, *Der Kampf*, p.70, where the custom is classified alongside those from Sweden and Denmark.

[181] Another possible parallel to such combats is found in certain Finnish autumn rites to do with the god Peko in which a fight (to the point of blood) annually took place to decide who was to look after the image of the god during the coming year, and take the role of the 'Peko-prest': see Olsen, *Kultminder*, pp.111–112.

[182] See Nilsson, *Årets folkliga fester*, p.95; Baskerville, 'Dramatic aspects', 33; and Eliade, *Patterns*, pp.319–320. Indeed, the fourteenth-/ fifteenth-century Swedish *Samtal mellan Jul och Faste*, which Ljunggren relates to Lent, might well have distant roots in a Scandinavian verbal custom of this kind: see Ljunggren, *Svenska dramat*, pp.133–134, and Beckman, 'Julens och fastans träta', pp.17–18. For examples and discussion of these competitive seasonal dialogues, see Liungman, *Der Kampf*.

[183] This idea was suggested as far back as 1822 by Finnur Magnússon, in *Den Ældre Edda*, II, pp.131–135, albeit in a somewhat exaggerated style. Regarding this form of two-man verbal contest in Scandinavia, see further *Chapter V, D.3-4*. Collinder, in *Den poetiska Eddan*, p.25, offers a further parallel for *Hárbarðsljóð* in another old folk tradition in which two groups of young people from Gagnef and Leksand in Sweden used to insult each other across the Österdalälven river.

[184] See Olaus Magnus, *Historia de gentibus septentionalibus* (Book XV, ch.23–25), pp.517–518; translated into Swedish in *Historia om de nordiska folken* III, pp.150–153. As Alford points out in *Sword dance*, p.115, the sword dance described in detail by Magnus is typical of the European dances in the same genre. The hoop dance, which here involves more circus-like acrobatics, is really a variant of the same thing. See further Alford, *Sword dance*, p.113.

[185] Cf. the *gothikon* dance discussed in *Chapter I, C.7*. See also *Chapter I*, notes 112 and 187.

C. Costumed Combat Traditions

Fig. 66. A *Jonsok* wedding (Balestrand, Sogn, 1931).

later form are known to have been directly associated with dramatic texts involving a king, a trial and a ducking. Dramatic implications are also found in Olaus Magnus' account in which the hoop dance is led by a figure called the 'king', and is accompanied by songs about heroes. Like the *gothikon*, the action of the hoop dance was clearly meant to be seen in a symbolic narrative context.[186]

---

[186] See Norlind, 'Svärdsdans', pp.738–756, for an examination of the later seventeenth-century texts and a discussion of the origin of the sword dance in Scandinavia. Norlind believes ('Svärdsdans', pp.753–756) that the dance originated in Germany c.1400, and like the text (which is in a mixture of Swedish, German and Latin and evolved later) was imported to Scandinavia during the sixteenth century. Nonetheless, Norlind is open to

2. The sword and hoop dances

Concerning the age of these dances, it is evident that Olaus Magnus was not describing a new tradition. Other reports of Scandinavian sword dances are known from Borgö in Swedish-speaking Finland, Copenhagen (1554), and Aalborg (1431) where the dance was already regarded as being an old custom.[187] There can be little dispute, however, that these particular dances are closely related to other variants of the same dance found elsewhere in Europe, especially in the Germanic countries. Many of these dances were also associated with folk plays.[188] Furthermore, as Alford has pointed out, all of the Swedish and Danish dances noted above seem to have been professionally organised, which increases the possibility that the custom was imported.[189] Certainly, the sword dance as such appears to have been unknown in Norway, Iceland and the Faroes.[190] It is therefore questionable exactly how 'native' Olaus Magnus' sword and hoop dances were.

Nonetheless, Hibbert's and Scott's references to a nineteenth-century dramatic sword dance tradition on Papa Stour in Shetland,[191] and the fact that sword dances in England tended to be found predominantly in those areas earlier colonised by the Vikings,[192] encouraged certain scholars in the past to argue that the sword dance must have been natural to Scandinavia, and that it must have been brought to the British Isles with the Viking settlers.[193] This argument, however, needs to be modified by several

---

consideration of the view that the dance became attached to earlier existing Spring traditions like the fight between Winter and Summer ('Svärdsdans', pp.754–755).

[187] See Alford, *Sword dance*, pp.115–116.

[188] Regarding these sword dance plays and their geographical distribution, see Alford, *Sword dance*, pp.97–135, and Chambers, *The English folk-play*, pp.200–204. Among other dances, Chambers refers to one from Lübeck (sixteenth – seventeenth century) which involves six champions and two fools, one of whom is named 'Sterkader' after the Scandinavian hero Starkaðr. On this play, see Chambers, *The English folk-play*, pp.203–204; Feilberg, *Jul*, II, p.227; and Alford, *Sword dance*, p.114.

[189] See Alford, *Sword dance*, pp.115–116. For a description of the Finnish hoop dance, see Norlind, 'Svärdsdans', pp.749–751.

[190] Alford, *Sword dance*, p.37 and p.116.

[191] See Scott, *The pirate* (originally published in 1822), pp.465–468; and Hibbert, *A description*, (originally published in 1822), pp.289–293. Both are commented on and discussed in Sharp, *The sword dances*, I, pp.21–22, and Brody, *The English Mummers*, pp.156–161.

[192] See especially Needham, 'The geographical distribution', 23–29 (and accompanying map); Cawte, Helm, and Peacock, *English ritual drama*, p.32; and Helm, *The English Mummers' play*, p.19 and map (fig.2) on p.20. As all of the above point out, the sword dance and play belong predominantly to the north-east of England, i.e. Yorkshire, Durham and Northumberland.

[193] In Scott's earlier account of the dance, in his diary (dated 7 August, 1814; quoted in Lockhart, *Memoirs*, IV, pp.217–219), he refers to a pamphlet which stated that the dance had originated with the Danish settlers. A similar idea was held at this time by the vicar of Whitby, who in 1817 suggested that the Yorkshire sword dance was introduced by the Danes: see Alford, *Sword dance*, pp.34–35. In 1851, Worsaae in *Minder*, pp.288–289, felt confident enough to state that the sword dance was a favourite Shetland amusement the origin of which 'almost certainly' went back to the Norwegian settlers in pagan times. Similar attitudes to English folk customs were still very much in vogue at the turn of the

D. The Seasonal 'Mock-Marriage'

important considerations. First of all, as was mentioned above, Olaus Magnus' account obviously relates to an organised courtly performance rather than one performed by the common people,[194] thus raising the likelihood that his dance had a fashionable foreign origin. Secondly, even if the Papa Stour *dance* had native roots (which is not certain), the same cannot be said for the *text* of the play provided by Scott and Hibbert which has an English origin.[195] Finally, as regards the origin of the English sword dance, several scholars have emphasised that the geographical distribution of this activity actually extends beyond the immediate area of the Danelaw,[196] opening the possibility that the distribution might be based on something other than a shared cultural background.[197] In general terms, therefore, even though there is some reason for assuming that a continuing tradition of seasonal combat existed in certain areas of Scandinavia, it is necessary to be extremely wary about assuming that the same thing applied to dramatic sword dances on the basis of the extant material.[198]

1. The winter marriage

D. The Seasonal 'Mock-Marriage' in Scandinavian Folk Tradition

1. The winter marriage

In the previous chapter (*sections C.2 and 5*), a brief examination was made of the evidence for some form of *hieros gamos* having taken place in pagan Scandinavia. It is therefore interesting to note the wide range of Scandinavian folkloristic material concerning seasonal mock-marriages and pairing activities in more recent times. Various aspects of these traditions should already be apparent from the evidence concerning the mid-winter *Lussebrud* traditions,[199] and perhaps also from the occasional appearance of the

---

century: see, for example, Ordish, 'English folk-drama', and Heanley, 'The Vikings', 40, where certain English Plough Monday troups are related to Óðinn's 'Wild Huntsmen', and the horse skull they carried associated with Óðinn's horse 'Gleipnir' (sic.).

[194] Olaus Magnus talks of an eight-day training period for the sword dancers: *Historia de gentibus septentionalibus* (Book XV, ch.23), p.517; translated into Swedish in *Historia om de nordiska folken*, III, p.150.

[195] See Brody, *The English Mummers*, pp.156–161; Helm, *The English Mummers' play*, p.21; and the detailed source material in Macleod Banks, *British calendar customs: Orkney and Shetland*, pp.93–101.

[196] See Alford, *Sword dance*, pp.35–37; Sharp, *The sword dances*, I, pp.34–35; and Chambers, *The mediaeval stage*, I, p.195.

[197] Alford, in *Sword dance*, pp.15–16, argues that the European distribution seems to reflect the occurrence of mining activities. See further the geographical distribution tables provided with Alford's book.

[198] However, on the possibility that the sword dance might be closely related to circle dances in general, like a 'ribbon' dance from the Faroe Islands, and a circle dance from Norway, see Norlind, 'Svärdsdans', p.751; Alford, *Sword dance*, pp.14–15; and Brody, *The English mummers*, p.97. These dances of course need not be associated with drama, but, in a general sense, they do provide echoes of the masked *gothikon* which also involved circle dances: see *Chapter I, C.7*.

[199] See *section B.1* above, and Celander, *Nordisk jul*, p.344, on the figures of the

II. Dramatic Activities, II: Folkloristic Evidence

1. The winter marriage

julebukk and *julegeit* as a pair.[200] These individual elements, however, are paralleled and emphasised by the wealth of other Scandinavian Christmas games that involved mock-marriages, or the pairing of members of the community.

Typical examples of such games are the Norwegian *Hindeleik* ('Hind game'), in which an 'old woman' paired all the 'stags' in the room with their chosen 'hinds'; and the *Giftarleik* ('Marriage game') which was similar but also involved a more formalised mock-marriage carried out by a 'priest' and 'sexton'.[201] This latter game is really a simplified variation of the better known Danish custom from south Sjælland of the *julebisp*, or 'Christmas bishop'. Here, a chosen boy was dressed in a white shirt, given a stick with burning candles on both ends to hold in his mouth, and then placed in a chair in the centre of the floor where he was offered nuts and apples, and 'ordained'. In many cases, this game then continued into the 'consecration' of mock marriages.[202]

There can be little question that the *julebisp* game belongs to the European Boy Bishop tradition, the likelihood being that this particular Danish custom developed within the Latin schools.[203] It is much less likely, however, that the same argument can be applied to the mock-marriages themselves since these seem to have led an independent existence amongst the common people in association with several other traditions such as that of the *gadebasse* and *gadelamme*.[204] Indeed, it is noteworthy that these particular marriage games seem to have developed in the face of (or as a result of) early church prohibitions in Scandinavia against the celebration of marriages at any time during the Christmas period.[205] The question must be raised as to whether these bans were merely a vain attempt to underline the solemnity of the Christmas festival or whether there was some other reason based on pagan belief and folk practices. Interestingly enough,

---

trettondagsbrud ('thirteenth-day bride': Småland); *tjugondagsbrud* ('twentieth-day bride': Österbotten); and *lappbrud* ('Lapp bride': Österbotten). See also Celander, *Stjärngossarna*, pp.434–436, for further examples of an *anndasbrur* ('second day bride': Värmland), *julbrudar* ('Christmas brides'), and other *Lussebrudar*.

[200] See Celander, 'Slakta julbocken', p.34, and Weiser-Aall, *Julenissen*, p.26. See also note 87, on the Trøndelag tradition involving the threat that girls could become the 'bride' of the *julebukk*. However, no recorded tradition involves the marriage of these goat figures.

[201] See Støylen, *Norske barnerim*, p.114 and pp.119–124; Berge, 'Norske brudlaupsleikar'; and Bø, *Vår norske jul*, pp.160–161. The *Hindeleik* was also known in Iceland and the Faroe Islands. See further below, *section G.2-3*. Regarding marriage games involving a priest figure from elsewhere in Scandinavia, see Celander, *Nordisk jul*, pp.294–295.

[202] On these and other related games involving the 'coronation' of a king and queen (the *Kongeleg*), see Nilsson, *Årets folkliga fester*, pp.264–265; Feilberg, *Jul*, II, pp.253–256; Celander, *Nordisk jul*, pp.295–296; Ellekilde, *Vor danske jul*, pp.300–302; and Bringéus, *Årets festseder*, pp.64–65. See also note 260 and 284 below for references to comparable Icelandic traditions.

[203] See, for example, Tydeman, *The theatre in the Middle Ages*, pp.16–17; and Sveinn Einarsson, *Íslensk leiklist*, I, pp.153–161.

[204] See above, *Chapter I, D.2*.

[205] See the references in note 25 above.

D. The Seasonal 'Mock-Marriage'

according to Saxby and several others, in Shetland 'all marriages were celebrated if possible during the three winter months'.²⁰⁶ Naturally, this might have been based on practical considerations alone,²⁰⁷ but considering the evidence given in the previous chapter, such a tradition might also have had roots in the postulated link between marriage ceremonies and the pagan winter festivals.²⁰⁸ Indeed, early this century in Fryksände, Värmland, Sweden, most marriage ceremonies are reported as having been performed on the second day of Christmas, that is to say, on the same day that costumed games took place in the community.²⁰⁹

2. The spring/summer marriage

2. The Spring/ Summer Marriage

Mock-marriages and bridal figures were not solely associated with the Christmas period in Scandinavia. They also played (and still play) a central role in the Scandinavian folk traditions related to the beginning of summer, and the summer solstice.²¹⁰ As in many other European countries, these traditions are commonly based around the marriage procession of one or two figures who, in many cases, bore crowns.

These bridal processions, and occasionally also weddings of figures known in Sweden as the *majgreve*, *majgrevinna* ('May Count and Countess'), *maibrud* ('May bride'), *Pingstbrud* ('Whitsun bride'), *blomsterbrud* ('flower-bride'), *kransdräng* ('wreath-boy'), and *kranspiga* ('wreath-girl');²¹¹ and in Denmark as the *gadebasse*, *gadinde*, *gadelamme*, *majgreve*, *majinde* ('May Countess'), *majkonge*, *majdronning* ('May King and Queen'), and *Pinsebrud* and *Pinsebrudgom* ('Whitsun bride and bridegroom')²¹² occur at different times during the stated period. In Sweden, for example, the activities tend to concentrate in the Whitsun

---

²⁰⁶ Saxby, *Shetland traditional law*, p.85. See also Macleod Banks, *British calendar customs: Orkney and Shetland*, p.13.
²⁰⁷ See Moffatt, *Shetland*, p.182.
²⁰⁸ See, for example, the saga references to the marriages taking place during the *vetrnætur*, given in *Chapter I*, note 65.
²⁰⁹ 'Alla bröllop firades om möjligt på annandagjul, då varjehanda upptåg med förklädningar förekommo': see Keyland, *Julbröd*, pp.100–101.
²¹⁰ See Hammarstedt, 'Karlevor', p.510, on this parallel occurrence of marriage traditions performed at mid-winter and mid-summer. In a wider sense, Eliade, in *Patterns*, pp.353–354, comments on the fact that certain aspects of agricultural festivals are often echoed at the winter solstice as part of a feast of the dead. In Scandinavia, the winter festival certainly seems to have been related to both a feast of the dead and fertility. See for example, de Vries, *Contributions*, p.24.
²¹¹ See Svensson, 'Årsfester', pp.68–69 (Easter weddings), pp.74–76 (Whitsun) and p.80 (Midsummer); and Bringéus, *Årets festseder*, pp.148–151 (Easter), pp.168–173 (the *majgreve* and *majgrevinna*), and pp.183–190 (Whitsun weddings). For the most detailed collection and classification of original material regarding the Whitsun 'Pingst' brides and weddings, see Granlund, 'Pingstbrud', 41–79, and especially the distribution map accompanying Granlund's article.
²¹² See Nilsson, *Årets folkliga fester*, pp.83–84; and Møller, 'Aarsfester' p.126, and pp.132–135, and 'Sommer', 97–132.

II. Dramatic Activities, II: Folkloristic Evidence

2. The spring/summer marriage

period (*Pinse*),[213] while in Denmark they are more commonly related to the first of May.

Some of the names mentioned above, such as those of the *majgreve* and *majgrevinna*, imply direct associations with the male 'kings' or 'lords' of May and Whitsun encountered in both Germany and England.[214] However, as several scholars have suggested, these names probably only represent a surface addition that was imported from Germany during the late fifteenth century, since the elements of folk marriage and election seem to have existed already in the older Danish traditions related to the *gadebasse* and *gadelamme*, and the *majkonge* and *majdronning*.[215]

An older stratum of the summer 'marriage' is possibly found in Norway, where such customs are more commonly associated with *Jonsok*, or St John's Eve (24 June), the date to which Ólafr Tryggvason deliberately moved the original midsummer festival at the end of the tenth century (see *fig.66*).[216] These *Jonsokbryllup* ('*Jonsok* weddings'), which are nowadays largely confined to the western fjords, have much less direct relation to any named 'king' or 'queen' figures than the Danish and Swedish traditions have.[217] As in the other countries, however, the *Jonsok* wedding is often linked to seasonal bonfires.[218] The nature of this particular link remains uncertain, but certain scholars earlier this century drew attention to the fact that many Norwegian bonfires used to bear a wooden figure known as a *kall* ('old man') or *kjerring* ('old woman'). This encouraged them to associate these figures and the bridal pair with old and new representations of fertility spirits.[219]

---

[213] Not all the descriptions of the above traditions mention a marriage. In Sweden and Denmark, the terms *bröllop/ bryllup* are only applied to the Whitsun ceremonies, and even then are limited to particular areas: see Møller, 'Sommer', 113, and the detailed information provided in Granlund, 'Pingstbrud', 68–79. Otherwise, it is more common that the 'bride' appears alone. However, as Bringéus points out in *Årets festseder*, p.189, it is possible that the single bride represents a degeneration in the tradition from an earlier 'marriage'. For further descriptions of these processions, see Olrik and Ellekilde, *Nordens gudeverden*, II, pp.638–639 and pp.678–681.

[214] See Nilsson, *Årets folkliga fester*, p.84, p.87, and pp.90–91; Troels-Lund, *Dagligt liv*, VII, pp.191–209; Bringéus, *Årets festseder*, p.187; and the description of the *majgreve* tradition in Olrik and Ellekilde, *Nordens gudeverden*, II, pp.629–638.

[215] See, for example, Olrik and Ellekilde, *Nordens gudeverden*, II, p.638; and Møller, 'Sommer', 123–129, and 'Aarsfester', p.133. See further Møller's map of the distribution of these traditions published in 'Sommer', 113. As Bringéus, points out in *Årets festseder* p.187, the *blomsterbrud* tradition seems to have preceded that of the *majgreve* and *majgrevinna* in Östergötland, in Sweden.

[216] See *Ágrip*, p.22.

[217] Naturally enough, the only reference to a *majgreve* festival in Norway is connected to the Hansa merchants in Bergen in the sixteenth century: see Bringéus, *Årets festseder*, p.151. Otherwise, unlike in Denmark and Sweden, the Norwegian custom tends to involve a bridal *pair*, and, as the name of the tradition suggests, is associated with a wedding: see Bondevik, 'Høgtider', pp.103–104, and Wyller, *Sankt Hans*, pp.109–118.

[218] On the dates of these bonfires, and their geographical distribution, see Olrik and Ellekilde, *Nordens gudeverden*, II, pp.663–664 and p.668; Campbell and Nyman, *Atlas*, II, 1, pp.46–47; and Bringéus *Årets festseder*, p.158.

[219] See Bugge, 'Bonfires' and 'St Hansbaal'; and Almgren, *Hällristningar*, pp.60–62. Almgren

D. The Seasonal 'Mock-Marriage'

Such an idea can be nothing more than speculation. However, it is undeniable that certain aspects of the tradition would seem to have deeper meaning. In most cases, as with the Yuletide processions, the bridal procession went from farm to farm, or through the town, the central figure of the bride usually being clad in bridal finery or national costume with a crown made of silver or birch, and flowers in her hair.[220] This deliberate use of leaves and flowers would seem to stress the symbolic nature of the bride, and such considerations are perhaps encouraged by an early account from Arboga in Sweden (1737) which describes one accompanying figure in such a procession as being dressed entirely in leaves.[221] A more recent account from Västmanland in Sweden goes further and states directly that this figure, who 'was dressed as a "leaf man" of giant proportions' ('var udklædt som "løvgubbe" i jættestörrelse'), was meant to be the bridegroom of the Midsummer bride.[222] Such costumes are reminiscent of the 'Green Man' traditions known in England, Germany and elsewhere,[223] and the leaf- and flower-clad *comes florialis* mentioned in Olaus Magnus' account of the combat between 'Summer' and 'Winter'. More native parallels are found in the enormous straw-men who appeared in Sweden at Christmas, such as *Halm-Staffan* and the *julegoppa*.[224] Accounts of such figures appearing in summertime, however, are extremely rare in Scandinavia, and in general, as Bringéus has concluded, it is very difficult to date the origin and background of the 'leaf men'. Conceivably, these figures might be very old, but they could equally well have been imported from abroad along with the other German May traditions mentioned above.[225]

Nowadays, the bride or bridal pair in these summer 'wedding' processions tend to be represented by children, but this was evidently not always the case. In Vangsnes, in Sogn, for example, the bridal couple were still being played by adults in the last century.[226] Furthermore, in many cases, the summer 'weddings' did not only involve processions, but were

2. The spring/summer marriage

---

notes certain parallels to the Swedish Bronze Age petroglyphs, in that on the west coast of Norway (especially in Ålesund) boats were sometimes burnt following a boat procession. Bondevik, in 'Høgtider', pp.100–101 and pp.103–104, is less certain of any direct connection, but accepts the possibility of links with a fertility belief. Regarding parallel European traditions involving seasonal bonfires, and the burning of similar figures in Germany, see Nilsson, *Årets folkliga fester*, pp.96–97 and pp.102–117.

[220] See Bondevik, 'Høgtider', p.103; Svensson, 'Årsfester', p.75; and Møller, 'Aarsfester', p.134.
[221] See Svensson, 'Årsfester', p.80, and Bringéus, *Årets festseder*, pp.200–201.
[222] Olrik and Ellekilde, *Nordens gudeverden*, II, p.680.
[223] On these German traditions, see Mannhardt, *Wald- und Feldkulte*, I, pp.316–341; Frazer, *The golden bough*, III, pp.207–211; and Rudwin, *The origin of the German carnival comedy*, pp.16–20.
[224] Regarding *Halm-Staffan* and the *julegoppa*, see above, *section B.2*. See also *section G.4* below on the the Shetland *skeklers* and *grøleks*.
[225] Regarding these Scandinavian midsummer *lövgubbar*, see further Bringéus, *Årets festseder*, pp.198–200; Olrik and Ellekilde, *Nordens gudeverden*, II, p.680; and Arill, 'Lövgubben'.
[226] See Wyller, *Sankt Hans*, p.110. On these points, see further Bondevik, 'Høgtider', p.103; Bringéus, *Årets festseder*, pp.188–189; and the tables provided by Granlund, in

2. The spring/summer marriage

also consecrated by another figure (a costumed boy or girl) who took the role of the priest.[227] Some sources even suggest that in certain cases the marriage was actually consummated (whether this was planned is not certain), which might help explain why, in later years, it was often difficult to find older girls to take on the role of the bride.[228] Such implications might also be echoed in the feeling expressed by some girls that the role of the 'bride' was degrading or shameful,[229] and in the superstition found in some areas that a girl chosen as a *Pingstbrud* would never wear white or have a legitimate child.[230] Of particular interest is the superstition revealed in certain Swedish accounts that the leading participants in the procession/wedding would never marry in later life, a belief that would appear to be based on the idea that the 'bride' was already seen as being married on the spiritual plane.[231] Such a concept, of course, might also lie behind the common incidence of the bride appearing alone.

The problem with dating this tradition is that the earliest Norwegian reference is from 1863 (Sogndal),[232] and that from Sweden was recorded in 1725 (Lund).[233] The *majgreve* and *majinde*, however, are first referred to as a pair in Danish Lenten festivities in 1670,[234] thus suggesting again that all

---

'Pingstbrud', 68–79, which show that in Sweden in earlier times, the bride and bridegroom tended to be young people aged 14–15 and older.

[227] See Wyller, *Sankt Hans*, pp.115–116, and the tables in Granlund, 'Pingstbrud'. Such marriage services naturally echo traditions like that of the *julebisp* referred to above in note 202.

[228] See, for example, the account from Rönneberga härad in Skåne (which may refer to a tradition reaching back to the eighteenth century) in Granlund, 'Pingstbrud', 48–49. An interesting parallel to the above is offered by Gudnitz who, in *Broncealderens monumentalkunst*, p.70, relates that in 1868, when faced by a catastrophic threat of drought and crop failure, people in one town in Dalsland fell back on an old superstition which suggested that 'there was only one way to achieve the desired result, namely to carry out certain prescribed ceremonies and have one couple copulate on the petroglyphs at Tisselskog where the images of several mating couples had been carved' ('der kun fandtes en måde til at opnå det ønskede resultat, nemlig ved at lade et par, under nærmere forskrevne ceremonier, indgå kønslig forbindelse på bergskråningerne ved Tisselskog, hvor der er indristet flere brudepar'). Apart from its being an interesting reference to superstitions concerning the petroglyphs, this account has special value in its demonstration of folk belief in the efficacy of the ritual marriage even at such a recent time.

[229] Similar attitudes are expressed in at least four of the accounts given in Granlund, 'Pingstbrud', 48, 79, and tables.

[230] See Granlund, 'Pingstbrud', 79 and tables.

[231] See Granlund, 'Pingstbrud', 79 and tables, and Nilsson, *Årets folkliga fester*, pp.81–83 (beliefs from Skåne, Södre Halland, and Östergötland in Sweden); and de Vries, *Contributions*, pp.17–18.

[232] See Wyller, *Sankt Hans* p.109, and Bondevik, 'Høgtider', p.103.

[233] See Olrik and Ellekilde, *Nordens gudeverden*, II, p.639. For other early references from the eighteenth century, see Svensson, 'Årsfester", p.75, and Granlund, 'Pingstbrud', 46–47. See Bringéus, *Årets festseder*, pp.185–186, for examples of church prohibitions of the custom from this period.

[234] See Møller, 'Aarsfester', p.132. The earliest Danish reference to the tradition of the 'bride' (*bruden*) occurs in a reference from Mathias Moth's dictionary (1680). See Granlund, 'Pingstbrud', 44.

D. The Seasonal 'Mock-Marriage'

of these marriage traditions might have originated in Germany. In consideration of these dates, however, Svensson concludes that 'all explanations of how the summer bridal couple entered Scandinavian folk tradition must be regarded as uncertain, since we have no knowledge about the existence of this tradition in older times.'[235] In spite of this, scholars have offered a variety of explanations for the origin of the tradition, ranging from hints that it had associations with a fertility belief,[236] to other suggestions that it was a means of raising alms,[237] or grew out of Christian ceremonial procession and the idea of holy marriage to the church itself.[238]

2. The spring/summer marriage

These last two arguments may well have played a central role in the evolution of the tradition in certain areas. Yet it must also be remembered that in some parts of Scandinavia (particularly in western Norway), the roles of the bride and groom were originally played by *adults* who do not seem to have collected money. Furthermore, the titles given to the bridal pair in the countryside of western Norway do not ever seem to have been linguistically related to those of the German folk brides or bridegrooms. These particular Norwegian customs evidently have deep roots in folk tradition, and their connections with the summer solstice encourage the view that they might well go back to a very early period. Indeed, it is worth noting that, until recent times, many of the elements of the 'wedding' ceremony were performed in the forests or away from the towns.[239] For example, in Ullensvang, in Hardanger, the *Jonsokbrur* used to be dressed at a particular stone outside the town known as the 'Ullaberstein'.[240] Furthermore, in Denmark the ceremonies often took place in close proximity to certain grave mounds, and as Møller comments, 'such festival sites might have roots in sites used for pre-Christian cult activities'.[241]

The winter and summer mock-weddings remain perplexing in spite of the more recent attempts to explain them in terms of foreign or Christian

---

[235] 'Varje förklaring på hur sommerbrudparet kommit att ingå i nordisk folksed, är överhuvudtaget osäker, då man icke vet något om dess existens här i äldre tid': Svensson, 'Årsfester', p.75.

[236] See references given in notes 219 and 231 above.

[237] This is possibly reflected in the reference from Moth's dictionary mentioned in note 234 above. See also Eskeröd, *Årets fester*, pp.90–91, and the references given in Svensson, 'Årsfester', pp.75–76 (Finland); Granlund, 'Pingstbrud', 42–44 (Sweden); and Møller, 'Sommer', p.129 (Denmark).

[238] See Granlund, 'Pingstbrud', 56–61, with particular reference to the Östergötland traditions which involve a single bride.

[239] This was the case in Balestrand, Sogn, for example, according to the older townspeople. See also Bugge, 'Bonfires', 150–151, on Norwegian traditions; Møller, 'Sommer', 130–131, and Olrik and Ellekilde, *Nordens gudeverden*, II, p.662, on traditions from Jylland; and Svensson, 'Årsfester', p.76, and Granlund, 'Pingstbrud', 46, 78, and tables, on Swedish customs.

[240] See Olsen, *Kultminder*, p.180.

[241] 'Saadanne Festpladser har mulig Rødder i førkristne Kultpladser': Møller, 'Aarsfester', p.135. See also Olrik and Ellekilde, *Nordens gudeverden*, II, p.663; Nielsen, 'Danse på Höj'; Uldall, 'Dansehøj'; and Møller, 'Sommer', 130–131.

influence. If the foregoing considerations are kept in mind, the possibility must remain that some of these folk marriage ceremonies have roots in a form of pagan *hieros gamos* like that proposed in the previous chapter.[242]

E. The Continuation of Pagan Ritual in Scandinavia?

It might be argued that the church would have endeavoured from the start to wipe out any examples of pagan ritual that were left over from earlier times,[243] and that there can be little possibility of pagan dramatic rituals surviving in Scandinavia to become seasonal folk 'games'. Yet at the same time, it must be considered that any early farmer who believed that a particular ritual aided his crops would be very unlikely to abandon it completely, merely on the basis of Christian advice. To his mind, it might result in him losing his entire means of subsidence for the following year. Indeed, the fact that certain local rituals *did* continue in mainland Scandinavia is attested by the numerous examples of offerings to spirits being placed on grave mounds and elsewhere on Thursdays and at particular holy times of the year, all of which testify to the strength and endurance of ancient superstition even in the face of the established law.[244] In short, while the early written sources may be silent regarding such performances as those suggested above in relation to the *julebukk* or mock-marriage, their silence does not necessarily mean that such beliefs and such rituals did not continue during the early Middle Ages.

Indeed, further support for a relatively early dating of the folk traditions examined above is provided by the fact that very close parallels to many of the customs examined above are known to have existed in the North Atlantic Viking colonies of Orkney, Shetland, the Faroe Islands, and even Iceland.

---

[242] Such a relationship is suggested indiectly by Olsen, in *Kultminder*, p.180; and supported by Phillpotts, in *The Elder Edda*, p.129; and Stumpfl, in *Kultspiele*, p.211.

[243] That it did attempt this is illustrated by the accounts of Ólafr Haraldsson's somewhat over-zealous missionary excursions described in *Heimskringla* and other works; and by the comment regarding Bishop Jón Ögmundarson's work in Iceland (see above *Chapter 1*, note 266). Nonetheless, it is also possible that these accounts should be viewed predominantly as examples of church propaganda, i.e. as warnings to the local farmer who was still engaged in various forms of folk ritual.

[244] See, for example, Olrik and Ellekilde, *Nordens gudeverden*, I, pp.229–249, and pp.302–303; Bø et al, *Norske segner*, p.165; and Birkeli, *Fedrekult*, pp.156–166. Regarding the importance of Thursdays in Scandinavian folk tradition, see also Grambo, *Norske trollformler*, pp.27–28. The early medieval Gulaþing law from western Norway specifically prohibited sacrifices from being made to grave mounds ('Vér skolom eigi blota heiðit guð. ne hauga'): *Norges gamle lov*, I, p.18.

F. The Transportation of Dramatic Folk Traditions

It is commonly assumed that folk traditions tend to disappear when people emigrate and leave the soil on which the traditions were originally created,[245] the supposition being that, if pagan customs and rituals of the kind mentioned in the first chapter ever existed in mainland Scandinavia, they would never have reached Iceland. As Phillpotts pointed out, for example, in Iceland there seem to have been 'no dancing around May-poles, no mock battles between Summer and Winter, no festivities at Midsummer bonfires.'[246]

Nonetheless, several recent folkloristic studies concerning emigrants to Newfoundland and Ireland have provided clear evidence of settlers taking their native dramatic folk customs with them and preserving them, rather than adopting foreign customs through contact with new neighbours, or creating wholly new customs on the basis of local conditions.[247] As Helm comments on the transportation of the English 'hero play' to Ireland, 'the fact that the actions did travel so widely is evidence that they were an accepted feature of the performers' seasonal life. Although they retained the basic pattern, what has emerged finally is a version which owes something to its place of origin and something to its new surroundings.'[248]

Of course, it is highly unlikely that beliefs and customs intrinsically bound to local rocks, springs, grave mounds and such like could be transported with emigrants, something that is well demonstrated by the absence in Iceland of the spirits like the *gardvord*, or *tomte*, who in mainland Scandinavia were closely bound up with the site of the original farm. On the other hand, settlers might well transport processional customs and religious rituals associated with wider concepts to do with the bestowal of luck, fertility, or protection on an area and its inhabitants. Such rituals are less geographically anchored or defined, and if not grounded in religious belief, tend to have strong roots in superstition and the sense of individual or communal identity.[249]

Considering the fact that the settlement of Iceland often not only

---

[245] See, for example, Phillpotts, *The Elder Edda*, p.84. As Helm shows in *The English Mummers' play*, p.19, this argument obviously applied to many English traditions which became lost with the breaking up of large estates, and the dispersal of tenants.

[246] Phillpotts, *The Elder Edda*, p.84. See also Olrik and Ellekilde, *Nordens gudeverden*, II, p.668, who note that spring and Midsummer bonfires also seem to have failed to take root in the Faroes. None of these scholars, however, consider the possibility that the lack of bonfires might have been related to the scarcity of disposable wood for burning in these parts in later years.

[247] See, for example, Halpert, 'A typology', p.38, and the other articles contained in Halpert and Story, eds, *Christmas mumming in Newfoundland*.

[248] See Helm, *The English Mummers' play*, pp.30–31, and p.8; and Gailey, *Irish folk drama*, pp.8–68. See also Alford, 'The Hobby Horse', 132, on Strömbäck's suggestion that the Icelanders adopted folk drama figures from abroad: see below, *sections G.2–3*.

[249] Regarding the social role of such dramatic folk customs, see Bregenhøj, *Helligtrekongersløb*, passim.

II. Dramatic Activities, II: Folkloristic Evidence

1. England and Ireland

involved people from the same family or same area settling in close proximity to each other, but also the immigration of men who had originally conducted religious ceremonies in Norway, there is no real reason to assume that such religious traditions as those presupposed above should not have been brought with the settlers. On the contrary, there is everything to be said for such traditions having been maintained in the form of a ritual or game. A simple example of such a transportation of religious custom is the ritual of circling land with fire which several Icelandic settlers seem to have practised in the late ninth century, if the Icelandic sources can be trusted to reflect actual events or folk beliefs.[250] Interestingly enough, this particular ritual is based on one of the central concepts lying behind many of the folk traditions examined in this chapter, namely the belief that circling one's land in a ritual fashion not only bestows some form of luck or protection, but also emphasises ownership, spiritual or otherwise.[251]

Bearing in mind the possibility of rituals and customs having been brought with the original Scandinavian settlers of the North Atlantic islands, it is interesting to note the numerous similarities in pattern between the dramatic traditions found in the one-time Scandinavian colonies and those referred to earlier in this chapter. It soon becomes apparent that the North Atlantic traditions not only widen the range of available Scandinavian folkloristic material, but also, perhaps, offer further clues as to the dating of the material that has already been examined. While the possibility of some later adoption of foreign customs into the islands can never be ruled out, various central aspects of the North Atlantic dramatic customs, especially as regards their names, general format, and seasonal association, point to the existence of a shared Scandinavian folk 'dramatic' tradition that must go back to a period prior to the Reformation. In all probability the roots are even older than that.

G. The Evidence for a Shared Tradition of 'Folk Drama' in the North Atlantic Scandinavian Settlements

1. England and Ireland

The western Viking expansion of the eighth, ninth and tenth centuries was obviously not limited to the North Atlantic islands. However, in the following examination folkloristic material from Ireland and England will be ignored for the most part, the Irish material because of the extreme difficulty in extricating the Scandinavian from the Gaelic traditions, and the

---

[250] See *Landnámabók*, pp.350–351; *Vatnsdæla saga*, pp.27–28; and *Eyrbyggja saga*, p.8.
[251] Regarding the tradition of circling land with fire and its relationship to Scandinavian belief, see Strömbäck, 'Att helga land', pp.142–151. For parallel traditions in Norway and Sweden in later times, see, for example, Bø, *Heilag-Olav*, pp.149–152, on the Christian adoption of this pagan tradition; and Granlund, 'Barfotaspringning'. For similar Icelandic traditions, see, for example, Jón Árnason, *Íslenzkar þjóðsögur*, II, p.569, and pp.572–573.

G. A Shared Tradition of 'Folk Drama'

1. England and Ireland

English material because it is impossible to ascertain what is of Scandinavian origin, and what originated with the Angles, Saxons, British, French, Celts or Gaels.

Certainly, as was mentioned above, the English sword dance play seems to be largely confined to the area of the Danelaw, and the same applies to costumed traditions involving *julebukk*-like figures such as the 'Old Tup' and the 'Wild Horse'.[252] It is easy to point to numerous other customs that might appear to have Scandinavian roots, such as the Lancashire procession involving a disguised figure drawn in a reed cart, an image that is strongly reminiscent of the ritual processions of Nerthus and Freyr.[253] Yet, however tempting these parallels might be, it would be foolhardy to place as much weight on them as other scholars have sometimes done in the past.[254] For the purposes of any examination of dramatic folk traditions of Scandinavia, English customs have potential value as comparative material, but rarely much more than that. The North Atlantic islands, however, provide more useful and more immediately revealing material, since they represent not only comparatively isolated communities, but also communities that are more obviously grounded in what was predominantly a Scandinavian culture.

---

[252] See Cawte, *Ritual animal disguise*, pp.110–117 (the sheep-like 'Old Tup'); pp.125–131 (the Cheshire 'Wild Horse'); pp.117–120 (the 'Old Horse'); pp.140–142 ('Old Ball'); p.94 ('Mari Lwyd'); p.120 (the Winster Horse); and p.123 (the Richmond Horse). All of these figures have a similar shape to that of the *julebukk*, albeit with the skull of a horse instead of the head of a goat (except in the case of 'Old Tup'). Regarding other similarities between 'Old Tup' and the *julebukk*, see above, note 110. See further the detailed geographical list given in Cawte, *Ritual animal disguise*, pp.228–249, and the distribution maps on p.128, p.133, and p.217. Regarding horse disguises in the Isle of Man, Cheshire, and Ireland, see also Alford, 'The Hobby Horse', 129–130; Brody, *The English Mummers*, p.64; Helm, *The English Mummers' play*, p.30; and Gailey, *Irish folk drama*, pp.89–90. It might be noted that skin and straw costumes are comparatively rare in England: only two examples of straw costumes (from southern England) are given in Hole, *A dictionary of British folk customs*, pp.286–287. Nonetheless, Helm, in *The English Mummers' play*, p.45, raises the question of whether the later strips of paper or material used by the Mummers perhaps replaced earlier use of skins and straw. When skins do occur, they again appear in the north of England, as in traditions from Lincolnshire and Yorkshire: see Dean Smith, 'The life cycle play', 252–253, and Helm, *The English Mummers' play*, p.40.
[253] See Helm, *The English Mummers' play*, pp.51–52, and 'The rushcart'.
[254] See, for example, Phillpotts' arguments regarding the Haxey 'Hood game' and the Lincolnshire 'Wild Worm', in *The Elder Edda*, p.132 and p.139. The former is linked to the death of the god Heimdallr, the latter regarded as being 'evidently a Scandinavian dragon' like all other English dragon figures. As Cawte points out in *Ritual animal disguise*, p.39, however, 'there is no example of a dragon in any traditional custom in the British Isles', the figure having almost certainly come into being as a derivation from the figure of St George. See also above, note 193 on other attempts to propose a Scandinavian origin for English folk traditions.

II. Dramatic Activities, II: Folkloristic Evidence

2. Iceland: The 'Vikivaki' Games

As was emphasised in the previous chapter, the Icelandic sagas contain very little direct evidence of dramatic activities over and above the enigmatic mention of the *leikgoði*, the *Syrpuþingslög*, and the occasional references to disguise. Even the various references to 'danz' ('dance'/ 'dance-songs') and 'danzleikar' ('dances'/ 'dance-games') provide little solid to go on. The only exceptions are the 'many dance-songs and many other kinds of joke' ('danza marga, ok margs-konar spott annat') made about Loftr Pálsson, according to *Íslendinga saga*, which would seem to have involved an element of satirical impersonation not only in words but also action, similar to the satirical 'háð' described in *Gunnlaugs saga*, and the offensive 'danzgörðir' ('new dance-songs') performed by Kolbeinn Arnórsson's men mentioned in *Íslendinga saga*.[255] It is nonetheless tempting to suppose that many of these medieval Icelandic dances, like the *gothikon*, and those from more recent times in the Faroe Islands, must have involved, in the very least, some elementary form of imitative movement.[256] Interestingly enough, the first unquestionable evidence of dramatic games taking place in Iceland points to the context of dance gatherings, or wakes, which seem to have been held predominantly during the Christmas period. Even more interesting is the fact that the disguise in question belongs firmly within the *julebukk* tradition, both in terms of the construction of the costume, and the loose connection between the acted figure and a legendary nature spirit. The account in question, written by Jón lærði Guðmundsson in 1644, describes an enacted creature that the writer saw in his youth in the late sixteenth century. Jón lærði begins his account by referring to the background of the 'Fingálpn', a legendary monster which had a reputation for trying to capture and defeat handsome men. He then comments that 'a wake-game was based around this. One man was chosen and dressed up along with the person who was supposed to be captured. I saw this in my childhood.'[257] The monster in question is clearly the same semi-bestial spirit otherwise known in Icelandic folklore as the *finngálkn*,

---

[255] For these particular references, see above *Chapter I*, note 260. For other references to dance and dance songs in the late twelfth and thirteenth and fourteenth centuries, see *Jóns saga helga hin elzta* and *Jóns saga hins helga* in *Biskupa sögur* (1858–1878), I, p.165 and p.237 ('mansaungs kvæði'; see further below, *Chapter V, D.5*); *Þorgils saga ok Hafliða*, in *Sturlunga saga* (1878), I, p.19 ('margs-konar leikar, bæði danzleikar, glímur og sagna-skemtan': 'many kinds of entertainments, including dances, wrestling and storytelling'); *Sturlu saga*, in *Sturlunga saga* (1878), I, p.63 ('vera/ slá skyldi hringleik[r]': 'a "circle" game should be held'); *Guðmundar saga biskups*, in *Guðmundar sögur biskups*, I, p.241 ('þá uar sleigen dans j stofunne': 'a dance was held in the room': see also *Biskupa sögur* [1858–1878], I, p.549, and *Sturlunga saga* [1878], I, p.293). See also *Íslendinga saga*, in *Sturlunga saga* (1878), II, p.225, p.245, and p.264; *Laurentius saga biskups* (1969), pp.101–102; and *Árna saga biskups* (1972), p.5. For the last two references, see also *Biskupa sögur* (1858–1878), I, p.849 and p.680. For a discussion of these references, see Jón Samsonarson, *Kvæði*, I, pp.ix–xxvi.
[256] See Thuren, *Folksangen*, pp.9–10. Regarding the *gothikon*, see *Chapter I, C.7*.
[257] 'Það skógarkrátýr vill gjarnan fanga og yfirkomast fríða menn velbúna. Þar eftir var gjörður einn leikur á vökunóttum. Var þar maður tilfenginn og forklæddur og hinn sem

G. A Shared Tradition of 'Folk Drama'

2. Iceland: The 'Vikivaki' games

which, like the spiritual *julebukk*, lived 'on the moors and in the woods' ('á heiðum og skógum').²⁵⁸

Jón lærði's account is not only valuable because of its age, but also because it describes an obviously dramatic game that was based on a simple narrative involving not one, but two costumed characters. The exact nature of the costume worn by the creature Jón saw is left up to the imagination, but the implications behind the name are that it must have been a mixture of beast and man. This is emphasised still further by the detailed descriptions of the 'þingálp' costume in later times, all of which underline that this figure is nothing other than the *julebukk* hiding behind an alias.²⁵⁹ According to *Niðurraðan*, written in the later part of the eighteenth century, the basis of the *þingálp* costume was a block of wood attached to a long pole, the wood being decorated with two ram's horns, sheep-skin cheeks, glass eyes and nostrils holding candles that were lit when the performer entered the room.²⁶⁰ The performer, who held the pole, was then covered with a bedspread of some kind. Especially striking is the fact that this particular version of the *þingálp* was equipped what seem to have been clacking jaws.²⁶¹

Two other slightly different descriptions of the *þingálp* exist, both of them worthy of note. According to Árni Magnússon in the early eighteenth century, the 'þingálpn' was 'a contraption in a Christmas game . . . a man

---

hún fanga skyldi. Ég sá þetta í barnæsku minni': quoted in Jón Samsonarson, *Kvæði*, I, p.clxxiv.

²⁵⁸ See Jón lærði Guðmundsson, quoted in Jón Samsonarson, *Kvæði*, I, p.clxxiv, and Jón Árnason, *Íslenzkar Þjóðsögur*, I, pp.613–614, where the *finngálkn* is defined as a beast conceived by two different breeds of animal. Regarding the habitat of the spiritual *julebukk*, see above, note 67. The idea of the *finngálkn* was clearly known in various forms as far back as the Middle Ages. It is referred to as a monster in *Örvar-Odds saga*, pp.348–350, and *Hjálmþés saga ok Ölvis*, pp.247–250. In Ólafr Þórðarson's *Þriðja málfræðiritgerðin*, from the mid-thirteenth century, the term 'finngálknat' is applied to the use of mixed metaphors in poetry (a reference, it would seem, to the *finngálkn*'s mixed ancestry): see Ólafr Þórðarson, *Málhljóða- og málskrúðsrit*, p.56. For other early references and discussion of the origin of the name, see Bugge, 'Mindre bidrag', 123–138; Örn Ólafsson, 'Finngálknað'; and Sveinn Einarsson, *Íslensk leiklist*, I, pp.87–90.

²⁵⁹ Various forms exist of the name *þingálp*. The *Crymogæa* translator writes of 'fingálfsleikur'; *Niðurraðan* of 'þingálp'; Árni Magnússon of 'fingálpn'; and Magnus Andrésson, in a letter to Sigurður Guðmundsson (1864), of 'þingálpið' or 'finngálknið'. For this last reference, see Jón Samsonarson, *Kvæði*, I, p.lxxiii. For the other accounts, see the references given below in this section.

²⁶⁰ *Niðurraðan og undirvísan hvurninn gleði og dansleikir voru tíðkaðir og um hönd hafðir í fyrri tíð*, published in Jón Samsonarson, *Kvæði*, I, pp.liii–lxiv, (translated into Danish by Blöndal, in 'Dans i Island', pp.169–176). For the *Niðurraðan þingálp* description, see Jón Samsonarson, *Kvæði*, I, pp.liv–lv. Regarding the dating of the *Niðurraðan*, see Jón Samsonarson, *Kvæði*, pp.l–lii.

²⁶¹ 'Fjöl er brúkuð fyrir neðan staurinn, föst við dýrshöfuðið. Henni skellir leikmaðurinn upp yfir alla í húsinu' ('A piece of wood is attached to the animal head below the place where the pole joins it. The performer "claps" this above everybody in the house'): *Niðurraðan*, in Jón Samsonarson, *Kvæði*, p.lv. Similar wording is used for the same phenomenon in a description from Hallingdal given in Lid, *Joleband*, p.39.

2. Iceland: The 'Vikivaki' games

II. Dramatic Activities, II: Folkloristic Evidence

Fig. 67. Wooden mask found at Stóraborg, by Eyjafjöll, Iceland.

in a monstrous costume, walking, so to speak, on all fours'.[262] A similar account is given by Magnus Andrésson, who writes in 1864 of the '*finngálkn* crawling on all fours' ('finngálkn skríðandi á fjórum fótum'), and describes the creature as being 'monstrous in all ways, covered in the ugliest rags it was possible to find, and clusters of shells which clattered and rattled.'[263] A living image of such a disguise might well be offered by the mysterious, full-sized wooden mask found recently at Stóraborg near Eyjafjöll in Iceland (see *figs 67–68*), probably the oldest wooden mask

---

[262] 'Þingálpn er ein machina í jólaleik . . . maður monstrosè út klæddur, gengur, so að segja, á fjórum fótum': quoted in Jón Samsonarson, *Kvæði*, I, p.clxxiii.
[263] 'Ófreskjulegt í alla staði, alþakið svo ljótum lörfum sem framast var unnt og skelja-klastri sem skrölti og hringlaði í': see Jón Samsonarson, *Kvæði*, I, p.lxxiii.

G. A Shared Tradition of 'Folk Drama'

2. Iceland: The 'Víkivaki' games

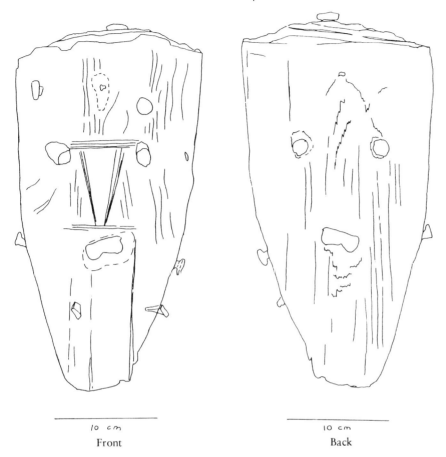

Fig. 68. Scale drawing of the Stóraborg mask.

known in the Nordic countries. The context and use of this object is unclear, but the possibility is that it was made in the sixteenth century. If that were so, it would support the early dating of Icelandic 'monster' disguises like that described by Jón lærði Guðmundsson.[264]

The appearance of the *þingálp* from *outside* the room in between dances was not accompanied by any song. The creature's main function was to cause a disturbance in between dances, and especially amongst the womenfolk. As Magnus Andrésson comments, the '*finngálkn* tried to go under the women's skirts, and also shook ash off its rags or body until the men

---

[264] See Mjöll Snæsdóttir, 'Andlitsmynd', pp.169–171. According to Mjöll in conversation, the mask may have been in the ground since 1600. It could itself be older than that. As regards the use of the mask, it is only possible to make guesses. The hole in the forehead *might* have been used for a single horn or candle, such as that used on the *þingálp*. The nails found on the mask were conceivably used to attach some material to it, yet no traces of leather or woven material were found nearby so it is impossible to be sure. Mjöll herself (in 'Andlitsmynd', p.170) raises the possibility of associations with the *víkivaki* dances. See further Cawte, *Ritual animal disguise*, p. 126.

2. Iceland: The 'Vikivaki' games

attacked it and drove it back out the same way that it had entered.'[265] Another characteristic of the *þingálp* is that it was usually accompanied by two other costumed figures known as *skjaldmeyjar* ('shield-maidens'),[266] or *valkyrjur* ('valkyries'), who, according to Jón Ólafsson frá Grunnavík's dictionary in Latin from the mid-eighteenth century, were played by young men dressed as women.[267]

The parallels with mainland Scandinavian dramatic traditions are obvious. The basic features of the costume and behaviour of the *þingálp* are exactly like those of the *julebukk*,[268] and the presence of the two costumed followers is strongly reminiscent of the mainland pairs of assistants like the 'father' and 'son' who accompanied the *julebukk*; the *hámenn* who accompanied *Stallo*; *Halm-Staffan*'s two followers; and the two *gadebassedrenge* or *gadebassesvende* ('gadebasse lads') who were chosen to accompany and assist the Jylland *gadebasse* elected at Christmas.[269] The presence of candles in the *þingálp*'s nostrils seems on the surface to offer close parallels with the Danish *julebukk*, *julevætte*, and *julebisp*, all of which are occasionally depicted as bearing 'candle sticks' in their mouths,[270] raising the possibility that this primitive, but effective 'lighting effect' was borrowed from Danish tradition. However, it is also worth noting a Christmas tradition from Shetland where on Christmas morning, a candle used to be placed in the eye socket of the skull of a recently slaughtered cow, which was then carried through the house and the byre to bestow 'Yule gude' on the inhabitants of the farm for the coming year.[271]

Whatever the origin of the candles, it is clear that the earliest reference to

---

[265] 'Finngálkn ... leitast við að fara upp undir kvenfólkið og hristi einnig upp á það öskuryk úr lörfunum eða skrokknum, unz karlmenn gerðu aðsúg að því og drífu það í burt sömu leið og það kom': quoted in Jón Samsonarson, *Kvæði*, I, pp.lxxiii–lxxiv.

[266] *Niðurraðan*, in Jón Samsonarson, *Kvæði*, I, p.lv. For a brief description of the costumes worn by these figures, see *Niðurraðan*, in Jón Samsonarson, *Kvæði*, p.liii. The same name is given to these figures by Eggert Ólafsson in the MS of his and Bjarni Pálsson's *Reise igiennom Island* (Sórey 1772). Eggert writes of 'Amazoner eller skioldmøer' ('Amazons or shield-maidens') which took part in these dances, which he terms as 'skuuespill' ('dramas'): see Jón Samsonarson, *Kvæði*, I, p.xlviii–lxxiv.

[267] Original text provided in Jón Samsonarson, *Kvæði*, I, p.clxix, note 3: 'Additæ sunt valkyrjur, seu virgines vestales, id est, juvenes longis vestibus & amictu muliebri ornati, circa eqvitem saltantes.'

[268] Regarding the *julebukk* costumes and their use of bells, see above, *section B.3*. Concerning the ribald behaviour of the *julebukk*, and other figures like *Stallo*, see above, notes 87–89 and 55. See also Cawte, *Ritual animal disguise*, pp.126–127 on the behaviour of the Cheshire horse. As regards the throwing of ashes and cinders, see for example, Lid, *Joleband*, pp.39–40; Feilberg, *Jul*, II, p.228; and Schager, *Julbocken*, p.88.

[269] See references given in notes 36 and 56–57 above, and *section B.3–5* on the *julebukk*; and Lid, *Joleband*, p.109, on the *gadebasse*. See also Keyland, *Julebröd*, pp.94–95, p.102, pp.129–130, and especially p.116 on a particularly comparable tradition from Orsala in Värmland, where the *julbock* was accompanied by two men dressed as women.

[270] See note 79 above; Feilberg, *Jul*, II, p.228, and p.254; Ellekilde, *Vor danske jul*, pp.300–301; and the description of the *julebisp* given above in *section D.1*.

[271] See Saxby, *Shetland traditional lore*, p.81 and p.83; and Macleod Banks, *British calendar customs: Orkney and Shetland*, p.82 and p.86 This tradition, linked with the

G. A Shared Tradition of 'Folk Drama'

2. Iceland: The 'vikivaki' games

the *þingálp* is almost contemporary to the earliest material concerning the *julebukk* from elsewhere in Scandinavia. It certainly predates the Danish descriptions of figures bearing candles. Even more revealing is the fact that in Iceland, this figure went under an independent name, and was related to a spirit that was intrinsically linked to older Icelandic folk belief. Furthermore, it is noteworthy that those people who wrote descriptions of this game never attempted to compare the *þingálp* with the *julebukk*. All of these features would seem to point to the joint existence of two parallel traditions that must go back to much older shared roots in Scandinavia, rather than to the Icelanders fashionably adopting a *julebukk* tradition from Denmark or Norway during the sixteenth century. At that time, surely the name of the creature would also have been adopted?[272]

The *þingálp*, however, was not the only costumed figure to appear in the Icelandic dance games. Arngrímur Jónsson's *Crymogæa* published in Latin in 1609 mentions various 'ludicra exercitia' practiced by the Icelanders, including dance ('staticuli') and *vikivaki* ('orbis saltatoris'), a particular kind of popular ring dance that was accompanied by songs and the dance games mentioned above.[273] The original Latin work provides little detailed information about the games themselves. However, an Icelandic translation of the first part of *Crymogæa*, made in the mid-seventeenth century, provides an additional list of 'dansleikir' ('dance-games') which includes not only the 'fingálfsleikur', but also 'hringbrot' ('Breaking the ring'); 'frantzensleikur'; 'Þórildarleikur' ('Þórhildur's game'); 'hindarleikur' ('The hind game'); 'Háu-Þóru leikur' ('Tall Þóra's game'); 'hestreiðarleikur' ('The horseriding game'); 'hjartarleikur' ('The stag game'); and other activities which are not named but are classed alongside dance and *vikivaki*.[274] As later accounts reveal, all of these 'games' were essentially associated with the Icelandic *vökunætur* ('wakes') which were commonly held during the Christmas and New Year period,[275] and began attracting the wrath of

---

elements of sacrifice and procession, has a number of interesting associations, and brings to mind Celander's and Burkert's suggestions about the relationship between costumed presentations (such as that of the *julebukk*) and sacrifice: see notes 74, 81, 133 and 168 above; and Simpson, 'Some Scandinavian sacrifices', p.191, on comparable traditions from sixteenth century England.

[272] The *Þingálp* is examined further in Ólafur Davíðsson, *Íslenzkar gátur*, III, pp.134–137; Jón Samsonarson, *Kvæði*, I, pp.clxxiii–clxxiv; and Sveinn Einarsson, *Íslenskt leiklist*, I, pp.99–102.

[273] See Arngrímur Jónsson, *Crymogæa*, p.148. Regarding the *vikivaki* dance, see Jón Samsonarson, *Kvæði*, I, pp.cxxviii–cxliii. On the origin and meaning of the word *vikivaki* (which is still uncertain), see Chesnutt, 'On the origin of Icelandic *vikivaki*'.

[274] Arngrímur Jónsson, *Crymogæa*, p.149. Regarding this account, see also Jón Samsonarson, *Kvæði*, I, pp.xxviii–xxxi. Regarding the date of the translation, see Jakob Benediktsson's introduction to *Crymogæa*, pp.51–52. All of these games are referred to in more detail below, except for 'hringbrot' and 'frantzensleikur'. Regarding these two games, see Jón Samsonarson, *Kvæði*, I, pp.clxiv–clxix, and p.ccxv.

[275] Regarding the particular seasonal dating of these gatherings, see, for example, Ólafur Davíðsson, *Íslenzkar gátur*, III, p.18, pp.20–22, and p.25; and Jón Samsonarson, *Kvæði*, I, p.xxxvii, p.xxxix, and pp.xlii–xliii. Árni Björnsson, in *Jól*, pp.122–123, like many of the original informants, defines all the games in question as being 'jólaleikir' ('Christmas

2. Iceland: The 'Vikivaki' games

the church in the later part of the sixteenth century.[276] Actual descriptions of the games, however, do not start appearing until the middle of the eighteenth century, in works like *Niðurraðan* and the writings of Jón Ólafsson frá Grunnavík.[277]

The so-called *vikivakaleikir* ('vikivaki games') have previously been examined in detail by Ólafur Davíðsson, Dag Strömbäck, Jón Samsonarson, and most recently Sveinn Einarsson.[278] Four of the games demand particular attention here, because, like the *þingálp*, they involved a strong element of costumed representation and used to occur in the form of an interlude in between dances. All four of these games appear to have roots in mainland Scandinavian tradition.

Two of the games in question, namely the *hestleikur* ('horse game') and the *hjartarleikur*,[279] centred upon the disguised animal figures of the 'horse' and the 'stag'. The *hestleikur*, which had a brief song attached to it,[280] seems to have involved a basic scenario in which the 'horse' was danced with, and then developed a limp which was cured by the other participants spitting on the animal and beating it. The proceedings ended with the creature being up-ended and thrown into the air.[281] As Strömbäck has pointed out, the descriptions of the animal costume in this game, constructed around a covered frame hanging from the performer's waist, suggest close affinities to foreign ritualistic disguises such as that of the English Padstowe horse and other horse costumes known in Basque tradition.[282] This of course raises the question of whether the game itself was native, or originally imported from England, or from Basque sailors.

The latter 'animal' game, the *hjartarleikur*, involved the impersonation

---

games'). He is nonetheless wary about automatically limiting the *vökunætur* to the Christmas period: see *Jól*, pp.101–102.

[276] See Jón Samsonarson, *Kvæði*, I, pp.xxxv–xxxix. It is perhaps this kind of dance-game that is referred in *Qualiscunque Descriptio Islandiae* which was possibly written by Bishop Oddur Einarsson in 1588–89: see Jón Samsonarson, *Kvæði*, I, p.xxxi. This work refers to certain gatherings of people on Christian holidays ('uigilijs sanctorum'), who 'between dances presented other play activities and ridiculous spectacles' ('et alternatim alias ludicras actiones et ridicula spectacula exhibendo'). This comment is emphasised still further by the later mention of the 'ridiculous, effeminate and lascivious activities' ('ridiculas, effæminatas et lasciuas actiones') that occurred at these gatherings: quoted in Jón Samsonarson, *Kvæði*, I, p.xxxiii.

[277] Regarding the information provided by Jón frá Grunnavík, see, for example, Ólafur Davíðsson, *Íslenzkar gátur*, III, pp.18–19; and Jón Samsonarson, *Kvæði*, I, pp.xxxiv–xxxv.

[278] See Ólafur Davíðsson, *Íslenzkar gátur*, III, 95–246; Jón Samsonarson, *Kvæði*, I, pp.ix–ccxliii; Strömbäck, 'Cult remnants', and 'Um íslenska vikivakaleiki'; and Sveinn Einarsson, *Íslensk leiklist*, I, pp.65–118. For translations of Strömbäck's articles see the *Bibliography*.

[279] Also called the 'hjörtleikur' and 'hjartleikur': Jón Samsonarson, *Kvæði*, I, p.clxxiv.

[280] See Jón Samsonarson, *Kvæði*, II, p.332.

[281] For further discussion of this game, see Ólafur Davíðsson, *Íslenzkar gátur*, III, pp.128–129, and Jón Samsonarson, *Kvæði*, I, pp.clxix–clxxiii.

[282] Descriptions of the *hestleikur* are given by Jón frá Grunnavík and in *Niðurraðan*: see Jón Samsonarson, *Kvæði*, I, p.clxix, note 3, and pp.liii–liv. A basic translation of the *Niðurraðan* text is given in Strömbäck, 'Cult remnants', 139–140, and 'Dramatic dances', 97. The Basque tradition is described in Strömbäck, 'Cult remnants', 142–143. Concerning

G. A Shared Tradition of 'Folk Drama'

2. Iceland: The 'Vikivaki' games

of a stag by a man bent forward and using two sticks as the forefeet.[283] The costume itself consisted of a decorative red cloth, on top of which was placed a wooden cross holding candles, a feature which conceivably replaced the earlier wearing of horns.[284] The game began with the 'stag' being led into the room by a scarf, after which the performer proceeded to herd the women present into a group in the centre of the room to the accompaniment of a 'stag song'.[285]

The two other costumed *vikivaki* games involved grotesque female figures. The former, *Háu-Þóru leikur*, which the author of *Niðurraðan* describes as a possible replacement for the *þingálp* game, centred upon the figure of a giant woman who, like the *þingálp*, appeared from outside the room accompanied by the two 'shield-maidens' (*skjaldmeyjar*).[286] Like the *þingálp*, the figure of *Háa-Þóra* was constructed around a large pole carried by the performer, but in this case the pole was held upright (see fig.69). According to *Niðurraðan*:

> This (pole) is topped with a tall woman's head-dress, and a white scarf is bound around this in such a way that the end is left trailing down. Another pole is then placed across the first one, and tied to it. A large bunch of keys is hung from this. After that, a long, black woman's coat is (placed around the frame, and) done up at the neck, and a man goes underneath. An apron is fixed to the front, and a decorative belt drawn over it. When the idol/ doll has been prepared in this way, a man goes under the dress, holds the pole and hammers at the stone or the floor.[287]

The hallmarks of the *Háa-Þóra* performance as recorded in the *Niðurraðan* account are violence and ribald behaviour, the figure

---

the Padstowe and Minehead horses, which appear on May Day, see Cawte, *Ritual animal disguise*, pp.157–177.

[283] *Niðurraðan* in Jón Samsonarson, *Kvæði*, I, p.lix. See other descriptions in Jón Samsonarson, *Kvæði*, I, p.lxxiii, p.lxxix, p.xcvi, and p.clxxvii (Jón frá Grunnavík).

[284] Ólafur Davíðsson, in *Íslenzkar gátur*, III, p.131, suggests (probably on the basis of a letter by Sigurður Guðmundsson, dated 1863) that horns were occasionally used instead of the cross, and that the candles were attached to them. See also Strömbäck, 'Um íslenska vikivakaleiki', 73. Jón Samsonarson, in *Kvæði*, I, p.clxxvi, note 1, disagrees with this idea, arguing that there is no evidence for such a custom, and that it would have been extremely difficult for the dancers to procure deer horns.

[285] See *Niðurraðan*, in Jón Samsonarson, *Kvæði*, I, p.lix.

[286] See *Niðurraðan* and the descriptions given by Magnús Andrésson and Brnjólfur Jónsson frá Minna-Núpi, in Jón Samsonarson, *Kvæði*, I, p.lxiii, p.lxxiii and p.xcvi. For further comment on this game, see Ólafur Davíðsson, *Íslenskar gátur*, III, pp.137–140, and Jón Samsonarson, *Kvæði*, I, pp.clxxxiv–clxxxv.

[287] 'Hönum er skautað, og yfir um hann er vafið með trafi, og lafir langt skott niður, því staur er látinn yfir hinn staurinn og bundinn fast við. Þar er og hengt á stórt lyklakerfi. Síðan er bundið um kragann á kvenhempu, og fer þar maður undir. Svunta er höfð að framan, og málindakoffur yfirdregið, og þegar goðið er so tilfansað, fer maður undir hempuna, heldur um staurinn og pikkar í hallinn eða gólfið': *Niðurraðan*, in Jón Samsonarson, *Kvæði*, I, p.lxiii. The costume described here is largely based on eighteenth-century Icelandic national costume. See, for example, the illustrations in Eggert Ólafsson and Bjarni Pálsson, *Ferðabók*, I, pp.4–5; and in Guðjónsson, *The national costume*, passim.

Fig. 69. A reconstruction of Háa-þóra used in the recent Icelandic productions of *Bandamannasaga* (1992–1993), written and directed by Sveinn Einarsson.

G. A Shared Tradition of 'Folk Drama'

2. Iceland: The 'Vikivaki' games

commencing by creeping between the dancers' legs and then suddenly standing up, instigating a general free-for-all. The Bacchanalian atmosphere is underlined by the fact that the performance was accompanied by the singing of 'defamatory and mocking songs' ('níð og narrarí').[288] All of these features were, of course, also found in the *þingálp* performance mentioned above.

Sexual connotations also figured in the other *vikivaki* game featuring costumed female characters acted by men: the *kerlingarleikur*, or 'Old hag game'.[289] This game involved four characters, the central pair being a mother known as 'the old hag' (*kellingin*), and her daughter who was dressed in finery of various kinds, and equipped, like both *Háa-Þóra* and the 'horse', with a bunch of keys to shake. The mother, on the other hand, bore a much closer resemblance to an ogress of some kind:

> She is dressed up in the following decorative fashion: first of all, a hairy dogskin bag is filled with flour, and this is forced onto her head and firmly bound under her chin. She is then clad in a ragged dress of horsehair sacking which reaches down to her backside. Apart from this, she is covered in old flour-bags, and other rags and tatters. A mask with spectacles on covers her visage. She has a fishskin bag on her back and some tattered seaman's gloves on her hands. Dressed like this, she totters along to the living-room door.[290]

Like the *hestur*, *þingálp* and *Háa-Þóra*, the old woman, who is known in *Niðurraðan* as 'Gunnhildur gríðarsterki' ('Gunnhildur the strong'),[291] has two servants. Here, though, they were known as 'Kári' and 'Benedikt langi' ('Tall Benedikt'), the last name probably implying yet another disguise. The *kerlingarleikur*, however, appears to be less primitive and more directly associated with a narrative dance than the other games, since it also involves a short dialogue between the daughter and the *kelling* about the nature of the ideal man, both 'women' being in search of a partner.[292] At the end of the conversation, the men 'throw . . . the old woman to the floor' ('slengja . . . kerlingunni á gólfið').[293] Various noisy antics, insulting verses and dances then ensue before both the old woman and her daughter are eventually forced to leave the premises.[294]

---

[288] See *Niðurraðan*, in Jón Samsonarson, *Kvæði*, I, p.lxiii. Regarding the background of *Háu-Þóru leikur*, see further Sveinn Einarsson, *Íslenskt leiklist*, I, pp.102–104.
[289] See *Niðurraðan*, in Jón Samsonarson, *Kvæði*, I, pp.lv–lix. This game is not mentioned in *Crymogæa*.
[290] 'Hún er so í skraut búin, að það er tekinn fyrst loðinn hundsbelgur og steyttur með mel, þrýstur síðan á hennar höfuð og reyrður niður um kjálkana. So er hún færð í vonda hærusekksdulu, og nær hún ofan á rassinn. Þar að auki er hún öll þakin með meltuskum, leppum og tirjum. Grímhetta með gleraugum er fyrir hennar ósjónu. Hún hefur og roðaveski á bak til ásamt vonda sjóvettlinga á hendi. Með þetta staulur hún til baðstofudyra': *Niðurraðan*, in Jón Samsonarson, *Kvæði*, I, pp.lv–lvi.
[291] *Niðurraðan*, in Jón Samsonarson, *Kvæði*, I, p.lvi.
[292] *Niðurraðan*, in Jón Samsonarson, *Kvæði*, I, pp.lvi–lviii.
[293] *Niðurraðan*, in Jón Samsonarson, *Kvæði*, I, p.lviii.
[294] See further Ólafur Davíðsson, *Íslenzkar gátur*, III, pp.124–128, and the discussion of

II. Dramatic Activities, II: Folkloristic Evidence

3. Possible Origins of the 'Vikivaki' Games

The origin of the *vikivaki* games has been the subject of some academic discussion, since, as with so many of the traditions mentioned in this chapter, it is impossible to be certain about their exact age or their original context and function. As regards the *vikivaki* games, apart from certain vague suggestions of a possible origin in more ancient medieval dance traditions from Scandinavia,[295] the general tendency in more recent times has been to look towards England and mainland Europe for a background. This approach began with Sigurður Guðmundsson's suggestion in 1864 that the *hjartarleikur* might have roots in England,[296] and was later strengthened by Ólafur Davíðsson's conclusion in 1894, following an extremely brief review of Danish Christmas customs such as that of the *julebukk*, that 'none of the games I am aware of bears any real resemblance to the Icelandic *vikivaki* games apart from *Hoffinnsleikur*' (which involves no costume).[297]

The most influencial scholar as regards the origin of the *vikivaki* games was Dag Strömbäck. In spite of arguing that the games represented 'cult remnants',[298] and briefly noting certain similarities between the 'death' of 'our Swedish *julbock*' and the limping of the 'horse'[299], Strömbäck came to be more attracted by the argument that animal disguise was a predominantly Celtic phenomenon.[300] His eventual conclusion, like that of his

---

these figures and their possible relation to certain other Icelandic verses, in Jón Samsonarson, *Kvæði*, I, pp.clxxxv–cxcii.

[295] Páll Vídalín suggested in 1727 that the *vökunætur* and dance games 'fyrir utan allan efa voru leifar heiðinna manna hátíðis-siða, og voru gleði kallaðar, eins og hjá þeim hétu blótveizlurnar mannfagnaður, sem Snorri vottar' ('were doubtless the remnants of pagan festivals, and were called *gleði*, or 'joy', just like they called sacrificial feasts *mannfagnaður* or "celebrations", as Snorri testifies'): Vídalín, *Skýringar*, p.268. A slightly more tentative approach is found in Sigurður Guðmundsson's suggestion in 1864 that the 'finngálknið' was probably related to medieval carnival traditions which, Sigurður believed, also had existed in Iceland, but was 'máske eldra' ('maybe even older'): quoted in Jón Samsonarson, *Kvæði*, I, p.lxxvi. Regarding the possibility of an earlier pagan origin to the dances and games, see also the references to Strömbäck's articles mentioned above in note 278, and most recently Sveinn Einarsson's detailed examination of the games in *Íslensk leiklist*, I, pp.111–115.

[296] See Jón Samsonarson, *Kvæði*, I, p.clxxxi.

[297] 'Einginn af þessum leikjum, sem ég þekki, er þó líkur íslenzku vikivakaleikjunum að marki, nema Hoffinnsleikur': Ólafur Davíðsson, *Íslenzkar gátur*, III, pp.145–146. Regarding *Hoffinnsleikur*, see Jón Samsonarson, *Kvæði*, I, pp.ccxii–ccxiv. It might be noted that séra Þorsteinn Pétursson in his attack on the *vikivaki* gatherings, written shortly after 1757 and making use of evidence from Denmark and Germany, had proposed origins for the games in these two countries: see Jón Samsonarson, *Kvæði*, I, p.clxxxi, and pp.xliii–xliv.

[298] See Strömbäck, 'Cult remnants', 141. Strömbäck argues here that even though the present form of the games may have been borrowed from abroad, 'it must be said that the ground was prepared, that a kind of substratum existed, and that the norsemen by no means were unacquainted with maskings and unbridled pageants of ritual character.'

[299] Strömbäck, 'Cult remnants', p.144. No mention is made here of the Norwegian *julebukk* tradition.

[300] See above, section B.5.

G. A Shared Tradition of 'Folk Drama'

3. Possible origins of the 'Vikivaki' games

predecessors, was that the Icelandic *vikivakaleikir* were probably imported from England during the later Middle Ages,³⁰¹ the figure of the limping 'horse' having distant roots in Basque customs which involved the gelding of a similar horse figure.³⁰² Strömbäck adds as an afterthought that he 'will not exclude that some dances may have come by way of Norway and Denmark, but the Norwegian and Danish material is very poor regarding masquerades, compared with that of England and the Continent.'³⁰³

This conclusion was later developed by Jón Samsonarson, who echoes Strömbäck's words,³⁰⁴ and proposes that the figure of *Háa-Þóra* might also go back to these same Basque roots.³⁰⁵ Furthermore, noting that several of the disguised figures share the characteristic of being accompanied by the two 'shield-maidens', he makes the logical suggestion that the 'shield-maidens', the 'horse', the *þingálp*, and *Háa-Þóra* should be regarded as 'a kind of associated group of figures, whatever route they may have taken to Iceland, and whenever that might have been'.³⁰⁶ Like Ólafur Davíðsson and Strömbäck, Jón notes that disguises similar to the *þingálp* existed in Denmark and Norway, but he makes very little of this.

In general, the current academic view is summed up succinctly by Vésteinn Ólason's cautious statement that 'these games may ultimately be of pre-Christian origin' (in Europe), but 'most likely . . . they were brought to Iceland in Christian times, probably sometime during the late Middle Ages.'³⁰⁷ Vésteinn rejects Strömbäck's earlier suggestion that cult dances might have existed in Iceland from the start, mainly because the word *danz* has a foreign origin, and because accounts of dance do not appear in Icelandic literature prior to 1100. Nothing is said, though, about the possible implications of the word *leikr*, or the visual evidence of dance in the Swedish petroglyphs, the Torslunda and Sutton Hoo plates, the gold foils or the Oseberg tapestry mentioned in the previous chapter. Nor is any mention made of how few references to native dances exist *anywhere* in northern Europe before 1100.³⁰⁸ In general, as Sveinn Einarsson has recently argued, there can be little question that some form of dance must have existed in the northern countries just as it has always existed everywhere else in the world.³⁰⁹ The Scandinavians obviously possessed an inherent sense of rhythm (testified to by the patterns of their poetry); they

---

301 Strömbäck, 'Um íslenska vikivakaleiki', 76.
302 See Strömbäck, 'Cult remnants', 141–145, and 'Um íslenska vikivakaleiki', 74–80. See further the discussion of the origin of the *hestleikur* in Sveinn Einarsson, *Íslenskt leiklist*, I, pp.81–90.
303 Strömbäck, 'Um íslenska vikivakaleiki', 76; translated in 'Icelandic dramatic dances', 96.
304 See Jón Samsonarson, *Kvæði*, I, p.cci, and pp.clxxxii–clxxxiv.
305 Jón Samsonarson, *Kvæði*, I, pp.cxcii–cxciii.
306 'Auðvelt væri að hugsa sér hestinn, skjaldmeyjar, þingálp og Háu-Þóru sem nokkuð samstæða fylkingu, hvernig svo sem leiðir hennar hafa legið til Íslands og hvenær á öldum sem það hefur gerzt': Jón Samsonarson, *Kvæði*, I, p.cxciii.
307 Vésteinn Ólason, *The traditional ballads*, p.41.
308 See Vésteinn Ólason, *The traditional ballads*, pp.35–42.
309 See, for example, the discussion of this question by Sveinn Einarsson, in *Íslenskt*

3. Possible origins of the 'Vikivaki' games

were interested in music and song (testified to by various accounts of harp players and other musicians); and, equally important, they made alcohol. The logical result of the above must surely have been that they indulged in dance of some kind.

Whatever the origin of the dance gatherings, the tendency of scholars to look south for an origin to the *vikivaki* games, rather than east to Norway is somewhat surprising, especially in the light of the unquestionably close relationship between the *þingálp* and the *julebukk*. In very general terms, even though the *vikivaki songs* may be related in some way to the English *carols*,[310] the entire context of the *games* would appear to be Scandinavian. This is exemplified by the presence amongst the *vikivakaleikir* of wooing games such as *Þórhildarleikur* and *hindarleikur*, both of which involved the pairing of couples and implied mock-marriage, a tradition also reflected in another Icelandic game entitled 'Drawing Christmas lads and Christmas maids' (*Að draga jólasveina og jólameyjar*).[311] As has been illustrated above, pairing activities of this kind were well known in mainland Scandinavian Christmas traditions such as those related to the *julebisp* and *gadebasse*; indeed, there is little doubt that both the Icelandic *hindarleikur* and *Hoffinnsleikur* must have originated in either Norway or Denmark.[312] The text of the *kerlingarleikur* might well be seen as a satire on such a tradition. Yet this is not all. As has been pointed out above, obvious parallels with mainland Scandinavian tradition are also found in the *julebukk*-like figure of the *þingálp*, and in the descriptions of the ribald behaviour of both this creature and *Háa-Þóra* which are sharply reminiscent of many accounts concerning the cavorting of the *julebukk* and *Stallo*.[313]

For these reasons alone, it ought to be natural to look first and foremost

---

leiklist, I, pp.71–73; and Árni Björnsson, in *Jól*, p.126, where similar conclusions are reached.

[310] See Vésteinn Ólason, *The traditional ballads*, pp.44–50.

[311] For descriptions and discussion of these wooing games see Ólafur Davíðsson, *Íslenzkar gátur*, III, pp.97–103, and pp.103–107; and Jón Samsonarson, *Kvæði*, I, pp.lix–lxiii (*Niðurraðan*) and pp.cxciii–ccxii, and II, pp.299–304, and pp.314–322 (the song texts). *Þórhildarleikur* is a marriage game led by a man dressed as a woman, who initiates the 'marriage' of mixed couples. Regarding the lottery pairing game, *Að draga jólasveina og jólameyjar*, see Jónas Jónasson, *Íslenzkir þjóðhættir*, p.210. On the tradition of 'mock-marriages' in Iceland in earlier times, see Árni Björnsson, *Jól*, p.124; and 'Sumardagurinn fyrsti', 114, on similar customs once associated with the first day of summer in parts of Iceland.

[312] Close parallels to the *Hindarleikur* are found all over Scandinavia, but especially in Norway and the Faroe Islands. See Jón Samsonarson, *Kvæði*, I, p.ccii; Berge, 'Norske brudlaupsleikar', 111–144, and note 201 above. Regarding *Hoffinnsleikur*, see references in note 297 above. Regarding the *julebisp* and *gadebasse* and other such traditions in Denmark and Sweden, see especially notes 202 and 203 above, and *Chapter I*, note 304. For faint English parallels to these traditions, see Baskerville, 'Dramatic aspects', 38, and 44–45, and more recently Brody, *The English Mummers*, pp.99–116, on the acted 'wooing ceremony' from Lincolnshire, Leicestershire, Nottinghamshire and Rutland.

[313] Regarding the behaviour of *Stallo* and the *julebukk*, see references given in notes 55, and 87–89 above.

G. A Shared Tradition of 'Folk Drama'

towards Scandinavia for relevant parallels and a possible origin for the *vikivaki* games. As the evidence provided earlier in this chapter reveals, such parallels are easily found. Concerning the costumed figures, it would seem clear that not only the *þingálp*, but also the 'horse' and the 'stag' belong to the same family as the *julebukk* in its various guises. The limping Icelandic 'horse', for example, fits in well alongside the 'dying' and 'leaping' Scandinavian *julebukk*, the resurrected 'Stephanus' and the kneeling or executed black-faced 'King of Morieland' found predominantly in Swedish *Stjärnspel*.[314] While it cannot be denied that the costume of the 'horse' as described during the seventeenth and eighteenth centuries is very similar indeed to certain English horse costumes, this need not imply that the basis of the tradition itself should have originated in the British Isles, any more than that the *julebukk* tradition should have come from Germany because that was the home of the earliest accounts of costumes with 'clacking jaws'.[315] Certainly, there is little detailed evidence to confirm the existence of a horse tradition in Scandinavia over and above the brief mentions of 'Arnaldus Jólahest', the Danish *Hvegehors*, the mysterious Faroese *jólhestur* ('Christmas horse'), and certain other questionable animal figures such as the 'Carrying horse' known in Shetland and Orkney.[316] These notices, however, should suffice to discourage researchers from ruling out the possibility that some sort of Scandinavian horse tradition might have existed in the distant past. At the same time, it might be noted that the actual nature of the creature in the Icelandic *hestleikur* is comparatively unimportant, since the dance verses accompanying the performance specify little about the species of the animal in question.[317]

The case of the 'stag' is similar. Like that of the *þingálp*, this guise bears obvious similarities to the candle-bearing Danish *julebisp* and *julebukk*

3. Possible origins of the 'vikivaki' games

---

314 See above, section B.4.
315 See note 80 above for a reference to the possible adoption of the 'clacking jaw' image of the *julebukk* from Germany.
316 Regarding 'Arnaldus Jolahest' and the *Hvegehors*, see references in *Chapter I*, note 247, and *Chapter II*, notes 92–93. Regarding the Faroese *jólhestur*, see below, note 359. Regarding the Orkney and Shetland 'Kyerrin Horse' (the 'fool' in a regular troupe of New Year disguised visitors who had the job of carrying the food and drink the group collected), see Alford, 'Some Hobby Horses', 229; Macleod Banks, *British calendar customs: Orkney and Shetland*, pp.22–36; Marwick, *The folklore of Orkney*, p.102 and pp.109–110; and Cawte, who in *Ritual animal disguise*, p.194, is more cautious about the links between this tradition and animal disguise. One account of this game from Orkney, however, describes how the 'carrying horse' was beaten by the rest of the group with knotted handkerchiefs, thus presenting a faint parallel with the treatment of the 'horse', the *julebukk*, and the black king in the *Stjärnspel*. For references to other Scandinavian traditions involving mock-horses, see above note 138; Alford, 'The Hobby Horse', 131–133; Møller, 'Sommer i by', 129; and Nilsson, *Årets folkliga fester*, p.83. Regarding Stefán Einarsson's unsuccessful attempt to find a reference to an acted horse figure in *Íslendinga saga* (*Sturlunga saga* [1878], I, p.230), in 'Horse dance', pp.290–293, see Almqvist, 'Midfjordingamärren'.
317 Considering the close parallels between the guise of the *julebukk* and the Northern English 'horse' figures (see note 252 above), it is easy to imagine a basic construction for animal disguise that altered in accordance with local conditions or beliefs.

3. Possible origins of the 'Vikivaki' games

which cannot be ignored.[318] It is certainly highly questionable whether this costume should be grouped apart from the other animal figures on the basis of the the beauty of the guise and the Christian connotations of both the stag figure itself and the 'cross' that was placed on the back of the animal.[319] In support of such a Christian interpretation, Jón Samsonarson cites an account of how the Devil supposedly appeared during a performance of the *hjartarleikur*, and ended up sinking into the floor, the implication being that Satan's defeat here was brought about by the wonderous presence of the holy 'stag'.[320] Such an argument, however, finds no support at all in the original text of this account. Indeed, if the common Danish and Swedish oral legends concerning the *julebukk* and other such figures are borne in mind, there is much more reason to assume that in the original legend, the Devil was *attracted* by the appearance of the horned 'stag', and eventually banished by some other external figure such as a local priest.[321] The usual context of the *vikivaki* games makes it even more unlikely that any of the costumed figures making an appearance would have been assumed to have any element of holiness. This is certainly supported by the stag's treatment of women which hardly belongs in any Christian scenario. In general, considering the Danish 'stag' tradition mentioned above (*section B.4*), and the use of two sticks for front legs which also occurs within the *julebukk* tradition,[322] it would seem much more logical to classify the *hjörtur* firmly alongside all the other *vikivaki* animal guises, well and truly within the boundaries of recognised Scandinavian tradition.[323]

As has been noted above, the two *skjaldmeyjar* assistants accompanying the 'horse' appear to have been a common feature of the *vikivaki* games, since they also appear with the figures of the *þingálp* and *Háa-Þóra*. These

---

[318] See references in notes 79, 202 and 260 above.
[319] See Jón Samsonarson, *Kvæði*, I, p.clxxvi, and most recently, Sveinn Einarsson, *Íslenskt leiklist*, I, p.80.
[320] Jón Samsonarson, *Kvæði*, I, p.clxxvi, and p.lxxvi, an account recorded by Sigurður Guðmundsson in 1864.
[321] See the references given in note 152 above. Numerous Scandinavian legends tell of appearances made by the Devil when people were dancing or playing cards and how Satan later had to be forcibly removed from the room, often by a famous local priest. See, for example, Bø et al., *Norske segner*, pp.172–175; Klinteberg, *Svenska folksägner*, pp.204–208; and Kvideland and Sehmsdorf, *Scandinavian folk belief*, pp.293–295. Sigurður Guðmundsson's account has all the signs of belonging to the same type of legend. He states that 'the moment the stag had been dressed, the Devil entered' (*'þegar búið var að klæða hjörtinn ... kölski gamli kóm þá inn'*: my emphases). Sigurður then adds that he could not find out what happened next, but the account he heard ended with the Devil sinking into the floor, leaving a hole that could not be filled (*'hvað þá gerðist gat eg ei fengið að vita, en endirinn varð sá, að kölski sökk ofan um baðstofugólfið, og er ekki hægt síðan að fella (í) það gat'*). No interpretation is given of these events in Sigurður's account.
[322] See the references given in note 161 above.
[323] See further Jón Samsonarson, *Kvæði*, I, pp.clxxvi–clxxvii, note 2, on the question of the 'stag' and women, and the suggestion of earlier links between this game and the *hindarleikur* made by Strömbäck in 'Um íslenska vikivakaleiki', 73–74. See also the comments on this custom given in Ólafur Davíðsson, *Íslenzkar gátur*, III, pp.129–132.

G. A Shared Tradition of 'Folk Drama'

figures have obvious parallels in other pairs of assistants found in mainland Scandinavian tradition. In a wider sense, however, the 'shield-maidens' might be classified alongside the *groups* of costumed figures such as the *stjärngossar* ('star-boys') and *Staffansdrängar* ('Staffan's lads'), all of whom tended to accompany a central figure or symbol, but were also set apart from the 'audience' by their masks or costumes.[324]

3. Possible origins of the 'Vikivaki' games

The same argument applies to the female figures, *Háa-Þóra*, and the *kelling* and her daughter. While the latter pair might be tentatively compared to similar figures found in the English 'wooing ceremony' plays,[325] there is equal reason to suggest that the central troll-like *kelling* herself might have originated in a house-visiting costumed ogress-figure like the Norwegian *Lussi*.[326] *Háa-Þóra* is more problematic, but very close parallels in costume are encountered, for example, in an Estonian figure known as the *lange gjente* (the 'tall girl') who used to appear on Shrove Tuesdays accompanied not only by two costumed female companions (one acted by a man), but also by a phallic *julebukk*.[327] Closer to home, the fact that the *Háa-Þóra* gulse was constructed around a long pole held by the performer suggests that this figure should be grouped alongside the *þingálp* and *julebukk*, especially since the *julebukk* was also sometimes equipped with a long extendable neck capable of reaching up to the rafters.[328] Indeed, strong similarities exist between the initial entrance of *Háa-Þóra* and that of at least one *julebukk* figure which apparently used to enter the room silently, and then crept 'along the floor' ('langsamt efter Golvet').[329]

The above comparisons are naturally little more than analogies, and as mentioned at the start of this chapter, it would be foolhardy to suggest that parallel customs separated by such a distance should necessarily originate from the same source. Yet, in very general terms, the likelihood of some

---

[324] The fact that the *skjaldmeyjar* were men disguised as women is not really important as a distinction from the other groups (see, however, note 269 above). Such a form of disguise has always been common throughout Europe and Scandinavia. Furthermore, female disguise was undoubtedly popular in Iceland and the other North Atlantic islands, as can be seen from *Háu-Þóru leikur*, the *kerlingarleikur*, *Þórhildarleikur*, and the traditions from the Faroe Islands and Shetland examined below.
[325] See, for example, Brody, *The Mummers and their plays*, pp.99–116.
[326] See above, *section B.1*.
[327] According to Lid, in *Jolesveinar*, p.89, the "*lange gjente*" had a cloth hung over her, 'og ho bar på toppen av ein stake ein figur, eit hovud med tvo armar, slik at gjenta på det viset syntest vera so lang at ho nådde heilt upp til taket' ('and on the top of a pole she bore a figure composed of a head and two arms, which made the girl seem so tall that she reached up to the roof'). One of her companions was constructed in a similar way, but had a bird's beak on top of the pole. Lid suggests a further parallel between this figure and the Bronze Age petroglyph from Ekenburg in Östergötland which depicts a linked procession drawing a giant-like figure similar to the carnival giants known in Flanders and elsewhere: see Lid, *Jolesveinar*, pp.152-154, and Almgren, *Hällristningar*, p.128 and pp.131–134.
[328] In several descriptions, the head of the goat is said to have been capable of reaching up to the roof or down to the cellar. See, for example, Lid, *Joleband*, pp.39–40, and Weiser-Aall, *Julenissen*, p.28, for examples from Hallingdal and Hordaland in Norway.
[329] See Lid, *Joleband*, p.40, on the bird-like *Kveldsjøgl* from Vest-Agder.

II. Dramatic Activities, II: Folkloristic Evidence

1. 'Grýla' in Icelandic, Faroese and Shetland seasonal custom

interrelation would seem to be strong. Furthermore, the fact that the *þingálp*, the *kelling*, the *hestur*, and *Háa-Þóra* all make an entrance from outside the room, and later leave it, not only emphasises the element of a deliberate 'performance', but also encourages the suggestion that these games might have grown out of earlier house-visits by disguised figures like *Lussi* and the *julebukk*.

Validating such an argument of Scandinavian origin, and deciding the actual age of these figures in Iceland are more problematic matters. On the surface, there are only hints to go on. A typical example of such a vague hint is the Icelandic superstition, still talked of nowadays, that those who are not given new clothes at Christmas will 'fara í jólaköttinn' ('dress up as the Christmas cat'/ 'become the 'Christmas cat'[330]). This curious expression raises the question of whether the cat was not also enacted at one time, especially when the Icelandic superstition has direct parallels in Norwegian beliefs related to the *julebukk*. As certain scholars have suggested, the relationship between these two figures, theoretically, may have very early roots, like those shared by the *þingálp* and the *julebukk*.[331]

4. 'Grýla' in Icelandic, Faroese and Shetland Seasonal Custom

There are, however, several more trustworthy pieces of evidence which suggest a tradition of costumed house-visits and procession *was* known in Iceland prior to the time of *vikivaki* games and the Stóraborg mask. This evidence not only provides a logical background for monstrous costumed female figures such as the *kelling* and *Háa-Þóra*, but also offers a firm link with early Norwegian tradition. The key figure here is the present day associate of the *jólaköttur*, namely *Grýla*, the legendary mother of the Icelandic *jólasveinar* ('Christmas lads'), who was supposed to visit farms at Christmas looking for badly behaved children to place in her sack, very much like the figure of Lussi in Norway.[332]

---

[330] See Jón Árnason, in *Íslenzkar þjóðsögur*, II, p.570, where the expression 'klæða jólaköttinn' ('dress the Christmas cat') is also mentioned; see also Árni Björnsson, *Í jólaskapi*, p.64. This particular aspect is taken up by Weiser-Aall who, in *Julenissen*, p.37, makes the suggestion that the expression 'að fara í jólaköttinn' originally implied 'å kle seg som julekatt' ('to dress as the Christmas cat').

[331] See Weiser-Aall, *Julenissen*, p.37, and Guðmundur Ólafsson, 'Jólakötturinn', 112–119. Guðmundur suggests that the costumed figure of the *jólaköttur* might originate in an Icelandic St Nicholas tradition reaching back to the early twelfth century, the cat, like the *julebukk*, being a development from a Devil figure. (On this questionable argument, see above, *section B.5*.) The link between the *jólaköttur* and *julebukk* is also noted by Árni Björnsson, in *Í jólaskapi*, p.64. Árni, however, argues that the Icelandic expression was probably borrowed from Norway within the last two hundred years, the name of the creature altering because of the scarcity of goats in Iceland.

[332] See Jón Árnason, *Íslenzkar þjóðsögur*, I, pp.218–219 (a description largely based on Guðmundur Erlendsson's *Grýlukvæði*; see below, note 418), and the various descriptions given of Grýla in the *Grýlukvæði* published in Ólafur Davíðsson, *Íslenzkar gátur*, IV, pp.111–148. See also Árni Björnsson, 'Hjátrú á jólum', 113–119. Concerning Scandinavian parallels to the figure of *Grýla*, in the form of *Lussi*, *Guro Rysserova* and the

G. A Shared Tradition of 'Folk Drama'

Grýla was clearly recognised as an ugly troll figure in Iceland at least as far back as the early fourteenth century when her name is listed among those of other ogresses ('trollkvinna') in the AM 748 manuscript of *Skáldskaparmál*.³³³ Of greater interest, however, is the earlier appearance of the names Steingrímr Skinngrýluson and Grýlu-Brandr in Sturla Þórðarson's *Íslendinga saga* (mid-thirteenth century).³³⁴ Some context for these names is provided by the following 'Grýla verse', supposedly uttered threateningly by Loftr Pálsson as he rode onto the enemy farm of Breiðabólstaðr in the summer of 1221:

4. *'Grýla'* in Icelandic, Faroese and Shetland seasonal custom

> Hér ferr Grýla í garð ofan
> ok hefir á sér hala fimmtán.³³⁵
>
> (Here comes Grýla down into the field
> with fifteen tails on her.)

This verse, recorded in *Íslendinga saga*, demands particular attention. Not only does it confirm that the modern belief about a tailed, animal-like Grýla coming *down* onto farms (from the mountains?) was already in existence in the thirteenth century; it also suggests, albeit indirectly, that Loftr was placing himself in the role of *Grýla* when he chanted or sang the verse. This latter suggestion might be regarded as an overstatement. However, if it is placed alongside another thirteenth-century expression from *Þorgils saga skarða*, describing how certain *men* (Þorgils Böðvarsson skarði and Þorvarðr Þórarinsson) had 'behaved like *grýlur* (been

---

Juleskrei, Stallo, and the Norwegian *julesveiner*, see, for example, Lid, *Joleband*, pp.51–57, and pp.60–62, and *Jolesveinar*, pp.44–48; Olrik and Ellekilde, *Nordens gudeverden*, II, pp.944–951; Bø, *Vår norske jul*, pp.90–96; and Eike, 'Oskoreia', passim.

³³³ *Edda* (1926), p.197.

³³⁴ See *Sturlunga saga* (1878), I, p.244, and II, p.171. As Guðbrandur Vigfússon notes here (I, p.244), one later paper MS replaces the name 'Skinngrýluson' with 'Skinngreifuson'. In the circumstances, this is no less interesting since, while it might considered a simple copying error, the new word reflects the copiest's understanding of the passage and its context. Regarding the dating of *Íslendinga saga*, see, for example, Jónas Kristjánsson, *Eddas and sagas*, p.194.

³³⁵ *Íslendinga saga*, in *Sturlunga saga* (1878), I, p.246. A further reference to the *movement* of Grýla is made in another verse contained in *Íslendinga saga*: 'Hvat er um? hví kveðum sæta? heim gengr sterkr af verki?/ Vitu rekkar nú nökkut nýlegs um för Grýlu?' ('What is going on? Why should we talk of making terms? Is Strong (a man) going home from his work?/ Have you warriors heard anything new about the passage of Grýlu?'): *Sturlunga saga* (1878), I, p.283. Considered in relation to the above verse, these lines with their unanswered questions raise an intriguing parallel to the verse accompanying the Theoderik version of the Kölbigk dance as it occurs in the *Old Swedish legendarium*, now placed in the context of a St Magnus legend in Orkney. The verse runs as follows: 'Redh(u) kompana redhobone jwer thiokka skogha/ Oc gildo mz synd venisto jomfrw/ hwi standom vi hwi gangom vi ey' ('The prepared company rode/ over thick forests/ And banqueted with their lovely maiden./ Why do we stand, why do we not move?') The original verse in Latin from the twelfth century runs: 'Equitabat Bovo per silvam frondosam,/ Ducebat sibi Merswinden formosam,/ Quid stamus? cur non imus?': Strömbäck, 'Den underbara årsdansen', 65; and *Ett forn-svenskt legendarium*, II, p.877. Regarding the figure of Bovo/ Bovi see further above, note 53.

4. 'Grýla' in Icelandic, Faroese and Shetland seasonal custom

threatening) during the summer',[336] and the evidence concerning Grýla's etymological relatives further south in the North Atlantic Islands, the pieces begin to fall into place. Indeed, the evidence in question from the Faroe Islands and Shetland also helps to explain why two *men* should have the element *grýla* in their names, and why in one case, this element is connected with animal skin ('Skinngrýla').

In the Faroe Islands, as in Iceland, 'Grýla' is known as an ugly, female supernatural being. Here, however, her bestial qualities seem to have more prominence since she supposedly bears more likeness to a two-legged sheep than to a woman, having 'a sheep's body, but walking upright like a man'.[337] This description is strongly reminiscent of other accounts of Scandinavian costumed figures, especially those concerning the *julebukk*,[338] and therefore it is perhaps of no surprise to find that in the Faroes, the word *grýla* is also applied to a 'a person (dressed as a troll or some such being) wearing a mask in front of his/ her face, who, at the beginning of Lent went from house to house.'[339] This acted *grýla* tradition continues to this day on the days preceding Lent, and especially on what used to be called *grýlukvøld* ('Grýla night'), the night of Shrove Tuesday.[340] On the evidence of Svabo's dictionary, the tradition was well known in the Faroes in the late eighteenth century, at which time the costumed figure was also known as 'Lengeføsta'/ 'langaføsta'/ 'Langefaste' ('long fast', meaning Lent), a name which might conceivably also have been related to a

---

[336] 'Sturla (Þórðarsson) . . . þótti þeir gört hafa sér grýlur um sumarit': *Sturlunga saga* (1878), II, p.213. The expression, 'gera grýla' is explained in *Sturlunga saga* (1946), II, p.307, as meaning 'sýna fjandskap, glettast til við' ('show enmity' or 'joke with'). See also *Þórðar saga hreðu*, p.188, where the plural word is used in a similar sense: 'Ekki hirði ek um grýlur yðrar' ('Your threats do not bother me'). The 'grýlur' in this case are again people, namely the brothers of the threatening party. Another reference of the same type is found in *Michaels saga*, in *Heilagra manna sögur*, I, p.683: 'Her hia fram kostar uvinrinn aa . . . at maðrinn . . . teli þat sem opptaz i huginn, at kristnir menn ok skirðir meghi ekki firirfaraz, þo at læ(r)ðir menn geyri grylur afheimis ok sege slikt, er þeim likar' ('Here, the Archenemy does his best . . . to make man . . . imagine that no Christian will ever suffer damnation, even if learned men *make threats/ ugly images* of the afterlife and say whatever they wish').

[337] Williamson, *The Atlantic islands*, p.248. See also Jakobsen, 'Ordsamling', p.97; Thuren, *Folksangen*, p.66; and Jacobsen and Matras, *Føroysk-Donsk orðabók*, p.131, where a *grýla* is described initially as 'et uhyre som man skræmte børn med' ('a monster that people frightened children with').

[338] See the reference to description of the two-legged *julebukk* given in note 84 above.

[339] 'Person (udklædt som trold el. lign) med maske for andsigtet, der i (begyndelsen af) fasten gik fra hus til hus': Jacobsen and Matras, *Føroysk-Donsk orðabók*, p.131. Regarding these figures, see further, Svabo, *Dictionarium*, p.290; Hammershaimb, 'Færøiske skikke', 308–309; Jakobsen, 'Ordsamling', p.97; Thuren, *Folksangen*, pp.65–66; Rasmussen, *Sær er siður*, pp.139–141; Williamson, *The Atlantic islands*, pp.247; Bregenhøj, *Helligtrekongersløb*, pp.87–89; Joensen, *Fólk og mentan*, pp.202–209; and Heinesen, 'Grylen'. Thuren notes in *Folksangen*, pp.65–66, that the tradition seems to have been dying out on Suðuroy in 1821. In spite of this, the tradition is still alive all over the Faroes today, albeit in a slightly diluted form.

[340] See Rasmussen, *Sær er siður*, p.140. Williamson, in *The Atlantic islands*, p.247, suggests that *grýlukvöld* took place on the Monday rather than the Tuesday.

G. A Shared Tradition of 'Folk Drama'

comparatively 'long' figure, like the Icelandic *Háa-Þóra*.³⁴¹ The costumes of the Faroese *grýla* figures, however, were variable, probably largely dependent on the material available to the performers. Nowadays, for example, shop-bought masks are used,³⁴² but in the past there was need for more imagination. For example, in one account from 1821, 'Langefasten' is described as having a 'large coat of seaweed which dragged behind her like a tail, a rusty black hook in each hand', and a great skin bag on her back which she rattled.³⁴³ Seaweed also formed the basis for the *grýla* costumes which Rasmus Rasmussen describes as having been used by two poverty-stricken young children from Miðvágur at the turn of the century. This brother and sister literally covered themselves in seaweed, which was hung on their shoulders, tucked into their belts, and wrapped around their heads like hair, as well as hanging behind them in the form of tails. In addition to the above, they had animal skin around their necks, fish guts drawn up upon their arms 'like muffs', and blackened faces.³⁴⁴ Like most Faroese *grýlur*, this desperate pair used to visit houses in the hope of collecting gifts such as meat and clothing.

The greatest, and most challenging enigma, however, is the costume described by William Heinesen in his short story 'Grylen' (1957) which describes the *Grýla* tradition on the fictional Faroese island of 'Stapa'. The single *Grýla* in this tale seems to be a predominantly feminine being, but her ancient costume is composed of horn, wool, fur, rags, a bottle, and, most important of all, a large wooden phallus ('Standaren').³⁴⁵ She ('hun') is described directly as having a 'horned head', and is 'huge, much like a stack of peats', dragging 'a long rustling tail behind her' which 'rattles and bumps like empty pots and kettles'.³⁴⁶ Occasionally, she 'stretches herself

4. *'Grýla'* in Icelandic, Faroese and Shetland seasonal custom

---

³⁴¹ The MSS of J. C. Svabo's *Dictionarium Færoense* were written between 1773–1800. Here *grýla* is spelled 'grujla', a related word being the adjective 'grûiliur', meaning 'abominable': Svabo, *Dictionarium*, p.290. Regarding 'langeføsta', see Hammershaimb, 'Færøiske skikke', 308; and Svabo, *Dictionarium*, p.491, where 'Lengaføsta' is described, like *grýla*, as a 'bugbear used to frighten children at Lent; a costumed figure' ('Bussemand hvormed man skræmmer Børn i Fasten. Manducus').

³⁴² See the photograph in Joensen, *Fólk og mentan*, p.202, and Bregenhøj, *Helligtrekongersløb*, p.88.

³⁴³ 'Stor Tangstakke, som slæbe bag after hende som Halen og en rustet sort Krog i hver Haand', and 'paa Bagen en stor Skindpose, som hun rasler med': Thuren, quoting a letter by J. H. Schrøter, in *Folksangen*, pp.67–68. This description echoes Hammershaimb's mention of a facial mask and a tail of seaweed ('maske for ansigtet, halen af tang o. lign') in 'Færøiske skikke' (1851), 308.

³⁴⁴ See Rasmussen, *Sær er síður*, p.140: 'Tari varð hongdur uttan á tær spjarrarnar, tey vóru í, nakað tvörtur um herðarnar, og nakað upp á eitt sterkt beltisband. Um hálsin hövdu tey ein bleytan skinnlepa, og upp á skövningarnar vóru drignir fiskamagar til muffur. Reipatari og hoytari varð vavdur upp á hövdið til hár. Gekkaskort hövdu tey ikki, men vóru málað svört við kjönnroyki, og síðst fingu tey ein tongul til hala.'

³⁴⁵ See Heinesen, 'Grylen', p.35: 'Det er her altsammen, skinde og klude, hovedet, flasken og standaren.' Translation by Brønner, from 'The night of the Gryla', p.17.

³⁴⁶ See Heinesen, 'Grylen', p.38: 'Hun løfter og sænker det hornede hoved... Stor er hun, som en tørvestak at se, en lang, raslende hale slæber hun efter sig, den runger og skramler som af tomme kedler og kasseroller.' See also p.33: 'Hun er meget lådden og bærer horn

4. 'Grýla' in Icelandic, Faroese and Shetland seasonal custom

full length with her snout to the ground', just like *Háa-Þóra* on her entrance into the room.³⁴⁷ Finally, at the lonely climax of her tour of the island settlement, she raises herself as high as possible and then temporarily falls to the ground as if dead.³⁴⁸ Direct associations with older fertility beliefs are implied by the supposed superstition that the 'Standaren' has the quality of being able to bestow fertility on barren women.³⁴⁹

Until recently, very little was known about the background of this unique account which bears so much resemblance to the descriptions of the costumed figures in both the Icelandic *vikivaki* games and the Scandinavian traditions examined above, and especially to the accounts of *Stallo* and the horned *julebukk*. The story itself is fictional, but Heinesen stated that it contained an authentic portrayal of 'pagan ritual' that was still being performed on one of the smaller islands in the Faroes in the nineteen fifties.³⁵⁰ This somewhat vague statement has since been supported by new evidence proving that Heinesen's story was based on a factual account concerning traditions on the small northerly island of Svínoy which Heinesen heard from Esmar Hansen, a wholesale merchant from the island.³⁵¹ While the details of Hansen's account are unknown, a recent Faroese television interview with several of the older inhabitants of Svínoy has confirmed that there only used to be one *Grýla* on Svínoy, and that this figure was usually performed by the same man who dressed in skins, kept a bag for offerings under his costume, and used a wooden mask, possibly like that found in Stóraborg in Iceland (see *figs 67–68*).³⁵² Heinesen's account, therefore, must be taken as having had a solid basis in fact, the story suggesting that the traditional Svínoy *Grýla* Hansen knew was not only skin-clad but also horned and equipped with a phallus.

It might be noted that neither the Svínoy *Grýla* nor the costumed children described by Rasmussen speak in their normal voices. For the most part, they make animal noises and use 'reverse speech' like the *julebukker*

---

og hale' ('She is very shaggy and has horns and a tail'). Translations by Brønner, from 'The night of the Gryla', p.19, and p.15.

³⁴⁷ Heinesen, 'Grylen', p.38: 'Undertiden standser Grylen, lægger sig udslettet med trynet i jorden.' Translation by Brønner, from 'The night of the Gryla', p.19.

³⁴⁸ See Heinesen, 'Grylen', p.43.

³⁴⁹ See Heinesen, 'Grylen', p.39.

³⁵⁰ Jones, *William Heinesen*, p.164. See also Joensen, *Fólk og mentan*, p.203.

³⁵¹ I am extremely grateful to Professor Jóan Pauli Joensen of the Faroese Academy for providing me with information about Heinesen's sources. According to Professor Joensen, the artist Bárður Jákupsson heard a different interview that was taken with Esmar Hansen by the late Professor Mortan Nolsøe, in which Hansen gave more information about the Svínoy *Grýla* than Heinesen includes in his story. In other words, Heinesen only describes part of the Svínoy tradition: as Professor Joensen writes in his letter dated 20 January 1994, 'Esmar nágreiniliga segði Mortan Nolsøe frá grýluni, og ... hann segð nógv meira enn tað, sum William Heinesen hevur skrivað, ið sostatt bert er ein partur av teimum "fænomenum", sum hoyrdu til ta veruligu grýluna.'

³⁵² An interview with Jukim frá Svínoy and two other men on the programme *Manna millum* shown by the Faroese television service (Sjónvarp Føroya) on 17 February 1991. The programme also shows a reconstruction of the original Svínoy *Grýla* costume, and pictures of Svínoy children in modern-day home-made *grýla* masks.

G. A Shared Tradition of 'Folk Drama'

described above.³⁵³ Heinesen's 'Grylen', however, occasionally sings, 'chanting old rhymes and dark refrains'.³⁵⁴ These 'old rhymes' are probably related to the fact that in earlier times the *langefaste* is said to have introduced herself with the following words, albeit spoken with a 'twisted voice' ('fordrejet mæle'):

4. 'Grýla' in Icelandic, Faroese and Shetland seasonal custom

> Oman kemur grýla frá görðum
> við fjöriti hölum,
> bjálg á baki, skálm í hendi,
> kemur at krivja búkin úr börnunum,
> ið gráta eftir kjöti í föstu.³⁵⁵
>
> (Down comes Grýla from the outer fields,
> with forty tails,
> a bag on her back, a sword/ knife in her hand,
> coming to carve out the stomachs of the children
> who cry for meat during Lent.)

The direct association between this verse and the costumed figure is emphasised by the shared characteristics of the tails and the bag which obviously form part of the traditional Faroese *grýla* costume. The use of the verse by a costumed figure also offers an interesting analogy to Loftr Pálsson's early thirteenth-century rendition of part of a closely related variation of this verse when approaching a farm.

The existence of this verse in the Faroes raises several pertinent questions. Was it brought to the Faroes from Iceland, or do both versions stem from an older common tradition? There seems little question that the Faroese did not regard Loftr as having been the composer of this well-known verse which has survived in Faroese oral tradition free of all contextual references to Loftr's attack on Breiðabólstaðr. Loftr was clearly quoting a verse that already existed in the oral tradition. Yet within what context did the verse survive in the oral tradition? Is it possible that it was always associated with a recognised seasonally acted figure that was regarded by many as a threat?³⁵⁶

---

353 See Heinesen, 'Grylen', pp.33–35, p.38, and p.43; the interview on *Manna millum*, and Rasmussen, *Sær er síður*, p.141. See also note 107 above, and note 374 below.
354 Heinesen, 'Grylen', pp.33–34: 'Undertiden synger hun også, kvæder gamle rim og forblommede omkvæd.' Translation by Brønner, from 'The night of the Gryla', p.15.
355 Hammershaimb, 'Færøiske skikke', 308. See also the discussion of translation in Thuren, *Folksangen*, p.65. Two slightly different variants of this song are contained in Williamson, *The Atlantic Islands*, pp.247–248, and in Rasmussen, *Sær er síður*, p.204, where the verse runs as follows: 'Oman kemur grýla *av* görðum/ við *fjöruti* hölum,/ *bjölg* á baki, *skölm* í hendi,/ kemur at *skera* búkin burtur úr börnum/ ið gráta eftir kjöti í föstu.' (My emphases.) Most recently, in another variation read on the Faroese television programme *Manna millum* (see above, note 352), the fourth line runs: 'kemur at skera *tungum* úr börnunum' ('coming to cut tongues out of the children').
356 In order to survive in the oral tradition, a piece of 'occasional verse' must have a particular value, purpose, or association to keep it alive. For example, it might contain some life philosophy (a piece of gnomic wisdom), or historical information, or might be associated with a particular poet or event. The *grýla* verse has none of the above. It is

4. 'Grýla' in Icelandic, Faroese and Shetland seasonal custom

Concerning the age of the Faroese tradition, it is impossible to ignore the fact that since the eighteenth century, at least, both the acted figure and the verse have been firmly linked to the Christian festival of Lent. Nonetheless, the figure of *Grýla* encountered in both the verse and the costumed tradition can hardly be envisaged as having had a Christian background. Bearing this in mind, it is interesting to note the appearance in the verse of the slightly archaic word *skálm(ur)*, meaning a 'short sword' or elementary form of halberd. Such an item would have fitted well into a more ancient context like that of Loftr's attack, and also makes *Grýla* faintly reminiscent of the stave- and sword-bearing horned figures depicted on both the Torslunda matrix and the Oseberg tapestry.[357] It should be also be noted that, like the Norwegian *julebukker*, the disguised *grýla* visitor always demands a form of offering. In general, as Thuren has suggested, the associations between the Faroese *Grýla* and Lent are probably superficial and comparatively recent; the likelihood must be that the *Grýla* tradition was linked originally to another period of the year.[358] Considering this, Joensen has recently suggested that the Faroese *grýlur* might have had earlier connections with other Faroese costumed traditions that were predominantly associated with Christmas dances, that is to say, with two mysterious figures known as the *jólhestur* ('Christmas horse') and *jólahøna* ('Christmas hen'). On the basis of the little information available on these two disguises, there would seem to be little doubt that they too belong firmly within mainland Scandinavian tradition, closely related to not only the *julebukk*, but also the *þingálp*, and the birdlike *julegoppa*.[359] Indeed,

---

simply about a spirit. This raises the possibility of the verse having existed within a particular living context like that of a regularly performed tradition.

[357] See further Thuren, *Folksangen*, p.65, note 4; and Jacobsen and Matras, *Føroysk-Donsk orðabók*, p.384. As Helga Kress has recently pointed out in *Máttugar meyjar*, 133–134, female trolls in the legendary sagas often appear armed with a *skálm* and a wooden trough, as in *Grettis saga*, p.212. Helga argues that a *skálm* was a kitchen utensil, half of a pair of scissors, which the troll primarily used to cut up the bodies of her male victims, the meat then being carried home in the trough. Whether it was primarily male meat that female trolls were after (as Helga suggests) is questionable, but this early picture of female trolls collecting meat and cutting it off with a *skálm* is interesting in the context of the Faroese and Shetland dramatic traditions under discussion here.

[358] Thuren, *Folksangen*, p.66. A comparable transference of tradition is found in the appearance of 'goat' figures in the Swedish carnival processions described by Olaus Magnus. See the reference given in note 96 above.

[359] Regarding these figures, see Joensen, *Fólk og mentan*, p.204; and Jacobsen, Matras and Poulsen, *Føroysk-Donsk orðabók: Eykabind*, p.102. On pp.197–198 of *Fólk og mentan*, Joensen notes that the *jólhestur* involved a person acting the role of a horse at dances, apparently as part of some game on the second day of Christmas in which the horse answered questions ('Jólhesturin var spurdur um ymist og mátti svara'). The costume was sometimes made of a genuine horse-skin, but the central feature seems again to have been the 'two blocks of wood', or 'clacking jaws' also found on the *julebukk* and *þingálp* ('tvær fjalir, sum hann læt dúgliga við til kjaft'). As with both of these figures, the *jólhestur* was especially known for disturbing women. The *jólahøna* is described in Matras, 'Fornur hugsunarháttur', 180–181, as a person covered in a woollen blanket, with two short sticks poking out in front and behind. The front stick was then used to pick at the ground in a hen-like fashion, similar to the behaviour of the Swedish

G. A Shared Tradition of 'Folk Drama'

while the Svinoy *Grýla* provides a possible 'missing link' between the *jule-bukk* and the *þingálp*, the appearance of the Faroese *jólhestur* at dances offers a tentative connection between the thirteenth-century figure of 'Arnaldus Jolahest' from Bergen,³⁶⁰ and the *hestleikur* of the Icelandic *vikivaki* games. It also emphasises the point made earlier about the danger of reading too much into the *form* of costume used by the 'horse' figure in Iceland: Joensen's *jólhestur* with the 'clacking jaws' could just as easily be seen as a *þingálp* or *julebukk* rather than a horse.

Interestingly enough, there is even further evidence concerning the *Grýla* tradition which not only supports the idea of an intrinsic link between the figure, the verse and costumed disguise, but also underlines the probability that the tradition must have been related originally to the winter months and must have had roots in mainland Scandinavia. Until very recently, a directly related name for a seasonal disguise, *grølek* (spelled variously as *grøli/ grölik/ grulek/ gruli/ grulick/ grulja/ grülik* and *grillock*), was also known on the islands of Unst and Mainland in Shetland.³⁶¹ The *grøleks* were a group of young men, who used to go 'hoosamylla' (between houses) wearing high, plaited-straw hats, veils, and 'dresses' of plaited straw³⁶² and/or black material.³⁶³ One of the group also used to carry a bag made from a complete sheep-skin, similar to that borne by the Faroese *Grýla*.³⁶⁴ These figures used to appear several times a year, on 'Winter Sunday' (14 October), All Saints' Day (1 November), during the Christmas period, and at Shrovetide.³⁶⁵

4. 'Grýla' in Icelandic, Faroese and Shetland seasonal custom

---

julegoppa. See above, note 139 on comparable Scandinavian bird-costumes. See also the description of *Háa-Þóra*'s behaviour in note 287 above, and Hammershaimb, 'Færøiske skikke', 309, on other Faroese dances and songs that seem to have involved animal costume.
³⁶⁰ See references given in *Chapter I*, note 247.
³⁶¹ See Jakobsen, *An etymological dictionary*, I, p.271 and pp.274–275; Saxby, *Shetland traditional lore*, p.77 and p.86; Macleod Banks, *British calendar customs: Orkney and Shetland*, p.75; Marwick, *The folklore of Orkney*, pp.106–107; Balneaves, *The windswept isles*, pp.230–231, and p.311; and Newall, 'Up-Helly Aa', 42–44. The relationship between the words *grýla* and *grølek* was first commented on by Jakobsen, in *Det norrøne sprog*, p.104 (see also *An etymological dictionary*, I, p.275) and has since been supported by Lid, in *Joleband*, pp.59–60, and *Jolesveinar*, pp.58–60; the *Scottish national dictionary*, IV, p.427; and most recently by Ásgeir Blöndal Magnússon, in *Íslenzk orðsifjabók*, p.284. In spite of this, to the best of my knowledge, no examination has ever been made of the relationship between the Faroese and Shetland costumed figures and the Icelandic Grýla, apart from a brief mention in Jón Samsonarson's 'Marghala Grýla', pp.52–54.
³⁶² See Jakobsen, *An etymological dictionary*, I, p.274; Saxby, *Shetland traditional lore*, p.77; and Newall, 'Up-Helly Aa', 42, who suggests that the oldest costumes were made of straw. The expression to go 'hoosamylla' is refered to in Macleod Banks, *British calendar customs: Orkney and Shetland*, p.75.
³⁶³ See Newall, 'Up-Helly Aa', 42, quoting an account which talks of two groups of 'Grulicks' on Unst, the White and the Black. The latter group wore black clothes, the former costumes of straw. The Black group, also known as 'Raiders', were known to burst into the room, while the others used to enter dancing.
³⁶⁴ Saxby, *Shetland traditional lore*, p.77 (Unst).
³⁶⁵ See, for example, Jakobsen, *An etymological dictionary*, I, p.274. 'Guizing', however,

II. Dramatic Activities, II: Folkloristic Evidence

4. 'Grýla' in Icelandic, Faroese and Shetland seasonal custom

On the other Shetland islands of Yell and Fetlar, masqueraders of a similar kind appeared under the name of *skeklers* (or *skekels*).[366] The *skeklers*, obviously belonging to the same tradition as the *grøleks*, appeared primarily at Hallowe'en (31 October – 1 November), Martinmas (11 November), Christmas,[367] and also at weddings,[368] led by a figure known as the *skudler* (*skudlar/ skuddler/ scuddler*).[369] Their costumes, like those of the *grøleks*, closely resembled that of *Halm-Staffan* described above (see *fig.70* and *fig.52*), involving a long straw 'petticoat' called a 'gloy', straw leggings, a short straw cloak, and a tall, pointed hat made of the same material, all of which tended to be decorated with ribbons.[370] Their faces were often covered with coloured handkerchiefs.[371] Other accounts, which might refer to either the *grøleks* or the *skeklers*, also

is also recorded as taking place during the Christmas and New Year period in Lerwick on Mainland, in Macleod Banks, *British calendar customs: Orkney and Shetland*, p.44, p.83 and pp.92–93. Saxby, in *Shetland traditional lore*, p.77, talks also of appearances on Up-Helly-A', 29 January; see also Marwick, *The folklore of Orkney*, p.106. This festival, in its present form, is relatively recent: see Newall, 'Up-Helly Aa', passim.

[366] See Jakobsen, *An etymological dictionary*, I, p.275, and II, pp.778–779; Marwick, *The folklore of Orkney*, p.91 and pp.115–117; and Newall, 'Up-Helly Aa', 42–44.

[367] See Hibbert, *Description*, p.289 and p.293; Edmondston, 'Notes', 470–472; Newall, 'Up-Helly Aa', 42–43; and Marwick, *The folklore of Orkney*, pp.115–117, where it is noted that it usually took the *skeklers* two or three nights to complete their round of visits.

[368] See Marwick, *The folklore of Orkney*, p.91, and Moffatt, *Shetland*, pp.181–184.

[369] See Hibbert, *Description*, p.293; Jakobsen, *An etymological dictionary*, II, p.778; Moffatt, *Shetland*, p.181; Marwick, *The folklore of Orkney*, p.91 and p.116; and Newall, 'Up-Helly Aa', 43. Saxby, in *Shetland traditional lore*, p.77, also talks of the 'Grüliks' (probably on Unst) as being led by a 'Skuddler', which offers a direct link between the two customs. According to Alfred Johnston, the 'Skudlar' had become known as the 'Supreme Chief Guizer' before 1889, and later (before 1911) adopted the more recognisable title of 'Guizer Jarl', an annually elected figure in charge of the 'Up-Helly Aa' activities: see Macleod Banks, *British calendar customs: Orkney and Shetland*, p.45.

[370] See Jakobsen, *An etymological dictionary*, II, p.778; Hibbert, *Description*, p.293; Edmondston, 'Notes', 472; Black and Thomas, *County folk-lore*, III, pp.210–211; Marwick, *The folklore of Orkney*, p.91; Mitchell, *Up-helly-aa*, pp.79–80 and p.119; and Moffatt, *Shetland*, p.183. Another photograph of the *Skeklers* as they appeared in 1939 is given in Mitchell, *Up-helly-aa*, p.80. Note also the description quoted in Black and Thomas, *County folk-lore*, III, pp.204–205, of the leader of a troup of New Year guizers (including a 'carrying horse') who wore 'a cap made of straw, with his name lettered on the front, a collar of straw round his neck, a belt of straw around his waist, and a band of straw round his right arm.' This figure, who has the role of 'the gentleman' and is never directly associated with the *skeklers*, must nonetheless belong to the same tradition. The similarities with *Halm-Staffan* are emphasised still further by Fergusson's account (1884) quoted by Marwick, in *The folklore of Orkney*, p.116, which describes the whole group as standing 'like so many statues'. One, however, 'was far above the rest, and of gigantic dimensions'.

[371] Edmondston, 'Notes', 472; Macleod Banks, *British calendar customs: Orkney and Shetland*, p.77; and Black and Thomas, *County folk-lore*, III, p.210, where a 'white cambric napkin' is mentioned.

G. A Shared Tradition of 'Folk Drama'

4. 'Grýla' in Icelandic, Faroese and Shetland seasonal custom

Fig. 70. A group of "Skakelers" from Fetlar, Shetland.

mention white shirts or 'dresses' being worn above, or over the straw petticoats,[372] and 'long staves with which they kept rapping the floor'.[373]

Like the *julebukker* and the Faroese *grýlur*, these straw figures did not speak in a normal fashion when they visited houses. Instead, they made animal-like grunting noises, or (more recently) used 'reversed speech', going out of their way to avoid recognition.[374] Furthermore, as with all the Scandinavian traditions examined so far, the *skeklers* used to demand some form of offering on their winter visits, most particularly meat like the Faroese *grýlur*.[375]

One of the earliest descriptions of the *skeklers* comes from 1822 when Hibbert described the 'guisards', led by the 'Scudler' ('the proper *arbiter elegentiarum* of his party'), appearing after the Christmas sword dance on Papa Stour, and dancing alternately with the women present.[376] At that

---

[372] See Hibbert, *Description*, p.293; R. M. Fergusson, quoted in Macleod Banks, *British calendar customs: Orkney and Shetland*, p.77; and Black and Thomas, *County folk-lore*, III, pp.210–211.

[373] R. M. Fergusson, quoted in Macleod Banks, *British calendar customs: Orkney and Shetland*, p.77.

[374] See Marwick, *The folklore of Orkney*, p.116, and p.91 (on the importance of hiding identity). In his account of a wedding, quoted in Black and Thomas, *County folk-lore*, III, p.210, Robert Jamieson notes that the 'scuddler' made 'a snore' when he entered. Laurence Williamson, quoted in Marwick, *The folklore of Orkney*, p.116, mentions that they 'gave a sneeze' on entering. Regarding the comparable disguising of speech by the *julebukker* and *grýlur*, see notes 107 and 353 above.

[375] See Marwick, *The folklore of Orkney*, p.116. Indeed, it is possible that the demand for meat might explain why the *grýlur* came to be connected with Lent in the Faroes.

[376] See Hibbert, *Description*, p.289 and p.293. (Regarding the sword dance, see above section C.2.) The earliest account of the *skeklers* is found in Edmondston's *A view . . . of*

4. 'Grýla' in Icelandic, Faroese and Shetland seasonal custom

time, the tradition can hardly have been new, and the comment about the 'Scudler' dancing might well reflect older, more superstitious associations between the straw figures and fertility. In this sense, these figures provide a very interesting parallel to the mainland Scandinavian accounts of women dancing with straw figures like 'Bovi' and the straw *julbock*.[377] As mentioned above, the straw-clad *skeklers* seem to have been a regular feature of Shetland weddings where they would make a point of dancing with the bride and her 'maidens', sometimes leaving a gift of 'hansel money' behind them on their departure.[378] In some accounts, however, the visit appears to have had more ritualistic overtones. For example, in one case the *skudler* is said to have appeared with a straw besom, and then alone, 'danced around the room making protective gestures with his besom over the bride and groom'.[379] On other occasions, the *skeklers* (here known simply as 'guizers') entered one by one, the *skudler* then 'beginning a kind of solemn dance in which he was joined by five companions'.[380] The role of the *skudler* in these accounts as a priest-like master-of-ceremonies provides an enlightening, living parallel to the 'games leader' figures previously discussed, such as the *gadebasse* and *leikgoði*.[381]

The above accounts, however, also stress the hybrid nature of these Shetland customs which contain an intriguing mixture of various Scandinavian and Gælic folk tradition. For example, the custom of 'strawmen' or 'strawboys', led by a 'captain', and dressed in 'leggings, skirt, cape or coat, and tall conical mask rising from shoulder level, all of straw' appearing at weddings and bringing 'luck' by dancing with the bride and other women present was once also well known on the west coast of Ireland.[382] Like the *skeklers*, these figures occasionally carried sticks and were known to wear white 'petticoats' or white shirts, and decorate their pointed hats with

---

the Zetland Islands (1809), II, pp.64–65. Walter Scott, in *The pirate*, pp.169–172, describes a group of disguised 'Shoupeltins' who appear at the door following the sword dance, 'grotesquely habited, with false hair, and beards made of flax, and chaplets composed of seaware interwoven with shells and other marine productions' (p.170). No sources, however, are given for this odd description which has the distinct flavour of a decorative Jacobean masque, and bears no relation to Edmondston's account or Scott's own diary entry (see references given in note 193 above). The word 'Shoupeltins', however, is drawn from the name of another Shetland sea spirit, the *shøøpiltie* or *shoopiltee* (c.f. *sjópiltur* which in Icelandic would mean 'sea boy'): see Macleod Banks, *British calendar customs: Orkney and Shetland*, p.15. There is no evidence of this spirit ever having been impersonated.

[377] See note 54 above.
[378] See Marwick, *The folklore of Orkney*, p.91.
[379] Marwick, *The folklore of Orkney*, p.91.
[380] Marwick, *The folklore of Orkney*, p.91. See also the similar account of a wedding by Robert Jamieson quoted in Black and Thomas, *County folk-lore*, III, pp.210–211.
[381] See above, Chapter I, D.2.
[382] See Gailey, *Irish folk drama*, pp.74–75 and pp.91–93, and Haddon, 'A wedding dance-mask', 123–124, on traditions from west Ulster, Fermanagh, Cavan, Leitrim, Mayo, Roscommon, and Limerick. On other Irish straw figures connected with Mummers' plays and the 'Wrenboys', see Gailey, *Irish folk drama*, pp.48–49, p.54, p.57, pp.82–87, p.94, pp.97–98. On the role of the Irish 'captain', see the same book, p.15.

G. A Shared Tradition of 'Folk Drama'

ribbons or streamers.[383] There seems little doubt that the wedding aspect of the *grølek/ skekler* activities belongs to the same tradition as that of the Irish 'strawmen', and the same may apply to the use of straw costumes in the Shetlands.[384] Yet these features should not detract from the strong Scandinavian element that also exists in the *grølek/ skekler* traditions, or from the possibility of other earlier links with Scandinavian straw figures like *Halm-Staffan* and the Danish Bovi. Such connections are stressed by the regular appearances of the *grøleks* and *skeklers* not only at Hallowe'en, but also on the more important Scandinavian festivals of 'Winter Sunday' (14 October) and Yuletide, with which the Irish straw figures had much less intimate connections.

In this context, it should be noted that while the *skeklers*' use of staves (especially the element of rapping them on the floor) arguably might have some relation to the originally English Papa Stour sword dance mentioned above, they also offer parallels to both the sword/ stave carrying Faroese Grýla, and the 'knocking' and 'pecking' sounds associated with other figures like *Knut*, *Háa-Þóra*, the Faroese *jólahøna* and Swedish *julegoppa*.[385] Furthermore, as has been shown above, the use of white 'dresses' and ribboned pointed hats was not limited to Ireland. They were also known in Denmark and Sweden. Indeed, the use of such costumes, and the fact that the name 'Judas' was supposedly given to one of the group who had a face 'as black as Hornie', and a basket on his back,[386] suggests that in the distant past the *grølek/ skekler* tradition must have adopted, and half-forgotten, a *Stjärnspel* tradition from Sweden.[387] Indeed, some faint memory of this might be betrayed by a note in a more recent account that the 'grillocks' were also known as 'Swedes'.[388] There can be little doubt, though, that this was a later addition which never really succeeded in supplanting the basis of the native tradition of disguise. No *Stjärnspel* can be found in recorded Shetland tradition. There is not even any sign of a 'star'.

Nonetheless, the strongest evidence that the *grølek* and *skekler*

4. *'Grýla'* in Icelandic, Faroese and Shetland seasonal custom

---

[383] See Gailey, *Irish folk drama*, p.52, p.81, p.87 and p.92. Gailey, however, feels that the white 'smock' did not originate in Ireland, but was imported from southern England with the Mummers' plays: *Irish folk drama*, p.52.

[384] On the fading of the tradition of straw costumes in the nineteenth century in Shetland, see Edmondston, 'Notes', 472. Regarding the scarcity of straw costumes in England, see the references given above in note 252.

[385] Regarding the sword dance, see *section C.2* above. On the image of the Faroese Grýla carrying a *skálm*, see note 355 above. Regarding *Knut*'s 'knocking out' of Christmas, see the references in note 8 above. As regards the action of rapping at the ground made by Háa-Þóra, the Færoese *jólahøna*, and the Swedish *julegoppa*, see notes 287 and 359 above.

[386] See Marwick, *The folklore of Orkney*, p.116; and R. M. Fergusson, quoted in Macleod Banks, *British calendar customs: Orkney and Shetland*, p.77.

[387] Regarding 'Judas' and the use of white costumes and decorated pointed hats by the *stjärngossar*, see, for example, Celander, *Stjärngossar*, pp.324–325 and pp.357–358, and pp.412–422. The costumes in the Danish *Helligtrekongerspill* were almost identical, but there Judas seems to have been a much rarer figure. See Schmidt, 'Helligtrekongersangere' passim.

[388] See Balneaves, *The windswept isles*, p.231.

4. 'Grýla' in Icelandic, Faroese and Shetland seasonal custom

traditions were neither wholly imported from Ireland, nor based on the remnants of an English sword dance play or a Swedish *Stjärnspel*, is found in the names of the traditions which testify to deeper connections with with Norwegian and Icelandic tradition. The word *skekler*, for example, might originate in words like *jólaskekil/ joleskjekel* (Faroese/ northern Norwegian), meaning a Christmas troll figure;[389] *joleskjekedl* (Norwegian), a dialect word from Sogn summing up the effect of Christmas food and drink on a fasting stomach;[390] *skulkar* (Norwegian), meaning a shirker, or party gate-crasher;[391] or, most likely of all, the word *kveldsjøgl/ kveldsgjøgla* which is an alternative name for a house-visiting *julebukk* figure in some areas of Norway.[392] Indeed, earlier links with an animal figure might be supported even further if the word *skekler* is related to the Old Icelandic word *skekill* in the sense of the 'shanks or legs of an animal's skin when stretched out'.[393] Such a link with a horned figure like the *julebukk* might also explain why the 'Judas' figure was more easily adopted than the other features of the *Stjärnspel*. Some support for this particular theory is found in at least one account which suggests that the 'Judas' character was sometimes known as the 'hind', which, if it is not related to the Norwegian noa-term 'Hinmannen' ('The Other One') used for the Devil, could refer back to some earlier horned figure like the Icelandic *hjörtur* or Heinesen's 'Grylen'.[394] A similar argument applies to the word *skudler*, which, as Árni Björnsson has pointed out, might be etymologically related to the Icelandic word *skolli* (pronounced 'skodli') which is used for the Devil. If these two words are related, then the likelihood must be that the *skudler* once bore a closer resemblance to the traditional Devil. Again, this might reflect some memory of the wearing of horns, or animal skins.[395]

The most direct link with traditions from elsewhere, however, is the word *grølek* which is not only directly related to the Icelandic and Faroese name *Grýla*, but also appears to be applied again to an essentially feminine, troll-like creature which was traditionally acted by men. Even more interesting is that the disguised figures in Shetland are also indirectly connected

---

[389] Lid, *Jolesveinar*, p.60, and *Joleband*, p.62. See also below, note 407.
[390] Sjur Bøyum, 'Gamler truer', p.97.
[391] See Eike, 'Oskoreia', 260. As might be apparent from the examples given above, this link to weddings would be particularly applicable in the case of the *skeklers*. See also Balneaves, *The windswept isles*, p.311, and Black and Thomas, *County folk-lore*, III, pp.213–214. Disguised party-crashing at weddings was also well-known in Norway.
[392] See Lid, *Joleband*, pp.40–41. See also Lid's examination of the etymology of the word *skekel* in *Jolesveinar*, p.63, and *fig.*55 above.
[393] Cleasby and Guðbrandur Vigfússon, *An Icelandic-English dictionary*, p.543.
[394] See Marwick, *The folklore of Orkney*, p.116. For an example of the expression, 'Hinmannen', see, for instance, Bø et al., *Norske segner*, p.215.
[395] See above *section B.5* on the clerical associations between the *julebukk* and the Devil. As Árni Björnsson has also pointed out in conversation (12 April 1991), this association might well offer an explanation for unique Icelandic name for Blind Man's Buff, i.e. *Skollaleikur*. (On this game, see Ólafur Davíðsson, *Íslenzkar gátur*, II, pp.103–105.) The name *Skollaleikur* has never been logically explained, but it might make more sense if it was originally linked to a masked figure like the *skudler*.

G. A Shared Tradition of 'Folk Drama'

to the 'Grýla verse', of which yet another variant was discovered on the island of Foula. One of the most revealing features of this particular verse, however, is the fact that here the ogress is not named Grýla, or even Grølek, but has instead been given the other, more common name for the equivalent acted figure in Shetland, namely 'Skekla'. In other words, this name, which is almost interchangeable with the word *grølek* concerning the acted tradition, has been substituted for *grølek* in the verse on the basis of local beliefs and traditions:

4. 'Grýla' in Icelandic, Faroese and Shetland seasonal custom

> Skekla komena rina tuna
> swa'rta hæsta blæta bruna
> fo'mtena (fjo'mtan) hala
> and fo'mtena (fjo'mtan) bjadnis a kwara hala.[396]

Loosely translated, this means 'Skekla (an ogress) rides into the homefield/ on a black horse with a white patch on its brow,/ with fifteen tails/ and fifteen children on each tail'. Jakobsen states nothing about the age of the verse, except that it is 'old'. Nor does he say anything about it having any direct relationship with the costumed *skeklers* who are not reported by name from Foula, although Foula is known to have had some form of costumed tradition related to New Year's Eve.[397] While Foula is relatively isolated, there is also a possibility that the verse was brought there by immigrants from other parts of Shetland.[398]

Apart from the intriguing alteration in the name of the creature and the substitution of 'tun' for 'garðr',[399] both of which testify to the verse's existence and transformation within the oral tradition, the Foula verse has additional interest because of how closely it echoes the Icelandic variants of the verse, while ignoring all the associations with Lent found in the Faroese versions. Here, for example, the number of tails remains fifteen, just as it was in Loftr Pálsson's rendition, rather than forty like in the Faroes. Furthermore, it is noteworthy that Skekla (like the Grýla in later Icelandic versions of the 'Grýla verse'[400]) is said to *ride onto* a farm, an impossible feat for a large straw-clad figure, but relevant a situation like Loftr Pálsson's attack on Breiðabólstaðr (even though, ironically, Loftr,

---

[396] Jakobsen, *Det norrøne sprog*, p.19.
[397] See Marwick, *The folklore of Orkney*, pp.102–104.
[398] Letter from Brian Smith, Shetland Archivist, dated 12 January 1994. As Smith points out in the same letter, there is also a possibility of some relationship between Foula and the Faroes before 1700. However, this would not explain the original features found in the Shetland version of the verse.
[399] According to Brian Smith, in the same letter referred to in the previous note, 'During the past 350 years or so I suspect the word "toon" has been used much less self-consciously than *garðr*. "Toon" has multiple meanings in Shetland, and is still used . . .; *garðr* only appears [albeit frequently] in place-names.'
[400] A version of the verse from 1582 runs: 'Gryla reið í gard ofan/ hafdi hala xv -/ enn í huorum hala/ hundrad belgi,/ enn í Belg huorum/ börn: 20' ('Grýla rode down onto the farm/ and had fifteen tails,/ and on each tail a hundred bags,/ and in each bag/ twenty children'): quoted in Jón Samsonarson, 'Vaggvisor', p.428.

4. 'Grýla' in Icelandic, Faroese and Shetland seasonal custom

who is on horseback, does not use the verb 'ride').[401] Indeed, the survival of this particular feature, which also defies all logic as regards the normal behaviour of Scandinavian trolls, raises the possibility of associations with either a mid-winter supernatural 'Wild Ride', or a living horse-riding tradition like that of the *Staffans reid*. Perhaps both traditions existed together and interrelated, just as both the legendary Grýla existed alongside the acted *grýlur* in the Faroes. Certainly, as Eike has pointed out, many features in Norwegian legends concerning the *Oskoreia* and the *julebukk*, seem to echo local practices related to Christmas horse-races and disguised house-visits.[402]

Shetland, however, does not mark the end of the tradition involving the acted female ogre, because yet another group of related figures is known to have existed on the island of Papa Westray in Orkney. Here, however, they were known as the *gyros*, probably from the Norn word *gyre* meaning an ogre/ogress.[403] According to a unique account of this tradition, these masked figures used to appear on *Gyro* night, some time in February (like the *grýlukvöld*?), dressed as old women, each wearing 'some grotesque headwear, then some woman's garment about the body, and about the legs he would have loose *simmans* tied around the waist by a piece of rope,' *simmans* being a rope made of straw or heather. According to the account in question, the costumes with their 'rags and tatters and *simmans*' were sometimes so cumbersome that the performers had difficulty running.[404]

As Lid points out, the words *gyro/gyre* are not only closely related to the word Old Icelandic word *gýgr* (also meaning a female giant or ogress), but are also reminiscent of the name 'Guro Rysserova', applied to the legendary horse-tailed leader of the Norwegian *Oskoreia* known in Telemark and Setesdal who shared a number of common features with the legendary figure of *Grýla* from Iceland and the Faroes.[405] Further links between the

---

[401] Nonetheless, as the previous note shows, the lines 'Grýla reið fyrir ofan garð,/ hafði hala fimmtán' ('Grýla rode above the field,/ had fifteen tails') were probably known in Iceland in the sixteenth century: Árni Björnsson, 'Hjátrú á jólum', 114.

[402] See Eike, 'Oskoreia', passim. See also notes 82 and 162 above for further references.

[403] Marwick, *The Orkney Norn*, p.65, where the expressions *gyre-karl*, and *gyre-karline/gy-karline* (from the Old Icelandic *kerling*, meaning 'old woman') are also found. Interestingly enough, as Lid points out in *Jolesveinar*, p.59, a tradition also existed in Fife concerning a female troll figure called 'Gy(re) Carlin' (*Gyre-karline*?) that was supposed to take any unspun flax from spinning wheels at New Year, as the Norwegian *Lussi* was supposed to do in some areas: see, for example, Alver, 'Lussi', pp.106–108. See further, Maclagen, 'Notes', 148–154, on the straw *Cailleach* ('Old Woman') from the Western Hebrides (Islay and Kintyre); and Flett and Flett, 'Some Hebridean folk dances', 114–117, and Gailey, *Irish folk drama*, pp.97–98, on an old dance known as 'Carlin of the Dust' (*Cailleach an Du'dain*), from Eriskay, Benbecula and Perthshire which involved an old hag (acted by a man) who fought her husband, was killed, lamented for, and then brought back to life.

[404] Drever, 'Papa Westray Games', 70, quoted also in Lid, *Jolesveinar*, pp.59–60. See also Marwick, *The folklore of Orkney*, p.107. The custom seems to have died out before the time of Drever's article of 1922.

[405] See Lid, *Jolesveinar*, pp.58–60. As Lid points out here, Guro was called 'Gyro' in some accounts from Setesdal.

G. A Shared Tradition of 'Folk Drama'

gyros, Grýla, 'Grylen', *Lussi* and the *julebukker* are found in the description of the supernatural 'gyre' in Orkney, which is also supposed to have boasted a number of horns and several tails.[406]

The connections between all of these traditions would appear obvious, especially because the majority of the North Atlantic guises are related to apparently female figures of some kind, all of which have legendary counterparts on the spiritual plane (two of them directly associated with Christmas).[407] At the same time, there is an interesting similarity in the terms used to describe the costumed activity. In the Shetlands, it is called to *geng in grøleks*,[408] or *geng in skeklin*[409] ('to go/ walk in *grøleks* or in *skekling*'), and in the Faroes, *at ganga grýla* ('to go/ walk *grýla*').[410] Such expressions are paralleled by the Norwegian *å gå julebukk* ('to go/ walk *julebukk*')[411] and the Danish *at gå Knut* ('to go/ walk *Knut*').[412] All of the above provide a challenging parallel for the present-day Icelandic expression *að fara í jólaköttinn*.[413]

The close relationship that these North Atlantic customs have with mainland Scandinavia, and especially with Norway, is obvious, not only because of the linguistic roots to the names, but also because most of the names have direct counterparts in Norwegian folk belief, in names and words like *Guro, joleskjekel, gygri* (ogress) and so on.[414] In addition to this, as will be shown below, there is evidence that the implications of the name Grýla must have been understood in Norway in the early thirteenth century. Even in more recent times, the word *grøkle* was regularly applied to a *julebukk* or "jolegjeite" in Kviteseid, Telemark.[415] This term would seem to come from the same root as the word *grølek*.

The above examination of these related North Atlantic traditions leads attention back to the Icelandic Grýla of the thirteenth century. The existence of this name in Iceland applied in later times to a female ogress who, like the Faroese *grýla*, visited farms to punish disobedient young people, suggests that logically the two figures must belong to the same tradition. Since this tradition was enacted both in the Faroes and in Shetland,

4. *'Grýla'* in Icelandic, Faroese and Shetland seasonal custom

---

[406] Marwick, *The folklore of Orkney*, p.32.
[407] In Yell and Fetlar, where the *skeklers* appear, a *grøli* is a 'bogey' figure, while on Unst, in the Faroe Islands, and in northern Norway, the term *skekel* or *jólaskekil/ joleskjekel* is applied to the same thing. See Jakobsen, *Det Norrøne sprog*, p.53, and *An etymological dictionary*, II, pp.778–779, and the references given above in note 385. According to Lid in *Joleband*, p.62, the Norwegian *joleskjekel* was a male troll figure, very similar to *Lussi*.
[408] Jakobsen, *An etymological dictionary*, I, p.274.
[409] Jakobsen, *An etymological dictionary*, I, p.275.
[410] See Jacobsen and Matras, *Føroysk-Donsk orðabók*, p.131, and Bregenhøj, *Helligtrekongersløb*, p.89.
[411] Lid, *Joleband*, p.39.
[412] Bregenhøj, *Helligtrekongersløb*, p.89.
[413] See references given in note 330 above.
[414] See above, notes 389–392, 403 and 405.
[415] See Weiser-Aall, *Julenissen*, p.80, note 100.

4. 'Grýla' in Icelandic, Faroese and Shetland seasonal custom

apparently linked in some way to the various 'Grýla verses', then vestiges of the same tradition ought to be found in Iceland as well. Was Loftr Pálsson referring to such a living tradition when he adopted the role of Grýla while riding onto the farm of Breiðabólstaðr?

A strong intimation that such a tradition was known or at least remembered in Iceland in the eighteenth century is found in Þorsteinn Péturssons's use of the expressions 'Grýlu andlit' ('Grýla faces/ masks'), 'Grýlu maður' (a 'Grýla man') and 'Grýlumynder' ('Grýla images') when attacking the *vikivaki* games and listing other devilish animal disguises that had earlier been used in mainland Europe.[416] These expressions imply that séra Þorsteinn must have understood the word 'Grýla' in the sense of a *male* costumed figure, be it in the form of an animal or a figure dressed in straw, and must have expected his readers to understand the word in the same way. Indeed, a parallel expression to the word 'Grýlumaður' is found in the term 'Grýlukallinn' ('Grýla-man') which appears in another relatively early Grýla poem.[417]

Séra Þorsteinn's application of the expression 'Grýlumaður' to *animal* guises abroad is especially interesting when considered alongside a seventeenth-century poem (contemporary with the *vikivaki* games) in which Grýla is described as being three-headed, with 'a ram's nose' ('hrútsnef'), a beard, jaws like a bitch ('kjaftinn eins og tík') and eyes like burning embers.[418] In the eyes of this particular poet, Grýla was therefore visualised as being almost identical to the *vikivaki þingálp* or *julebukk*, and it would appear that séra Þorsteinn must have imagined her in the similar way. Indeed, one wonders whether such a description arose from a personal memory of the *vikivaki* games, or some oral tradition based on a

---

[416] *Manducus eður leikfæla*: MS JS 113 8to, fols 43(42)v, 47(46)v, and 48(47)v (the numbering of the pages is questionable). The former expression, used with regard to disguises in general, can be found in Jón Samsonarson, *Kvæði*, I, p.xliii: 'jólaleikir, föstugangs kæti og narrabúningar, þá menn forklæða sig, taka upp annarra myndir, grýlu andlit og gikkerí . . .' ('Christmas games, carnival antics and clownish costumes, when people dress themselves up, take on disguises, *grýla* faces/ masks and other such vanities'). The other two expressions are used in a section of Þorsteinn Péturssons's book dealing with the use of disguises abroad. The word *Grýlumaður* is applied to a man acting a satyr or 'wildman' ('skógvættur') wearing a costume made of flax and hemp ('hör og hamp') covered with tar and resin. The expression *grýlumynder* (meaning 'Grýla guises') is used in a general sense for such costumes. Both expressions are given in Ólafur Davíðsson, *Íslenzkar gátur*, III, p.23, without any context, along with a further expression, 'Grýla eða gríma ásjóna' ('Grýla or facial mask') which I have not been able to trace in the MS.
[417] Ólafur Davíðsson, *Íslenzkar gátur*, IV, p.147.
[418] Stefán Olafsson, 'Grýlukvæði', in *Ljóðmæli*, pp.18–20. This description might be compared with the statements in Guðmundur Erlendssons's 'Grýlukvæði' (1650), that Grýla, who has 'horns like a goat's' ('horn eins og geit'), goes about in 'the tatters of a hairy skin-coat' ('loðnu skinnstaks tetri'), bearing 'her impure iron rod' ('sína rauðbrota staung'). 'Her ears lay on her shoulders, close up to her nose' ('eyrun lágu á öxlunum . . . áföst við nef'), and 'there was hair upon her chin/ like unwoven knotted wool' ('Svo var hár um hökuna/ sem hnýtt garn á vef'), her 'teeth enclosed in a filthy mouth' ('voru tennur í óhreinum kjapt'): quoted in Ólafur Davíðsson, *Íslenzkar gátur*, IV, pp.114–115.

G. A Shared Tradition of 'Folk Drama'

memory of an enacted *Grýla* that took the shape of a goat, similar perhaps to the *Lussia* depicted above in *fig.51*.[419]

4. *'Grýla' in Icelandic, Faroese and Shetland seasonal custom*

The possibility that such a *Grýla* tradition was also known in Iceland as far back as the thirteenth century is supported by the evidence of *Íslendinga saga*, which in the light of the information given above, would now seem to make much more sense. Of particular interest is the figure of Steingrímr Skinngrýluson from the isolated western fjords of Iceland, who was one of Loftr Pálsson's principal targets in the battle following Loftr's dramatic arrival at Breiðabólstaðr in 1221, and was almost certainly one of the 'Breiðabólstaðr men' who had earlier not only 'made mocking verses about Loftr', but also 'many dance-songs and many other kinds of joke'.[420] As Finnur Jónsson has stressed, the name of Steingrímr's father (or mother?), Skinngrýla, must be a by-name, probably meaning 'skin-monster'.[421] Considering Loftr Pálsson's use of the 'Grýla verse' at this time, and the other evidence presented above, everything would seem to indicate that a *skinngrýla* must have been a *Grýla* figure clad in animal skins that visited farms at a particular time of the year (probably in winter time), and was seen as threatening (especially by children).[422] It is also important to stress that the name Skinngrýla here probably refers to a *male*, in other words, a *grýlumaður*. Such a direct link between a male and the essentially female Grýla is supported still further by the other Grýla name mentioned in *Íslendinga saga*, namely that of Grýlu-Brandr, who was one of the followers of Ásbjörn Illugason in 1254; and also by the earlier mentioned references to men 'behaving like *grýlur*'.[423]

Interestingly enough, there is evidence that at least the supernatural connotations of Grýla as a figure must have also been understood by some people in Norway during the mid-thirteenth century, when the title of *Grýla* was given to the first section of *Sverris saga*, written by Karl Jónsson apparently under the supervision of King Sverrir himself. The earliest extant manuscript states that this name is based on the fact that 'as the book

---

[419] The question must arise whether the modern Icelandic Christmas pantheon of the spiritual *Grýla*, *jólaköttur*, and *jólasveinar* might not reflect a distant memory of an enacted group that used to visit farms at Christmas time, just as certain descriptions of the spiritual *julebukk* and *Oskoreia* seem to be based on originally acted traditions. See Weiser-Aall, *Julenissen*, pp.52–53; and Eike, 'Oskoreia', passim.

[420] '. . . færðu Breiðbælingar Lopt í flimtan, ok gördu um hann danza marga, ok margskonar spott annat': *Sturlunga saga* (1878), I, pp.245–246. See also note 255 above. Steingrímr is described elsewhere (p.246) as personally making verbal attacks on Loftr, and in the battle, Loftr singles Steingrímr out for a particular onslaught that leads to the latter's death: *Sturlunga saga* (1878), I, p.247.

[421] 'Skind-uhyre' or 'skind-skræmsel': Finnur Jónsson, 'Tilnavne', 347.

[422] The presence of such a figure as Steingrímr Skinngrýluson amidst the insulting jokes and dances conducted during the winter at Breiðabólstaðr conjures up the image of a wake with costumed games like the *vikivaki* gatherings known in later times.

[423] Regarding Grýlu-Brandr, see *Sturlunga saga* (1878), II, p.171. Finnur Jónsson, in 'Tilnavne', 328, also links this name to Grýla, but suggests here that if it is not related to the 'skræmsel' ('bugbear'), it might have something to do with a name for a fox. On the expression, 'at gera sér grýla' ('to behave like Grýla'), see note 336 above.

5. The dating of the North Atlantic seasonal customs

proceeds his (Sverrir's) strength increases'.[424] This, however, is somewhat vague, unless reference is being made to some form of *Grýla* procession. Considering everything that has been stated above about Grýla, the more likely explanation would appear to be that given in *Flateyjarbók*, where it is explained that the title was chosen because 'many people felt that they (King Sverrir and his men) had caused a great deal of fear and terror'.[425] Such qualities seem to have been the hallmark of Grýla and her relatives throughout the North Atlantic islands.

In general, there is good reason to believe that some form of *Grýla* tradition comparable to that found in the other North Atlantic islands must have existed as far back as the thirteenth century in Iceland, thus giving birth to the curious by-names met in *Islendinga saga*, and the later expressions used by Þorsteinn Pétursson, and helping to ensure the survival of the 'Grýla verse' in the Icelandic oral tradition. Indeed, considering the similarities between the figures of the *þingálp*, *kelling*, and *Háa-Þóra* in the Icelandic *vikivaki* games, and the descriptions of *Grýla* in Faroese customs and the seventeenth-century Icelandic Grýla poems, the possibility must exist that over time the Icelandic Grýla tradition blended into the *vikivaki* games, which were hardly a new phenomenon in the sixteenth century.[426] Considering the worsening of the Icelandic climate during the later Middle Ages, the weather at Christmas would have been hardly supportive of a tradition of disguised house-visits like those known in mainland Scandinavia or England. Appearances at a single centralised gathering, however, would have been a different matter entirely.

5. The Dating of the North Atlantic Seasonal Customs

In general terms, a core tradition of seasonal dramatic performance involving the costumed enactment of supernatural figures during the mid-winter period can be assumed to have run across Scandinavia from Sweden to

---

[424] See *Sverris saga*, p.1: 'Oc sua sem a liðr bokina vex hans styrkr. oc segir sa hinn sami styrkr fyr[ir] hina meiri luti. kalloðu þeir þan lut bocar fyrir þui Grylu.'

[425] *Flateyjarbok* (1860–1868), II, p.534: 'Kolluðu menn þui enn fyrra lut bokarinnar grylu at margir menn tolodu at þa efnadiz nockurr otti edr hræðzla sakir mikils strids ok bardaga enn mundi skiott nidrfalla ok allz eingu verda.' Comparisons might also be made between Sverrir's early life as a semi-outlaw figure in the woods and that of Grýla in the mountains (cf. the *julebukk* which lived in the woods, and the *finngálkn* that lived 'á heiðum og skógum': see references above in notes 67 and 258). Regarding the two prologues, see further Sverrir Tómasson, *Formálar*, pp.388–394; Holm-Olsen, *Studier*, pp.42–43, and pp.53–54; and Blöndal, *Um uppruna Sverrissögu*, pp.53–73.

[426] It seems clear that most of the early commentators on the *vikivaki* games considered them as being the end result of a much older tradition that was dying out. See Jón Samsonarson, *Kvæði*, I, p.xxxiv (*Qualiscunque descriptio Islandæ*, 1588), and p.xlii (Þorsteinn Pétursson, late eighteenth century); Ólafur Davíðsson, *Íslenzkar gátur*, III, p.19 (Jón frá Grunnavík, mid-eighteenth century); and Eggert Ólafsson and Bjarni Pálsson, *Ferðabók*, I, p.205 (a translation of *Reise igiennom Island*, originally published in 1772). Þorsteinn Pétursson also comments that the games were kept secret amongst the common people (see Jón Samsonarson, *Kvæði*, I, p.xlii), but it is of course open to debate how much this statement can be trusted.

H. Conclusion

Iceland from at least as early as the sixteenth century, and, in all probability, as far back as the thirteenth century.⁴²⁷ At the very least, there is good reason to believe that the shared traditions from the North Atlantic islands, closely connected with traditions from Norway, must have been firmly established before the time of the Reformation. After that time, the close links between Norway, Shetland and Iceland broke down.⁴²⁸ Indeed, bearing in mind the thirteenth-century Icelandic references to *Grýla*, *grýlur*, and *skinngrýla*, and the echoes of the much older enacted pagan rituals involving winter processions, ritual marriage and both horned and animal skin costumes which appear in the *vikivaki* games and the traditions from the Faroes and Shetland, the possibility must exist that the North Atlantic dramatic traditions had much earlier roots.

As Strömbäck argued, even if the *vikivaki* games traditions were adopted from abroad during the later Middle Ages, it must be assumed that they did not enter a void, but instead were surplanted on top of a native tradition that already existed,⁴²⁹ and was associated essentially with the mid winter period. In this context, it should be borne in mind that the original figure of Grýla certainly did not originate in England or Ireland. Nor is there very much likelihood that she was instituted by the Christian church.

5. The dating of the North Atlantic seasonal customs

H. Conclusion

Returning to the question of the silence of the sagas on the existence of dramatic ritual or folk custom, it might be noted that of all the references given above to the folk traditions of the sixteenth to early twentieth century, only three have been drawn from fictional works.⁴³⁰ Literature alone can never be trusted to provide a complete and accurate social picture of

---

⁴²⁷ The same assumption is made by Bregenhøj in *Helligtrekongersløb*, pp.89–90, on the basis of a comparison between the Faroese and Danish traditions. Bregenhøj, however, says nothing about the Icelandic *Grýla*.

⁴²⁸ Jón Samsonarson argues this point with regard to the shared tradition of *Grýla* verses from the Shetlands, the Faroes and Iceland. See Jón Samsonarson, 'Vaggvisor', p.428. Contact with Norway, however, was weakening even in the fifteenth century, Iceland having come under the Danish crown with Norway in 1380, and the English and Germans beginning to surplant Norwegian trade with Iceland from 1413 onwards: see Björn Þorsteinsson and Guðrún Ása Grímsdóttir, 'Norska öldin', p.117, pp.177–179, p.235 and p.247. Furthermore, as Brian Smith, the Shetland Archivist, has stressed in a letter (dated 12 January 1994), 'In the late eighteenth and early nineteenth centuries there were very few contacts between Shetland and any part of Scandinavia, at any level: economic or intellectual.'

⁴²⁹ See above, notes 298 and 309.

⁴³⁰ I.e. Scott's *The pirate*; Holberg's *Julestuen*; and Heinesen's 'Grylen', none of which can be said to give a strictly accurate portrait of the customs in question.

II. Dramatic Activities, II: Folkloristic Evidence

the lives and beliefs of the common people at any given time.[431] Nonetheless, the evidence presented above should emphasise, if nothing else, that semi-dramatic and dramatic cult activities of the kind examined in the previous chapter appear to have continued in Scandinavia in the form of popular games and costumed house-visits even after the advent of Christianity, their existence being prolonged largely on the basis of custom and superstition. It can be assumed, furthermore, that in one form or another, these traditions were originally brought to the Viking colonies by the original settlers.

Naturally, individual examples of folk customs and beliefs should never be taken to represent the beliefs of an entire people. Yet from the examinations made of the evidence of Scandinavian dramatic customs found in archaeological, literary and folkloristic sources in the last two chapters, it is possible to extract a general core of traditions, predominantly involving customs related to the periods around the winter and summer solstice. Both sets of traditions contain traces of a mock-marriage and the elements of a procession and/ or house-visits. The winter customs involve, in particular, the elements of disguise (often in the form of a horned animal figure, an ogress, or a walking 'idol' such as *Halm-Staffan*), and in some areas this figure may also have taken part in a combat, a mock death, and/ or a marriage. Assuming that such core elements existed in ritual and/ or games during the Viking Age, there is little question that they could have provided a context for the dialogic Eddic poems that will be discussed in the following chapters. Many of these poems feature disguise as a central motif. It is not hard, for example, to imagine associations between *Skírnismál* and a tradition of folk marriage; between *Hárbarðsljóð* and an enacted poetic contest, or *mannjafnaðr*, involving figures representing Winter and Summer; or between *Fáfnismál*, *Vafþrúðnismál* and the costumed initiation ceremonies suggested by Arent with regard to the Torslunda matrices, and Weiser-Aall with regard to the *julebukk*.[432] In this sense, the dialogic Eddic poems, if they were originally performed dramatically, would fill in the temporal gap between the archaeological and the folkloristic evidence, and help to illustrate both.

As pointed out in the *Introduction*, however, consideration of ritualistic thematic elements alone is not enough. Nor does the material presented in the previous two chapters *prove* that such a dramatic tradition existed in Scandinavia at the time that the Eddic poems were recorded. All that it provides is a probable, and valuable context. The following chapter, therefore, contains an examination of the dialogic poems themselves to

---

[431] See also *Chapter I*, note 263.
[432] See references given above in *Chapter I*, note 174, and *Chapter II*, note 170. *Fáfnismál*, of course, also contains the additional feature of the battle with the monster. Both poems involve the elements of gnomic question and answer common to initiation ceremonies. As was noted above in note 359, the Faroese *jólhestur* also used to take part in a game of questions and answers.

H. Conclusion

investigate how much their extant form reveals about the way in which they were originally performed. In short, is there any reason at all to regard the dialogic Eddic poems as *dramatic* works, rooted in the semi-dramatic traditions described in the last two chapters, rather than merely as fine examples of ancient mythological poetry?

CHAPTER III

The Eddic Poems and Drama

A. The Eddic Poems as Oral Poetry

Central to the discussion that follows is the basic premise that, for the most part, the extant versions of the Eddic poems represent records of works that were originally presented and preserved orally.[1] Of course, this is an accepted fact, but it is often taken too much for granted without deeper consideration of the manifold implications involved. Amongst other features, it raises the possibility that until the time they were recorded, and perhaps even afterwards, the Eddic poems, like other oral works, were continually being 'recreated' by their performers who would have made use of a basic framework and a fund of formulas and thematic patterns.[2] Yet the fact that a work lived within the oral tradition also places additional

---

[1] It is believed by a number of scholars, among them being Wessén in 'Den isländska eddadiktningen', 7, and Einar Ólafur Sveinsson, in *Íslenzkar bókmenntir*, p.195, that *Grípisspá* is the only poem in the corpus that was composed with pen in hand. In *Litteraturs historie*, I, p.268, Finnur Jónsson suggests that the poem was written to provide a summarising preface to the Brynhildr/ Sigurðr anthology of poems. In this sense, it plays a similar introductory role to that of *Helgakviða Hundingsbana I* and *Völuspá*. See further Finnur Jónsson's theory of the 'summary principle' ('oversigtsprincip') in 'Eddadigtenes samling', 223–225. For a detailed examination of *Grípisspá*, see R. L. Harris, 'A study of Grípisspá'. More recently, Söderberg, in 'Lokasenna', 79, has concluded that *Lokasenna* must also be a literary product. There are, however, several flaws in this argument: see further below, *section G.2*.

[2] For examinations of the patterns and demands of oral composition, see, for example, Lord, *The singer of tales*; and Finnegan, *Oral poetry*, pp.139–153 in particular. For brief comparisons of the Yugoslavian oral tradition examined by Parry and Lord, and that within which the Eddas seem to have been preserved, see Harris, 'Eddic poetry as oral poetry'; and 'Eddic poetry', pp.111–126. On the subject of formulas and stock patterns in the Eddic poems, see also Söderberg, 'Formelgods'; Meletinsky, 'Commonplaces', and Gurevic, 'The formulaic pair'. On the question of compositional thematic units, particularly those employed in formalised verbal conflicts (the *senna* and *mannjafnaðr*), see Harris, 'The senna'; and Clover, 'Hárbarðsljóð', and 'The Germanic context'. A clear illustration of the conflict at present raging about the relevance of the 'oral theory' to Eddic study is shown in the recent heated discussion on the subject conducted by Gísli Sigurðsson and Einar Már Jónsson in *Tímarit Máls og menningar*: see Einar Már Jónsson, 'Góður veðurviti', 'Heilsurækt fræðanna' and 'Heilsurækt fræðanna – Niðurlag'; and Gísli Sigurðsson, 'Fordómur fáfræðinnar', and 'Munnmenntir og staða fræðanna'. See also Jónas Kristjánsson, 'Stages', pp.146–147; and Sørensen, 'Loki's senna', p.259.

A. The Eddic Poems as Oral Poetry

emphasis on the element of performance, the form of the work at any given time being dependent on the dating, place and nature of the presentation in question.[3] Between the time of Phillpotts and the Chadwicks[4] and the last decade, this subject was unfortunately granted very little detailed academic attention, largely because of the limited amount of concrete evidence available on the performance of the Eddic poems.[5]

Most people nowadays encounter the Eddic poems in printed form, and thus tend to approach them, and indeed the entire Old Icelandic corpus, first and foremost as *readers* rather than as a listening, watching audience. Our perception of these works is thus necessarily somewhat different to that 'intended' by the original oral presenters of these works, not least because our societies, experiences and expectations are of a totally different nature to those of the original Scandinavian listeners. Essentially, though, what the reader has lost is the original element of the performance itself. As Jeff Opland points out:

> An oral poet performing before an audience enjoys a unique relation with them at the time of the performance. He is there and the audience can see him, they can hear his voice and the rhythmical cadences of his delivery. He moves before them with facial expressions and gestures ... The words he utters are only one aspect of the poet's performance: the impact on the audience is aural, visual and emotional. They experience a totality of performance, a unique sequence that can never be repeated. All these facets of the performance are necessarily lost when an oral poem is committed to paper...[6]

The borderline between such an oral performance and drama is extremely vague. As *readers* of the texts of such oral works we are left in a position similar to that of a blind person listening to a film.

Careful examination of the texts of the Eddic poems, however, can reveal a great deal about the setting and the mode of performance both directly and by implication, in the same way that the texts of medieval and Tudor drama provide valuable information about the nature of early theatrical presentation. The following examination, which concentrates largely on the question of performance, will be examining in particular the question of whether it would have been possible for a single performer to have presented the dialogic Eddic poems *without* moving into the realms of dramatic performance as defined in the *Introduction*.

---

[3] See Finnegan, *Oral poetry*, p.17.
[4] See Chadwick and Chadwick, *The growth of literature* (1935–1940), I, pp.576–582.
[5] Exceptions to this rule are the work of Stefán Einarsson and others on the question of 'alternate singing' (see further below, Chapter V, D.2), and the work of Lönnroth, particularly on the question of the 'double scene' related to the time and place of performance: see Lönnroth, 'Hjálmar's death song', 'Skírnismál', 'The double scene', and *Den dubbla scenen*, pp.53–80. A detailed examination of the evidence concerning the performance of oral poetry amongst the early Germanic peoples is given in Opland's *Anglo-Saxon oral poetry*.
[6] Opland, *Anglo-Saxon oral poetry*, pp.12–13; see also pp.80–86. A similar point is made by Harris in 'Eddic poetry', p.115.

III. The Eddic Poems and Drama

B. The Dating of the Extant Texts of the Eddic Poems

The Eddic poems in their present form are found in the following manuscripts: the *Codex Regius* (Gml.kgl.saml.2365 4to) (R), dating from the period around 1270; the AM 748 4to fragment (A) from c.1300; the *Codex Wormianus* (AM 242 fol.) from the mid-fourteenth century; and *Flateyjarbók* (Gml.kgl.sml.1005 fol.) from between 1380 and 1390.[7] Scholars agree that neither of the main collections of poems contained in the *Codex Regius* and the AM 748 manuscripts represents a wholly original collection of individual poems. Both appear to be compilations made up from earlier smaller collections that are now lost. The question of the manuscripts will be referred to again in more detail later in this book, but for now it is enough to accept the likelihood that if most of the poems contained in these collections were in existence in the oral tradition prior to the time that the original manuscripts came to be written, then the extant manuscripts must ultimately contain more or less accurate textual transcripts of oral performances of these poems.[8] It is logical to assume that these directly transmitted oral performances cannot have taken place much earlier than the time at which the earliest extant Scandinavian manuscripts were written. In short, the manuscripts versions reflect the state of the poems as they existed in the oral tradition in the mid-twelfth century, at the very earliest.[9]

---

[7] Regarding the dating of these MSS, see, for example, Wessén, 'Den isländska eddadiktningen', 2; Lindblad, 'Poetiska Eddans förhistoria', 166; and Jón Helgason, ed., *Eddadigte*, II, p.v, and pp.x–xi.

[8] This, of course, only concerns those poems that were not actually composed pen in hand, and have been preserved in what appears to be an almost complete form. The case of *Grípisspá* is mentioned in note 1 above. Certain other poems, like *Reginsmál*, *Helgakviða Hundingsbana II*, and *Helgakviða Hjörvarðssonar*, in their extant form, appear to represent a composite of various poems and pieces of prose patched together by a redactor at an early stage in the process of collection. It would be hard to say whether these poems existed in a complete form at the time of the original collection or not. Certainly, even the supporters of a mixed verse-and-prose form would not argue that the extant form of these particular poems represents the original word-for-word transcript. See further below, *section D*. Regarding the question of transcription of the other poems, it must be accepted that the recorded performance might have been stilted owing to the unusual conditions of recording line by line: see Lord, *The singer of tales*, pp.124–128, and Gísli Sigurðsson, 'Munnmenntir', 20. Nonetheless, the possibility also exists that the recorder learnt the poems off by heart before writing them down, as Wessén suggests in 'Den isländska eddadiktningen', 11. Similarly, it cannot be ruled out that some of the more sacred mythological poetry, like the ritual poems of the Zuñi and Navajo indians, might have remained strictly intact in transmission. See the *Introduction*, note 93; and Ong, *Orality and literacy*, pp.57–68, on the memorization of texts in other oral cultures. On the question of transmission in Scandinavia, see further, Lönnroth, 'Hjálmar's death song', 17–20; and Harris, 'Eddic poetry as oral poetry', pp.212–213 and pp.231–233. In both articles, however, the poems discussed are heroic poems. The variations encountered in mythological Eddic verse show much less alteration on the whole.

[9] 1150 is the date of the so-called *Fyrsta málfræðiritgerðin* (First grammatical treatise) which names neither the sagas nor Eddic poetry as individual genres. On the basis of

C. The Forms of Eddic Poetry

Any examination of the implications of the form of the poems must refer primarily to the presentation of these poems during this particular period. Bearing in mind the possibility of textual and structural alteration in performance like that which occurs in other oral cultures,[10] it is difficult to make any definite statements about the precise textual form, or the dating of the 'original' poems before that time. All that it is possible to be certain about prior to this period are the broad outline of the action, the poetic form itself, and certain details concerning the natural surroundings depicted in the poems.[11]

1. General grouping

C. The Forms of Eddic Poetry

1. General Grouping

As was stated at the start of this book, the term 'Eddic poetry', used to cover the body of poetic work contained in the Codex Regius and AM 748 manuscripts, is slightly misleading. The works in question can hardly be considered as belonging to a single genre. While the poems obviously belong to a particular culture, they clearly did not all originate from the same 'hand' or a rigid homogeneous tradition. Apart from noticing the differences in subject matter and metre, readers also become aware of the essential difference between those poems containing third-person narrative, and those others, much more dramatic in tone, that convey their material entirely through the medium of dialogue or first-person monologue. Over and above this, poems like *Völuspá*, *Hamðismál*, *Skírnismál* and *Oddrúnargrátr* betray glaring differences not only in style and approach but also as regards sensitivity and characterisation.

A variety of internal classifications of the Eddic poems have been effectively employed by scholars for different purposes. With regard to the structural nature of the poems, however, matters appear to be relatively straightforward. Einar Ólafur Sveinsson, for example, classified the poems according to nine varying stylistic categories:

a. *Dialogic poems* in which the subject matter is conveyed entirely through the medium of dialogue involving two or more characters. These poems can in turn be grouped into three main types:

---

examinations of the *Codex Regius*, Lindblad suggests that certain particularly old-fashioned features dating back to c.1200 can be detected in the handwriting techniques used in *Vafþrúðnismál*, *Hymiskviða*, 'Frá dauða Sinfjötla' and *Helgakviða Hjörvarðssonar*: Lindblad, 'Poetiska Eddans förhistoria', 162. Lindblad suggests here that the original recording probably took place between that time and 1240. This supports the dating suggested for the earliest collections by Müllenhoff, Heusler, and Wessén. See further below, notes 82–83.

[10] See references above in note 2.

[11] A similar attitude to the dating of the poems is expressed by Sørensen, in 'Loki's senna', pp.239–243; and most recently by Vésteinn Ólason, in 'Kveðskapur', pp.47–50, and 'Eddukvæði', pp.77–78. For an examination of the 'natural' references in the poems, see Einar Ólafur Sveinsson, *Íslenzkar bókmenntir*, pp.163–174.

III. The Eddic Poems and Drama

1. *General grouping*

a.i. *Dialogic poems with an epic structure*, such as *Skírnismál*, *Fáfnismál*, *Grógaldr* and *Fjölsvinnsmál*. The poems in this group tend to be more interspersed with prose passages than those in the two following groups.[12]

a.ii. *Senna* or *mannjafnaðr* poems, such as *Lokasenna* and *Hárbarðsljóð*, which are essentially confined to a single setting and centre predominantly on the verbal duel (the *senna* or *mannjafnaðr*[13]).

a.iii. *Mnemonic poetry* in which knowledge is conveyed through the medium of a life-and-death verbal contest of wisdom, as in *Vafþrúðnismál*, and *Alvíssmál*. Only one narrative strophe can be found in the poems of any of these three groups, namely *Vafþrúðnismál*, st.5.

b. *First-person monologues*, such as *Hávamál*, *Völuspá*, *Grímnismál*, and *Sigrdrífumál*, most of which again tend to be gnomic or mnemonic.

c. *Narrative poems*. Purely *narrative poems* (c.i) are limited to *Rígsþula* which has no more than one strophe of pure speech. The rest can be generally placed under the heading of *epic-dramatic* poems because they all make effective use of monologue or dialogue as part of the poetic narrative, but never to the degree encountered in the dialogic poems.[14] Einar Ólafur Sveinsson divides these *epic-dramatic* poems into four groups according to their apparent stages of development. The oldest (c.ii), such as *Hamðismál*, *Hlöðskviða*, and *Völundarkviða*, cover a large amount of material and long periods of the hero's life at a fast pace. These poems were succeeded by another group (c.iii) including works like *Atlamál* and *Sigurðarkviða in skamma* which display a greater interest in psychological states, more attention to small detail, and a larger proportion of dialogue. The third stage (c.iv) is reflected in poems such as *Oddrúnargrátr* and *Guðrúnarkviða in forna* which show even further limitation of the amount of epic material, and a growing emphasis on individual human emotion and states of grief, depicted in particular in the character of the central figures about whom the poems are constructed. This form, in turn, leads to what Einar Ólafur sees as being the last stage (c.v) in which the narrative verse itself finally disappears to be replaced by first-person verbal expressions of grief primarily given in the form of monologue, as in poems like 'Hjálmar's death song'.[15]

Certain details here are open to dispute, but Einar Ólafur's suggested grouping of poems for the most part reflects the variety of poetry and song shown by historical sources to have been in existence among the Germanic

---

[12] This latter feature does not apply to *Grógaldr* or *Fjölsvinnsmál*, neither of which contains any prose. These two poems, however, only survive in a much later MS from the seventeenth/ eighteenth century. It is thus questionable whether they should be grouped with the other poems. Neither work is included in the tables given below.
[13] Regarding the *senna* and *mannjafnaðr*, see further below, Chapter V, D.3.
[14] See the statistical tables in given in *Table I* concerning the degree of direct speech in the poems.
[15] Einar Ólafur Sveinsson, *Íslenzkar bókmenntir*, pp.200–202. The divisions given here largely echo those made in Heusler's *Die altgermanische Dichtung*, 2nd ed., p.27; and de Vries' *Literaturgeschichte*, 2nd ed., I, pp.12–34. For 'Hjálmars death song', see *Örvar-Odds saga*, pp.328–330.

C. The Forms of Eddic Poetry

tribes as far back as the early Iron Age. As Opland has shown in his examination of the source material on oral performance among the early Germanic tribes, a number of different types of poetry and song must have existed from an early point in time, each of which was not only artistically different, but also relevant to a particular given performance situation.[16] Opland clarifies this by citing Heusler's own vision of a 'multiform' tradition of poetry in early times, ranging from the magical, to the gnomic, to the mnemonic, to the communal, to the societal, all in which existed in addition to the traditional epic, heroic and mythical forms.[17] As both Opland and Heusler point out, each type seems to have had its own style and form of presentation, ranging from an individually chanted or sung performance to a choral, communal effort. It is only natural, in the absence of material on Eddic presentation, to apply the same suggestions about different modes of performance to the various types of Eddic poems in their earlier manifestations.

2. The use of direct speech

2. The Use of Direct Speech in Different Forms of Eddic Poetry

Table I below, based on Neckel and Kuhn's edition of the *Edda*, contains statistics about the amount of direct speech and prose in the various Eddic poems. The categorisation of the Eddic poems in the table is directly related to the information provided in the table itself. For the main part, it reflects Einar Ólafur Sveinsson's classification of the poems, although for practical purposes, the classification here has been limited to four general types (dialogue, monologue, 'framed' monologue, and epic-dramatic), primarily on the basis of the structure and form of the poems. The figures in the table add little that is new regarding the grouping of the poems. They do, however, clearly emphasise the sharp distinction between the form of the monologic and dialogic poems, and those classified above as epic-dramatic.

Considering the information assembled in *Table I*, it is possible to make the following basic observations:

    a. Those poems containing a large proportion of pure narrative verse also tend to contain a number of strophes in what can be termed a 'blended' narrative-speech form, the narrative of the strophe usually forming a brief descriptive introduction to the character uttering the lines of speech that follow (see further *Table III* below).

    b. Those poems which are almost entirely composed of pure speech strophes (90% or more pure speech) are devoid of this 'blended' strophe

---

[16] Opland, *Anglo-Saxon oral poetry*, p.38. See also below, *Chapter V, C*. Nonetheless, as Turville-Petre points out in *The origins*, p.15, 'There is nothing to show that mythological lays comparable to those of the *Edda* were known among Germanic tribes other than those of Scandinavia, and nothing to suggest that those which we now possess originated amongst people other than the Norwegians and Icelanders.'
[17] See, for example, Heusler, *Die altgermanische Dichtung*, pp.26–27.

TABLE I

THE PROPORTION OF SPEECH, 'BLENDED STROPHES'
AND PROSE IN THE EDDIC POEMS

Abbreviations for types: D: Dialogic M: Monologic FM: 'Framed' monologue ED: Epic–dramatic

POEM	TYPE	NARRATIVE		'BLENDED'		SPEECH			PROSE LINES (Neckel)	
		Narrative strophes	Narrative sts: lines	Narr/spch strophes	Narr/spch sts: lines	Pure spch strophes	Pure spch sts: lines	Pure spch sts: %	At start and end	Internal
Vsp.	M	–	–	–	–	66	538	100%	–	–
Háv.	M[18]	–	–	–	–	164	1087	100%	–	–
Vm.	D	1	6	–	–	54	325	98.18%	–	–
Grm.	M	–	–	–	–	54	360	100%	36: 7	–
Skm.	D	–	–	–	–	42	264	100%	6: –	8
Hrbl.	D	–	–	–	–	60	256	100%	2: –	–
Hym.	ED	24	188	10	53/39[19]	5	36	11.3%	–	–
Ls.	D	–	–	–	–	65	396	100%	17: 9	7
Þrk.	ED	10	86	15	46/72	7	52	20.3%	–	–
Vkv.	ED	16	130	7	26.5/22.5[20]	18	150	45.5%	17: –	7
Alv.	D	–	–	–	–	35	247	100%	–	–
HH.I	ED	26	214	6	31/17	24	194	42.5%	1: –	–
HHv.	D	1	8	–	–	42	310	97.4%	16: 1	48
HH.II	D	3	16	–	–	48	422	96.3%	12: 6	63
Grp.	ED/D[21]	–	–	3	10/14	50	400	94.3%	5: –	–

[18] It is naturally questionable whether *Hávamál* should be regarded as a single entity or not. Nonetheless, in *Hávamál I*, a mysterious 'ek' ('I') appears in sts 14, 39, 47, 49, 67, 70, and 78, suggesting the existence of a personalised narrator. Whether 'ek' can be called a 'character' or not is open to question. Even if 'ek' becomes Óðinn in the later strophes of the poem, it is debatable whether the two 'ek's are one and the same person. In the later strophes, however (i.e. *Hávamál II, III and V*, where Óðinn is undoubtedly 'ek'), one is more obviously dealing with a 'role'. The same can probably also be said of the 'þulr' educating Loddfáfnir in *Hávamál IV*: a frame situation (though not an enacted scene) has been created. As for *Hávamál VI*, even though the master of the 'ljóð' (spells or magical incantations) is a clearly different character from the homely lower-class wanderer of *Hávamál I*, it would be difficult to argue that the reciter is necessarily taking on a role. See further the reference to a recent lecture on this subject by Richard North in the *Conclusion*, note 1.

[19] The figures given for *Hymiskviða* include two irregular 'blended' strophes in which the speech *precedes* the narrative. One (st.17) is a 4:4 line strophe (see, however, Neckel and Kuhn, ed., *Edda*, p.91), the other (st.32) a very rare form in which the speech is interspersed by a narrative line in which a new speaker is named.

[20] *Hymiskviða* and *Völundarkviða* are the only Eddic poems to contain a strophe in which speech is interrupted by a *poetic* insert naming the speaker. In *Völundarkviða*, st.29, the words 'kvað Vǫlundr' are placed at the end of the first line following the initial words of Völundr's speech.

[21] Certainly *Grípisspá* is largely dialogic, written like *Alvíssmál* and *Vafþrúðnismál* in the form of question-and-answer. However, the presence of the three 'blended' narrative-speech strophes (sts 4–6) is so totally alien to the pure dialogic form that the poem has been tentatively included among the epic-dramatic poems.

POEM	TYPE	NARRATIVE Narrative strophes	NARRATIVE Narrative sts: lines	'BLENDED' Narr/spch strophes	'BLENDED' Narr/spch sts: lines	SPEECH Pure spch strophes	SPEECH Pure spch sts: lines	SPEECH Pure spch sts: %	PROSE LINES (Neckel) At start and end	PROSE LINES (Neckel) Internal
Rm.	D	–	–	–	–	26	176	100%	20: –	33
Fm.	D	–	–	–	–	44	279	100%	9: 7	17
Sd.	FM/M[22]	–	–	–	–	37	251	100%	11: –	13
Br.	ED	4	32	7	22/42	8	64	40%	– :14	–
Gðr.I	ED	9	64	8	18/52	10	80	37.3%	6: –	–
Sgk.	ED	19	146	9	26/56	43	337	59.6%	7: –	–
Hlr.	FM	–	–	–	–	14	108	100%	5: –	–
Gðr.II[23]	M/ED?	(24)	(191)	(2)	(8/8)	(18)	(142)	40.6%	21: –	–
Gðr.III	ED	2	12	2	8/8	7	52	65%	3: –	–
Od.	FM	6	46	–	–	28	204	81.6%	4: –	–
Akv.	ED	21	165	7	24/34	15	126	36.1%	4: –	–
Am.	ED	40	290	11	45/61[24]	19	363	17.6%	1: –	–
Ghv.	FM	3	24	2	4/16	16	129	74.5%	11: –	–
Hm.	ED	10	64	10	30/48	11	78	35.4%	– : 1	–
Bdr.	ED/D	4	32	–	–	10	82	68.4%	–	–
Rþ.	Narr.[25]	45	351	1	2/4	1	8	2.1%	4: –	–
Hdl.	FM	–	–	–	–	50	390	100%	1: –	–
Grt.	ED	4	30	3	12/14	17	126	69.2%	(34): –	–
Hlð.	ED[26]	3	22	1	4/4	30	190	86.3%	***[27]	***

[22] *Sigrdrífumál* could logically also be regarded as being dialogic, or a 'framed' monologue. However, very little real dialogue takes place between Sigrdrífa and Sigurðr, and considering the late dating of most of the other 'framed' monologue poems (see *Table II*), and their general style, the poem would also seem out of place amongst them. In general, as Noreen has shown in 'Studier, III', 28–32, *Sigrdrífumál* differs in a number of ways from the normal pattern and form of the other ljóðaháttr poems. However, there is reason to believe that the initial awakening of Sigrdrífa could be linked to the previous poem, *Fáfnismál* (see *section G.4a*). The monologue attributed to Sigrdrífa which follows (with the exception of one strophe placed in Sigurðr's mouth) then stands comfortably alongside parts of *Hávamál* and *Grímnismál*.

[23] *Guðrúnarkviða II* is a slight oddity in its present state. The poem begins 'in role' with Guðrún acting as primary narrator, giving a monologue. However, as the poem progresses, the monologue begins to take on all the stylistic traits of epic-dramatic verse listed above, including the 'blended' narrative-speech verse. For practical purposes, therefore, the poem is counted as being essentially epic-dramatic here.

[24] In two of the 'blended' strophes in *Atlamál* (i.e. sts 20 and 48) the speech precedes the narrative.

[25] *Rígsþula* stands out from the rest of the Eddic poems by nature of the fact that it has only two strophes containing direct speech.

[26] Even though 86.3% of *Hlöðskviða* as a poem comes in the form of speech would be extremely difficult to argue for its being a dialogic or monologic poem, if only because of its generally fragmentary state and almost total lack of anything that could be termed either 'dialogue' or 'monologue'.

[27] Figures for the prose connected to *Hlöðskviða* have been left out for the obvious reason that the poem forms part of *Hervarar saga ok Heiðreks*.

2. *The use of direct speech*

form. In those cases where an alternative type of strophe does occur in this type of poem, as in *Vafþrúðnismál*, st.5, or *Helgakviða Hundingsbana II*, it always takes the form of pure narrative verse, rather than 'blended' narrative-speech. This results in the strophe becoming an almost self-reliant, dispensable unit which might be considered to be an addition to the original poem.[28] Indeed, such a possibility is hardly unlikely considering the degree of editorial activity involved in the some parts of the collection of Eddic poems.[29]

c. The amount of prose connected to the various poems appears on the whole to be in proportion to the amount of pure speech they contain. Prose inserts occur particularly in dialogic poems with an epic structure, that is to say *Skírnismál*, *Reginsmál*, *Fáfnismál*, and the *Helgakviður*. In direct contrast to this, hardly any prose interpolations occur in the epic-dramatic poems. Many scholars have thus concluded that the prose accompanying the dialogic poems might often replace lost narrative strophes.[30] Such an argument, however, must be considered unlikely for two reasons. Firstly, in certain poems, such as *Fáfnismál*, prose is used to describe the most climatic pieces of action, material that is unlikely to have been forgotten in poetic form.[31] Secondly, the high proportion of narrative prose in the dialogic poems is balanced by the almost total absence of narrative or 'blended' strophes. As Wessén succinctly puts it, 'It would be an odd coincidence if it were only those strophes containing dialogue that were well preserved, while every one of the narrative strophes was forgotten and lost'.[32]

d. Different poetic metres appear to have been used for different types of poem (see *Table II* below). It is especially noteworthy that the majority of poems in dialogic or monologic form tend to have been composed in the *ljóðaháttr* metre ('the metre of chants/ incantations') rather than that known as *fornyrðislag* ('the rhythm of ancient words').

Bearing this last point in mind, it is worth taking a brief look at the chief characteristics of the three main metres encountered in the Eddic poems.

---

[28] This certainly applies in the case of *Vafþrúðnismál*, st.5, which only serves to indicate the transition of time and scene (see further below, *section G.6*). St.14, st.15 and st.17 in *Helgakviða Hundingsbana II* are shown by the redactor of the MS to be an interpolation since they all appear together as part of an inserted quotation from 'Völsungakviða in forna'.

[29] On the question of editorial activity, see the following section.

[30] See further below, *section D*.

[31] In certain cases, both the prose and the poetry seem to ignore such action: see Phillpotts, *The Elder Edda*, pp.103–106.

[32] 'Det vore en underlig tillfällighet, om just de strofer, som innehålla samtal, skulle ha blivit väl bevarade, men alla berättande strofer undantagslöst ha blivit glömda och gått förlorade': Wessén, 'Den isländska eddadiktningen', 28. Jónas Kristjánsson answers this statement in *Eddas and sagas*, p.49, by suggesting that the collectors may have summarised certain narrative parts of the poems in prose, but 'thought it less fitting to tamper with the words uttered by the heroic actors in the drama'. This is, of course, possible in the case of the *Helgakviður*. However, considering the near complete lack of narrative verse in the dialogic *ljóðaháttr* poems, this argument is not terrible convincing.

C. The Forms of Eddic Poetry

TABLE II

THE EDDIC POEMS: VERSE FORMS, DATING, THE PROPORTION OF SPEECH/ NARRATIVE, TRANSITIONS IN SPEAKER, AND NUMBER OF SPEAKING ROLES

Explanation of terms used in column headings

Verse form	Predominant verse form used in poem: F: *Fornyrðislag* L: *Ljóðaháttr* M: *Málaháttr*
E.Ó.S. dating:	Generalised dating allotted to the poem by Einar Ólafur Sveinsson in *Íslenzkar bókmenntir*: O: Older R: More recent
Strophes: Sp./Tot.:	The proportion of speech strophes to the total number of strophes in the poem.
Narr.sts:	The total number of narrative strophes.
Dialogue changes:	The number of times the poem passes directly from one speaker to another *without* an intervening narrative introduction to the new speaker being given as part of the strophe.
Spoken roles:	The number of direct speakers in the poem.
General class:	Four main categories have been given here: NS: Narrative with speech D: Dialogue M: Monologue FM: Framed monologue (the number of strophes in the central monologue also given in this column).

Poem	Verse form	E.Ó.S. dating	Strophes: Sp./Tot.	Narr. sts	Dialogue changes	Spoken roles	General class
Vsp.	F	O?	66/66	–	–	1	M
Háv.1	L	O	83/83	–	–	1	M
Háv.2	L	O	19/19	–	–	1	M
Háv.3	L	O	8/8	–	–	1	M
Háv.4	L	O	27/27	–	–	1	M
Háv.5	L	O	8/8	–	–	1	M
Háv.6	L	O	19/19	–	–	1	M
Vm.	L	O	1/55	1	52	3	D
Grm.	L	O	54/54	–	–	1	M
Skm.	L	O	42/42	–	25	5	D
Hrbl.	F? L?	O	60/60	–	59	2	D
Hym.	F	R	5/39	10	2	5	NS
Ls.	L	O?	61/61	–	61	16	D
Þrk.	F	O?	7/32	15	4	6	NS
Vkv.	F	O	18/41	7	8	6	NS
Alv.	L	R	35/35	–	33	2	D
HH.1	F	R	24/56	6	10	7	NS
HHv.	F(L)	O	42/43	–	34	8	D(N)
HH.2	F	O	48/51	–	27	8	D
Grp.	F	R	50/53	3(beg)	50	3	NS/D

191

III. The Eddic Poems and Drama

Poem	Verse form	E.Ó.S. dating	Strophes: Sp./Tot.	Narr. sts	Dialogue changes	Spoken roles	General class
Rm.	L(F)	O(R)	26/26	–	17	7	D
Fm.	L(F)	O(R)	44/44	–	33	4–10	D
Sd.	L(F)	O(R)	37/37	–	4	2	FM16+16
Br.	F	O	8/19	7	2	5	NS
Gðr.1	F	R	10/27	8	1	5	NS
Sgk.	F	R	43/71	9	2	4+GROUP	NS/FM20
Hlr.	F	R	14/14	–	3	2	FM 10
Gðr.2	F	R?	44/44 (18)	(2)	(14)	4	M(NS)
Gðr.3	F	R	7/11	2	1	2	NS
Od.	F	R	28/34	–	5	3	FM 20
Akv.	F	O	15/43	7	3	5	NS
Am.	F/M	R	49/103	14	29	6+GROUP	NS
Ghv.	F	R	16/21	2	–	2	FM 11
Hm.	F	O	11/31	10	3?	7	NS
Bdr.	F	O?	10/14	–	8	2	D(NS)
Rþ.	F	O	1/47	1	–	–	N?
Hdl.	F	R	50/50	–	8	2	FM 17
Grt.	F	O	17/24	3	3	3	NS
Hlð.	F	O	30/32	1	6	6–7	NS

Fornyrðislag and *málaháttr* ('the metre of speeches') are closely related to other forms of other early Germanic poetry in that they involve alliterating pairs of double-stressed lines. Both metres, however, were strophic. The lengths of the *fornyrðislag* strophes seem to have varied initially, but over time they became regulated to eight lines, each of which contained, on average, four or five syllables. Good examples of *fornyrðislag* are found, for example, in the poem *Völuspá*. The main distinguishing feature of *málaháttr* was that each of the eight lines had to be five syllables long. *Ljóðaháttr*, on the other hand, involved a six-line strophe, composed of two three-line units. The length of the lines in *ljóðaháttr* was more variable than those in *fornyrðislag*. However, the first and second (and fourth and fifth) lines, had two stresses each, and formed alliterating pairs. The third and sixth lines (often called 'full lines') tended to be longer, with two or three stressed syllables. These lines were also independent to the degree that they were internally alliterating (see most of the strophes quoted in this chapter).[33]

[33] For more detailed general reviews of the Eddic metres in English, see, for example, Foote and Wilson, *The Viking achievement*, pp.319–326, and Jónas Kristjánsson, *Eddas and sagas*, pp.33–36. See also Einar Ólafur Sveinsson, *Íslenzkar bókmenntir*, pp.103–121.

C. The Forms of Eddic Poetry

2. *The use of direct speech*

The differences in strophe length and metre, however, are not the only points of differentiation between those poems in *fornyrðislag* and *ljóðaháttr*. As Phillpotts pointed out, *ljóðaháttr* seems to be only used for speech, and the poems in *ljóðaháttr* seem to have a more 'popular' approach and a higher proportion of formulaic features such as incremental repetition.[34] These characteristics were also noted by Noreen, who went even further and lucidly pointed out a number of other important differences between the two metres, over and above the obviously looser syllabic count of *ljóðaháttr* lines:

a. *Ljóðaháttr* hardly occurs anywhere outside Eddic poetry.
b. There is less strict control of alliterative patterns in *ljóðaháttr* poems.
c. *Kenningar* (a particular form of skaldic metaphor) are used noticeably less in *ljóðaháttr* than in *fornyrðislag* poetry.
d. Variation (according to Noreen) does not occur in its true form in the *ljóðaháttr* poems.
e. Word order is, in general, much more natural in the *ljóðaháttr* poems than in those composed in *fornyrðislag*.[35]

The choice of using *ljóðaháttr* rather than *fornyrðislag* for the dialogic poems of course might be related as much to the magical/mythical subject matter of the poems in question as to the suggestion that *ljóðaháttr* was more naturally suited to speech than *fornyrðislag*.[36] Yet at the same time, Phillpotts' and Noreen's observations about the important stylistic differences between the *ljóðaháttr* poems on one hand and the epic-dramatic poems in *fornyrðislag* on the other cannot be ignored. It would seem that these two metres and the poems composed in them must have originated and been used in different milieu.

This idea would seem to be supported by the form of the poems themselves. Dispensing temporarily with the middleground of the monologic and 'framed' monologic poems, both of which involve primarily a *single* speaker, like an external narrator albeit 'in role', the reader is faced with two glaringly different types of poem:

a. The epic-dramatic poem in *fornyrðislag* which communicates its narrative solely via poetic means, employing an external omniscient primary narrator who dominates the story, and in some cases steps forward

---

[34] Phillpotts, *The Elder Edda*, pp.26–27, pp.41–42, and pp.88–99.
[35] See Noreen, 'Några anteckningar', 44–50, 'Eddastudier', 33–38, 'Studier, III', 5–18, and *Den norsk-isländska poesien*, pp.41–42. With regard to the more natural word order used in *ljóðaháttr* poems, it is worth bearing in mind two exceptions to this rule noted by Noreen, both of which seem to be particularly common in *ljóðaháttr*: firstly, the reversal of the word order in the case of certain prepositions, as in lines like 'horfa heimi ór' (*Skírnismál*, st.27); and secondly, the separation of the possessive pronoun from the noun it governs, especially when the possessive pronoun precedes the noun in question: e.g. 'gakk at beiða/ okkarn mála mǫg' (*Skírnismál*, st.1). See, for example, Noreen, 'Eddastudier', 36–37, note 1.
[36] See, for example, de Vries, *Literaturgeschichte*, 2nd ed., I, pp.25–26, and Einar Ólafur Sveinsson, *Íslenzkar bókmenntir*, p.201.

III. The Eddic Poems and Drama

2. *The use of direct speech*

to introduce, conclude and comment on the progress of the narrative to his listening audience, as in *Guðrúnarhvöt*, sts 1 and 21. In these poems, the characters are continuously being described for the audience/ reader, especially in the descriptive narrative introductions of the 'blended' narrative-speech strophes.

b. The dialogic poem, where the physical presence of the narrator as part of the poem is more open to discussion. Here, it would seem that rather than being told about a past event, the audience actually witness the action of the poem as it progresses; in short, they are not temporally distanced from the speech of the characters by the presence of the narrator. The lack of the narrator results also in the absence of direct character description of the kind encountered in the epic-dramatic poems. All character description and indication of setting and action have to be gleaned from the actual speech of the characters (and the prose interpolations).[37] Obviously, this kind of work has a great deal in common with drama.

It might be argued, of course, that the prose passages in the dialogic poems serve to replace the external narrator, and thus remove the essential difference between these two types of poem. This is indeed true, to some degree, in the case of the extant manuscripts. Nonetheless, as the following section will show, it is highly questionable whether the prose passages should be considered an intrinsic part of the poems as they were originally performed in the twelfth and thirteenth centuries.

D. The Prose in the Eddic Poems

Table I above illustrates the amount of prose connected to the various poems in the Eddic corpus. Most of this occurs in the form of introductions to certain poems, in particular to *Grímnismál*, *Reginsmál*, and *Guðrúnarkviða II* (the account entitled 'Dráp Niflunga').[38] Of these, the *Grímnismál* introduction is so complete in itself that it could have been drawn from a separate source in the form of an independent prose tale, or *þáttr*.[39] The other two long introductions would appear to have evolved either as the result of editorial emendation (especially 'Dráp Niflunga') or

---

[37] For a detailed examination of this 'einseitige' form in relation to the use of dialogue in other early Germanic poetry, see Heusler, 'Der Dialog', pp.611–689.
[38] The long prose section, 'Frá dauða Sinfjötla', which follows on from *Helgakviða Hundingsbana II*, would appear to be completely independent and has therefore not been included here.
[39] See Finnur Jónsson, 'Eddadigtenes samling', 225–226. In this article, Finnur revises his earlier suggestion that the *Grímnismál* prose was partially based on the poem itself (Finnur Jónsson, 'Sigurðarsaga', 16). He now observes that the prose before and after *Grímnismál* forms a complete story (minus one sentence which has been replaced by the poem) which was probably taken from another prose work. Wessén, in 'Den isländska eddadiktningen', 18, generally agrees, but points out that Snorri obviously had both the prose and poetic parts of *Grímnismál* combined in front of him when he composed the *Prose Edda*.

TABLE III

THE 'BLENDED STROPHES': NARRATIVE/ SPEECH PROPORTIONS

The following table illustrates the form of the 'blended' narrative-speech and speech-narrative strophes, which, as the table shows, do not occur in the dialogic *ljóðaháttr* poems. It also emphasises another common feature of these strophes, that is the tendency of the poets/ performers to begin mixed strophes with narrative, which is usually used for no more than half the strophe (2–4 lines, or *vísuorð*). These narrative passages usually form an introduction to the speaker, and often take an almost formulaic form, in which the speaker is named in the first line (e.g. 'Þá kvað Þrymr': 'Then Þrymr said'), the second (or second to third) line(s) providing an additional adverbial or adjectival phrase (e.g. 'Þursa dróttinn': 'Lord of the giants': *Þrymskviða*, sts 22, 25, and 30).

Abbreviations

N:S: Narrative:speech (in that order)
Blended sts: 'Blended' strophes (total).
Other forms: Unless otherwise stated, the figures here apply to a narrative/speech proportion, and are followed by the number of strophes in this form if there are more than one.
Other forms: SN = speech/narrative
              NSN = narrative/speech/narrative
              SNS = speech/narrative/speech

Poem	Blended sts	'Blended' strophes: Narrative:speech line proportions					Other forms
		N:S 2:6	N:S 4:4	N:S 2:8	N:S 4:6	N:S 2:4	
Vsp.	–	–	–	–	–	–	–
Háv.	–	–	–	–	–	–	–
Vm.	–	–	–	–	–	–	–
Grm.	–	–	–	–	–	–	–
Skm.	–	–	–	–	–	–	–
Hrbl.	–	–	–	–	–	–	–
Hym.	10	–	4	–	–	–	6/2: 2 SN 4/4: 3 NSN 4/1/3
Ls.	–	–	–	–	–	–	–
Þrk.	15	5	6	–	1	2	6/4, 6/2 4/2, 3/2
Vkv.	7	–	1	–	–	1	NSN 3/1/4 and st.29
Alv.	–	–	–	–	–	–	–
HH.1	6	–	1	–	–	1	6/2 7/1 8/2 SN 4/4
HHv.	–	–	–	–	–	–	–
HH.2	–	–	–	–	–	–	–
Grp.	3	1	2	–	–	–	–

III. The Eddic Poems and Drama

Poem	Blended sts	'Blended' strophes: Narrative:speech line proportions					Other forms
		N:S 2:6	N:S 4:4	N:S 2:8	N:S 4:6	N:S 2:4	
Rm.	–	–	–	–	–	–	–
Fm.	–	–	–	–	–	–	–
Sd.	–	–	–	–	–	–	–
Br.	7	2	4	–	–	1	–
Gðr.1	8	2	1	2	–	–	2/10,2/4 NSN 2/4/2
Sgk.	9	2	4	1	–	–	2/10: 2
Hlr.	–	–	–	–	–	–	–
Gðr.2	2	–	2	–	–	–	–
Gðr.3	2	–	2	–	–	–	–
Od.	–	–	–	–	–	–	–
Akv.	7	1	2	2	–	–	1/2,6/2
Am.	14	3	5	1	–	2	6/2 SN6/2,4/4
Ghv.	2	–	–	2	–	–	–
Hm.	11	2	4	1	1	1	2/2
Bdr.	–	–	–	–	–	–	–
Rþ.	1	–	–	–	–	1	–
Hdl.	–	–	–	–	–	–	–
Grt.	3	–	–	–	–	2	NSN2/2/2
Hlð.	1	–	1	–	–	–	–

were also borrowed from other independent prose sources, such as the 'ancient tales' ('fornum sǫgum') referred to in the prose introduction to *Rígsþula*. Indeed, Finnur Jónsson suggested that a majority of the prose passages in the section of the *Codex Regius* manuscript between *Helgakviða Hundingsbana II* and *Guðrúnarkviða I* were taken from a lost prose work about Sigurðr Fáfnisbani known as 'Sigurðar saga'.[40] Whatever the truth may be, there is good reason to doubt whether any of the above pieces of prose is essential to the poems that they introduce. The question now is whether the same applies to the other shorter passages of prose in the manuscripts containing the Eddic poems.

In general, later editorial emendation would seem to explain a majority

---

[40] See Finnur Jónsson, 'Sigurðarsaga'. This idea has since been supported by several scholars: see Jón Helgason, *Eddadigte*, III, pp.xiii–xiv; and Jónas Kristjánsson, 'Sigurðar saga'. See also further below in this section, and note 59. In 'Sigurðarsaga', 18, Finnur Jónsson shows how 'Dráp Niflunga' appears to be built on material contained in *Guðrúnarkviða II* and the poems dealing with Atli. This passage, interestingly enough, does not appear in *Völsunga saga* which is otherwise largely based on the poems contained in the heroic section of the *Codex Regius*.

D. The Prose in the Eddic Poems

of the prose interpolations, particularly those found in the latter part of the *Codex*. It is immediately apparent, for example, that many of these shorter prose passages belong to a completely different moral and temporal climate to that of the poems. In them, the author of the prose actively distances himself from the setting, sources, and particularly the folk beliefs of his material. This is especially relevant to the *Helgakviður* prose, where, concerning the question of the supposed reincarnation of Helgi Hjörvarðsson and Sváva, and Helgi Hundingsbani and Sigrún, the prose writer goes out of his way to emphasise his impartiality in statements like '*It is said that* Helgi and Sváva were reborn' (*Helgakviða Hjörvarðssonar*, following st.43),[41] and '*It was believed in ancient times that* people were reborn, *but that is an old wives' tale*. Helgi and Sigrún are *said to have been* reborn. He was then called Helgi Haddingiaskati, and she was named Kára, daughter of Hálfdan, *as is told in Káruljóð*; she was a *valkyrja*' (*Helgakviða Hundingsbana II*, following st.51).[42] The same attitudes and temporal distancing are also found in the prose comment preceding st.1 of *Fáfnismál* that '*It was believed by people in ancient times that* the words of a doomed man had great power, especially if he cursed his enemy by name.'[43]

Similar distancing references with regard to sources occur in the following statements from the introductions to *Guðrúnarkviða I* (the passage entitled 'Frá dauða Sigurðar') and *Helreið Brynhildar* respectively: '*People say that* Guðrún ate some of Fáfnir's heart, and understood the language of birds',[44] and '*It is said that* Brynhildr rode to Hel in the wagon'.[45] The same occurs in the longest prose passage, 'Frá dauða Sinfjötla', where the reader is informed that 'Sigurðr was the greatest of all, and *all men in ancient tales state that* he stood above all others, and was the noblest of military kings'.[46] Certainly, the reference to other men here is used to emphasise Sigurðr's fame. However, once again the word 'ancient' ('forn') emphasises a temporal separation between writer and subject.

The final distancing reference to be mentioned in this context occurs in the passage following the fragment of *Sigurðarkviða* ('Frá dauða Sigurðar')

---

[41] 'Helgi ok Sváva er *sagt at væri* endrborin'. All the emphases here and in the following passages from the Eddic poems and the *Prose Edda* are my own.

[42] '*Þat var trúa í forneskio at* menn væri endrbornir, en *þat er nú kǫlluð kerlingavilla*. Helgi ok Sigrún er *kallat at væri* endrborin. Hét hann þá Helgi Haddingiaskati, en hón Kára Hálfdanar dóttir, *svá sem kveðit er í Károlióðom*, ok var hón valkyria.' It is debatable whether the author of this prose comment has inserted the reference to 'Káruljóð' at this point to emphasise further his personal independence from this belief, or whether he simply forgot to make the comment about the *valkyrja* until the end. Even then, however, it would betray an immediacy of writing unrelated to any exact or careful memorial rendering of the prose as part of the poem.

[43] '... þat var trúa þeira í forneskio at orð feigs mannz mætti mikit, ef hann bǫlvaði óvin sínom með nafni.'

[44] '*Þat er sǫgn manna*, at Guðrún hefði etið af Fáfnis hiarta oc hon scildi því fugls rǫdd.'

[45] '*Svá er sagt, at* Brynhildr óc með reiðinni á helveg ...'

[46] 'Sigurðr var þó allra framarstr, ok *hann kalla allir menn í fornfræðom* um alla menn fram ok gǫfgastan herkonunga.'

III. The Eddic Poems and Drama

where the redactor, who apparently has difficulties reconciling the different accounts of Sigurðr's death given in the previous poem and in those that follow, lapses into a confused bout of excuses about his earlier sources:

> *This poem tells* about the death of Sigurðr, and implies that they killed him out of doors. Yet *some say* that they killed him when he was sleeping in his bed. But *some Germans say that* they killed him outside in a forest. *And then the old Guðrúnarkviða says* that Sigurðr and the sons of Gjúki had ridden to the *þing* and that he was killed there. But *everybody also says* that they betrayed his trust, and killed him while he was lying down and unprepared.[47]

This last quotation displays not only temporal objective distancing, but also an academic editorial approach to the poems which are named and referred to as separate entities, alienated from the prose comment. The same tone is encountered in the editorial introductory comments that have been affixed to *Atlakviða, Atlamál, Helgakviða Hundingsbana I, Völundarkviða*, and even *Rígsþula* where the prose comment encompasses all of the distancing devices met so far:

Atlakviða: 'As *is well known*, Guðrún Gjúkadóttir avenged her brothers . . . *This poem deals with these events.*'[48]

Atlamál: 'But *Atlamál in groenlensku tells (of this) even more clearly.*'[49]

Helgakviða Hundingsbana I: '*Now commences a poem* about Helgi Hundingsbani and Höðbroddr.'[50]

Völundarkviða: 'King Níðuðr had him taken prisoner, *as is recounted in this poem.*'[51]

Rígsþula: '*In ancient tales people say* that one of the Æsir gods named Heimdallr was out travelling . . .' and '*this poem is based on that story.*'[52]

These distancing techniques are not the only reasons for considering the prose comments to be separate entities from the poems themselves. Several of the prose passages quoted above also contain short or more detailed summaries of the material dealt with in the poem(s) that follow. Such an approach implies foreknowledge of one or more of the poems on the part of the prose 'narrator', who can be said to be actively presenting the poems as a form of flashback. This is particularly relevant in the case of the two

---

[47] 'Hér er sagt í þessi qviðo frá dauða Sigurðar, oc vícr hér svá til, sem þeir dræpi hann úti. Enn *sumir segia svá*, at þeir dræpi hann inni í reccio sinni sofanda. Enn *þýðverscir menn segia svá*, at þeir dræpi hann úti í scógi. Oc *svá segir í Guðrúnarqviðo inni forno*, at Sigurðr oc Giúca synir hefði til þings riðit, þá er hann var drepinn. Enn *þat segia allir einnig*, at þeir svíco hann í trygð oc vógo at hánom liggianda oc óbunum.'

[48] 'Guðrún, Giúca dóttir, hefndi bræðra sinna, svá *sem frægt er orðit*. . . *Um þetta er siá qviða ort.*'

[49] 'Enn segir gleggra í Atlamálom inom grænlenzcom.'

[50] 'Hér hefr upp kvæði frá Helga Hundings bana þeira ok H(ǫðbrodds).'

[51] 'Níðuðr konungr lét hann hǫndom taka, *svá sem hér er um kveðit.*'

[52] '*Svá segia menn í fornum sǫgum* at einhverr af ásum, sá er Heimdallr hét, fór ferðar sinnar . . .' and '*Eptir þeiri sǫgu er kvæði þetta.*'

D. The Prose in the Eddic Poems

long prose passages, 'Frá dauða Sigurðar' (mentioned above), and 'Dráp Niflunga' which precedes *Guðrúnarkviða II*. Both of these passages take on the introductory 'summary' ('oversigt') role postulated by Finnur Jónsson with regard to the role and placing of *Völuspá*, *Helgakviða Hundingsbana I* and *Grípisspá* in the *Codex Regius*.[53] In the case of 'Dráp Niflunga', for example, the reader is informed of Gunnar's death in the snake pit three poems before it evenually occurs in *Atlakviða*. The 'Dráp Niflunga' prose thus links all of the following poems leading up to *Atlakviða* (*Guðrúnarkviða II and III* and *Oddrúnargrátr*) in the form of a continuous narrative where all events appear to be guided by an inexorable fate towards a foreseen end.

All of these points, and more (such as the prose connecting *Hymiskviða* and *Lokasenna* in the *Codex Regius*),[54] would appear to support the suggestion originally made by Finnur Jónsson that the ordering of the poems of the *Codex* was guided by a redactor who had some overall concept in mind.[55] By reordering and linking the poems, according to what Finnur calls the 'story principle' ('sagaprincip') and 'summary principle' ('oversigtsprincip'), he created for the reader a form of continuous narrative that arguably stretched throughout the *Codex*.

The above points, however, raise another question more directly relevant to the argument being made in this present book. Since such a large number of the prose statements in the *Codex Regius* (particularly those in the later part of the manuscript, from *Sigrdrífumál* onwards) can obviously be attributed to editorial emendation, can the same conclusion be broadly applied to *all* the prose in the Eddic collection? In particular, is it possible to say the same thing about the prose connected to the dialogic poems in *ljóðaháttr*, few of which (apart from two brief references to *Fáfnismál* and *Lokasenna*) have been mentioned in the above references?

The most detailed examinations of the prose passages in the *Codex Regius* are those conducted by Sijmons, Finnur Jónsson, Heusler and Wessén,[56] all of whom were attempting to estimate the prehistory and formation of the *Codex Regius* from the content and context of the prose. All of these scholars are in agreement about the presence of external and unnecessary editorial comment in the prose passages, particularly in the final section of the manuscript commencing with 'Dráp Niflunga'. Otherwise, the extent of this later interpolation appears to be under dispute.

---

[53] See references above in note 1.
[54] The back-reference to *Hymiskviða* at the start of *Lokasenna* does not appear to have preceded *Lokasenna* until the *Codex Regius* was assembled. See further below, *section F.2*.
[55] See Finnur Jónsson, 'Eddadigtenes samling', 223–225. This idea is supported by most scholars. See, for example, Wessén, 'Den isländska eddadiktningen', 3–4; Lindblad, 'Poetiska Eddans förhistoria', 142–143; and Klingenberg, *Edda*, pp.37–41.
[56] Sijmons, 'Einleitung', pp.cliii–clxii; Finnur Jónsson, 'Sigurðarsaga', and 'Eddadigtenes samling', 216–233; Heusler, introduction to *The Codex Regius*, p.19; and Wessén, 'Den isländska eddadiktningen', 11 and 15–31. See also Phillpotts, *The Elder Edda*, pp.100–110; and Jónas Kristjánsson, 'Sigurðar saga', and *Eddas and sagas*, pp.48–49.

III. The Eddic Poems and Drama

Finnur Jónsson believed an almost complete collection of the poems was in existence as early as c.1200,[57] and both he and Barend Sijmons regarded all the prose as totally extraneous. Some of it they felt was an unnecessary rewording of strophes still extant in the poems, as in the cases of the internal prose in *Skírnismál*, *Lokasenna*, and *Völundarkviða*, and in the introductions to *Hárbarðsljóð* and the poems following 'Dráp Niflunga'. They suggest that the prose elsewhere reflects an editorial approach which arose from the splicing together of extant poetry and prose saga, as seems to have applied in the cases of *Grímnismál* and the Sigurðr poems (the section running from *Reginsmál* to *Sigrdrífumál*[58]). As a source for the prose comments accompanying the Sigurðr poems, both scholars point to the assumed prior existence of the 'Sigurðar saga' mentioned above.[59] This latter suggestion is supported by Heusler.[60] Wessén is slightly more sceptical, but suggests that the extant prose comments in the Helgi poems (the *Helgakviður*) and those in the early Sigurðr poems probably originated from the same source.[61]

There is unfortunately no space in this present book to deal in any detail with the complex matter of the *Helgakviður* which are so central to Phillpotts' argument. However, a brief examination of the academic approaches to the prose sections of these poems is of particular interest for the present examination. It might be noted that the scholars mentioned above are in agreement that the section of the *Codex* containing the *Helgakviður* bears all the signs of complex editorial work, so much so that it is impossible to say whether the poems were originally wholly dialogic or not.[62] Regarding the prose in this section of the manuscript, however, Finnur Jónsson suggests that the redactor approached his material in a similar way to the creator of the later *Völsunga saga*, strophes being removed from the poems and substituted by prose wherever possible.[63] Heusler, like Müllenhoff,[64] believed that the *Codex* in the main represented the joining together of four previous collections of poems, one of them being that containing the *Helgakviður*. Heusler disagreed with some of the suggestions made by Finnur Jónsson about the development of the prose, but he did envisage an editor of 'helpless incapacity' as being the master-

---

[57] Finnur Jónsson, 'Eddadigtenes samling', 221.
[58] Sijmons, in 'Einleitung', pp.lxii–lxxiv, and p.clx, considers that this approach goes as far as the prose introduction to *Helreið Brynhildar*.
[59] 'Sigurðar saga' is mentioned in *Norna-Gests þáttr*, in *Flateyjarbok* (1860–1868), I, p.353, and in *Háttatal*, in *Edda* (1926), p.163. For further references, see above, note 40.
[60] Heusler, introduction to *The Codex Regius*, p.29. See also note 82.
[61] Wessén, 'Den isländska eddadiktningen', 27–29.
[62] There are no wholly dialogic poems in *fornyrðislag* outside the *Helgakviður* apart from *Helreið Brynhildar* and *Hyndluljóð*, both of which have to be seen as 'framed' monologues rather than pure dialogue. It is equally impossible to assume, as Phillpotts does in *The Elder Edda*, pp.53–54, p.58 and pp.79–81, that the *Helgakviður* or *Hyndluljóð* originally existed in *ljóðaháttr*, in a comparable form to works like *Skírnismál* and *Fáfnismál*.
[63] Finnur Jónsson, 'Eddadigtenes samling', 228–232.
[64] Müllenhoff, *Deutsche Altertumskunde*, V, p.158 and p.235.

D. The Prose in the Eddic Poems

mind behind the existing form of the Helgi section. The *Helgakviður* for him represented the 'patching together of complete and fragmentary lays, and probably *lausavísur* (individual verses) as well, held together by prose passages of unusual length and frequency, causing the literary genre of certain verse passages to remain uncertain.'[65] To Heusler's mind, therefore, the prose here originates in several ways: in some places it is mere editorial emendation for the purpose of linking fragments, but elsewhere it simply replaces lost verses.[66] De Vries took both Heusler's and Finnur Jónsson's arguments regarding editorial work one step further in his suggestion that when writing out *Helgakviða Hundingsbana II*, the redactor or collector used prose to summarise those passages in which the poetic text was a duplicate of the first Helgi poem. *Helgakviða Hundingsbana II* thus sums up Helgi's birth in prose (since this was covered in *Helgakviða Hundingsbana I*) but included a poetic account of certain other events not previously mentioned in the other poem.[67]

Not everybody was content to put the origin of the prose solely in the hands of an editor. Wessén, for example, dismissed Heusler's idea of the prose replacing lost verses as a romantic misconception. For him, 'the idea that the individual strophes and strophe series contained in *Helgakviða Hundingsbana II* should have been preserved without any form of connecting narrative is totally absurd . . . No fundamental alteration took place during the process of transformation from the oral account to that which now exists in written form. A mixed form (of poetry and prose) was still necessary.'[68] Wessén's concept of a mixed prose/ verse form has been supported in more recent years by other scholars such as Holm-Olsen and Jónas Kristjánsson who suggests this particular possibility, alongside those of the prose replacing lost strophes, or being a method employed by the original collectors to summarise narrative sections of the text.[69] Indeed, both this proposed mixed prose/ verse form and the use of prose to replace forgotten verses find support from the evidence of other oral cultures, and

---

[65] Heusler, introduction to *The Codex Regius* , p.27.
[66] In his introduction to *The Codex Regius*, p.20, Heusler notes that the prose of the *Helgakviður* displays 'the telegraphic style which Icelandic sagas often shew as a result of compression'. He also draws attention here to the fact that Sváva and Sigrún are said to be *valkyrjur* only in the prose sections of the poem, something that again implies some difference between the poem and the prose. Phillpotts, in *The Elder Edda*, p.100, reaches a similar conclusion to Heusler.
[67] De Vries, 'Die Helgilieder', 123–125. Harris, in 'Eddic poetry as oral poetry', p.215, comments that 'this explanation . . . calls for qualification in several respects, but the principle of complementarity probably did have an effect on the form of *HHII*.'
[68] 'Att dessa stofer og strofföljder, som ingå i HHu II, skulle ha kunnat bevaras utan att ingå i en sammanhängande berättelse, är en rätt orimlig tanke . . . Någon principiell förändring har icke skett vid övergången från muntlig saga til skriftlig framställning. En blandad form var fortfarande nödvändig': Wessén, 'Den isländska eddadiktningen', 22–23; see also 28.
[69] See Holm-Olsen, *Edda-dikt* (1985), p.9, and Jónas Kristjánsson, *Eddas and sagas*, p.49. Regarding the idea of the mixed prose/ verse form, see further below, *sections E.3 and F.5*.

III. The Eddic Poems and Drama

particularly from those of Mongolia which bear several close resemblances to the poetic form at present under discussion. Oral performers of the Mongol epics, for example, habitually summarise in prose any passages they cannot remember in verse form. They also reveal a tendency, similar to that posed by Wessén for the *ljóðaháttr* poems, of presenting speeches and, above all, monologues in verse while giving the narrative passages in prose.[70]

The dispute about the origin of the prose accompanying the *Helgakviður* (the verse of which is predominantly dialogic) leads on to the question of the prose accompanying the other dialogic poems which are found primarily in the mythological section of the *Codex Regius*. Here, while some organisation of the poems is evident (unlike in the AM 748 manuscript), there is no obvious overall narrative 'sagaprincip' at work as there seems to have been in the case of the Helgi or Sigurðr poems. Nor are there as many obvious external editorial comments as in the latter part of the *Codex*. Given this latter feature alone, it would seem evident that a different editorial style and approach was employed in this section of the manuscript and/ or its forerunner.

Before proceeding to examine the prose accompanying the mythological poems, it is worth briefly summing up the possible origins that scholars have suggested for the prose accompanying the other Eddic poems:

a. The prose represents purely unnecessary editorial rewriting of existing strophe material for the sake of narrative clarity.

b. The prose originated with the redactor and was either 'intended to explain the passages in verse' or to 'open up a wider perspective'.[71]

c. The prose replaced lost verses, an argument Heusler held on to firmly, albeit with the slight reservation that 'this is less frequently the case than used to be supposed'.[72]

d. The prose replaced existing verses perhaps for the sake of brevity, an argument supported in particular by both Finnur Jónsson and Jónas Kristjánsson.[73] Indeed, there is evidence of this approach being employed by the 'author' of *Völsunga saga*, and by Snorri Sturluson in his *Prose Edda*, albeit for differing ends.

e. The prose replaced earlier prose passages that already existed alongside the verse in the oral tradition, but, which, according to Wessén, was not as stable or decided as the verse.[74] Many scholars, including Einar Ólafur Sveinsson and Jónas Kristjánsson, have echoed Wessén's belief in the existence of this blended prose/ verse form which will be discussed in more

---

[70] See Bawden, 'Mongol', p.272, pp.278–282, and pp.292–293.
[71] Heusler, introduction to *The Codex Regius*, p.19.
[72] Heusler, introduction to *The Codex Regius*, p.19.
[73] Finnur Jónsson, 'Eddadigtenes samling', 229, and Jónas Kristjánsson, *Eddas and sagas*, p.49.
[74] Wessén, 'Den isländska eddadiktningen', 23.

E. The Dialogic Poems in 'Ljóðaháttr'

detail below.[75] Both Wessén and Heusler stress furthermore that the collectors were most interested in collecting the verse passages, and took less care about the prose for the reason that the prose had always been variable.[76] As a result, according to Wessén, the prose is much more telescoped than it would have been originally.[77]

Which of the above explanations would appear to apply in the case of the prose in the dialogic *ljóðaháttr* poems? Can these works be regarded as having been prose/verse compositions from the start, as Wessén, Heusler and Einar Ólafur Sveinsson suggest, or were they, as Finnur Jónsson, Sijmons, and Phillpotts argue, originally free of all prose comments?[78] As regards the form of the original performances of these works, and the dividing line between drama and pure poetry, this question is highly important.

1. 'Skírnismál', 'Hárbarðsljóð', 'Vafþrúðnismál', 'Lokasenna' and 'Fáfnismál': General Relationships

The rest of this chapter will be devoted to a closer examination of one particular group of dialogic poems that stand apart from the other poems of the Poetic Edda, not only because of their form, but also, and perhaps most importantly, because of the way they are presented in the *Codex Regius* and AM 748 manuscript. The poems in question are *Skírnismál*, *Lokasenna*, *Fáfnismál*, *Hárbarðsljóð*, and *Vafþrúðnismál*.

These works have a number of common features in addition to the facts that they are all dialogic, and that four of them are in *ljóðaháttr* (*Hárbarðsljóð* being a strange mixture of prose, *fornyrðislag*, *málaháttr*, and *ljóðaháttr* with the odd line of prose appearing here and there[79]). As

---

[75] See Heusler, introduction to *The Codex Regius*, p.19; Einar Ólafur Sveinsson, *Íslenzkar bókmenntir*, p.200 and p.276; Söderberg, 'Lokasenna', 83; Jónas Kristjánsson, *Eddas and sagas*, p.49; and Steinsland, *Det hellige bryllup*, p.43.

[76] This approach would find some support in *Norna-Gests þáttr*, pp.349–356. See further section F.5 below.

[77] In 'Den isländska eddadiktningen', 13–15, Wessén suggests that prose introductions and interpolations similar to those found in the other poems must have once existed alongside *Völuspá*, *Alvíssmál* and *Hamðismál*. In his opinion, the prose introductions to poems like *Grímnismál* have survived largely because they are so well supported by the verse material of the poems themselves.

[78] Phillpotts, in *The Elder Edda*, pp.100–110, limits the types of prose to three basic forms: that added in the form of introductions or conclusions to the poems; that which replaces lost verses (as in the case of the *Helgakviður*, and, to her mind, *Grímnismál*); and that which acts merely as a 'prose aside', describing action implied by the verse (i.e. the short prose statements found particularly in the *ljóðaháttr* poems discussed below). In the long run, Phillpotts regards all of the prose as having been written in Iceland by the collector of the poems or the redactor of the *Codex Regius*.

[79] Finnur Jónsson conveniently saw *Hárbarðsljóð* as being primarily a *málaháttr* poem, interspersed with additional fragments in other verse forms: see Finnur Jónsson,

III. The Eddic Poems and Drama

1. 'Skírnismál', 'Hárbarðsljóð', 'Vafþrúðnismál', 'Lokasenna' and 'Fáfnismál': General relationships

Lindblad has pointed out, in manuscript form *Skírnismál* and *Hárbarðsljóð* display a large amount of orthographical and paleographical similarities.[80] It would thus appear that they were originally transcribed together, separately from the other poems in the mythological part of the *Codex*.

Other isolated 'groupings' identified by Lindblad in the *Codex*, are, interestingly enough, the section containing *Helgakviða Hjörvarðssonar* and *Helgakviða Hundingsbana II*, and the *Reginsmál/ Fáfnismál* section. Each of these parts of the *Codex* would also appear to have led an independent existence prior to the assembly of what Lindblad sees as being the prototype volume of heroic poems.[81] The identification of these groupings forms part of Lindblad's argument for a step-by-step development towards the *Codex* which has since been accepted by most scholars, and is worth bearing in mind for the argument that follows below. Lindblad's proposal, similar in many ways to the earlier arguments of Müllenhoff and Heusler, is that the extant collection of Eddic poems began to take shape in the early thirteenth century centring around two smaller main collections: a collection of Sigurðr poems (a 'Sigurðar saga' which included both Heusler's so-called 'Hortlied' and 'Vaterrachelied'); and a small collection of mythological poems that perhaps began with *Grímnismál* and *Vafþrúðnismál*, the two poems which Snorri Sturluson would seem to have had at hand in their extant form when he was writing the *Prose Edda*; and which possibly also included *Völuspá* and *Hymiskviða*.[82] Lindblad believes that poems were added gradually to both collections, the 'heroic collection' taking in other Guðrún and Brynhildr poems, and eventually also the previously assembled group of poems that centred around the figure of Helgi. This 'Völsungr' collection then joined the by now virtually complete 'mythological collection' (which at an earlier stage would appear to have resembled the AM 748 collection). This now placed the Sigurðr story in a slightly tenuous mythological context, the links between Sigurðr's family and

---

'Hárbarþsljóþ', and *Litteraturs historie*, I, pp.154–155. See further below in *section G.5* for comment on this. Noreen, in 'Studier, III', 15, and *Den norsk-isländska poesien*, p.77, is less decisive, but believes that the relatively loose *ljóðaháttr* form has probable genetic connections with the highly variable poetic form of *Hárbarðsljóð* which he places alongside Sievers' 'Sagdichtung', an early Germanic verse form used for 'lagvers', proverbs, and so on. See also Noreen, 'Eddastudier', 37–38, on Eduard Sievers, *Die altschwedischen Upplandslagh nebst Proben formverwandter germanischer Sagdichtung*.

[80] Lindblad, *Studier*, p.262, and 'Poetiska Eddans förhistoria', 162.
[81] See Lindblad, *Studier*, pp.267–268, and 'Poetiska Eddans förhistoria', 162. As Lindblad shows in *Studier*, p.268, *Reginsmál* and *Fáfnismál* are particularly close, but other close similarities are also found in *Sigrdrífumál* which may have joined them at an early stage. See further below. In general, as Lindblad points out in 'Poetiska Eddans förhistoria', 162, all three poems seem to have existed together in an early collection along with the prose 'Frá dauða Sinfjötla' and *Grípisspá*.
[82] See Lindblad, 'Poetiska Eddans förhistoria', 144–147 and 159–166, and *Studier*, p.265; Müllenhoff, *Deutsche Altertumskunde*, V, p.158 and p.235; and Heusler's introduction to *The Codex Regius*, p.19. Regarding the *Hortlied* and *Vaterrachelied*, see below, *sections D and G.4a*.

E. The Dialogic Poems in 'Ljóðaháttr'

1. 'Skírnismál', 'Hárbarðsljóð', 'Vafþrúðnismál', 'Lokasenna' and 'Fáfnismál': General relationships

Óðinn being given additional weight.[83] This suggestion of a gathering together of smaller collections naturally emphasises the possibility that different sections of the *Codex* manuscript might contain different editorial approaches.

Orthographical and paleographical similarities, however, are not the only points of comparison regarding the five poems under discussion. More recently, Söderberg has made a thorough and objective investigation of the textual and stylistic similarities between *Lokasenna* and the other Eddic poems, and concludes that a particularly close relationship seems to have existed between *Lokasenna*, *Hárbarðsljóð* and *Skírnismál*.[84] To some extent, this supports the previous observations of Bugge, Olsen, and, in particular, those made by Guðbrandur Vigfússon and Powell, who postulated that all three poems were written by the same poet, their 'Western Islands' Aristophanes'.[85] On the surface, Söderberg agrees with this, commenting that superficially, at least, these three poems would definitely appear to 'go back to one and the same person, if not the "Western Aristophanes", then perhaps an Icelandic Lucian.'[86]

Guðbrandur Vigfússon and Powell, however, went further than this,

---

[83] Lindblad's argument would appear to disprove conclusively the earlier arguments favouring a very long and complicated process of collection (see, for example, Sijmons, 'Einleitung', p.clii), or the early dating of the initial collections, as supported by Sijmons (see above), and Finnur Jónsson, in 'Eddadigtenes samling', 223, and *De gamle Eddadigte*, p.viii. It also refutes the 'single-leaf' argument posited by Wessén in 'Den isländska eddadiktningen', 1–12. Wessén is against the idea of earlier minor collections, suggesting instead that the poems were recorded and preserved individually. For him, the semi-organised form that the poems now have in the *Codex Regius* only took shape in the final editing of the MS.

[84] Söderberg, 'Formelgods', 50–79. See also Bibire, who, in 'Freyr and Gerðr', p.22, also talks of close links between *Skírnismál*, *Lokasenna* and *Helgakviða Hjörvarðssonar* 'which could indicate literary relationship . . . or which could also indicate the precise and specific literary convention used in these texts.'

[85] Guðbrandur Vigfússon and Powell, *Corpvs Poeticvm Boreale*, I, p.lxvii, and pp.100–123; see also the *Introduction*, note 23. These scholars concentrated on word similarities, emphasising in particular the occurrence of word compounds based on the word *gamban* which are only found in these poems, i.e. *gambanreiði* (*Skírnismál*, st.33), *gambantein* (*Skírnismál*, st.32 and *Hárbarðsljóð*, st.20), and *gambansumbl* (*Lokasenna*, st.8). See also Bugge, 'Iduns Æbler', 4, and Olsen, *Edda-og-skaldekvad*, I, p.86. Bugge suggests that *Lokasenna* and *Skírnismál* had the same author, Olsen that *Lokasenna* and *Hárbarðsljóð* were closely connected.

[86] '. . . alla tre dikterna återgår på en och samma person, om inte de västliga öarnas Aristofanes, så kanske dock en isländsk Lucianos': Söderberg, 'Formelgods', 78. Nonetheless, in the second of her articles on *Lokasenna* ('Lokasenna', 79), Söderberg proceeds to date *Lokasenna* to the Age of the Sturlungar (c.1152–1262) which, considering Noreen's suggestion about the possibility of *Skírnismál* having been composed before 700, could mean a space of four centuries between the 'composition' of the two poems (if they are taken as having ever been 'composed' in the ordinary sense of the word). On the question of dating, see also Jónas Kristjánsson, *Eddas and sagas*, p.30 and p.39, on the likelihood of *Lokasenna* also being a pre-Christian work. Even if there is an age difference, this does not devalue the importance of the similarities between the poems, which could still suggest that all three poems belonged to a particular tradition or were being preserved in a limited geographical area at the time of collection.

2. The marginal speaker indications in the Edda manuscripts

suggesting that 'The Old Wolsung Play' (*Reginsmál/ Fáfnismál/ Sigrdrífumál*) alone shows parallelisms to the other three.[87] In this argument they were supported by Olsen,[88] but do not win much favour with Söderberg who notes the parallels but does not find them convincing enough to suggest direct borrowing or close textual similarity. Söderberg, however, illustrates close links between *Lokasenna*, *Vafþrúðnismál* and *Hávamál*, and suggests that the first poem deliberately satirises elements borrowed from the other two.[89]

Nonetheless, the most obvious common feature linking all five of the aforementioned poems is something that is apparent only in the *Codex Regius* and AM 748 manuscripts, and diplomatic editions made of them, namely the way in which the various individual speakers in the dialogic poems were originally identified for readers.

2. The Marginal Speaker Indications in the Edda Manuscripts[90]

In most editions of the Eddic poems, editors have adopted the style of presentation employed by playwrights, placing the names of the speakers in the dialogic poems in full either above or beside their words. However, this is a somewhat misleading approach because it differs radically from the form employed in the actual manuscripts. Certainly, in some poems in the *Codex*, it is possible to see the speaker named in a normal, virtually unabbreviated fashion within the body of the manuscript text itself, as occasionally occurs in *Reginsmál*, *Völundarkviða*, *Helreið Brynhildar*, and *Helgakviða Hundingsbana II*, for example. Yet what is more common and even more interesting is that in long passages of dialogue, the names of the speakers are often dropped completely, as occurs, for example, in the manuscript versions of *Alvíssmál*, *Grípisspá*, and most of the epic-dramatic poems where the audience is often given some other form of direct guidance within the poetic text itself about who is speaking at any given time.

Considering the previous statement, it might be noted that those sections of the *Codex Regius* manuscript containing the epic-dramatic poems display a variety of methods for indicating the names of speakers for the

---

[87] Guðbrandur Vigfússon and Powell, *Corpvs Poeticvm Boreale*, I, p.lxvii, note 1.

[88] Olsen, *Edda-og-skaldekvad*, I, p.86, and II, p.53.

[89] Söderberg, 'Formelgods', 56–79. In this context, it is also worth noting Kragerud's observation in 'De mytologiske spørsmål', 21, that in *Fáfnismál* there seems to be a peculiar tendency to place 'universal statements' alongside particulars, i.e. general proverbial statements meant to be applied to the concrete situation. This tendency, Kragerud points out, also occurs in *Vafþrúðnismál*, *Skírnismál*, *Hárbarðsljóð*, *Lokasenna* and *Hávamál*.

[90] See the following editions of the MSS: *Håndskriftet nr.2365 4to gl. kgl. Samling*, ed. Wimmer and Finnur Jónsson (1891); *The Codex Regius*, ed. Heusler (1937); *Håndskriftet nr.748, 4to, bl.1–6*, ed. Finnur Jónsson (1896); and *Fragments of the Elder and the Younger Edda*, ed. Wessén (1945). See also Jón Helgason, *Eddadigte*, II, pp.xii–xiv, and *Eddadigte*, III, p.xvii, and pp.20–21, on the markings.

E. The Dialogic Poems in 'Ljóðaháttr'

reading or listening audience, all of which could have been used effectively with the dialogic poems:

a. The earlier mentioned 'blended' narrative-speech verse form, where speakers are named in verse usually at the start of the strophe. Here two-line narrative introductions are sometimes found preceding what are already regular eight-line speech strophes in *fornyrðislag* (see Table III above). In these cases, it could reasonably be argued that a redactor, scribe, or even the original performer has *added* these lines to the poem in order to clarify who is speaking the strophe. As was pointed out above, however, such a method never occurs in *ljóðaháttr* poems, perhaps because the poetic form offers less flexibility, but possibly also for other reasons that will be discussed in more detail below.

b. The placing of a statement like, for example, 'kvað Vǫlundr', as an integral part of a speech strophe, as in *Völundarkviða*, st.29.

c. The clear naming of the speaker as part of a preceding prose passage, the speaker's name usually being given in full in the manuscript (rather than abbreviated), at least on his/ her first appearance. This approach is very common, and is also employed in the poems under discussion.

d. The clear naming of the speaker within the body of the manuscript text, yet outside the framework of the actual poetry, as occurs several times in *Reginsmál*,[91] where, on three occasions, the abbreviated name of the speaker accompanied by a speech verb appears in the middle of the first line of a speech strophe (st.3, st.9 and st.11).[92] Nonetheless, there is little question in metrical terms that these statements must have been regarded as additions to the poetic strophes. This is quite different from the example of *Völundarkviða*, st.29.

It is noteworthy that in the case of *Skírnismál*, *Vafþrúðnismál*, *Lokasenna*, *Fáfnismál*, *Hárbarðsljóð*, and six early strophes of *Helgakviða Hjörvarðssonar*,[93] a completely original approach to the naming of speakers is encountered in both the *Codex Regius* and the AM 748 manuscripts. While the speakers certainly do appear to have been regularly named in the sections of the manuscripts containing these poems, the

2. The marginal speaker indications in the Edda manuscripts

---

[91] Regarding the relationship between *Reginsmál* and *Fáfnismál*, and whether the two should be counted as a single entity, see further *section G.4a* below.

[92] *Codex Regius*, p.57, l.27 ('q.l.') and l.33 ('q.h.'); and p.58, l.5 ('q.h.').

[93] I.e. *Helgakviða Hjörvarðssonar*, sts 1–4, and sts 7–8 on pp.43–44 of the *Codex Regius*. The use of the notation here is an intriguing anomaly, suggesting the possibility that notation may have been used throughout the poem originally, but was later lost through the cutting of the sheets. Owing to the impossibility of knowing any more about this, this poem will not be included in the following discussion. Nonetheless, when considering the question of the later addition of the prose, it is interesting to note that the MS gives a double indication of the speaker for st.1 of this poem, which is uttered by a bird. Not only is the notation 'h.q.' ('hann qvað'; 'he said') found at the end of the prose introduction, but the letters 'f.q.' ('fuglinn qvað'; 'the bird said') have also been placed in the margin. This raises the question of which came first, the prose or the notation, since the mistake implies that one of the two must have been added at a later stage in the various redactions of this work.

III. The Eddic Poems and Drama

2. The marginal speaker indications in the Edda manuscripts

naming was obviously not regarded as being an integral part of the poems themselves. Nor does it usually occur within the actual body of the manuscript text. Instead, apparently scribal shorthand notes (for example, '.l.q.' [Loki qvað; Loki said], '.s.q.' [Skírnir qvað; Skírnir said] and so on) have been placed almost consistently alongside the text to indicate the names of those characters who begin speaking in the lines in question (see *figs 71–73 and 75*). These notes are usually placed in the outer margin, at least half an inch away from the actual text of the poems, and seldom directly precede the speeches themselves. This is seen, for example, in *fig.72*, l.2, where Vafþrúðnir's words 'Ór Ymis holdi', commencing at st.21 of *Vafþrúðnismál*, are only accredited to Vafþrúðnir with the marking 'v.q.' in the *right-hand* margin parallel to the start of the speech. There is no doubt that the notation accompanying these poems was deliberately written at the same time as the rest of the text in both manuscripts.[94] Indeed, the notation on fol.2v of the AM 748 manuscript even appears to have been originally decorated with red ink.[95] Because of its position, much of the original marginal notation has been cut away, or reduced to single letters, as in *fig.71* (left-hand margin). In many cases, however, in poems such as *Alvíssmál*, it appears that the names of the speakers were never written at all.

In the *Codex Regius*, the aforementioned system appears to have been regular in *Vafþrúðnismál* (pp.14–16[96]), *Lokasenna* (pp.29–33,[97] the only exception being st.43 where Byggvir is named in full in the text[98]), *Skírnismál* (pp.21–23,[99] except before sts 2,10 and 15[100]) and *Fáfnismál* (pp.59–62[101]).[102] *Hárbarðsljóð* (pp.24–26[103]) seems to have used the same system, but additionally includes two instances of a new speaker being named in mid-line, before st.2 (p.24), and before st.32 (p.25). The first instance is possibly due to direct copying from the original manuscript on which the

---

[94] I am grateful to both Sverrir Tómasson and Jónas Kristjánsson for confirming this point for me with regard to the notation in the *Codex Regius*; and to Jonna Louis-Jensen for examining the AM 748 MS notation with me.
[95] Red ink is not used for the notation on the later folios.
[96] The notation has obviously been cut away on p.15.
[97] The notation has been cut away on pp.32–33.
[98] Notably, Byggvir's name here is not accompanied with the speech verb, 'qvað'. This raises the question of whether the verb in the notation was considered wholly necessary, or whether it was merely an additional element attached to the names of the speakers.
[99] The notation has been cut away on p.23.
[100] I.e. '**Scirn q.**' before Skírnir's first speech (wholly unnecessary since it was clear from the previous speech that Skírnir was being addressed); '**Sc.ml.v.hestin**' ('Skírnir mælti við hestinn': 'Skírnir spoke to the horse') before the speech to the horse, which could almost be seen as a prose comment; and finally '**Ambǫt q.**' ('the bondwoman said') before the servant's speech to Gerðr, a note that needs to be made since there is no statement anywhere in the poem or the prose passages about the existence of such a character.
[101] The notation has been lost on p.59 and p.62.
[102] Neckel (in *Edda*) seems to have missed these notes for sts 13–15 and 17–21, just as he misses the notation for *Helgakviða Hjörvarðssonar*, sts 7–8. He also ignores the *Codex Regius* numbering of the 'iðtur' (the numbers ll–llll are visible). With regard to preciseness, Jón Helgason's text in *Eddadigte*, III, is much closer to that contained in the MS.
[103] The notation has obviously been cut away on p.24.

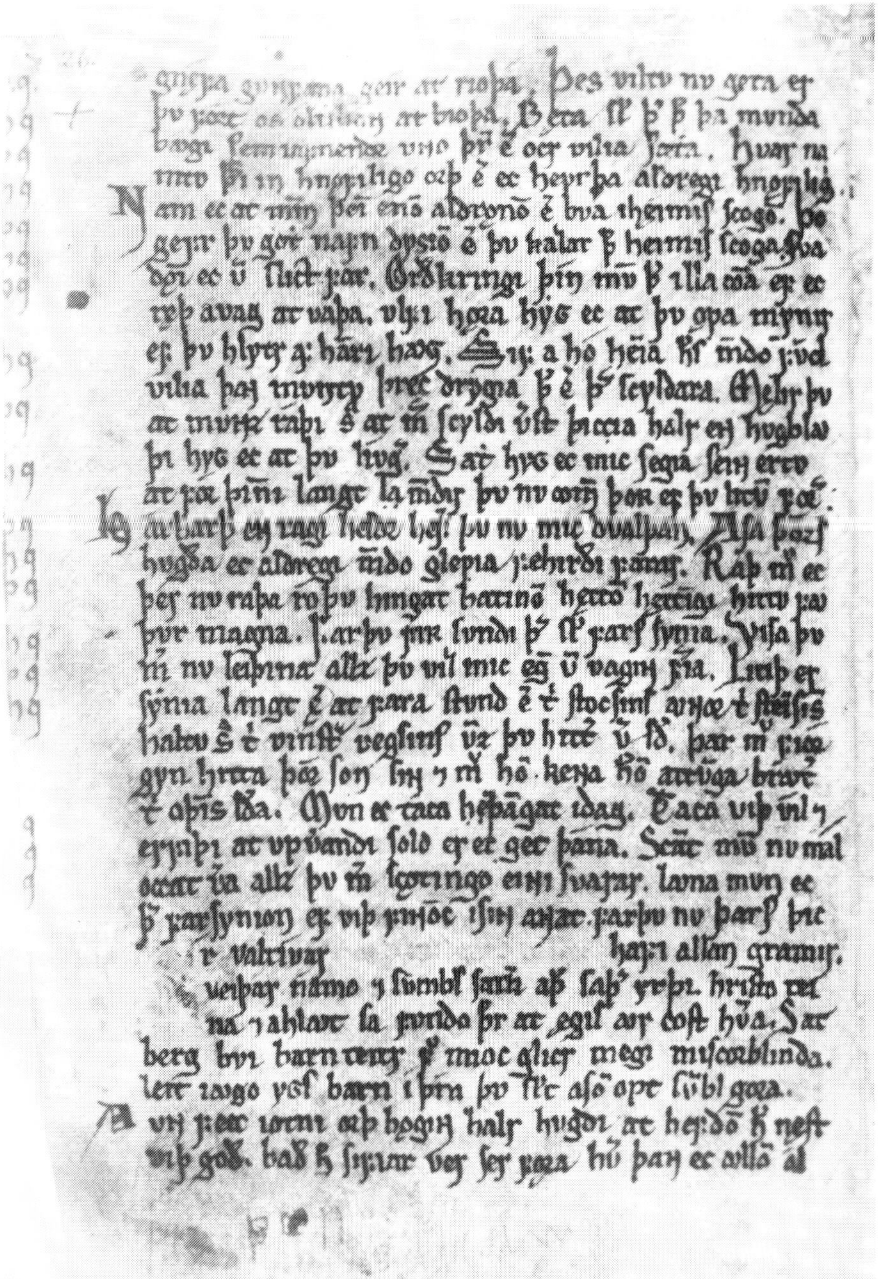

Fig. 71. *Codex Regius*. Gl.kgl.sml.2365, 4^(to), p.26 (c.1270).
Hárbarðsljóð, st.40 – end. *Hymiskviða*, start.

III. The Eddic Poems and Drama

2. The marginal speaker indications in the Edda manuscripts

AM 748 was based (see further below). In the second instance, however, two changes of speaker take place on the same line of the manuscript, thus necessitating some new way of indicating a second speaker, since two notes side by side in the margin would only create misunderstanding. Thus, the first new speaker is named at the *end* of the line, the second in the text itself (see *fig.73*, l.24). Indeed, when the same thing happens earlier in st.11 (p.24), the second speaker is named in shorthand on the *inner* margin. These exceptions, of course, not only prove that p.24 must have also contained some form of notation, but also emphasise that the marginal notation cannot have been a later addition. The scribe was obviously working to a set pattern.

Interestingly enough, the approach found in the *Codex Regius* seems to be a development on that employed in the AM 748 manuscript where all of the notation for *Hárbarðsljóð* (fols 1r–1v) is placed within the body of the text (see, for example, *fig.74*).[104] However, half-way through *Skírnismál* (which follows *Baldrs draumar*, on fols 2r–2v), the scribe (or the scribe of the original manuscript being copied) suddenly decides to alter his approach. On fol.2r, he employs the same system as that used previously in *Hárbarðsljóð*.[105] On the following page, however, with the exception of the full naming of Gerðr and her servant inside the body of the text when they first speak (sts 14 and 15), the scribe changes his mind and takes up the same system as that described earlier for the *Codex Regius* (see *fig.75*, left-hand margin, the inner-textual markings being on l.8 and l.10). This approach is then maintained throughout *Vafþrúðnismál* (fols 3r–3v).[106]

The deliberate use of this system of marginal notation has important implications, as will be shown in more detail below in *Chapter IV*. In terms of the actual text of the poems, however, it stresses that the naming of speakers was seen by the redactor or scribe as something completely extraneous to the text of the poems themselves. Had the original performer of the poems inserted statements like 'kvað Loki' throughout, then surely these statements would have been continuously inserted into the manuscript text itself, as occurs, for example, in *Helreið Brynhildar* (both in the

---

[104] It seems, however, that some attempt may have been made in places to thicken the letters indicating the speakers in order to differentiate them from the other abbreviations. See Finnur Jónsson's diplomatic version of the MS text, *Håndskriftet nr.748, 4to*, bl.1–6, p.1.

[105] *Baldrs draumar*, which comes between *Hárbarðsljóð* and *Skírnismál* in the AM 748 MS, and is also largely dialogic, clearly lacks any indications of speakers in the margin or inside the text. This makes it even more likely that the redactor saw a difference between this poem and the two works on either side of it.

[106] The difference (and development) of the notation systems in the two MSS could be seen as further proof for the suggestion that the AM 748 MS might have been a copy of the original collection of mythological poems used by the redactor of the *Codex Regius*: see Lindblad, 'Poetiska Eddans förhistoria', 161. This would explain the reason for the initial naming of Hárbarðr inside the text at the start of *Hárbarðsljóð* in the *Codex Regius*, and why a more regular system of notation was used in that MS, the scribe of the *Codex* being aware of the system that was taken up on the later folios of the original of the AM 748 MS.

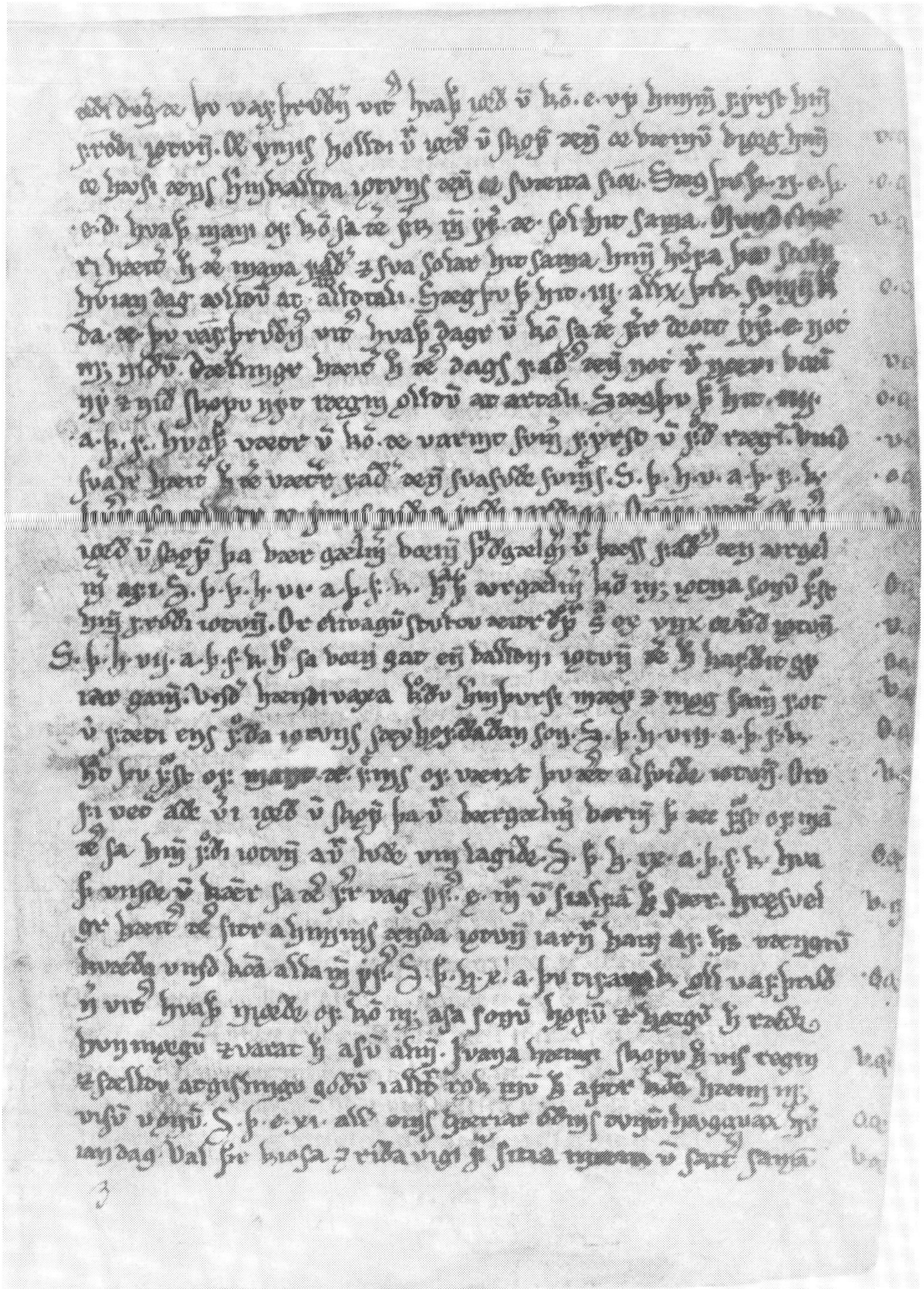

Fig. 72. AM 748 I, 4to, fol.3r (c.1300). *Vafþrúðnismál, sts 20₂ – 41.*

3. The question of the blended prose-and-verse form

Codex text, and that apparently performed by Norna-Gestr as recorded in *Flateyjarbók*.¹⁰⁷) In short, the notation is primarily a silent *reader's* aid (or perhaps, more interestingly, meant for guidance in a spoken recitation), placed there by the scribe or redactor in the form of an 'editorial' comment that was felt to be necessary, in spite of the fact that most of the notation is superfluous for any careful reader. The original poems themselves, however, almost certainly lacked these external indications of character which would have continuously interrupted the poetic flow of any performance. It is logical to assume that the poems under discussion must have been continuous pieces of dialogue, similar in form to *Alvíssmál*.¹⁰⁸

Yet before such a statement can be made with any certainty, it is necessary to return to the question of the extant prose passages in the poems under consideration. As was illustrated in the previous section, there is a much greater amount of prose attached to the dialogic poems (and the *Helgakviður*, which are also predominantly dialogic) than to any other poems in the *Codex Regius*. It has also been noted that much of the prose in that part of the manuscript which follows on from *Sigrdrífumál* betrays obvious evidence of editorial emendation, and would seem to be the work of the compiler of the original 'heroic collection'. The question now is whether the same can be said regarding the prose in the mythological poems at present under discussion, or whether, as has been suggested above, they were in fact totally free of all interpolation?

3. The Question of the Blended Prose-and-Verse Form

As has been mentioned above, with the exception of two examples in *Lokasenna* and *Fáfnismál*, there is little direct evidence of temporal or moral distancing, or obvious foreknowledge in the prose accompanying the dialogic *ljóðaháttr* poems and *Hárbarðsljóð*. The origin of the prose here is therefore more open to discussion.

Several scholars have suggested that a development was under way during the early twelfth century whereby narrative strophes in the Eddic poems were being turned into prose, a stepping-stone in the development towards the prose-with-verse *fornaldarsaga* tradition.¹⁰⁹ In many ways this is a development of Heusler's suggestion that some of the prose passages

---

107 See *Norna-Gests þáttr*, pp.355–356.
108 A similiar view is taken by Söderberg who is apparently the only other person to have paid any close attention to the implications of the marginal speaker indication: see Söderberg, 'Lokasenna', 68–69. In 'Den isländska eddadiktningen' 14–15, and 'Hávamál', p.23, Wessén argues that poems such as *Alvíssmál* and *Völuspá* (and even *Hávamál I*) originally must have had prose introductions containing a clear indication of the speakers to come and thus removing any difficulty in understanding. This, of course, is possible, but can be nothing more than a theory. As will be shown below, such an approach would still not have covered all the difficulties that would have arisen in oral performance.
109 See Brown, 'The saga of Hrómund Gripsson', 61–64; Lönnroth, 'Hjálmar's death song', 5–10; Davíð Erlingsson, 'Icelandic legendary fiction', p.382; and indirectly, Jónas Kristjánsson, *Eddas and sagas*, p.49.

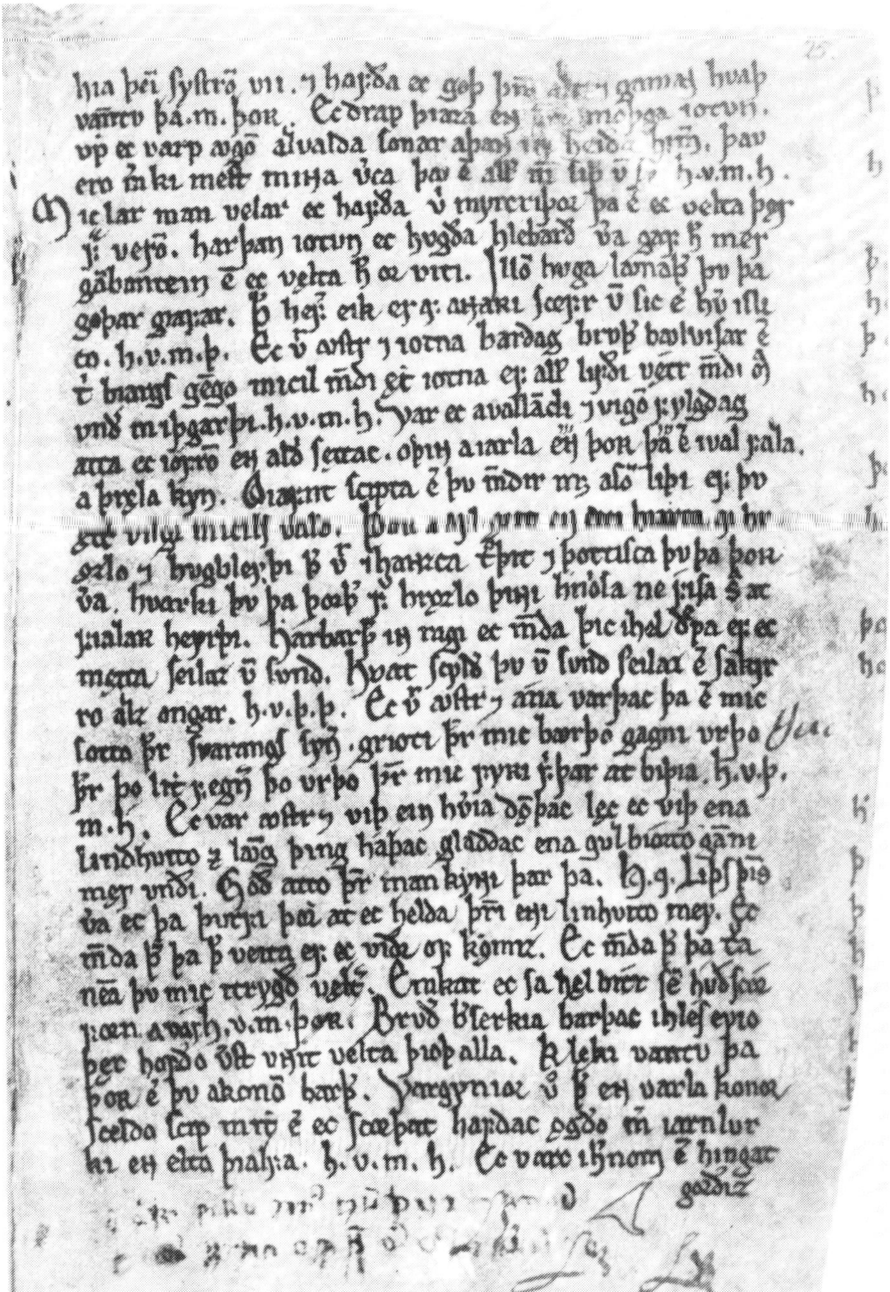

Fig. 73. *Codex Regius*. Gl.kgl.sml.2365, 4^(to), p.25 (c.1270). *Hárbarðsljóð*, sts 18 – 40.

III. The Eddic Poems and Drama

3. *The question of the blended prose-and-verse form*

served to replace lost narrative strophes.[110] Heusler's argument would seem to be applied not only to works like the *Helgakviður*, but also to the poems at present under discussion, where the prose clearly serves a narrative purpose, largely limited to describing situation and action.

Another suggestion, already mentioned above, is that explanatory passages in prose had always accompanied Eddic poems such as those under discussion. As Wessén states regarding the prose in *Skírnismál*, for example,

> The prose here admittedly has a subordinate role, but it is nonetheless necessary to indicate scene changes and connect the various different conversations . . . Such narrative interludes in prose must have existed also in the oral tradition. I am inclined to believe that these would have been more numerous and more detailed than they are in the written sources.[111]

Similar attitudes were voiced even earlier by Heusler, and also by Ker, who in *Epic and Romance* argued that in the dialogic poems like *Skírnismál* and 'The Old Play of the Wolsungs', there really is 'much more need for an interpreter to act as a chorus in the intervals between the dialogues' in the form of prose, and that, in many cases, prose explanations must have accompanied the verse from an early stage.[112]

Over and above this, Davíð Erlingsson has recently gone so far as to suggest that true dialogic verse, lacking in narrative, was a comparatively late invention, the offspring of the development in which narrative was becoming prose, and dialogue was supposedly breaking loose to become a form in its own right.[113] With regard to this latter point, however, it should be remembered that four of the poems at present under discussion are in *ljóðaháttr*, a poetic form that does not appear to have been used outside western Scandinavia,[114] and which was used almost solely for dialogic and

---

110 See above, *section D*.

111 'Här är prosan ett visserligen underordnat, men dock nödvändigt element för att ange scenväxlingen och för att förbinda de olika samtalen med varandra . . . Det måste ha funnits sådana berättande mellanspel på prosa redan i den muntliga traditionen. Snarast får man tro, att de ha varit flera och fylligare än i den skriftliga formen': Wessén, 'Den isländska eddadiktingen', 18. In the same article, 12–31, Wessén makes similar comments about the prose connected to the other poems under discussion. Comparable ideas are expressed by Einar Ólafur Sveinsson, in *Íslenzkar bókmenntir*, p.200.

112 Ker, *Epic and romance*, pp.112–115 (the original edition was published in 1896). See also Heusler, introduction to *The Codex Regius*, p.19.

113 See Davíð Erlingson, 'Icelandic legendary fiction', p.382. This suggestion, which echoes the much earlier ideas of Bergmann, in *Le message de Skirnir*, pp.64–91, and *Poëmes*, pp.21–24, is interesting, but is unfortunately neither developed or explained. It demands another question in return: if the narrative poetry became the saga, what happened to this posited new dialogic form?

114 On this question, see further Malone, 'Plurilinear units', 201–204, and Sievers, *Altgermanische Metrik*, pp.145–146. Phillpotts, in *The Elder Edda*, p.47, goes even further in limiting the sphere of *ljóðaháttr*, when she states that 'the chant metre verse . . . never took root in Iceland – except in a late imitative work or two'. In further defence of her claim, she suggests that 'Icelandic poets were so little accustomed to compose in this metre, that they interpolate old-lore metre strophes into such a poem as *Grímnismál*':

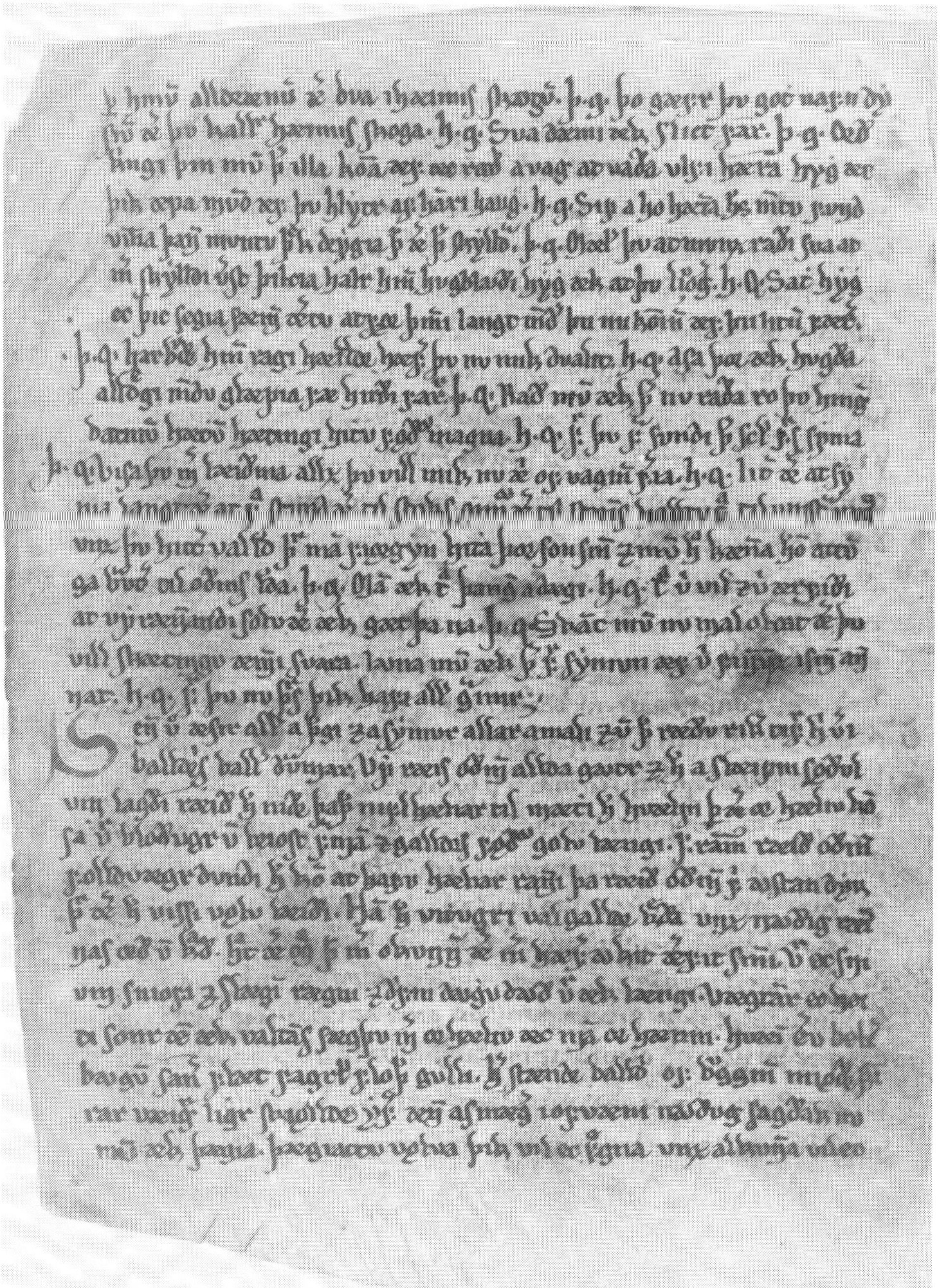

Fig. 74. AM 748 I, 4^(to), fol.1v (c.1300). *Hárbarðsljóð*, st.44 – end.
Baldrs draumar, start – st.8.

monologic poetry (with the exception of *Vafþrúðnismál*, st.5). Yet there is nothing at all to suggest that *ljóðaháttr* as a verse form was a recent development. On the contrary, Noreen's examinations of the extant *ljóðaháttr* poems suggest that there is nothing against some of the poems in this metre having been in existence even before the period of syncope in the Germanic languages was complete, that is to say in c.700.[115] Furthermore, as Einar Ólafur Sveinsson points out with regard to *Skírnismál*, 'People have sometimes suggested that the dialogic form represents an imitation of heroic poetry in which narrative and dialogue alternate. That seems highly unlikely. Poems like *Skírnismál* appear to be the mature end product of a long and independent process of development of this type of poetry'.[116]

In general, regarding the question of the prose replacing lost strophes in these poems, it would seem logical to argue that if there had been any lost strophes then they too would have been in dialogic or monologic speech form, rather than narrative, or blended, since narrative strophes are virtually unknown in *ljóðaháttr*. Concerning the other argument about the development towards the saga form, it is a little suspicious, to say the least, that conjectured narrative strophes should have had prose substituted for them in the *ljóðaháttr* poems, while little or no prose appears in the larger body of more obviously narrative epic-dramatic poems in *fornyrðislag* in the *Codex Regius*, poems where one would logically expect to find numerous examples of prose having been substituted for narrative verse.[117]

Phillpotts, *The Elder Edda*, p.47. For Phillpotts (pp.47–48), *ljóðaháttr* was a wholly Norwegian form. Hollander, in 'Recent studies', 121, fully supports these ideas.

[115] In 'Eddastudier', 2–18, Noreen reexamines an argument advanced by Sophus Bugge regarding the general rule that the long lines in *ljóðaháttr* poems commonly end in a two-syllabled word in which the first syllable is short. Bugge felt that because of this rule, no *ljóðaháttr* poem could have existed in its present form before the period of syncope. Noreen, however, demonstrates that in the cases of *Skírnismál* and *Vafþrúðnismál*, there would be remarkably few departures from the metrical format suggested by Bugge if these poems had existed in primitive Norse, and had then over time been transposed into Old Norse. As Noreen himself notes, this could be nothing more than a coincidence. However, to his mind, *ljóðaháttr* has its roots in early Germanic memorial poetry ('Eddastudier', 38).

[116] 'Stundum má sjá menn láta liggja orð að því, að samtalskvæðasniðið sé stæling á hetjukvæðunum, þar sem frásögn og samtöl skiptast á. Þetta virðist með öllu ólíklegt. Kvæði eins og *Skírnismál* virðast fullþroskaður ávöxtur langrar og sjálfstæðrar þróunar þessa kvæðasniðs': Einar Ólafur Sveinsson, *Íslenzkar bókmenntir*, p.277. A similar attitude regarding the age of the *ljóðaháttr* form is expressed by Hollander in 'Notes', 46. On the dating of *Skírnismál*, see further Nerman, 'De äldsta Eddadikterna', 22–24. Equally worthy of note is Meletinsky's argument in 'Commonplaces', pp.28–31, regarding the existence of semantic parallels and parallelism of short lines which predominate in parts of the mythological poetry, as opposed to parallelism of long lines, strictly organised by alliteration, which occurs more often in the heroic Eddic poems. These features, for Meletinsky, confirm the relative antiquity of the mythological poems.

[117] The exceptions here are of course the extant versions of *Helgakviða Hjörvarðssonar*, *Helgakviða Hundingsbana II*, and *Völundarkviða*, all of which are individual cases. The first two poems, for all anyone knows, may well have acquired their present form in the hands of a redactor who had the express intention of writing a prose-with-verse saga, similar in form and approach to *Völsunga saga*. As Lindblad has shown (see references

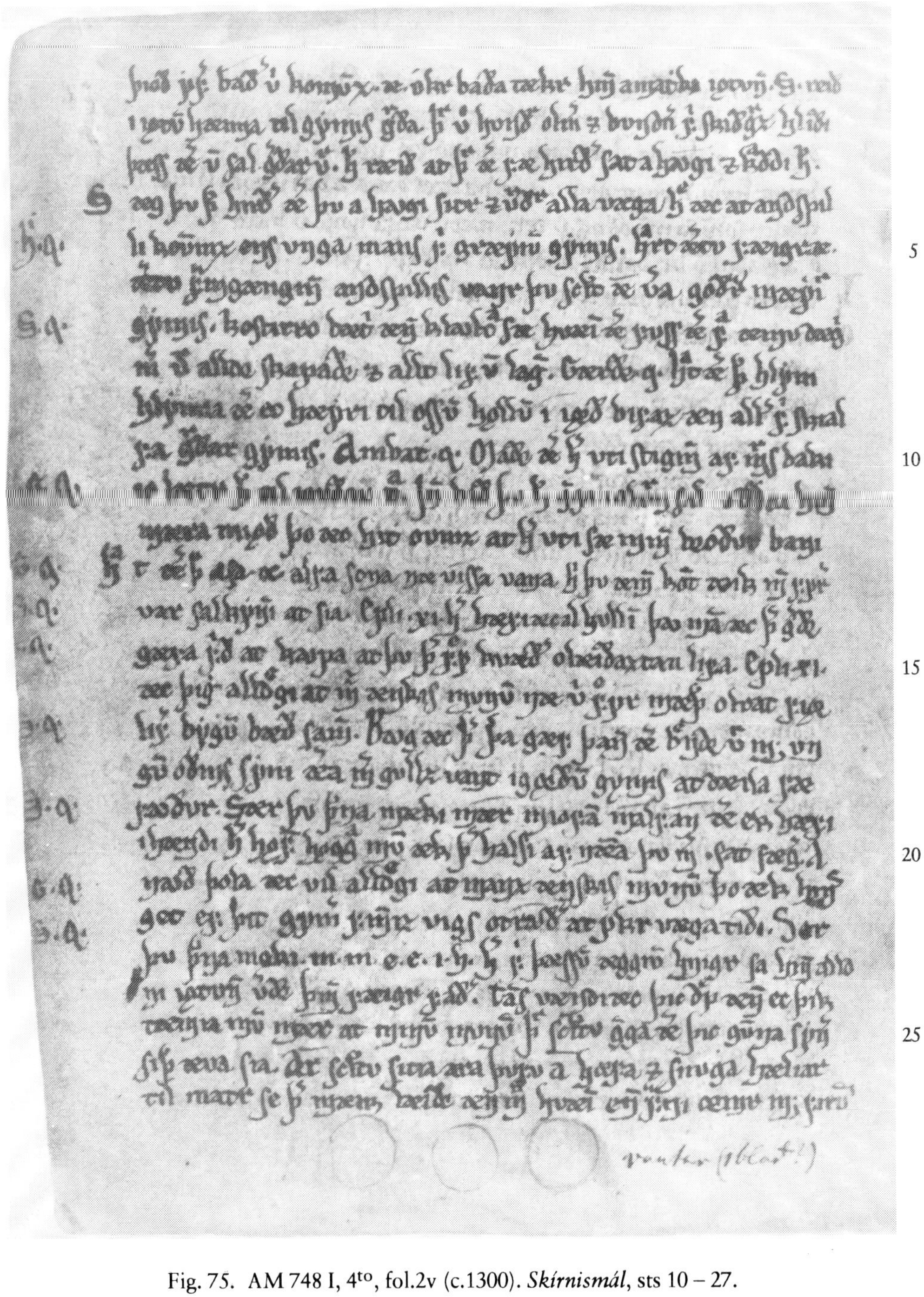

Fig. 75. AM 748 I, 4to, fol.2v (c.1300). *Skírnismál*, sts 10 – 27.

4. Snorri Sturluson, the dialogic poems and the 'Prose Edda'

While it is possible to accept that there was an obvious academic tradition at work in the thirteenth century involving the rewriting of certain *fornyrðislag* poems to create prose-with-verse *fornaldarsögur* (something one can see clearly in process behind the creation of *Völsunga saga*), it is also worth noting that *ljóðaháttr* strophes do not appear in these later sagas, in spite of the fact that the legendary *fornaldarsögur* take place to a large extent in 'ancient' Norway.[118] The prose in the *ljóðaháttr* poems, therefore, does not seem to have replaced lost or abandoned narrative strophes.

Can the prose interpolations in the poems under discussion be considered, then, as purely later emendations, like the marginal speaker notation, or is it possible to accept the relatively theoretical notion that some prose had always existed with the poems in the oral tradition? As was mentioned above, both Sijmons and Finnur Jónsson felt that *the bulk* of the prose in the *Codex Regius* was added by the redactor or scribe. Finnur's argument, which is really a development on that made earlier by Sijmons,[119] is that both the mythological and heroic collections of poems in the Codex follow the same main principles, and bear witness to the fact that the volume was assembled by a single editor who both arranged the order of the poems, and added the prose interpolations.[120] As mentioned above, Finnur Jónsson's dating of the original collections of the Eddic poems and his notion of a single original redactor have to some extent been challenged by Lindblad, but this does not detract from the argument that the prose is the work of a redactor (or redactors), rather than an intrinsic part of the poems. In general, Finnur argues that there is next to nothing original in the prose connected to these poems. For him, the prose evolved in two main ways. In many cases, it is merely a rewriting of the material already existing in the poems, but otherwise must have originated in a separate source, such as 'Sigurðar saga'. This last suggestion that the prose could have been borrowed from earlier sources raises another important question, namely the relationship between the prose in the poems under discussion and the text of Snorri Sturluson's *Prose Edda*, which contains numerous striking similarities.

4. Snorri Sturluson, the Dialogic Poems and the 'Prose Edda'

Like most other scholars, Finnur Jónsson noted the close similarities between the text of the *Prose Edda* (PE) and the prose accompanying some of Eddic poems, but to his mind they resulted either from Snorri's use of an

---

given above in note 81), these two poems apparently came from a different source to the rest. As regards *Völundarkviða*, which is highly fragmentary, even Wessén, in 'Den isländska eddadiktningen', 21, accepts that the extant prose is based entirely on the substance of what remains of the poem itself.

[118] Certainly Snorri Sturluson also took up rewriting in prose, and made use of *ljóðaháttr* material, but neither the purpose behind his work nor his approach can be directly compared to the creation of the *fornaldarsögur*.

[119] Sijmons, 'Einleitung', pp.cliii–clxii.

[120] Finnur Jónsson, 'Eddadigtenes samling', 225.

E. The Dialogic Poems in 'Ljóðaháttr'

earlier complete Eddic collection, or from his knowledge of similar sources.[121] This question of where Snorri's *Prose Edda* stands in relation to the *Codex Regius* has often been under discussion during the years since Finnur wrote his *Litteraturs historie*. It is nowadays generally agreed, however, that the *Prose Edda* was composed c.1220, some twenty or thirty years before the finalised version of the *Codex Regius* came to be written.[122] This has led certain scholars to suggest that Snorri either initiated the collection of Eddic poems himself,[123] or, more likely, that his work inspired the collection of poems that eventually resulted in the *Codex Regius*.[124] It seems probable, though, that Snorri did not know all the poems extant in the *Codex*. For example, as Jón Helgason has pointed out,[125] there is no evidence that he ever knew of the verbal conflict between Þórr and Óðinn depicted in *Hárbarðsljóð*. Similarly, although Snorri was obviously aware of the myths behind *Hymiskviða* and *Þrymskviða*, there is nothing to suggest that he knew those particular poems; indeed, the fact that a poem exists in one of the extant manuscripts cannot be taken as a necessary indication of its widespread popularity or importance.[126]

In general, critics are agreed that when Snorri Sturluson composed the *Prose Edda*, he must have had in front of him versions of *Grímnismál* and *Vafþrúðnismál* similar to those found in the extant manuscripts, and a version of *Völuspá* that was somewhat different.[127] It also seems that he was aware of the existence of certain other Eddic poems including the other three *ljóðaháttr* works at present under discussion, that is to say,

4. Snorri Sturluson, the dialogic poems and the 'Prose Edda'

---

[121] Finnur Jónsson, 'Sigurðarsaga', 26–30 and 35–36, 'Eddadigtenes samling', 221 and 226–228, and *Litteraturs historie*, I, pp.178–179 and p.183.
[122] See Lindblad, 'Snorre Sturlason', 18, and 'Poetiska Eddans förhistoria', 162.
[123] See Wessén, 'Den isländska eddadiktningen', 6–9 and 11.
[124] See Lindblad, 'Centrala eddaproblem', 14–20, 'Snorre', 18–34, and 'Poetiska Eddans förhistoria', 166.
[125] Jón Helgason, 'Norges og Islands digtning', p.29.
[126] It is worth considering Opland's discussion about why so much Anglo-Saxon poetry concerns Continental rather than local heroes. Opland queries whether this was because most travelling performers came from abroad, or simply a result of an inherent 'belief that Englishmen would always remember their own heroes', and that therefore there was less reason to record stories about them: Opland, *Anglo-Saxon oral poetry*, p.97. That the Scandinavians were also eager to record foreign material is testified to by, for example, the transcription of the Low German *Þiðriks saga* in Bergen, and Saxo's comment about how the Icelanders 'regard it a real pleasure to discover and commemorate the achievements of every nation': Saxo Grammaticus, *Gesta Danorum*, p.5; trans. in *The history of the Danes*, p.5. Bearing this in mind, any of those Eddic poems that lack strong Icelandic links of the kind found in *Völuspá*, and are not referred to in a way that suggests general possession, could just as logically have been recorded from a single traveller who was based in an isolated community in the north of Norway or Sweden.
[127] Müllenhoff, in *Deutsche Altertumskunde*, V, p.232, suggests that Snorri possessed written versions of these three poems, but does not note exactly how much Snorri's version of *Völuspá* differs from that found in the *Codex*. Indeed, Müllenhoff's conclusion is supported by Heusler, in the introduction to *The Codex Regius*, p.25, and Sijmons, in 'Einleitung', p.cxlvi. See, however, Wessén, 'Den isländska eddadiktningen', 6–8; Jón Helgason, 'Norges og Islands digtning', p.28; Lindblad, 'Snorre', 29, and 'Poetiska Eddans förhistoria', 162; and Vésteinn Ólason, 'Eddukvæði', pp.95–96.

4. Snorri Sturluson, the dialogic poems and the 'Prose Edda'

Fáfnismál, *Lokasenna* and *Skírnismál*. It is equally obvious, however, that he did not know these particular poems in their extant form.

For example, while Snorri clearly knew the story of Sigurðr, and general features of both *Reginsmál* and *Fáfnismál*, he quotes nothing of the latter poem in context apart from two of the *fornyrðislag* strophes of the nuthatch prophecy (the 'igðaspá': sts 32 and 33).[128] Out of context, *Fáfnismál*, st.13, is quoted in *Gylfaginning*, with reference to the various types of 'nornir',[129] and it is also possible that Snorri made use of *Fáfnismál*, st.15 in his description of the collapse of the rainbow bridge, Bifröst, at Ragnarök.[130] Both of these strophes, however, come from the mnemonic section of *Fáfnismál* which some scholars have regarded as being an addition to the original *ljóðaháttr* poem (the *Hortlied*).[131] As will be discussed in more detail below, there is good reason to believe that the extant *Fáfnismál* contains strophes drawn from two older poems, one in *fornyrðislag* (known as the *Vaterrachelied*) and one in *ljóðaháttr* (the *Hortlied*). Considering the above, there is nothing to indicate that Snorri ever knew the original *Hortlied* poem as a whole; indeed, he makes no mention at all of the conversation between Fáfnir and Sigurðr that forms the centrepiece of the poem.[132]

It is also worth comparing the two treatments of the relationship between Reginn and Sigurðr after Fáfnir's death. Snorri introduces the heart-roasting scene in the following way: 'Then Reginn came over and said that he (Sigurðr) had killed his (Regin's) brother, and suggested he (Sigurðr) could *make up for this* by taking Fáfnir's heart and roasting it at the fire.'[133] The *Codex* version of *Fáfnismál* makes no suggestion of Reginn getting Sigurðr to roast the heart as a form of reparation ('að sætt'). Certainly, Reginn states to Sigurðr, 'you have fatally wounded my brother' ('bróður minn/ hefir þú beniaðan'), but he then immediately adds, 'and I am partly to blame' ('ok veld ek þó siálfr sumo': st.25), thus admitting his own involvement in the act. Sigurðr agrees:

> You arranged   Þú því rétt,
> that I should ride here   er ek ríða skyldak
> over the holy mountains;   heilog fioll hinig;

---

[128] *Skáldskaparmál*, in *Edda* (1926), p.104.
[129] *Edda* (1926), p.22.
[130] See Jón Helgason, *Eddadigte*, III, p.64. St.15 reads 'Bilrǫst brotnar,/ er þeir á brot fara,/ ok svima í móðo marir'. In *Gylfaginning*, the passage reads: 'þá mun hon brotnar, þá er Muspellz-megir fara ok ríða hana, og svima hestar þeira yfir stórar ár': *Edda* (1926), p.18. The relationship between these two can hardly be taken as proven.
[131] See, in particular, de Vries, 'Om Eddaens visdomsdigtning', 17. Kragerud, in 'De mytologiske spørsmål', 11–20, refutes this idea, seeing a close connection between these stophes and those preceding them in the poem. Yet there is nothing to suggest that the strophes could not also have led a life of their own outside the framework of the poem.
[132] See *Edda* (1926), p.103.
[133] 'Kom þá Reginn at ok sagði, at hann hefði drepit bróður hans, ok bauð honum þat at sætt, at hann skyldi taka hjarta Fáfnis ok steikja við eld': *Skáldskaparmál*, in *Edda* (1926), p.103.

E. The Dialogic Poems in 'Ljóðaháttr'

riches and life,	fé ok fiǫrvi	4. Snorri
the shining serpent would still own,	réði sá inn fráni ormr,	Sturluson, the dialogic poems and
if you had not worked me up to this.	nema þú frýðir mér hvaz hugar (st.26)	the 'Prose Edda'

Indeed, the poem makes no suggestion of reparations, violent or otherwise, prior to st.33 of the nuthatch prophecy from the *fornyrðislag Vaterrachelied* which Snorri quotes.[134] Even this strophe, however, makes no suggestion of any peaceful settlement having been made. On the contrary, the birds suggest that Reginn is still planning revenge for his brother: 'vill bǫlva smiðr/ bróður hefna'.[135] On the basis of the above, it can be assumed that if Snorri did possess a copy of 'Sigurðar saga' containing both prose and verse as Finnur Jónsson suggests, this work cannot have contained a 'complete' version of the *Fáfnismál* now extant in the *Codex Regius*.[136]

Concerning *Lokasenna*, all that Snorri quotes of the poem is a strange composite of three strophes, which is not only out of context, but is also said to have sprung in its entirety from Óðinn's lips.[137] In the *Codex* version of *Lokasenna*, the same words appear scattered amongst speeches uttered by Óðinn, Freyja and Heimdallr (sts 21, 29, and 47). Admittedly Snorri refers elsewhere to a problem at Ægir's party in *Skáldskaparmál*, stating that 'then Loki disputed with the all of the gods, and killed Ægir's slave, who was named Fimafengr; another slave of his was named Eldir'.[138] It should be noted, though, that this murder only occurs in the prose of *Lokasenna*, not the words of the poem. Furthermore, Snorri does not place the mangled strophe mentioned above in the context of the *senna* itself. Indeed, he does not link his 'quotation' to any poem by name, and may never have associated the words with any poem named *Lokasenna*. Certainly, the poem itself is never named in the *Prose Edda*.

Snorri's knowledge of the extant *Skírnismál* is similarly scanty. His only quotations from the poem come in the form of a close prose rewriting of sts 1–3, and a variation on the final strophe which follows a summarised prose version of the Freyr-Gerðr myth:

---

134 Regarding the *Vaterrachelied*, see below, *section G.4a*.
135 Indeed, in the *fornyrðislag Vaterrachelied*, it would seem that Sigurðr in killing Reginn acts either out of self protection or in response to his companion's planned betrayal. In the *ljóðaháttr* strophes of the *Hortlied*, however, it seems that Sigurðr acts out of pure greed. In answer to the birds' suggestion that if he cut Reginn's head off, 'þá mundu fiár/ þess er Fáfnir réð/ einvaldi vera' ('then the riches/ that Fáfnir ruled/ would be under your sole control': st.38), he immediately decides that Reginn shall join his brother on the road to Hel (st.39).
136 See Lindblad, 'Snorre', 22; and Finnur Jónsson, 'Sigurðarsaga'.
137 *Gylfaginning*, in *Edda* (1926), p.25: 'Ærr ertu nú Loki/ ok ørviti,/ hví né lezkaþu Loptr;/ ørlǫg Frigg/ hygg ek at ǫll viti,/ þótt hon sjálfgi segi' ('You are mad, Loki/ and out of your mind,/ why won't you let things be?/ Frigg knows/ all fate, I believe,/ though she does not state it herself').
138 'Þá senti Loki þar við ǫll goð ok drap þræl Ægis, þann er Fimafengr hét; annarr þræll hans er nefndr Eldir': *Edda* (1926), p.96.

4. Snorri Sturluson, the dialogic poems and the 'Prose Edda'

R: One night is long,	PE: One night is long
two are long,	another is long
how will I bear three?	how can I bear three?
I have often thought	I have often thought
a month seemed less	a month seemed less
than half this wedding eve.	than half this wedding
(st.42)	eve.[139]

Other loose similarities between Snorri's prose and the text of the initial strophes of the poem are as follows:

a. Njörðr (not Skaði as in the poem) asks Skírnir to find out why Freyr is 'so angry' ('svá reiðr'), an expression which echoes Freyr's description as a 'wildly angry man' ('ofreiði afi') in the poem.

b. Skírnir agrees to go to Freyr but is 'not willing' ('eigi fúss'), since he feels that he 'can expect a bad answer from him' ('illra svara vera ván af honum'). This is reminiscent of Skírnir's words in st.2: 'I can expect/ bad words from your son' ('Illra orða/ er mér ón at ykrom syni').

c. Freyr's words regarding Gerðr's looks in st.6, that 'her arms gave off light/ and from them/ all the air and water too' ('armar lýsto/ en af þaðan/ alt lopt ok lǫgr') are paralleled in Snorri's comment that when she went out 'her arms gave off light both into the air and water, and all the worlds radiated because of her ('þá lýsti af hǫndum hennar bæði í lopt ok á lǫg ok allir heimar birtusk af henni').

That, however, is as far as Snorri goes.[140] His account lacks the entire Skírnir/ Gerðr episode, and instead accentuates the eschatological motif of how Freyr's missing sword brought about his death at Ragnarök, a feature that has little, if any, importance in the poem.[141]

Snorri's acquaintance with the *verse* of *Fáfnismál*, *Lokasenna*, and *Skírnismál* as preserved in the *Codex Regius* and AM 748 manuscripts would thus appear to have been highly limited. It is a different matter, however, if the wording of the *prose* passages in the poems under discussion is compared with that contained in the relevant passages of

---

[139]
R: Lǫng er nótt,	PE: Lǫng es nótt
langar ro tvær,	lǫng es ǫnnur
hvé um þreyiak þriár?	hvé megak þreyja þríar?
opt mér mánaðr	opt mér mánuðr
minni þótti	minni þótti
en siá hálf hýnótt.	an sjá hǫlf hýnótt.

See *Gylfaginning*, in *Edda* (1926), pp.37–38. Jón Helgason, in *Eddadigte*, II, p.ix, concludes that Snorri's strophe must come from a different version of the poem to that contained in the *Codex Regius*.

[140] See *Gylfaginning*, in *Edda* (1926), pp.37–38, and Finnur Jónsson, *Litteraturs historie*, I, pp.178–179. Possibly on the basis of this, Jónas Kristjánsson concludes that Snorri must have known *Skírnismál* in complete form, and 'probably even more of it than is preserved in the Codex Regius': Jónas Kristjánsson, 'Stages', p.152. Unfortunately, Jónas provides no explanation for this belief.

[141] Indeed, there is nothing in the poem to indicate that Freyr does not get his sword back from Skírnir after the trip.

F. *The Prose in the Mythological Dialogic Poems*

Snorri's *Prose Edda*. Such a comparison reveals not only very close textual similarities, but also the fact that the material of the *Codex* and AM 748 prose passages rarely strays beyond the framework set by Snorri.

1. *'Fáfnismál'*

F. *The Prose in the Mythological Dialogic Poems*

1. *'Fáfnismál'*

Fáfnismál (in Neckel's edition) has thirty-three lines of prose, seventeen occurring within the body of the poem itself, the remaining sixteen coming in the form of a narrative introduction and conclusion. As was mentioned above in *section D*, some of the explanatory internal prose (such as that preceding st.2) shows clear signs of having been added at a much later stage than the poem. Elsewhere, as in the case of the prose preceding st.23, the material is little more than an echo of what is stated in the verse. Nonetheless, the greater part of the prose displays a number of distinct similarities to the way in which this story is treated in the *Prose Edda*. The introductory prose section of *Fáfnismál* runs as follows:

> R: *Sigurðr and Reginn went up onto Gnitaheiði* (Gnita heath) and found the trail used by Fáfnir when *he crawled to get water*. Sigurðr made *a great ditch in the path*, and Sigurðr went into that. And *when Fáfnir crawled* off his gold, he spewed poison, and that dropped onto Sigurðr. Then, *as Fáfnir crawled over the ditch, Sigurðr thrust his sword* into Fáfnir's heart.[142]

Snorri relates the same events in a very similar style:

> PE: After that *Sigurðr and Reginn went up to Gnitaheiði*, and then Sigurðr dug *a ditch in Fáfnir's path*, and *sat down in that*. And *when Fáfnir crawled to get water*, and came *over the ditch, Sigurðr thrust his sword* through him (Fáfnir), and that caused his death.[143]

Following st.27 and st.32 in the poem, the prose reads:

> R: Then Reginn went over to Fáfnir and cut his heart out with a sword which was called Riðill, and then afterwards drank the blood from the wound.
>
> Sigurðr took Fáfnir's heart and *roasted it* on a spit. And *when he thought that it was fully roasted, and the juice was foaming out of the heart, he took some on his finger*, and *checked whether it was fully*

---

[142] 'Sigurðr ok Reginn fóro upp á Gnitaheiði ok hitto þar slóð Fáfnis, þá er *hann skreið til vaz*. Þar gørði Sigurðr *grof mikla á veginom*, ok gekk Sigurðr þar í. En *er Fáfnir skreið* af gullino, blés hann eitri, ok hraut þat fyr ofan hǫfuð Sigurði. En *er Fáfnir skreið yfir grofna, þá lagði Sigurðr hann með sverði* til hiarta.'

[143] 'Eptir þat *fóru þeir Sigurðr ok Reginn á Gnitaheiði*, þá gróf Sigurðr *grof á veg Fáfnis* ok settisk þar í. En *er Fáfnir skreið til vats* og hann kom *yfir grofna, þá lagði Sigurðr sverðinu* í gǫgnum hann, ok var þat hans bani': *Edda* (1926), p.103.

1. 'Fáfnismál'

roasted. He burnt himself, and put his finger into his mouth. But *the moment the blood of Fáfnir's heart touched his tongue, he could understand the language of the birds.*[145]

Snorri's account of the events runs in the following way:

Reginn lay down and drank Fáfnir's blood and lay down to sleep. And when Sigurðr *was roasting the heart* and *he thought that it would be fully roasted*, and felt with his finger (lit. *took on his finger*) how hard it was, and when the *foam/ juice flowed out of the heart* onto his finger, *he burnt himself and stuck his finger into his mouth*, and *when the blood of the heart touched his tongue, then he knew the language of the birds.*[145]

The two texts are not exactly the same, but the similarities in wording are striking enough to suggest that closer links existed between the *Prose Edda* and the *prose* of Fáfnismál, than those between between the *Prose Edda* and the poetic substance of the *ljóðaháttr* strophes of this poem.

The remaining prose attached to the poem also covers the same ground as that covered in the remainder of Snorri's account, albeit in slightly more detail. The prose of the *Codex Regius*, for example, provides more information than the *Prose Edda* about Fáfnir's remarkably human underground hideout which is made of wood and iron. It also states more about the amount of gold and treasure found in this lair, including Fáfnir's famed 'helmet/ mask of terror' ('ægishiálmr'). In Snorri's account, the helmet is forgotten as soon as its power has been described and it is said to have been in Fáfnir's possession. It might be noted, however, that the *ljóðaháttr* poem places a great deal of importance on this helmet, sts 16–17 being centred around it. Once again, this would seem to suggest that Snorri did not know the *ljóðaháttr* Hortlied in any detail.

In conclusion, it would seem that either the editor of *Fáfnismál* made deliberate use of Snorri's work, or, as Finnur Jónsson and Heusler suggest, both men were using the lost 'Sigurðar saga'.[146] Whatever the truth may be, it would seem evident that the extant prose of *Fáfnismál* and the

---

[144] 'Þá gekk Reginn at Fáfni ok skar hiarta ór hánum með sverði er Riðill heitir, ok þá drakk hann blóð ór undinni eptir. . . . Sigurðr tók Fáfnis hiarta ok steikði á teini. (En) *er hann hugði at fullsteikt væri, ok freyddi sveitinn ór hiartano, þá tók hann á fingri sínom ok skyniaði hvárt fullsteikt væri. Hann brann ok brá fingrinom í munn sér. En er hiartblóð Fáfnis kom á tungo hánom, ok skildi hann fuglsrǫdd.*'
[145] 'Reginn lagðisk niðr ok drakk blóð Fáfnis ok lagðisk at sofa. En er Sigurðr *steikði hjartat* ok *hann hugði, at fullsteikt myndi*, ok *tók á fingrinum*, hvé hart var, en er *frauðit rann ór hjartanu á fingrinn, þá brann hann ok drap fingrinum í munn sér*, en *er hjartablóðit kom á tunguna, þá kunni hann fugls-rǫdd*' : *Edda* (1926), p.103. Snorri has previously mentioned the name of Reginn's sword, but calls it 'Refill' rather than Riðill (p.103).
[146] Finnur Jónsson, 'Sigurðarsaga', 28–29 and 35–36, and Heusler, introduction to *The Codex Regius*, p.29. However, in 'Den isländska eddadiktningen', 29, Wessén concludes that all the prose here must have been written by the editor of the *Codex Regius*, and notes close similarities between the style of the *Fáfnismál* prose and that included in the *Helgakviður* section of the *Codex*.

F. The Prose in the Mythological Dialogic Poems

ljóðaháttr strophes of the poem were *not* together in 1220. Certainly, if he was himself borrowing material, Snorri does not appear to have had both the prose and the verse in front of him. It is hardly likely that he would remember only the prose section correctly while forgetting large parts of the poem.[147] Bearing the above points in mind, it is possible to proceed to the prose attached to the other poems under discussion. Once again, strong support is found for Sijmon's and Finnur Jónsson's hypothesis that the extant prose is a later addition to the poems and that the original poems lacked any form of prose narrative.

2. 'Lokasenna'

In Neckel's edition, *Lokasenna* has thirty-three lines of prose, most of them coming at the start and finish of the poem, while seven lines occur within the text itself. As in the previous examination, there is little reason to believe that any of the extant prose originally formed part of the poem. Indeed, as Lindblad has shown on the basis of language and writing, the prose conclusion to *Lokasenna* was definitely a recent addition to the poem, probably the most recent piece of text found in the entire *Codex*.[148]

Lindblad's argument is backed up by many other pieces of evidence which suggest that all the prose in *Lokasenna* must have originated elsewhere, not the least being the present form of the first sentence of the introduction. Here, a back-reference is made to the previous poem in the *Codex* manuscript, *Hymiskviða*, highlighting the problems of a redactor desperately trying to link the poems into a chronological narrative (Finnur Jónsson's 'sagaprincip' mentioned above): 'Ægir . . . had made ale for the Æsir gods, after receiving the great cauldron *as was described just now*' ('Ægir . . . hafði búit ásom ǫl, þá er hann hafði fengit ketil inn mikla, *sem nú er sagt*'). As various scholars have noted, this statement obviously cannot have always existed in this form, because in the AM 748 manuscript *Hymiskviða* is followed not by *Lokasenna*, but by *Völundarkviða*.[149] As Jón Helgason writes, 'If *Lokasenna* ever formed part of the AM 748 manuscript, the words "sem nú er sagt", must have taken another form, such as "sem áður er sagt" ("as was mentioned earlier") or something of that kind.'[150]

However obvious or petty such a comment may seem, it gives good justification for wondering whether further scholarly editorial emendation might have taken place elsewhere in the poem. Certainly, it is hard to

---

[147] Certainly, there are even closer links between *Völsunga saga*, pp.37–42, and both the prose and the poetry of *Fáfnismál*, but it seems to be clear from the high degree of textual similarity between the *Codex* texts of the twelve older Völsunga poems and that of *Völsunga saga* that the author of the saga must have possessed a collection of the Sigurðr/Brynhildr poems in a form closely resembling that found in the *Codex*.

[148] Lindblad, *Studier*, p.286, and 'Poetiska Eddans förhistoria', 159 and 162.

[149] See for example, Finnur Jónsson, *Litteraturs historie*, I, pp.179–180, and 'Eddadigtenes samling', 223; and Wessén, 'Den isländska eddadiktningen', 21.

[150] 'Ordene "sem nú er sagt" . . . må, hvis *Lokasenna* har stået i A, have haft en anden form (f.eks. "sem áður er sagt" el lign.)': Jón Helgason, *Eddadigte*, II, p.vii.

2. 'Lokasenna'

ignore the number of glaring inconsistencies between the facts provided in the introductory prose and those suggested by the poem. For example, if, as the prose suggests, Loki had only just been expelled from the hall in which he had previously been a guest ('Æsir . . . elto hann braut til skógar'), he certainly would not describe himself in the poem as having come 'a long way' ('um langan veg': st.6). Nor would he need to question Ægir's servant, Eldir, about what is going on in the hall before he enters (st.1). It might also be argued that the gods would be unlikely to be shocked into silence as they obviously are in st.7 ('Hví þegið ér svá,/ þrungin goð,/ at þér mæla ne megoð?') if they had only recently ejected Loki to the accompaniment of shield-clashing and shouting as the prose suggests ('skóko æsir skioldo sína ok æpðo at Loka').[151]

In general, there is every reason to assume that the material of both the introduction and conclusion of *Lokasenna* must have come from a different source to the poem. Indeed, the poem is perfectly capable of standing alone without the help of either prose passage. The origin of these prose passages, however, has been under much discussion. Jón Helgason, for example, argues that the material contained in the introduction largely originates from the passage in *Skáldskaparmál* describing the gods' drinking parties in Ægir's hall.[152] The situation is the same, and the names of those present given in the *Prose Edda* and the prose introduction to *Lokasenna* would seem to be based on a similar tradition.[153] Furthermore, both accounts share similar smaller details, such as the mention of the 'light-gold' or 'gold-oil' ('lýsigull') used for firelight, the self-serving ale, and the killing of Fimafengr, a character who is never mentioned in the poem, despite the fact that, according to the prose, it was his murder which had resulted in Loki's previous removal from the hall.[154] In spite of the above, however, there are far fewer direct textual similarities between the *Prose Edda* and the introductory prose than are to be found elsewhere in the more obvious echoes of Snorri's writing. Indeed, Finnur Jónsson, van Hamel, Wessén and Söderberg all suggest that the introduction must be based partly on material contained in the poem itself and partly on a totally separate source used by both Snorri and the original editor of *Lokasenna*.[155]

---

[151] Van Hamel, 'The prose frame of Lokasenna', 205.
[152] Jón Helgason, *Eddadigte*, II, p.x, regarding *Edda* (1926), p.96. The same argument has been made recently by Clunies Ross in *Skáldskaparmál*, p.140. See also above, *section E.4*.
[153] Interestingly enough, Snorri includes Gefjun who is named in the poem but not in the prose introduction. However, he neglects to mention the slightly mysterious Byggvir and Beyla who appear in the poem. Both texts ignore the presence of Heimdallr.
[154] Certainly, the story of the death of Fimafengr in the prose introduction contradicts the poem in several other ways, since it suggests that the gods have already reacted in a violent way towards Loki, whereas in the poem, as Sørensen has shown in 'Loki's senna', p.245 and pp.248–257, they are doing their very best not to break the sanctity of Ægir's hall, a symbol of cosmic unity between the gods and giants and 'a great place of sanctuary' ('griðastaðr mikill') as even the prose writer emphasises. On the question of Fimafengr, see also Gurevich, 'On the nature of the comic', 131.
[155] According to Finnur Jónsson, in 'Eddadigtenes samling', 227, much of the introduction

F. The Prose in the Mythological Dialogic Poems

2. *'Lokasenna'*

On the surface, the origin of the prose conclusion to *Lokasenna* would seem to be a much more clear-cut question. Several scholars see clear links between this and the passage in *Gylfaginning* relating the binding and punishment of Loki following the death of Baldr.[156] There is little question that the prose in the *Codex Regius* covers the same material in the same order as *Gylfaginning*, albeit in what is at first a much simplified version. The final section of the prose, describing how Loki is bound below a poisononous snake which drips poison into his face, is particularly worth closer examination:

R: Loki's wife, Sigyn, sat there and held a bowl under the poison. But when the bowl was full, she carried out the poison, and meanwhile, the poison dripped onto Loki. Then he jerked so hard that the entire earth shook; that is now known as an earthquake.[157]

PE: But his wife, Sigyn, stands beside him *and holds a bowl under the drops of poison; and when the bowl is full*, she goes and *throws out the poison, and meanwhile the poison drips* onto his face. Then he jerks so hard that the entire earth shakes – *you call that an earthquake*.[158]

Apart from the interesting, conscious change in tense in the prose written later in the *Codex Regius*, there seems little doubt about direct borrowing here. Furthermore, as Einar Ólafur Sveinsson has argued, the *Codex* description of how Loki was bound only makes sense if it is looked at from the viewpoint of Snorri's version of the same events.[159] The *Codex Regius* states somewhat mysteriously that Loki 'was bound with the intestines of his son, Nari; and his son Narfi became a wolf' ('Hann var bundinn með þǫrmom sonar (síns) Nara. En Narfi, sonr hans, varð at vargi'). Snorri's version, proceeds as follows: 'Loki's sons, Váli and Nari or Narfi, were taken. The Æsir transformed Váli into a wolf, and he tore his brother Narfi apart. Then the Æsir took his intestines and bound Loki . . .'[160]

and all of the internal prose is based on the information given in the poem itself, an idea supported by Einar Ólafur Sveinsson, in *Íslenzkar bókmenntir*, p.318. For further discussion of this question, see Van Hamel's 'The prose frame', 204–214; Söderberg, 'Lokasenna', 82–93; Wessén, 'Den isländska eddadiktningen', 20; and Sørensen, 'Loki's senna', pp.244–247.
[156] See Wessén, 'Den isländska eddadiktningen', 20; Einar Ólafur Sveinsson, *Íslenzkar bókmenntir*, p.188 and p.319; Jón Helgason, *Eddadigte*, II, p.x; Lindblad, 'Snorre', 33; and Harris, 'Eddic poetry', p.76.
[157] 'Sigyn kona Loka sat þar ok helt munnlaug undir eitrit. En er munnlaugin var full, bar hón út eitrit; en meðan draup eitrit á Loka. Þá kiptiz hann svá hart við, at þaðan skalf iǫrð ǫll; það ero nú kallaðir landskiá(l)ptar.'
[158] . . . en Sigyn, kona hans, stendr hjá honum *ok heldr mundlaugu undir eitrdropa; en þá er full er mundlaugin*, þá gengr hon ok *slær út eitrinu, en meðan drýpr eitrit í* andlit honum; þá kippisk hann svá hart við, at jǫrð ǫll skelfr – *þat kallið þér landskjálpta* . . .: *Edda* (1926), pp.61–62.
[159] Einar Ólafur Sveinsson, *Íslenzkar bókmenntir*, p.188.
[160] 'Þá váru teknir sønir Loka, Váli ok Nari eða Narfi; brugðu æsir Vála í vargs líki, ok reif hann í sundr Narfa, bróður sinn; þá tóku æsir þarma hans ok bundu Loka . . .': *Edda* (1926), p.61.

2. 'Lokasenna'

It seems clear that this section must be based, albeit somewhat clumsily, on the *Prose Edda*. Söderberg, however, like several other scholars suggests again that even here both Snorri and the editor of the *Codex Regius* were making use of an earlier mythological prose source.[161] The only problem with this argument, as with that regarding the introduction to *Lokasenna*, is that no other written prose works dealing with myths about the gods are known of apart from academic works such as the *Prose Edda*, and Saxo's *Gesta Danorum* from the thirteenth century, and the short introduction to *Sörla þáttr* (also known as *Heðins saga ok Högna*) which was recorded in *Flateyjarbók*. It must be regarded as questionable whether such mythological prose works as those suggested by Söderberg and others ever existed *in manuscript form* prior to the writing of the *Codex* and its forerunners. Bearing this point in mind, it is most unlikely that both Snorri's work and that of the prose writer should display such close textual similarities on the basis of a shared prose source that existed in oral form and was recorded by both of them some thirty years apart. The most likely answer has to be that the prose writer borrowed from the *Prose Edda*.

Concerning the internal prose of *Lokasenna*, as both Finnur Jónsson and Phillpotts point out,[162] there is little that could not be argued to have originated from the facts contained within the poem itself. The first passage, preceding st.6, ('Then Loki went into the hall; and when they saw who had entered, they all fell silent'[163]) is little more than a rephrasing of sts 6 and 7: 'Thirsty I came/ to this hall' ('Þyrstr ek kom/ þessar hallar til': st.6) and 'Why so silent,/ you swollen gods,/ that you cannot utter a word?' ('Hvi þegið ér svá,/ þrungin goð,/ at þér mæla né megoð': st.7). As mentioned above, this description would seem to conflict with the atmosphere of the introductory prose. The second internal prose passage, preceding st.11, ('Then Víðarr arose, and poured a drink for Loki . . .': 'Þá stóð Víðarr upp ok skenkti Loka . . .') is implied by st.10, in which Óðinn tells Víðarr to stand, and by st.11, which commences with Loki toasting the Æsir, thus implying he has received a drink.[164] The prose preceding sts 53 and 54 states that 'Sif stepped forward and presented Loki with mead in a frosted glass' ('þá gekk (Sif) fram ok byrlaði Loka í hrímkálki mioð'), and adds that Loki then 'received the horn and drank from it' ('tók við horni ok

---

[161] See Söderberg, 'Lokasenna', 87–93; van Hamel, 'The prose frame', 211; and Bibire, 'Freyr and Gerðr', p.35. Söderberg, like Finnur Jónsson in 'Eddadigtenes samling', 227–229, rejects the idea of direct borrowing from the *Prose Edda* on the grounds that the two accounts differ with regard to Loki's sons, and points out that the prose writer seems to have missed out a number of potentially useful details from Snorri's account. Her final view is that both Snorri and the editor of the *Codex* must have used an earlier prose work dealing solely with the death of Baldr, something for which Loki is not blamed in the poem.

[162] Phillpotts, *The Elder Edda*, p.102, and Finnur Jónsson, 'Eddadigtenes samling', 227.

[163] 'Síðan gekk Loki inn í hollina. En er þeir sá, er fyrir vóro, hverr inn var kominn, þognoðo þeir allir.'

[164] Indeed, Víðarr's pouring the drink would seem unnecessary on the basis of the statement in the prose that 'siálft barsk þar ǫl' (lit. 'the ale bore itself') which is echoed in the *Prose Edda*.

F. The Prose in the Mythological Dialogic Poems

drakk af'),[165] all of which is implied by Sif's formal offering of the *hrímkálkr* ('frosted glass') in st.53. The final piece of internal prose, preceding st.57 ('Then Þórr came in and said . . .': 'Þá kom Þórr at ok kvað . . .') is similarly superfluous. Þórr's arrival was previously announced by Beyla in st.55, and he then speaks in st.57 (and is named in st.58), thus fulfilling Beyla's prophecy, without any need of the prose.[166]

In conclusion, as in the case of *Fáfnismál*, all the extant prose linked to *Lokasenna* would seem to be extraneous. It can hardly be considered an essential explanatory feature of the poem itself. On the contrary, it causes more problems than it solves, since it often appears to contradict the information provided by the strophes.[167] Much of it probably represents a later attempt to manipulate the material of the work towards some given end, applying it, for example, to a new external narrative context such as the death of Baldr and the coming of Ragnarök.[168]

3. 'Skírnismál'

With regard to *Skírnismál*, which has no more than fourteen lines of prose in Neckel, the question would seem to be even simpler. Nonetheless, the prose here has given rise to even more dispute than that associated with *Lokasenna*, largely because the six introductory lines have such importance for certain individual interpretations of the poem. Jón Helgason once again relates these lines to the material given in Snorri's *Gylfaginning*,[169] and there is little question that most of the additional pieces of information which appear in the prose introduction but find no support in the poem itself all appear in the *Prose Edda*.

Most importantly, the prose echoes Snorri's suggestion that Freyr had seen the wondrous sight of Gerðr while sitting in Óðinn's seat, Hliðskjálf:

PE: Freyr had gone into Hliðskjálf and seen across all the worlds.

R: Freyr, the son of Njörðr, had sat in Hliðskiálf and seen over all the worlds.[170]

---

[165] The discrepancy between the 'hrímkálkr' which would have been made of glass (see Nerman, 'De äldsta Eddadikterna', 23–24), and the 'horn' which Loki receives is interesting, although it is difficult to say whether it was the performer of the poem who misunderstood the word *hrímkálkr*, or the prose writer.

[166] As will be shown in *section G.2*, the direct naming of Þórr in the prose conflicts with the pattern of the poem, in which the audience consistently is left to guess the names of the speakers until after they speak.

[167] See notes 154, 164 and 165 above with regard to Fimafengr's death, the ale, and the inconsistency concerning the *hrímkálkr*.

[168] See further Söderberg, 'Lokasenna', 86–88.

[169] Jón Helgason, *Eddadigte*, II, p.x; see also Bibire, 'Freyr and Gerðr', p.35. Bibire recognises the likeness, but is nore wary about suggesting direct borrowing. However, as he notes, it cannot be ruled out.

[170] PE: 'Freyr hafði gengit í Hliðskjálf ok sá of heima alla': *Edda* (1926), p.37; R: 'Freyr, sonr Niarðar, hafði setzk í Hliðskiálf ok sá um heima alla.'

III. The Eddic Poems and Drama

3. 'Skírnismál'   In *Gylfaginning*, this clearly forms part of the eschatological pattern. According to Snorri, 'his (Freyr's) presumption at having sat in this holy seat was punished because he walked away full of sorrow.'[171] This leads to Freyr's search for Gerðr, and the ultimate loss of his sword, which finally results in the god's death at Ragnarök. The poem itself, however, merely comments that Freyr 'saw' ('sá') Gerðr (st.6). Nothing is stated about how or where he managed this. Nor is there any suggestion that he had committed any crime in doing this, by temporarily usurping Óðinn's seat (and power?). On the contrary, all that Njörðr and Skaði are worried about in st.1 is his health, and why he is so upset. In spite of this, scholars still continue to see the mention of Hliðskjálf as a central component of the poem and its theme.[172]

Another minor point, but one that is worth attention, is the fact that both the prose accompanying *Skírnismál* and the *Prose Edda* describe Gerðr as being in the process of going somewhere when Freyr began spying on her. In the poem, all that Gerðr is doing is walking 'on Gymir's farmstead' ('í Gymis gorðum'. st.6). In the *Prose Edda*, Freyr looks down and saw 'on one farm, a large and beautiful building, and towards this building was walking a woman.'[173] The prose introduction to the poem also visualises her approaching a door, since she 'was walking from her father's longhouse to a storehouse' ('hón gekk frá skála foður síns til skemmo'). The parallel, if it exists here, is a little uncertain, and of course, this is a logical explanation of what any woman might have been doing outside during the Viking period. Finnur Jónsson, however, in line with his belief about an early complete Eddic collection, sees Snorri's account here as a conscious development of that contained in the *Codex Regius* and AM 748 manuscripts, possibly going back to a common source.[174]

The final direct likeness is found in the suggestion that Skírnir is Freyr's 'skósveinn', something stated in both in the *Prose Edda* and the prose introduction. This would seem to conflict with Skírnir's comment in st.5 which suggests a relatively close relationship between him and Freyr,

---

[171] '... og svá hefndi honum þat mikillæti, er hann hafði sezk í þat et helga sæti, at hann gekk í braut fullr af harmi': *Edda* (1926), p.37.

[172] See, for example, Olsen, 'Fra gammelnorsk myte og kultus', 20; Sahlgren, *Eddica et scaldica*, 219–223, and 'Sagan om Frö och Gärd', 4–5; Lönnroth, 'Skírnismál', 166; Randlev, 'Skírnismál', 138; and most recently, Steinsland, *Det hellige bryllup*, pp.40–43, and pp.66–86. A typical, if somewhat exaggerated example of this process is seen in Guðbrandur Vigfússon and Powell's edition of the poem in *Corpvs Poeticvm Boreale*, I, p.110. Here, the prose introduction is dropped entirely, and substituted with a picturesque summary of Snorri's account (with emphasis placed on the eschatological overtones), which frames a brief introductory outline of the events about to be described in the poem.

[173] '... sá hann á einum bæ mikit hús ok fagrt, ok til þess húss gekk kona': *Edda* (1926), p.37.

[174] See Finnur Jónsson, in 'Eddadigtenes samling', 226–227, and *Litteraturs historie*, I, pp.178–179. A similar argument is advanced by Steinsland in *Det hellige bryllup*, p.43, and pp.66–67. Wessén, in 'Den isländska eddadiktningen', 19, accepts that the introduction could be based on the *Prose Edda*, but also raises the possibility of a common source, i.e. the oral tradition.

F. The Prose in the Mythological Dialogic Poems

3. 'Skírnismál'

similar to that between Helgi and Sinfjötli (in *Helgakviða Hundingsbana II*), and Helgi Hjörvarðsson and Atli (in *Helgakviða Hjörvarðssonar*); in other words, a kind of blood-brotherhood. As Skírnir says, '. . . we were young together/ at the dawn of time (in ancient times?);/ two men can trust each other well' ('. . . ungir saman/ várom í árdaga;/ vel mættim tveir trúask').[175]

The information given in the prose introduction to *Skírnismál* would thus again seem to be immaterial,[176] and in a way disruptive. Apart from the near contradiction just mentioned, the introduction also suggests, like Snorri, that '*Njörðr* asked him (Skírnir) to speak to Freyr' ('Njǫrðr bað hann kveðia Frey máls'), which would be quite acceptable if it were not followed by the words, 'Then *Skaði* said:' ('Þá mælti Skaði:') which directly precede the first strophe. It would thus appear to be Skaði, rather than Njörðr, who initiates the conversation in st.1, by asking Skírnir to see Freyr. The poem itself gives no comment either way apart from the suggestion that the speaker or speakers are discussing '*our* . . . lad' ('*okkarn* . . . mǫg') which could suggest *both* parents are present. Whatever the answer, the conflicting statements here would appear to point to a rather clumsy attempt to link two different traditions, namely the prose and the verse.

In general, as Finnur Jónsson suggests, at some time or other the poem itself gives or implies most of the other information found in the introduction. And indeed, like *Hárbarðsljóð* and *Fáfnismál*, *Skírnismál* has a perfectly good opening line of its own that is somewhat weakened by the addition of the prose introduction.

The internal prose of the poem comes in two parts. Both simply inform the reader about Skírnir's ride to and from Jötunheimar. In the first passage, preceding st.11, the additional information over and beyond the actual journey, is that on Gymir's land, 'ferocious dogs were tied to the gate of the enclosure that ran around Gerðr's hall',[177] and that 'a herdsman sat on a mound' ('féhirðir sat á haugi'). These statements would appear to be nothing more than slightly elaborated versions of what Skírnir himself says in st.11:

Tell me, herdsman,	Segðu þat, hirðir,
sitting on the mound,	er þú á haugi sitr
and watching all roads,	ok varðar alla vega,
how I can get to converse	hvé ek at anspilli
with the young woman,	komumk ens unga mans
past Gymir's hounds?	fyr greyiom Gymis?

---

[175] Steinsland, in *Det hellige bryllup*, p.42, suggests that the word 'skósveinn' can apply to both a friend and servant. Olsen, in *Edda-og-skaldekvad*, VII, pp.27–28, proposes that Skírnir was possibly given to Freyr as a teething gift ('tannfé') along with the world of Álfheimr. Finnur Jónsson, in *Litteraturs historie*, I, p.179, suggests, more logically, that here Snorri deliberately chose to ignore the comradeship between Skírnir and Freyr that is displayed in the poem.

[176] See, for example, Heusler, in 'Der Dialog', p.626, and Noreen, in *Den norsk-isländska poesien*, p.63. Other scholars, such as Dronke, in 'Art and tradition', and Motz, in 'Gerðr', choose to ignore the prose completely.

[177] 'Þar vóro hundar ólmir, ok bundnir fyrir skíðgarðs hliði, þess er um sal Gerðar var.'

4. 'Vafþrúðnismál' and 'Hárbarðsljóð'

In the second internal prose passage, the additional information is that when Skírnir returned home, 'Freyr stood outside' ('Freyr stóð úti') something that is also perhaps implied in the poem, if it is accepted that whoever is talking to Skírnir as he dismounts from his horse (st.40) has to be outside. However, as will be illustrated below, there is no obvious indication in the poetry that it is *Freyr* who is outside. In general, his sudden movement seems to detract from the static position and almost awesome power that mark Freyr's character in the first part of the poem. Indeed, this piece of prose suddenly transforms the brooding fertility god into the mythological equivalent of the rustic pipe-smoking kings who seem to spend their time waiting for visitors outside their farmhouses in Asbjørnsen and Moe's Norwegian fairy tales.

In general terms, the internal prose attached to *Skírnismál* effectively supports Phillpotts' argument that the prose in the mythological poems is 'superfluous in a majority of cases, and where it is not superfluous it is inadequate', because of the important implied actions that it fails to mention.[178] As Phillpotts suggests, 'where the action is obscure or liable to be overlooked, it will constantly be found that there is no prose statement to elucidate or emphasize it.'[179] In the case of *Skírnismál*, for example, no mention is made of the fact that Skírnir must at some stage have crossed the 'sure and flickering flame' ('víss vafrlogi': sts 8, 9, 17 and 18) to reach Gerðr. Nor is there any explanation of Gerðr's suggestion that Skírnir is her 'brother's slayer' ('bróðurbani' st.16), which some commentators have seen as proof that Skírnir must have killed the herdsman (or someone else who is Gerðr's brother) on the way in to her abode.[180]

4. 'Vafþrúðnismál' and 'Hárbarðsljóð'

Vafþrúðnismál and *Hárbarðsljóð* are somewhat different to *Fáfnismál* and *Skírnismál* in that they are more limited in setting, and concentrate on simple, largely static two-man dialogue. Perhaps in consequence of this, the prose in both cases is fairly limited. Indeed, in *Vafþrúðnismál*, it is totally absent, although it might be argued that the narrative st.5 is equivalent to the superfluous prose comments in the other poems. As will be shown below, the information provided in the strophe is again based on the verse surrounding it.

In *Hárbarðsljóð*, the only prose comes in the form of a two-line introduction[181] stating that 'Þórr was returning from the east and came to a

---

[178] Phillpotts, *The Elder Edda*, p.106.
[179] Phillpotts, *The Elder Edda*, p.101. In the same book, pp.104–106, Phillpotts points to similar omissions in *Grímnismál* (sts 42–45), *Hyndluljóð* (throughout), *Vafþrúðnismál* (the end), and *Alvíssmál* (the end).
[180] See further below, section G.3.
[181] Those spoken lines in the poem which appear to take on a prosaic form (i.e. sts 21, 36, 41, 44–46, 57 and 60) are not included here, since these are not only totally different from the earlier narrative prose that has been under examination, but can also be seen as an

F. The Prose in the Mythological Dialogic Poems

sound. On the other side of the sound was a ferryman with his boat'.[182] As in the case of the internal prose of *Lokasenna* and *Skírnismál*, nothing is stated here that cannot be found (or heard) within the first nine strophes of the poem itself. Indeed, the lines are almost unnecessary, since everything stated about the situation, that is to say, the presence of the 'sound' and the 'ferryman with his boat', is reiterated within the first five lines of the poem. Nonetheless, it is interesting to note that if the introduction was absent, the question of who exactly is speaking to whom would remain a puzzle for a further seven strophes. It is not until st.9 that the audience gets to know that the ragged, bare-legged character who eats oats and herring and is making all the noise is, in fact, 'The son of Óðinn,/ brother of Meili,/ and father of Magni,/ the powerful ruler of the gods' ('Óðins sonr,/ Meila bróðir,/ en Magna faðir,/ þrúðvaldr goða'). Bearing this in mind, it might be argued that the introduction removes what was originally intended as a shock-factor deliberately designed to provoke laughter.[183]

5. Conclusion

In conclusion, the following can be stated about the prose passages in the dialogic poems under discussion:

   a. Although the prose of all of these poems but one (*Lokasenna*) has been shown to have formed part of the manuscript versions of the poems from probably quite an early stage,[184] it would appear not to be an intrinsic part of the text of any of the works in question. Whether any of these works originally contained a different form of prose, as some scholars suggest, is another question that will be discussed further below.[185]

   b. Most of the extraneous prose material that is not already suggested by the poems themselves would seem to contain echoes of material given in the relevant sections of the *Prose Edda*. In some places, the similarities are so close that they point to either direct borrowing from Snorri's work, or, alternatively, joint use of parallel sources external to the poems. The former suggestion, however, would be quite natural if it is accepted that Snorri's work inspired the written collection of the mythological Eddic poems.[186] The similarities in wording are particularly apparent in the cases of the prose accompanying *Fáfnismál*, *Lokasenna* and probably also

---

essential, albeit abstract ingredient of the poetic structure of the poem: see Clover, 'Hárbarðsljóð', 63–81.

[182] 'Þórr fór ór austrvegi ok kom at sundi eino. Qðrom megom sundzins var feriokarlinn með skipit.'

[183] Nonetheless, Wessén again argues in 'Den isländska eddadiktningen', 15–16, that the poem must have always had a prose introduction of some kind, probably longer than the existing one.

[184] Lindblad, *Studier*, pp.284–286. The prose is almost completely identical in the two thirteenth-century MSS of *Skírnismál*.

[185] See also above, *section D*, and note 68 above.

[186] See *section E.4* above.

III. The Eddic Poems and Drama

5. Conclusion

Skírnismál, three poems about which Snorri apparently had limited detailed knowledge.[187] The overall impression given of the prose writer(s) is that of a scholarly editor using an approach similar to that depicted in the *Prose Edda* itself or even *Völsunga saga*, both of which reveal academics at work, building upon, rather than merely echoing and recording, the resources available to them.

c. As was mentioned in b., much of the remaining prose material involves a simple rewriting of information already given in the poems in a direct or clearly implied form. As Phillpotts and others have argued, these prose passages are to a large extent superfluous to the poems. As in the case of the material taken from Snorri, this again seems to indicate that the extant prose was largely an editorial addition to what was already there.

d. The most interesting aspect of the prose that remains after the removal of those extraneous additions that could well have originated in the *Prose Edda* and/ or the lost 'Sigurðar saga' or indeed, in some other theoretically lost work, is that it generally consists of lines indicating simple action or movement. Typical examples here are the lines indicating Skírnir's trip to Jötunheimar, or Freyr's appearance outside his hall, both of which are in any case already loosely implied by the relevant parts of the poetic text.[188] It was precisely this feature that led Phillpotts to suggest that the internal prose asides resemble 'stage directions' of some kind.[189]

This brings one back to the suggestion made by Wessén, Einar Ólafur Sveinsson, Söderberg and others, all of whom accept that much of the extant prose is borrowed or unimportant, but argue that some form of prose must have always accompanied these poems in question in performance.[190] On the surface, such an argument might be defended by the fact that in *Norna-Gests þáttr*, Norna-Gestr uses prose in his presentation of *Helreið Brynhildar* and part of *Reginsmál* to account for his presence on the scene of the action. While the poems presented by Gestr are almost word-for-word copies of the *Codex* versions of the poems, the prose is different, and this might appear to suggest that for performers, while the poetic sections of a work were seen as being largely sacred, the prose was

---

187 See *section E.4* above.
188 Indeed, as Phillpotts points out in *The Elder Edda*, pp.109–110 (echoed by Hollander, in 'Recent studies', 119–120), the *ljóðaháttr* poems under discussion display surprising skill in their portrayal of movement through the medium of direct speech.
189 Phillpotts, *The Elder Edda*, pp.107–108. Nonetheless, as Phillpotts herself shows earlier in her book (see references given above in notes 178–179), the prose does not cover all the actions implied by the poems, and it is thus unlikely that the extant prose represents a description of a performance. Regarding the close resemblance in form between the internal prose and stage directions in plays from the early Middle Ages, see below, *Chapter IV, D.7.*
190 See Wessén, 'Den isländska eddadiktningen', 16, 18–20 and 28; Söderberg, 'Lokasenna', 83–84; and Steinsland, *Det hellige bryllup*, p.43. For other references to Wessén, Ker, Heusler, and Einar Ólafur Sveinsson, see *section D*, and notes 68–70, and 74–75 above.

F. The Prose in the Mythological Dialogic Poems

flexible within limits.¹⁹¹ Nonetheless, it is important to remember that *Norna-Gests þáttr* was composed in c.1300, and could thus be said to reflect only a local performance style at that particular time. Furthermore, it cannot be overstressed that the numerous similarities between the text of the poems as presented by Norna-Gestr and that preserved in the *Codex* suggest that the *þáttr* has a background in a literary tradition rather than an oral one, the words of the fictional performance not being based on a real performance but rather a literary text. This implies also that the style of the supposed mixed prose-and-verse presentation might owe more to literary works involving prose-and-verse like the *Prose Edda* and *Völsunga saga* rather than to live performance techniques.¹⁹²

The hypothesis of a mixed prose and poetry tradition can never be ruled out, but in the case of the five poems under discussion, it should be borne in mind just how little original material is found in the extant prose passages over and above that provided by the poems themselves and in the *Prose Edda*. Surely, if some form of prose account had accompanied the poems in the 'performances' from which they were recorded, then a much greater amount of original material would have been found in the prose of the *Codex Regius* and AM 748 manuscripts?¹⁹³

5. Conclusion

In conclusion, there is strong reason to assume that the poems in question must have conveyed their storyline and verbal confrontations to their audiences without the benefit of any third person narration, since they appear to have originally lacked both prose interpolations and speaker indications. In other words, in written form, they would originally have resembled the *Codex Regius* form of *Alvíssmál*. The similarities to dramatic texts are obvious. However, before it can be stated that these works *were* dramatic, it is necessary to examine them from the viewpoint of performance. The rest of the chapter will therefore be devoted to an examination of the texts of these poems as *purely* dialogic works to see whether they could have been adequately and effectively performed by a static solo performer along the lines of Egill Skallagrímsson's performance of *Höfuðlausn* or Þormóðr Bersason's performance of *Bjarkamál*, or whether, for the sake of clarity, the performer(s) would have needed to move into the area of dramatic performance. Indeed, would a solo performance have been possible?

---

191 See *Norna-Gests þáttr*, pp.349–357, and Lönnroth, 'Hjalmar's death song', 6–8 and 19.
192 On the background of the *þáttr*, see Harris and Hill, 'Gestr's 'prime sign''. See also note 76 above, and *Chapter V, A*.
193 Wessén's suggestion in 'Den isländska eddadiktningen', 18–19, that the collectors were interested, first and foremost, in collecting the poetry still does not explain this lack of original material of which the collector would surely have remembered at least the core.

III. The Eddic Poems and Drama

G. The Difficulties Involved in a One-man Performance of the Dialogic Poems

1. Introduction: Rules for the Performance of Dialogue by a Single Performer

Central to the discussion that follows is the very relevant observation made by Lars Lönnroth that 'a text which is going to be performed orally must be easy to understand and survey. The audience does not have the same possibility available to a reader of looking back into the text at will, of carefully analysing sentences, of analysing the meaning of the text in peace and quiet.'[194] This is an obvious point, but one that is often overlooked in respect of the question of whether the five poems under discussion should be regarded as dramatic texts or not.[195]

Dialogic presentation by a solo performer is, in itself, neither impossible nor unusual. Demands for such a presentation occur continuously in ballads, and even here and there in the epic-dramatic Eddic poems. However, in all of these cases the audience is usually given some indirect aid towards understanding exactly who is speaking and what is going on at any given time. This is done in several ways:

a. *Tagging*.[196] The dialogue can be preceded by a stretch of narrative verse which indicates both the situation and the speakers. As has been shown, this does not occur in the dialogic *ljóðaháttr* poems. It is often found in the epic-dramatic poems, however, and occurs in exemplary fashion in *Baldrs draumar*.

b. *Partial context marking*. Speakers often immediately give some indication of whom they are talking to, thus limiting the situation, and helping the listener guess by a process of elimination exactly who is talking at a given moment. This happens constantly in the Eddic corpus, and often occurs in the poems under discussion. The most common technique is for a speaker to name the person he is talking to at the end of the first line, or *vísuorð*,[197] thus promptly removing any unnecessary period of bewilderment for the listener. For example, when Skírnir arrives in Jötunheimar, he commences his conversation with the herdsman he meets with the following words (st.11):

---

[194] 'En text som skall framföras muntligt måste vara lätt att uppfatta och överblicka. Publiken har inte den möjlighet som en läsare har att gå tillbaka i texten efter behag, långsamt analysera meningarna, i lugn och ro analysera betydelsen': Lönnroth, *Den dubbla scenen*, p.12.
[195] To the best of my knowledge, the only scholar to have made any close investigation of the complications arising from a solo oral performance of these texts as they would be without the extant prose and marginal notation is Söderberg, in 'Lokasenna', 68–71.
[196] The terminology used in this section has been borrowed from Lowe's 'Discourse analysis and the þáttr'.
[197] The positioning of the name-tag at the end of the first line is not a set rule, but its common occurrence here would appear to indicate that it represents a recurring formulaic pattern.

G. One-Man Performance of the Dialogic Poems

Tell me, *herdsman*,	Segðu þat, *hirðir*,	**1. Introduction: rules for the performance of dialogue by a single performer**
sitting on the mound,	er þú *á haugi sitr*	
and watching all roads ...	ok varðar alla vega ...	

There can be no doubt about who is speaking or about who is likely to answer in the following strophe. There is similarly little doubt about the setting of the speech.

c. *Question-and-answer/ statement-and-reaction.* There is also relatively little difficulty in understanding who is talking if the verse form is regular, and contains a pattern of either clear question-and-answer or order-and-reaction or simply statement-and-reaction. The first two are particularly helpful for understanding, especially if they occur in alternate strophes, and are aided by direct naming, as under b. above, or by repetitive two- or three-line formulæ. Both occur, for example, in *Vafþrúðnismál* where both Óðinn's and Vafþrúðnir's questions and answers begin with formalised set patterns. For example, in sts 11–18, strophes commencing with the formula:

Tell me/ Say, *Gagnráðr*,	Segðu mér/ þat, *Gagnráðr*,
since you wish to stand	allz þú *á golfi* vill
and try your skill,	þíns um freista frama,
what [X] is called ...	hvé [X] heitir ...

are all answered by a strophe commencing, '[Y] is the name ...' ('[Y] heitir ...').

With such a regular pattern, comprehension is little problem, and on the whole, *Vafþrúðnismál* would not pose much difficulty for most solo-performers. However, although this alternate statement-reaction/ question-answer form is also employed in the other poems under discussion, it does not occur enough to solve all the problems that arise. Certainly, it does not occur in such a regular fashion as in *Vafþrúðnismál* where forty-eight strophes out of fifty adopt this approach, most of them in the highly stylised and formal fashion described above.

The simplistic two-man format is, of course, a reflection of Olrik's 'Law of two to a scene' (the 'totalslov'), which suggests that in oral narrative, 'an account only reluctantly places more than two speaking characters together at the scene of the action. If two have been conversing, and a third appears, one of the first two will fall silent or totally disappear.'[198] This rule is followed, for the most part, in the Eddic poems.

d. *Context markers.* These are other pointers that require more thought than those so far mentioned, but which nonetheless offer some indication of character. Context markers range from the indications implied by the gender of adjectives to slightly more subtle pointers like Skírnir's suggestion that the person on the receiving end of his curse will end up 'weeping for pleasure' ('grát at gamni ... hafa': *Skírnismál*, st.30),

---

[198] 'Sagnet vil nødig have mere end to handlende personer på sin scene. Hvis to har været i samtale og en tredje så optræder, skal en af de to gå over til stum person eller helt forsvinne': Olrik, 'Episke lov', 70–71. See also Olrik, *Principles*, p.43.

2. 'Lokasenna': The difficulties of performance

tears being a feminine characteristic in the world at present under discussion. Of course, it is also necessary to reckon with a wider mythological knowledge on the part of the contemporary audiences that would have listened to these poems, and would have understood contextual references to mythological personal attributes like Þórr's hammer, and to family relationships, as in Þórr's reference to himself as 'The son of Óðinn,/ brother of Meili,/ and father of Magni' ('Óðins sonr,/ Meila bróðir,/ en Magna faðir') in *Hárbarðsljóð*, st.9.[199]

The techniques listed above are all commonly encountered in oral accounts where a single storyteller or performer is presenting a dialogue alone. To some extent, these approaches save the performer from having to resort to *impersonating* characters, something which would immediately represent a movement into the realms of dramatic performance. As has been shown above, most of these techniques are also employed at some stage in the poems at present under discussion. Yet as the following examination demonstrates, the techniques are not used consistently. All the poems in question, with the possible exception of *Vafþrúðnismál*, make radical departures from the rules stated above. This feature has important implications.

2. 'Lokasenna': The Difficulties of Performance

Lokasenna has a total of sixty-five strophes composed in *ljóðaháttr*, describing, in short, Loki's arrival outside Ægir's hall where the gods are partying, his subsequent entry and verbal duel (*senna*) with the gods, and his eventual ejection from the building by Þórr. A total of sixteen speakers utter words during the progress of the poem, involving any solo performer in the difficulty of clearly conveying no fewer than sixty-one transitions between different speakers.[200]

The performer is helped to a large extent in this poem by the fact that *Lokasenna* is remarkably consistent in its presentation of place and time. Indeed, it observes Aristotle's unities. Here the only movements implied are:

a. Loki's movement into the building between sts 5 and 6, something clearly implied by st.6.
b. Víðarr's giving up his place to Loki (st.10).
c. The two toasts implied by sts 11 and 53.

---

[199] All the same, the knowledge and intelligence of audiences should not be too conveniently overestimated. Pagan religious beliefs and later folk beliefs in early medieval Scandinavia can hardly have been clear-cut or homogeneous, particularly in view of the size and landscape of the area in question. It is therefore a radical mistake to take Snorri's *Prose Edda* with the same degree of trust as the Bible might be taken nowadays, as a mirror of beliefs, and a collection of stories known and accepted by all: see, for example, Vésteinn Ólason, 'Eddukvæði', pp.81–82.
[200] See *Table II*, above.

G. One-Man Performance of the Dialogic Poems

d. Þórr's arrival, which, it might be noted, does not immediately follow on from Beyla's announcement that she has heard his approach (st.55), but occurs a strophe later, thus realistically allowing Þórr time to descend from his wagon and enter.

e. Loki's departure which must follow on from st.64.

2. 'Lokasenna': The difficulties of performance

The poem thus contains none of the greater distances implied by *Fáfnismál*, *Skírnismál* and *Vafþrúðnismál*. In setting, it utilises nothing more than an 'outside' (indicated in st.1) and an 'inside', where the gods are situated.

Further help is given in the fact that *Lokasenna*, like *Vafþrúðnismál*, for the most part displays a very clear, patterned structure,[201] commencing with the *introduction* (Loki and Eldir, sts 1–5) which involves a clear cut question-and-answer/ statement-and-reaction form, Eldir being named from the start (st.1), while Loki remains an anonymous 'other' throughout. The *senna* itself (sts.12–56) also often takes on a very clear four-strophe pattern in which:

St.A: An 'anonymous' god/ goddess enters the fray, clearly distinguishing him- or herself from the previous two (or three) speakers by mentioning both of them in some way. For example, Óðinn, on entering the *senna*, breaks in on Gefjun and Loki with the following words (st.21):

You are mad, *Loki*,	Ærr ertu, *Loki*,
and out of your mind,	ok ørviti,
trying to provoke *Gefjun*,	er þú fær þér *Gefion* at gremi,
for I believe she knows	þvíat aldar ørlǫg
the fate of mankind,	hygg ek at hón ǫll um viti
just as well as I do.	*iafngǫrla sem ek*.

St.B: Loki replies beginning with the characteristic formula, 'Shut up' ('Þegi þú'), which is followed directly by clear identification of the previous speaker, rendering his adversary no longer 'anonymous' to the audience.

Sts C and D: The god/ goddess that spoke *st.A* is given a chance to reply to Loki's insult, and this in turn is answered with a clear additional insult by Loki, at which point another god intervenes and the pattern is repeated.

The *conclusion* (the *senna* between Loki and Þórr, sts 57–63) also adopts an obvious pattern, with Þórr apparently incapable of doing anything other than preceding all statements with 'Shut up, you effeminate worm!/ My mighty hammer, Mjöllnir/ will put an end to your prattle' ('Þegi þú, rǫg vættr,/ þér skal minn þrúðhamarr,/ Miǫllnir, mál fyrnema'), and Loki uttering somewhat wary responses.

Should the whole poem follow this pattern mechanically, there would be little problem for the performer or the audience, aside from the question of

---

[201] See Söderberg, 'Lokasenna', 32-35. As Söderberg shows, the poem seems to follow closely the general pattern employed in other *sennas*. See further Clover, 'The Germanic context', 452–459, and Harris, 'The senna', 66.

2. 'Lokasenna': The difficulties of performance

'initial anonymity' already mentioned in connection with the A-strophes. This element of anonymity, however, is something that seems to be a deliberate ploy, and is totally lost if the extant prose interpolations and marginal notation of speakers are taken to be an essential part of the poem. Indeed, it should be stressed that in the poetic text, even Loki retains anonymity for nine strophes. The audience is provided with no name for the newly-arrived visitor, only suggestions from Eldir and Loki himself that he is not only held in contempt by the gods inside ('no one speaks warmly of you': 'mangi er þér í orði vinr'; st.2), but is also eager to cause trouble: 'Discord and strife/ I bring the sons of the Æsir,/ I'll stir misfortune into their mead' ('ioll ok áfo/ færi ek ása sonom,/ ok blend ek þeim svá meini mioð': st.3). Loki then announces himself on his entry to the hall as 'Loptr' ('The lofty one': st.6). His real name is not mentioned until Óðinn offers him a seat in st.10. Once again, this seems to be a deliberate move on the part of the 'performer-composer'. Even though, as Söderberg has argued, the clues given *suggest* the visitor is Loki, they do not prove it.[202] For the uncertain audience, this malevolent character could just as easily be one of the *jötnar* or a vengeful dwarf of some kind. Loki would not be the only likely evil candidate. Indeed, in other poems and myths, he often acts as a friend and companion to the other gods, his role in Northern mythology being closer to that of a trickster than a devil.

Regarding the question of regular speaker anonymity in the A-strophes, it is perhaps not illogical to compare the *senna* to a form of mythological guessing game that has been set up for the audience. Each time a new 'round' begins, the audience is initially left to guess who speaks the first strophe, with the occasional aid of a mythological clue, as in the above quotation of Óðinn's words from st.21 which include a reference to the speaker's well-known omniscience.[203]

Similar obvious clues to the speaker's identity occur in Iðunn's first speech (st.16), where she refers to her and Bragi's children (they were married), and perhaps also in the first speeches by Njörðr (st.33), who was known for his somewhat lax moral attitudes; Skaði (st.49), who as the daughter of the slaughtered giant Þjazi has some reason for wanting a particularly cruel revenge on Loki; Heimdallr (st.47), who was perhaps known for his dry moral didacticism; and Sif (st.53), who appears to suggest that she alone has reason to consider herself faultless. Other clues might be provided by the way that subsequent speakers are often related: Iðunn follows her husband Bragi, Frigg follows her husband Óðinn, Njörðr follows on from his daughter (and perhaps occasional mate) Freyja, Byggvir follows his master Freyr and so on. However, this pattern is not completely logical throughout. Skaði, for example, is clearly separated

---

202 Söderberg, 'Lokasenna', 69.
203 Söderberg in 'Lokasenna', 71, reaches a similar conclusion, regarding the poem as 'a kind of playful, riddling poem, an allusive literary game' ('ett slags lekfull gåtdikt, ett alluderande vittert skämt').

G. One-Man Performance of the Dialogic Poems

from her husband Njörðr, and Beyla is separated from her mate Byggvir, to mention just a few aids to confusion.[204]

As mentioned above, the mystery of the identity of the speaker of the A-strophe is usually resolved by Loki's revelation of the name in his B-strophe riposte. However, up until that point the audience is left slightly in the dark. They are not even allowed to rest assured that the speaker of the A-strophe is definitely someone that has not previously been encountered: both Bragi and Óðinn take the stage twice (sts 8 and 12, and sts 10 and 21 respectively), thus, from an early stage, introducing the possibility that an earlier speaker might return to the dispute at any moment. This substantially weakens the basis for Olrik's 'Law of two to a scene', and stresses the necessity for any solo performer presenting the poem to have a stock of up to sixteen different 'voices', if only to remove this essential complication.

Apart from these difficulties, it should be noted that the audience cannot even rely on the four-strophe pattern of interchange in *Lokasenna*. By no means all the encounters last for four strophes. Those with Gefjun (sts 19 and 20), Freyr (sts 41 and 42), Heimdallr (sts 47 and 48), Sif (sts 53 and 54) and Beyla (sts 55 and 56) last no more than two strophes, thus adding an element of confusion for the audience when they encounter the subsequent anonymous A-strophe at a time when they were expecting a second comment from the last god (a C-strophe). This problem is particularly relevant to st.49 (spoken by Skaði), which, although it names Loki as most A-strophes do, could be just as attributable to Heimdallr (the previous contender in st.47) as it is to Skaði. The same could be said for st.55 where Beyla anonymously announces the arrival of Þórr; it would be much more natural to assume that Sif (the previous opponent in st.53) would announce the homecoming of her husband. The other resulting complication, of course, is that these occasional brief two-strophe conflicts break down the audience's inner trust in a four-strophe pattern. Can they always trust that the C-strophe riposte *is* a riposte rather than the entry of another speaker?

A further minor difficulty is that not all the 'anonymous' speakers are directly named by Loki in his B-strophe answer. This applies especially in the cases of Freyr (sts 41–42), Skaði (sts 49–52), and Sif (sts 53–54), where basic mythological clues are all that are provided for the audience.

2. *'Lokasenna'*: *The difficulties of performance*

---

[204] Söderberg, in 'Lokasenna', 71, goes even further, suggesting that for the audience there is a logical progression from Gefjun to Óðinn (st.21), Týr to Freyr (st.41), and Heimdallr to Skaði (st.49) on the basis of partnership and close friendship. McKinnell, in 'Motivation', 243, 248–249, and 253–254, also sees some logic in the progression in these cases, the first on the basis of the fact that Loki's words to Gefjun echo *Hávamál*, st.108, regarding Óðinn's encounter with Gunnlöð, the second because Freyr has been the subject of conversation for several strophes prior to his entry. McKinnell, however, is somewhat uncertain about the third transition, and indeed, all of the above suggestions, however logical they may be academically, must be seen as being somewhat tenuous in terms of an oral performance. Regarding the motivation of the other characters, see further McKinnell, 'Motivation', 240–258.

III. The Eddic Poems and Drama

**2. 'Lokasenna':
The difficulties of
performance**

Byggvir's identity (sts 43–46) is also left open to discussion until he names himself in the C-strophe (st.45).[205]

Worse still is the fact that not all encounters even follow an alternating strophe pattern. In one case (st.19), one adversary gives way to another without Loki uttering the customary insult in between. This would be bound to cause difficulty for both audience and performer, not least because it makes an obvious break in the clear 'two-speaker' format. Matters here, however, are even more complicated: in st.18, Iðunn makes her second speech to Loki, but employs the usual introductory A-strophe form, naming both Loki and Bragi again in what is an obvious echo of her first speech (st.16). Yet, in spite of the fact that Iðunn is semi-repeating her earlier words when she states 'I will not utter/ insults against Loki/ in Ægir's hall' ('Loka ek kveðka/ lastastǫfom/ Ægis hǫllo í'; st.18; cf. st.16), the listener might still be tempted to believe that a new speaker has come onto the scene. In the Eddic poems, the repetition of words is never a guarantee that the person who originally uttered them is speaking again.[206] This slight problem in st.18 is then further complicated by the fact that Loki does not answer Iðunn. Instead, her words are followed by an A-strophe from Gefjun (st.19), which refers, as Iðunn has previously done, to 'you two Æsir' ('it æsir tveir'), the word 'Æsir' implying two *male* gods. For all the audience knows from the first half of Gefjun's speech, st.19 could well be an extraordinary continuation of Iðunn's (or some other god's) words from the previous strophe. It is only when the latter half of the strophe is reached, with its reference to 'Lopzki' (Loki) in the third person, that the immediate difficulty would seem to be resolved, since this form suggests that a new speaker has become involved.[207]

Yet another problem is that not all new speakers make clear reference to the presence of the two previous speakers (Loki and his last adversary),

---

[205] As was mentioned above in this section, in retrospect it is possible to see a logical progression from Freyr to his servant. However, in the performance situation, it must be regarded as highly unlikely that an audience member would immediately have leapt to the conclusion that it was Byggvir (a minor god) who was speaking rather than somebody else. Even Loki seems puzzled (st.44).

[206] Both Óðinn (st.21) and Freyja (st.29) begin their speeches with the same words, 'You are mad, Loki' ('Ærr ertu, Loki'), Heimdallr's initial words in st.47, 'You are drunk, Loki,/ so you are out of your mind', ('Ǫlr ertu, Loki,/ svá at þú er(t) ørviti') also forming a conscious echo of Óðinn's outburst in st.21, quoted above. See further *section G.6* below on the use of the 'Fjǫlð ek fór' formula in *Vafþrúðnismál*.

[207] As Söderberg suggests in 'Lokasenna', 70, this complication could be the result of text corruption. The only problem is that, whatever the case may be, the speaker still refers to two other male Æsir – presumably Bragi and Loki if the ordering of the poem has not been altered. The strophe is definitely of the A-variety; and if it is meant to refer to Bragi and Loki, then it would seem unlikely to follow a further (lost) riposte from Loki which ought logically to be an answer to Iðunn, and would remove the figure of Bragi from the present focus of attention (at least if the poem is being presented by a solo performer; if it were performed dramatically by several performers, there would be no problem at all). The only other imaginable solution is that the Heimdallr sequence (sts 47–48) originally preceded Gefjun's outburst, something that would at least allow a slightly more logical progression from Byggvir to Skaði later in the poem.

G. One-Man Performance of the Dialogic Poems

2. 'Lokasenna': The difficulties of performance

thus again in places allowing the audience to question whether the previous opponent is continuing or not. This is something that becomes particularly common as the poem progresses. Difficulty might well occur in the following places:

a. St.19, where Gefjun takes over from Iðunn, but does not refer to *Iðunn* and Loki but rather 'you two Æsir' ('it æsir tveir'), that is to say, *Bragi* and Loki, thus apparently suggesting the continuing presence of not three gods but *four*. This again shatters the idea of any clear-cut adherence to Olrik's 'Law of two to a scene'.

b. St.33, where Njörðr takes over from Freyja. Once again, there is no back-reference to the previous contender, although Loki is referred to in the third person ('the effeminate god/ who has come in': 'áss ragr/ er hér inn of kominn') rather than as 'you' ('þú'), the use of the third person for Loki (usually his name) being a common feature of the A-strophes. All the same, if the performer does not alter his voice, it is possible that a member of the audience might mistakenly attribute the first half of Njörðr's strophe to Freyja, since the words 'It is of little importance/ if women get themselves a husband,/ a lover or both' ('Þat er válítit,/ þótt sér varðir vers fái,/ hós eða hvárs') sound much more pertinent in her mouth than that of her father (even if he is a fertility deity).

c. St.37, where Týr follows on from Njörðr in defending Freyr against Loki. This strophe contains no reference to either Njörðr or Loki, and could be equally attributable to anybody.[208] Logically, the most likely candidate for the following words would be Njörðr, rather than Týr:

Freyr is the best	Freyr er beztr
of all bold horsemen	allra ballriða
in the home of the gods;	ása gǫrðum í;
he makes no maiden weep	mey hann né grætir
nor husband's wife,	né mannz kono,
and frees all from their bonds.	ok leysir ór hǫptum hvern.

d. St.41, in which Freyr himself enters the conflict, but makes no mention of Týr, the previous speaker. Loki, however, is referred to in the third person later in the strophe as the 'creator of misfortune' ('bǫlvasmiðr'). All the same, a listener could imagine that Týr is still addressing Loki here, since the strophe is largely an echo of Týr's earlier words concerning Ragnarök and the binding of Fenrir in st.39. St.41 runs as follows:

| I see a wolf lying | Úlf sé ek liggia |
| by the mouth of a river | árósi fyrir, |

---

[208] Söderberg's suggestion mentioned above in note 204 that Týr speaks because he is a friend of Freyr can hardly be said to be convincing. Indeed, as a god of war, he might be seen as Freyr's opposite. McKinnell's suggestion in 'Motivation', 247, that Týr is following his recognised role as an arbitrator might be logical in retrospective analysis, but by no means helps the audience to draw the conclusion immediately that he, rather than anybody else, should be speaking at this point.

2. 'Lokasenna': The difficulties of performance

until the gods shall fall;	unz riúfaz regin;
and thus will you next	því mundu næst,
– unless you shut up –	nema þú nú þegir
be bound, creator of misfortune!	bundinn, bǫlvasmiðr!

As in the case of the previous quotation, the only way to enable the audience to distinguish between speakers here is for the performer to employ a change of voice. The listener is not even given a direct clue to the identity of the speaker, prior to Loki's answer in st.42.[209]

e. St.47, spoken by Heimdallr, also lacks any reference to the previous adversary, but arguably suggests by its direct addressing of Loki that someone other than Loki or Byggvir (the previous speaker) must be talking. Nonetheless, the phrase used, 'You are drunk, Loki,/ so you are out of your mind' ('Qlr ertu, Loki,/ svá at þú er(t) ørviti') closely resembles those introductions made earlier by both Óðinn and Freyja in sts 21 and 29.[210]

f. St.49, spoken by Skaði can also lead to initial confusion if the audience does not appreciate the implication of the direct third person reference to Loki by name, and does not recognise the possible mythological clue to Skaði's identity in the speaker's particularly ugly description of Loki's future punishment, bound to a sharp rock with his son's entrails. Otherwise, there is nothing to prevent the audience from believing that Heimdallr is still speaking, especially when he has only spoken one strophe prior to this.[211]

g. St.53, Sif's offering of the horn to Loki, also contains a third person reference to Loki but no mention of his previous opponent. The only clue that a new speaker has taken over from Skaði is that suggested by Sif's words that '*she*' alone (spoken of in the third person) is without fault: 'Rather let her alone/ amongst all the Æsir/ be faultless' ('heldr þú hana eina/ látir með ása sonom/ vammalausa vera'). Exactly who 'she' is, however, is far from clear at this point.

h. St.55, already mentioned, where Beyla takes over from Sif and announces that Þórr is approaching. Once again, no back-reference is made to Sif, and thus if the performer makes no obvious change of voice, the audience's immediate reaction will be to attribute these words to Sif

---

[209] As mentioned above in note 204, both Söderberg's suggestion that the progression is governed by a close friendship between Týr and Freyr, and McKinnell's more logical argument that Freyr is a probable candidate on the basis of the fact that he has been the subject of conversation in sts 32, 35 and 37, have to be dismissed as aids to recognising the character change here. Indeed, there are any number of other gods who could just as logically be speaking these lines, Óðinn, Frigg and Heimdallr being the most obvious candidates.

[210] Possibly, as suggested above in note 207, this strophe, accompanied by Loki's riposte, should precede st.19. Such an alteration, however, would not solve the present problem. McKinnell, in 'Motivation', 251–252, is also unsure of why Heimdallr should intervene at this point, but, interestingly enough, suggests possible theatrical business that might be used to explain the transition.

[211] McKinnell, in 'Motivation', 253–254, is also uncertain about why Skaði should enter the conflict at this particular point.

G. One-Man Performance of the Dialogic Poems

rather than anybody else; after all, Þórr is her husband. St.56 with Loki's response to Beyla, rather than to Sif, will come as a thoroughly disorientating surprise.[212]

2. 'Lokasenna': The difficulties of performance

So much for the complications of the actual *senna*. The greatest difficulty, however, arises much earlier in *Lokasenna*, at the point when Loki enters the hall and the audience suddenly finds itself outside the reassuringly obvious two-man question-and-answer/ statement-reaction format that was established in the introductory strophes. Loki enters and comments on the silence in the room (st.7). His comment is then clearly answered in st.8 with the following semi-echo of his words from the previous strophe:

A bench and a place at the drinking feast the Æsir	Sessa ok staði velia þér sumbli at
will never choose for you, for the Æsir know which men they should invite to a glorious feast.	æsir aldregi, þvíat æsir vito, hveim þeir alda scolo gambansumbl um geta.

According to the marginal notation in the *Codex Regius* ('**Bra**'), Bragi is meant to be the speaker here. Lacking this information, however, the listening audience is left completely in the dark, especially when Loki's reply in st.9 begins 'Do you remember, Óðinn' ('Mantu þat, Óðinn'). Óðinn in turn makes a clear response to Loki, by telling *Viðarr* to give up his seat to the new arrival (st.10). Loki then makes a toast, followed by yet another speech from Bragi (st.12) in which he attempts to bribe Loki into a more peaceable approach. However, Bragi does not name himself in this strophe until the third line ('and Bragi adds an ring': 'ok bætir þér svá baugi Bragi'), thus leaving the audience puzzled for two half-lines: is it Óðinn (unlikely), or Víðarr, or even Freyr who is speaking? Indeed, the first words 'A horse and a sword, I give you from my possessions' ('Mar ok mæki/ gef ek þér míns fiár') contain an faint echo of Freyr's words in *Skírnismál*, st.9. Perhaps if Olsen's reasoning that Bragi was the recognised receiver of guests in Valhöll is followed,[213] the problem of st.8 might be somewhat resolved, but Loki's reference to Óðinn in st.9 does not help confirm any such guess based on uncertain mythological knowledge. Bragi's supposed role as doorkeeper does not help solve the problem of st.12 either.

In conclusion, *Lokasenna* poses a very large number of difficulties if it is

---

212 McKinnell, in 'Motivation', 256, suggests that there is some logic in Beyla following Sif, because she was possibly a servant of Sif's, in the same way that Byggvir serves Freyr. This, however, is mere conjecture, and again, does not answer the problem cited above.
213 Olsen, in *Edda-og-skaldekvad*, II, p.6, suggests that, amongst the gods, Bragi usually had the role of speaking for the others whenever a guest arrived. In support of this, he makes particular reference to *Hákonarmál*, st.14, and *Eiríksmál*, sts 3–4 (see *Den norsk-islandske skjaldedigtning*, A.I, pp.174–175, and pp.66–67; B.I, pp.164–165, and p.59). Yet there is reason to question in return whether this was not merely a feature of skaldic belief. Bragi is believed to have been a late addition to the family of gods. Would a common audience immediately have expected these words to be his?

2. 'Lokasenna': The difficulties of performance

assumed that the work was supposed to be presented in its present form by one speaker. Apart from the fact that such a presentation would demand a very wide range of clearly different 'voices', and probably actions as well to accompany the toasts in sts 11 and 53, and perhaps Þórr's wielding of Mjöllnir in the final strophes, there are other almost insurmountable problems.[214]

None of these problems would occur if it were accepted that the various figures were 'acted' by different people, perhaps working within the framework of a limited improvisation.[215] Such an improvised approach is suggested, and aided, by the common feature of speakers beginning their words with a set formula or a semi-repetition of words spoken by the previous speaker. Such a system would give performers time to formulate a riposte. Regarding the idea of several performers, it is worth bearing in mind what was stated above about Gefjun's speech in st.19, which seems to suggest the presence of at least four characters in front of the audience. The idea that the poem *was* presented before an audience, and that the 'presenters' were 'aware' of this fact in an almost Brechtian fashion, is perhaps also implied by Frigg's warning to Loki and Óðinn in st.25 that 'Your fates/ you should never/ tell men of' ('Ørlǫgom ykrom/ skylið aldregi/ segia seggiom frá'). The word 'seggiom' here would not appear to apply to the various gods, since throughout the poem a clear distinction is made between the Æsir and men. 'Men', or rather 'warriors', it might be implied, are within earshot of what is being said by the gods and goddesses.

Naturally, it is possible to argue that the poem must have become disordered since its original conception, and that the extant version lacks what might have been more explanatory strophes which would have solved all the problems mentioned above. Yet, as was stated above in *section B*, the poem *was* recited in this form by somebody to a scribe, which suggests that at that point it had this shape, and that it had been recently presented like this. However, while a solo dictator may have been capable of stopping and continuously explaining various difficulties to the scribe, the same cannot be said of the larger scale performances that must surely have recently preceded this.

With regard to Söderberg's alternative conclusion that *Lokasenna* is

---

[214] It is enlightening to note that Gregor Hansen, in his recent solo dramatic performances of *Lokasenna* and other Eddic poems, found it necessary to add speaker indications and additional character descriptions in prose throughout his presentation: see the *Introduction*, note 5.

[215] Indeed, it could be argued that Loki's comment in st.44 about Byggvir's size and the sound of his voice ('mundu æ . . . und kvernom klaka': 'you will always . . . be chirping around the mill stones') might suggest that some sort of comic vocal impersonation, if nothing else, was employed with Byggvir's words. This would of course add humour to Byggvir's wish that he could grind Loki into the dust (st.43). See also *Chapter II, section B.3* above, on the suggestion that Byggvir's description here might be related to the large straw figures known in Scandinavian, Shetland and Irish folk tradition.

G. One-Man Performance of the Dialogic Poems

essentially 'a literary product' ('en litterär produkt'),[216] it is important to note the many departures from the set four-strophe structure mentioned above, and Söderberg's own suggestion of possible textual corruption in st.19.[217] Furthermore, it should be remembered that the only strophe quoted by Snorri and containing material drawn from *Lokasenna* seems to be totally muddled, and that in written form (especially in the extant manuscript form with the accompanying marginal notation) the poem loses its implicit element of forcing listeners to guess the identification of speakers. All of these features point to a poem that must have been presented and passed down orally like all the other works under discussion.[218] Whatever the dating, and whatever the apparent lack of direct antecedents or later stylistic offspring, the poem has to be regarded as being essentially an orally transmitted work that needed to be presented in some dramatic fashion – if nowhere else, then amongst the circles of learned academics in the thirteenth century.[219] Certainly, as recent attempts at acting *Lokasenna* have shown, the poem lends itself particularly well to dramatic production.[220]

3. 'Skírnismál': The difficulties of performance

3. 'Skírnismál': The Difficulties of Performance

Skírnismál is composed of a total of forty-two strophes in *ljóðaháttr*, all of them pure speech, and deals with Skírnir's expedition to Jötunheimar to win over Gerðr, the daughter of the giant Gymir, for his childhood friend, the god Freyr. The poem has apparently six speakers, and would involve the solo-performer in conveying twenty-five direct transitions from one

---

[216] Söderberg, 'Lokasenna', 79.
[217] Söderberg, 'Lokasenna', 70.
[218] See most recently, Jónas Kristjánsson, *Eddas and sagas*, p.30 and p.39; Sørensen, 'Loki's senna'; and Vésteinn Ólason, 'Eddukvæði', pp.98–104. Jónas argues that the poem is pagan. Both Sørensen and Vésteinn Ólason make the same argument as that made in this book about the question of dating (see above, *section B*; and Vésteinn Ólason, 'Kveðskapur', pp.47–50 and 'Eddukvæði', pp.77–78) and are thus less prepared to make a definite stand. Sørensen, however, concludes that the strophe quoted by Snorri in *Gylfaginning* must confirm that 'the eddic poems were undergoing transformation up to the time in which they were written down. We must therefore view the poem as we have it in written form . . . as the *last* manifestation of a tradition which transmitted the myth and theme involved down to the 13th century': Sørensen, 'Loki's senna', p.259. Vésteinn, in 'Eddukvæði', pp.100–102 and p.104, sees no reason why the poem should not have originated in a pagan world.
[219] See Noreen, 'Studier, III', 22–23. Noreen, after suggesting that *Lokasenna* is the only poem clearly to break Olrik's 'Law of two to a scene' reaches the conclusion that 'Lokasennas diktare . . . synes härvidlag ha varit en nyskapare, men några efterföljare känna vi icke till, eljest kunde kanske en verklig dramatisk litteratur ha uppstått' ('the composer of Lokasenna . . . seems to have been an innovator in his field, but we know of nobody who followed on from him, otherwise real dramatic literature might have come into being'). See further the ideas of Bergmann and other early scholars about this poem referred to in the *Introduction*.
[220] See the references to the performances of *Lokasenna* given in the *Introduction*, note 5.

III. The Eddic Poems and Drama

3. 'Skírnismál': The difficulties of performance

character to another (if the marginal notation was not spoken aloud); a small matter perhaps in comparison to *Lokasenna*. Nonetheless, considering the difficulties of performance, and the necessity of comprehension, *Skírnismál* is a much more complex piece of work, notably for the following reasons.

First of all, while *Lokasenna* involved only two settings in close proximity to each other, *Skírnismál* moves between at least five: Njörðr and Skaði's hall, Freyr's hall, the mountains, a mound in Jötunheimar, and Gymir's hall. To these, it is possible to add a further setting of the area *outside* Freyr's hall if the intimations of the final strophes are accepted. The essential difficulty here is a temporal one. In short, it takes *time* to move between these places. As will be shown below, *Skírnismál* appears to ignore those unities encountered (and much more easily accommodated) in *Lokasenna*. Here, characters leap from one place to the other in the time it takes to move between strophes. This is something even the epic-dramatic poems rarely do in the middle of a piece of pure dialogue.

Secondly, while *Lokasenna* kept to an essentially 'paired-strophe' formula, involving a system of statement-and-reaction between alternating characters, *Skírnismál* occasionally moves between such a system and longer, more independent speeches in such a way that the audience simply cannot be sure whether an alternate strophe belongs to a new speaker or not. At the same time, *Skírnismál* has far fewer cases of partial context marking of the kind generally met in the A- and B-strophes of *Lokasenna*. In fact, only seven strophes involve clear naming of the listener in the usual position at the end of the first half-line. More often, the suggestion that another speaker has started talking is simply implied by the fact that a reaction is being made to a previous statement, a feature that is often underlined by the new speaker semi-repeating the words of the previous strophe.

In the case of *Skírnismál*, it is impossible to separate the difficulties into clear categories, since they tend to occur in close relation to each other, one problem resulting in another. In consequence, a form of critical commentary has to be employed to put each complication into its wider perspective:

The work opens in sts 1–2 where apparently Skaði and/ or Njörðr command Skírnir to go to their son and discover what is ailing him. The immediate problem is that although it is clear from st.1 that Skírnir is being spoken to, and that he must be replying in st.2 (a near repetition of st.1), it is not evident from the poetry alone exactly who is giving him his orders. As was shown above in *section F.3*, this difficulty is somewhat compounded by the prose introduction which first suggests that Njörðr does the ordering, and then goes on to attribute the words to Skaði. The only clue offered by the *poem* is that Skírnir is being sent to 'our . . . lad' ('*okkarn . . . mǫg*'), which could imply that *both* parents of whoever is being discussed are present. That the speakers are 'rulers' is also suggested by the fact that they can order Skírnir to take on this task. It should be stressed, however, that neither Freyr nor his parents have been mentioned

G. One-Man Performance of the Dialogic Poems

by name at this point in the poem. The subject of the quest is named indirectly as 'enn fróði', meaning 'the wise' or 'the fertile' (st.1), but it is questionable whether this relatively common epithet would be enough to result in the immediate identification of Freyr.[221]

3. 'Skírnismál': The difficulties of performance

Sts 3–9 apparently take place elsewhere in Freyr's hall (or wherever he is situated) which would seem to be some walkable distance from the previous setting: Skaði/ Njörðr have stipulated to Skírnir earlier, 'go/ *walk over* and ask/ for an audience with our son' ('*gakk at beiða*/ okkarn mála mǫg': st.1), something echoed by Skírnir in the following strophe in the words 'if I go/ *walk over* and ask for an audience with the son' ('ef ek *geng at* mæla við mǫg'). However, in the extant version of the poem, sts 3–9 follow on from the first two strophes without even a break for prose.[222] The immediate reaction of the unknowing listener must be that the action is still continuing in the same place as before. Indeed, when st.3 commences with the words, 'Tell me, Freyr' ('Segðu þat, Freyr'), it could easily be imagined that Skírnir, or even the third person present implied by the word 'inn' ('okkarn')[223] is continuing his answer to the speaker of st.1, who might appear from this to have been Freyr. Indeed, the speaker of the first strophe has still not been named. Even more probable, however, would be the mistaken belief that st.3 is spoken by the anonymous speaker of st.1, thus following the normal alternate strophe pattern. Indeed, the audience has very good reason for *not* imagining that the strophe should be uttered by *Skírnir* who is talking *elsewhere* to Freyr. Apart from the fact that no indication has been given about Skírnir's movement, it should be noted that in st.2, he appeared to have turned down the order, stating: 'I can expect/ bad words from *your* son/ *if* I go and ask for an audience with the lad.'[224] It is not until st.4, when clearer indication is given that Freyr must be talking to the 'young warrior' ('seggr enn ungi'), Skírnir, rather than to his parents, that the problem is almost resolved.

Sts 3–5 otherwise cause little difficulty, being clearly linked into a pattern of statement-and-reaction by a series of semi-repetitions:

St.3: '*Tell me*, Freyr . . .'
St.4: 'Why should I *tell you*, young warrior . . .'
    '. . . the elven beam lights up . . ./ and not according to *my desire*.'
St.5: '*Your desire*/ I believe is so not great/ that you, warrior, will not tell me (about it).'[225]

---

[221] Interpretations of the name 'enn fróði' in this context have certainly varied. See, for example, Dronke, 'Art and tradition', p.253 ('wise . . . fruitful'); Lönnroth, 'Skírnismál', p.167 ('den vise' : 'the wise'); Motz, 'Gerðr', 127 ('skillful, valiant'); and Randlev, 'Skírnismál', 139 ('vis': 'wise').
[222] As mentioned above in *section F.3*, Wessén argues in 'Den isländska eddadiktningen', 19, that a prose comment must have originally existed here as in the other places mentioned below where action is supposed to take place, i.e. the leaving of the hall, the crossing of the flame wall, and so on.
[223] This is another conflict with the 'Law of two to a scene'.
[224] 'Illra orða/ er mér ón at *ykrom* syni,/ *ef* ek geng at mæla við mǫg.'
[225] St.3: '*Segðu* þat, Freyr. . . .' St.4: '*Hví um segiak þér*,/ seggr enn ungi . . ./ . . . álfrǫðull/

3. 'Skírnismál': The difficulties of performance

Sts 6–7, however, while being clear to someone well acquainted with the story, could cause further slight confusion if it was expected that the system of statement-and-reaction would continue. Is it Freyr or Skírnir who, in st.6, describes Gerðr walking on 'Gymir's farmstead' ('Gymis gǫrðom')? The strophe itself gives no indication of whom is being addressed. The same occurs in st.7, which the unknowing listener, expecting an alternate strophe pattern, might temporarily accredit to Skírnir. No immediate indication is given of who is speaking here until the end of the first half-strophe where Gerðr is said to be dearer to the speaker than 'any young man from the dawn of time' ('mann(i) hveim/ ungom í árdaga'), a direct response to Skírnir's words in st.5 that he and Freyr were 'young together/ at the dawn of time' ('ungir saman/ várom í árdaga'). All of these difficulties would be even more complicated if the listener still assumed, not illogically, that he/ she were still in the presence of Njǫrðr and Skaði.

Sts 8–9 are clearer, since they involve, first of all, an obvious response to the strophe that precedes them (whether that be st.7 or the missing strophe proposed by certain scholars on the basis of *Gylfaginning*[226]) in the words, 'Give me a horse, *then*' ('Mar gefðu mér *þá*') in the first half-line of st.8. St.9 is then an almost word-for-word repetition response to st.8, beginning with 'That horse I give you' ('Mar ek þér þann gef').

St.10, however, is again likely to cause problems if it is presented without the brief prose interpolation that 'Skírnir spoke to the horse' ('Skírnir mælti við hestinn'). First of all, the poetic text suddenly informs the audience that Skírnir and someone (or something) else are apparently outside, and are about to move, or are moving 'over misty mountains/ over the country of the giants' ('úrig fiǫll yfir,/ þyria [A: þursa] þióð yfir'). The listeners also discover that it is night-time ('It is dark outside': 'Myrkt er úti'). Are they to assume that another jump in time has taken place without any warning, or that the whole poem up to this point has taken place at night, something that could be implied by the opening words of the poem, 'Arise now, Skírnir' ('Rístu nú, Skírnir': st.1)? Certainly the purpose of the strophe, which is to suggest movement and the passing of time, is successful, but it is

---

Ísir . . . / ok þeygi at *mínom munom.*' St.5: '*Muni þína*/ hykka ek svá mikla vera/ at þú mér, seggr, né segir.'

[226] See Jón Helgason, in *Eddadigte*, II, p.24, and Lönnroth in 'Skírnismál', p.169, with regard to Freyr's ordering Skírnir to visit Gerðr, and his offer of a reward for his services in *Edda* (1926), p.38. On the other hand, see also Finnur Jónsson, *Litteraturs historie*, I, p.179. Bibire, in 'Freyr and Gerðr', p.37, makes the sensible suggestion that such an order from Freyr would be a contradiction in his character at this point, and that the sword in the poem should be seen as functional rather than in terms of a financial reward leading to Freyr's later downfall at Ragnarök (an idea emphasised by Snorri). Certainly, such an additional strophe is unnecessary. As a childhood friend, asked to find out what is wrong with Freyr, Skírnir may equally well be acting in response to the challenge implied in Freyr's words that 'nobody wants/ us to be together' ('þat vill engi maðr/ at vit sát [A: samt] sém': st.7).

questionable whether it will work as it was designed to do in a static one-man performance.²²⁷

Even more confusing is the fact that Skírnir is talking to someone else, since he states, 'it is the time for *us* to go' ('mál kveð ek *okr* fara') The immediate reaction is that either he has supporters with him, or, more obviously, that Freyr is accompanying him. No formal parting between the two friends has taken place.²²⁸ The idea that Skírnir should have chosen to start conversing with his horse is frankly the last one that would spring to mind.

Sts 11–13 cover Skírnir's brief conversation with the herdsman on the mound. Since these three strophes involve clear name-tagging, and sum up the setting and situation in an obvious question-and-response format, they pose no difficulty.

Sts 14–18, however, are again likely to cause misinterpretation. The scene has now apparently moved to Gymir's hall or farmstead, and, since it is stated in st.17 (echoed in st.18) that Skírnir 'alone came/ over the raging fire' ('þú einn um komt/ eikinn fúr yfir'), the implication must be that he has already crossed the 'sure and flickering flame' ('vísan vafrloga') implied in sts 8–9. He must have also succeeded in getting past the hounds at the gate mentioned by both him and the herdsman in sts 11–12, and possibly he killed Gymir's son (the herdsman?) at the same time.²²⁹ It is noteworthy that neither the prose nor the verse provides any description of these lively events actually taking place.²³⁰

The audience also has to face the difficulty of who is speaking the following words in st.14:

What is that resounding din	Hvat er þat hlym hlymia
that I can hear now	er ek (hlymia) heyri nú til
within our walls?	ossom rǫnnom í?
The earth trembles,	iǫrð bifaz,
everything quakes,	en allir fyrir
all Gymir's buildings.	skiálfa garðar Gymis.

3. 'Skírnismál':
The difficulties of
performance

---

²²⁷ See Phillpotts, *The Elder Edda*, pp.108-110, and Lönnroth, 'Skírnismál', p.170. Both scholars stress the dramatic features of this strophe.

²²⁸ In fact, for the uninformed member of the audience there is nothing to suggest that Freyr himself is not speaking these words to Skírnir, having perhaps chosen to come some of the way with him.

²²⁹ See Gerðr's words in st.16, 'I am also worried/ that outside here is/ the slayer of my brother' ('ek hitt óumk/ at hér úti sé/ minn bróðurbani'). Several scholars believe this means that Skírnir must have killed Gerðr's brother on the way in: see, for example, Wessén, 'Den isländska eddadiktningen', 19; Hollander, trans. and ed., *The Poetic Edda*, p.68, note 12; Randlev, 'Skírnismál', 145; and Lönnroth, 'Skírnismál', p.171. Lönnroth suggests that since this act is not described in the text, it was probably mimed as part of a dramatic performance, thus removing the need for any further textual explanation. See further Dronke, 'Art and tradition', 260–263, where Gerðr's 'bróðurbani' is interpreted as being Freyr himself, seen in prophetic terms; and Steinsland, *Det hellige bryllup*, p.89, where the expression is simply explained as meaning an enemy of Gerðr's race.

²³⁰ See Phillpotts, *The Elder Edda*, p.103.

III. The Eddic Poems and Drama

3. 'Skírnismál':
The difficulties of
performance

The natural reaction is that these words must be spoken by Gymir himself, rather than Gerðr, since apart from the implications of the powerful alliterative speech ('Hvat er þat *hlym hlymia/* er ek [*hlymia*] *heyri*), it is Gymir who has been set up as being the principal menace throughout the poem so far. Skírnir, for example, previously made it a condition of his going that he received Freyr's sword which 'fights by itself/ against the race of *jötnar*' ('siálft vegiz/ við iotna ætt': st.8). Similarly, in st.10, in his statement to the horse, he commented, 'Both of us will make it,/ or both be taken/ by *the all-mighty jötunn*' ('báðir vit komumk,/ eða okr báða tekr/ *sá inn ámátki iotunn*'). The dogs were described as '*Gymir*'s hounds' ('greyiom Gymis': st.11), and apparently they are not the only dangers awaiting Skírnir, since according to the herdsman, 'you will never ever be/ granted free conversation/ with *Gymir*'s good daughter' ('anspillis vanr/ þú skalt æ vera/ góðrar meyiar *Gymis*': st.12), the stress again being placed on Gymir rather than Gerðr. Everything leads the audience to expect the sudden arrival of the *jötunn* at any moment. Gerðr herself is not named as being present until the end of the first half of st.19, and certainly there is nothing in her words, or in Skírnir's replies up until that point, that could not be attributed to Gymir.

The following strophe, st.15, forms an obvious reply to 'Gerðr's' question:

There is a man out here	Maðr er hér úti
dismounted from his horse,	stiginn af mars baki,
he's sending the horse to graze.	ió lætr til iarðar taka.

According to a note inserted into the body of the text in both manuscripts, these words are spoken by a serving woman. Yet once again, there is nothing in the actual text of the poem informing the audience of this fact. Indeed, the natural reaction from the audience would be that Gymir/ Gerðr is calling from the hall, and is answered by the shepherd, who was unquestionably 'out here' ('hér úti') earlier, and was speaking with Skírnir earlier in st.12. Once again, the listening audience is faced with a situation involving *three* active characters, if not four.

Sts 16–26 cover a much more straightforward piece of dialogue. In st.16, 'Gerðr' orders the 'servant woman' to invite her visitor in, and then, in st.17, attempts to elicit exactly what sort of person he is: 'What are you? Of the elves,/ or a son of the Æsir/ or the wise Vanir gods?' ('Hvat er þat álfa/ né ása sona/ né vís(s)a vana?') As in all the other poems under discussion, the visitor remains unnamed at first,[231] his clear reply in st.18 being a semi-repetition of the question. The same repetitive form is employed in sts 19–20 and sts 21–22, in which Skírnir makes various offers to Gerðr, all of which are formally declined, until Skírnir begins to intimate violence in st.23. At that point, Gerðr in turn takes to threatening him with her father

---

[231] See further *sections G.2, 4c, 5, and 6.*

G. One-Man Performance of the Dialogic Poems

(st.24). Like Skírnir in the strophe that follows ('before this blade/ the aged *jǫtunn* will fall': 'fyr þessom eggiom/ hnígr sá inn aldni iǫtunn'; st.25), the audience is again made to expect the giant's arrival, and this should be borne in mind throughout the magical strophes that follow.

3. 'Skírnismál': The difficulties of performance

The following strophes (sts 26–36) are supposedly continuous incantations by Skírnir, and contain several suggestions of accompanying action, similar to those pointed out already in *Lokasenna*. In fact, suggestions of gesticulation and movement are found even earlier in *Skírnismál*, in st.23 and st.25, where Skírnir points out his sword to Gerðr in a remarkably immediate fashion: 'Do you see *this sword*, maid,/ slim and inlaid,/ that I *have here in my hand*?' (st.23).[232] Such intimations of action become even more common in Skírnir's ritualistic curse of Gerðr:

- St.26: '*I strike you* with a taming rod' ('Tamsvendi ek þik drep').
- St.29: '*Sit down!*' ('Seztu niðr').
- St.32: 'To a copse *I went/ walked,*/ and to green wood/ to make a wand of power,/ a wand of power was made' ('Til holtz ek gekk/ ok til hrás viðar,/ gambantein at geta;/ gambantein ek gat').
- St.36: '*I carve* the Þurs rune,/ and three other signs' ('Þurs ríst ek þér/ ok þriá stafi').

It should be noted, furthermore, that st.32 implies yet another apparent temporal break to allow Skírnir to go in search of wood, although this presents less of a problem than the temporal difficulties met earlier. For the audience, this comment in the past tense might even refer to an action that is supposed to have taken place in the more distant past at some time during the journey (although this has not been previously mentioned in either the prose or the verse).

Sts 37–39, which follow on from this curse, are relatively straightforward. They begin with Gerðr's formalised submission to Skírnir, which again includes an implication of some form of living movement or gesticulation: '*Receive* the frosted glass,/ full of ancient mead' (*Tak við* hrímkálki,/ fullom forns miaðar': st.37). The first of these strophes opens by making a pointed break from Skírnir's speech, and is clearly addressed to Skírnir by somebody else (Gerðr): '*Better* to wish you good health, *lad*' ('Heill ver þú nú *heldr, sveinn*'). Skírnir then obviously replies in st.38, demanding an answer before he rides home. He is given this reply in st.39, Gerðr agreeing to meet Freyr in the holy grove of Barri 'which is known to *both* of us' ('er vit *bæði* vitom'), the word *bæði* ('both' in neuter plural) pointing to a mixed pair (Skírnir and Gerðr).

Following this, the *Codex Regius*[233] contains a piece of prose stating that 'then Skírnir rode home. Freyr stood outside and greeted him and asked for

---

[232] 'Sér þú þenna mæki, mær,/ mióvan, málfán,/ er ek hefi í hendi hér?/ hǫfuð hǫggva/ ek mun þér hálsi af,/ nema þú mér sætt segir': st.23.
[233] The fragmentary AM 748 manuscript lacks the folio containing the last part of *Skírnismál* (from st.27).

3. 'Skírnismál': The difficulties of performance

news'.[234] The only support for this in the *poem*, however, is that the speaker of the following strophe (st.40) asks Skírnir (by name) for news:

Tell me Skírnir	Segðu mér þat, Skírnir,
before you throw the saddle off your horse,	áðr þú verpir sǫðli af mar
and take a step forward,	ok þú stígir feti framarr,
what you fulfilled	hvat þú árnaðir
in Jötunheimar	í iǫtunheima
in terms of your or my desire.	þíns eða míns munar

There is nothing in the strophe to state that it is Freyr who is speaking; for the audience, at first it could just as well be Njörðr or Skaði, or indeed, somebody else that Skírnir happened to meet on the way home. Certainly the use of the word *muni* (desire) by the speaker of st.40 is reminiscent of Freyr's use of the word earlier in the poem in st.4. However, it is not until the end of the first half of st.42 that Freyr's presence is emphasised, his words here forming a clear personal reaction to the message conveyed by Skírnir in st.41.

Skírnismál is thus a highly complex matter if considered in terms of a solo presentation in its present form. First and foremost, if it is to be fully understood, it demands more narrative interpolations than it already has in prose, if only to give some indication of changes in time, situation, and other kinds of movement. Nonetheless, as has been suggested above, it is highly unlikely that such interpolations in verse or prose ever accompanied *ljóðaháttr* poems of this kind, outside a basic prologue.[235] Apart from this, an exact prior background knowledge of the events of the poem is often needed for the audience to understand who is speaking at any given time. Without this, numerous disruptions must be made to the flow of the poem in order for the non-dramatic performer to indicate the various transitions between speakers. The only other possibility, as has been suggested in connection with *Lokasenna*, is that the original performer made use of different voices or physically *enacted* the roles, something that again would bring the presentation immediately into the field of drama. Such a form of presentation, of course, is given further support by the textual indications of movement that have been listed above, all of which would provide any performer with an impulse to employ at least minor forms of gesticulation.

Yet none of the above problems would occur if one were prepared to accept the use of an even more dramatic mode of performance involving more than one speaker, and movement across a limited acting area containing several *mansions* (settings) of the kind encountered in medieval religious drama from the eleventh century onwards.[236] In drama of that kind, all that was needed to explain distance and time was a symbolic move

---

[234] 'Þá reið Skírnir heim. Freyr stóð úti ok kvaddi hann ok spurði tíðinda.'
[235] See above, *sections D and F*.
[236] See, for example, Tydeman, *The theatre in the Middle Ages*, pp.57–63, pp.67–70, pp.144–156, and pp.160–162; and Kolve, *The play called Corpus Christi*, p.23.

G. One-Man Performance of the Dialogic Poems

3. 'Skírnismál': The difficulties of performance

from one *mansion* to another, accompanied by an explanatory speech like that given in *Skírnismál*, st.10. Such a form of presentation for *Skírnismál* would make it possible for characters to walk quickly from one 'hall' to another in a moment, and for them to be both 'inside' and 'outside' at the same time, as when Skírnir leaves for Jötunheimar. It would also make it possible for Freyr to remain static in his seat 'inside', and still talk to Skírnir as he dismounts from his horse 'outside', in st.40.[237]

This consideration of the practical demands of *Skírnismál* leads to another observation about the work, namely the fact that if Freyr's later move outside his hall mentioned in the prose is disregarded, as has been suggested, then Skírnir and the horse are the only characters that physically move from one place to another. This odd feature gives further weight to the suggested system of *mansions* in which the various characters, by their mere presence at separate sites, 'represent' or 'imply' different settings. Indeed, the lack of movement by 'holy' figures (sometimes represented by statues) has close parallels in medieval drama where the figure of God often remained static, while the characters moved about him.[238] In terms of *Skírnismál*, this idea brings back to mind the concepts of the talking statues of Freyr and Þórr mentioned *Chapter I*.[239]

Possibly the strongest indication that *Skírnismál* must have been acted is the fact that the climax of the poem, which all the text has been leading up to, is missing: that is to say, the actual meeting of Freyr and Gerðr.[240] This event is described in neither verse nor prose, but is arguably essential for the poem, and must have originally formed part of the work. Since no words are ever spoken between Freyr and Gerðr, the event must have been given prominence in some other way. Mere narrative in prose is again unlikely. If a prose conclusion *had* been used, it would have been a great disappointment after the build-up to the event provided by the poem itself. The likelihood must be that action was used, at least of a symbolic kind.[241]

---

[237] On the basis of the experimental outdoor production of *Skírnismál* directed by the author in 1992 (see *Introduction*, note 5), it should be stated that *Skírnismál* is particularly well suited to this form of medieval presentation.
[238] See further Kolve, *The play called Corpus Christi*, pp.9–10, p.26, and pp.30–31, on the subject of the spiritual dangers of playing characters such as God or the Devil in medieval drama. As Kolve shows, this problem was avoided in certain cases by the use of a constructed image, or mask, or merely a detached voice.
[239] See *Chapter I, C.5*.
[240] Whether this 'union' should be seen as a wedding or not is beside the point here.
[241] It is difficult to imagine such a scene being lost, unless it was removed for reasons of taste, or out of religious zeal.

III. The Eddic Poems and Drama

4. 'Fáfnismál': The Difficulties of Performance

a. The text

Owing to the extant shape of *Fáfnismál* in the *Codex Regius*, it is necessary to make some decisions about which strophes should be considered as constituting the *original* recorded work before an examination of the performance difficulties regarding this poem can be undertaken.

In the *Codex Regius*, *Fáfnismál* forms part of a large unbroken passage of verse and prose which has been divided by most editors into three 'poems': *Reginsmál*, *Fáfnismál* and *Sigrdrífumál*. In the manuscript, no clear divisions are made between the individual poems, and none of them are given a title.[242] This feature, and the facts that all three poems in their present form are predominantly in *ljóðaháttr* (a metre rarely employed in any of the other heroic poems of the Edda) and display numerous other similarities in theme, approach, attitude, choice of vocabulary and more, has naturally led some scholars in the past to argue that the poems should not be considered separately from each other.[243] Nonetheless, for reasons that will be given presently, there is good cause to believe that the larger part of *Fáfnismál* must have existed originally as an individual entity.

This leads to the question of precisely which strophes make up the original body of *Fáfnismál*. For practical purposes (and partly on the basis of later paper manuscripts), the *Fáfnismál* section of the body of poetry mentioned above is seen as beginning either at the start of the prose passage which follows st.26 of *Reginsmál*,[244] or after the second sentence of this prose, beginning with the words 'Sigurðr ok Reginn fóro upp á Gnitaheiði . . .' ('Sigurðr and Reginn went up onto Gnitaheiði . . .').[245] The prose thus serves as an introduction to the verse of *Fáfnismál*, which itself commences after the minor heading of 'Frá dauða Fáfnis' ('Concerning the death of Fáfnir').[246] The *Sigrdrífumál* section, which comes last, is considered by most editors to begin with the words 'Sigurðr reið upp á

---

[242] The present titles stem from a much later date. The name *Reginsmál* was originally coined by Bugge in *Norroen fornkvæði* (1867), p.212. The paper MSS, from which the names *Fáfnismál* and *Sigrdrífumál* were drawn, suggested the title 'Sigurðarkviða Fáfnisbana önnur'.

[243] See, for example, Guðbrandur Vigfússon and Powell, *Corpvs Poeticvm Boreale*, I, pp.30–44, and pp.155–158; Ussing, *Om det inbyrdes forhold*, pp.64–81; Heusler, 'Jung Sigurd', pp.28–29 in particular; Finnur Jónsson, 'Sagnformen', 34–53; de Vries, 'Om Eddaens visdomsdigtning', 16–21; Einar Ólafur Sveinsson, *Íslenzkar bókmenntir*, pp.458–462; and Andersson, *The legend of Brynhild*, pp.82–93, all of which are referred to in more detail below. None of these scholars, apart from Finnur Jónsson ('Sagnformen', 48), sees the *ljóðaháttr Fáfnismál* as forming a separate entity. All postulate firm links between various strophes in *Fáfnismál* and other strophes belonging to one or both of the other two poems in question.

[244] See, for example, Neckel and Kuhn, *Edda*, p.180.

[245] See, for example, Bugge, *Norroen fornkvæði*, p.219, and Jón Helgason, *Eddadigte*, III, p.61.

[246] This title is emphasised by being written in red ink in the manuscript. Interestingly enough, it separates the final words of the prose, 'fáfnir q.' ('Fáfnir said'), and the first words of the poem. This could perhaps be read as yet another sign that the speaker

G. One-Man Performance of the Dialogic Poems

Hindarfiall' ('Sigurðr rode up onto Hindarfjall'), in the middle of the prose that follows st.44 of *Fáfnismál*.

In their present form, each of these three poems consists of a number of strophes composed in *ljóðaháttr* and a number in *fornyrðislag*, in addition to a comparatively large amount of prose (see *Table I*, above). This has led to any number of speculations, the most common being that the majority of the *ljóðaháttr* strophes (the so-called A-strophes) of *Reginsmál* and *Fáfnismál* form an almost complete poem which deals essentially with the early events of a tale about the curse of Andvari's gold. Heusler named this poem the *Hortlied*, a title which has since remained in use.[247] Most of the *fornyrðislag* strophes in these two poems, on the other hand, are generally regarded as having originated in a later poem that dealt with the same subject but concentrated more on the theme of filial revenge: the *Vaterrachelied*.[248]

In very general terms, Heusler's proposal has been accepted by many scholars.[249] Yet beyond these basic points of agreement, there are numerous other differences of opinion about precisely which *ljóðaháttr* strophes constituted the original *Hortlied*, and which ones should be disregarded on the basis of their being later additions.[250] Heusler, for example,

4. 'Fáfnismál': The difficulties of performance

---

indications (and the prose) had a separate origin to the poem, and that the scribe did not regard them as being part of the same entity.

[247] Heusler, 'Jung Sigurd', p.165. Heusler's ideas are reflected most clearly in Genzmer's translation of the poems into German: *Edda*, ed. Neider, with notes by Heusler (1914–1920), I, pp.113–124 ('Das Lied von Drachenhort'). Here, largely on the basis of the reordering made by the writer of *Völsunga saga*, the *Hortleid* is presented in the following form: *Reginsmál*, sts 1–2, 6–7, 8 (now spoken by Loki), 9–10 and 12, and *Fáfnismál*, sts 1–10, 16–25, 28–30, 26–27, and 32–39. Sts 11–15 and st.31 of *Fáfnismál* are thus dropped, in addition to the whole Hnikarr episode of *Reginsmál*. At the same time, several 'lost' lines from *Völsunga saga* are 'restored' to the half-strophes of sts 3, 18, and 21 of *Fáfnismál*, and a whole strophe is inserted after st.30 (Reginn being credited as the speaker). In later editions, this pattern alters slightly. For example, sts 11–15 have now been returned to the poem, and the *fornyrðislag* strophes uttered by the birds removed. See most recently *Die Edda*, trans. into German by Genzmer, with notes by Schier (1981), pp.249–257.

[248] The *Vaterrachelied* was originally seen as consisting of *Reginsmál*, sts 13–18, 23, 26, and 24, but later had seven further strophes from *Völsunga saga* added to it, all of them dealing with Sigmundr, Hjördís and the sword. The remaining *fornyrðislag* strophes of the 'nuthatch prophecy' from *Fáfnismál* were seen by Heusler as forming a collection of independent verses, or *lausavísur*: 'Die Vogelweissagung'. All in all, there are certain obvious weaknesses in this suggested pattern, not least because *Reginsmál*, st.5 and st.11 in Heusler's *Hortlied* are both in *fornyrðislag*.

[249] See, however, Andersson, *The legend of Brynhild*, pp.82-93. Andersson, on the whole, takes a similar attitude to Heusler, but suggests the prior existence of three poems rather than two, i.e. two *Hortlieder* (the second being a later version in *fornyrðislag* based on the first, and including *Reginsmál*, st.5 and st.11, and the bird strophes), and then the *Vaterrachelied*.

[250] Before Heusler's time, other scholars had seen the original *ljóðaháttr* poem as extending all the way from *Reginsmál* to *Sigrdrífumál*. See, for example, Guðbrandur Vigfússon and Powell, *Corpus Poeticvm Boreale*, I, pp.32–44, and pp.155–158, where the united *ljóðaháttr* 'Old Play of the Wolsungs' is clearly separated from the fragmentary *fornyrðislag* 'Western Wolsung Lay'; and Ussing, *Om det inbyrdes forhold*, pp.64–81. More

III. The Eddic Poems and Drama

4. 'Fáfnismál': The difficulties of performance

deletes not only those strophes of *Reginsmál* which deal with Sigurðr's meeting with Hnikarr, but also st.31 of *Fáfnismál*.[251] On the other hand, de Vries, following Müllenhoff's earlier example, cuts sts 12–15 (and then more tentatively sts 32–39) with the argument that these seem to be totally out of context, the earlier gnomic strophes probably originating in a lost catechetic mythological poem similar to *Vafþrúðnismál*.[252] Many of these arguments have since been contested by other scholars.[253]

Another dispute relates to the ordering of sts 26–31. Müllenhoff, for example, suggested, on the basis of *Völsunga saga*, that sts 28–30 should precede st.26, while Finnur Jónsson felt that they should directly follow this particular strophe, preceding st.27 as they seem to do in *Völsunga saga*.[254] Ussing, somewhat more logically, made the suggestion that st.27 and st.31 should be substituted for each other, st.31 thus being placed in the mouth of a different speaker (Reginn).[255] Heusler, nine years later, went on to make a further contribution to the argument, very similar to Müllenhoff's, except that he now added another strophe (drawn from *Völsunga saga*) between st.30 and st.26.[256]

For the purposes of the following study, the intention is to concentrate solely on the *ljóðaháttr* strophes belonging to *Fáfnismál*, examining them in the order in which they are found in the *Codex Regius*, although the postulated alternatives mentioned above will also be included in the discussion. The few *fornyrðislag* strophes found in the extant text of the poem will not be included for the simple reason that no convincing argument has yet been made for a mixed *ljóðaháttr/fornyrðislag* form of poetry, and as

---

recently, Ussing's argument was supported by Einar Ólafur Sveinsson, in *Íslenzkar bókmenntir*, pp.459–60, with the slight reservation that the whole should be seen as a form of cycle of poems, or 'kvæðaflokkur', made up of various components from different periods, rather than an original poem. On the other hand, Finnur Jónsson had argued that 'both' parts of *Reginsmál* (the *ljóðaháttr* and the *fornyrðislag* parts) must have been written before *Fáfnismál* and *Sigrdrífumál* which Finnur saw as constituting totally separate poems: see Finnur Jónsson, *Litteraturs historie*, I, pp.65–66, and 'Sagnformen', 48.

[251] A similar opinion was held by both Bugge, in 'Efterslæt', 268, and Finnur Jónsson, in 'Sagnformen', 43, on the grounds, it would seem, that the strophe does not exist in *Völsunga saga*. The same, however, could be argued for st.19 and st.26.

[252] See Müllenhoff, *Deutsche Altertumskunde*, V, p.160 and p.364, and de Vries, 'Om Eddaens visdomsdigtning', 17–18.

[253] Müllenhoff's ideas were rejected by Finnur Jónsson, and de Vries was in turn challenged by Ström and Kragerud on the grounds that the visionary strophes on the subject of the *nornir* and Ragnarök follow up Fáfnir's mention of the 'judgement of the *nornir*' ('nornadóm') in st.11. Ström argues that it was believed in medieval Scandinavia that the dying gained visionary prophetic powers and that, in this sense, the verses are structurally in perfect context. Kragerud goes further, convincingly suggesting that the strophes are central to the idea of inescapable fate that runs through the poem. See Finnur Jónsson, *Litteraturs historie*, I, pp.274–276; Ström, 'Den döendes makt', 27–28, and 68; and Kragerud, 'De mytologiske spørsmål', 9–20. More recently, see also Quinn, 'Verseform', 120–124, and 126–127.

[254] Müllenhoff, *Deutsche Altertumskunde*, V, p.160, note, and p.365; and Finnur Jónsson, *Litteraturs historie*, I, p.275. See also *Völsunga saga*, p.40.

[255] Ussing, *Om det inbyrdes forhold*, pp.75–77.

[256] See note 247 above.

G. One-Man Performance of the Dialogic Poems

the scholars mentioned above have shown, these particular strophes appear to be repetitive and unncessary.[257] The *ljóðaháttr* strophes of *Reginsmál* will also be ignored for three central reasons that have not been stressed enough in the past:

First of all, the action contained in all the other extant *ljóðaháttr* poems is strictly limited in terms of time and space. None of these poems covers the extent in time implied if the episodes of *Reginsmál* dealing with the otter and Hnikarr are linked to that of Fáfnir's death in *Fáfnismál*. Indeed, this later event must logically occur a number of *years* later than those described in *Reginsmál*.[258]

Secondly, it should be noted that in *Norna-Gests þáttr*, Norna-Gestr totally ignores the details of *Fáfnismál* after his performance of parts of *Reginsmál*, contenting himself by saying simply that 'Sigurðr then killed Fáfnir and Reginn because he (Reginn) wanted to betray him.'[259] It would therfore seem that the writer of this *þáttr* did not envisage *Reginsmál* and *Fáfnismál* as forming an inseparable unit.

Finally, there is no evidence that *Reginsmál* in the Codex Regius ever included the same kind of marginal speaker notation as that found alongside *Helgakviða Hjörvarðssonar*, *Fáfnismál* and the other poems under discussion. In *Reginsmál*, phrases like 'Hreiðmarr said' ('Hreiðmarr sagði', before st.7), 'Reginn answered' ('Reginn svaraði', before st.17) and 'Hnikarr said' ('Hnikarr kvað', before st.20) are all written within the body of the poetic text. In *Fáfnismál*, on the other hand, such internal speaker indications only occur at the end of the prose interpolations. All other speaker indications appear to have been totally relegated to the margin. This, of course, raises the possibility that these works were recorded independently of each other.

Regarding the question of the links between *Sigrdrífumál* and the *ljóðaháttr* strophes of *Fáfnismál* suggested by Guðbrandur Vigfússon and others,[260] it is necessary to bear in mind that *Sigrdrífumál* seems to have

4. 'Fáfnismál': The difficulties of performance

---

[257] Judy Quinn's argument for such a mixed form of verse in 'Verseform' is interesting, and might be applicable to the literary text of the poem. However, it fails to note the implicit associations of the *ljóðaháttr* and *fornyrðislag* metres as they seem to have existed in the oral tradition: see *section C* above.

[258] It is suggested in the prose passage which introduces *Reginsmál* that the early section of the poem concerning Hreiðmarr and the 'otter-payment' is all part of a narration given by Reginn for Sigurðr's benefit. This comment, however, has to be considered as the work of the editor who, as elsewhere in the heroic section of the *Codex*, is trying to bind various elements into a comprehensible, logically narrative whole. In 'Sagnformen', 37–38 and 43, Finnur Jónsson even postulates a family relationship between Fáfnir and Sigurðr (Lyngheiðr or Loftheiðr supposedly being Sigurðr's grandmother), something which Finnur feels is suggested by *Reginsmál*, st.10. The Fáfnir and Sigurðr who appear in *Fáfnismál*, however, seem to have no knowledge of this relationship. In *Fáfnismál*, st.4, Sigurðr states, 'Ætterni mitt/ kveð ek þér ókunnikt vera/ ok mik siálfan it sama' ('My family,/ I would say, is unknown to you/ and the same can be said about me').

[259] 'Sidan drap Sigurðr þa Fafni ok Regin þuiat hann uillde suikia hann': *Norna-Gests þáttr*, p.353.

[260] See above, note 250.

4. 'Fáfnismál': The difficulties of performance

originated at a different time from *Fáfnismál*.[261] Nonetheless, *Sigrdrífumál* does provide a logical extension of events described in *Fáfnismál*, and its addition to that poem would not result in any departure from the usual format of the *ljóðaháttr* works under discussion.

It can be concluded that while obvious links in tradition exist between parts of *Reginsmál* and *Fáfnismál*, this does not necessarily mean that these individual parts originally belonged to the same poem. On the other hand, it is possible, and logical, that something of the nature of *Sigrdrífumál* might have once followed on directly from the events related in the *ljóðaháttr* strophes of *Fáfnismál*. All the same, there seems to be good reason to be wary of regarding the extant text of *Sigrdrífumál* as having originally been a direct continuation of *Fáfnismál*.

b. Difficulties in speaker identification in an oral performance of the 'ljóðaháttr' strophes of 'Fáfnismál'

The *ljóðaháttr* poem, *Fáfnismál*, can thus be said to comprise a total of thirty-five strophes. These can be divided into three distinct 'scenes', the first being the slightly mystical conversation between Sigurðr and the mortally wounded Fáfnir (sts 1–22), the second being that between Sigurðr and Reginn (sts 23–31), and the final episode the scene between Sigurðr and the nuthatches (st.34, and sts 37–39). In performance, the extant *ljóðaháttr* strophes would involve the presenter in clearly distinguishing between no fewer than five characters for the listening audience: Fáfnir, Sigurðr, Reginn and (at least) two birds which could perhaps be considered as speaking in 'chorus'. Indeed, the marginal notation in the manuscript implies that individual speeches were made by up to seven birds,[262] but this conflicts with the iconographic tradition represented by the illustrations on the Hylestad and Vegusdal portals, the Ramsundsberg petroglyph, the Halton Cross and perhaps also those illustrations on the Ockelbo stone and the Värsås church door in Sweden, all of which seem to show only two birds talking to Sigurðr.[263] Even in its simplest form, *Fáfnismál* demands

---

[261] See, for example, Noreen, 'Studier, III', 26–32. On the basis of his examination of the words occurring at the end of each half-strophe, Noreen suggests that *Sigrdrífumál* as a whole cannot be considered as being authentically old. For a summary of more recent attitudes, see Einar Ólafur Sveinsson, *Íslenzkar bókmenntir*, pp.466–467; and Vésteinn Ólason, 'Eddukvæði', p.146. Einar Ólafur himself saw the various component parts of *Sigrdrífumál* as originating at different periods in time.

[262] This includes, interestingly enough, four *fornyrðislag* strophes: sts.32–33, and 35–36. The notation has been lost on p.62 of the manuscript, but on p.61, which contains sts 32–35 of the poem, the birds are numbered in the margin against their speeches ('ll','lll', and 'llll'), implying that these numbers must have originally continued on the following page. However, for the final prophecy (sts 40–44 in *fornyrðislag*), the manuscript seems to suggest a more choral presentation, introducing the words of the birds with the prose statement that 'Þá heyrði Sigurðr hvar igðor mælto' ('Then Sigurðr heard the nuthatches speak').

[263] See Schück, *Litteraturhistorie*, 2nd ed., I, p.116, and Blindheim, *Sigurds saga*, pp.21–34. Finnur Jónsson nonetheless believed that the *fornyrðislag* strophes pointed to the

G. One-Man Performance of the Dialogic Poems

that any solo performer must successfully make at least thirty clear transitions in character between speeches.

Interestingly enough, Olrik cites the action of *Fáfnismál* as living proof of the 'Law of two to a scene', commenting on the fact that Reginn does not talk to Sigurðr until Fáfnir is clearly dead, and that the birds do not speak indirectly to Sigurðr until Reginn has conveniently gone to sleep.[264] Nonetheless, if the poem is examined carefully, it becomes obvious that Olrik's rule is also broken here (perhaps even more radically than in the case of *Skírnismál*), and especially in the scene in which Sigurðr listens to the birds, who were seen by the redactor/ scribe as talking individually.[265] This is further complicated by the fact that Reginn must also be sleeping in the near vicinity. Certainly, he says, 'I will go off to sleep' ('ek mun sofa ganga': st.27), but any early audience would have envisaged his sleeping place as being somewhere close to the fire over which Sigurðr is roasting the heart of Fáfnir when he hears the voices of the birds.

On the whole, the first two scenes of the poem (sts 1–31) would offer little difficulty for the solo performer, since the speeches mainly alternate between two speakers in a clear system of question-and-answer or statement-and-reaction. Indeed, these strophes tend to be tightly linked into pairs by theme or inter-strophe alliteration (as in the case of sts 8–9). In addition to this, the initial scene between Sigurðr and Fáfnir (sts 1–22) contains numerous examples of partial context marking in the form of direct or indirect self-identification, or identification of the other person present, most of them occurring either in the traditional fashion at the start of the strophe, or in the first line of the second half of the strophe: Fáfnir, for example, refers to himself directly twice (st.1 and st.22), elsewhere giving indirect reference to himself by talk of his poison (st.18), the fact that he is dying (st.5 and st.22, which refer back to st.1), and the jewels he used to lie on (st.16). He is named directly by Sigurðr three times (sts 8, 12, and 14), and indirectly once, as 'the mighty serpent' ('inn rammi ormr') in st.19. Sigurðr, meanwhile, is directly named only once by Fáfnir (st.20) who otherwise indicates the hero by reference to his age (sts 1, 5 and 7). Sigurðr only names himself directly once, and then not until st.4.

As with the other poems under discussion, all would be well and good if such speaker indication was obvious throughout, and if speeches were limited to this alternating strophe pattern. Problems occur for audience understanding the moment that this trustworthy system is disrupted, and even in the first scene of *Fáfnismál*, the pattern is broken twice. In st.16, for example, Fáfnir continues his speech into a second strophe, making a statement that is completely unrelated to his words in st.15. The earlier strophe (st.15) had formed the answer to Sigurðr's question concerning the small isle on which the giant Surtr and the Æsir will fight at Ragnarök:

4. 'Fáfnismál': The difficulties of performance

---

existence of at least three birds, since one of them talks of 'you sisters' ('yðvar systra') in st.35: Finnur Jónsson, *Litteraturs historie*, I, p.276.
[264] Olrik, 'Episke love', 70–71; *Principles*, p.43.
[265] See note 262 above.

4. 'Fáfnismál': The difficulties of performance

> It is called Óskopnir,
> and there all the gods
> will engage in spear-play;
> Bilröst will break,
> as they leave,
> the horses will swim in the great river.

> Óskópnir hann heitir,
> en þar oll skolo
> geirom leika goð;
> Bilrost brotnar,
> er þeir á brot fara,
> ok svima í móðo marir.

St.16 then runs as follows

> Ægishiálmr (the helmet/ mask of terror)
> I bore amongst the sons of men
> while I rested on riches;
> mightier than others
> I believed myself to be,
> I never found many real men.

> Ægishiálm
> bar ek um alda sonom,
> meðan ek um meniom lág;
> einn rammari
> hugðomk ollom vera,
> fanka ek marga mogo.

According to the established pattern in the poem up to this point, Sigurðr should speak in st.16. For that reason, it is somewhat surprising that the strophe gives no indication that Fáfnir is speaking rather than Sigurðr prior to the statement in the third line about the riches Fáfnir lay on. From the audience's point of view, this is somewhat late, especially when the talk of helmets would be much more likely to spring from Sigurðr's lips than from those of a supposed serpent like Fáfnir. (The talk of being amongst 'the sons of men' could apply to either character.) More important is the fact that, as in *Lokasenna* and *Skírnismál*, the double strophe breaks the expected underlying pattern for the listener, thus allowing for further complications later, especially in those places where names and other partial context markers are completely absent from the speeches.

Such a case arguably occurs in st.23, when Reginn appears on the scene with the following words:

> I now wish you health, Sigurðr,
> now you are victorious
> and have despatched Fáfnir;
> of the men
> who walk the earth
> I pronounce you to be the bravest.

> Heill þú nú, Sigurðr,
> nú hefir þú sigr vegit
> ok Fáfni um farit;
> manna þeira
> er mold troða,
> þik kveð ek óblauðastan alinn.

If one ignores the interim prose interpolation stating that Reginn has returned, this strophe sounds very similar in tone to the previous strophe (st.22) which was unquestionably uttered by Fáfnir: 'I think that Fáfnir will/ lose his life;/ yours was the greater strength.'[266] This half-strophe not only displayed Fáfnir admitting Sigurðr's victory (as in the words 'Now you are victorious' in st.23), but also contained an example of the 'serpent'

---

[266] 'Fiǫr sitt láta/ hygg ek at Fáfnir myni;/ þitt varð nú meira megin.'

4. 'Fáfnismál':
The difficulties of
performance

talking of himself in the third person. Other indications that might lead a listener to imagine that Fáfnir rather than Reginn is speaking in st.23 are the faint echo of Fáfnir's earlier words in st.20, 'Ræð ek þér nú, Sigurðr' ('I advise you now, Sigurðr'), and the further reference to the concept of bravery (of being 'hvatr' or 'blauðr') which was earlier raised by Sigurðr in st.6. Furthermore, it might be noted that on several other occasions in the *ljóðaháttr* poems, the word 'heill' ('hail' or 'good health') is used in the sense of respect by figures who have been defeated. A typical example is Gerðr's speech in *Skírnismál*, st.37, at the point when she finally acknowledges Skírnir's dominance: 'Heill ver þú nú heldr, sveinn,/ ok tak við hrímkálki . . .' ('Better to wish you good health, lad;/ receive the frosted glass').[267] For the listening audience, the speech in *Fáfnismál*, st.23, would certainly not have been understood immediately as an obvious greeting by a newly arrived person.

Furthermore, it is noteworthy that Reginn is never directly named in the scene between him and Sigurðr.[268] The first real sign that somebody other than Fáfnir and Sigurðr is present, a character who according to tradition has to be Reginn, is in st.25, where the speaker refers to Sigurðr wiping his sword on the grass, and adds 'you have fatally wounded/ my brother,/ and I am partly to blame' ('bróður minn/ hefir þú beniaðan,/ ok veld ek þó siálfr sumo'). For the audience lacking the prose, and listening to a non-dramatic solo recitation, this section of the poem could well be highly puzzling.

Even if the problem of identity in sts 23–24 can be explained away by the suggestion of prose having always existed alongside the verse of *Fáfnismál*, the same cannot be said about the much-discussed st.31, which some scholars have tried to disregard totally.[269] Here, where the audience would logically expect to hear an answer or reaction from Reginn, Sigurðr continues speaking into a second strophe, closely echoing his previous words in st.30:

Spirit is better	Hugr er betri
than the might of the sword,	en sé hiǫrs megin,
when men fight in battle,	hvars (v)reiðir scolo vega,
because a brave man	þvíat hvatan mann
I see winning a hard fight	ek sé har(ð)liga vega
even with a dull sword.	með slævo sverði sigr. (st.30)

---

[267] See Sif's similar offer in *Lokasenna*, st.53; and Frigg's words in *Vafþrúðnismál*, st.4, following another lost dispute: 'Heill þú farir,/ heill þú aptr komir,/ heill þú á sinnom sér!' ('May you leave in good health,/ may you return in good health,/ may you travel in good health!'). In this latter case, the words represent a farewell, but since Óðinn has disregarded Frigg's advice not to visit Vafþrúðnir, they might also be regarded as representing Frigg's acceptance of defeat. In *Vafþrúðnismál*, st.6, the same word is used as a welcome: 'Heill þú nú, Vafþrúðnir!' ('Good health to you now, Vafþrúðnir!')
[268] Reginn's name is mentioned earlier by Fáfnir in st.22, and by both the birds and Sigurðr in the final scene (sts 37 and 39).
[269] See note 247 above, with regard to Heusler's suggestions concerning *Fáfnismál* (the *Hortlied*).

4. 'Fáfnismál': The difficulties of performance

To be brave is better	Hvǫtom er betra
than to lack in courage,	en sé óhvǫtom,
in the game of battle;	í hildileik hafaz;
to be joyful is better	glǫðom er betra
than to be faint-hearted,	en sé glúpnanda,
whatever should come to pass.	hvat sem at hendi kømr. (st.31)

As has been pointed out above, Ussing suggested that st.31 should be be switched with st.27, in which Reginn orders Sigurðr to roast Fáfnir's heart while he sleeps. This would make good sense in that it would remove the problem of Reginn bidding goodnight (st.27) and then deciding to indulge in a renewed spate of conversation (sts 28–31). It would also remove the problem of the double-strophed speech, while adding a new angle to the conversation.[270] However, the parallel form of the two strophes, so common elsewhere in the dialogue poems,[271] surely suggests that these two strophes were meant to stand together, and that they had existed in this order when the poem came to be recorded in the twelfth or thirteenth century. Indeed, the use of the word *hvatr* ('bravery'/ 'courage') is particularly common in *Fáfnismál*, and, to some extent, the ideas in st.31 reflect those already expressed in, for example, st.10 and st.24. The only problem for the listening audience is that in most other cases the parallel strophe is uttered by the other speaker in the conversation, and as Ussing's suggestion makes clear, there is nothing in the second strophe to suggest that it should not stem from Reginn's mouth.[272]

The final, and possibly greatest problem arises in connection with the *ljóðaháttr* speeches uttered by the birds. As has been shown above, these strophes have to be considered as part of the original *Fáfnismál*, if only on the basis of the wood and stone carvings depicting the story.[273] The text of the verse, however, never provides the listeners with any indication about who is speaking or where the voices come from.[274] In spite of this, all three *ljóðaháttr* strophes (st.34, and sts 37–39) make it evident that they are not being spoken by any of the previous three characters, all of whom are named as subjects of the conversation. Working this out, however, demands that the audience should understand by elimination and attention to context that Sigurðr is the 'he' ('hann') referred to in these strophes, and are prepared to associate Reginn with epithets like 'the ancient sage(?)' ('inn hára þul': st.34) and 'the ice-cold *jötunn*' ('inn hrímkalda iǫtun': st.38). In addition to this, the verse provides no indication about whether

---

[270] Ussing, *Om det inbyrdes forhold*, pp.75–77.
[271] See sts 5–6, sts 16–17 and sts 20–21 in *Fáfnismál* alone.
[272] In this section (p.61) of the MS, the marginal notation is relatively clear, the names of the speakers remaining evident, while the speech verb has been cut away. However, the possibility cannot be ruled out that the scribe forgot to write Reginn's name beside this strophe.
[273] See references in note 263 above.
[274] The prose only mentions 'igðor klǫkoðo i hrísinom' ('the nuthatches sang in the bushes'), but gives no indication of how many.

G. One-Man Performance of the Dialogic Poems

the birds are meant to speak as a chorus, or about which individual bird (if there are only two) was supposed to utter which strophe. Sigurðr, in fact, *never* acknowledges that the birds (or any other creatures apart from himself, Reginn and Fáfnir) have ever been present on the scene when he 'responds' to their words in st.39, a strophe which presents yet another difficult transition since it offers no obvious clues to stress that the speaker is not one of the birds until the third line: 'Fate will never be so rich/ as to allow Reginn/ to pronounce *my* death sentence' ('Verðra svá rík skǫp/ at Reginn skyli / *mitt* banorð bera').

As regards the various deletions and changes in strophe-order suggested by scholars in the past,[275] it is clear that none of them would remove any of the presentation difficulties implicit in *Fáfnismál*, except, perhaps, in the case of st.31 which several critics have attempted to drop.[276] Müllenhoff's reordering, for example, still leaves Sigurðr with two consecutive strophes (st.30 and st.26). Heusler's suggestion of taking the same course but adding a theoretical 'missing', but apparently repetitive strophe by Reginn concerning his involvement in his brother's death in between sts 30 and 26 is more acceptable, but only to a limited degree.[277] Finnur Jónsson's approach fits the pattern better (as long as st.31 is dropped), in that at least it retains the related sts 25–26, even if it results in Sigurðr making another double-strophed speech (st.26 and st.28). While this longer speech would disrupt the pattern of alternate speakers, it nonetheless manages to avoid confusing the listening audience, since both strophes give clear indication, in one way or another, that they are spoken by Sigurðr rather than Reginn. Finally, the suggestion made by all the scholars mentioned above, that st.27 (where Reginn states he is going off to sleep) should be placed at the end of the scene between Sigurðr and Reginn has more to recommend it than any of the other changes, both in terms of sense and practical considerations. Nonetheless, it is questionable why the strophes should have got so disordered in the first place.

c. Setting, movement and other dramatic elements in 'Fáfnismál'
Like *Skírnismál* and *Hárbarðsljóð*, *Fáfnismál* takes place outside, and involves, it would seem, at least two relatively closely placed settings: the site

4. 'Fáfnismál': The difficulties of performance

---

[275] See above, in the previous section.
[276] As with the other cuts, de Vries' removal of sts 12–15 still results in a double strophe by Fáfnir, including yet another abrupt change of subject from his curse of the 'judgement of the *nornir*' ('norna dóm') in st.11 to his discussion of the 'helmet of terror' ('ægishiálmr') in st.16. This is no more helpful than the original double-strophed speech (sts 15–16) discussed above.
[277] First of all, it is doubtful whether the existing strophe pair of sts 25 and 26 can be broken up since they display a natural progression: see Finnur Jónsson, *Litteraturs historie*, I, p.275. The question might also be raised as to whether the compiler of *Völsunga saga* did not himself make a mistake when he had Reginn repeat the words 'Bróður minn hefir þu drepit, ok varla má ek þessa verks saklauss vera' ('You have killed my brother, and I can hardly be considered totally innocent of that myself') with minimal variation: *Völsunga saga*, p.40.

4. 'Fáfnismál': The difficulties of performance

where Fáfnir is killed, and some other nearby location beneath a tree where Sigurðr grills Fáfnir's heart over the fire. It should also be considered that both the poem (st.34 and st.38) and the accompanying prose interpolations imply that after despatching Reginn, Sigurðr, accompanied by his horse Grani, proceeds to Fáfnir's lair ('bæli'), in the near vicinity to collect the monster's treasure which, according to the prose, includes the famed 'helmet/ mask of terror', the 'ægishiálmr'.

It is interesting to note that, as in *Skírnismál* and perhaps also *Vafþrúðnismál*, the most important actions of *Fáfnismál* (the killing of Fáfnir and Reginn, and the collecting of the treasure which forms a satisfactory conclusion to the poem) occur *outside* the framework of the spoken text which, nonetheless, depends on these actions having occurred, or taking place in the near future. At the same time, the direct speech of the poem once again includes a number of interesting implications of gesture, and physical movement or position, many of which would seem almost unnecessary for the course of the action:

St.25:	You are happy now, Sigurðr, and victorious, *as you wipe Gramr*[278] *on the grass* . . .	Glaðr ertu nú, Sigurðr, ok gagni feginn, *er þú þerrir Gram á grasi* . . .
St.27:	*You sit now*, Sigurðr, and I *will go* off to sleep; *hold* Fáfnir's heart in the fire!	Sittu nú, Sigurðr, en ek mun sofa *ganga*, ok *halt* Fáfnis hiarta við funa!
St.37:	. . . there where Reginn *is lying*.	. . . þar er Reginn liggr.[279]

With regard to the action of the poem, it might be noted that *Fáfnismál* is the only poem at present under consideration in which the prose interpolations provide information about actions that are *not* directly implied by the extant words of the poem. For example, the poetic text makes no mention of the all-important action of how Sigurðr, checking to see whether the heart was fully roasted, 'burnt himself, and put his finger into his mouth' ('brann ok brá fingrinom í munn sér'), a motif which, on the basis of certain wooden church carvings in Norway and other rock carvings in Sweden, appears to have played an essential part in the story of Sigurðr's killing of Fáfnir.[280]

---

[278] Gramr was the name of Sigurðr's sword.
[279] To these examples might be added sts 32–33 in *fornyrðislag* which give a very immediate picture of both Sigurðr and Reginn in the vicinity of the tree: '*þar sitr Sigurðr/* sveita stokkinn' ('There sits Sigurðr/ splattered with blood'), and '*Þar liggr Reginn/* ræðr um við sik' ('There lies Reginn/ deliberating').
[280] All that the poem reveals (in *fornyrðislag* in st.32) is that Sigurðr is 'splattered with blood' ('sveita stokkinn': st.32). The *ljóðaháttr* strophes state nothing at all. Regarding the carvings, see, for example, the illustrations on the Hylestad and Vegusdal portals, the

G. One-Man Performance of the Dialogic Poems

4. 'Fáfnismál': The difficulties of performance

Furthermore, the poem (both the *ljóðaháttr* and *fornyrðislag* strophes) only implies that Sigurðr should kill Reginn and then visit Fáfnir's lair. The prose, on the other hand, makes this a clear fact, stating simply that 'Sigurðr followed Fáfnir's tracks to his lair' ('Sigurðr reið eptir slóð Fáfnis til bælis hans'). The same thing can be said about the information regarding the setting of the poem. Apart from the mention of the fire (st.27) and the nearby heather where Reginn lies (st.28 and st.29), the poem gives no indication of the prose suggestions that Sigurðr 'made a great ditch in the path, and ... went into that' ('gørði ... grǫf mikla á veginom, ok gekk ... þar í') in order to kill Fáfnir, or that Fáfnir was on his way 'to get water' ('til vaz'), the water in question therefore being somewhere in the near vicinity. Nor does the poem make any mention of the bush ('hrís') or tree in which the birds sit, a feature very evident in the Scandinavian carvings at Hylestad, Vegusdal, Ramsundsberg, not to mention the Gök and Ockelbo stones and the Halton cross near Lancaster.[281] Naturally, all of these points would appear to suggest that, in the case of *Fáfnismál*, the prose has an essential role (at least in the present literary form of the poem).[282]

Yet in relation to this point, and the question of performance, it might be noted that if the prose is dispensed with, the initial anonymity of characters becomes as much a characteristic of *Fáfnismál*, as it is of the other poems under discussion. Here, while Fáfnir announces his own identity in st.1, Sigurðr remains anonymous and mysterious until st.4. Initially, in st.2, he introduces himself as 'gǫfugt dýr' (lit. 'noble animal'), a feature that closely parallels the situation in *Lokasenna* and *Harbarðsljóð* (and possibly also *Vafþrúðnismál* if the introductory framework is removed) where the visiting 'aggressor' initially disguises his real name.[283] In *Fáfnismál*, an attempt is made to explain Sigurðr's action in the prose inserted between st.1 and st.2 which states that 'it was believed by people in ancient times that the words of a doomed man had great power,

---

Ramsundsberg stone, the Halton cross, and the Ramsey and Malew crosses in the Isle of Man, all of which give almost identical pictures of the thumb-sucking motif: see Blindheim, *Sigurds saga*, pp.21–29, and Schück, *Litteraturhistorie*, 2nd ed., I, pp.108–111.

[281] See Blindheim, *Sigurds saga*, pp.21–29, and Schück, *Litteraturhistorie*, 2nd ed., I, p.106, pp.108–109, pp.111–112, and p.115.

[282] See recently Jónas Kristjánsson, *Eddas and sagas*, p.57.

[283] Regarding the choice of the name, 'Göfugt dýr', and its logic, see, for example, Finnur Jónsson, 'Sagnformen', 42–43; Kjær, 'Zu Fáfnismál str.2'; Olsen, 'Göfugt dýr'; Ólafur M. Ólafsson, 'Sigurðr duldi nafns síns'; and Gade, 'Sigurðr – Göfuct dýr'. Of all of these, Finnur Jónsson's suggestion that the words mean simply 'man' makes the most immediate sense. Olsen's attempt to make a connection between the name Sigurðr and the words Siggi and *sigg* (i.e. a thick pig skin), thence to a boar as the 'noble animal' seems somewhat far-fetched, and Ólafur Ólafsson's highly complex suggestion that the word is a form of anagram is even more dubious. Gade's development of Kjær's ideas, suggesting that the name is a circumlocution for the name Hildisvíni (thence to the name 'Sigrøðr') is more logical. However, Olsen's proposal that the words might also relate to a decorated helmet would make good sense in terms of a performance, and particularly one originating in animal disguise.

4. 'Fáfnismál': The difficulties of performance

especially if he cursed his enemy by name.'[284] That this superstition existed, there is little doubt. However, since Sigurðr reveals his real name (in st.4) so quickly after having tried to disguise it, there is reason to question whether the superstition was the original reason for why Sigurðr used an epithet for himself in this poem.[285] The probability has to remain that the motif of the 'disguised visitor' was a traditional element in the *ljóðaháttr* poems, just as it is in some of the *fornaldarsögur*. This motif also had a role to play in the structure of *Fáfnismál*, but as with the other poems, the prose introduction and marginal notation remove this element of mystery for the reading audience.

d. Conclusion

On the surface, *Fáfnismál* is much simpler in form than the poems previously discussed, yet there is good reason to believe that for an effective performance of this poem at least two performers would be needed – even if prose interpolations of some kind were always attached to the poetic text. (Indeed, the use of the prose comments might have demanded a third performer in the role of narrator.) Nonetheless, as has been pointed out above in *sections E.3*, and *F.5*, there is good reason to doubt the existence of a mixed *ljóðaháttr* verse-and-prose form, and it is highly questionable whether the prose has replaced earlier lost narrative strophes in *ljóðaháttr*. As in the case of *Skírnismál*, it is an intriguing fact that the poetry seems to ignore the most dramatic actions implied by the poem, relegating them to the far more everyday level of the prose passages. There is thus good reason for examining this feature in a little more detail. Indeed, if the prose accompanying *Fáfnismál* was removed, and the idea accepted that much of the *content* of the prose would have been conveyed originally through the medium of basic movement and gesticulation, then one would be faced with the likelihood of an astonishingly active performance that even two individual performers would have had difficulty in carrying out effectively.[286]

---

[284] '... þat var trúa þeira í forneskio at orð feigs mannz mætti mikit, ef hann bǫlvaði óvin sínom með nafni.'

[285] Certainly, the superstition may have some part to play in the poem, and is reflected perhaps in the later curses (in st.9, st.11 and st.20), but it is somewhat doubtful that Sigurðr, young as he may be, should remember to protect himself at one moment, and then immediately forget this in st.4. Regarding the superstition and the poem, see Ström, 'Den döendes makt', 26–28.

[286] Examples have been given above of how the text seems to imply certain basic physical movements. From this point of view, it is worth considering that certain actions implied by the prose, such as Sigurðr digging the ditch, burning his thumb, and killing Reginn, would have been difficult to present in direct speech in a form like Skírnir's conversation with his horse. Reginn, of course, could have been provided with a dying speech after the event like that given to Fáfnir, but otherwise, Sigurðr is totally alone, and none of the *ljóðaháttr* poems contain examples of pure soliloquy. Even monologues like *Grímnismál* and *Hávamál* are directed towards another character, fictive or real. This, too, might be taken to imply that solo action of the kind mentioned above would have had to be carried out physically; in other words, acted in some way.

G. One-Man Performance of the Dialogic Poems

Apart from two slayings, one of which involves a giant semi-human serpent figure who apparently often wears a terrifying helmet or mask of some kind, there is the drinking of the blood and the roasting of the heart, the burning of the finger, and the overhearing of two (or more) speaking 'birds' before the implied move to Fáfnir's hideout, and then, perhaps (if a possible development into the material of *Sigrdrífumál* is included) a further move to another spot containing the sleeping, fire-encircled *valkyrja*. Such a performance resembles nothing less than large-scale outdoor drama of the kind mentioned above in relation to *Skírnismál*. Moreover, the use of disguising headwear, implied possibly by the monstrous 'helmet of terror' ('ægishiálmr'), and Sigurðr's by-name, 'noble animal' ('gǫfugt dýr'), which Olsen suggests might have been also related to a helmet (or possibly mask?),[287] raises some interesting direct parallels with the Scandinavian dramatic ritual and folk traditions illustrated in *Chapters I and II*. Certainly, as the various Scandinavian carvings of the legend of Sigurðr and Fáfnir illustrate, the active motifs of *Fáfnismál* seem to have had a surprisingly *visual* impact on the Scandinavian mind.

5. 'Hárbarðsljóð': The Difficulties of Performance

Amongst all the other Eddic poems, *Hárbarðsljóð* is somewhat of an anomaly for various reasons. First of all, the verbal confrontation between Þórr and Óðinn (in the role of Hárbarðr, or 'Grey-beard') contained in the poem is not mentioned anywhere else. Snorri neither names the poem, nor makes any obvious borrowings from it, thus suggesting that either he did not know the poem (most likely) or simply that he did not deem it worthy of note.[288]

Secondly, the extant poem does not keep to any one metre, but appears on the surface to be a confused jumble of *fornyrðislag*, *málaháttr* and *ljóðaháttr* interspersed with several lines that lack any poetic metre at all. This led Finnur Jónsson to declare that the extant poem 'totally conflicts with the early concepts of demands relating to poetic form' and that it should be regarded as corrupt.[289] Finnur's resulting attempt to 'restore' what he saw as the original *málaháttr* poem by removing the *ljóðaháttr* verse, the prose, and all 'unnecessary' lines, words and articles has been ignored by most scholars with good reason. Indeed, in attempting to restore one rule, Finnur broke numerous others. For example, apart from the fact that there is no evidence of any other mythological dialogic poem

---

[287] See above, note 283.
[288] Þórr's exploits with the giants Hrungnir, Þjazi and Fjalarr mentioned in the poem (sts 15, 19, and 26) are known elsewhere. However, the episode involving Svarangr's sons (st.29) remains mysterious, as do all of Hárbarðr's exploits. Einar Ólafur Sveinsson, in *Íslenzkar bókmenntir*, p.294, feels it likely that these exploits were all the product of an author's imagination.
[289] Hárbarðsljóð 'står . . . i fuldstændig strid med oldtidens opfattelse af de fordringer, som man stillede til et digts form': Finnur Jónsson, 'Hárbarþsljóþ', 149.

5. 'Hárbarðsljóð': The difficulties of performance

existing in *málaháttr*,²⁹⁰ Finnur's version of the poem also includes six strophes containing one or more transitions between speakers. Such changes in speaker midway through a strophe are extremely rare, and indeed, unlikely to have occurred in such purely dialogic, orally performed poetry as that now under discussion.²⁹¹ In terms of performance, Finnur Jónsson's version of *Hárbarðsljóð* would create many more problems than it resolves.

More recently, scholarship has come to accept that while *Hárbarðsljóð* in its present form may be an anomaly, it represents the form in which the poem existed at the time it was recorded, and in which it was meant to be performed. Given what we know of performance and poetic tradition at the time,²⁹² there is no reason for the poem to be in its present state as a result of decay. Had words become lost, they could easily have been replaced by others in the same metre dealing with the same subject matter, in a comparable fashion to the way that professional actors of Shakespeare, in the case of forgotten lines or missed cues, have been known to 'ad-lib' fluently in perfect iambic pentameter for several minutes with little difficulty. The rhythm becomes second nature. For an experienced poet/ performer, surely *málaháttr* would not have caused any greater problem. Nor would there have been much sense in replacing lost lines with new lines in a completely different metre.

The answer must be that the poem was either composed in this way, or more probably, that it had this kind of loose format from the start. Jón Helgason, for example, explains the informal poetic form of *Hárbarðsljóð* by suggesting that it can be 'best understood as a little comedy. One might imagine two men dividing the parts among themselves and using certain prepared jokes with other improvised passages in between.'²⁹³ More recently, Carol Clover has argued quite convincingly that the breakdown in poetic form plays a designated role in the comedy of the poem in which Óðinn flouts the rules of the verbal duel (*senna/ mannjafnaðr*) that Þórr depends on.²⁹⁴

Both Clover and her challengers, Bax and Padmos, have given good, if differing arguments for the poem being based essentially on a clear, recognised pattern similar to that encountered in *Lokasenna*, involving a

---

290 The only similarities are found in the early skaldic poems *Eiríksmál* and *Hákonarmál* which belong to a somewhat different genre.
291 An exception might be *Helgakviða Hjörvarðssonar*, st.2, containing words by both Atli and the bird. It is questionable, however, whether the extant version of this poem represents its original form, and extremely difficult to draw conclusions about whether the poem was originally totally dialogic or not.
292 See above, *section A*.
293 'Digtet forstås bedst som en lille komedie; man kan tænke sig at to mænd har delt rollerne mellem sig og sagtens også lavet løjer og tilføjet improvisationer ind imellem': Jón Helgason, 'Norges og Islands digtning', p.35. Jón does not provide any further information about the art form he is suggesting here, or its origins. Regarding the general support scholars have given to this idea, see the references given in the *Introduction*, note 56.
294 Clover, 'Hárbarðsljóð', 124–145.

G. One-Man Performance of the Dialogic Poems

5. 'Hárbarðsljóð': The difficulties of performance

regular, recurring four-strophe sequence, with additional material appearing as the poem progresses.[295] On the basis of this and the fact that, as with *Vafþrúðnismál*, there are only two characters to be distinguished between, there would seem on the surface to be little problem for a solo entertainer to carry off a performance of the poem. Yet this is, once again, far from the truth. Whether the poem followed recognised rules or not, the problems of speaker identification and the overall poetic form of the work remain, and these would cause any solo performer enormous difficulties.

As was mentioned above, *Hárbarðsljóð* is made up of sixty 'strophes' that not only vary in metre, but also range in length from one prose line up to thirteen lines of verse, something that, as Holm-Olsen has pointed out, 'must have made it (the poem) particularly vulnerable to alteration in the oral tradition.'[296] Nonetheless, the setting of verbal conflict beside water is clear, and is emphasised regularly throughout the poem, with mentions of the 'sound' ('sund') or 'fjord' ('vágr') occurring in sts 1, 2, 3, 8, 13, 27, 28, 47, 54 and 55. The same is implied by numerous other indirect references to the presence of the boat and so on. Similarly obvious from the start is the fact that the two men are supposed to be standing on opposite sides of the water. Yet despite this apparent clarity, there are problems for the listening audience right from the start of the poem.

The first difficulty is one that has been encountered in the other poems previously discussed, namely that in performance, in order to identify speakers, the listener needs name references, and clear indications of changes of speaker through a pattern of question-and-answer, or statement-and-obvious-reaction, or some other regular system of alternating speakers helped by a regular sequence of lines and strophes. In *Hárbarðsljóð*, even though the speakers alternate, there is little regularity in the length of each speech. The listener therefore has to be ready for a change of speaker at almost any moment (unless some use of dramatic alteration in voice for each speaker is employed by the performer). Syntactic indications occur in the actual *senna/ mannjafnaðr* part of the poem, but these are by no means obvious throughout. Finally, to make matters worse, partial context markers in the form of names placed in the traditional position at the start of strophes are comparatively rare in *Hárbarðsljóð*.

As has been noted in *section F.4*, *Hárbarðsljóð* follows the tradition encountered in several of the other poems under discussion in that neither of the characters here reveals his name until sts 9–10. At the start, all that the audience knows (if the prose introduction is removed) is that there are

---

[295] See Bax and Padmos, 'Two types of verbal duelling', 164–165 in particular; and Clover, 'Hárbarðsljóð', 134. Clover's four-strophe pattern is typified by sts 14–17 and sts 18–21, and involves three strophes of verse followed by one speech in prose. Bax and Padmos, on the other hand, posit sts 15–18 and sts 19–21 as typical units involving a system of claims, rejections and counter-claims.

[296] 'Den løse metriske formen må ha gjort det særlig utsatt for endringer i den muntlige overlevering.' Holm-Olsen, ed., *Edda-dikt* (1985), p.321.

5. 'Hárbarðsljóð': The difficulties of performance

two figures, one apparently young, 'the lad of lads' ('sveinn sveina') mentioned in st.1, and one old, 'the gaffer of gaffers' ('karl karla') referred to st.2). It should be stressed that without the prose or speaker notation, it is not clear at this point which of these two is Þórr and which is Hárbarðr. Furthermore, it should be stressed immediately that the deliberate comedy involved in Þórr's naming the grey-bearded Hárbarðr 'sveinn sveina' could only succeed if the recipient of Þórr's insult was, or *appeared* to be, a character of marked old age. Another thing that is not clear to the listening audience at the start of the poem is which of these two characters is meant to be the ferryman. In the introductory harangues that are a feature of the other comparable verbal duels that are conducted over water in the Eddic poems,[297] it is the static character in the role of a look-out man on land who calls first. The arriving character (commonly on board ship) is the one who answers. This may not always have been the case, but it is enough to demonstrate that the audience cannot rely on any established tradition to help them with *Hárbarðljóð*. For that reason, it might be argued that, in the mind of many listeners, the following first four lines of st.3 could be attributed to either 'the gaffer of gaffers' or 'the lad of lads':

Ferry me over the sound,	Ferðu mik um sundit,
and I will feed you tomorrow;	fæði ek þik á morgun;
I have a basket on my back,	meis hefi ek á baki,
there is no better food;	verðra matrinn betri;

Furthermore, since the first two strophes make it clear that speeches do not necessarily last the normal six or eight lines, listeners might also be drawn into wrongly supposing that the last four lines of st.3,

I ate while resting,	át ek í hvíld,
before I left home,	áður ek heiman fór,
herring and oats,	síldr ok hafra,
and I am still full	sáðr em ek en þess

are a sarcastic reply to the previous statement, uttered by the ferryman who, whether he is old or young, has already been insulted in sts 1–2. Living by the fjord, he might naturally be expected to be the one who is the enthusiastic eater of herring.

From the above, it should be clear that by st.4, the audience of a colourless, undramatic recitation of the poem would already be in great difficulties. It is no longer certain who is saying what, or which character is what age, and no additional help is given in the three strophes that follow. It would, for example, be totally logical for the traveller who has had the chance to pick up news (Þórr) to be the one who reveals the death of the *ferryman*'s mother in st.5. It would also make sense for the ferryman, who is the one supposed to be offering services, to be the poorest and thus the recipient of the following words rather than the mighty Þórr: 'Bare-legged

[297] See, for example, *Helgakviða Hundingsbana I*, st.32, *Helgakviða Hjörvarðssonar*, st.12, *Helgakviða Hundingsbana II*, st.19, and perhaps also *Reginsmál*, st.16.

G. One-Man Performance of the Dialogic Poems

you stand/ and have the garb of a vagabond;/ you don't even seem to have your breeches on' (st.6).[298] Yet any listener making such logical assumptions is wrong.

It is not until st.7 that the audience is again allowed to feel certain that they must be listening to the traveller, when he commands the ferryman to 'Steer that dugout over here!' ('Stýrðu hingat eikionni'). This speech, however, does not help to clarify the previous strophes, since, for the confused listener, this rather superior speaker who adds that they intend to 'teach you your position' ('mun þér stǫðna kenna': st.7) might well be referring back to the ferryman's apparently insolent reply in the second half part of st.3 (if that had been previously misconstrued). The traveller's air of superiority in this strophe also reflects the tone of st.4 and st.6, thus adding weight to any mistaken thoughts being entertained by the audience that he might have spoken these particular strophes rather than the ferryman.[299]

From this point, the poem becomes much clearer. The following eight strophes contain clear syntactic indications of who is speaking, and these are aided still further by the two characters at last naming themselves in st.9 and st.10. The problems of performance, however, are still not totally resolved. As has been demonstrated above, the performer of the first nine strophes would have *had* to distinguish audibly between the two characters by using changes in voice, and maybe altering his posture. Now, however, he has to maintain these characters for a spate of three very short alternating strophes (sts 10–12).

As might be expected, the section containing the actual *senna* or *mannjafnaðr*[300] flyting (sts 15–40) is much clearer, since each speech takes the form of a question, statement, reply or reaction, reactions being marked in particular by the use of the word 'þá' ('then'), as in sts 21, 31, 32, 33, 34 and 38. Further help is occasionally provided by direct naming in sts 24, 26 and 27, and through recognisable mythological or character references: Þórr, for example, continually boasts of victories in warfare, while Hárbarðr counters with a list of victories over women. For the performer, however, there are still a large number of short replies in prose, notably those from Þórr, and a particularly difficult passage running from st.31 to st.38 in which only two speeches are more than two lines long.

5. 'Hárbarðsljóð': The difficulties of performance

---

[298] 'Berbeinn þú stendr/ ok hefir brautinga gervi,/ þatki at þú hafir brækr þínar.'
[299] In fact it is Þórr who speaks sts 1, 3, 5, and 7, and Hárbarðr, the ferryman, who utters the others.
[300] Opinions differ about how the verbal duel in *Hárbarðsljóð* should be classified. For example, Finnur Jónsson, in *Litteraturs historie*, I, p.152, and Harris, 'The senna', 67, call it a *senna*, while Jón Helgason, in 'Norges og Islands digtning', p.35; Einar Ólafur Sveinsson, in *Íslenzkar bókmenntir*, pp.293–294; and Lönnroth, in *Den dubbla scenen*, p.68, rank it alongside other *mannjafnaðir*. More recently, Bax and Padmos, in 'Two types of verbal duelling', 151, go one step further and find both forms in the same poem. Most sensible of all, Clover, in 'Hárbarðsljóð', 124–126, and 'The Germanic context', 445, ignores the dispute completely and talks of a joint genre, the 'senna-mannjafnaðr', or simply 'flyting'.

5. 'Hárbarðsljóð': The difficulties of performance

The speed of response rises in the final part of the poem, at the conclusion of the flyting (sts 40–60). Indeed, this passage of twenty-one strophes involves eleven speeches of three lines or less. Seven of the speeches are no more than single-line prose comments, three of which occur in the last four speeches. Especially worth noting is the speed of riposte in sts 40–46. In this section of the poem, there are only two questions (st.43 and st.57), and therefore everything depends on the audience recognising the difference between statement and reaction. For the most part, this is relatively clear since implications of character are comparatively numerous, even if they do not always come at the start of the speeches. Direct naming, for example, occurs in sts 50–53, and st.56, Þórr's hammer and his wife are mentioned in sts 47–48, and there are several clear references by Þórr to Hárbarðr's insulting behaviour.

In spite of these aids, the essential problem remains as whether any performer would have the ability to perform *Hárbarðsljóð* successfully alone, even with the use of basic dramatic skills. As was pointed out above, the difficulties of the introductory strophes demand dramatic use of voice if only to identify who is speaking at any given time, and from that point onwards, the performer naturally has to maintain this style of presentation. It is highly doubtful whether most solo performers could effectively cope with the speed of many of the verbal exchanges in this manner. Apart from the difficulty of a performance of this kind, which involves so much direct conflict and would be nothing if not clumsy, the medieval performer would also have found himself placed in direct comparison with the other much more lively, popular, improvised, two-man verbal contests that were almost certainly a recognised feature in his society.[301]

There can be little doubt that in practical terms, *Hárbarðsljóð* needs two participants, as Jón Helgason suggested. It probably also demands the wearing of a disguise by the person acting Hárbarðr, and most likely also a beggarly costume for the performer acting Þórr. Furthermore, Þórr's threats of violence in st.27 and st.47 would be likely to encourage the performer to make use of suitably vehement gesticulation. A performance of this kind would again be well within the field of drama.

With regard to the original setting of *Hárbarðsljóð*, it is naturally unlikely that such performances would have taken place across a river of the size that needed a boat to cross it (although if a small river was used this might have added to the comedy). Nonetheless, as with *Vafþrúðnismál* (see below), some degree of spacial separation between performers would have been necessary to enable the performance to achieve the desired effect. Certainly, both poems could have been performed in any large homestead. However, for the original performances of *Hárbarðsljóð*, an outdoor setting of some kind would probably have been be the most appropriate.

---

[301] See below, *Chapter V, D.3*.

G. One-Man Performance of the Dialogic Poems

6. *Vafþrúðnismál*: The Difficulties of Performance

Vafþrúðnismál consists of fifty-five strophes in *ljóðaháttr*. In simple terms, the poem describes Óðinn's visit to the *jötunn* Vafþrúðnir to gain knowledge, and the subsequent verbal competition between these two powerful figures. In form, there are obvious similarities between this poem and other knowledge contests such as *Alvíssmál*, and *Gátur Gestumblinda* ('The riddles of Gestumblindi') which is contained in *Hervarar saga ok Heiðreks*. Of all the five poems under discussion, *Vafþrúðnismál* is the simplest in terms of performance, because although it again involves a change in setting and three characters, it is built for the most part around a highly formalised structure which is rigidly adhered to.

After the introductory strophes of the poem (sts 1–10) which create a framework and setting for the gnomic contest between Vafþrúðnir and Óðinn (here under the pseudonym 'Gagnráðr' or 'Gangráðr'[302]), the formal pattern of question-and-answer is extremely clear. The first section of the poem, sts 11–18, involves Vafþrúðnir questioning Gagnráðr, and receiving answers in alternate strophes. All of Vafþrúðnir's questions here are preceded by the formula:

>   Tell me/ say, Gagnráðr,   Segðu mér/ þat, Gagnráðr,[303]
>   since on the floor you wish   allz þú á golfi vill
>   to test your skill,   þíns um freista frama,
>   what [X] is called ...   hvé [X] heitir ...

Apart from providing a partial context marker in the use of Gagnráðr's name set in the usual place at the end of the first line, this formula also serves to emphasise Vafþrúðnir's opponent's physical position in the room.[304] The answer, which is consistently given in the next strophe, takes on a comparable formulaic pattern, in that it begins with the words: '[Y] is the name ...' ('[Y] heitir ...').

St.19, the turning point in the poem, depicts Vafþrúðnir's recognition of his guest's undoubted knowledge, and his subsequent invitation for Gagnráðr to 'come ... to the *jötunn*'s bench,/ and we will talk together on the seat' ('far þú á bekk iotuns,/ ok mælomk í sessi saman'), the stakes now being raised to that of life. As Vafþrúðnir says, 'our heads/ we will wage here in the hall,/ guest, on our wisdom.'[305]

The remaining section of the poem (sts 20–55) contains Gagnráðr's questioning of Vafþrúðnir, the first twelve questions being numbered and clearly addressed to Vafþrúðnir by name. Again the strophes begin with a basic formulaic pattern which has slight variations in the second and third lines, largely according to the demands of alliteration:

---

[302] See Ejder, 'Eddadikten Vafþrúðnismál', 11–13, and Machan, *Vafþrúðnismál*, p.75, for summaries of the discussions regarding these names which mean, consecutively, 'the decider of victory' and 'he who wishes to travel'.
[303] The first question, in st.11, is prefixed by the words 'Segðu mér ...' ('Tell me ...'). The rest begin with 'Segðu þat ...' ('Say ...').
[304] See Machan, *Vafþrúðnismál*, p.34.
[305] 'Hǫfði veðia/ vit skolom hǫllo í,/ gestr, um geðspeki.'

III. The Eddic Poems and Drama

6. 'Vafþrúðnismál: The difficulties of performance

Say this first (second, third etc.),	Segðu þat it eina (annat, þriðia etc.),
if your mind stands the test,	ef þitt æði dugir, (st.20 and st.22)
and you, Vafþrúðnir, know ...	ok þú, Vafþrúðnir, vitir ...[306]

For the last six questions which deal predominantly with Ragnarök, Gagnráðr adopts another set formula to introduce his questions, a form that is first encountered in Óðinn's words to Frigg at the start of the poem in st.3:

Much have I travelled,	Fiǫlð ek fór,
many have I tested,	fiǫlð ek freistaða,
many great ones have I tried ...	fiǫlð ek reynda regin ...

Noticeably, there is no naming of the questioned party here, the reliance being presumably on the strength of the alternating strophe pattern (when the form is used first, it is Óðinn's turn to speak), the fact that Óðinn used these words earlier (and possibly that they were traditionally associated with him), and finally the knowledge that Ragnarök was a prime concern of his.

As can be seen above, *Vafþrúðnismál* has such a consistent format that there is little confusion about who is speaking at any given time. In fact, the pattern is so consistent that even if the poem is considered as being a loose collection of mythological fragments placed within a framework, as Müllenhoff and certain other scholars have suggested, this would make little difference to the ease of understanding. Whatever order the questions came in would not affect the formulaic framework.[307] There are, however, three minor exceptions worth noting, two of which are connected to the 'Much have I travelled' ('fjǫlð ek fór') formula which lacks any obvious partial context marker. The first example occurs in the introductory

---

[306] The other third lines are 'allz þik svinnan kveða' ('since you say you are wise': sts 24, 30, and 32); and 'allz þik fróðan kveða' ('since you say you are knowledgeable': sts 26, 28 and 34). In st.38 and st.42, the third and fourth lines run 'allz þú tíva rǫk/ ǫll, Vafþrúðnir, vita' ('since you know, Vafþrúðnir/ of the fate of the gods'); and 'hví þú tíva rǫk/ ǫll, Vafþrúðnir, vita' ('why you know, Vafþrúðnir,/ the fate of the gods'). St.40 ('ið ellipta'), which lacks three lines including the last two of the formula, could be expected for reasons of alliteration to take the same form as that used for sts 20 and 22. However, as sts 24, 34 and 36 show, not all strophes follow the same alliterative pattern, and at this point in the mounting power of the contest, 'ef þitt æði dugir' is out of place, set as it is between the questions of sts 38 and 42. What should have stood there was clearly a problem for the reciter, and has to remain open for scholars too. On this question, and the various approaches taken to it by scholars, see Machan, *Vafþrúðnismál*, p.85.

[307] See Müllenhoff, *Deutsche Altertumskunde*, V, p.246, and by nature of reply, de Vries, 'Om Eddaens visdomsdigtning', 11-15. Ejder, in 'Eddadikten Vafþrúðnismál', 15-20, is less certain than de Vries, and gives good reason (based on the rubric in the MS) for seeing the entire section of Óðinn's questions to Vafþrúðnir as having originated elsewhere. See also the complex attempts at reordering the strophes made by Boer, in *Die Edda*, II, pp.53-56, and Machan's examination of these arguments and the structure of the poem as a whole in Machan, *Vafþrúðnismál*, pp.27-30 and pp.33-38.

G. One-Man Performance of the Dialogic Poems

section of the poem which has the role of providing the wisdom contest with an external epic framework.

In many ways, this external framework created by the first five strophes seems to be totally unnecessary to the main business of the poem, and many scholars have viewed this introductory section as being a later interpolation.[308] There can be little doubt that this is true with regard to the narrative st.5 which tells of Óðinn's journey to Vafþrúðnir's hall. This is the only purely narrative *ljóðaháttr* strophe in existence, and like many of the prose passages in the Edda manuscripts, it appears to be totally superfluous.[309] However, the first four strophes of the poem, in which Frigg tries to dissuade Óðinn from leaving, have so many direct links to the main body of the poem itself that they appear to have been an essential feature of the work from an early stage. As was mentioned above, the first three lines of st.3 with the 'Much have I travelled' formula are later echoed numerous times in the final section of the poem. Furthermore, the first half of st.1 seems to be an obvious variation on the form of the questioning formulæ later to be employed by both Vafþrúðnir and Óðinn in sts 11–17, and sts 24–38:

6. '*Vafþrúðnismál*: The difficulties of performance

> Advise me now, Frigg,   Ráð *þú mér nú*, Frigg,
> since I wish to go   *allz mik* fara tíðir
> to visit Vafþrúðnir;   at vitia Vafþrúðnis;[310]

If the four-strophe introduction is accepted as being original, it adds several new aspects to the poem, not least being the addition of a third

---

[308] De Vries, for example, in 'Om Eddaens visdomsdigtning', 15, notes certain incongruities in this introductory scene, not least being the fact that Óðinn asks Frigg for advice which he then blatantly refuses to follow. Nonetheless, de Vries does not rule out the idea that the present form of the poem might represent an original whole composed by a poet who was making use of an earlier question-and-answer poem. Machan, in *Vafþrúðnismál*, p.33, argues against de Vries' suggestion on the grounds that the introductory strophes are 'well integrated with the rest of the poem'.

[309] As usual in *ljóðaháttr* verse, Óðinn's journey is made abundantly clear by the conversation in st.4, where Frigg bids Óðinn farewell with the words 'May you leave in good health' ('Heill þú farir'), and st.6, where Óðinn greets Vafþrúðnir with the words 'Good health to you now, Vafþrúðnir!/ Now I have arrived in the hall,/ to see you myself' ('Heill þú nú, Vafþrúðnir!/ nú em ek í hǫll kominn,/ á þik siálfan siá . . .'). Furthermore, at least half of st.5 is composed of words and expressions found elsewhere in the poem, as in the case of the words 'orðspeki' ('words of wisdom': cf.st.55); 'að freista' ('to test or try') which recurs throughout the poem; and the epithet used for Vafþrúðnir, 'inn alsvinni iǫtunn' ('the all-wise *jötunn*') which occurs in both st.1 and st.42.

[310] See above, and note 306. Also worth noting are the mention of 'fornom stǫfom' ('ancient letters': st.1), later echoed in st.55, and the use of the expression 'æði þér dugi' ('your mind will stand the test': st.4), which is an obvious variation on 'ef þitt æði dugir' ('if your mind stands the test') in st.20 and st.22. Furthermore, the epithet for Vafþrúðnir, 'inn *alsvinna* iǫtun' ('the all-wise *jötunn*': st.1), re-occurs later in st.42, and receives numerous echoes in the word *svinnr* ('wise') which is consistently applied to Vafþrúðnir in sts 24, 30, 32 and 36. As opposed to the case of st.5, which contains little originality, the first four strophes seem deliberately and artistically to make use of variations on later themes.

6. '*Vafþrúðnismál*: The difficulties of performance

speaker, Frigg, and a second setting (presumably Ásgarðr) from which Óðinn has to travel to reach the *jötunn*'s hall. The minor problem that it might add is related to the first use of 'Much have I travelled' formula which here follows directly on from Frigg's statement (st.2) that 'no *jötunn*/ have I considered equal in might/ to Vafþrúðnir' ('engi iotun/ ek hugða iafnramman/ sem Vafþrúðni vera'). For the audience, who have not yet been introduced to the pattern of alternate speakers, it would make sense for these words to continue into the statement in st.3, 'Much have I travelled,/ many have I tested,/ many great ones have I tried . . .' (see above). The fact that it is Óðinn who is speaking here does not become clear until the second half of the strophe, when he adds that 'I also want to know/ what Vafþrúðnir's/ hall is like' ('hitt vil ek vita,/ hvé Vafþrúðnis/ salakynni sé').

The same problem for the listening audience could logically occur in st.44 when the same formula is employed for the first time in the wisdom contest. Here, it might be argued that from the point of view of the audience there would be good reason to believe initially that it is Vafþrúðnir rather than Gagnráðr who poses the question in this strophe. Óðinn has already asked twelve questions, and logically, it is time for Vafþrúðnir to begin the next round; after all, he only granted himself four questions in the first part of the contest. Bearing this in mind, the unwitting listener might momentarily take the unprecedented alteration in the form of questions in st.44 to reflect the expected change of speaker. This idea would receive further support from the fact that in the previous strophe (st.43), *Vafþrúðnir* was the one to speak of having travelled widely:

. . . I have entered every world;	. . . hvern hefi ek heim um komit;
nine worlds I entered	nío kom ek heima
below Niflhel,	fyr Niflhel neðan,
where those men who	hinig deyia ór helio
die in Hel go.	halir.

It would hardly be illogical for the 'Much have I travelled' ('fjǫlð ek fór') sequence to be initially attributed to Vafþrúðnir rather than Óðinn, even if it does break the alternating pattern. Since no characters are directly named from this point until the end of the poem, such a misunderstanding would give a confused listener an entirely different angle on the final stages of the verbal combat. Ironically, it would ultimately involve Óðinn being asked about his own slayer and mode of death.

The third possible stumbling-block for the audience occurs even before this, soon after Óðinn's arrival in Vafþrúðnir's hall. In the brief introductory sequence, both characters are introduced by name (Vafþrúðnir in st.6, and 'Gagnráðr' in st.8), and the setting is made vividly clear, the hall being described as a 'hǫll' in sts 6–7, and a 'salr' in sts 7–9. Once again, the two characters commence speaking alternately in an obvious pattern of statement-and-reaction (sts 6–7) or question-and-answer (sts 7–8, and sts 9–10). Yet in spite of this initial clarity, there has to be some possible doubt for the listening audience as to who speaks the words in st.10. Although

G. One-Man Performance of the Dialogic Poems

Vafþrúðnir asks a question in the first half of st.9 ('Why are you, Gagnráðr,/ speaking from the floor?/ Take a seat in the hall!'[311]), he proceeds to follow it up with a statement: 'Then we will test,/ who knows the more,/ the guest or the old sage(?).'[312]

6. 'Vafþrúðnismál: The difficulties of performance

St.10 is neither an obvious answer nor reaction to this, and as an independent universal statement with no element of even partial context marking, it could be attributed to either character:[313]

A man without wealth	Óauðigr maðr,
who comes to a rich man,	er til auðigs kømr,
should either talk or be silent.	mæli þarft eða þegi;
Too much speech,	ofrmælgi mikil
I believe, brings no good,	hygg ek at illa geti,
when you come up against	hveim er við kaldrifiaðan
the cold-hearted.	kømr.

While such a mistaken assumption conflicts with the regularity of the alternating strophe pattern which by this point has been established in *Vafþrúðnismál*, it must also be remembered that the patterns are regularly broken in the Eddic poems. The final two points examined here therefore give good reason to argue that any solo performer of *Vafþrúðnismál* would also have had to adopt some elementary dramatic change of voice to underline the transitions between the two main characters, if only to avoid any momentary confusion in the minds of the audience.

While *Vafþrúðnismál* is unquestionably simpler and more rigidly structured than the other poems under discussion, it shares a number of common features with them implying that they all belong to a similar tradition. The first is that *Vafþrúðnismál* also involves the element of initially disguised identity encountered in *Lokasenna*, *Fáfnismál*, *Harbarðsljóð*, and so many of the other *ljóðaháttr* poems such as *Grímnismál* and *Hávamál*. Here, admittedly, if it is accepted that the introductory scene between Óðinn and Frigg forms an integral part of the poem, then Óðinn's identity has already been made clear to the audience by implication in these initial four strophes, where his wife, Frigg, names him 'The father of armies' ('Heriafǫðr': st.2) and 'The father of men' ('Aldafǫðr': st.4). Yet in the hall itself, Óðinn retains his guise of 'Gagnráðr' until the final strophe (st.55), at which point Vafþrúðnir realises that he must have been competing 'with Óðinn' ('við Óðin'). This secondary level of anonymity is similar to *Skírnismál*, where Skírnir never reveals his name to Gerðr, in spite of her initial questions in st.17.

Other similarities have to do with setting and implied physical movement. As in the case of *Lokasenna* (and *Grímnismál*), the main setting of *Vafþrúðnismál* is the interior of a hall, which implies the presence of a fire.

---

[311] 'Hví þú þá, Gagnráðr,/ mæliz af gólfi fyrir?/ farðu í sess í sal!'
[312] 'Þá skal freista,/ hvárr fleiri viti,/ gestr eða inn gamli þulr.'
[313] There is nothing to prevent anyone considering that Vafþrúðnir might be talking of himself in the third person when the mention is made in the strophe of coming up against a 'kaldrifiaðan' (lit. 'cold-ribbed', i.e. 'cold-blooded') character.

6. 'Vafþrúðnismál: The difficulties of performance

Of particular interest, however, is the emphasis placed on physical position and movement in the poem. First of all, there is the movement between Ásgarðr and Vafþrúðnir's hall which must occur in the space vacated by st.5. Yet if that strophe is dropped, as has been suggested above, nothing exists to replace it as a means of stressing and bridging the jump in time and place. *Vafþrúðnismál* contains nothing like *Skírnismál*, st.10, to describe the movement between settings, or to imply the passage of time involved in such a move. At the very least, a solo presenter would have to pause briefly between strophes in order to indicate this change in position.

It should also be noted that once inside the hall, Gagnráðr is shown to be separated spatially from Vafþrúðnir, who talks of his visitor speaking 'from the floor' ('af gólfi': st.9). In the same strophe, Vafþrúðnir invites Gagnráðr to take a seat in the hall ('farðu í sess í sal'), thus indicating that Gagnráðr has been standing up for the last three strophes. Yet Gagnráðr, for some reason, appears to ignore this offer, since when Vafþrúðnir questions him in the next strophes (sts 11, 13, 15, and 17), the *jötunn* continues to refer to him as being 'on the floor' ('a golfi'). This raises the question of why Gagnráðr refuses to take a seat? Is it possible that the reasons were practical, and related to the necessity of his being visible to an audience? The next move seems to occur in st.19 when Vafþrúðnir invites Gagnráðr to come up 'to the *jötunn*'s bench,/ and we will talk together on the seat' ('far . . . á bekk iǫtuns,/ ok mælomk í sessi saman'), as a gesture of respect. Yet once again, the action is only implied. Neither character ever confirms that the move has been made. It has to be *shown*. The same applies to the final action of the poem which must be the death of Vafþrúðnir who wagered his own head in st.19, and admits that he is doomed in st.55: 'From fated lips/ I spoke ancient lore/ and of Ragnarök' ('feigom munni/ mælta ek mína forna stafi/ ok um ragna røk'). Yet the act itself, which is taken for granted, is described in neither prose nor verse. As with the other poems under discussion, for some reason such essential climactic action appears to be deliberately ignored.

In conclusion, *Vafþrúðnismál* in its present form *could* conceivably be presented by one man. Nonetheless, strophes like st.3, st.10 and st.44 would appear to demand elementary dramatic changes of voice to avoid momentary confusion for an audience. In addition to this, the implied actions demand some dramatic use of pause or, more likely, actual movement. The deliberate spatial separation of Vafþrúðnir and Gagnráðr in the hall, and the problematic implied movement of Gagnráðr to the upper bench cannot be ignored. Both have to be solved in some way. Since the form of the knowledge contest, like that of the *senna/mannjafnaðr*, has its origin in religious rituals and popular games involving more than one participant,[314] the most likely answer is that two individual performers would have also been utilised here.

---

[314] See further below, *Chapter V, E*.

H. Conclusion

On the basis of the examinations conducted in this chapter, it is possible to conclude the following:

1. There is good reason to examine the Eddic poems in *ljóðaháttr* solely in their poetic form, that is to say, *without* considering the information provided by the marginal speaker notation and prose comments. Neither of these features can be taken for granted as originally having accompanied the poems in oral performance. Indeed, it seems likely that the original recorded texts of the dialogic poems in *ljóðaháttr* must have resembled the extant version of *Alvíssmál* in the *Codex Regius* which lacks both prose comments and marginal notation.

2. Bearing in mind that from the point of view of the audience listening to an oral performance, immediate understanding of who is speaking and where they are situated is necessary, it must be concluded that any solo performers of *Lokasenna*, *Skírnismál*, *Fáfnismál*, *Hárbarðsljóð* and probably also *Vafþrúðnismál* would have had to employ various dramatic techniques in performance. Indeed, in most cases they would have needed to be highly talented actors.

3. If only for practical reasons, the greater likelihood is that each 'poem' was originally performed (at the time of its recording and earlier) by more than one person, and that these persons wore costumes and/ or masks of some kind, used gesticulation, and moved between various points of the acting area as part of their performance.

4. In short, it is logical to call these works elementary *plays* rather than poems, although it is questionable whether the Scandinavians of the twelfth and thirteenth centuries would have had the terminology to differentiate between the two forms of art, or would have even regarded them as belonging to different genres.

It is naturally impossible for any twentieth-century reader to *prove* this argument on the basis of the Eddic poems alone, since as was mentioned at the start of the chapter, the possibility can never be ruled out that the texts of the poems themselves altered in transmission, and were possibly recorded under somewhat unreal conditions. Nonetheless, the conclusions arrived at in this chapter receive yet further support from the system of marginal speaker notation that was employed in the original manuscript versions of these poems. As the following chapter will demonstrate, the form of this notation offers a highly revealing insight into the way that the redactor and/ or the scribes of the thirteenth century viewed the material they were dealing with.

CHAPTER IV

Marginal Speaker Notation in the Edda and Early Manuscripts of Drama

A. *The Marginal Notation in the Edda Manuscripts*

As has been illustrated in the previous chapter, the extant form of the dialogic poems of the Poetic Edda suggests the necessity of some form of dramatic presentation. This leads one to examine further the way in which these works were recorded in the *Codex Regius* and AM 748 manuscripts, and in particular the original practice of indicating the speakers in dialogic works with brief notation *in the outer margins* of the text.

This feature has been described in detail in *Chapter III, E.2*, where it was used as evidence to suggest that the marginal indications were regarded as being external to the text of the poems in question. The use of the margin for speaker notation, however, is even more revealing because the scribes evidently made a conscious decision to use it, and because such a form of marginal notation exists in no other Scandinavian manuscripts up to or during the period in question. These points, largely uncommented on by earlier scholars, obviously deserve further attention.[1]

To review briefly the form of the marginal notation which is most clearly preserved in the AM 748 manuscript, it is clear that the complete form of the notation is a single letter abbreviation of the speaker's name followed consistently by the past tense verb *kvað* ('said'/ 'uttered'), written as 'qvað', again in abbreviated form. These letters are kept at a regular distance of c.15mm from the text. Often the speaker's name is both preceded *and* followed with a full stop (see, for example, *fig*.72, l.10 and l.15). The 'q.' indication is similarly followed by a full stop (see, for example *fig*.75, l.5). As Hreinn Benediktsson has pointed out, this system of abbreviation is by no means uncommon in Scandinavian manuscripts.[2] However, in this instance, the stop following the 'q.' seems to be often deliberately placed in a superscript form *above* the line (see, for example, *fig*.75, l.7 and l.19), a feature worth bearing in mind during the argument that follows.

---

[1] None of the earlier cited works on the Eddic poems and their MSS go any further than pointing out the existence of the notation.
[2] Hreinn Benediktsson, *Early Icelandic script*, p.87.

B. *Other Early Medieval Scandinavian Manuscripts Containing Dialogues*

In terms of *literary form*, the closest parallel to the totally dialogic Eddic poems contained in Scandinavian manuscripts is that of the theological or moral dialogue, typified by the *Dialogues* of Gregory the Great and Honorius Augustodunesis' *Elucidarius*. Both of these popular and influential works existed in translated form in Iceland long before the *Codex Regius* came to be written,[3] and would in normal terms have been expected to have provided the scribes of the Poetic Edda with a textbook model for transcribing dialogue, and especially dialogue of the form encountered in *Vafþrúðnismal*. An examination of the manuscripts of these works and others, however, reveals a completely different tradition to that taken up by the scribes of the Edda manuscripts. Indeed, as has been shown above (in *Chapter III, E.2*) it is evident that at least one scribe of the Eddic poems for some reason deliberately abandoned the earlier theological model for transcribing dialogue in the midst of writing.

There are nearly twenty extant manuscript examples of moral and theological colloquys translated in Iceland and Norway during the twelfth, thirteenth and early fourteenth centuries. Honorius' *Elucidarius* exists in fragmentary form in three Icelandic manuscripts from this period, all of which show strong traces of Norwegian orthography:[4] the AM 674 4to fragment (twelfth century) and two other fragments both extant in *Hauksbók* (AM 675, fols 1r–16v, and AM 544, fols 10b–12a; fourteenth century).[5] No less widely-read were the translations of Gregory's *Dialogues* which are found in three other fragmentary Icelandic manuscripts from this time: the AM 677 4to, fols 49–82 (dated shortly after 1200); the AM 655 XV 4to, a single leaf fragment from the later half of the thirteenth century; and a number of single leaf fragments which Hreinn Benediktsson has established as originating from the same late thirteenth-century manuscript (AM 921 4to IV 1,1; AM 921 4to IV 1,2: NRA 72; NRA 72 b; and NRA 71).[6]

Another popular pedagogic work written in colloquy form is the

---

[3] The AM 677 MS of Gregory's *Dialogues* was written shortly after 1200. The oldest version of *Elucidarius*, the AM 674 MS, is from the twelfth century: see further below in this section. Regarding the influence of these works, see Firchow and Grimstad, eds., *Elucidarius*, p.xxvi, and Sverrir Tómasson, 'Erlendur vísdómur', pp.549–552.

[4] See Finnur Jónsson, ed., *Hauksbók*, p.XXXI and pp.LVII–LVIII, and Firchow and Grimstad, eds., *Elucidarius*, pp.xxiii–xxiv, and pp.xliv–xlv.

[5] For facsimiles of the MSS, see *The Arnamagnæan manuscript 674 A 4to*, ed. Jón Helgason, and *Hauksbók*, ed. Jón Helgason. For the texts of all three versions, see *Elucidarius*, ed. Firchow and Grimstad.

[6] For facsimiles of the MSS, see *The Arna-Magnæan manuscript 677, 4to*, introduced by Seip; Hreinn Benediktsson, *Early Icelandic script*, plate 66 (AM 655 XV); and *The life of St Gregory*, ed. Hreinn Benediktsson, for the remaining fragments. For the original texts, see *Heilagra manna sögur*, I, pp.179–255 (AM 677) and pp.228–229 (AM 655 XV); and Hreinn Benediktsson, ed., *The life of St Gregory*, for the text of the other fragments.

IV. Marginal Speaker Notation

Norwegian *Konungs skuggsjá*, or *Speculum regale* ('The King's mirror'), dealing with the ideal 'skills and manners' of merchants and rulers in Norway. *Konungs skuggsjá* was probably composed in about 1250 at the instigation of King Hákon the Old, and exists in no less than five Norwegian manuscripts from the period in question: AM 243 b α (late thirteenth century); NRA 58 A (three leaves: c.1270); NRA 58 C (four leaves) and the Ny kgl.saml.235g 4to (one leaf) which belong together (c.1270); and two other fragments (AM 1056 IX and NRA 58 B) which were written about, or shortly after 1300.[7]

In addition to the above, there are four manuscript versions of shorter theological dialogues in translation from this period. The Norwegian *Viðræða líkams ok sálar* ('The debate of the body and soul'), which probably originated from the Old French poem, *Un samedi par nuit*, is found in the *Gamal norsk homiliebok* (AM 619 4to, fols 75b–78a; c.1200).[8] Hugo of St Victor's *Soliloquium de arrha animæ* exists under the mistaken title of *Viðræða líkams og sálar* in *Hauksbók* (AM 544, fols 61b–68b; fourteenth century), where it is preceded by a complete version of *Ældri senna ok hugrekki* ('The debate between fear and courage'; fols 60a–61b), a translation of a work by Guillaume de Conches.[9] This last work is also found in fragmentary form in another thirteenth-century manuscript from Norway (Uppsala, De la Gardie, nr.4–7, fol. 6r).[10]

The body of material contained in these manuscripts provides a clear picture of the accepted method of indicating speakers in dialogues at the time when the Eddic poems were recorded. The speaker indications in the above works sometimes take the form of simple initials, as in the AM 677 manuscript of the *Dialogues* and the AM 674 and AM 544 manuscripts of *Elucidarius*.[11] Elsewhere, however, they become longer statements of speech. In the case of the AM 243 b α manuscript of *Konungs skuggsjá*, the scribe occasionally makes use of the space available at the end of the

---

[7] For coloured facsimiles of these MSS see *Konungs skuggsjá*, introduced by Holm-Olsen (1947). For the original text of these MSS, see *Konungs skuggsjá*, ed. Holm-Olsen (1945). Icelandic MSS of the *Konungs skuggsjá* also exist, but all come from a much later date and are thus less relevant to the present examination.

[8] For a facsimile of this MS, see *Gammelnorsk homiliebok*, introduced by Knudsen. Text published in *Gamal norsk homiliebok*, ed. Indrebø, pp.148–153. Regarding the text, see Widding and Bekker-Nielsen, 'A debate of the body and soul'. Regarding these minor religious dialogues in general, see Sverrir Tómasson, 'Erlendur vísdómur', pp.560–561.

[9] For facsimiles of the MSS of these two works, see *Hauksbók*, ed. Jón Helgason. For the texts, see *Hauksbók*, ed. Finnur Jónsson, pp.303–330. On the original of the latter dialogue see T. Olsen, 'Den høviske litteratur', p.109.

[10] See *Elis saga*, introduced by Tveitane.

[11] Considering the size of the spaces left vacant in the extant texts, it can be assumed that the same system was used in the AM 655 and AM 675 MSS of these works, where no speaker indications remain. In both cases, if the indications were ever filled in, they were probably written in red ink which has since faded: see Hreinn Benediktsson, *Early Icelandic script*, p.xliv; Jón Helgason, ed., *Hauksbók*, p.XXII; and *Elucidarius*, ed. Firchow and Grimstad, pp.38–39. The AM 1056 IX MS and NRA 58 B fragments of *Konungs skuggsjá* are so short that they contain no speaker indications of any kind.

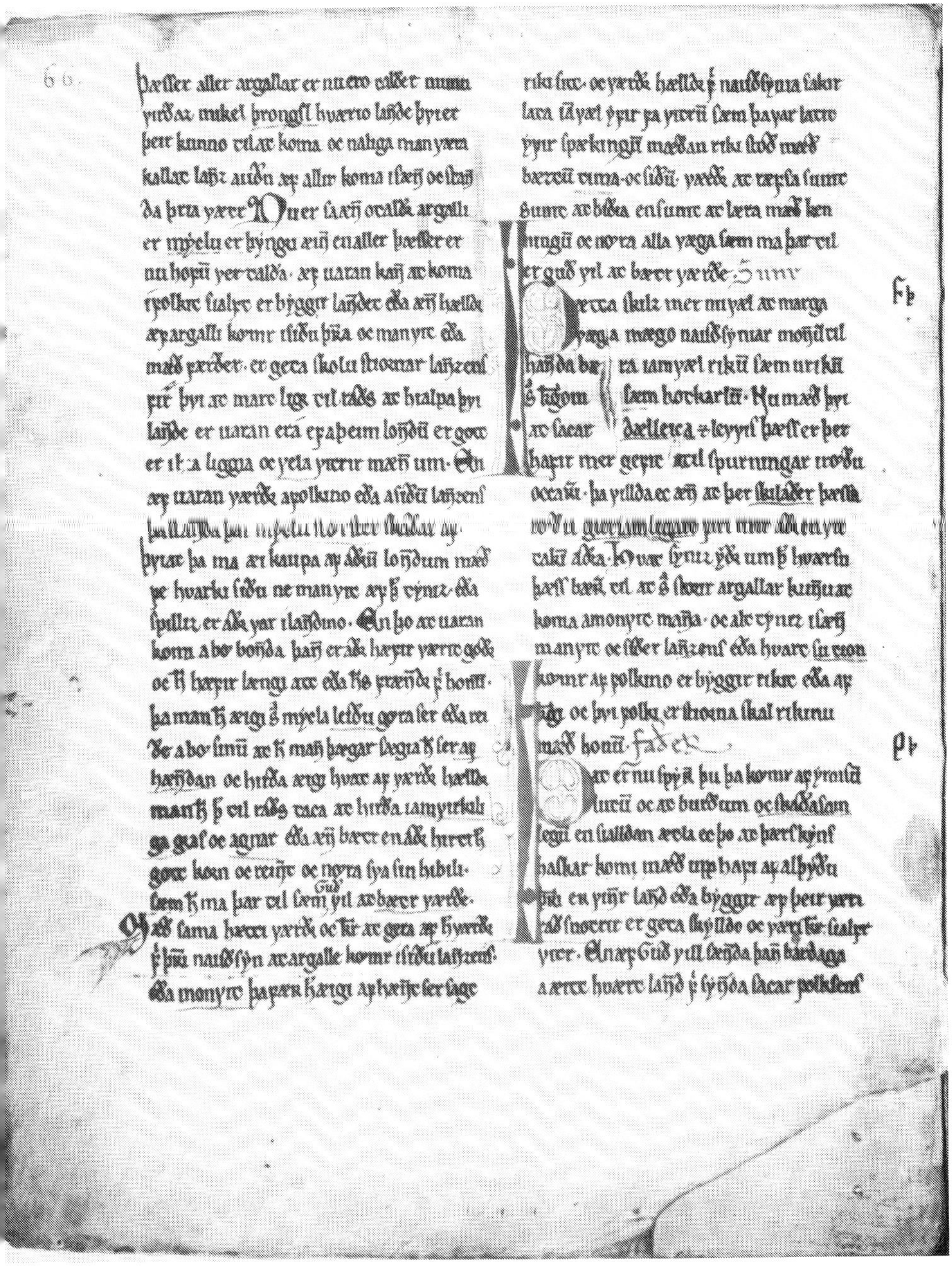

Fig. 76. *Konungs skuggsjá*. AM 243 b α fol., p.66
(late 13th century: south-west Norway).

IV. Marginal Speaker Notation

previous speech to add some description of the tone of wisdom accompanying the words that follow: for example '**sunr talar snotrlega**' ('the son speaks courteously'; fol.29a), '**faðer svarar froði harðla**' ('the father answers very wisely'; fol.29b) and '**faðer taler fullvitur**' ('the father speaks knowledgeably'; fol.44a). In the case of the *Konungs skuggsjá* fragments NRA 58 C and Ny kgl.saml.235g, unnecessary mention is made of whom the speaker is talking to: for example, '**pat ad f**' ('pater ad filium'; 'father to son': fol.1ra) and '**fili ad patreo**' ('son to father'; fol.4ra). In the AM 619 manuscript of the Norwegian *Viðræða líkams ok sálar*, the speaker indications become so full that they form complete prose sentences: for example, 'En salan þa er hon sa þat. þa toc hon at ræðasc ok øymde sec ok mælte sva . . .' ('When the soul saw this, it became fearful and weak, and said . . .').[12]

In all cases, however, the speaker indications are kept within the body of the text. Sometimes, when there is a system in which new speeches commence on a new line, the speaker indications are deliberately placed in the space at the end of the preceding line, as in the manuscripts of *Konungs skuggsjá* mentioned above (see *fig.76*, right, l.7 and l.22).[13] Otherwise, the abbreviated initials (such as '.M.' for Magister, and '.D.' for Discipulus in the *Elucidarius* manuscripts) occur wherever appropriate in a text which runs in a solid body like that in the Edda manuscripts (see, for example, *fig.77*, l.18 and l.24, and *fig.78*, l.7 and l.8). In both cases, though, scribes are often encountered making a clear differentiation between the speaker indications and the speeches by using red or even blue ink for the former.[14] The margins, however, are never utilised for speaker indications, the scribes presumably keeping within the manuscript traditions of the original Latin and French texts. The only occasions on which initials do appear in the margins of these manuscripts is when they are meant to act as reminders for the rubricator, marking those lines in which coloured lettering was to be added at a latter stage. Examples of such are found in the AM 243b α manuscript of *Konungs skuggsjá* (pp.2–3 and p.66; see *fig.76*) where marginal reminders in Latin are evident beside those lines containing rubricated speaker indications.[15] This was obviously not the intention behind the marginal notation in the Edda manuscripts. As has been illustrated in the previous chapter, the scribe of the AM 748 manuscript of the Eddic poems (or the scribe of the manuscript he was copying) starts by using a system of speaker notation very similar to that found in the manuscripts of Gregory's *Dialogues* and *Elucidarius*, but then proceeds to

---

12 See *Gamal norsk homiliebok*, ed. Indrebø, p.153.
13 See also the AM 921 IV 1, 1 and NRA 72 fragments (*Dialogues*), and the AM 544 *Viðræða líkams ok sálar*. A variation on this system exists in certain MSS where the speaker indication, be it a single name or something more extensive, is occasionally deliberately placed at the end of the line on which the speech begins. See NRA 71v (*Dialogues*) and AM 544 (*Hauksbók*), fols 61b–62a (*Viðræða líkams ok sálar*).
14 As in AM 677 (Gregory's *Dialogues*), and the fragments of another MS of the same work assembled by Hreinn Benediktsson (see above, note 6); the AM 544 *Viðræða*; and the AM 243b α MS, and NRA 58 C and NRA 58 A fragments of *Konungs skuggsjá*.
15 See further Finnur Jónsson, ed., *Hauksbók*, p.XVI.

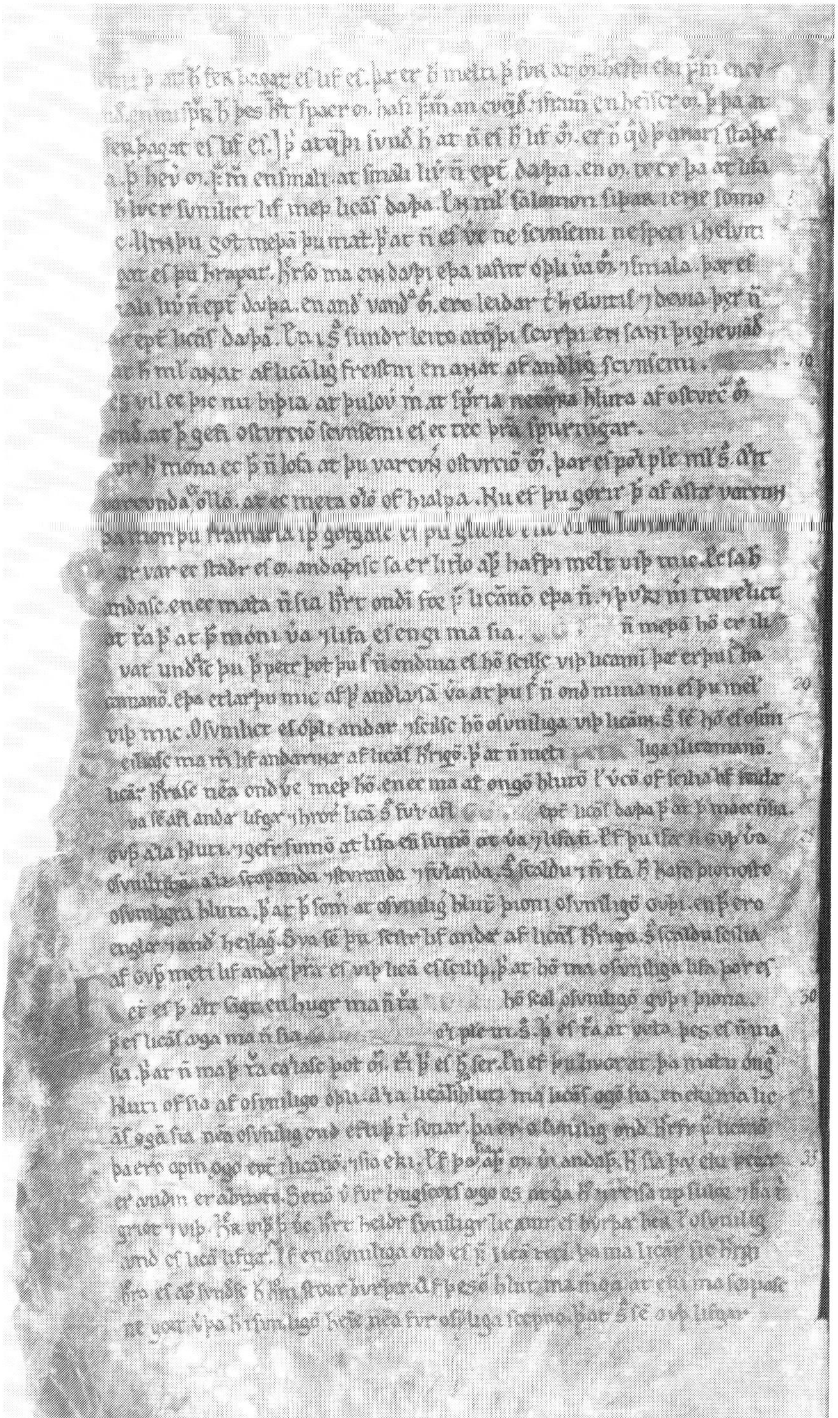

Fig. 77. *The dialogues of Gregory the Great.* AM 677, 4to, fol.36v
(shortly after 1200: Iceland).

IV. Marginal Speaker Notation

abandon it in favour of marginal notation. Since they deliberately chose to turn their backs on the existing and fairly widespread approach used in the presentation of other purely dialogic material, it seems clear that the scribes of the Eddic dialogues must have felt that they were working with a very different kind of tradition. Similar conclusions can be drawn from the fact that the later scribes of the rhetorical dialogues seem to have decided against using the more space-saving Eddic form of notation. The question thus arises as to why marginal notation came to be employed solely with the dialogic poems of the Edda.

In the absence of comparable Scandinavian manuscript traditions to that employed in the Edda manuscripts, it is necessary to look elsewhere for an original model. And it is no real surprise to discover that the only truly comparable material during this period comes from northern France and England, an area that exerted considerable influence on the Norwegian and Icelandic scribes and saga writers during the thirteenth and fourteenth centuries, not only in terms of literary style, but also scribal techniques.[16] What *is* noteworthy, however, is that when marginal notation is used in manuscripts from these parts, it does not occur in works containing simple poetical or rhetorical dialogue,[17] but rather in those manuscripts that contain early 'dramatic' works, that is to say, works that all appear to have been 'performed' by at least one actor in a dramatic style.

Two works that at first glance might seem to be exceptions to the above rule are the twelfth-century Irish manuscripts of the *Táin Bó Cúailnge*,[18] and the eleventh-century German manuscript of *Ruodlieb*. Both works are largely narrative, but contain occasional brief passages of dialogue that are sometimes accompanied by marginal speaker markings.[19] The purpose behind this notation is unclear, but it has recently been suggested that the marginal markings in the Irish manuscripts might be 'not descriptive but prescriptive', that is to say, meant as indications for the oral performance of the work rather than information to be read aloud.[20] A similar argument

---

[16] See below, notes 91–92.

[17] Bennett and Smithers, when commenting on the notation in *Dame Sirith* (see below, section D.1), can only refer to the Latin *comediæ*: see Bennett and Smithers, eds, *Early Middle English verse and prose*, p.78.

[18] Two different kinds of sporadic marginal speaker notation are found in the *Lebor na Huidre* MS (Royal Irish Academy; early twelfth century) and the *Book of Leinster* (TCD MS 1339 4to; mid-twelfth century). Regarding the former MS and its echoes in the later *Yellow book of Lecan*, see *Leabhar na H-Uidhri*, ed. Gilbert, pp.66–67; *Lebor na Huidre*, ed. Best and Bergin, pp.170–171; *Táin Bó Cúailnge*, ed. O'Rahilly (1976), pp.33–38; and *Táin Bó Cúailnge*, ed. Strachan and O'Keefe, pp.36–41. On the markings, see Mac Cana, 'On the use of the term Retoiric', 79–81, and most recently Tranter, 'Marginal problems', p.228. For the markings in the *Book of Leinster*, which are closer to those discussed above, see *Táin Bó Cúailnge*, ed. O'Rahilly (1967), pp.72–74.

[19] Münchener Staatsbibliothek Handschrift M (Clm 19486). The marginal speaker indications occur in certain isolated passages of dialogue, where confusion might arise as to who is speaking: see *Ruodlieb: Faksimile-Ausgabe*, ed. Haug and Vollmann, I.ii, p.77, p.115 and p.137; II.i, p.67, p.125 and p.173.

[20] Tranter, 'Marginal problems', p.239.

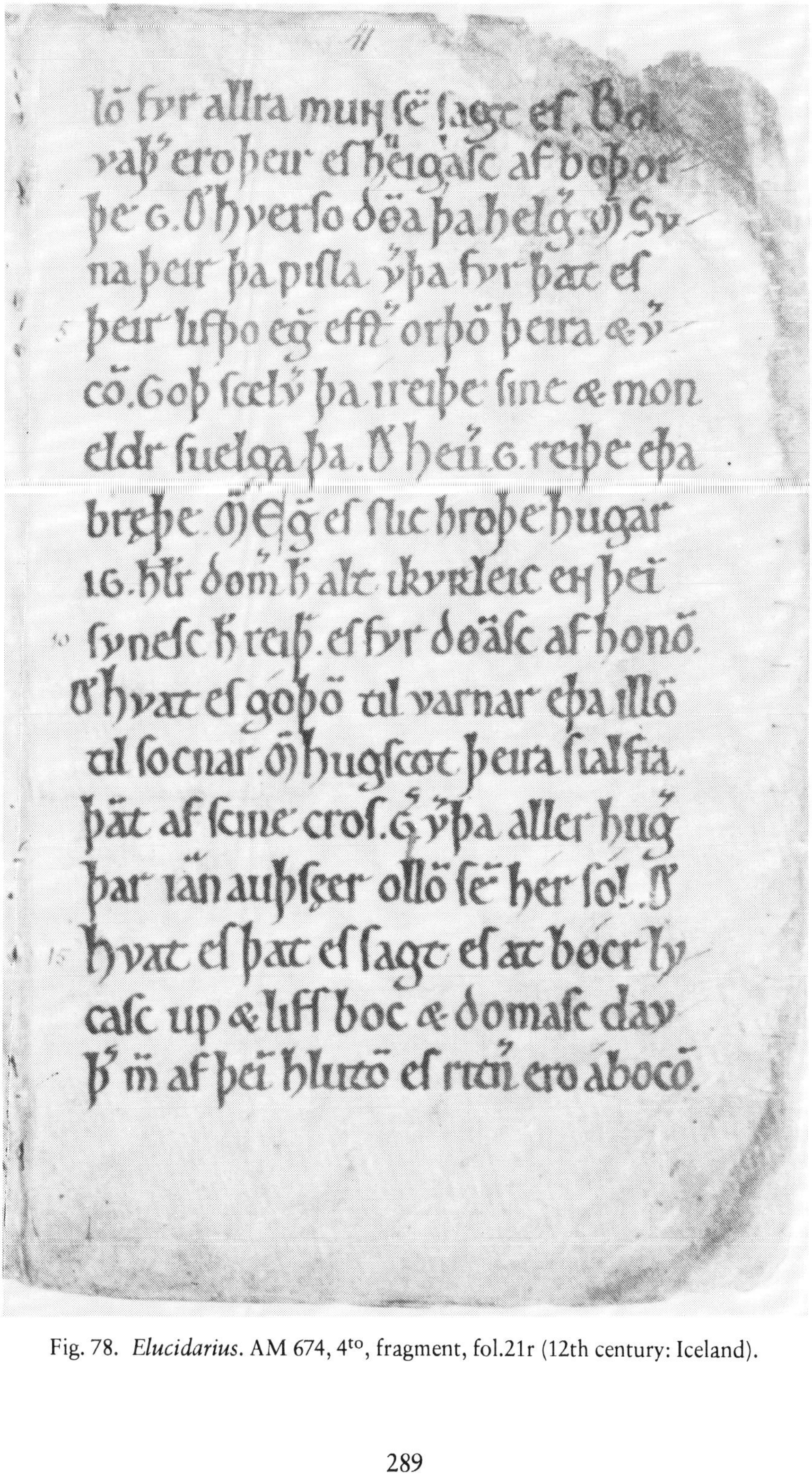

ló fyr allra muñ sē sagt ef. Bœ
vað ero þeir ef hēigasc af boþor
þe G. Ö hverso dőa þa helg. vi) Sv
na þeir þa pisla. yþa fyr þat ef
þeir lifþo eg efñ orþő þeira æ·y
cō. Goþ scælv þa ireiþe sine æ mon
eldr suelga þa. Ö heii G. reiþe eþa
breþe. ō) Eg ef slic hroþe hugar
16. hlr dom h alt ikyrleic en þei
synesc h reiþ. ef fyr doäsc af honō.
Ö hvat ef goþō til varnar eþa illō
til socnar. ō) hugscot þeira sialfra.
þat af sine crof. g̃ yþa aller hug
þar ian auþsęer ollō sē her sol. ý
hvat ef þat ef sagt ef at bœcr ly
casc up æ liff boc æ domasc dav
þ ḿ af þei hlutō ef rtn̄ ero aboco.

Fig. 78. *Elucidarius*. AM 674, 4to, fragment, fol.21r (12th century: Iceland).

IV. Marginal Speaker Notation

1. The problem has been made by Peter Dronke with regard to the *Ruodlieb* manuscript which was probably written by the author himself. Concerning the markings here, Dronke writes, 'These suggest to me that the poet intended his poem to be read aloud with different readers for different roles and inserted the directions when the text alone didn't make clear who was speaking.'[21] The use of marginal speaker notation in these manuscripts would thus appear to have a similar function to that found in the manuscripts of more obviously dramatic works discussed below. They point to a strong dramatic element in the spoken performance of the works in question, either in the sense that various speakers were expected to take the different roles in these dialogues, or that the single performer 'acted' the different roles in the very least by altering his voice for different characters.

The manuscripts of most interest in comparison with those of the Eddic poems are those containing the following works: the Latin *comedia*, *Babio*; the Anglo-Norman Passion play, *La seinte resureccion*; the Middle English religious play, *The harrowing of Hell*; and the Anglo-Norman religious drama, *Le mystere d Adam*. *Babio* and *Le mystere d Adam* both exist in manuscripts from the mid- to late twelfth century, while *La seinte resureccion* is recorded in two manuscripts from the late thirteenth century. The most recent work is *The harrowing of Hell*, which in the form under discussion occurs in one manuscript from the early fourteenth century. All of these manuscripts show striking similarities to the manuscripts of the dialogic poems of the Edda which were written during the same period.[22]

It should be stressed, however, that not all manuscripts of medieval plays used this system. More probably, marginal speaker notation represents a logical development of the method of speaker indication that had been used in earlier manuscripts of drama in Latin. A brief summary of the manuscript traditions for transcribing drama that surrounded and preceded the works in question is thus necessary in order to explain the context of this development and isolate the probable milieu within which it occurred.

C. European Manuscripts of Dramatic Works, 1000–1300

1. The Problem

By its nature, drama demands a different manuscript approach to that used for normal prose or poetry, since in performance it relies solely on the spoken word and accompanying action. In writing, therefore, its demands extend beyond the mere *text* of the performance which might be incomprehensible or difficult for the reader (or later performers) if it lacked any indication of the actual speakers of the words in question. These external indications, therefore, have to accompany the text, but since they *are* additional to the actual body of the text 'as performed', they need to be

---

[21] Letter from Peter Dronke, dated 10 June 1990.
[22] Regarding these mainland European MSS, see below, *sections D.2–5*.

C. European Manuscripts of Dramatic Works, 1000–1300

somehow set apart from the text, along with any stage directions which are not meant to be read aloud, but are instead intended as directions for the performers or as an external aid for the reader who will need help in visualising the proceedings.

2. Terence and his imitators

It might be assumed that the margin would be the natural setting for such additional comments. However, as was mentioned above, the use of margins for speaker indications during the early Middle Ages was by no means common practice. It rather represents a stage en route towards the later, more common medieval English format found in the manuscripts of the fifteenth-century York and Townley cycles of mystery plays, for example, where speeches are separated by a horizontal line drawn across the page and ending in the right-hand margin with the name of the next speaker.[23] One of the earliest examples of this particular system is found in the fragmentary manuscript of the *Interludium de clerico et puella* (British Library, MS Add.23986) from the late thirteenth century.[24]

However, prior to and even during this period when the manuscripts of the Eddic poems were written, it is almost impossible to talk of any 'common' system being employed in manuscripts of drama. Drama as a formal genre was in the throes of emerging from the chaos and clerical animosity of the early Middle Ages, and just as the academics and clerics of the time were in doubt as to what term should be used to define a medieval play,[25] so too were the scribes unsure as to what approach should be employed when recording dramatic texts. Nonetheless, in general terms, prior to and contemporary with the Edda manuscripts and those of *Babio, La seinte resureccion, The harrowing of Hell* and *Le mystère d'Adam*, it is possible to talk of three broadly based 'genres' of drama in Europe. All of these are reflected in what are often very different styles of manuscript writing, few of which make use of the margin.

2. Terence and his Imitators

It might be thought that the most natural models for the manuscript writing of plays would have been the manuscripts of the plays of Terence (written c.186–159 B.C.). The Latin comedies of this Roman dramatist were extremely popular as text books and stylistic models in medieval

---

[23] See the facsimiles in *The York play*, introduced by Beadle and Meredith, and *The Towneley cycle*, introduced by Cawley and Stevens. In spite of this ever-increasing agreement about methods of indicating speakers, there was evidently still some confusion as late as the fifteenth and sixteenth century, as can be seen in certain of the N-Town mystery plays, and in Oxford, Bodley, MS Digby 133 which contains the Digby plays. See, for example, the Digby plays of *Mary Magdalene* (Digby 133, fols 95r–157v) and *The Conversion of St Paul* (fols 37r–50v) and *The killing of the children of Israelle* (fols 148r–157v). See also *The Digby plays*, introduced by Baker and Murphy, pp.x–xi, and p.xiii, and *The N-Town plays*, introduced by Meredith and Kahrl, pp.xix–xxi.
[24] See the facsimile in *Non-cycle plays* (1979), ed. Davis, pp.9–12.
[25] See Woolf, *The English mystery plays*, pp.34–35, and Wickham, *Medieval theatre*, pp.36–40.

IV. Marginal Speaker Notation

2. Terence and his imitators

schools in Europe where students from Iceland would certainly have encountered them.[26] They were also highly influential as regards the development of works like *Babio* and the religious *comediæ* of the Benedictine Abbess, Hrotsvitha of Gandersheim (c.935–c.1002). Terence's works and the various imitations of them, such as *Querolus* (eleventh century), may well have been performed in one fashion or another during the early Middle Ages, possibly read aloud by one man and simultaneously imitated by a group of mimes. Nonetheless, the evidence for such entertainments is limited, and probably such performances were rare.[27] It is also questionable whether these works were associated with the type of drama that was being performed in the villages and churches of Europe during the early Middle Ages.

The fact that the plays of Terence were usually regarded as works of literature rather than scripts of drama for performance is emphasised perhaps by the way in which they were recorded.[28] In their manuscript form, these works and those of Terence's imitators such as Hrotsvitha are marked by an approach to dialogue very similar to that used in the Scandinavian manuscripts of *Elucidarius*: the abbreviated speaker indications tend to remain within the confines of the text itself, unless they occur at the start of the line where they are occasionally placed slightly out into the margin (see, for example *fig*.79, l.22, **SYM, DAV**; *fig*.80, l.6, **.S., .M.**). No stage directions are given. The only real distinguishing feature from works like *Elucidarius* is the list of characters that is given at the start of each scene as part of the text.[29]

---

[26] As part of his examination of the classical works studied by students at this time, Sverrir Tómasson cites the *Ars lectoris*, written by a French cleric named Aimeric in the late eleventh century. Aimeric grades the material that is read, and places the works of Terence in the highest 'gold' class: see Sverrir Tómasson, *Formálar*, p.18. See further Woolf, *The English mystery plays*, pp.25–26: copies of Terence's works existed in at least six religious houses in England. MSS of Plautus' plays seem to have been less common.

[27] See Woolf, *The English mystery plays*, pp.26–28; Axton, *European drama*, pp.24–29; and Tydeman, *The theatre in the Middle Ages*, pp.27–28, and pp.48–50. Regarding the performance of the works of Hrotsvitha, see also Zeydel, 'Were Hrotsvitha's dramas performed?', 443–456, and Dronke, *Women writers*, pp.58–59.

[28] The chief extant MSS are the fourth-/ fifth-century *Codex Bembinus* (Vatican Library 3226); the ninth-/ tenth-century *Codex Parisinus* (Bibliothèque Nationale, fonds latines 7899) and *Codex Vaticanus* (Vatican Library, MS 3868), and the twelfth-century *Codex Dunelmensis* (Bodleian Auct. F.213) all three of which which are closely related; and finally the ninth-/ tenth-century *Codex Victorianus* (or *Laurentianus*) (Laurentian Library, Florence MS XXXVIII, 24) which represents another family of MSS. Regarding the speaker indications in these MSS, see *The comedies of Terence*, ed. Ashmore, pp.40–41, pp.60–64, and Notes, 4. Example facsimiles of Terence MSS are given in *P.Terenti Afri, Comediae*, ed. Prete.

[29] Exactly the same system of speaker notation was employed by the various imitators of Terence, such as the writer of *Querolus* (BN, f.lat. 8121A, fols 11v–27r; eleventh century) and Hrotsvitha. The main MSS of Hrotsvitha's works from the period under discussion are the Munich Bayerische Staatsbibliothek MS Clm 14485 (early eleventh century); Cologne, Historisches Archiv MS W* 101 (late twelfth century); and the Munich Bayerische Staatsbibliothek MS Clm 2552 (early thirteenth century). For example facsimiles from these MSS, see Harrsen, 'The manuscripts'.

ut tu sis sciens. nisi puerum tollis iam ego hunc in mediam uiam puol uam æque
ibidem puol uam in luto MYS tu pol homo non es sobrius DAV fallacia alia aliam
trudit iam susurrari audio ciuem atti cam esse hanc CRI hem DAV coactus legibus eam
uxorem ducet MYS eho obsecro annon ciuis est CRI tocularium immalum insciens
pæne incidi DAV quis hic loquitur o chreme per tempus aduenis ausculta CHR audiui
omnia DAV an hæc tu omnia CHR audiui inquam a principio CHR audis tem
obsecro 'hem scelera. hanc iam oportet incruciatum abripi hic est ille non te credas
dauum ludere MYS me miseram nihil pol falsi dixi MYS senex CRI no ut omnem rem
es sermo intus DAV est MYS neme at tingas scelesta si pol glycerio non omnia hæc   10
eho inepta nescis quid sit actum MYS quis ciam DAV hic socer est alio pacto haut poterat
fieri ut sciret hæc quæ uolumus MYS præ diceret DAV paulum interesse consefs & animo
omnia ut fere natura facies inde indu stria,

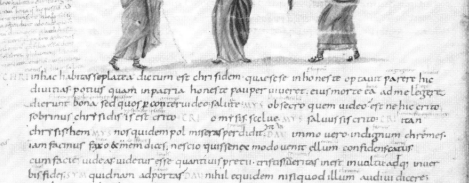

CRI in hac habitas replate a dictum est chrisidem quæ sese in honestæ optauit parere hic   15
diuitias potius quam in patria honestæ pauper uiueret. eius morte ea ad me legere
dierunt bona sed quos p contra ui deo salute MYS obsecro quem uideo est ne hic erito
sobrinus chrysidis is est crito CRI o mysis scelue MYS saluus sis crito CRI tan
chrysishem MYS nos quidem pol miseras perdidit DAV immo uero indignum chremes
iam facinus faxo &mem dices, nescio quis senex modo uenit ellum confidens satis
cum facie uideas uidetur esse quanti uis preciu en satis ueras inest in ualtu adqu inuer   20
bis fides SYM quidnam adportas DAV nihil equidem nisi quod illum audiui diceres
SYM quid ait tandem DAV glycerium se scire ciuem esse atticam SYM hem dromo
dromo DAV quid est SYM dromo DAV audi SYM uerbum si addideris dromo
DAV audi obsecro DRO quid uis SYM sublimem intro rape hunc quantum potes

Fig. 79. Terence, *Andria*, 775–803; 854–861. *Codex Vaticanus*,
Vatican Library, MS 3868, fol.15v (9th–10th century).

ingressi sunt? S. Nonne precepi ut rebelles dox
ad locū t'pruditnis traheretis? M. Precepisti. nos q́; tuis
preceptis opam dedim'. isplendo s. sup uenere duo iuuenes iuuenes. asserentes se ad hoc a te missos. ut in
renā ad cacumē montis p̄ducerē. S. Ignorabā. M.
Agnosc̄m. S. Quales fuerē. M. amictū splendidi ē-
uultu ad modū reuerendi. S. Hū sequabamini
illos? M. Sequebam. S. ad fecerē? M. Adexteram q'
hirene se collocauerē. 7 nos huc direxerē. q̃ te et n̄
rei n̄ lateret. S. Restat ut ascenso eq̃. pgā. 7 q̃ fuerint
q̃ nostram libet'tlusert'. pq̄trā. M. Probabim's parte. S.
Heu ignoro q̃d agā. pessum data sum maleficiis xp̄icolax
en montē circueo 7 semitam aliq'ciens repiens non as-
sensum cop̄hendere n̄ reditū q̃o reposco. M. Aduersis mo-
dis om'sillicitū nimiaq; lassitudine fatigam. uix
sanū caput uiuere sustines? te ipsum 7 nos p̄def. S.
Si q's es mox strennue exrende arcū. iacta sagittam.
p̄fode hanc maleficā. M. Decet. h. Erubesce i felix sisin-
ni. erubesces teq; t'put uictū ingemisce. q'm tenelle
infancie uirguncule. absq; armorū aparatu nequisti
superare. S. Quicq'd decoris accidit tollero.
qm̄ te moriturā haut dubito. h. hinc m̄ maxi-
me gaudendū t'u dolendū qa p̄rue malignita-
tis seueritate in tartara dampnaberis. ego aut
martirii palmā uirginitatisq; recepta coronā in-
tr bo etherū 7 eterni regis thalamū cui ē honor 7 gla ī
Calimac̄. Drusiana. Amicē. p̄scta sclox an-
fortunas. S. Ioh'n. Andromac̄. Calimac̄. Pauci uos ami-
ci nolo. A. Vtere quantū libet n̄ro collo q'o. C. Si egre
n̄ accipitis malo uos int'im sequestrim. alio x̄ a collegio.
A. Quid t'uidet' comodū. nob est sequentium. C. Acceda-
m' in secretiora loca. nequis sup ueniens int'rupat dicen-
da. A. Vt iubet. Am'iū ducē. q'ue sustinui dolorem
quē uēro consilio releuari posse sp̄o. A. Equū est ut com̄u-
nicata in uicē copassione paciam q̄eq'd unicuiq; n̄rm
utriq; euentu fortune ingerat. C. O utinā uoluisses
meā passionē copaciendo mecū partiri. A. Pn̄ uolea

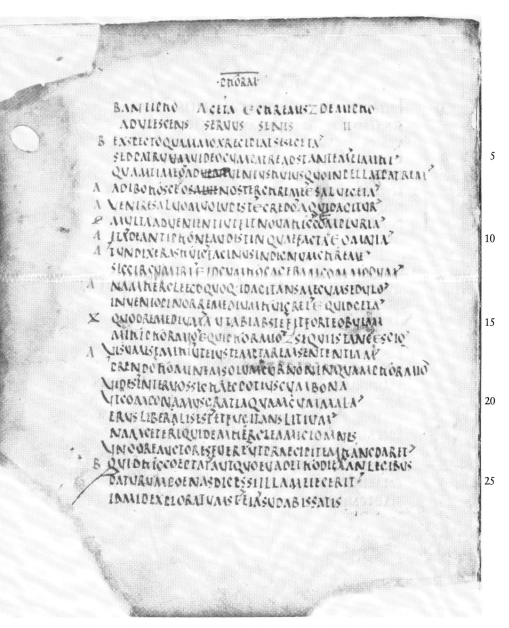

Fig. 81. Terence, *Phormio*, ll.606–628. *Codex Bembinus*, Vatican Library, MS 3226, fol.66v (4th/ 5th century).

3. The drama of the church

An intriguing exception to this rule, however, is found in the earliest manuscript of Terence's plays, the early Italian *Codex Bembinus* from the fourth or fifth century, written in rustic capitals. In this manuscript, Greek initials for the speakers are placed in the left-hand margin close to the text, unless two speakers occur in the same line. On such occasions, the initial for the second speaker is placed within the text preceding his/ her words (see *fig.81*).[30] This naturally offers parallels to the manuscripts of the Eddic poems, but considering the age and provenance of the *Codex Bembinus*, it would seem unlikely that the tradition followed by the scribe of this manuscript had much influence further north in Europe. Indeed, such a conclusion is supported by the fact that the scribes of the later Terence manuscripts avoid using the margins.

3. The Drama of the Church

Alongside the texts of Terence and his imitators, there was, from the eleventh century onwards, an ever-increasing number of manuscripts containing Latin liturgical drama. However, as was mentioned above, it is unlikely that the writers of these works saw a resemblance between what they were creating and any plays of Terence that they might have read. The drama of the church arose out of the liturgy, and therefore a method had to be found in which the normal method of writing liturgical texts could be altered in order to accommodate stage directions and speaker indications. This information was not meant to be read aloud and had to be differentiated in some way from the main text. A wide variety of methods was used, but one of the most typical is that represented by the thirteenth century *Fleury play-book* from northern France, where the text is accompanied by music, and the speaker indications and stage directions are separated from the text and music by being placed in interlinear 'boxes' marked off by vertical lines (see *fig.82*).[31] As with the Eddic dialogues, it is not uncommon that a speech verb is found accompanying the names of the speakers in these manuscripts, although usually in the present subjunctive rather than the past tense.[32]

The whole range of manuscript approaches to the naming of speakers stretches from something resembling the Terentian format (as in the

---

[30] See the complete facsimile contained in *Il Codice di Terenzio Vaticano Latino 3226*, ed. Prete. As with the other Terence MSS, the names of the characters in each scene are listed across the page at the start of the scene. Here, however, each name is accompanied by a letter (e.g. **A** GETA) which is used to indicate the speaker in the text and the margins below. The letters are not followed by full stops.

[31] Comparable to the works in the *Fleury play-book* are the Rouen *Play of the shepherds* (BN, f.lat.904, fols 11v–14r; thirteenth century), and the Salisbury *Visitatio sepulchrum* (Bodleian Rawlinson Lit. D.iv, fols 130r–132r; fourteenth century). A complete facsimile of the *Fleury play-book* is contained in *Sacre rappresentazioni*, ed. Tintori, pp.86–103. For the Salisbury MS, see Chambers, *The mediaeval stage*, II, frontispiece.

[32] See further below, *section D.9*.

Fig. 82. *The play of the conversion of St Paul. The Fleury play-book*, Orléans, Bibliothèque de la Ville, MS 202 (178), p.230 (13th century).

4. The travelling entertainers

Strassburg *Play of the Magi*, c.1200[33]) to other methods in which the speaker indications are underlined (as in the early fourteenth-century *Play of the Prophets* from Rouen[34]), or placed in the line at the end of the previous speech, similar to the approach used in certain Scandinavian manuscripts such as those of *Konungs skuggsjá* mentioned above. Such an approach is evident, for example, in the eleventh-/ twelfth-century *Sponsus* from Limoges.[35] In certain other cases, no differentiation is made at all between the speaker introductions and the text (as in the fourteenth-century Barking Easter play and Hilarius' twelfth-century *Ludus super iconia Sancti Nicolai*.[36] It is noticable, however, that margins are not employed for speaker names in liturgical works in Latin until the early fourteenth century (see below, *section D.1*). It is thus evident that the system of marginal notation employed in the manuscripts of the Eddic poems did not originate in liturgical drama.

4. The Travelling Entertainers

The manuscripts of liturgical drama demonstrate some of the earliest attempts to make a clear differentiation between the names of the speakers and the text itself. The logical next step was to separate the two completely. This is demonstrated in the use of marginal notation, but also in the evolution of another system during the thirteenth century, wherein the names of the speakers were placed separately *above* their lines (see *fig.83*, l.18: **Theophiles**). Initially, this method seems to have been largely restricted to the new genre of vernacular dramatic writing which grew out of the French troubadour tradition and was centred particularly in Arras. Such an approach is found in the manuscript of *Le miracle de Théophile* (c.1261) by the Parisian *trouvère*, Rutebeuf,[37] and also those containing the works of the Arras poets Jean Bodel (*Le jeu de Saint Nicolas*; c.1199–1201[38]) and Adam de la Halle (*Le jeu de la feuillée*, c.1275 and *Le jeu de Robin et Marion*, c.1283[39]). In later years, this approach was to become

---

[33] See Young, *DMC*, II, facing p.64.
[34] See Young, *DMC*, II, facing p.154.
[35] See Young, *DMC*, II, facing p.364.
[36] See Young, *DMC*, I, facing p.384, and II, facing p.338.
[37] BN, fonds francais 837, fols 298v–302v (mid-thirteenth century). For a facsimile of this MS, see Omont, *Fabliaux*, pp.596–604. Also contained in this compendium are a short extract from Adam de la Halle's *Le jeu de la feuillée* (see note 39) which uses the same system, and the only MS of another early play, *Courtois d'Arras* (c.1225), which, on fols 63r–66v (Omont, *Fabliaux*, pp.125–132), completely lacks any kind of speaker indication.
[38] BN, f.fr.25566 (Ancien fonds Lavallière no.81), fols 68r–83r. The MS was written c.1300.
[39] The main redactions of *Le jeu de la feuillée* and *Le jeu de Robin et Marion* are preserved in the same MS as *Le jeu de saint Nicolas* (c.1300): BN, f.fr.25566, fols 48v–59v and fols 39r–48v, where this system is used. The same system was probably meant to be employed in the short passage of *Le jeu de la feuillée* contained in BN, f.fr. 837, fols 251v–252r, (the same MS containing *Théophile*) where spaces for the names have been left above the speeches. A different, unique approach is encountered in the two other MSS of

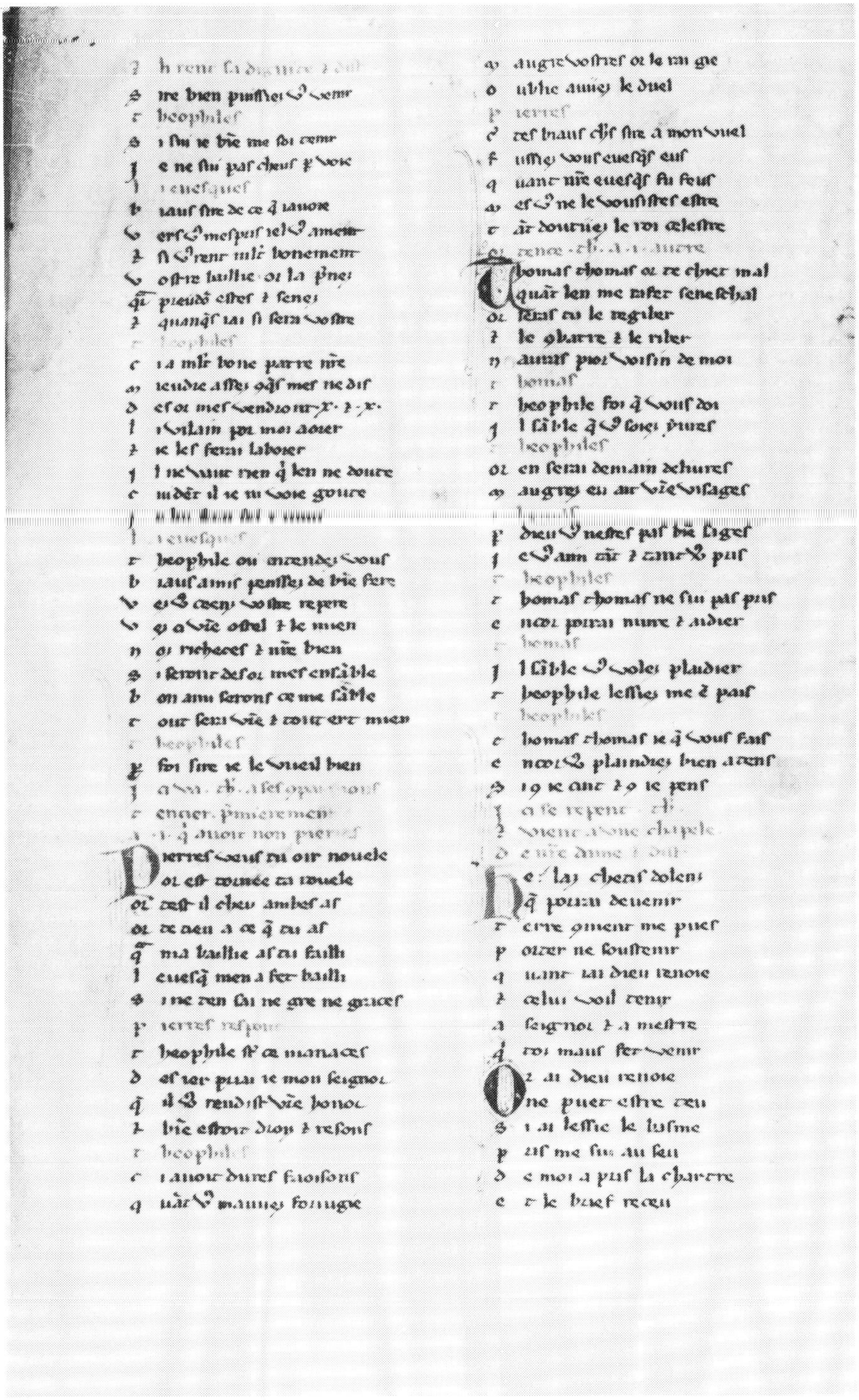

Fig. 83. Rutebeuf, *Le miracle de Théophile*. Paris, Bibliothèque Nationale, fonds francais 837, fol.300v (mid-13th century).

IV. Marginal Speaker Notation

1. General more widespread in Europe,[40] and is, of course, commonly used in printed editions of plays today.

This costly, space demanding technique of placing names above speeches was possibly a development of the system mentioned above in which new speakers' names were placed at the end of the previous line of speech, often in rubricated form. Nonetheless, the individuality of approach reflects the fact that the works in question represent an independent genre that was directly related to neither the church nor the academic tradition. Written in the vernacular, these works were much closer to the laity and their amusements and traditions, and much more directly naturalistic. They show some of the first steps taken towards a popular form of written drama.[41] Such a system of speaker indication as that employed here, however, would have never been considered for the cramped, abbreviated manuscripts containing the Eddic poems.

D. The Use of the Margin to Indicate Speakers in Dramatic Manuscripts

1. General

As with the system of speaker indication described above, the use of margins for speaker indications in manuscripts of dramatic works must be seen as a development away from the restrictions of the liturgical and Terentian approach. Marginal notation, however, seems to have been the earliest of these two systems to evolve since it was obviously in use in northern Europe as early as the eleventh century. Unlike the system of placing speaker names above speeches, it had the advantage of saving valuable manuscript space. It also allowed the names to be isolated from the text, and simultaneously made them more immediately visible. As was mentioned above, it is apparent that no strictly liturgical manuscripts make use of this approach until the fourteenth century when it is encountered in the Cividale *Planctus Mariæ* from Italy (see *fig.84*, right-hand margin).[42] Marginal speaker

---

Le jeu de Robin et Marion: BN, f.fr.1569, fols 140–144; and Bibliothèque Mejanes à Aix en Provence MS 572, fols 1–11. Here the names of the speakers (abbreviated in the Mejanes MS) are placed to the left of the body of the text. However, the same thing is also done with the initial letters of succeeding lines: see *Le jeu de Robin et de Marion*, ed. Varty, facing p.96 and p.81, with an example of the BN f.fr.25566 MS (*Robin et Marion*) facing p.80. For a facsimile example of the BN f.fr.25566 MS of *Le jeu de la feuillée*, see *Le jeu de la feuillée*, ed. Rony, facing p.18. For a facsimile of the BN f.fr.837 MS of the same work, see Omont, *Fabliaux*, pp.502–503.

[40] See for example note 23 above regarding the Digby and N-Town plays, and *section D.4* below concerning the Auchinleck MS of *The harrowing of Hell*.

[41] Regarding these works, see Axton and Stevens, ed. and trans., *Medieval French plays*, pp.xi–xix; and Axton, *European drama*, pp.131–158.

[42] Cividale, Reale Museo Archeologico, MS CI, fols 74r–76v. A photograph of fol.75r of this MS is provided on the cover of *Planctus Mariæ*, transcribed and translated by Smolden. A possible exception to this argument are the so-called 'Shrewsbury Fragments' from c.1300. These unique fragments (Shrewsbury School MS. VI, fols 38r–42v) contain

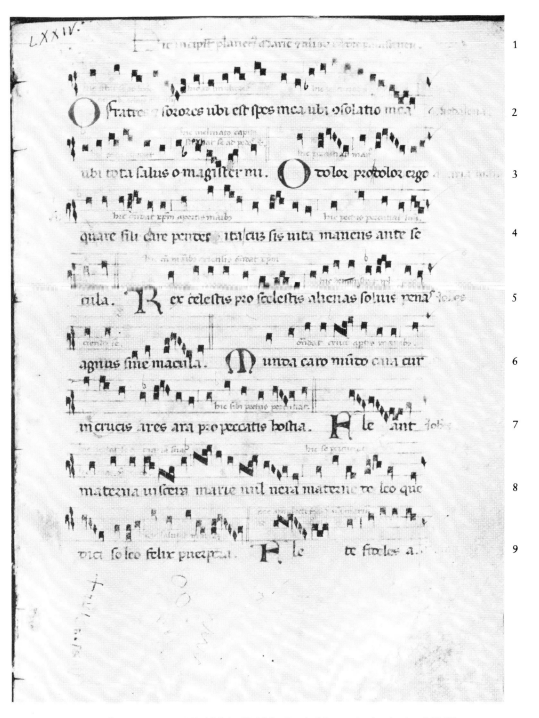

Fig. 84. *Planctus Mariæ* (Cividale). Cividale, Reale Museo Archeologico MS CI, fol.74r (14th century).

IV. Marginal Speaker Notation

1. General notation would thus appear to have its origins in a different milieu to that of the church. This particular system demands closer examination especially because of the similarities encountered in the Edda manuscripts.

With the exception of the *Codex Bembinus*, the earliest use of marginal speaker notation appears to be found in the late eleventh-century Latin manuscript of *Semiramis* from the north of France (BN, f.lat.8121A, fols 30r–32v).[43] This incomplete work describes an augur's summoning up of the spirit of Semiramis who was raped by Jupiter in the form of a bull. With the exception of the first nineteen lines, which form a kind of prologue to the action that follows, the poem is wholly dialogic. In the manuscript, the three speakers are almost always indicated with single letters placed in the left-hand margin, 'A' standing for Semiramis' brother, the Augur, 'a' for the god Apollo, and 'S' for Semiramis (see *fig.85*, left-hand margin). On the basis of the form of the poem and its strongly visual elements, Dronke suggests that it was meant to be declaimed by several readers who would have taken separate roles and perhaps also enacted certain stage business. In its simplest form such a performance would resemble a modern radio drama being presented live in front of an audience.[44]

Almost one hundred years later, marginal speaker indications were again used in the earliest fragmentary manuscript of the Latin *comedia De nuntio sagaci* ('The shrewd messenger'), also known as *Ovidius puellarum* ('The girl's Ovid') (British Museum MS. Add.49368, s.XIII[1], fols 47r–50v; c.1200).[45] This work is essentially a first-person account dealing with the seduction of a girl by a poet, but in spite of this, it is composed largely of dialogue. Once again, the deliberate system of marginal notation takes the form of single letters, 'p' (Puella) and 'n' (Nuncius) which are only found in the right-hand margin alongside the passages of dialogue on fols 47v, 48r and 48v (see *fig.86*, ll.14–16, for example).[46] Interestingly enough, the

---

one actor's speeches accompanied by his cue lines for three Latin liturgical plays. The cue lines are placed in the right-hand margin parallel to the end of the previous speech. The start of each new speech, however, is indicated by a paragraph marker placed in the left-hand margin: see *Non-cycle plays and fragments* (1970), ed. Davis, frontispiece and pp.1–7.

[43] The text, with translation, is given in Dronke, *Poetic individuality* (1986), pp.66–75.

[44] See Dronke, *Poetic individuality* (1986), pp.xxix–xxx. No discussion is made here about the speaker indications.

[45] For the text of this work, see *De nuntio sagaci*, ed. Rossetti, in *Commedie latine*, ed. Bertini, II, pp.11–125.

[46] The markings are occasionally placed a line too early or late, and seem to be missing in certain other places where it might be expected that they would be found. They are lacking completely on the final four folios of the MS. However, the fact that marginal speaker notation is also found in certain other later MSS, such as Oesterreichische Nationalbibliothek; Vienna, Codex Vindobonensis 303 (Novus 392), fols 112v–115v (late fourteenth century), suggests that such marginal notation might have been a common feature of certain MSS of *De nuntio sagaci*. See Rossetti, ed., *De nuntio sagaci*, pp.51–61, and the examples from the various MSS given in the same volume between p.127 and p.129.

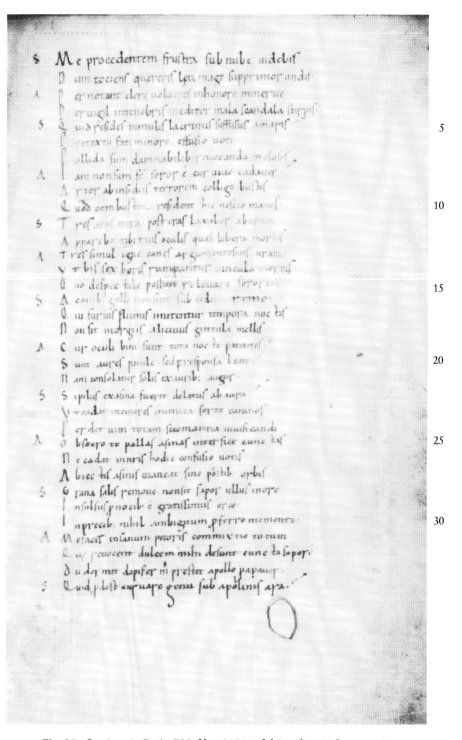

Fig. 85. *Semiramis*. Paris, BN, f.lat. 8121A, fol.31r (late 11th century).

IV. Marginal Speaker Notation

1. General markings also occur in places where the narrative transitions have already made it clear who is speaking, a feature also encountered in the *Codex Regius* at the start of *Helgakviða Hjörvarðssonar* (see above Chapter III, note 93). Both this and the unique use of arrows in the left-hand margin at those points where action seems to be required have encouraged Dronke to argue that the markings (in the original manuscript of which this was a copy) were not intended for the reader, but rather for a performance of the work. This could possibly have been carried out by a single speaker, but more probably the work was presented by more than one man in a lively dramatic fashion similar to that described by Arnulf of Orléans with regard to a late twelfth-century performance of another Latin *comedia*, *Pamphilus*.[47]

The same approach to speaker names is found, albeit less obviously, in the manuscripts of two other works closely related in theme to *De nuntio sagaci* and *Pamphilus*: the Middle English *Dame Sirith* and the French *Gilote et Johane*, both of which contain passages of narrative in addition to dialogue. As in the cases of *De nuntio sagaci* and *Semiramis*, scholars have recently begun to argue that these works must have been performed in a dramatic fashion.

Dame Sirith (MS Digby 86, fols 165r–168r; late thirteenth century) has a similar storyline to that of *Pamphilus* and *De nuntio sagaci*, and must have roots in a similar tradition.[48] It is a brief comedy about the seduction of a virtuous young wife by a lovelorn clerk who gains the cunning assistance of an older, more experienced bawd. After a brief introduction, the work becomes largely dialogic, and once again, the only direct indication of who is speaking at any given time is a small letter usually placed to the right of each speech. The notation, 'T' for the Narrator (or perhaps, according to Dronke, for *thymelicus*, or 'theatre musician'[49]), 'C' for Clericus, 'V' probably for Vxor, and 'F' for Femina, does not continue throughout the entire text. When the letters do occur, they usually appear at the *end* of the first line of each speech like the Edda speech indications on *recto* folios, but sometimes are placed beside the last line of the previous speech (see *fig.87*, l.24 and l.27, left column). In three cases, when space is lacking, the notes are placed above the last word of the first line. All of this suggests that they were added to the text after it was written, as an afterthought.

There is every reason to believe that *Dame Sirith* was performed

---

[47] Dronke, 'Narrative and dialogue', pp.104–109; and 'A note on Pamphilus', 225–230. Arnulf states in his gloss on Ovid's *Remedia Amoris* in explanation of the fiction of the theatre: '. . . like Pamphilus, and like the others who are brought on in a comedy as characters (*persone*); people become inflamed, because the more they see these entertainments, the more they are aroused by the love-making of the characters.' 'Saltantur' ('who are mimed') is then explained as meaning 'represented by means of leaping (*saltationes*) and gesturing': translation by Dronke in 'A note on Pamphilus', 226.

[48] Text published in Bennett and Smithers, *Early Middle English verse and prose*, pp.80–95. Regarding the relationship between *Dame Sirith*, The *Interludium de clerico et puella* and the Latin *comediæ*, see Dronke, 'Narrative and dialogue', passim.

[49] Dronke, 'Narrative and dialogue', pp.110–111.

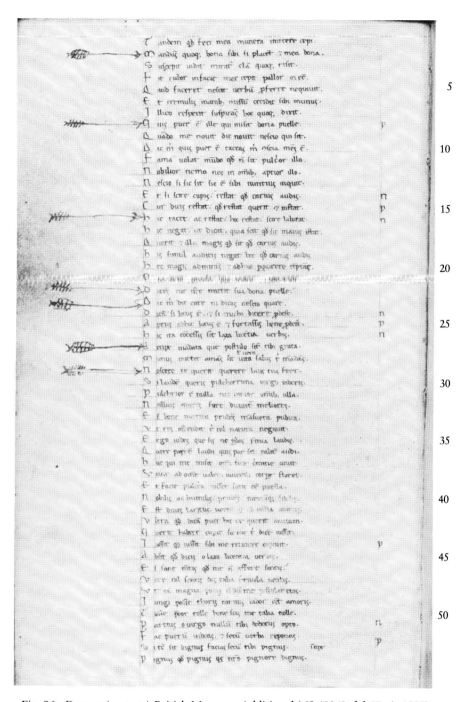

Fig. 86. *De nuntio sagaci*. British Museum, Additional MS 49368, fol.47v (c.1200).

IV. Marginal Speaker Notation

1. General

dramatically like its contemporary, the *Interludium de clerico et puella* which not only covers the same tale in a very similar way, albeit without any third person narrative, but also makes use of marginal notation (see above, *section C.1*). The main discussion in recent years has been whether such a performance of *Dame Sirith* could have been carried out alone. Using a similar method of practical analysis to that employed in the previous chapter, Richard Axton has pointed out that the text of *Dame Sirith* demands certain stage business with a weeping dog, as well as dramatic characterisation for it to make sense in performance.[50] Peter Dronke and Brian Moore have taken this argument even further. Dronke considers the work to be a 'fully-fledged play' for three characters and a narrator, partly for the same reasons given by Axton, but also because of the marginal notation.[51] Moore is in full agreement, adding the practical comment that certain passages of the work (like *Lokasenna* and *Hárbarðsljóð*) involve such fast alteration in roles that 'the characterization would depend entirely on voice modulation', so that the ' "single minstrel" hypothesis would demand . . . a feat of (scarcely credible) vocal legerdemain'.[52] The text of *Dame Sirith* also seems to contain cues for gestures that 'demand the presence of different actors'.[53] Furthermore, like *Fafnismál*, *Skírnismál*, and *Lokasenna*, *Dame Sirith* appears to break Olrik's 'Law of two to a scene'.[54]

Similar conclusions have been made about *Gilote et Johane* which is contained in British Museum, MS Harley 2253, fols 67v–68v (early fourteenth century).[55] This work is somewhat different in that it involves more narrative, centring around a debate between two women, Gilote and Johane, on the merits of sensual delights as opposed to that of virginity. Gilote, the advocate of the former wins, and the two embark on a tour of the country preaching their new gospel.

In spite of the presence of the narrative, the dialogue sections are accompanied by an intriguing system of notation. For the main part of the text, changes of speakers are marked not only with small initials in the outer margins of the folio parallel to the beginning of speeches ('**J.**' for Johane, '**G.**' for Gilote, and '**UX.**' for Vxor), but also with paragraph markers placed in the left-hand margin (see *fig.88*, l.21 and l.31).[56] As Carter Revard has pointed out, some of the paragraph markers are not

---

[50] See Axton, *European drama*, pp.21–23.
[51] Dronke, 'Narrative and dialogue', pp.109–113.
[52] Moore, 'The narrator within the performance', 23.
[53] Moore, 'The narrator within the performance', 21–24.
[54] Moore, 'The narrator within the performance', 22–23.
[55] See *Facsimile of British Museum MS.Harley 2253*, introduced by Ker. For the text of *Gilote et Johane*, see Jubinal, ed., *Nouveau recueil de contes*, II, pp.28–39.
[56] The markings only occur on fols 67*r–68r. On fol.67*r, the letters are placed in the outer margins of the folio, on fol.68r they occur only on the left-hand side. On fol.67*r, the letters are always accompanied by paragraph markers. Regarding the use of paragraph markers for the start of speeches, see also note 42 above, and notes 64 and 69 below.

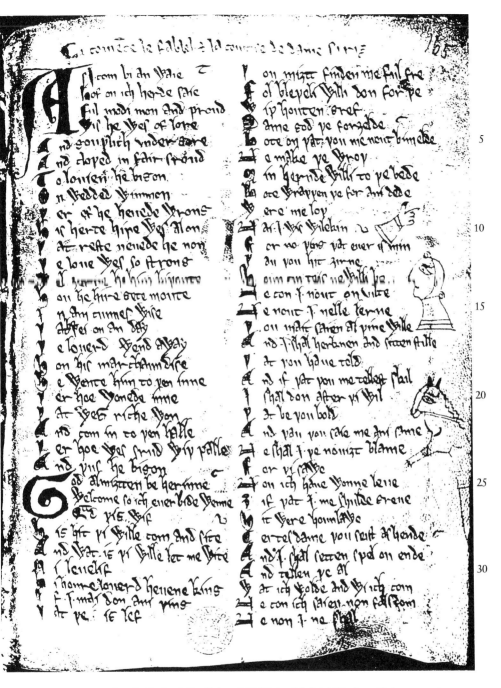

Fig. 87. *Dame Sirith*. Oxford, Bodleian, MS Digby 86, fol.165r (late 13th century).

IV. Marginal Speaker Notation

2. *'Babio'* placed beside dialogue but instead indicate where the Narrator takes over from the speakers. This point and the existence of the markers encourage Revard reach the logical conclusion that '*Gilote et Johane* was copied either from or as an *interlude* or mime-piece, in which the various parts were to be "played", either by an accomplished mime (or reader), or by several actors (or readers).'[57]

In spite of the similarities with regard to the use of marginal speaker indication, it is naturally impossible to say that any of the above works represents a deliberate manuscript policy. In the case of all of these works (especially *Dame Sirith* and *Gilote et Johane*), it might be argued that the initials were placed in the margins as a necessary afterthought for the sake of clarity, rather than during the process of writing. The same, however, cannot be said for the manuscripts of the Eddic poems, or those of *Babio*, *La seinte resureccion*, *The harrowing of Hell* and the *Le mystère d'Adam* (*Ordo repræsentationis Adæ*).

2. '*Babio*'[58]

Babio is a Latin work from the late twelfth century, possibly composed in England. It was evidently popular since it exists in no less than five manuscripts in Britain, France and Germany from the thirteenth and fourteenth centuries: Oxford, Bodleian, MS Digby 53, fols 35r–43v (late twelfth century); MS P.Codices latini phillipici, Royal Library, Berlin, fols 55v–60r (thirteenth century); Codex Lincolniensis, Lincoln Capit.105, fols 89v–90v, and 117r–118v (two closely related versions of *Babio* from the late thirteenth/ early fourteenth century); British Library, Cotton Titus MS A XX, fols 132v–137v (fourteenth century); and Oxford, Bodleian MS 851, fols 94vb–97va (late fourteenth/ early fifteenth century).[59]

Generally classed as one of the Latin *comediæ*, alongside works like *Pamphilus*, *De nuntio sagaci* and Vitalis' *Geta* and *Aurularia*, *Babio* has a Plautan-style plot in which a lecherous old man is fooled by his wife and her lover. The work nonetheless stands apart from the other *comediæ* because it appears to be English,[60] and because it is totally dialogic, whereas the other works make deliberate use of narrative to a greater or lesser extent. As Malcolm Brennan and Peter Dronke have shown, there is very good reason to believe that *Babio* was performed dramatically. Using

---

[57] Carter Revard, 'Gilote et Johane', 126. As Revard points out (126–127), *Gilote et Johane* has several thematic similarities to *Dame Sirith* and the *Interludium de clerico et puella*, and may well belong to a similar tradition.

[58] Text given in *Three Latin comedies*, ed. Bate, pp.35–60. See also *Babio*, trans. and ed. Brennan.

[59] It is known that versions of *Babio* also existed in the libraries of the monastery at Rievaulx in Yorkshire, and the Abbey of St Augustine in Canterbury: Brennan, *Babio*, p.3. For example facsimiles of the various MSS, see *Commedie latine*, ed. Bertini, II, between p.127 and p.129.

[60] See Bate, *Three Latin comedies*, p.1. Many of the other *comediæ* have closer links with the Loire area.

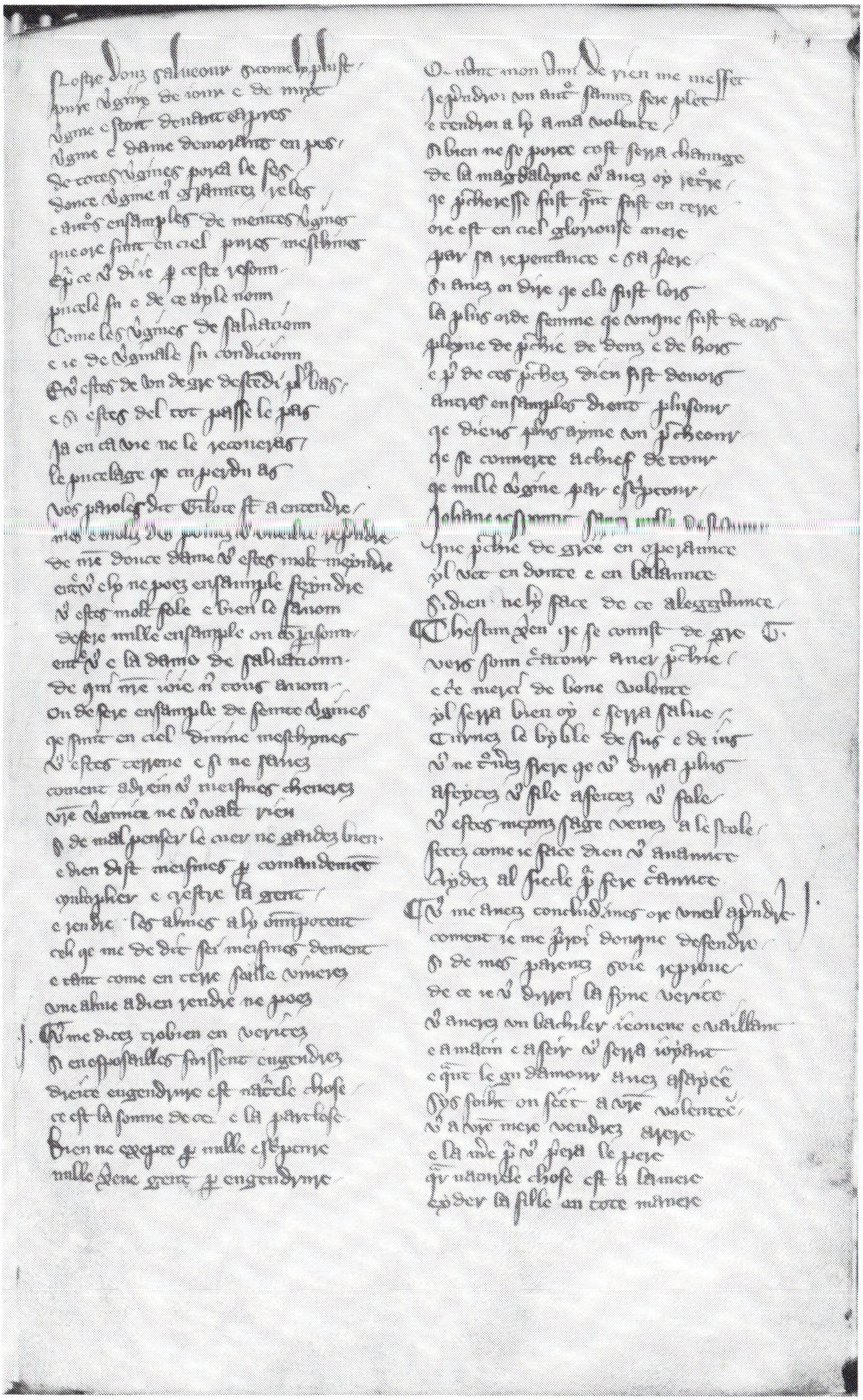

Fig. 88. *Gilote et Johane*. British Museum, MS Harley 2253, fol.67*r (early 14th century).

IV. Marginal Speaker Notation

2. 'Babio' the same method as that used in the previous chapter, Brennan demonstrates that the play demands not only more than one speaking performer, but also several non-speaking performers, the possibility of 'asides', and three adjacent settings for it to make sense to its audience.[61]

As Axton has pointed out, both the indecency of this work (which ends with the castration of Babio) and its grammar point to its having originated within the milieu of a school, something which also applies to *De nuntio sagaci*.[62] As in the case of *De nuntio sagaci*, however, the scribes of *Babio* appear to have turned their backs on the Terentian tradition of placing speaker indications in the text. Instead, when they give these indications, they consistently transfer them out into the margins in a style very similar to that used in the manuscripts of the Poetic Edda, in that the name or abbreviated name (which is often little more than a single letter) is often both preceded and followed by a full stop, occasionally in superscript form. For instance '.B.' is used for Babio and '.f.' for Fodius (see *fig.89*, ll.1, 3, and 5 for example; and especially l.25; see also *fig.90*).

In the Digby 53 manuscript, the speaker indications are consistently placed in the left margin, except on the final page where the text changes into two columns, at which point the indications are moved strangely to the right-hand margin (that is, in the centre of the page). In the first version of *Babio* in the Lincoln Capit.105 manuscript (fols 89v–90v), the text is written in two columns, and the notation is always placed in the outer margins, written in red ink for emphasis.[63] In the Cotton Titus A XX manuscript, the names are placed to the right of the text. The Codex Berol.Phillippicus manuscript has far fewer speaker indications, but when these occur they are placed far out into the left margin, which suggests that many of them may have been lost.[64]

Particularly worthy of attention is that fact that at several points in the Digby 53 manuscript, when two or more changes in speaker take place in one line, the additional speaker indications are moved into the body of the text, and placed in abbreviated form above the new speech as on fols 39v, 41r and 42v (see *fig.90*, markings in left-hand margin, additional markings above the text of fol.39v in l.18 [.**fo.** and .**B.**], l.20 [.**f.** and .**B.**], l.22 [.**fo.**] and l.28 [.**fo.**]). This approach is reminiscent of that employed in the *Codex Bembinus* of Terence's works, and brings to mind the similar predicament

---

[61] See Brennan, *Babio*, pp.9–31, and Dronke, 'Narrative and dialogue', p.113. Brennan's argument is supported by Axton in *European drama*, pp.29–31. All three scholars disagree with Faral's suggestion in *De Babione*, pp.xliv–l, that Babio was a 'poème comique' intended for one performer.

[62] Axton, *European drama*, pp.29–30.

[63] According to Dr M. Bateson of the Hallward Library in the University of Nottingham, the second version of *Babio* in Lincoln Capit.105, fols 117r–118v, seems to be a later copy of the first version of the work contained in the same manuscript, but this second version lacks any marginal speaker notation.

[64] Both the Cotton Titus and Codex Berol.Phillippicus MSS also make use of paragraph markers like those found in the MSS of *La seinte resureccion* and *Gilote et Johane*. The Bodleian 851 MS has no marginal indications.

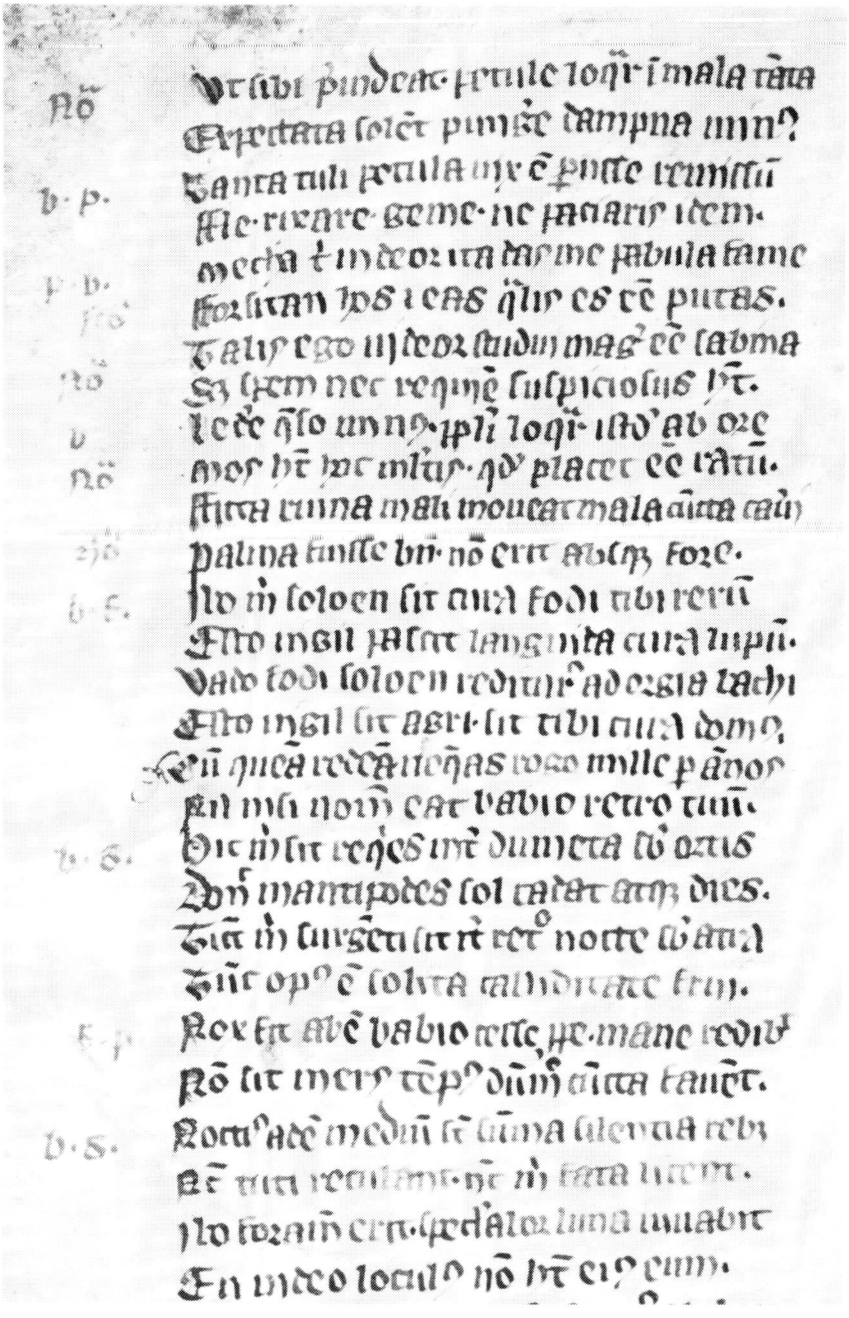

Fig. 89. *Babio. Codex Lincolniensis*, MS Lincoln Capit.105, fol.90v (late 13th/
early 14th century). (Enlargement of the top left half of the folio.)

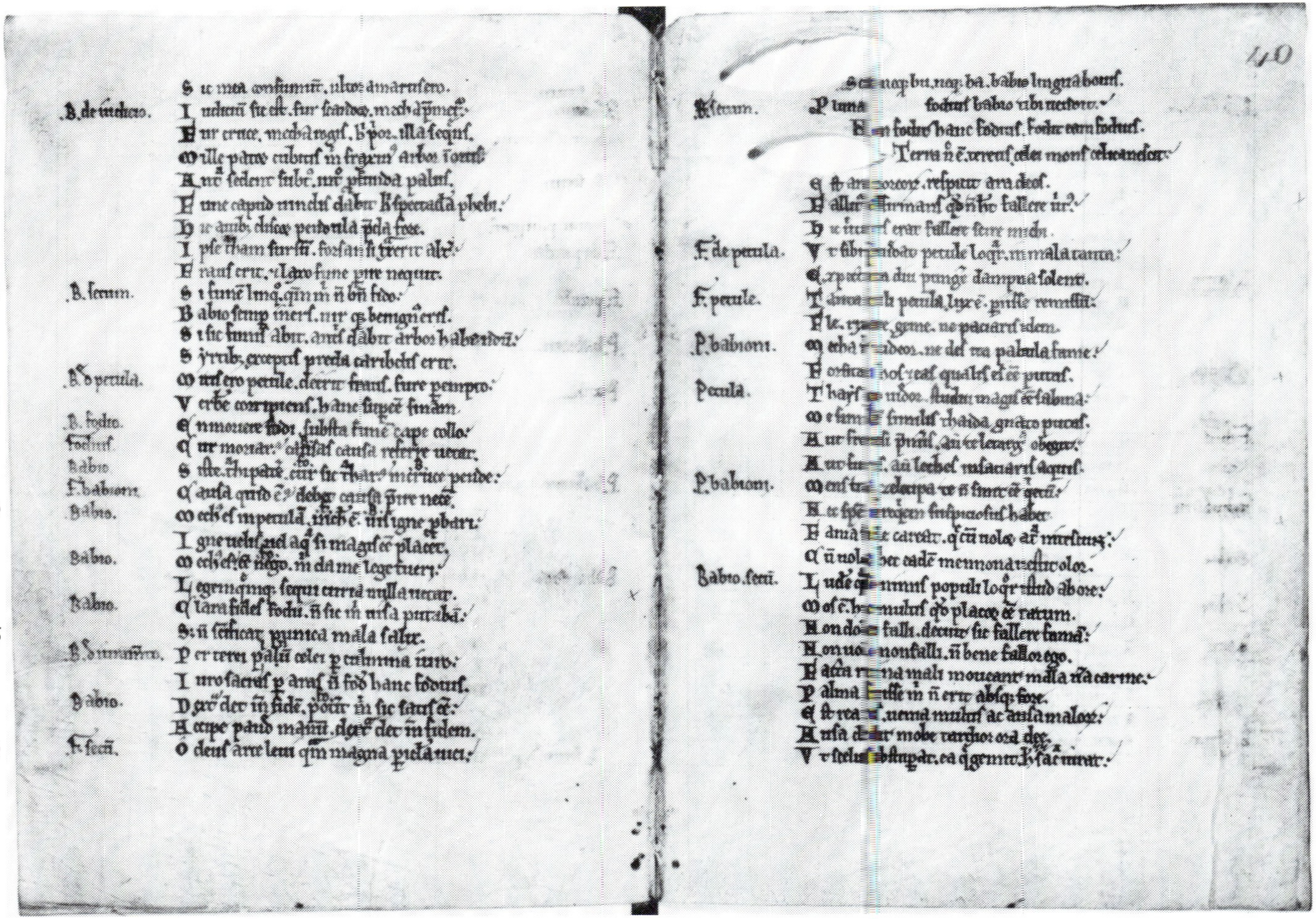

Fig. 90. *Babio*. Oxford, Bodleian, MS Digby 53, fols 39v–40r (late 12th century).

D. The Use of the Margin in Dramatic Manuscripts

faced by the Eddic scribe when dealing with the equally fast repartee of *Hárbarðsljóð*.⁶⁵

3. 'La Seinte Resurreccion'

The main differences between the *Babio* manuscripts and those of the Eddic poems are that the speaker indications in the former lack any verb of speech, but instead are often accompanied by an indication of whom is being spoken to (for example, '**Babio secum**', '**Babio ad femina**' and so on).⁶⁶ Such an approach is commonly found in manuscripts of liturgical drama⁶⁷ and even in the R 58 C and Ny kgl.Saml.235g fragments of *Konungs skuggsjá* (see above, *section B*).

3. 'La Seinte Resureccion'

Written c.1175, and extant in two incomplete Anglo-Norman manuscripts from the latter part of the thirteenth century (BN, f.fr. 902, fols 97ra–98rb, and British Museum, Additional MS 45103), *La seinte resureccion* is a Passion play written in the vernacular possibly in England.⁶⁸ There is little doubt that the work was designed for a full-scale dramatic performance since it is preceded by clear and complex instructions regarding the 'mansions' or settings needed for the production, and demands no less than forty-two performers.

The shorter *Canterbury* manuscript, written at Christ Church monastery in Canterbury, lacks any indications as to who is speaking at any given time. In the slightly more recent *Paris* manuscript from Northern France, however, the names of the speakers are consistently transferred to the outer margins of the text which is in two columns. The names, which soon diminish into two-letter abbreviations (often followed by a superscript full stop), are preceded by a paragraph marker ¶, which is also used to mark the start of each new speech and occasional Biblical glosses that appear in the text (see *fig.91*, outer margins and to the left of the text). Of additional interest here is the fact that the play lacks stage directions, but instead has a

---

⁶⁵ Regarding *Hárbarðsljóð*, see *Chapter III, G.5*. Interestingly enough, similar confusions occur in the MS of the English N-Town plays (fifteenth century), fol.43v, l.3; fol.39v, l.6; and fol.54, l.9, where the scribe faces a similar problem to the scribes of *Hárbarðsljóð* and *Babio*, where two speakers occur on the same line. The problem is resolved in a similar fashion: the name of the speaker of the shorter speech is inserted into the text before the speech, while the main speaker is named in the right-hand margin. See *The N-Town plays*, introduced by Meredith and Kahrl, pp.xix–xxi. See also further below with regard to the MS of *Le mystère d'Adam*.
⁶⁶ In the Digby 53 MS, speakers' names are often repeated every two lines in the longer speeches.
⁶⁷ As in the Freising *Nativity play* (eleventh century); the Strassburg *Play of the Magi* (c.1200); Hilarius' plays, *The raising of Lazarus* and *The play of Daniel* (twelfth century) and more. See Young, *DMC*, II, pp.93–97, pp.64–66, pp.212–218, and pp.276–286.
⁶⁸ The Paris MS would appear to be a copy of an early thirteenth-century MS. Both MSS are incomplete. For the text of the work, comments on the MSS, and a commentary, see *La seinte resureccion*, ed. Jenkins and Manly. Translations and further comments are given in Bevington, *Medieval drama*, pp.122–136, and *Medieval French plays*, ed. and trans. Axton and Stevens, pp.47–70.

IV. Marginal Speaker Notation

4. 'The Harrowing of Hell'
series of narrative passages which are given as part of the text, and are written in the past tense, very much like the prose sections of the Poetic Edda (for example, 'Quant il vindrent devant la cruis,/ Joseph criat od halte voiz ...'). Owing to the practical nature of the work as a whole, and the fact that these passages are also preceded with a ¶ marking (but lack any speaker indication in the margin), most scholars have agreed that the narrative must have been spoken aloud as part of the performance, possibly like the narrative sections of *Dame Sirith* and *Gilote et Johane*.[69]

4. 'The Harrowing of Hell'

The Middle English *Harrowing of Hell* exhibits a number of similar features to *La seinte resureccion*, especially in its use of a narrative prologue and conclusion that appear to have been spoken aloud as part of the performance.[70] This work, which is otherwise totally dialogic, exists in three manuscripts, the most important for the present examination being MS Harley 2253 which also contains the earlier mentioned Interlude, *Gilote et Johane*.

The earliest recension of *The harrowing of Hell* is contained in the late thirteenth century MS Digby 86[71] which lacks speaker indications, but instead has occasional past-tense prose statements such as 'þenne spak him satanas' which occur in the first part of the text.[72] In the two later manuscripts, Harley 2253 (British Museum, MS Harley 2253, fols 55v–56v; early fourteenth century),[73] and the *Auchinleck MS* (National Library of Scotland, Advocates' MS.19.2.1, fols 35vb–37ra; c.1330–1340),[74] such prose statements are deliberately absent after the narrator's initial introduction to Jesus: 'þe he com þere þo seide he,/ asse y shal nouþe telle þe.'[75] In the *Auchinleck MS*, the speaker names, accompanied by a present-tense speech verb (for example, '**Satanas dixit**'), are consistently placed above the speeches in the same style as that found in the manuscripts of dramatic works by the French wandering entertainers (see above, *section C.4*). In the *Harley MS*, these indications, which are underlined and crossed out,[76] are

---

[69] See, for example, Woolf, *English mystery plays*, p.52; and Bevington, *Medieval drama*, pp.122–123: Bevington also raises the possibility that these passages were added for the benefit of the reader. Nonetheless, as Grace Frank notes in *Medieval French drama*, p.89, the fact that the same narrative exists in both MSS suggests that it was probably part of the author's own conception. On use of such paragraph markers in other dramatic works during this period, see above regarding certain MSS of *Babio* (note 64), the MS of *Gilote et Johane* (note 56), and the *Shrewsbury fragments* (note 42).
[70] See Moore, 'The narrator within the performance', 29–34.
[71] MS Digby 86, fols 119r–120v.
[72] *The harrowing of Hell*, ed. Hulme, p.8 (l.71). The texts of all three MSS of *The harrowing of Hell* are contained in Hulme's edition.
[73] See *Facsimile of British Museum MS Harley 2253*, introduced by Ker.
[74] Facsimile in *The Auchinleck manuscript*, introduced by Pearsall and Cunningham.
[75] *The harrowing of Hell*, ed. Hulme, p.5: Harley MS text, ll.41–42.
[76] The same approach is found in the MS of *Querolus*: see note 29 above. Perhaps the crossing out was meant to emphasise that these names should not be read aloud.

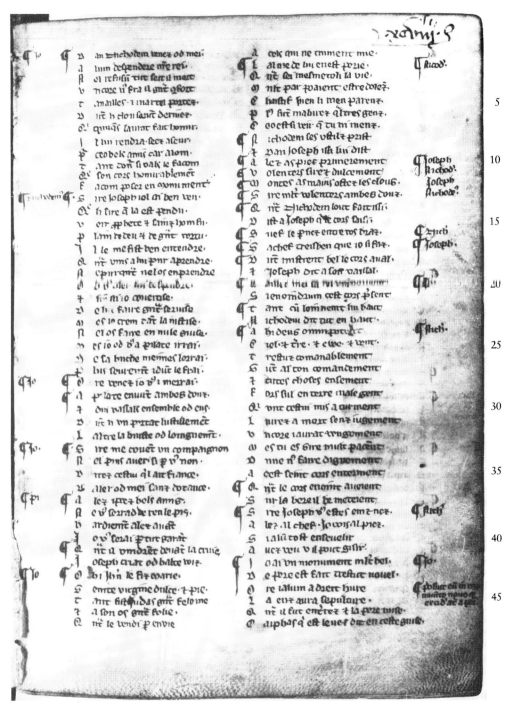

Fig. 91. *La seinte resureccion*. Paris, BN, f.fr. 902, fol.98r (late 13th century).

IV. Marginal Speaker Notation

5. *'Le Mystère d'Adam'*

transferred to the margins. On fols 55vb and 56va–b, they are consistently placed to the right of the two-columned text, usually (but not always) in line with the end of the previous speeches, something which perhaps suggests a development of the widespread manuscript tradition commented on earlier in which new speakers' names were placed in the text in the available space at the end of previous speeches.[77] On fol.56r, however, the notation is placed in the outer margins of the folio (see *fig*.92, left, ll.6 and 15 for example) in the same way as in the Paris manuscript of *La seinte resureccion*, the right-hand indications being placed at a level slightly higher than the line on which the speech begins. Here, in a similar form to the manuscripts of the Eddic poems, the first two notes are accompanied by a verb of speech ('**Sathan ait**' and '**Dominus ait**'), but after that most of the names are given alone in abbreviated form (for example, **Do·** [Dominus] and **Sath·** [Sathan]).

In the past, it was argued on the basis of the narrative that *The harrowing of Hell* must have been presented by a solo performer.[78] However, in recent years, scholars have pointed out that both the wordings and the practical demands of the text make it more probable that this work, too, was acted as a play or interlude by several actors.[79] As with the manuscripts of *Babio*, the presence of speaker indications in the *Auchinleck MS* of *The harrowing of Hell* emphasises that they were not a mere later addition, but were considered a necessary accompaniment to the text.

5. *'Le Mystère d'Adam'*

The closest parallels to the marginal speaker indications in the Edda manuscripts are found in *Le mystère d'Adam*, an Anglo-Norman religious drama dealing with the Fall of Man and the prophecies of the coming of Christ. The earliest extant religious drama to have been composed entirely in the vernacular, this work is preserved in a single, incomplete paper manuscript written in the middle of the twelfth century: Bibliothèque Municipale de Tours, MS 927, fols 20r–40r.[80]

As with *La seinte resureccion*, there is little doubt that this work was meant to be performed because it commences with clear instructions as to the stage setting, the costumes, and even the method of presentation. The

---

[77] See above, notes 35 and 42, and *fig*.76.
[78] See Chambers, *The mediaeval stage*, I, p.83, and II, p.74.
[79] See Revard, 'Gilote et Johane', 128–129, and Moore, 'The narrator within the performance', 21 and 28–34. As Moore points out (32), in performance the dialogic nature of the text engenders difficulties in comprehension that can only be solved by the use of more than one performer.
[80] A complete facsimile of the MS is provided in *Le mystère d'Adam*, ed. Sletsjöe. For translations and valuable comments on the text, see, for example, Muir, *Adam*, pp.149–204; Bevington, *Medieval drama*, pp.78–121; Studer, ed., *Le mystère d'Adam*, pp.xxix–xxxii; and Aebischer, ed., *Le mystère d'Adam*, introduction. According to Muir, p.155, the MS was probably written c.1150, possibly in England, but the work seems to have been composed originally in south-eastern France.

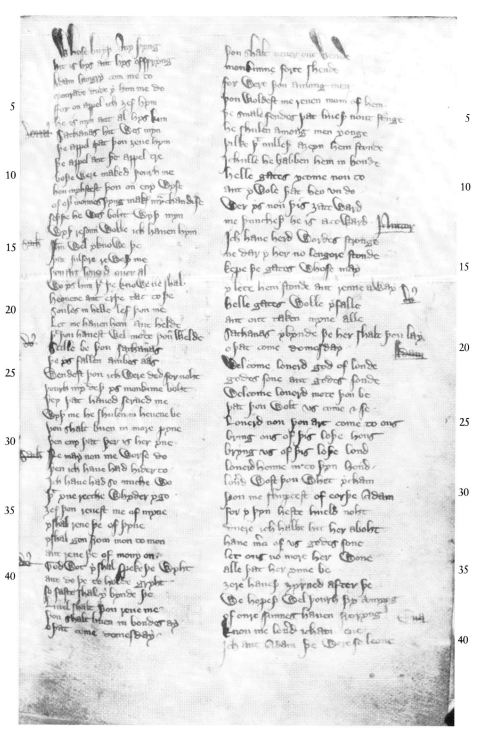

Fig. 92. *The harrowing of Hell*. British Museum, MS Harley 2253, fol.56r (early 14th century).

IV. Marginal Speaker Notation

5. *'Le Mystère d'Adam'*

likelihood is that such a performance, like that of *La seinte resureccion*, would have taken place outside a church building. Both plays, however, would seem to be rooted in the vernacular tradition rather than that of the liturgy. This is apparent not only from the variety and realism of the dialogue and the psychological depth of the characters, but also because the story of the Genesis does not seem to have formed part of Latin liturgical drama at that time.[81]

The manuscript of *Le mystère d'Adam* was written by a single scribe, who uses two very different approaches as regards the system of line division and the placing of the speaker notation.[82] At first, he presents the work as a solid, unbroken text, the names of the speakers appearing within the text in a similar fashion to the Terence and *Elucidarius* manuscripts, and those of Gregory's *Dialogues* in Scandinavia. The names of the speakers are given in full when they first occur, but after that they are reduced to single initials which are preceded and followed by full stops in the same way as that encountered in the Eddic texts (for example, '.D.' for *diable*, and '.a.' for 'Adam'; see *fig.93*, l.6). The most valuable point about this section of the manuscript is that it proves that the speaker notation itself was not a later addition as could be the case in certain of the texts mentioned above such as *Semiramis*, *Gilote et Johane* and *Dame Sirith*.

On fol.25v, however, the scribe adopts a new system of writing in which each line of verse is written separately unless a new speaker takes over mid-line, in which case the second half-line is usually also written separately. At the same time, there is a near-consistent transference of speaker indications into the right-hand margin (see *fig.94*, ll.8, 13, 14, 15 and so on).[83] As with much of *The harrowing of Hell*, however, the speakers' initials are placed in line with the end of the *previous* speech, rather than the new one.

Of particular interest is the section of dialogue written on fols 33v–34r, where the scribe temporarily drops the system of beginning a new line in the manuscript whenever a new speech commences in mid-line in the verse. As a result, he immediately runs into similar problems to those encountered by the scribes of the *Codex Bembinus* manuscript of Terence's works; the Digby 53 version of *Babio*; and the *Codex Regius Harbárðsljóð*: in short, there is sometimes a need for two speaker indications on the same line. When such occurs here, the scribe of *Le mystère d'Adam* resorts to exactly the same approach as that used by the scribes of the manuscripts

---

[81] See Axton and Stephens, *Medieval French plays*, pp.xiv–xvi.
[82] Aebischer, ed., *Le mystère d'Adam*, pp.13–14.
[83] The one obvious exception occurs in the last three lines on fol.32r where the names of 'Chaim' and 'abel' (twice) are again placed within the text in a somewhat puzzling fashion. Here, momentarily, the system of writing single verse lines separately is dropped. The name of 'abel', who speaks the first line here is placed slightly apart on the right of the first line (but not in the margin) in the middle of the speech. 'Chaim''s name then appears in full before his answer which lasts two lines. His speech is then followed by the 'abel''s name (in full). This indication, however, applies to Abel's speech which follows on the next page. Perhaps the confusion here stems from the scribe copying an earlier text in which the names were placed within the text, preceding the speeches.

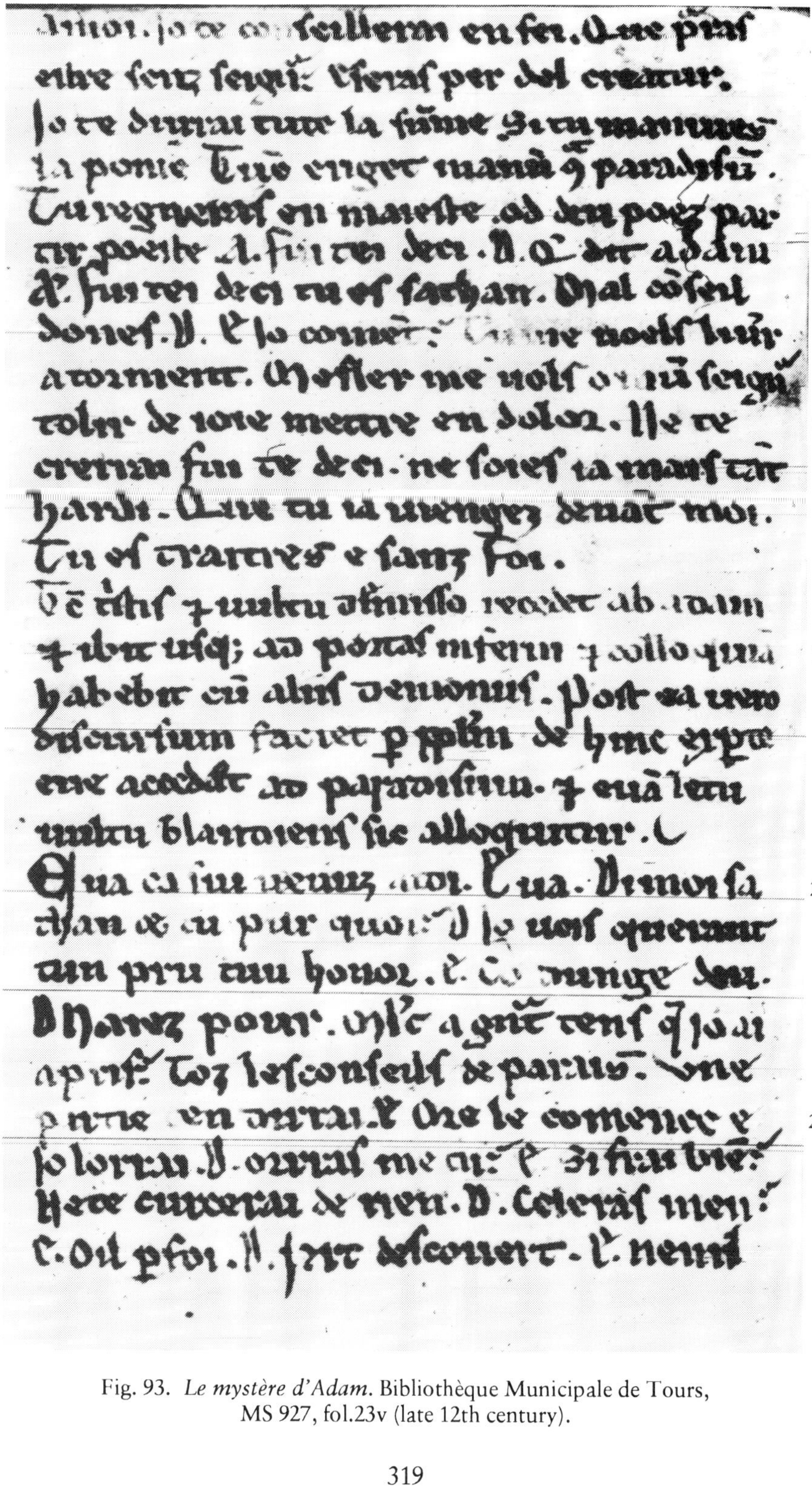

Amor, jo te conseillerai en fei. One plus
estre sentz sequit. Eseras per dol creatur.
Jo te dirrai tute la sume. Si tu manuues
la pome. Tu iès en grant mand ǧ paradysu.
Tu regneras en maieste. od deu poez par- 5
tir poeste. A. fui tei deci. D. O. dit adam
R. fui tei deci tu es sathan. Dial cosail
dones. D. E lo comet?... ne uols huy
atormentr. Oster me uols ... mi seign
tolir de ioie mettre en dolor. Ne te 10
creirai. fui te deci. ne soies tan mais tant
hardi. Ains tu la uengez deuant moi.
Tu es traitres e sanz fei.
Dē tc̄ ifs ꝑ uultu ōmisso redeat ab adam
ꝯ ibit usq; ad portas mferm ꝯ collo qui a 15
habebit cū aliis demonibus. Post ea uero
discursium faciet p̄ pplm de hinc expre
ire accedit ad paroisium. ꝯ eua leticia
uultu blandiens sic alloquatur. C
Eua ca iūs uenez moi. Eua. Dimei sa- 20
than de ce pur quoi? D. Jo uois quere un
tun prou tun honor. E. co mange deu.
Maunt pour. un lo a grā tens ǧ jo ai
aprīs. Toz les conseuls de parais. vne
partie en dirrai. E. Ore le comence y 25
jo l orrai. D. orras me tu? E. Si fiaubiē
He te curocerai de rien. D. Celeras mei.
E. Oil pfoi. D. frat descouert. E. neul

Fig. 93. *Le mystère d'Adam.* Bibliothèque Municipale de Tours, MS 927, fol.23v (late 12th century).

IV. Marginal Speaker Notation

6. The origins and provenance of the system of marginal speaker notation

mentioned above:[84] The indication for the second speaker is placed in the text itself, immediately preceding the relevent words of the speech (see *fig.94*, l.9 [.c.], l.23 [.a. and .c.] and l.27 [c. and .a.] for example). Apart from this passage, the aforementioned system of initials in the right-hand margin is retained.[85]

The manuscript of *Le mystère d'Adam* presents a picture of a scribe facing similar dilemmas to those faced by the scribe of the AM 748 manuscript (or perhaps the scribe of the manuscript he was copying) and adopting similar solutions. For the works being dealt with, it was felt to be wrong or inappropriate to place the speaker indications within the body of the text. For one reason or another, the margin was considered to be a more correct setting for the indications, perhaps because it obviously detached them from the text, at the same time making them more visible for the performer(s) or reciter(s).

6. The Origins and Provenance of the System of Marginal Speaker Notation

On the basis of the evidence available, it is possible to draw several tentative conclusions regarding the use of marginal speaker notation in manuscripts. First of all, as pointed out above, marginal notation would seem to be limited to works that were performed in some dramatic fashion, and appears to represent, in part, a development the older system of placing speakers names in the text at the end of previous speeches. This, however, would not totally explain the use of the left-hand margin (as in the manuscript of *Semiramis*), an approach that might have roots in much older dramatic manuscripts, now lost, which took the form of the *Codex Bembinus*. The use of outer margins, like that found in *Le seinte resureccion* and the Edda manuscripts, would be a development from one, or both, of the above approaches.

The system would appear to have gained ground during the late thirteenth century when the Eddic poems were recorded, and seems to have been centred in Northern France and England. Indeed, the emphasis is on the latter area where marginal speaker notation would appear to represent a stage on the way towards the more regulated system employed in the several of the English cycles of mystery plays from the later Middle Ages (see above, *section C.1*). It is also noteworthy that the system of marginal notation differs essentially from those methods used in most manuscripts of Terence's plays, and in those containing liturgical drama. It appears to have developed in a schools milieu,[86] and to have been adopted primarily by writers interested in working in the vernacular, and with connections to

---

[84] See further above, *sections C.2 and D.2*, and also note 65.
[85] The earlier system of new lines for each speaker is taken up again in the dialogue on fols 39r–39v.
[86] See, for example, Thomson, 'Latin "elegiac comedy" ', pp.54–55 and pp.62–63, on the provenance of works like *Babio* and *De nuntio sagaci*.

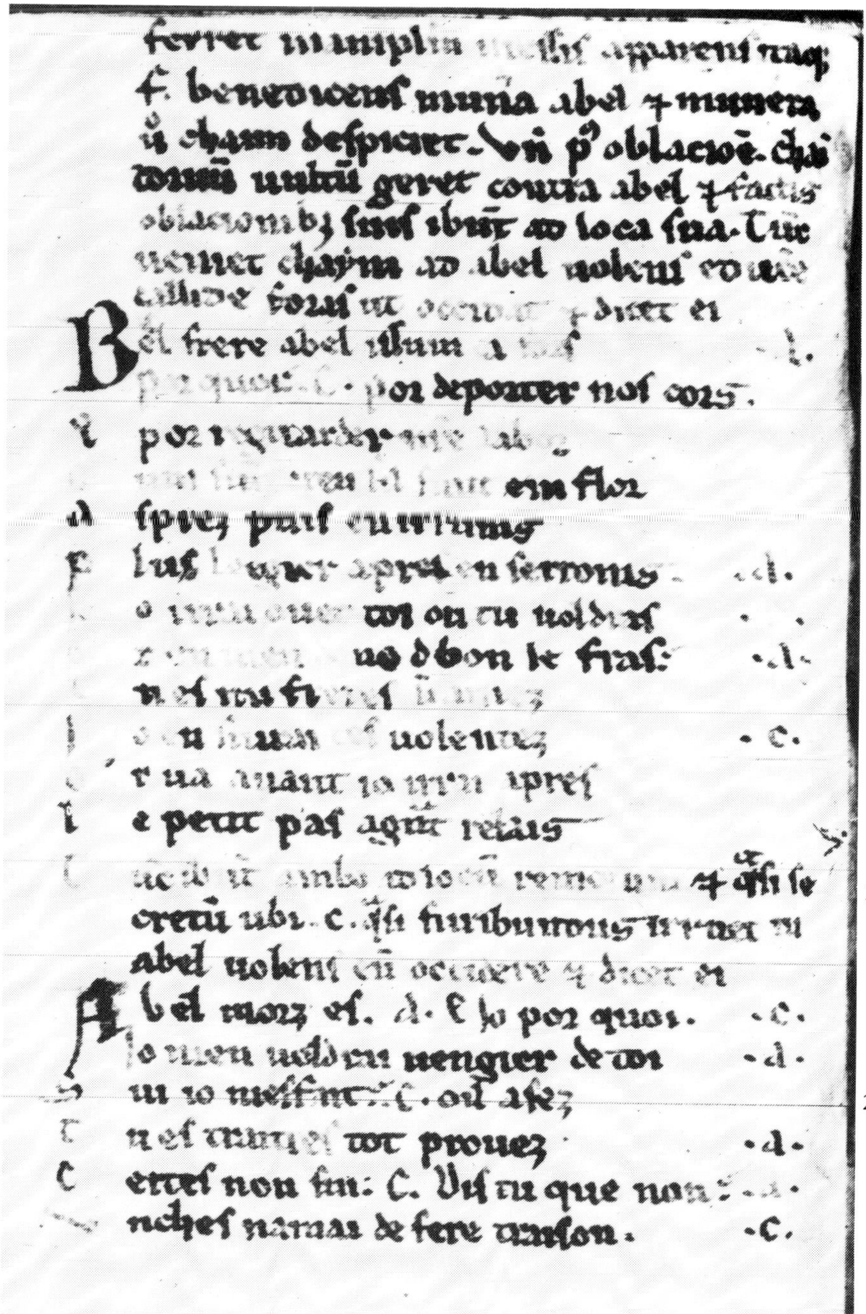

ferret maniplis [...] apparent nsq̃
f. benedicens munia abel ⁊ munera
ŭ chaym despicet. Vñ p oblacõe chi
toīmi unltū geret contra abel ⁊ fratris
oblacioibj suis ibiit ad loca sua. Tūc
veniet chaym ad abel volens co[...]
[...] [...] [...] dicet ei

Bel frere abel oiium a [...]
[...] quoi. C. poi depoiter nos cors.

poi [...]
[...] [...] en flor
spies pail eu [...]
lus [...] apres en serrons   .d.
o [...] tos [...] noldras   ...
[...] no d bon le fias: .d.
n el [...] [...]
[...] [...] uolentus   . c.
r na anaīt io [...] ipres
e petit pas agūt relais
[...] ambs coioss reine [...] ⁊ [...] se
cretii ubi. c. ssi furiburrons [...]
abel volens eū occidere ⁊ dicet ei

Abel mors es. d. e io poi quoi.   .c.
Io men volden venger de toi   .d.
ui io nessu[...] C. ou ses
n el [...] tot proues   .d.
eties non su: C. Uis tu que non   ...
[...] namai de fere rançon.   .c.

Fig. 94. *Le mystère d'Adam*. Bibliothèque Municipale de Tours,
MS 927, fol.33v (late 12th century).

7. Differences from the Edda MSS

popular and professional forms of entertainment, like that reflected in *Dame Sirith* and the *Interludium de clerico et puella*.

The links between the above and the dialogic poems of the Edda might appear to be somewhat vague. However, the dialogic poems also belonged to a popular vernacular tradition, and appear to demand some form of dramatic presentation. The humour in *Lokasenna* and *Hárbarðsljóð* would certainly have attracted the readers of the *comediæ*, and in very general terms, it would be possible to draw a parallel between the storyline of *De nuntio sagaci*, *Dame Sirith* and *Interludium de clerico et puella* on one hand, and *Skírnismál* on the other. All of these works tell of a lovelorn male achieving his aim with a virtuous lady through the help of a middle party. Furthermore, *Skírnismál* is also distinguished for its elements of what appears to be ancient magic ritual, similar to that encountered in *Semiramis*. One can understand an Icelandic scribe or editor who had studied abroad drawing vague parallels between the material in question, both in terms of theme and methods of presentation.

7. *Differences from the Edda Manuscripts*

It might be said that in spite of the similarities in scribal method and material mentioned above, there is one central difference between the notation used in most of the manuscripts from France and England and that accompanying the Eddic poems, namely that the Edda notation also includes the verb of speech (for example, '.l.q.':'Loki *qvað*') given in the past tense like the prose interpolations.

Concerning this minor feature, it is necessary to keep the following points in mind. Firstly, as has been noted in *Chapter III, D*, there is good reason to believe that the compilers of the Edda manuscripts were attempting in places to transform the poems into a chronological narrative in which the prose provides continuity and explanation. The verb of speech is thus natural in such a saga-like setting.[87] Similarly, as has also been noted in *section B*, there is a certain tendency reflected in the Scandinavian manuscripts of the various theological and moral dialogues of adding a verb of speech, and more, to the name of the speaker when space allows. This is illustrated particularly well in the cases of the two *Viðræður líkams ok sálar*, the two *Æðru senna ok hugrekki* manuscripts, the *Dialogues* fragments, and also in certain manuscripts of the *Konungs skuggsjá*. In the case of the marginal notation in the Edda manuscripts, there was obviously enough space to add a brief note of a speech verb in the same way.

Furthermore, the use of the speech verb certainly does not rule out the comparability of the relevant sections of the *Codex Regius* and AM 748 manuscripts to European dramatic manuscripts from this period. As has been pointed out, all three manuscripts of *The harrowing of Hell* use verbs of speech in places, and the same phenomenon is often encountered in

---

[87] See, however, *Chapter III*, note 98.

D. The Use of the Margin in Dramatic Manuscripts

manuscripts of liturgical Latin dramas which commonly employ verbs of speech, albeit most commonly in the present subjunctive or future (the latter relatively rare form being used consistently in the plays of Hilarius).[88] These indications, for words like *respondeant*, *respondeat*, and *responsio* are often given in the form of an abbreviated single 'R', much like the Icelandic 'q' for 'qvað'.

7. Differences from the Edda MSS

As has been shown above, the use of the past tense was certainly not alien to medieval dramatic works either. *De nuntio sagaci*, *Dame Sirith*, *Gilote et Johane* and *The harrowing of Hell* all contain passages of narrative in past tense that appear to have been spoken aloud. The past tense is also used in the certain speech indications (as in the Digby 86 *Harrowing of Hell*) and in the stage directions of plays like *La seinte resureccion* and the longer Passion play contained in the *Carmina Burana* manuscript.[89] Indeed, as late as the fifteenth century, this approach is found in the early Swedish play *De uno peccatore qui promeruit gratiam* ('The play of the sinner who found mercy'), which employs a strange mixture of both the past and the present. Here, for example, one encounters stage directions like 'vratislaus svarade', and 'Her sätther han vdden pa brystit tha gik jomfru maria fram ok fik om hans hender ok sagde swa . . .'[90] The same applies to the Brome mystery play *Abraham and Isaac* from the same period: 'Her Abraham drew his stroke and þe angell toke he sword in hys hond soddenly', and 'Here Abraham leyd a cloth over Ysaacys face thus seyying . . .'[91] The Edda manuscripts' past-tense verbs of speech are therefore hardly out of place in terms of medieval dramatic traditions. Indeed, the above evidence reopens the possibility suggested by Phillpotts that some of the terse prose 'asides' in the dialogic poems of the Edda might be regarded as the counterparts of stage directions in a play.[92] Yet it might also be remembered that the narrative sections of *La seinte resureccion*, if they were not a later addition for readers or performers, were probably meant to be read aloud by a narrator.[93] Considering the dramatic traditions of the time, it cannot be ruled out that the same thing occurred with the dialogic poems of the Edda.

---

[88] See Young, *DMC*, II, pp.212–218, pp.276–286, and pp.338–341.
[89] See below, note 93.
[90] 'Vratislaus answered'/ 'Here he places the point (of the knife) against his breast; then the Virgin Mary went forward and took his hands, and said.' MS: AM 191 fol. (The Askaby Codex), fols 89r–93r. For text, see *Sveriges dramatiska litteratur*, ed. Klemming, pp.1–6. Regarding the background of this play, see also Wright, 'The oldest Swedish play', 49–72.
[91] *Non-cycle plays and fragments* (1970), ed. Davis, pp.51–52. Another work that has a tendency to slip into the past tense in stage directions is the fifteenth century morality play, *The castle of perseverance* (Folger Library MS Va 354). See Bevington, *Medieval drama*, pp.799–900, and notes p.1069 (regarding ll.1766–1863).
[92] Phillpotts, *The Elder Edda*, pp.106–108.
[93] See above *section D.3*. Narrative passages of this kind are also encountered in the eleventh-century *Nativity play* from Freising, and twelfth-century Beauvais *Danielis ludus*, and the thirteenth-century text of the longer Passion play in the *Carmina Burana* from Bavaria, where past-tense narrative is accompanied by musical notation. See Young,

IV. *Marginal Speaker Notation*

E. *Scandinavian Contact with European Dramatic Manuscripts*

1. *Literary Contacts with England and France*

Considering the degree of contact between England, northern France and western Scandinavia (particularly Norway)[94] during the period in question, there would be nothing against Scandinavian scribes having gained the idea of marginal notation from abroad after coming into contact with manuscripts of the kind described above.

There is no doubt that Scandinavian scribes were influenced by English and Anglo-Norman paleography in other ways during the twelfth and thirteenth centuries.[95] It is also certain that the Scandinavians encountered, and were attracted by popular works from the area in question like *Babio* and *De nuntio sagaci*. During the thirteenth and fourteenth centuries, numerous Anglo-Norman works were being translated into Old Norse in the scriptoria of Norway and Iceland, among them *Alexanders saga Tristrams saga*, and the *Strengleikar* collection of the *lais* of Marie de France.[96] There was also interest in the Latin *comediæ* that came from the same area. This is confirmed by the existence of a translation of *Pamphilus* which is found in one late thirteenth-century Norwegian manuscript.[97] *Pamphilus* commences as a first person account and becomes predominantly dialogic, and, as has been mentioned above (*sections D.1 and D.2*) has close links with the tradition that which gave birth to *Babio*, *De nuntio sagaci*, and *Dame Sirith*. Like these other works, *Pamphilus* would appear

---

DMC, I, pp.432–437, and II, pp.92–97 and pp.290–301. The effectiveness of these passages in dramatic performance has recently been demonstrated in the performances of *Danielis Ludus* by the Polish company, *Bornus Consort*, in Europe during 1989–1990. On the question of the narrative passages in medieval drama, see Dronke, 'Narrative and drama', pp.105–107, and Moore, 'The narrator within the performance', passim.

[94] Naturally Norway and Iceland were also closely linked in more ways than one. Influences in writing were mutual, and at this time scribes and manuscripts seem to have been commonly on the move between the two countries, particularly through the influence of the church. This has led to a number of open-ended disputes about the origins of particular MSS, including that of the *Codex Regius*. See, for example, Seip, 'Har nordmenn skrevet opp Edda-diktningen?', 3–33, and 'Om et norsk skriftlig grunnlag', 81–207. See also Einar Ólafur Sveinsson's comments on Seip's theories in *Íslenzkar bókmenntir*, pp.188–189.

[95] See Seip, *Palæografi*, p.13 and pp.68–70.

[96] See Leach, *Angevin Britain*, pp.382–383, for a list of works probably imported to Norway from England or France during this period. See also Olsen, 'De høviske litteratur', pp.102–117; Jónas Kristjánsson, *Eddas and sagas*, pp.314–331; and most recently, Tulinius, 'Kynjasögur', pp.195–217.

[97] MS: Uppsala, De la Gardie 4–7, fols 3r–5v. This MS also contains *Elís saga*, *Strengleikar* and one of the fragments of the *Æðru senna ok Hugrekki*. The text and a facsimile are given in Holm-Olsen, ed., *Den gammelnorske oversettelsen av Pamphilus*. As Holm-Olsen shows, this MS was apparently written in the late thirteenth century, probably at the monastery of Lyse, near Bergen, which had close contact with Fountains Abbey in England. *Elís saga*, for example, was translated by a Bishop Roðbert who might have been one of the abbots of Fountains Abbey (Holm-Olsen, pp.83–84). This version of *Pamphilus* is fragmentary, and contains no speaker indications of any kind.

E. *Scandinavian Contact with European Dramatic Manuscripts*

to have been performed dramatically, if only in France during in the twelfth century.[98]

The interest in this kind of Latin material is supported furthermore by an account regarding Klængr Þorsteinsson, later bishop of Skálholt, who was reprimanded by Bishop Jón Ögmundarson for reading *Ovidius de arte amandi* while studying at the cathedral of Hólar in the early twelfth century.[99] The more ascetic men of the church, like the fanatical Bishop Jón, might have despised these works, but for others they held attractions, not only for their themes, but also for their literary qualities. Indeed, the romantic comedies of Terence were esteemed in European monastic schools for similar reasons.[100]

2. Knowledge of the concepts of drama

2. Scandinavian Knowledge of the Concepts of Drama

There can be little doubt that learned Icelanders were just as aware of the classical concepts and themes of drama as their European counterparts. They must have also known of practical performances in Europe during the early Middle Ages. Like so many other academic establishments in Europe at this time, the libraries of the Icelandic monasteries contained copies of the *Etymologiæ* of Isidore of Seville (570–636), a work which includes essentially historically correct definitions of the words *tragoedi*, *comoedi*, *mimi*, *histriones*, *scena* and *theatrum*, all of which were closely associated with the classical theatre.[101] Another popular book existing in both Norwegian and Icelandic libraries was Honorius Augustodunesis' highly influential *Gemma animæ* (c.1100) which at one point deliberately compares the Catholic Mass to a classical tragedy: after explaining the meaning of tragedy by stating that 'It is known that those who recited tragedies in the theatres represented to the people, by their gestures, the actions of conflicting forces,'[102] Honorius goes on to state that the priest can be seen as a 'tragicus' who acts in 'theatro ecclesiae'.[103]

That the Icelanders must have understood this kind of terminology and must have been well aware of the existence of dramatic performers is

---

[98] See also Roy, 'Arnulf of Orleans', 258–266.
[99] See *Jóns saga helga hin elzta*, in *Biskupa sögur*, (1858–1878), I, pp.165–166. See further Sverrir Tómasson 'Veraldleg sagnaritun', pp.272–273.
[100] See above, note 26.
[101] Isidore of Seville, 'De theatro', in *Etymologiæ*, Book XVIII, chs 42–49, in *Patriologiæ*, series Latina, LXXXII, pp.657–659. The *Etymologiæ* is named in the registers of both Hólar (1396) and Viðey (1397). See *Diplomatarium Islandicum*, III, p.613, and IV, p.110. Regarding the quality of Isidore's definitions, see Marshall, 'Theatre in the Middle Ages', 8–12.
[102] 'Sciendum quod hi qui tragoedias in theatris recitabant, actus pugnantium gestibus populo repraesentabant'. English translation by Bevington, in *Medieval drama*, p.9.
[103] Honorius Augustodunensis, 'De Tragoediis' in *Gemma Animæ*, Book I, ch.83, in *Patrologiæ*, series Latina, CLXXII, p.570. Honorius's book is named amongst other works in the Viðey register of 1397: see *Diplomatarium Islandicum*, IV, p.111. Regarding the popularity of the *Gemma animæ* in Norway during the period in question, see further Gjerløw, *Adoratio Crucis*, p.105.

IV. Marginal Speaker Notation

3. Knowledge of European liturgical drama

suggested by the translation of Honorius' *Elucidarius* (see above, *section B*). Here, for example, it is stated that entertainers ('ioculatores'), translated as 'leikarar' ('players'), are doomed to abide in Hell: 'Have entertainers/ actors any hope? – None, because they are the servants of the Devil and, as it is written, those who mock will be received with mockery' ('Hava leikarar nøkora vonn? – Enga þvi at þeir ero þionar fiandans ok taka þeir sem melt er haðvng er haðong veita').[104] The translator clearly understood what *ioculatores* meant, and simultaneously expected the readers of the book to know what he meant by *leikarar*, since no additional glosses are provided in the extant translations. Furthermore, the readers must have understood why *leikarar* were worthy of such condemnation.

3. *Scandinavian Knowledge of European Liturgical Drama*

Even if some of the terms used in the aforementioned books were not associated by readers with contemporary practical dramatic activities, it is near certain that many Scandinavian students who went abroad must have come into contact not only with the works of Terence, but also with practical drama of various kinds in the churches, monasteries and town squares of Europe. Among these students from Iceland, it is possible to mention influential figures such as Sæmundr Sigfússon (1056–1135) who is assumed to have studied in Paris or the Rhineland,[105] and the Skálholt bishops, Ísleifr Gizurarson and his son Gizurr, who studied in Saxony, all of them during the eleventh century at a time when liturgical drama was in its earliest stages.[106] Þorlákr Þórhallsson, another bishop of Skálholt, spent six years studying in Paris and Lincoln c.1160, at the time when the earliest religious plays in the vernacular such as *Le mystère d'Adam* and *La seinte*

---

[104] *Elucidarius*, ed. Firchow and Grimstad, p.109. Regarding the question of professional *leikarar* in Scandinavia, see the *Appendix*.
[105] *Íslendingabók*, p.21, states that Sæmundr returned from 'Frakkland', Gunnlaugr Leifsson's *Jóns saga hins helga* (*Biskupa sögur* [1858–1878], I, pp.227–228) merely mentioning that Sæmundr was 'í útlöndum' ('abroad') and was visited by Jón Ögmundarson 'þar sem hann var' ('where he was'). The only mention of Paris occurs in the sixteenth-century MS of *Oddverja annáll*, p.471, which refers to Sæmundr's return in 1077. Regarding the actual location of Sæmundr's schooling, which might have been in the Rhineland, see further Foote, 'Aachen, Lund, Hólar', pp.114–118. This article as a whole (pp.101–120) contains a detailed and valuable examination of the subject of Icelandic students studying in mainland Europe during the Middle Ages.
[106] Ísleifr studied at Herford ('Herfurða') c.1030–1040, and his son (b.1042) studied in the same area somewhat later: see *Kristni saga*, *Húngrvaka*, and *Jóns saga helga hin elzta*, in *Biskupa sögur* (1858–1878), I, p.27, pp.60–61, p.66, p.151 and p.153. See also Sverrir Tómasson, *Formálar*, pp.19–20, for further information regarding the sources and variations in this material. It might be noted that Herford had close links with the monastery of Hildesheim which has provided a manuscript containing two of the earliest plays of St Nicholas from the eleventh or twelfth century. See Young, *DMC*, II, pp.311–316, and pp. 324–330. It is also worth bearing in mind that Hildesheim and Gandersheim (where Hrotsvitha had been based in the late tenth century) are both named as being on one of the main routes used by Icelandic pilgrims going to Rome in the mid-twelfth century: Foote, 'Aachen, Lund, Hólar', p.118.

E. Scandinavian Contact with European Dramatic Manuscripts

resureccion were being written and performed.[107] Paris, by this time, was surrounded by cathedrals and monasteries like those at Beauvais, Rouen and Laon, all of which were producing mature forms of liturgical drama. Lincoln houses one of the extant manuscripts of *Babio*, and according to Woolf, quite possibly had its own Easter play by the time of Þorlákr's visit.[108]

3. Knowledge of European liturgical drama

Less information is available regarding Norwegian students, but it would appear that there was even greater contact between Norway and England. Indeed, Leach infers that numerous Norwegian students must have studied in England during the twelfth and thirteenth centuries.[109]

A majority of the early Icelandic monasteries and abbeys (those at Þingeyrar, Þverá, Hítadalur, Kirkjubær and Reynisstaður) were Benedictine. It is clear that the tradition of liturgical drama flourished particularly within this order, and that close communications existed between the various Benedictine and Augustine monasteries in Europe at this time.[110] Furthermore, a number of European clerics (many from England) spent time working in Norway and Iceland during the period in question, men who would naturally have carried not only manuscripts but also the knowledge of their own experiences of dramatic works and activities.[111] Indeed, up until the end of the thirteenth century, the Norwegian church appears to have been closer to the English church than to that of any other country,[112] and had been reorganised in 1152 at the hands of an Englishman, Nicholas Breakspeare, then Cardinal Archbishop of Albano.[113] Other close ties existed between the Benedictine monastery of Holm near Trondheim in Norway, the Norwegian crown itself, and the monk,

---

[107] See *Saga Þorláks biskups hin elzta* and *Þorláks saga helga hin yngri*, in *Biskupa sögur* (1858–1878), I, p.92 and p.267. According to Sverrir Tómasson, in *Formálar*, p.23, Þorlákr possibly spent his time in Paris at the monastery of St Victor. Þorlákr was followed to England by his nephew, Páll Jónsson, who possibly stayed at the same institutions. See *Páls saga biskups*, in *Biskupa sögur* (1858–1878), I, p.127.

[108] See Woolf, *The English mystery plays*, pp.18–19. As Woolf points out (p.14), Lincoln was under strong influence from Rouen which had a tradition of liturgical drama dating back to the early twelfth century, if not before. Evidence also points to an Easter play having existed in the Benedictine monastery of Eynsham before 1196. Eynsham was under the patronage of the Bishop of Lincoln, and as Woolf points out (p.18), 'it seems likely that Eynsham adopted an Easter play through the influence of Lincoln.' Nonetheless, the first definite proof that Lincoln was producing drama does not appear until the early fourteenth century.

[109] Leach notes in *Angevin Britain*, p.101, that as late as 1309, there is a record of an absent Norwegian canon being engaged in study in England.

[110] See Young, *DMC*, I–II, and in particular, Wright, *The dissemination of the liturgical drama*, passim, for a detailed examination of the influence of, and relationship between, the various institutions and orders in France during the Middle Ages.

[111] See Leach, *Angevin Britain*, pp.85–113, and Hans Bekker-Nielsen, 'Den ældste tid', p.14.

[112] Leach, *Angevin Britain*, p.85. From the end of the thirteenth century, France took over as the main sphere of influence on the Norwegian church: Leach, pp.108–109.

[113] Leach, *Angevin Britain*, p.89.

3. Knowledge of European liturgical drama

Matthew Paris, who came to Norway c.1248–1251 from St Albans which probably had a growing tradition of liturgical drama from the twelfth century onwards.[114]

In the case of Iceland, there seems to have been originally a closer relationship with Saxony and the Rhineland than France, influences from France being filtered through England, Lotharingia and the Rhineland rather than coming directly from France itself. This, however, altered after c.1150.[115] This variation in influence is partly reflected in the places in which the Icelanders studied, and also in the various nationalities of the foreign clerics said to have visited Iceland during the early Middle Ages. Among those mentioned in *Íslendingabók* and *Hungrvaka*[116] are several Germans, two men from Ermland, one from Ireland, and possibly two from England, if the figure includes Bishop Hróðolfr who spent nineteen years in Iceland (in the mid-eleventh century), and may well have died as the Abbot of Abingdon in Berkshire in 1052.[117] According to *Hungrvaka*, Hróðolfr came from 'Rúðu or Englandi' ('Rúða in England'). 'Rúða', however, is usually interpreted as being Rouen, and drama was in all probability practised there from a very early period.[118]

As regards firm evidence of Scandinavian awareness of the development of practical drama in this period, it seems clear that the Norwegians knew of, and possessed copies of Æthelwold's *Regularis Concordia* (965–975) which contains the first extant proof that dramatic presentation was taking place in Benedictine monasteries in England.[119] In addition to this, while there is no evidence that the Norwegians or Icelanders developed any form of liturgical drama themselves during the early Middle Ages,[120] it is

---

114 See Leach, *Angevin Britain*, pp.98–105, and Woolf, *The English mystery plays*, pp.17–18. It is also worth noting Archbishop Eysteinn's sojourn at Bury St Edmunds in 1181–1182: Leach, *Angevin Britain*, pp.89–94.

115 Foote, 'Aachen, Lund, Hólar', pp.107–112 and p.118.

116 *Íslendingabók* (late eleventh/ early twelfth century) names twelve foreign bishops who had visited the country between the initial stages of the conversion and the time of writing; *Hungrvaka* names six. See *Íslendingabók* p.18, and *Húngrvaka* in *Biskupa sögur* (1858–1878), I, pp.64–65.

117 See Foote, 'Aachen, Lund, Hólar', p.106.

118 See Woolf, *English mystery plays*, p.14.

119 A fragment exists in Norway (NRA, *Lat. frag. no.208* [7]r, [*Mi1 fragment*]) which originally belonged to an eleventh-century English MS, and contains three prayers prescribed in the *Adoratio Crucis* of the *Regularis Concordia*. Further indications of the influence of the *Regularis Concordia* exist on a fragment of a twelfth-century missal (NRA, *Lat. frag.* 311 and 728. [*Mi 12*]): see Gjerløw, *Adoratio Crucis*, p.14, pp.48–49 and pp.69–70. As Gjerløw points out (p.68), the existence of the fragments does not prove that the *Regularis Concordia* was taken up anywhere in Norway at this time. On the other hand, the fragments establish how close links were with the English monasteries, and stress that some Norwegians must have been aware of the dramatisation of the liturgy in the eleventh or twelfth century. For the complete text of the *Adoratio Crucis*, see Young, *DMC*, I, pp.118–120.

120 See, however, Sveinn Einarsson, *Íslensk leiklist*, I, p.145, and Jørgensen and Vésteinn Ólason, 'Fyrirlát mér jungfrúin hreina', p.187, on the question of whether an elementary Norwegian Christmas play can be assumed on the basis of the *Nidaros Ordinary* from the early thirteenth century.

F. Conclusion

fairly certain that the Swedes did, since there are no less than three extant manuscripts of Easter plays which were probably performed in Linköping and in the Stockholm area during the thirteenth century.[121]

In the light of the facts given above, it is by no means strange that the Scandinavians should have been interested in, and come in contact with, manuscripts of religious works like *The harrowing of Hell*, *La seinte resureccion*, and *Le mystère d'Adam*, or those of light comedies like *Babio*, *De nuntio sagaci*, or *Dame Sirith*, any of which would have provided a natural model for the transcription of vernacular dramatic material in the thirteenth century.

F. Conclusion

On the basis of the material presented above, the following can be surmised:

Firstly, since the scribes of the *Codex Regius* and AM 748 manuscripts deliberately chose not to follow the normal Scandinavian manuscript traditions for indicating the speakers in a dialogue, it must be assumed that they felt they were dealing with a form very different from that of the theological dialogues (which of course would also have been read aloud for others).

Secondly, the alternative form of notation the scribes chose is found only in connection with the dialogic poems of the Edda manuscripts and in certain manuscripts from northern France and England containing obviously dramatic works, or works which, like the dialogic Eddic poems, arguably needed to be performed in a dramatic fashion to be understood properly. This has to be more than a coincidence. Since the scribes deliberately chose to make use of marginal notation, they must have been aware of the similarities in form between the works they were dealing with and other European works using the same method of speaker notation. In short, they must have regarded the dialogic poems as a kind of popular vernacular drama, designed for performance by more than one speaker.

---

[121] Svenska Riksarkivet, Värmland, 1589, No.12; SRA, Småland 1574, No.3:2; and SRA, Dalarna 1575, No.14. See Davidson, ed. and trans., *Holy Week and Easter ceremonies*, pp.1–61, and plates 4–6 for photographs of the MSS, all of which keep to the pattern for liturgical dramatic MSS described above. See also Schmid, 'Mysteriespel', p.103, and Kjellén, 'Några undersökningar', 10–18. See further *Chapter II*, note 11, on the possible influence of religious drama on later folk traditions.

CHAPTER V

Performances of Poetry and Song Involving More that One Participant in Early Medieval Scandinavia

A. The Evidence Regarding Solo Performance

In spite of Phillpotts' argument, and the evidence of the dramatic form of the Eddic poems presented in the last two chapters, the general consensus amongst scholars has still tended to be that all the Eddic poems, like those of the skalds, must have been presented by a single performer. Even when Lönnroth reached the somewhat radical conclusion in 1971 that 'it seems quite likely that the dramatic speech poems were intended to be performed in a semi-theatrical fashion,' he felt bound to add the words 'by one performer only'.[1]

The problem with this affirmation is that Lönnroth, like many others, bases his argument on the evidence of *Norna-Gests þáttr* which describes the performances of a visiting ancient harpist and oral storyteller at the court of King Ólafr Tryggvason. Yet, as has been pointed out earlier in this book, it has to be remembered that what Norna-Gestr performs for his audience are almost word-perfect renditions of the *Codex Regius* versions of the heroic poems *Reginsmál* (in part) and *Helreið Brynhildar*, neither of which can be said to be directly comparable to the purely dialogic *ljóðaháttr* poems that have been discussed above: *Helreið Brynhildar* is predominantly a monologic poem composed in *fornyrðislag*, while *Reginsmál*, in its extant form, seems to be little more than a prose-connected conglomeration of two or more poems drawn from several different sources rather than an original complete poem. All in all, it is necessary to be highly cautious about regarding the evidence of Norna-Gestr's performance as conclusive for the Eddic corpus as a whole.[2]

---

[1] Lönnroth, 'Hjálmar's death song', 6. More recently, the same idea of a single composer and performer has been strongly advocated by Einar Már Jónsson in 'Góður veðurviti', 383–384. It should be noted, however, that since this earlier article, Lönnroth has changed his stance slightly. In 'Skírnismál', p.166 and pp.170–171, he seems to propose a more dramatic, 'pantomimic' form of presentation for *Skírnismál*.
[2] See further *Chapter III, F.5*.

B. Outside the Germanic Peoples

The same must be said about the account of Þormóðr Bersason's performance of *Bjarkamál in fornu* ('The ancient *Bjarkamál*') for King Ólafr Haraldsson and his army before the battle of Stiklastaðir in 1030.[3] Certainly, *Bjarkamál* can be considered dialogic in the sense that the poem seems to have been composed entirely of speeches which are uttered by more than one person. However, *Bjarkamál* was not composed in *ljóðaháttr*, and the dialogue itself is hardly as fast-moving as that contained in the Eddic poems discussed in *Chapter III*; for the main part, the poem appears to have been made up of eight long exhortations and monologues uttered by the two main characters, Hjalti (Hialto) and Bjarki (Biarco). Apart from this, as Harris has recently argued, it is quite possible that Þormóðr's supposed performance of this poem was a borrowed literary motif, rather than a historical fact.[4]

As has been illustrated in *Chapter III*, the extant form of the poems under discussion suggests either that any solo performer presenting them must have been an exceptionally skilled actor as Lönnroth is perhaps suggesting in the reference given at the start of this chapter, or, more likely, that more than one person must have taken part in the performances. As has been shown in *Chapter IV*, this latter argument would appear to be supported by use of marginal notation alongside these works in the earliest extant manuscripts. The question therefore remains as to whether there is any evidence at all to support the suggestion that 'poetry' might have been performed by more than one person in Scandinavia during the thirteenth century or earlier.

B. Oral Performance Involving More than One Participant Outside the Germanic World

Considering the evidence of cultures elsewhere in the world, the concept of more than one person participating in the oral presentation of a poem is neither original nor particularly surprising. Numerous examples exist of oral traditions in which two or more poets act jointly in the composition and/ or presentation of a poem. Group singing, for example, takes place all over the world in a variety of contexts ranging from religious gatherings to drunken revelry. In most cases, the group learns the songs from repeated experience, or through careful prior organisation.[5] However, in some cultures, much more complicated improvised group singing is known to

---

[3] See *Fóstbræðra saga*, pp.261–264, and *Eddica minora*, pp.21–32. Apart from a few strophes, the original version of the poem is now lost. Saxo Grammaticus' Latin translation of this poem is contained in Saxo Grammaticus, *Gesta Danorum*, Book II, pp.53–61; trans. in *The history of the Danes*, pp.56–63.

[4] See Harris, 'Eddic poetry', pp.118–119, where Harris also considers the other examples of solo poetic performance described in Saxo's work.

[5] See, for example, the case of the rehearsed choral performances of poetry carried out by the Gilbert Islanders, noted in Finnegan, *Oral poetry*, pp.156–157.

V. Performances of Poetry and Song

have taken place, as in the case of Indian Toda poetry, which is presented as follows:

> All the performers will have a good knowledge of the technique and what is being sung about. The first unit, even the first syllable of the first unit that is uttered by the chief performer almost always gives a certain clue to the limited possibilities of the two-dimensional structures that he intends to use; a quick intelligence on the part of his accompanists does the rest.[6]

One of the most common forms of group singing is antiphony which involves the group singing a refrain on alternate lines. This technique, also used in the Toda songs, often involves improvisation, and is often known to have occurred, for example, amongst certain African and Native American tribes and in Negro prison gangs.[7] Of particular interest in the present context is the argument that antiphonal recital of this kind was also used in the performance of the sacred *Rig Veda* hymns from India (c.1200–900 B.C.), many of which, like the Eddic poems, are wholly dialogic in form.[8]

Choral performances of the kind mentioned above naturally involve a greater degree of social organisation, and are more likely to be limited to particular large-scale social gatherings. The same, however, need not apply to the more common types of poetic performance involving several performers such as duets, organised poetry competitions, and, most relevant of all, poetic duels which Finnegan feels 'can be interpreted as resulting in a single poetic composition, produced jointly by two composers.'[9] Competitions or duels of this kind are encountered all over the world amongst a wide variety of races, and apart from their artistic value, often have an important social function as the expression or resolution of conflicts between individuals or groups.[10] As will be shown below, there is little question that the same applied in Scandinavia. Indeed, considering the account of the oral flyting reported as having taken place at the Reykhólar wedding in twelfth-century Iceland (see below, *section D.3*), it is especially interesting to note that poetic duels or competitions in other cultures often tend to be associated with weddings.[11] Amongst the Greenland Inuit, for example, such poetic duels are known to have turned into 'long and biting

---

6   M. B. Emeneau, quoted in Finnegan, *Oral poetry*, p.85.
7   See Finnegan, *Oral poetry*, pp.102–103 and pp.154–155.
8   Berthold, in *A history of world theatre*, p.48, argues that because of this, such performances would have remained in the realms of 'sophisticated poetry' rather than theatre. O'Flaherty stresses, however, that the actual form of presentation remains open to discussion, her own opinion being that the conversational poems 'may have been part of a special ritual performance involving actors and dancers': O'Flaherty, ed., *The Rig Veda*, p.245.
9   Finnegan, *Oral poetry*, p.85.
10   Finnegan, *Oral poetry*, p.223.
11   See, for example, Finnegan, *Oral poetry*, p.223; Owen, *Welsh folk customs*, pp.163–166; Shklovsky, *In far north east Siberia*, pp.55–58; and Davidson, 'Insults and riddles', p.41, for information about such activities amongst the Welsh, Russians and Greenland Inuit. For information regarding similar behaviour at weddings in the Tatra mountains of Poland, I am grateful to my friends Stanisław and Barbara Szczycinski.

B. Outside the Germanic Peoples

poems of derision', although, as Finnegan notes, 'one can surmise that entertainment and amusement are *also* likely to play a part in such performances.'[12]

The logical next step from such traditional systems of bandying verse is the formally organised poetry or song competition which has been reported from places as far apart as Polynesia, Russia, Japan, and Tanzania, and naturally might also have taken place amongst the skalds at the medieval Norwegian court. As with poetic duels, many of these competitions have political or tribal implications,[13] although in most cases, the emphasis tends to be 'on display and poetic accomplishment rather than on resolving or maintaining hostilities.'[14]

The kind of multiple-performer events described above need have little to do with drama over and above the dramatic quality of the visual 'event'. They merely provide the possibility of performers taking on roles. Certain other oral poetic traditions, however, come much closer to the traditional forms of drama. In this regard, Finnegan mentions so-called 'dialogue poems' which are sometimes composed and performed in cooperation by two men. While these have certain similarities to the two-poet duels mentioned above, here the element of conflict is not essential. As examples of this kind of poetry, Finnegan cites the ballad form, which commonly involves dialogues between lovers or antagonists, and then a particular kind of 'conversation song' known to have existed in Mongolia. Such 'conversation songs' were usually performed 'in the narrow confines of the Mongol tent, where several performers sometimes took part, "acting" as they sat by facial expression or gestures; at other times all the parts were played by one performer.'[15]

For the people of Northern Europe during the early Middle Ages, it is unlikely that such forms of presentation as those briefly listed above would have seemed strange. For instance, in the setting of the larger Catholic churches and monasteries of this period, people would have regularly encountered several types of multiple-performer presentation. The most

---

[12] Finnegan, *Oral poetry*, p.223. See also Hoebel, *The law of primitive man*, pp.93–99; and Day, *The sky clears*, pp.43–47, for examples and a description of these so-called Inuit 'nith-songs'. Particularly interesting is Hoebel's observation in *The law of primitive man*, pp.98–99, that these song contests often act as 'judicial instruments' in place of court proceedings. See also below, note 78. Weddings, however, are not the only situations in which such contests of poetic derision take place. For instance, in *The sky clears*, pp.54–56, Day quotes examples of material from boasting competitions practised by the northwest Pacific coast Indians as part of their potlatch ceremonies. In Ireland, similar activities have been known to take place at wakes: see Ó Suilleabháin, *Irish wake amusements*, pp.56–58.

[13] See, for example, Chadwick and Zhirmunsky, *Oral epics*, p.329, on the Kirghiz families.

[14] Finnegan, *Oral poetry*, p.158.

[15] Finnegan, *Oral poetry*, p.117; see also p.15 and p.124. See also Bawden's introduction to Mongolian poetry, and the Mongolian dialogic song, 'Prince Sumiya' in *The Penguin book of oral poetry*, p.41, and pp.58–63. As Finnegan points out in *Oral poetry*, p.117, dialogue as a medium is naturally more effective orally than in the written form.

V. Performances of Poetry and Song

common, of course, was the system of responses included in the Mass, but other varieties of antiphony involving a soloist and a responding choir were becoming relatively widespread in monasteries throughout Europe before 900. The tenth and eleventh centuries then witnessed the evolution of certain systems of these responses into the dramatic *Quem Quaeritis* tropes of Easter and Christmas, both of which represented major stepping stones in the development of liturgical drama.[16] During the same period, there is also strong evidence to suggest that monastic and court 'readings' of dramatic and semi-dramatic texts were taking place in a 'radio-drama' style reminiscent of that employed with the Mongolian 'dialogue songs', except that the monks and their pupils or the members of the court would have been reading their parts aloud, rather than improvising the words as they went along.[17] The seeds of dramatic presentation had been well and truly sown in the Catholic church, and, as pointed out in the previous chapter, it is unlikely that the scriptorium clerics of Scandinavia, or even the travelling skalds who must have stayed in such monasteries alongside all-round entertainers such as the *mimi* and *histriones* (see the Appendix) were unaware of this continuous development. Indeed, it is not unlikely that similar elementary dramatic activities would also have been encountered in the larger monasteries of Scandinavia.

C. Oral Performance Involving More than One Participant Among the Germanic Peoples

Activities like those mentioned above were taking place in the church all over mainland Europe throughout the early medieval period. Yet variety in forms of poetic presentation was not limited to the sphere of the church. With regard to secular activities, it must be assumed on the basis of the extant evidence that the early Germanic peoples (the Scandinavians included) could boast of as many forms of poetic performance as any other race in the world. As elsewhere, the presentation of song and poetry amongst the Germans was not limited to solo performance. For example, according to Tacitus and other classical historians such as Ammianus Marcellinus, Priscus and Jordanes, choral/ group singing or chanting seems to have been common practice amongst the early German tribes, especially

---

[16] See Young, *DMC*, I–II, for the most detailed examination of this process and the original texts. See also Tydeman, *The theatre in the Middle Ages*, pp.32–45, for an effective summary of this development in its early stages. The first definite indication of monks actually presenting an elementary Easter 'play' based on the *Quem Quaeritis* tropes, and involving both imitation and role play, appears in Æthelwold's *Regularis Concordia* (955–975).

[17] See Dronke, 'A note on Pamphilus', 225–230; *Woman writers*, pp.57–63; and *Poetic individuality*, pp.xxix–xxx. For evidence of a similar kind of dramatic reading of religious texts in monasteries, see Tydeman, *The theatre in the Middle Ages*, p.31, and Young, *DMC*, II, pp.133–138.

D. In Scandinavia

in the context of battle and at funerals.[18] Similarly noteworthy, and of particular interest with regard to early Scandinavian tradition, is the observation made by Giraldus Cambrensis in the late twelfth century about the inhabitants of the area near the south Yorkshire border in England. Giraldus notes that these people used 'the same kind of symphonious harmony' practised by the Welsh 'choirs' he had previously encountered, 'but with less variety, singing only in two parts, one murmuring in the base, the other warbling in the acute or treble.' 'The English,' he adds, 'do not adopt this mode of singing, but only those of the Northern countries.' Giraldus proceeds to suggest, perhaps from personal experience, that this kind of song was 'contracted' from the 'Danes and Norwegians'.[19] The striking resemblance between the mode of song described by Giraldus, and the original native two-voice harmony (*tvísöngur*) encountered even today in Iceland suggests that this kind of delivery must have had a long tradition in western Scandinavia. The likelihood is that it was brought to England with the Scandinavian immigrants during the ninth and tenth century. Interestingly enough, the sagas make no obvious mention of any such tradition.[20]

1. '*Seiðr*'

D. *Oral Performances Involving More than One Participant in Scandinavia*

1. '*Seiðr*'

With regard to Scandinavia during the Viking period, the sagas give good reason to believe that joint or group performances of secular poetic material must have continued in a variety of contexts. Group singing or chanting, for example, probably occurred as a central feature of magical

---

[18] See Tacitus, *The annals*, Book I, ch.65, in *The histories. The annals*, II, pp.354–355; *The histories*, Book II, ch.21, Book IV, ch.18, and Book V, ch.15, in *The histories, The annals*, I, pp.194–195, and II, pp.34–35 and pp.202–203; and *Germania* (chs 2, 3, 7 and 8), pp.130–131, pp.132–135 and pp.142–143. See also Ammianus Marcellinus, XVI, 12.43, in *Rerum gestarum libri qui supersunt*, I, pp.286–289; and Priscus, *Fragmenta*, and Jordanes, *Getica*, ch.49, in *The fragmentary classicising historians*, II, pp.286–287 (Priscus), and pp.316–319 (Jordanes). For a detailed analysis of all the extant evidence regarding poetic performance and song amongst the Germanic tribes, see Opland, *Anglo-Saxon oral poetry*, pp.40–73. For discussion of the works mentioned above, see in particular pp.41–53.

[19] Giraldus Cambrensis, *Descriptio Kambriæ*, ch.XIII, in *Opera*, pp.189–90. Translation: Giraldus Cambrensis, *The itinerary through Wales*, p.175.

[20] A faint possibility exists that Bishop Laurentius of Hólar's complaint in the early fourteenth century about 'tripla' ('three-voice harmonies') or 'tvísöngr' might relate to this variety of song: Einar Haflíðason, *Saga Laurentius Hólabiskups*, in *Biskupa sögur* (1858–1878), I, p.847 and p.903; also *Laurentius saga biskups* (1969), p.99. Nonetheless, if this comment is genuine, the greater likelihood is that the bishop was referring to the fashion of choral trope-singing mentioned above, whereby the old system of plain-chant, in which each syllable had had a single note, was being replaced by a new system in which a whole melody could be assigned to the last syllable of a line: see Tydeman, *The theatre in the Middle Ages*, p.34.

V. Performances of Poetry and Song

1. 'Seiðr'   rites such as that known as *seiðr*, which was used both for divination and as a means of wielding harmful influence. Indeed, as Strömbäck has shown, the use of the word *seiðr* in kennings such as 'suerða seiða' ('the *seiðr* of swords': battle) would seem to suggest that in later times the word had come to be associated more with the mode of singing that took place in these ceremonies than with any other part of the ceremony.[21]

In this connection, the account given in *Eiríks saga rauða* concerning the prophetess Þorbjörg lítil-völva's performance of *seiðr* in Greenland has particular interest,[22] not least because of the details given of Þorbjörg's shaman-like costume of various animal skins and stones, and the fact that when she sits on her raised platform, or *seiðhjallr*, she is surrounded by a circle of apparently dancing women ('slógu þá konur hring um hjallinn').[23] In this case, the 'kvæði' ('poem/ song') performed in the ceremony is 'kveðið' ('spoken/ chanted/ sung') by only one woman in a group. However, the implication is that usually the 'kvæði' would have been performed by all the women involved since Þorbjörg 'asked to have *those women* who had mastered the skill needed for the *seiðr*, which was called Varðlokur. But *those women* were nowhere to be found' (my emphases).[24]

That group singing or chanting was a regular feature of the *seiðr* ritual is supported by other references to this practice in *Örvar-Odds saga*, and *Laxdæla saga*. In the former account, a description is given of a 'prophetess and witch woman' ('völva ok seiðkona') named Heiðr, who, like Þorbjörg, seems to have had a particular costume,[25] but was now accompanied by 'thirty people, fifteen young men and fifteen young women. It was a large chorus (*raddlið*), because wherever she was, there were supposed to be great chants.'[26] In *Laxdæla saga*, the 'chanting' is performed not only by the sorcerer Kotkell, but also by his wife and two sons. They ascend the

---

21 See Strömbäck, *Sejd*, pp.118–120.
22 See *Eiríks saga rauða*, pp.206–209. As Strömbäck suggests in *Sejd*, pp.49–60, there is good reason to be wary about the historical accuracy of this section of the saga. Nonetheless, the account still has importance if only because of its detailed nature which suggests some traditional knowledge on the part of the author, however misunderstood it may have been.
23 *Eiríks saga rauða*, p.208. On the basis of this quotation, it might be questioned whether the women were actually dancing. However, the verb 'slógu' ('formed') implies movement, and considering the evidence of most other cultures in the world, and the mention of the song/ chant that accompanied the ritual, it seems highly unlikely that the women merely formed a ring and then proceeded to stand still while they sang.
24 'Hon bað ok fá sér *konur þær*, er kynni fræði þat, sem til seiðsins þarf ok Varðlokur hétu. En *þær konur* fundusk ekki': *Eiríks saga rauða*, p.207. Regarding the 'Varðlokur' or 'Varðlokkur' chant and its purpose, see further Olsen, 'Varðlokur', and Strömbäck, *Sejd*, pp.124–139.
25 When she leaves, Heiðr specifically asks somebody to collect some special clothing other than that which she is wearing: 'Taki fǫt mín . . . ok vil ek á braut fara': *Örvar-Odds saga* (1888), p.14; cf. *Örvar-Odds saga* (FN I), p.289.
26 'Hon hafði með sér XXX manna, XV sveina ok XV meyjar. Þat var raddlið mikit, þvíat þar skyldi vera kveðandi mikil, sem hon var': *Örvar-Odds saga* (1888), p.11. The word *raddlið* is not used in all the versions of this saga. See, for example, *Örvar-Odds saga* (FN I), pp.286–289.

D. In Scandinavia

seiðhjallr together and 'there chanted powerful incantations; they were magic spells'.²⁷ As in the case of the Greenland account, the sound of the 'chanting' by Kotkell and his family is said to have been beautiful: 'fǫgr var sú kveðandi at heyra'.²⁸

1. *'Seiðr'*

Considering the mention of the large chorus, or *raddlið* accompanying Heiðr in *Ǫrvar-Odds saga*, it is also worth noting the 'eighty sorcerers' ('átta tigu seiðmenn') who are said to have been killed alongside King Haraldr hárfagri's son Rǫgnvaldr réttilbeini, and the 'sorcerers and other people skilled in magical arts' ('seiðmenn ok annat fjǫlkynngisfólk') who were supposedly drowned with Rǫgnvaldr's grandson, Eyvindr kelda. While these accounts from *Heimskringla* make no mention of group singing or chanting, they emphasise the thirteenth-century belief that pagan magical rituals were essentially a group activity.²⁹

These suggestions of group participation and group chanting in magic ritual offer intriguing parallels to another account dealing with a supernatural experience that might conceivably have had some basis in early pagan practice, namely the dream image of the performance of *Darraðarljóð* described in *Njáls saga*. Like the *seiðr* ritual in Greenland, this performance seems to involve a group of women singing or chanting together. The introduction to the poem stipulates that 'they (the women) then sang/ chanted some verses' ('þær kváðu þá vísur nǫkkurar'), and this is perhaps backed up by the plural verbs in the poem itself, as in the repeated lines 'Let us wind, let us wind,/ the web of Dörruðr' ('Vindum, vindum/ vef darraðar').³⁰ Yet, just before being presented with the vision of the women chanting the poem, the reader is informed that 'twelve men rode together to a women's bower, and all of them disappeared' ('menn riðu tólf saman til dyngju nǫkkurrar ok hurfu þar allir'). The question remains as to whether these men provided the heads and entrails used for the ghoulish weaving that apparently accompanied the singing of the poem inside the bower; whether they are involved in the action elsewhere; or whether they somehow 'became' the 'women' singing the song, as Gunnarr helmingr 'became' Freyr, and Þorleifr jarlsskáld 'became' the 'stafkarl'.³¹

---

²⁷ 'Þau kváðu þar harðsnúin fræði; þat váru galdrar': *Laxdæla saga*, p.99.
²⁸ *Laxdæla saga*, p.106.
²⁹ See *Haralds saga ins hárfagra*, in *Heimskringla*, I, p.139 and p.312.
³⁰ *Brennu-Njáls saga*, pp.454–457. It is probable that the form of *Darraðarljóð* reflects weaving songs that were sung together by women during the early Middle Ages, just as the poem *Grottasǫngr* might have a basis in actual corn-grinding songs: 'They chanted a cacophony,/ never-silent:/ "Let us set up the stand,/ let us lift the stones!"/ . . . They sung and slung/ the whirling stone . . .' ('Þær þyt þulu/ þǫgnhorfinnar;/ "leggium lúðra,/ léttum steinum!"/ . . . Sungu ok slungu/ snúðga steini . . .'): *Grottasǫngr*, sts 3–4. See Holtsmark, 'Arbeidssanger', p.202.
³¹ See also Strömbäck, *Sejd*, p.195, where reference is made to a foreign shamanistic practice in which men dressed up as women; and *Chapter I, C.4* on the figure of the 'bearded woman' on the Gallehus horn, and for other early references to similar ritualistic behaviour. Regarding Gunnarr helmingr and Þorleifr jarlsskáld, see *Chapter II, C.5 and D.1*.

V. Performances of Poetry and Song

2. Alternate singing?

Indeed, while the act of *seiðr* was considered to be an essentially feminine activity closely associated with the goddess Freyja, it was supposedly originally introduced by Óðinn who was a recognised master of this craft.[32]

2. Alternate Singing?

In connection with the group performances of ritualistic chants like *Varðlokur* and *Darraðarljóð*, it is worth examining briefly the case for 'alternate singing' or 'víxlkveðandi' that Stefán Einarsson tried to establish on the basis of evidence contained in the accounts surrounding three other intriguing 'dream verses' (*draumavísur*) quoted in *Íslendinga saga* and *Guðmundar saga*.[33]

In the first example, a man has a dream in which 'it seemed to him that he came into a large house; in there sat two women; they were covered in blood and were continuously rowing; blood seemed to be raining through the sky-lights. One of the women chanted . . .'[34] In the second example, which is also said to have occurred shortly after the battle at Víðines in 1208, a man dreams that he is in a small room where he sees two men dressed in black, with loose hoods on their heads. They 'held hands, each sitting on his own bench, and they rowed. Their arms hit the walls so hard that they (the walls) were on the point of collapsing. They then chanted the following verse, each chanting alternate lines/ words: . . .'[35] The third and final example quoted by Stefán involves a dream in which two ravens are heard to chant a verse. As in the previous example, they 'chanted alternate lines/ words' ('kvóðu þetta, sítt orð hvárr').[36]

The common feature of all these verses is that they seem to be performed jointly by two participants. Stefán Einarsson's belief was that this type of performance parallels a recorded shamanistic ritual practice known amongst the Lapps in which two people would shut themselves up alone inside a building (something also suggested by two of the Icelandic examples given above, and perhaps also *Darraðarljóð*), and then chant or

---

[32] On *seiðr*, see further, Strömbäck, *Sejd*, passim; Ström, *Nordisk hedendom*, pp.223–227; and Davidson, *Gods and myths*, pp.117–122, and 'Hostile magic'. Regarding Óðinn's connections with *seiðr*, and its 'unmanly' reputation, see *Ynglinga saga*, pp.19, and *Lokasenna*, st.24.

[33] See Stefán Einarsson, 'Víxlkveðandi'; 'Alternate recital' (an English version of 'Víxlkveðandi'); 'Dæmi um víxlkveðandi'; and 'Harp song'.

[34] 'Hann þóttisk koma í hús eitt mikit; þar sátu inni konur tvær blóðgar ok réru áfram. Hónum þótti rigna blóði í ljórana. Önnur konan kvað . . .': *Íslendinga saga*, in *Sturlunga saga* (1878), I, pp.219–220.

[35] 'Hann þóttisk kominn í litla stofu, ok sátu uppi tveir menn svart-klæddir, ok höfðu grár kollhettur á höfði; ok tókusk í hendr; sat á sínum bekk hvárr, ok réru. Þeir ráku hendrnar svá fast á veggina, at þá reiddi til fallz. Síðan kváðu þeir vísu þessa; ok kvað sítt orð hvárr: . . .': *Íslendinga saga*, in *Sturlunga saga* (1878), I, p.220. Both this description and the previous one are given in almost identical terms in *Saga Guðmundar Árnasonar*, in *Biskupa sögur* (1858–1878), I, pp.497–498; see also *Guðmundar sögur biskups* (1983), p.161 and p.259.

[36] *Íslendinga saga*, in *Sturlunga saga* (1878), I, p.372.

D. In Scandinavia

'sing' a song/ poem/ magical incantation. In the original form of this ritual suggested by Stefán Einarsson, the two performers would have sat opposite each other, held hands and rocked to-and-fro, each participant chanting alternate lines of the 'poem'. Drawing comparisons between this practice and a similar form of oral presentation known in Finland, and used with the 'runo chants', Stefán went on to link both methods of performance to shamanism and the singing/ chanting involved in *seiðr* ritual.[37]

2. Alternate singing?

Stefán Einarsson's argument was that, at one time, this system of 'alternate song' might have been more widespread in the Germanic world. In support of this proposal, he referred to other earlier sources such as the apparently joint performance of a song by Widsith and 'Scilling' mentioned in the Anglo-Saxon poem *Widsith* (ll.103–108),[38] and Priscus' description of an entertainment offered by Attila to his guests in 448 in which two barbarians are said to have recited poems before the king and his followers.[39] Neither of these examples, however, can be regarded as solid evidence of 'alternate singing'. As Stefán himself had suggested earlier, the poet of *Widsith* might just as well have been describing a form of duet or *tvísöngur* rather than any system of 'alternate singing'.[40] An even more likely proposal is the suggestion that 'Scilling' was Widsith's harp.[41] Similarly, there is no evidence in Priscus' account to suggest that the two barbarians ever actually sang together. As Opland argues, 'we probably have to see this as a description of separate, individual performances.'[42] The same probably applies to yet another account contained in the *Life of Ethelbert* (early twelfth century) which also mentions two 'singers' performing at approximately the same time.[43]

---

[37] Regarding the Finnish practice, see Andersson, 'Framförandet av Kalevalarunorna'. Andersson sees this practice as having originated in a ring dance involving a lead singer and chorus. Interestingly enough, a year later, Andersson went on to suggest a close connection between *fornyrðislag* and the Kalevala metre which he imagines was often presented in this form of 'tvesang': see Andersson, 'Kalevalameter – fornyrðislag'. More recently, the same argument is taken up by Mustanoja, in 'The presentation of ancient Germanic poetry'. Regarding the possible origin of this type of poetic performance in Lapp shamanistic ritual, see particularly Stefán Einarsson, 'Alternate recital', 59–83, which contains an English translation of most of Andersson's material, as well as a translation of an eighteenth-century account of Lapp shamanism from Dean Johann Berthold Ervast's *Descriptio Lapponiae* which contains clear echoes of the practice in question. In a later article, Stefán went on to argue that this form of presentation probably originated amongst the Germanic people, and was used by them as far back as the Bronze Age: Stefán Einarsson, 'Dæmi um víxlkveðandi', 115–129.
[38] See *Widsith*, ed. Malone, pp.87–88 and p.184; the Chadwicks', *Growth of literature*, I, p.574 and pp.589–590; and Stefán Einarsson, 'Harp song, heroic poetry', 14–17.
[39] See Priscus of Panium, *Fragmenta*, in *The fragmentary classicising historians*, II, pp.286–287, and Stefán Einarsson, 'Harp song', 16–17.
[40] See Stefán Einarsson, 'Víxlkveðandi', 129–130.
[41] See Opland, *Anglo-Saxon oral poetry*, p.211, and Malone, ed., *Widsith*, p.184, for further references. Harris, in 'Eddic poetry', p.116, feels that the *Widsith* example is related more to a form of poetic competition than a combined performance of any kind.
[42] Opland, *Anglo-Saxon oral poetry*, pp.51–52.
[43] See James, 'Two lives of St Ethelbert', 238; Moisl, 'Anglo-Saxon genealogies', 231 and 239; and Opland, *Anglo-Saxon oral poetry*, pp.148–149.

V. Performances of Poetry and Song

2. *Alternate singing?*

In general, Stefán Einarsson's arguments are interesting and reasonable insofar as they present some useful foreign parallels for the strange style of poetic performance illustrated in relation to the *Íslendinga saga* dream verses. However, as Stefán himself admits, there would appear to be large differences between this form of presentation and that suggested for *seiðr* in Norse sources.[44] Indeed, since the word *seiðr* is used in kennings to describe the noise of battle,[45] it must be assumed that it involved several voices chanting at one time, rather than any system of alternate singing. At the same time, even if rowing actions like those described in *Íslendinga saga* commonly occurred in shamanistic activities amongst the Lapps, there is nothing to say that the same methods were ever used in shamanistic activities elsewhere. A more logical solution, in view of the fact that in two of the examples the performers are described as 'rowing',[46] is the suggestion made by Holtsmark and Perkins that this system of singing/ chanting alternate lines should be directly associated with rowing chants, for which a number of foreign parallels exist.[47]

Nonetheless, as both Holtsmark and Harris have pointed out, the main difficulty for anyone trying to suggest that the three accounts from *Íslendinga saga* might reflect a popular practice is the fact that all of the verses contained in them have to be classified as 'spook verses', that is, verses spoken by ghosts.[48] Furthermore, even if such a form of oral presentation as that described by Stefán Einarsson, Holtsmark and Perkins *did* exist at one time (according to Stefán Einarsson, at the time of *Widsith* if not earlier) and later died out in popular practice,[49] it still does not provide a logical explanation for the form of the Eddic poems that have been examined in the previous chapters.[50] A performance of *Skírnismál* in such a

---

[44] Stefán Einarsson, 'Alternate recital', 73. Regarding *seiðr*, see the previous section.
[45] See reference given above in note 21.
[46] See notes 34–35 above.
[47] See Holtsmark, 'Arbeidssanger', pp.201–203; and Perkins, 'Rowing chants', 184–187. Perkins presents yet another verse as support for this system of alternate singing involving either two men, or a lead singer and a chorus, i.e. a *lausavísa* from *Bárðar saga Snæfellsáss* attributed to a 'trǫllkona' named Hetta, which involves a refrain on every other line: see *Bárðar saga Snæfellsáss*, p.127. As Perkins comments, this is the only example of such a verse from this period.
[48] Holtsmark, 'Arbeidssanger', p.202, and Harris, 'Eddic poetry', p.116. Indeed, *Darraðarljóð*, *Grottasǫngr*, and the verse from *Bárðar saga* can also be said to have supernatural implications: see previous note and note 30 above. Nonetheless, it is worth remembering that two of the examples from *Íslendinga saga*, and the performance of *Darraðarljóð*, are said to take place inside a building, away from general public view, similar perhaps to the *álfablót* that the poet Sigvatr Þórðarson was not allowed to see when he was travelling in Sweden: see *Heimskringla*, II, p.137. This suggests that the practice in question (if it is authentic) was hardly a daily social occurrence in early Christian Iceland, and that there was some reason to keep it out of public view if not out of the public mind. Whatever the case, concerning the rowing movement, it must be assumed that the contemporary listening or reading public understood exactly what was being talked about.
[49] Stefán Einarsson, 'Alternate recital', 81.
[50] Interestingly enough, Stefán Einarsson does mention the dialogic poems of the Edda

D. In Scandinavia

fashion as that described in the *Íslendinga saga* accounts would create more problems than it would solve. The same can be said perhaps regarding the ring-dance singing/ chanting accompanying *seiðr*.[51] Nonetheless, the evidence in both cases does give good reason to believe that the presentation of poetic works and songs by more than one person *did* take place, and would have been recognised by, and acceptable to the reading and/ or the listening audience.

This idea is supported still further by the existence of four other 'dialogic' verse forms mentioned in Icelandic literature from the early Middle Ages, namely the types of flyting known as the *senna*, and *mannjafnaðr*; the tradition linked to the expression *að ljóða á*; and finally, the *mansöngsvísur* mentioned in *Jóns saga helga*. All of these oral forms have much more direct relevance to the question of the performance of the dialogic Eddic poems, not least because all of them are based essentially upon a poetic conflict between two or more characters, rather than any form of combined presentation.

3. The 'Senna' and 'Mannjafnaðr'

In general terms, the two individual forms of verbal conflict known as the *senna* and *mannjafnaðr* have obvious similarities to the earlier mentioned popular poetic duels and contests encountered in the oral cultures of other countries.[52] Furthermore, they appear to have been particularly well known in early Scandinavia, since they occur in all forms of Old Norse literature ranging from the mythological[53] to the heroic and legendary[54] and the semi-historical.[55] As Heusler, Harris and others have argued, formal

---

and Þorbjörn hornklofi's poem *Hrafnsmál* (also known as *Haraldskvæði*) in 'Harp song', 19, but he never makes any attempt to explain these poems in terms of the practice he envisages for alternate singing.

[51] Nonetheless, the existence of an organised *raddlið* or 'chorus' opens the possibility that the group could have taken part in other organised pagan activities.

[52] See above, references in notes 11–14.

[53] I.e. *Hárbarðsljóð* (to some extent), and *Lokasenna*.

[54] I.e. *Helgakviða Hjörvarðssonar*, sts 12–30 (*Hrímgerðarmál*), *Helgakviða Hundingsbana I*, sts 32–46, and *Helgakviða Hundingsbana II*, sts 19–24. See also Ketill hængr's conflicts with Gusir and Forað (troll women) and Böðmóðr in *Ketils saga hængs*, pp.253–255, pp.259–261, and pp.263–264; Grímr loðinkinna's argument with another troll woman named Kleima in *Gríms saga loðinkinna*, pp.270–272; and the *mannjafnaðr* between Sjólfr, Sigurðr and Oddr in *Örvar-Odds saga* (*FN*, I), pp.369–376. Comparable encounters are also found in Saxo Grammaticus' *Gesta Danorum*: Gro and Gram (Book I); Eiricus Dissertus and Grep (Book V); and perhaps Eiricus Dissertus and Gøtwara (Book V) and Starcatherus and Hatherus (Book VIII): see Saxo Grammaticus, *Gesta Danorum*, pp.14–17, pp.112–114, p.118 and pp.224–228; trans. in *The history of the Danes*, pp.16–19, p.127, pp.132–133 and pp.247–251.

[55] For example, those contests depicted in *Þorgils saga ok Hafliða*, in *Sturlunga saga* (1878), I, pp.17–19; *Bandamanna saga*, pp.347–357; and *Ölkofra þáttr*, pp.90–93. See further Clover, 'The Germanic context', 446–447, note 9, for a list of other examples of 'flytings' to be found in the sagas.

3. The 'Senna' and 'Mannjafnaðr'

encounters of this kind probably had an origin in daily life.[56] Indeed, it has been suggested that both forms had legal origins, the *senna* being 'a verbal effort on the part of one person to prove the guilt of another', the *mannjafnaðr* 'an effort on the part of surviving relatives to assess the cash value of slain men'.[57] The evidence of the sagas, however, suggests that these poetic disputes also took place on less formal occasions whenever people gathered together, the *senna* being in essence a battle of exaggerated insults, the *mannjafnaðr* an exchange of boasts.

Eyrbyggja saga, for example, describes how on one occasion, 'there was a drinking session; and there was talk about comparing men, about who was the noblest man in the district, or the greatest chieftain; and people were not entirely in agreement about this as usually happens when men are compared.'[58] A similar introduction is given for the *mannjafnaðr* between the kings Sigurðr and Eysteinn in *Heimskringla*. The men at their joint feast are silent, and in order to brighten up the proceedings Eysteinn says, 'There is another better tradition associated with drinking, namely that men create some form of entertainment for themselves. Let us have a few drinking games. That will liven everything up. My brother Sigurðr, everyone will think it fitting for the two of us to make a few light speeches.'[59] Eysteinn then proposes that the two kings should engage in *mannjafnaðr*, which was evidently a recognised tradition. As he says, 'It is a common drinking custom for men to choose others to compare themselves with. I want that to be done here.'[60]

No *senna* is ever introduced in such recognisable formal terms,[61] but that a such contests of verbal insult regularly took place socially, and were recognised by everybody like any other form of communal 'game', seems evident from the account of the *senna* recorded as having occurred at the wedding in Reykhólar in 1119. The parallels here with the foreign wedding

---

[56] See, for example, Heusler, *Die altgermanische Dichtung*, pp.105–108; Harris, 'The senna', 69–70; and Clover, 'The Germanic context', 444–445.

[57] Clover, 'The Germanic context', 444–445. See also Holtsmark, 'Mannjevning', p.325. As Holtsmark points out, the word 'mannjafnaðr' is used in this sense in *Grænlendinga þáttr*, in *Flateyjarbok* (1860–1868), III, p.453. See further Hoebel's and Day's comments about Greenland Inuit duels referred to in notes 12 and 79.

[58] 'þar var ǫlteiti mǫrg; var þar talat um mannjǫfnuð, hverr þar væri gǫfgastr maðr í sveit eða mestr hǫfðingi; ok urðu menn þar eigi á eitt sáttir, sem optast er, ef um mannjǫfnuð er talat': *Eyrbyggja saga*, p.98.

[59] 'Hitt er ǫlsíðr meiri, at menn geri sér gleði. Fám oss ǫlteiti nǫkkura. Mun þá enn á reitask gaman manna. Sigurðr bróðir, þat mun ǫllum sæmst þykkja, at vit hefim nǫkkura skemmtanarræðu': *Magnússona saga*, in *Heimskringla*, III, pp.259.

[60] 'Sá ǫlsíðr hefir opt verit, at menn taka sér jafnaðarmenn. Vil ek hér svá vera láta': *Magnússona saga*, in *Heimskringla*, III, pp.259. The dispute that ensues after this is covered on pp.259–262. See also *Morkunskinna*, pp.186–187.

[61] For example, when in *Njáls saga* Gunnarr says to his wife Hallgerðr, 'it is most fitting that you argue (*sennir*) with the people of your own farm, but not in other people's homes' ('er þat makligast, at þú sennir við heimamenn þína, en eigi í annarra manna híbýlum') he is not referring to any organised bout of insults that follow an established pattern. 'All' that has happened is that Hallgerðr and Njáll's wife, Bergþóra, have insulted each other briefly: see *Brennu-Njáls saga*, p.91.

D. In Scandinavia

customs noted above in *section B* are striking: 'They drink heavily, and every one of them becomes a little intoxicated; they start talking too much, and it might be said that each one of them aims a few choice cutting words at the others; little will be quoted of their satirical jibes in this account.'[62] In spite of the pointed nature of the remarks that are bandied about here by Þórðr Þorvaldsson, Óláfr Hildisson, Ingimundr Einarsson and others, there is obviously a mutual sharing of amusement, at least in the initial stages of the conflict. Everyone, even Þórðr who is at the receiving end of most of the insults, seems to take the *senna* more as a game of skill rather than as something personal.[63]

As Clover, Harris and Lönnroth in particular have demonstrated, the *senna* and *mannjafnaðr* often come very close to overlapping, so close in fact that it has been suggested that both should be classified simply as forms of *flyting*.[64] Both types of contest clearly shared many common structural elements, and there is good reason to suspect that, like most games, they often followed particular rules. There is little question that they deserve to be considered as a poetic genre, or genres in their own right.[65]

The common features encountered in both the *senna* and *mannjafnaðr* range from the actual format of the confrontation, its introduction, development and conclusion, to various recurrent formulæ and themes. For example, it is striking that the disputes in question often take place in a particular setting which prevents the participants from concluding the conflict with physical violence, as in the case of *Hárbarðsljóð* where Þórr and Óðinn are separated by water. Another interesting feature is that the participants are sometimes representatives, or 'seconds', for other people, and are often accompanied by a third external character who has the role or ability of drawing the verbal duel to a conclusion, as occurs in the *Helgakvidur*). It might be noted that this element of 'representation' is only a short step away from drama, where instead of merely 'representing' them, the participants 'become' the leading figures in the dispute.

4. 'Að ljóða á'

As suggested above, the most characteristic feature of the *mannjafnaðr* and *senna* is that they tend to be conducted in verse form. This element raises the possibility of a faint, distant relationship with yet another form of

---

[62] 'Þeir drekka nú ákaft, ok fær á þá alla nökkut; görask nú málgir; ok má kalla, at hverr styngi annan nökkurum hnæfil-yrðum; ok er þó fátt hermt af þeirra keski-yrðum í þessari frásögn': *Þorgils saga ok Hafliða*, in *Sturlunga saga* (1878), I, p.17.
[63] See *Þorgils saga ok Hafliða*, in *Sturlunga saga* (1878), I, pp.17–19.
[64] Clover, 'The Germanic context', 445.
[65] See Harris, 'The senna', 65–74; and Clover, 'Hárbarðsljóð', 124–145, and 'The Germanic context', 444–468. See also, Holtsmark, 'Mannjevning', pp.325–326, and 'Senna', pp.149–152; and Lönnroth, *Den dubbla scenen*, pp.53–80 (dealing with the structure of the Sigurðr-Eysteinn conflict in *Heimskringla*), and 'The double scene', pp.94–109, with particular reference to *Örvar-Odds saga*.

V. Performances of Poetry and Song

1. *'Að ljóða á'*

two 'man' poetic conflict that was known from the same period, but which seems to have been more closely related to magic, namely the tradition implied by the expression *að ljóða á* (lit. 'to chant at') somebody or something. This expression goes back at least as far as the fourteenth century, and has certain echoes in traditions known to this day. As will be shown below, the sense of *ljóð* in this particular context is closest to that in which Óðinn uses the word in *Ljóðatal* (*Hávamál* sts 146–163); in other words, it is used in the sense of 'a magical incantation' rather than in the usual simple meaning of 'a poem'.

A good description of one aspect of this tradition as it existed in the late nineteenth century is recorded in the chapter on 'Acts of magic' ('Töfrabrögð') contained in Jón Árnason's collection of Icelandic folk tales and legends. In connection with methods of self-defence against the attacks of a ghost or the Devil, Jón writes that 'people believed that if they (a ghost or Satan) *ljóðuðu á* (chanted at) somebody first, and that person was not ready to answer them in verse, then the person in question would go mad or fall into their power; but if the person succeeded in replying with a verse promptly, then the attack would be in vain, and they (the evil spirit) would rush off in shame.'[66] In the legends that Jón cites to accompany this statement, various types of rhyming verse are employed, including one which bears an intriguingly close resemblance to *ljóðaháttr*. The first part of this particular poem, spoken by a spirit, runs as follows:

> Much lives in the fog; Margt býr í þokunni,
> ease back the bolt, þokaðu úr lokunni,
> my sweet, faithful maid. lindin mín ljúf og trú.

The farmer's daughter then immediately replies:

> My people miss me, Fólkið mín saknar,
> my father is waking; og faðir minn vaknar;
> he watches as well hann vakir svo vel, sem
> as you. þú.[67]

As in this example, the first three or four lines of this type of magical verse are usually spoken by the malevolent spirit, and they are then countered with a similar number of lines composed by the person under attack, which serve to complete the strophe in a parallel poetic format.

At first sight, this form of poetry and the tradition associated with it appears to be identical to another Icelandic poetic custom related to the expression *að kveðast á* ('to exchange verses') which also involves a contest in verse, and often occurs in a similar situation. However, *að kveðast á*

---

[66] 'Menn hafa haft þá trú, að ef þeir *ljóðuðu á mann* að fyrra bragði, og maður væri ekki viðbúinn að svara þeim aptur í ljóðum, þá yrði sá maður vitlaus og kæmist á vald þeirra; en gæti maður svarað þeim aptur samstundis vísu, yrðu árásir þeirra árangurslausar, og þeir sneyptust við það burtu' (my emphases): Jón Árnason, ed., *Íslenzkar þjóðsögur*, I, p.464.

[67] Jón Árnason, ed., *Íslenzkar þjóðsögur*, I, p.464

D. In Scandinavia

seems to be a more recent term than *að ljóða á*, and has a much wider range of applications, varying from the magical to the mundane. It is also a reflexive verb. The same cannot be said for *að ljóða á* which seems to retain its magical associations in all accounts.

4. '*Að ljóða á*'

The magical associations of *að ljóða á* are particularly clear in certain other tales in Jón Árnason's collection, where the expression seems to be applied to a distinct, recognised form of poetry. A good example occurs in a tale from Húnavatnssýsla in Iceland, called 'Skinnpilsa'. In this case, the versifying is initiated by a human being, a young poet called Niels who, while staying with a farmer, decides to deal with a rather unpleasant female spirit named Skinnpilsa that has been troubling the household: 'He started to *ljóða á* her, and she went into the wall with Niels after her. Nobody knows exactly how the "game" went, except that Niels returned, and nobody ever heard of Skinnpilsa again after that time.'[68]

In a more daily context, Jón Árnason also makes use of the expression in connection with some verse uttered by an old man on the island of Flatey in Breiðafjörður on the occasion of Jón's wedding there in 1866. Regarding this man, Jón writes in a letter that 'he *ljóðaði á* (chanted a poem for?) me and my bride and several others who said poems for us there.'[69] The implication here is that the old man's method of chanting poetry was different to that of the others, and perhaps seen as being more potent.

As mentioned above, this form of poetry had particular associations with magical incantation. Even more noteworthy is the fact that that the earliest extant reference to this term occurs in *Norna-Gests þáttr*, where it is used by Norna-Gestr to describe the way in which Brynhildr is challenged by the female giant (*gýgr*) when on her way to Hel at the start of the Eddic poem *Helreið Brynhildar*. According to Gestr, the poetic encounter begins with the *gýgr* (dressed in a skin-coat, and bearing a staff) challenging Brynhildr with the following words:

> I want to direct this at your burning, Brynhildr. It would have been better if you had been burnt alive for the evil deeds you carried out when you had that excellent man, Sigurðr Fáfnisbani, killed. I often gave him my support. For that act, I mean to chant these words of revenge at you ('hlioda a þig') so that everyone who hears mention of you will view you with hatred.[70]

Following this, Brynhildr and the giantess are said to 'hliodazst ... a',

---

[68] 'Fór hann þá að *ljóða á* hana, en hún gekk inn í veginn, og Niels á eptir henni. Einginn veit, hvernig þar hafa farið leikar með þeim, nema það eitt, að Niels kom aptur, en einginn varð var við Skinnpilsu siðan' (my emphases): Jón Árnason, ed., *Íslenzkar þjóðsögur*, I, pp.376–377.
[69] 'Hann *ljóðaði á okkur* bruðhjónin ásamt fleirum, sem þar kváðu til okkar' (my emphases): letter to Konrad Maurer, dated 6 September 1866, in Jón Árnason, *Úr förum Jóns Árnasonar*, II, p.114.
[70] 'Þessu uil ek bæina til brennu þinnar Brynhilldr. ok uæri betr at þu uærir lifande brend firir odadir þinar þær at þu letzt drepa Sigurd Fafnisbana sua agætan mann. ok oft var ek honum sinnut. ok firir þat skal ek *hlioda a þig* med hefnndarordum þeim at ollum ser þu at læidare er slikt heyra fra þer sagt': *Norna-Gests þáttr*, p.355.

V. Performances of Poetry and Song

5. 'Mansöngsvísur' and the poem commences, the first five strophes involving an alternation between the two characters, one of them wholly supernatural. In general terms, the similarities between this situation and the later legends mentioned above are obvious, and even more so when it is considered that one character (the *gýgr*) is deliberately trying to lay a curse on the other. Even if the same system of one character composing the first part of a strophe and the other completing it does not occur here, there are still enough parallels to suggest that the expression *að ljóða á* in the sense of a semi-magical confrontation between two people in verse was recognised and understood in popular tradition even at this time. It is tempting to consider whether the *senna* conflicts in poetry were at one time believed to have had as much magical efficacy. Similarly, the words of the expression raise the question of whether the term *ljóðaháttr*, used for the metre of the dialogic poems of the Edda, might not originally have been related to a some ritualistic custom related to the expression in question. Certainly, all the *ljóðaháttr* poems that have been discussed in this book involve a powerful alternation, and the danger of a curse of some kind often lurks behind the words, especially in the cases of *Skírnismál* (Skírnir and Gerðr) and *Fáfnismál* (Fáfnir and Sigurðr). Furthermore, the expression *að ljóða á* in the sense suggested above is particularly fitting as a description of Loki's trial of strength with the gods in Ægir's hall in *Lokasenna*.

5. 'Mansöngsvísur'

The idea of poetic conflict and that of efficacious poetry being chanted at a wedding leads to yet another piece of evidence concerning the presentation of poetry and song by more than one person in early medieval Iceland. The evidence in this case relates to another type of *leikr* that seems to have been popular during the twelfth and thirteenth centuries.

Gunnlaugr Leifsson's *Jóns saga helga*, of which only the Old Icelandic translation survives, was composed in Latin at the beginning of the thirteenth century, and includes the following statement:

> Before the holy Jón (Ögmundarson) became bishop, there used to be a popular game in which, as part of a dance, a man would sing erotic and obscene verses to a woman, and a woman love-verses to a man; he had this game stopped and strongly prohibited. He did not want any love-songs to be heard, or composed, but he did not entirely succeed in putting a stop to this.[71]

---

[71] 'Leikr sá var kærr mönnum, áðr en hinn heilagi Jón varð biskup, at kveða skyldi karlmaðr til konu í dans blautlig kvæði, ok regilig, ok kona til karlmanns mansöngsvísur; þenna leik lét hann af taka ok bannaði styrkliga. Mansöngskvæði vildi hann eigi heyra, né kveða láta, en þó fékk hann því eigi af komit með öllu': Gunnlaugur Leifsson, *Jóns saga helga*, in *Biskupa sögur* (1858–1878), I, p.237. Two other versions of the same passage, with minor differences in wording, are also given in *Biskupa sögur* (1858–1878), I, p.165:
a. 'Leikr sá var mönnum tíðr, er úfagrligr er, at kveðast skyldu at: karlmaðr at konu, en

D. In Scandinavia

As other scholars have suggested, this account seems to contain fashionable echoes of similar reports found in the biographies of other churchmen which were written in Europe during this period.[72] Nonetheless, as Strömbäck has argued, this fact should not rule out the possibility that the account was based on fact, and that it might point to an earlier Scandinavian dance-song tradition involving alternating verses like the Icelandic *vikivaki* of later times which was so closely connected with dramatic games of various kinds.[73] Indeed, as Jón Samsonarson has pointed out, even though this account has foreign parallels,

5. '*Mansöngsvísur*'

> (the game is) described in such a strange way that it seems unlikely to be pure fiction without any basis in reality. Gunnlaugur is either describing a game that he knows, or his description is based on a model found in some foreign literary work. And as long as it continues to be impossible to point to any comparable account in a work that Gunnlaugur might have known, then it must be expected that the game in question actually took place, either in his own time, or before it, or both.[74]

The critical comment made in the saga that the bishop 'did not entirely succeed in putting a stop to this' ('fékk . . . því eigi af komit með öllu') would seem to support this idea. As both Liestøl and Vésteinn Ólason have emphasised, 'the customs mentioned must . . . have been fairly well known about 1200, for otherwise the anachronism would have been too striking' for the readers.[75]

The form of poetry used in Gunnlaugr's *mansöngsvísur* was probably quite different from Eddic poetry, and much closer to the style of poetry later encountered in the Icelandic *rímur* and other dance-ballads. Yet in spite of this, the description given above has importance for the present discussion if only because it points once again to the fact that physical movement (*dans*) and 'poetry' (*kvæði*) were associated at this time, just as they are in the account of *seiðr* given above. The account also emphasises,

---

kona at karlmanni, klækiligar vísur ok hæðiligar ok óáheyriligar, en þat lét hann af takast ok bannaði með öllu at gera . . .'
b. 'Leikr sá var mönnum tíðr í þann tíma, er heldr var ófagr, at bera bottatilldi, þar skyldi karlmaðr kveða at konu, ok svo kona at kona at karlmanni, klækiligar vísur ok ótilheyrilegar með mansaungs sneiðíngi ok sámyrði. Þá forneskju lét hann af takast.'
[72] See Blöndal, 'Dans i Island', pp.165–166.
[73] See Strömbäck, 'Cult remnants,' 133–137. See further Ólafur Davíðsson, *Íslenzkar gátur*, III, p.9; Liestøl, 'Til spørsmålet', 69–70; and Jón Samsonarson, *Kvæði*, I, pp.ix–xii. Both Ólafur Davíðsson and Strömbäck see the tradition in question as having close links with the later *vikivaki*, and Jón Samsonarson is not averse to this idea. All of these scholars see the account as having some validity at least for the period around 1200, if not earlier. Regarding the *vikivaki* games, see *Chapter II, G.2–3*.
[74] '. . . er honum (leiknum) lýst svo sérkennilega, að ekki verður gert ráð fyrir, að lýsingin sé rakalaus uppspuni. Annað hvort er Gunnlaugur að lýsa leik sem hann þekkir til eða hann hefur fyrirmynd að lýsingunni úr erlendum ritum. Og á meðan ekki tekst að benda á hliðstæðu í ritum sem Gunnlaugur hefði getað þekkt, verður að gera ráð fyrir, að leikurinn hafi raunverulega tíðkazt um daga hans eða fyrir hans daga eða hvort tveggja': Jón Samsonarson, *Kvæði*, I, p.xi.
[75] Vésteinn Ólason, *Traditional ballads*, p.36, echoing Liestøl, 'Til spørsmålet', 70.

V. Performances of Poetry and Song

once again, that poetic traditions in which several people participated in presenting a song or poem must have been well known in Scandinavia during the early Middle Ages.

E. Conclusion

It is possible to draw several conclusions from the material collected above, the most obvious being that solo performance and creation of poetry was not the only method of performance for the Scandinavians of the early medieval period. Admittedly, the evidence presented is somewhat scant, covers a wide period of time, and is drawn from a variety of places, the Icelandic material having the greatest prominence primarily because Iceland provides the greatest amount of early literary source material. As with all evidence drawn from the sagas, there must remain an element of doubt about the exact historicity of what is written. Nonetheless, these stories were read for or by living people during the thirteenth and fourteenth centuries, and it must be assumed that the accounts made sense to these people on the basis of what they knew.

In other words, traditions like the *senna* and *mannjafnaðr* involving an impromptu competitive performance of poetry by two or more participants must have been recognised in daily life during the thirteenth century and earlier. These forms of poetry appear to have loosely followed a system of unwritten rules, and to have had a recognised pattern which the participants followed when they took part in the '*leikr*', although the mere nature of the game appears to have been such that real personal offence might easily occur, thus transforming 'game' into dangerous reality as occurs in the case of *Þorgils saga ok Hafliða*.

The origin and age of these two poetic forms is uncertain, but it is logical to consider the possibility of an earlier relationship between the *senna* and *mannjafnaðr* and preparations for battle. Indeed, according to Tacitus, the Germanic tribes often indulged in such bouts of insults as a prelude to battle, just as children and adolescents do in our own time.[76] Other natural early contexts for such conflicts are weddings, where, as in other countries, poetic contests between families seem to have been a common phenomenon,[77] and then the law courts which sat during the sacred *þing* meetings.[78] In the latter context, it is interesting to consider the role and context of the comparable Inuit 'nith-song' or 'drum-song' which are:

> the Eskimo's way of replacing a law-court by a public poetry contest . . .
> Since among the Eskimos there was no tribal police force for carrying out the

---

[76] See Tacitus, *The histories*, Book II, ch.21, in *The histories. The annals*, I, pp.194–195; and Harris, 'The senna', 69–70. Certainly, such a context would be relevant for the *sennur* between Sinfjötli and Guðmundr in *Helgakviður Hundingsbana I and II*.
[77] See above, note 11.
[78] As in the case of *Bandamanna saga* and *Ölkofra þáttr*. See also above, note 55.

E. Conclusion

laws, and individual revenge was expected, this bloodless way of settling feuds did have great social value. This form of verbal tournament . . . was often so successful that the loser, publicly shamed by his sharp-tongued opponent, left the neighborhood to avoid remaining a laughingstock.[79]

The choice of using of poetry as a medium for these verbal contests amongst the native Scandinavians suggests that at one time, perhaps, the duels were seen as being even more efficacious, and of having the capability to bestow protection or a curse along the lines of the tradition that lies behind the expression *að ljóða á*. In later times, however, it seems clear that competitions of this kind had entered the realm of 'games', and were often regarded simply as an established form of social entertainment, rather than anything magically dangerous.

The description of the *mansöngsvísur* given in *Jóns saga helga* suggests yet another form of *leikr* involving song or poetic performance conducted by two or more people of different sexes, probably in association with a circle-dance. As such, this account might even provide a bridge between the more religious pagan circle-dance hinted at in the account of *seiðr* given in *Eiríks saga rauða*, and the later circle-dances of the *vikivaki*, so closely connected with costumed games activities.

The only thing that is lacking in the above references is a detailed description of a performance of a *pre-composed* poem by more than one person. With the exception of *Varðlokur/ Varðlokkur* which formed a recognised part of the *seiðr* ritual, and possibly also the *mansöngsvísur*, all of the other accounts refer to poems, songs, or chants that seem to have been improvised on the spot. Nonetheless, the relationship between poems like *Lokasenna*, *Hárbarðsljóð* and *Skírnismál* and the popular, improvised *senna/ mannjafnaðr* traditions is unquestionable. It is also logical to suggest indirect links between these competitive traditions and the contests of knowledge encountered in poems like *Vafþrúðnismál*, *Alvíssmál*, and *Gátur Gestumblinda*, which centre upon two main contestants and are closely linked to the popular oral form of the riddle competition.[80] The only real difference in shape between the Eddic poems and those that are depicted as taking place in daily life is that none of the popular forms involves the active presentation of a fictional narrative framework for the contest. Yet the distance between a stylised 'game' involving two speakers competing in inventing fictional accounts about themselves or their opponents and an 'acted' performance of a preconceived 'poem' involving

---

[79] Day, *The sky clears*, pp.42–43. See also Hoebel, *The law of primitive man*, pp.98–99.
[80] See Machan, *Vafþrúðnismál*, pp.24–25. As Machan suggests, it can argued that *Vafþrúðnismál* draws on the traditions of the both *senna* and (in particular) the *mannjafnaðr*. The mythological form of these Eddic contests also raises the possibility of earlier links with initiatory rituals. Regarding the links between the form of riddle poem encountered in the Eddic poems and *Heiðreks saga* and those existing in religious poems like the *Rig Veda*, see Jón Hnefill Aðalsteinsson, 'Gátur', pp.428–433. Regarding comparable forms of mythological and genealogical instruction in puberty and shamanistic initiation ceremonies, for example, see Eliade, *Rites and symbols*, p.3, p.16 and p.87.

V. Performances of Poetry and Song

similar elements is extremely short. Even closer to drama is *seiðr*, with its platform, its animal skin costumes, its other magical props, and its particular chant. Indeed, considering these features and the fact that numerous rituals throughout the world involve the retelling of sacred myth in order to reinvoke the power of 'sacred time',[81] there cannot have been a great difference between a performance of *seiðr* and a semi-dramatic group performance of a monologic poem like *Völuspá*.

The question of which came first, the Eddic 'flytings' or the popular improvised form of the *senna* is a kind of chicken and egg problem. Most likely, influences were mutual. Yet the existence of both has to lead back to the question of the actual performance of the Eddic poems. According to Lönnroth, for example:

> The *mannjafnaðr* gives opportunities for an oral performer to act out, in an amusing manner, conflicts which are likely to be present in a Norse audience consisting of drinking party guests. By playing the roles of contesting and quarrelsome heroes, who belong to the world of myth but behave as if they were members of the audience, the performer is able to bridge the gap between the heroic dream and the considerably less heroic reality of the drinking table.[82]

Such may have been possible in the case of a prose account in which a verbal duel is firmly couched in a large body of narrative, as in the case of the sagas. Yet as has been demonstrated in *Chapter III*, the wholly dialogic Eddic poems present a very different problem. Apart from the immense difficulties that a live rendition of *Hárbarðsljóð* and *Lokasenna* would impose on any solo performer, it must be considered that the audience in question would have been used to similar 'live' competitions in daily life, performed by two or more men. In contrast with such two-man performances, a clumsy one-man presentation of the fast verbal fencing involved in these two Eddic poems would have been rather tame, to say the least.

---

[81] See the *Introduction, section C*, and especially note 96.
[82] Lönnroth, 'The double scene', p.98.

Conclusion

In the *Introduction* to this book, reference was made to the three questions posed by Andreas Heusler in 1922 in response to Bertha Phillpotts' argument in *The Elder Edda and ancient Scandinavian drama* that some form of ritual drama had existed in pagan Scandinavia, and that it was possible to find the remnants of this drama in the dialogic poems of the Poetic Edda. Heusler was highly sceptical, feeling that there was little real evidence to support such an argument. His attitude has since coloured the way in which many other academics have approached the question of 'Eddic drama' over the last seventy years.

The aim of the present study was simply to gather together all the available evidence for ritual and popular drama having existed in early Scandinavia, and to re-examine both this and the dialogic poems of the Poetic Edda with fresh eyes, and most particularly with the eyes of a performer. On the basis of the detailed evidence that has been presented above, it should now be clear that Heusler was far too hasty in his condemnation of Phillpotts' argument which, in spite of being over-theoretical and somewhat exaggerated, was obviously not so very far from the truth. Some form of ritual drama certainly seems to have existed in pagan Scandinavia, and there is good reason for believing that some of the Eddic poems in *ljóðaháttr* must have evolved within such a tradition.

As the archaeological and literary evidence assembled in *Chapter I* demonstrates, elementary dramatic activities of the kind defined in the *Introduction* must have been taking place in pagan ritual in Scandinavia at least as far back as the Bronze Age. Furthermore, the images depicted on the Oseberg tapestry and on other finds from the Iron Age imply that these ritual activities must have continued to exist in Norway and Denmark into the late ninth century. If the accounts written by Saxo Grammaticus and Adam of Bremen are to be trusted, these activities may well have gone on in Uppsala up until the time of the Conversion in the eleventh century. Subsequently, as in other countries in Europe, it is probable that many of these early ritualistic activities were transformed into seasonal dramatic folk 'games', such as those associated with the *julebukk*, *Halm-Staffan*, the midsummer folk weddings in mainland Scandinavia, and other related traditions like those involving the *þingálp*, the *grøleks*, *Grýla* and the *jólhestur* in the North Atlantic islands. All of these customs appear to be native to Scandinavia, and as has been demonstrated in *Chapter II*, there is good reason to believe that some of them go back at least as far as the thirteenth and fourteenth centuries.

On the basis of the examination made into the dialogic poems of the Poetic Edda and the marginal notation found accompanying their texts in the original manuscripts in *Chapters III–IV*, there would appear to be little doubt that the dialogic poems in *ljóðaháttr* must have been presented in a dramatic fashion somewhere in western Scandinavia as late as the twelfth or thirteenth centuries. The probability is that these presentations were not carried out by a solo performer, but by *at least* two people working together. This supposition would appear to be confirmed not only by the extant form of the poems, but also by the deliberate use of the system of marginal speaker notation in the manuscripts.

Bearing in mind the fact that four of the five Eddic works examined above were 'composed' in *ljóðaháttr*, a verse form used solely for direct speech in the form of dialogue and monologue, there is good cause to consider whether *all* the works in this metre were originally 'acted' in a similar fashion. In other words, is it possible that *ljóðaháttr* was not only closely associated with the use of speech, but also with the mode of presentation? Considering the nature of the other poems in this metre, this must be a distinct possibility. *Alvíssmál*, for example, lacks any marginal notation in the manuscript, but is wholly dialogic and displays many similarities and comparable problems to the five poems discussed in *Chapter III, G*. Furthermore, while there is no denying that *Grímnismál*, *Sigrdrífumál* and *Hávamál* are all essentially monologic works, it must also be considered that none of these works is a pure soliloquy. All three imply the necessary presence of another listening figure; that is, Agnarr in *Grímnismál*, Sigurðr in *Sigrdrífumál* and Loddfáfnir in *Hávamál IV* (sts 111–137). This feature takes the reciting figure of each work out of direct communication with the audience in the present time, and places the performer in a more distanced, 'acted' situation.[1]

The implication is that the use of *ljóðaháttr does* point to the use of some form of dramatic presentation, just as the use of *fornyrðislag* seems to have been associated with epic-dramatic works that employed an external third-person narrator. For this latter reason alone, it is impossible to assume automatically that works like *Helgakviða Hjörvarðssonar*, *Helgakviða Hundingsbana II*, and *Þrymskviða* should have been dramas too, just because they contain a lot of dialogue and several ritualistic motifs. The fact remains that they are composed largely in *fornyrðislag*, and they therefore have to be classified with the other epic-dramatic *fornyrðislag* poems, rather than alongside the 'dramas' composed in *ljóðaháttr*.

As has been pointed out in *Chapter V*, even though the sagas contain no direct evidence of dramatic activities, it seems clear that the involvement of more than one participant in the performance of 'poetry' in Scandinavia during the early Middle Ages was hardly unknown, particularly in the field of popular traditions such as the *senna* and *mannjafnaðr*, and magical ceremony. A two-man performance of a work like *Hárbarðsljóð* would not have taken a thirteenth-century audience by surprise.

The essential difference, however, is that any such performance of the dialogic Eddic poems would have immediately represented a move into the

---

[1] On the question of *Hávamál*, see further North, 'How was Hávamál performed', pp.160–162.

Conclusion

field of drama, since the audience would not have been able to avoid associating the individual performers with the roles they were reciting or improvising. Furthermore, the roles contained in the extant versions of the works in question are far from being totally static, characterless symbols. Parts like Þórr (in Hárbarðsljóð and Lokasenna), Óðinn (in Hárbarðsljóð in particular), Loki (in Lokasenna), Sigurðr and Fáfnir (in Fáfnismál), Freyr (in Skírnismál), Byggvir (in Lokasenna), and Frigg (in Vafþrúðnismál) all involve strong elements of emotion and/or characterisation which would encourage any solo performer to go beyond mere monotonous chanting. Once emotion has been added to a recital of any of these poems, direct 'acting' is just a tone or arm movement away.[2] Indeed, considering the examinations of Skírnismál and Fáfnismál in Chapter III, it is probable that many dramatic performances must have gone even further than this, and been much closer in form to present-day folk drama, or medieval drama in its more rudimentary stages. The works are so complex that in the unlikely event of their having been presented by a single performer, he or she would have had to be a highly talented actor, comparable in skill to the professional foreign *mimi* or *histriones* that were traversing Europe during the period in question (see the Appendix).

Of course, the festivals that provided the context for the dramatic and semi-dramatic rituals and the later folk *leikar* discussed in Chapters I and II might also have provided a context for the performances of these postulated Eddic dramas. However, the actual link between the Eddic poems and these games and rituals must remain vague. Here, it is necessary to step tentatively into the realm of informed speculation. Certainly, it is highly unlikely that these small dramas had any deep ritualistic function when they were recorded in the thirteenth century, although, as has been suggested in Chapter V, the possibility cannot be ruled out that at that time the *ljóðaháttr* metre may have still had certain magical associations in particular situations. The greater likelihood is that when works like Skírnismál, Hárbarðsljóð and Lokasenna were recorded, they were merely regarded as varieties of folk *leikar* with ancient roots.[3]

Bearing this in mind, it might be noted that the enacted seasonal 'marriage' reflected in Skírnismál and Gunnars þáttr helmings has close parallels in later Scandinavian folk tradition like the mock-weddings discussed in Chapter II, D. Furthermore, as has been suggested in Chapter I, C.5, the figure of the static, talking god reflected in these two works finds a logical counterpart in straw figures like Halm-Staffan, the thirteenth-century Danish Bovi, and the Shetland *grøleks*. Indeed, as has been pointed out elsewhere in this book (Chapter II, B.2), an enormous straw guise of this kind might well be envisaged as lying behind the description of Byggvir given in Lokasenna, sts 44 and 46.

Another interesting parallel between the dialogic poems and later folk games is found in Finnur Magnússon's logical suggestion that the verbal

---

[2] On characterisation in Vafþrúðnismál, see Machan, ed., Vafþrúðnismál, pp.31–32.
[3] See the examination of the word *leikr* in Chapter I, B.1.

conflict in *Hárbarðsljóð* might have had an origin in the popular flytings (and possibly combats) that used to be conducted in Scandinavia and elsewhere between seasonal figures representing the Summer and Winter. The possibility that such seasonal flytings and combats were taking place in Scandinavia from a very early point in time cannot be ruled out.[4]

Finally, Óðinn's names Grímr and Grímnir,[5] Fáfnir's 'ægishiálmr' ('helmet/ mask of terror'), and Sigurðr's possible guise of the 'gǫfugt dýr' ('noble animal') in *Fáfnismál* would all make good sense if they were viewed in the context of disguised seasonal figures like the *julebukk*, the *þingálp* and *Grýla*. Indeed, these last-named figures are all closely associated with the winter period, and, like many of the other house-visiting Yuletide traditions discussed in *Chapter II, B*, they also offer interesting parallels to certain aspects of poems like *Vafþrúðnismál*, *Grímnismál*, and *Lokasenna* in their use of initial disguise, and their instigation of guessing games aimed at trying to establish the true identity of the visiting figure.[6]

A context for the dialogic *ljóðaháttr* poems within this kind of semi-dramatic Scandinavian folk tradition in the twelfth and thirteenth centuries would certainly make sense. The question of whether these postulated Eddic dramas had their origin in pagan ritual as Phillpotts suggested is naturally more problematic. The conclusions here must of necessity be more tentative and less wide-ranging than those made by Phillpotts, if only because the present author does not believe that poems like the *Helgakviður* or *Þrymskviða* can be included in the evidence for discussion. As was pointed out above, in their present form, these latter works must be classed as essentially as myths, rather than dramas.[7] Similarly, considering the possible implications of the oral tradition in which the dialogic poems were preserved,[8] it is impossible to say for certain what the texts of the postulated *ljóðaháttr* plays would have been like during the pagan period (if, of course, these works existed at that time). The core motifs, the structure and the overall format of the poems, however, are another question.

Considering the probable stability of these features, there is little doubt that dramatic performances of works like *Skírnismál*, *Vafþrúðnismál*, *Grímnismál*, *Fáfnismál*, *Sigrdrífumál*, and *Hávamál V and VI* would have had a strongly ritualistic flavour. *Skírnismál*, for example, involves not only an implied encounter in a grove between the god of fertility and a *jötunn* maiden who has close associations with natural forces of one kind

---

[4] See *Chapter II, C.1*.
[5] See *Chapter I, D.1*.
[6] See, for example, the references given in *Chapter II*, notes 107, 353, and 374.
[7] See the *Introduction, section C*.
[8] See *Chapter III, A*. Nonetheless, it should be borne in mind that a 'play' preserved orally might well have kept its form for a longer period than a poem, since apart from the fact that the performers as a group learn the play and can thus help individual members (new or otherwise) to remember the text, it is also important that the different performers know what cues to expect from their fellow actors.

Conclusion

or another,[9] but also Skírnir's extended curse involving a 'gambantein' ('a wand of power') and the carving of runes which, to judge from a rune stick found in Bergen, were still seen as having magical efficacy even in the late fourteenth century.[10] In addition to this, one notes Gerðr's formalised offering of a cup or horn to Skírnir at the end of the curse (st.37). This particular motif also occurs in a ritualistic context on one of the Gallehus horns, as well as on a number of Viking Age rock carvings from Sweden.[11] Interestingly enough, it is also encountered in *Sigrdrífumál* (st.5), where the offer of the cup is again accompanied by an apparently magical incantation, and in *Lokasenna* (st.53), where it is possibly a borrowing.

Another recurring element in the works that have been discussed is the presence of fire. Skírnir, for example, has to leap over the flame wall surrounding Gerðr, an act that is paralleled by Sigurðr in *Sigrdrífumál*, and which, in real terms, finds close analogies in various European folk traditions connected with the Whitsun or midsummer bonfires, where people used to regularly jump over the flames for good luck or fertility.[12] At the same time, one notes the importance of fire for Grímnir's torment and shamanistic revelations in *Grímnismál*, and Sigurðr's ritualistic roasting of the heart in *Fáfnismál*, a poem that not only demands the presence of fire, but also the existence of a tree (or bush), water, and a hidden building as part of its surroundings.[13] *Fáfnismál*, of course, does not only involve the image of the roasting of the heart, but also the powerful motifs of both Reginn and Sigurðr tasting Fáfnir's blood. Furthermore, the expressions 'gǫfugt dýr' and 'ægishiálmr' which were mentioned above in connection with later animal disguises like that of the *julebukk*, might also be seen in terms of older, more ritualistic masks and costumes like those depicted on

---

[9] There is a great deal of dispute about the question of the relationship between *Skírnismál* and the seasonal marriage suggested by Olsen in 'Fra gammelnorsk myte og kultus', and later supported by Schück (see *Introduction*, note 29); Phillpotts, in *The Elder Edda*, p.137; Dronke, in 'Art and tradition'; and Talbot, in 'The withdrawal of the fertility god'. The movement against this idea was led by Sahlgren, initially in *Eddica et Skaldica*, pp.209–303. Even though Sahlgren's ideas have never been wholly accepted, similar doubts have been voiced by Motz, in 'Gerðr', 129–131, and 'Sister in the cave', 180; Polomé, in 'Etymology', 834; Randlev, in 'Skírnismál', 155; and most recently by Steinsland, in *Det hellige bryllup*, pp.30–38. Noreen, in *Den norsk-isländska poesien*, p.65; Lönnroth, in 'Skírnismál', p.178; and Bibire, in 'Freyr and Gerðr', p.29, are more ambivalent, but open to the possibility that *Skírnismál* might have an origin in ritual. For the present author, the likelihood that this myth was *acted* places it in a much more directly ritualistic context. See further the discussion of myth and ritual given in the *Introduction, section C*.
[10] See Leistøl, 'Runer frå Bergen', 41–49.
[11] See *Chapter I, B.4*.
[12] See, for example, Macleod Banks, *British calendar customs: Orkney and Shetland*, pp.51–52 and pp.55–57, on the traditions associated with the Beltane and Johnsmas fires in Shetland.
[13] All four features can be regarded as having potential ritual significance. The same applies to the 'haugr' (gravemound?) that the shepherd sits on in *Skírnismál*, st.11, close to Gerðr's flame wall and the site of Skírnir's incantation and rune carving. Naturally, the contest of wisdom contained in *Vafþrúðnismál* also takes place inside a 'hall' in firelight.

the Oseberg tapestry and the Torslunda matrices.[14] Indeed, in dramatic terms, *Fáfnismál* has all the traits of a formal initiation ceremony. In a wider context, it might be remembered that gnomic interrogation and knowledge contests like those encountered in *Fáfnismál*, *Vafþrúðnismál*, *Alvíssmál*, and perhaps also *Grímnismál* and parts of *Hávamál*, are often known to play a central role in religious ritual, and especially those rituals related to initiation ceremonies which tend to involve a number of dramatic elements.[15]

In general, the possibility cannot be excluded that, as acted works, certain of the *ljóðaháttr* poems might have evolved out of dramatic or semi-dramatic pagan rituals like those discussed in *Chapter I*. The notable exception is perhaps *Lokasenna*, which lacks any obvious ritualistic elements at its core, and which, as some scholars have argued, might have begun to take shape (perhaps as an improvised seasonal game) at a somewhat later date than the other works discussed in this book.[16] In spite of this, there is little question that *Lokasenna* belongs to, and almost certainly owes much to the proposed early Scandinavian dramatic tradition. Indeed, it might logically be regarded as the first Scandinavian dramatic work to evolve, or be created without any obvious *direct* link to earlier pagan ritual.

The above hypotheses raise one highly interesting and pertinent question. If, as has been suggested, the dialogic poems (or at least variations on them) *were* originally performed both as part of earlier ritual and later folk tradition and entertainment somewhere in Scandinavia, why then did the tradition never evolve? In answer to this, it must be stressed that it is impossible to say exactly how widespread the dramatic performances of these works would have been, if they ever took place at all. The likelihood is that by the early Middle Ages their distribution and frequency of performance would have been highly limited. If these dramas *did* evolve out of ritual, which seems a logical assumption, then such ritual would have had to have been on a relatively large scale, at a venue the size of a seasonal sacrifice or a *þing* meeting.[17] After the Conversion, such activities would have been reduced to a much smaller scale, and largely kept out of the view of the more zealous officials of the church. In time, just like folk games in other countries, these performances would have diminished in scope leaving nothing but the essential features of the costumed figures and basic action. These essential features might then have formed the basis for certain of the seasonal costumed folk traditions known in later times.

At the same time, it is worth noting that all of the extant dramatic works in question are associated directly or indirectly with the pagan gods and pagan religious belief. This emphasises the fact that these works cannot

---

[14] See *Chapter I, C.7 and D.1*.
[15] See further *Chapter I, C.7* and *Chapter V, E*.
[16] See *Chapter III, G.2*.
[17] Of course, less complex works like *Hárbarðsljóð* or *Vafþrúðnismál* could have evolved under simpler circumstances.

Conclusion

have been composed in the twelfth or thirteenth century. It is one thing to write a poem using pagan imagery, but quite another to write a play in which actors are expected to bring the pagan gods 'to life', utter curses and carve runes. In the moral climate of the early Middle Ages where there was little distinction between the actor and the role, such would have been out of the question.

At the same time, a dramatic tradition rooted in such beliefs and such seasonal contexts would not have been likely to inspire the development of purely secular works, or Christian dramas based on Biblical events. The tradition was bound to die out if it could not radically transform itself. Lacking any large-scale public venues which might have encouraged its development in other directions, such a dramatic tradition was certain to take the former course.

As mentioned above, these latter speculations can be nothing more than tentative. The fact remains, however, that drama in the sense defined in the *Introduction* must have existed in early medieval Scandinavia, and that some of the Eddic poems should also be seen in the context of dramatic performance, whatever their origin may have been. Indeed, the *Codex Regius* and the AM 748 appear to contain some of the earliest dramatic works written in the vernacular in northern Europe. If nothing else, these considerations require that some radical re-thinking be done about not only the nature and genre of the *ljóðaháttr* works themselves, but also our ideas concerning the depth and speed of the Conversion in Scandinavia which allowed such simple pagan dramas as these to remain in existence for so long.

APPENDIX

The *Leikarar* in Scandinavia

There can be little doubt that when Saxo Grammaticus referred to the 'womanish movements, the clatter of the *mimi* on the stage' at Uppsala,[1] and when he described Starcatherus' various other encounters with *mimi*, *ioculatores*, *histriones*, *scurræ* and *parasiti* in Book VI of *Gesta Danorum*,[2] he had in mind a particular type of multi-talented dramatic performer that he must have commonly encountered in Denmark in the early thirteenth century; a breed of performer that, in fact, would have been highly unlikely to have taken part in pagan ritual activities in Scandinavia. Saxo tends to use the above terms knowledgeably, if interchangeably and always negatively, to describe certain court entertainers. However, when writing about Uppsala, he was primarily using the word *mimi* as an image that his contemporaries would have recognised. As has been shown in this book, there was no other terminology available to him to describe a dramatic performer or dancer. Nonetheless, it is important for modern readers to make a clear distinction between the real *mimi* and any native Scandinavians who might have performed the Eddic poems.

The *mimi* and *histriones* and their counterparts were predominantly solo travelling performers whose roots can be traced directly back to the classical Roman theatre which had been formally dissolved in the late sixth century under pressure from the church.[3] The potential skill of these performers is demonstrated by the oft-quoted epitaph of the *mimus* Vitalis who appears to have died in the early ninth century:

> I used to mimic the face, manner and words of those talking,
> so that you would think many people spoke from one mouth.
> The subject, presented with a twin image of himself before his eyes,
> would tremble to see a more real self existing in my faces.

---

[1] 'Effeminatos corporum motus scænicosque mimorum': see references in *Chapter I*, note 215.
[2] See Saxo Grammaticus, *Gesta Danorum*, Book VI, pp.154–155, p.162, and pp.168–169; translated in *The history of the Danes*, pp.172–173, p.180, p.186. For other references to 'theatrical behaviour' in Saxo's history, see *Gesta Danorum*, Book III, p.72, and Book V, p.113; translated in *The history of the Danes*, p.78 and p.127.
[3] On the appearance and influence of these figures in medieval Europe, and their classical background, see Nicoll, *Mimes, masks and miracles*, pp.83–175; Chambers, *The mediaeval stage*, I, pp.1–86; Ogilvy, 'Mimes, scurræ, histriones'; Hunningher, *The origin of the theatre*, pp.71–93; Axton, *European drama*, pp.17–32; and Tydeman, *The theatre in the Middle Ages*, pp.22–27. Regarding the various attacks on the theatrical arts made by the Church Councils, see Nicoll, *Masks, mimes and miracles*, pp.136–150, and Chambers, *The mediaeval stage*, I, pp.12–17.

Oh, how often a lady saw herself in my performance,
and blushed for shame, horribly embarrassed.
Thus, as many human forms as were seen in my body
were snatched away with me by the dismal day of death.[4]

These street and court performers not only played instruments and performed tricks of various kinds, but also sang and presented simple dramatic scenes. They seem to have begun moving into northern Europe at the time the Roman theatre was dissolved,[5] and by 679, were apparently reaching England in sufficient numbers to warrant the Rome Council on English affairs issuing an ineffectual warning against the harbouring of plays ('iocus ludos') by monasteries.[6] In 797, Alcuin wrote a letter to Higbald, bishop of Lindisfarne, warning him of the dangers of 'istriones' and 'citharistem'. This clearly had little effect: King Edgar still complains in his *Oratio* in 969 about how monasteries are becoming houses of 'histrionum', resulting in '*mimi* singing and dancing in the squares' about the decadence of these institutions.[7] As Ogilvy points out, these performers actually seem to have prospered in the wake of the first Danish invasions of England during the second half of the tenth century.[8]

That performers known as *histriones* were still prevalent in England, and still closely associated with dramatic presentation during the thirteenth century when the sagas were being written and the Eddic poems recorded is demonstrated by the evidence contained in Thomas de Cabham's *Penitential* (c.1213), and *Thurkill's vision of Hell*, written by Ralph of Coggeshall in the early thirteenth century.[9] De Cabham writes knowledgeably of how some *histriones* 'transform and transfigure their bodies with lewd dancing and postures, either by stripping off their clothing, or by putting on dreadful masks,' and complains of the 'numberless evils' caused by other male and female dancers 'who act in shameless representations' ('ludunt in imaginibus inhonestis').[10] *Thurkill's vision of*

---

[4] Translation by Richard Axton in *European drama*, p.1, where the original text of Vitalis epitaph is also given. See also Nicoll, *Mimes, masks and miracles*, p.95.

[5] For example, Attila is said to have been entertained by a Moorish buffoon in c.448: see Chambers, *The mediaeval stage*, I, pp.34–35, and Opland, *Anglo-Saxon oral poetry*, pp.51–52, and the references given in note 3 above.

[6] See Chambers, *The mediaeval stage*, I, pp.31–32.

[7] Alcuin's *Epistolæ*, 124; Edgar's *Oratio Edgari Regius pro monachatu propoganda*, and a similar statement from canon 58 in Edgar's *Canons* (c.960) are referred to in Chambers, *The mediaeval theatre*, I, p.32, notes 3 and 5. See also Ogilvy, 'Mimes, scurræ, histriones', 609, on other references made by Alcuin to these entertainers (as in *Epistolæ*, 175). On Edgar's account in the *Oratio*, see further Ogilvy, 'Mimes, scurræ, histriones', 613–614.

[8] Ogilvy, 'Mimes, scurræ, histriones', 613–614.

[9] See also John of Salisbury's *Polycraticus*, written c.1159, and quoted in Tydeman, *The theatre in the Middle Ages*, p.187, which seems to display an unusually strong understanding of classical dramatic performance.

[10] Translation given in Tydeman, *The theatre in the Middle Ages*, pp.187–188. See also Nicoll, *Mimes, masks and miracles*, p.152. The original text is given in Chambers, *The mediaeval stage*, II, pp.262–263.

Appendix

Hell contains the image of a large iron amphitheatre in Hell containing several playing areas or 'plateæ' in which sinners are forced to re-enact their former crimes: a 'proud man' presents an exaggerated mimed image of himself, and a crooked lawyer enters the 'theatrical games' by recreating his corrupt deals with people. There is little question that these images, too, were based largely on the style of entertainment offered by contemporary entertainers like the *pantomimi* and *histriones*.[11] The likelihood is that it was solo performers of this kind who would have presented works like *Dame Sirith* and the *Interludium de clerico et puella* (see *Chapter IV, D.1*).

One route north for this tradition and this kind of entertainer ran through France from Italy. The other natural route was through Russia and Germany, from Constantinople where the Scandinavians in the Varangian Guard would have encountered several types of living professional theatre even in the tenth and eleventh centuries.[12] Frescoes containing images of such performers close by that of the 'Fight of the guisers' (see *Chapter I, C.7*) on the stairway of Hagia Sophia Cathedral in Kiev.[13] Considering all of the above, it is not altogether surprising that these kinds of foreign entertainer should also have begun appearing in Scandinavia perhaps as early as the late ninth century; or that by the twelfth century, they were becoming so popular that they were posing a serious threat to the position of the Icelandic skalds at the Norwegian and Danish courts.[14]

That the Scandinavians knew of the professional *mimi*, *histriones* and *ioculatores*, and understood the meanings and associations of these words, is evident not only from the way they consistently translated these terms and concepts with their own words *leikari*, *loddari* and *trúðr*,[15] but also

---

11 Original text given in Loomis and Cohen, 'Were theatres in the twelfth and thirteenth centuries?', 94–95. A translation from the Latin is given by Loomis, in 'Some evidence for secular theatres', 38–39. On this account, see Tydeman, *The theatre in the Middle Ages*, p.47 and p.189; Marshall, 'Theatre in the Middle Ages', 377–378; and Woolf, *The English mystery plays*, pp.31–34.
12 See Nicoll, *Masks, mimes and miracles*, p.148, pp.159–160, and pp.202–212; and La Piana, 'The Byzantine theatre'. Regarding Germany, it is worth noting the *present tense* description of the *pantomimi* in Hamburg written by Adam of Bremen in c.1070, in *Gesta Hammabergensis ecclesiæ pontificum*, Book III, ch.39, pp.180–181; trans. in *The history of the Archbishops of Hamburg-Bremen*, p.147.
13 See Nicoll, *Mimes, masks and miracles*, pp.159–160.
14 See Einar Skúlason's complaint in *Knytlinga saga*, p.275, that 'danskr harri metr dýrra,/ dugir miðlung þat, fiðlur,/ . . . ok pípur' ('The Danish ruler values more highly fiddles . . . and pipes;/ it is not good enough!'). On this comment, see also Frank, *Old Norse poetry*, p.102.
15 See the references given in *Chapter I*, note 28, and *Chapter IV*, note 104. See also *Stjórn*, p.505, where 'trúðr' is used to translate the word 'scurris' in *Vulgata* (*Samuel* 6,20); *Maríu jartegnir*, in *Maríu saga*, II, p.789, where the word 'leikarasongum' almost certainly applies to the songs of the *histriones* in England, like those referred to in Edgar's *Oratio* (see note 7 above); and *Ynglinga saga*, p.42, where reference is made to King Hugleikr's 'leikara, harpara ok gígjara ok fiðlara'. These are evidently the same figures referred to in the words 'mimos ac ioculatores', 'mimorum greges', 'histrionibus', 'scurrarum', and 'iocularis ministrii' in the description of Hugleicus' court in Saxo

The 'Leikarar' in Scandinavia

from the references to the *leikarar*, *loddarar* and *trúðar* that occur in their own compositions. Considered alongside the European evidence of the time, these references prove that the *leikari* and *loddari* in Old Norse had particular associations with dramatic performance that were new, and quite different from the more traditional, native forms of drama referred to in this book. They also emphasise that, like the *mimi*, the *leikari* in Scandinavia was much more than a mere 'juggler', 'jester', 'spillemand', 'gjøgler' or 'gaukler'.[16] As elsewhere in Europe, the multiple talents of this figure should not be underestimated, nor his/ her capacity for transmitting foreign influences and foreign material.

No thorough examination has ever been made of the figure of the *leikari* in Old Norse literature, and unfortunately there is no space to remedy this situation completely here.[17] It must suffice for now to present a brief, general review of the main sources of material on the *leikari*, and indicate the general conclusions that can be drawn about this figure.

Many of the references to *leikarar* and *loddarar* in Old Norse literature take the form of borrowed literary motifs or formulæ that are commonly found in European religious works and romances of the early Middle Ages. These motifs are naturally less trustworthy as sources on the native Scandinavian world, but provide given some insight into the general attitudes regarding these entertainers. The first common reference finds the *leikarar* and *loddarar* appearing as elements in the lists of disreputable types and sinful pursuits often mentioned in connection with wastrels and other dissolutes, a typical example being the description of the corrupt court of King Hugleikr given in *Ynglinga saga*.[18] In the second common

---

Grammaticus' *Gesta Danorum*, Book VI, pp.154–155; trans. in *The history of the Danes*, pp.172–173. See also the twelfth-century Latin-Icelandic glossary, MS Gl.kgl.saml.1812 4to. Here the word 'leikari' is used as a gloss for 'parasitus', which was one of the two names for a stock clown character in the old Roman mimic theatre: see Scardigli and Raschellà, 'A Latin-Icelandic glossary', p.306; Chambers, *The mediaeval theatre*, I, p.5; and Welsford, *The fool*, p.4, pp.7–8, p.19, and p.26. See also Ogilvy 'Mimes, scurræ, histriones', 607, on Isidore's definition of *scurra*. Another possible example of a translated concept is found in *Nikolaus saga erkibyskups II*, p.154, with regard to an antiphone that certain monks wish to sing about the life of St Nicholas, and which was seen by their prior as mere 'leikara læti' ('histrionic behaviour'). The word 'leikaraskapr' seems to be apply to the same phenomenon in *Laurentius saga Hólabiskups*, in *Biskupa sögur* (1858–1878), I, p.847. For references to comparable complaints about priests acting like 'tragedians' and using histrionic techniques, made in the twelfth canon of Clovesho (747), and by Ailred of Rievaulx (c.1160), see Ogilvy, 'Mimes, scurræ, histriones', 607: Loomis and Cohen, 'Were there theatres in the twelfth and thirteenth centuries?', 93; and Axton, *European theatre*, p.31.

[16] See, for example, the entries on *leikari* and *loddari* in Cleasby and Guðbrandur Vigfússon, *An Icelandic-English dictionary*, p.382 and p.396; Fritzner, *Ordbog over det gamle norske sprog*, II, p.471 and p.550; Sveinbjörn Egilsson and Finnur Jónsson, *Lexicon poeticum*, p.367, and de Vries, *Altnordisches etymologisches Wörterbuch*, p.362.

[17] For earlier examinations, see Olrik, 'Middelalderens vandrende spillemænd'; Holtsmark, 'Leik og skjemt'; Seip and Wallén, 'Leikarar'; Lindow, 'The two skaldic stanzas'; and most recently, Sveinn Einarsson, *Íslensk leiklist*, I, pp.13–16 and pp.31–34.

[18] Regarding *Ynglinga saga*, see above note 15 above. For further examples of this motif, see the references to *Rómverja saga* and *Thomassaga erkibiskups* in Chapter I, note

Appendix

formula, *leikarar* are regularly mentioned in the sense of 'musicians' or 'players' in traditional descriptions of entertainments at the courts of kings and princes in thirteenth and fourteenth century romances, where they are added primarily to help create an impression of grandeur.[19]

The most useful references to *leikarar*, however, are those which must be based, to some degree, on real life. The most trustworthy are the growing number of Scandinavian laws containing articles concerning the rights and treatment of *leikarar*. These demonstrate not only the changing attitudes to these figures who are sometimes ridiculed, and sometimes made the recipients of fine clothes used at weddings, but also their growing importance in Scandinavian society.[20]

Of equal value, if less clear in their implications, are the verses composed by skalds at the Norwegian and Danish courts, which deal with *leikarar*. The oldest, perhaps from c.900, is Þorbjörn hornklofi's *Haraldskvæði*, which tells of how King Haraldr hárfagri kept 'players and clowns' ('leikurum ok trúðum') at his court in Norway. Þorbjörn goes on to describe one particular *leikari* named Andaðr who supposedly 'makes the king laugh, when he dangles his crop-eared dog, and plays the fool', while other 'heel-kicking fellows (?) pass burning pieces of wood across the fire (juggling?) and have phalluses (or ass's ears?) tucked under their belts.'[21]

---

28. See also *Nikolaus saga erkibyskups II*, p.133, and *Maríu jartegnir II*, in *Mariu saga*, I, p.282.

19 See, for example, *Kirialax saga* (c.1350), p.72: 'Þar kvomu framm loddarar margir ok leikarar, fremiandi margskonar gledi, sumir blesu i pipur, adrir haufdu bumbur, gigiur edr sallterium edr haurpur.' For other similar descriptions, see *Rémundar saga keisarasonar* (fourteenth century), p.16 and p.340; *Konráðs saga keisarasonar* (c.1300), p.16; *Dínus saga dramblâta* (fifteenth century), p.88; *Sigurðar saga þǫgla: the shorter redaction*, p.44; and *Sigurðar saga þǫgla* (1963: the longer redaction) p.258 (the original saga was probably written in 1350–1400). All of the above are romances written in Iceland. See also *Alexanders saga*, p.83. This earlier work is a loose translation of Gautier de Châtillons' *Alexandreis*, possibly made by Brandr Jónsson in c.1250, and provided a model for the style of many of the romances. Stylistically related to the above works is another Icelandic romance, *Nikulás saga leikara* from the same period. The title of this work is apparently explained by the statement that King Nikulás 'iðkaði leikara-íþrótt' ('practiced the art of the *leikari*'), but it is never made clear which art this is supposed to be: see *Sagan af Nikulási konungi leikara*, p.6.

20 Swedish laws: see *Äldre Vestgötalagen* ('lecara rætar', c.1200); *Östgötalagen* ('Drapa balkær', XVIII, c.1300); *Konung Magnus Erikssons landslag* ('Giftobalker', VII, fourteenth century); and *Konung Christoffers landslag* ('Giptamala balker', VII and VIII, fourteenth century), in *Samling af Sweriges gamla lagar*, I, p.67; II, p.62; X, p.58; and XII, pp.64–66. Norwegian laws: see *Kong Haakon Magnussöns förste retterbod om klædedragten* (21 October 1314); and *Kong Haakon Magnussöns anden retterbod om klædedragten* (8 December 1315), in *Norges gamle lov*, III, pp.109–110 and p.116.

21 'At leikurum ok trúðum/ hefi ek þik lítt fregit:/ hverr es ørgáti/ þeira Andaðar/ at húsum Haralds?'// 'At hundi elskar Andaðr/ ok heimsku drýgir/ eyrnalausum/ ok jǫfur hlægir;/ hinir eru ok aðrir,/ es af eld skulu/ brennanda spón bera,/ logǫndum húfum/ hafa sér und linda drepit/ heldræpir halar': *Fagrskinna*, p.64. Naturally, there has been some discussion about the words 'logǫndum húfum' (lit. 'burning caps'), but Magnus Olsen's suggestion that they were probably originally 'logǫndum stúfum', or 'burning phalluses' is not as strange as it may seem in the light of the evidence regarding the costumes of early

There is much in this strophe that is unclear. However, it is interesting to note that the first named *leikari* in Scandinavia appears to have been foreign.[22]

Another pair of sarcastic strophes supposedly composed by the Icelandic skald Máni in the late twelfth century about two *leikarar* at the court of King Magnús Erlingsson demonstrates the growing disdain felt by the poets for the *leikarar*. Emphasis is placed here on the musical skills of the performers who play a 'giga', pipe, and drum as well as having a small red dog leap over a stick ('reccr lætr rauða bickiu . . . yfir staf laupa'). The particular interest of these verses, however, is the mention of exaggerated facial expression ('Vndr er hvæ augum vændir' and 'kiapt oc blasna hvapta'), the note of what might be white make-up of some kind ('leicarar bleikir), and the suggestion that the performers use trickery ('gin'), grotesque antics ('skripa lat'), and satire ('skaup').[23] As with the description of Andaðr, these verses seem to contain many of the trademarks of a traditional *mimi* performance, especially when the accompanying prose describes how the audience made a ring around the *leikarar*, creating an elementary 'playing area'. The final poetic reference to the *leikarar* in mainland Scandinavia is found in verse composed by Einar Skúlason in the twelfth century about a *leikari* named Jarlmaðr who played the fiddle and was whipped for stealing a goat kid.[24] Once again, one notes that the name of the performer seems to be foreign.

All the information given above points to the fact that the *leikarar* were essentially foreign performers who had started coming to Scandinavia in the early tenth century, and had all-round skills like those of the *mimi* and *histriones* described elsewhere, their acts involving costumes, music, tricks, grotesque physical movement and satire. A good detailed contemporary description of such an entertainer, which must have been understood by the Scandinavian audience, is that given of Isungr, the leading player ('havvð loddari'), in *Þiðriks saga* which was translated from German in Norway. Isungr boasts that he can sing/ chant, play a harp, a fiddle and a 'giga' and all sorts of stringed instruments ('ec kann qveða. ec cann sla harpv oc draga fiðlv oc gigiv oc allzkonar strengleica'). He is said to have freedom of movement between all courts, can sew perfectly, and is the ideal person to ask about deceptive tricks ('vel og brögð'). He also carries

---

Greek and Italian comic performers: see Olsen, 'Til Haraldskvæði', 381–382; and Nicoll, *Masks, mimes and miracles*, p.26, p.62, p.91 and p.163. Blöndal's suggestion that the words were 'lafandum húfum' ('dangling caps') might also make sense considering the traditional asses' ears often worn by the *mimi*: see Blöndal, 'Some remarks', and Nicoll, *Masks, mimes and miracles*, pp.160–161.

[22] According to Sveinbjörn Egilsson and Finnur Jónsson, *Lexicon poeticum*, p.11, the name Andaðr is German.
[23] *Sverris saga*, p.91.
[24] See *Morkunskinna*, p.227.

Appendix

out an effective performance at King Osantrix's palace, which involves a man dressed up in a bear costume.[25]

It is much less certain whether the foreign *mimi* and *histriones* ever reached Iceland. The only evidence for such is the mention of *trúðar* ('clowns') in the later of the two manuscripts containing the Icelandic law *Grágás* (*Staðarhólsbók*, c.1280), and in a verse apparently composed by Kári Sölmundarson in *Njáls saga* describing how Skafti Þóroddsson was drawn 'into a booth to a clown' ('inn í búð til trúðar') when wounded at the Alþingi soon after the burning of Njáll's farm.[26] Both references, however, stress the difference between the *leikarar*/ *mimi* performers and those people who performed the Eddic poems. The latter would never have been regarded as *trúðar*; nor is it likely that any Scandinavian poet or poetic performer would have been as little respected or trusted in the law as the *leikarar* were.

If there were any connection between the professional *leikarar* and the popular dramatic tradition in Scandinavia examined in this book, it is unlikely to have been before the time of the first official reference to a secular play being performed in Scandinavia, a tantalising eddict issued by Cardinal Gregorius de Cresendio in Schleswig, in c.November 1222, stating simply that 'ring dances, games, and unseemly plays are forbidden in the church, along with fighting.'[27] By this time, the dialogic poems of the Elder Edda had already taken shape, and been performed in one form or another for several hundred years.

---

[25] See *Þiðriks saga af Bern*, I, p.242, and pp.261–267. Regarding the performance with the bear, see also the quotation given in *Chapter I*, note 29.

[26] See *Grágás* (1879: *Staðarhólsbók*), art. 311, p.347; and *Brennu-Njáls saga*, p.410. Interestingly enough, *trúðar* are not mentioned in the *Konungsbók* MS of *Grágás* which was written c.20 years before *Staðarhólsbók*. For comparison, see *Grágás* (1850–1870: *Konungsbók*) art.101, I, p.176. The *Staðarhólsbók* version of this article, however, which disqualifies *trúðar* from being able to stand as witnesses in the case of a killing reflects the tone of Charlemagne's *capitulum* from 789, and ultimately the Roman *Corpus Iuris Civilis* from the time of the republic and the early Empire. These laws place performers alongside slaves and other outsiders, denying them any legal rights: see Ogilvy, 'Mimi, scurræ, histriones', 608; Chambers, *The mediaeval stage*, I, pp.8–9; and the other legal references given above in note 20. Such laws are based not only on the fact that these performers often had no legal home, but also because, logically, they could not be trusted to tell the truth. It might also be noted that a figure named Án trúðr is mentioned in *Droplaugasonar saga*, p.143 and pp.148–149, but no explanation is given of Án's by-name.

[27] 'Ringdanse, lege eller usømmelige skuespil bør ikke finde sted i kirken, og heller ikke slagsmål': *Danmarks riges breve*, I.5, nr.209, p.185.

Bibliography

In the following, all sources, whether primary or secondary, have been listed together for practical reasons. Unless they use a family name, all Icelandic authors are listed under their Christian names. Abbreviations for the titles of journals are provided in the *List of abbreviations*.

Aarne, Antti and Thompson, Stith, *The types of the folktale: A classification and bibliography*, FF Communications, 184, 2nd ed. (Helsinki 1961)
Aasen, Ivar, *Norsk ordbog* (Christiania, 1873)
Abrahams, Roger D., 'Folk drama', in *Folklore and folklife*, ed. Richard M. Dorson (Chicago, 1972), pp.351–362
Adam de la Halle, *Le jeu de la feuillée*, ed. Jean Rony (Paris, 1969)
Adam de la Halle, *Le jeu de la feuillée*, ed. Jean Dufournet (Paris, 1989)
Adam de la Halle, *Le jeu de Robin et Marion*, ed. Jean Dufournet (Paris, 1989)
Adam de la Halle, *Le jeu de Robin et de Marion*, ed. Kenneth Varty (London, 1960)
Adam of Bremen, *Gesta Hammaburgensis ecclesiæ pontificum*, in *Scriptores rerum Germanicarum*, ed. Bernhard Schmeidler, 3rd ed. (Hanover, 1917)
Adam of Bremen, *The history of the Archbishops of Hamburg-Bremen*, trans. Francis J. Tschan (New York, 1959)
Alexanders saga, ed. Finnur Jónsson (København, 1925)
Alford, Violet, 'The Hobby Horse and other animal masks', *Folklore*, 79 (1968), 122–134
Alford, Violet, 'Some Hobby Horses of Great Britain', *The journal of the English folk dance and song society*, III, iv (1939), 221–240
Alford, Violet, *Sword dance and drama* (London, 1962)
Almgren, Bertil, 'Hällristningarnas tro. Til tolkningen av de svenska hällristningarna från bronsåldern', *Saga och sed* (1977), 69–108
Almgren, Oscar, *Hällristningar och kultbruk*, Kungl. Vitterhets Historie och Antikvitets Akademiens handlingar, 35 (Stockholm, 1926–1927)
Almqvist, Bo, 'Midfjordingamärren: En folklig satir från Sturlungatiden og dess bakgrund', *Kungl. Humanistiska Vetenskaps Samfundet. Årsbok* (1969–70), 5–20
Alver, Brynjulf, 'Lussi, Tomas og Tollak: Tre kalendariske julefigurar', in *Nordisk folktro: Studier tillägnade Carl-Herman Tillhagen*, ed. Bengt af Klintberg, Reimund Kvideland and Magne Velure (Lund, 1976), pp.105–126
Ammianus Marcellinus, *Rerum gestarum libri qui supersunt*, 3 vols, trans. John C. Rolfe, rev., Loeb classical library (London, 1950)
Andersson, Otto, 'Framförandet av Kalevalarunorna', *Budkavlen* (1936), 65–80
Andersson, Otto, 'Kalevalameter – fornyrdislag', *Budkavlen* (1937), 84–100
Andersson, Theodore M., *The legend of Brynhild*, Islandica, XLIII (Ithaca, 1980)
Andersson, Theodore M., and Miller, William Ian, *Law and literature in medieval Iceland. Ljósvetninga saga and Valla-Ljóts saga* (Stanford, California, 1989)

Bibliography

Arent, A. Margaret, 'The heroic pattern: Old Germanic helmets, Beowulf, and Grettis saga', in *Old Norse literature and mythology: A symposium*, ed. Edgar C. Polomé (Austin, 1969), pp.130–199

Arill, David, 'Lövgubben i Uddevalla', in *Nordiskt folkminne: Studier tillägnade C. W. von Sydow*, ed. Åke Campbell, Waldemar Liungman and Sigfrid Svensson (Stockholm, 1928), pp.9–12

Aristotle, *The poetics*, ed. and trans. W. Hamilton Fry, in *Aristotle in twenty three volumes*, in the Loeb classical library, revised (London, 1932)

The Arnamagnæan manuscript 674 A 4º, Manuscripta Islandica, IV, ed. Jón Helgason (Copenhagen, 1957)

The Arna-Magnæan manuscript 677, 4to, introduced by Didrik Arup Seip, Corpus Codicum Islandicorum Medii Aevi, XVIII (Copenhagen, 1949)

Arngrímur Jónsson, *Crymogæa: Þættir úr sögu Íslands*, ed. Jakob Benediktsson and Helgi Þorláksson, trans. into Icelandic by Jakob Benediktsson, Safn Sögufélags, II (Reykjavík, 1985)

Ashmore, Sidney G., ed., *The comedies of Terence*, 2nd ed. (New York, 1908)

The Auchinleck manuscript, National Library of Scotland, Advocates' MS. 19.2.1, introduced by Derek Pearsall and I. C. Cunningham (London, 1977)

Auden, W. H., and Taylor, Paul B., trans., *Norse poems* (London, 1983)

Axton, Richard, *European drama of the early Middle Ages* (London, 1974)

Axton, Richard, 'Popular modes in the earliest plays', in *Medieval drama*, ed. Neville Denny, Stratford-upon-Avon studies, 16 (London, 1973), pp.13–40

Axton, Richard, and John Stevens, ed. and trans., *Medieval French plays*, (Oxford, 1971)

Ágrip af Nóregskonungasögum, in ÍF XXIX, ed. Bjarni Einarsson (Reykjavík, 1984), pp.1–54

Árna saga biskups, ed. Þorleifur Hauksson (Reykjavík, 1972)

Árni Björnsson, 'Hjátrú á jólum', *Skírnir*, 85 (1961), 110–128

Árni Björnsson, *Í jólaskapi* (Reykjavík, 1983)

Árni Björnsson, *Jól á Íslandi* (Reykjavík, 1963)

Árni Björnsson, 'Smalabúsreið', *Árbók hins íslenzka fornleifafélags* (1983), 69–82

Árni Björnsson, 'Sumardagurinn fyrsti', *Árbók hins íslenska fornleifafélags* (1970), 87–123

Árni Björnsson, *Þorrablót á Íslandi* (Reykjavík, 1986)

Ásgeir Blöndal Magnússon, *Íslenzk orðsifjabók* (Reykjavík, 1989)

Babio, trans. and ed., Malcolm M. Brennan, Citadel monograph series, 7 (Charleston, S. Carolina, 1968)

Balneaves, Elizabeth, *The windswept isles: Shetland and its people* (London, 1977)

Baker, Donald C., and Murphy, J. L., introduction, *The Digby plays: Facsimiles of the plays in Bodley MSS Digby 133 and e Museo 160*, Leeds texts and monographs, Medieval drama facsimiles, III (Leeds, 1976)

Bandamanna saga in ÍF VII, ed. Guðni Jónsson (Reykjavík, 1936), pp.291–363

Baskerville, Charles Read, 'Dramatic aspects of medieval folk festivals in England', *Studies in philology*, 17 (1920), 19–87

Bate, Keith, ed., *Three Latin comedies*, Toronto medieval studies (Toronto, 1976)

Bibliography

Baur, Grace van Sweringen, 'The disguise motif in the Germanic hero-sagas', *SS*, 4 (1917), 220–239

Bawden, C. R., introduction to Mongolian poetry in *The Penguin book of oral poetry*, ed. Ruth Finnegan (Harmondsworth, 1982), pp.37–42

Bawden, C. R., 'Mongol: the contemporary tradition', in A. T. Hatto, ed., *Traditions of heroic and epic poetry*, 2 vols (London, 1980–1989), I, 268–299

Bax, Marcel, and Padmos, Tineke, 'Two types of verbal duelling in Old Icelandic: The interactional structure of the senna and the mannjafnaðr in Hárbarðsljóð', *SS*, 55 (1983), 149–174

Bay, Svend Aage, 'Nogle bemærkninger om guldhornenes billeder', *DS* (1948), 1–20

Bárðar saga Snæfellsáss, in *ÍF* XIII, ed. Þórhallur Vilmundarson and Bjarni Vilhjálmsson (Reykjavík, 1991), pp.99–172

Beckerman, Bernard, *Theatrical presentation: Performer, audience and act*, ed. Gloria Brim Beckerman and William Coco (New York, 1990)

Beckman, Bo, 'Julens och fastans träta', in *KLNM*, VIII (Reykjavík, 1963), pp.17–18

Bede, *The ecclesiastical history of the English people*, ed. and trans. Bertram Colgrave and R. A. B. Mynors (Oxford, 1969)

Bekker-Nielsen, Hans, 'Den ældste tid', in Hans Bekker-Nielsen, Thorkil Damsgaard Olsen, and Ole Widding, *Norrøn fortællekunst* (Copenhagen, 1965), pp.9–26

Bennett, J. A. W., and Smithers, G. V., eds, *Early Middle English verse and prose* (Oxford, 1966)

Bentley, Eric, *The life of the drama* (London, 1965)

Berge, Rikard, 'Norske brudlaupsleikar', *Norsk folkekultur*, 11 (1925), 111–144

Bergmann, F. G., ed. and trans. into French, *Le message de Skirnir et Les dits de Grimnir* (Strasbourg, 1871)

Bergmann, F. G., ed. and trans. into French, *Poëmes Islandais (Voluspa, Vafthrudnismal, Lokasenna)* (Paris, 1838)

Berthold, Margot, *A history of world theatre*, trans. Edith Simmons (New York, 1972)

Bertilsson, Ulf, 'Bohuslän', in Sverker Janson, Erik B. Lundberg and Ulf Bertilsson, eds, *Hällristningar och hällmålningar i Sverige* (Helsingborg, 1989), pp.82–120

Bevington, David, ed. and trans., *Medieval drama* (Boston, 1975)

Bibire, Paul, 'Freyr and Gerðr: The story and its myths', in *Sagnaskemmtun: Studies in honour of Hermann Pálsson*, ed. Rudolf Simek, Jónas Kristjánsson and Hans Bekker-Nielsen (Wien, 1986), pp.19–40

Bibliorum Sacrorum: Iuxta Vulgatam Clementinam, ed. Aloisius Gramatica (Mediolani, 1922)

Bing, Just, 'Helleristningsstudier', *Oldtiden*, III (1913), 77–116

Bing, Just, 'Rock carvings of the Norse Bronze Age', *Saga-Book*, 9: 1914–1918, part II (1920–1925), 275–300

Birkeli, Emil, *Fedrekult i Norge: Et forsøk på en systematisk-deskriptiv fremstilling*, Skrifter utgitt av det Norske Videnskaps-Akademi i Oslo II. Hist.-filos. klasse, 1938, no.5 (Oslo, 1938)

Bibliography

Biskupa sögur, ed. Jón Sigurðsson and Guðbrandur Vígfússon, 2 vols (Kaupmannahöfn, 1858–1878)

Bjarni Aðalbjarnarson, ed., *Heimskringla*, ÍF XXVI, 3 vols (Reykjavík, 1941–1951)

Bjarni Aðalbjarnarson, ed., *Ynglinga saga*, in ÍF XXVI: *Heimskringla*, 3 vols (Reykjavík, 1941–1951), I, pp.8–83

Björn Bjarnason, *Íþróttir fornmanna á Norðurlöndum* (Reykjavík, 1908)

Björn Þorsteinsson, and Guðrún Ása Grímsdóttir, 'Norska öldin', in *Saga Íslands*, IV, ed. Sigurður Lindal (Reykjavík, 1989), pp.61–258

Black, G. F., and Thomas, Northcote W., ed., *County folk-lore*, III: *Examples of printed folk-lore concerning the Orkney and Shetland Islands*, Publications of the Folk-lore Society, XLIX (Nendeln,1967); originally published in 1901

Blindheim, Martin, ed., *Sigurds saga i middelalderens billedkunst* (Oslo, 1972)

Blom, Ådel Gjøstein, *Ballader og legender fra norsk middelalderdiktning* (Oslo 1971)

Blöndal, Lárus H., *Um uppruna Sverrissögu* (Reykjavík 1982)

Blöndal, Sigfús, 'Dans i Island', in *Nordisk kultur*, XXIV. *Idræt og leg. Dans*, ed. Johan Götlind and H. Grüner Nielsen (København, 1933), pp.163–179

Blöndal, Sigfús, 'Some remarks on Haraldskvæði 23', *Acta philologica Scandinavica*, 2 (1927–1928), 59–65

Blöndal, Sigfús, *Væringjasaga* (Reykjavík, 1954)

Boberg, I. M., 'Lussegubben', *DS* (1951), 64–70

Bodel, Jean, *Le jeu de Saint Nicolas*, ed. F. J. Warne (Oxford, 1972)

Boer, R. C., ed., *Die Edda mit historisch-kritischem Commentar*, 2 vols (Haarlem, 1922)

Bohannan, Laura, 'Shakespeare in the Bush', *Natural history*, 75 (August/September 1966), 28–33

Bondevik, Kjell, 'Høgtider i Noreg og på Island', in *Nordisk kultur*, XXII: *Årets höjtider*, ed. Martin P:n Nilsson (København, 1938), pp.89–112

Bord, Janet and Colin, *Earth rites: Fertility practices in pre-industrial Britain* (St Albans, 1982)

Borgfors, Erik Olof, 'Sockennamnet Leksand', *Namn och bygd*, 80 (1992), 91–106

Bósa saga ok Herrauðs, in *FN* II, pp.30–497

Bregenhøj, Carsten, *Helligtrekongersløb på Agersø* (Copenhagen, 1974)

Brennan, Malcolm, ed. and trans., *Babio*, Citadel monograph series, 7 (Charleston, S. Carolina, 1968)

Brennu-Njáls saga, ÍF XII, ed. Einar Ólafur Sveinsson (Reykjavík, 1954)

Brewer, Derek, *English gothic literature*, in the Macmillan history of literature (London, 1982)

Briem, Ólafur, *Heiðinn siður á Íslandi*, 2nd ed., rev. (Reykjavík, 1985)

Bringéus, Nils-Arvid, *Årets festseder* (Stockholm, 1976)

Brody, Alan, *The English Mummers and their plays* (Philadelphia, 1970)

Brot úr miðsögu Guðmundar biskups Arasonar, in *Biskupa sögur*, ed. Jón Sigurðsson and Guðbrandur Vigfússon, 2 vols (1858–1878), I, 559–618

Brown, Ursula, 'The saga of Hrómund Gripsson and Þorgilssaga', *Saga-Book*, 13 (1946–1953), 51–77

Bruce-Mitford, Rupert, *Aspects of Anglo-Saxon archaeology: Sutton Hoo and other discoveries* (New York, 1974)

Bibliography

Brøgger, A. W. and Schetelig, Haakon, *Osebergfundet*, 4 vols published (Oslo, 1917–)

Buchholtz, Peter, 'Shamanism: The testimony of Old Icelandic literary tradition', *Mediaeval Scandinavia*, 4 (1971), 7–20

Bugge, Alexander, 'Tingsteder, gilder og andre gamle mittpunkter i de norske bygder', *Historisk tidsskrift* (Kristiania), 5 række, 4 bind (1917–1918), 97–152, and 195–252

Bugge, Kristian, 'Bonfires in Norway', *Folklore*, 31 (1920–1921), 147–151

Bugge, Kristian, 'St Hansbaal i Norge', *Rig* (1921), 155–161

Bugge, Sophus, 'Efterslæt til min udgave af Sæmundar Edda', *Aarbøger* (1869), 243–276

Bugge, Sophus, 'Iduns æbler', *ANF*, 5 (1889), 1–45

Bugge, Sophus, 'Mindre bidrag til nordisk mythologi og sagnhistorie', *Aarbøger* (1895), 123–138

Bugge, Sophus, ed., *Norroen fornkvæði* (Christiania, 1867)

Burkert, Walter, 'Greek tragedy and sacrificial ritual', *Greek, Roman and Byzantine studies*, 7 (1966), 87–121

Burkert, Walter, *Homo necans: the anthropology of ancient Greek sacrificial ritual and myth*, trans. Peter Bing (Berkeley, 1983)

Burkert, Walter, *Structure and history in Greek mythology and ritual*, Sather classical lectures, 47 (Berkeley, 1979)

Bærings saga, in *Fornsögur Suðrlanda*, ed. Gustaf Cederschiöld (Lund, 1884), pp.85–123

Bø, Olav, *Heilag-Olav i Norsk folketradisjon* (Oslo, 1955)

Bø, Olav, 'Julehøgtida', in *Gilde og gjestebod*, ed. Halvor Landsverk (Oslo, 1967), pp.91–101

Bø, Olav, *Vår norske jul* (Oslo, 1970)

Bøthun, Per H., *Leikanger bygdebok* (Leikanger, 1965)

Bøyum, Sjur, 'Gamle truer og skikkar i Balestrand prestegjeld', in Jon Andreas Laberg, *Balestrand: Bygd og ætter* (Bergen, 1934), pp.60–145

Campbell, Joseph, *The way of animal powers: Historical atlas of world mythology*, vol.I (London, 1983)

Campbell, Åke and Nyman, Åsa, eds, *Atlas över Svensk folkkultur*, II: *Sägen, tro och högtidssed* (Uppsala, 1976), 1 (Kartor) and 2 (Kommentar)

Cawte, E. C., *Ritual animal disguise: A historical and geographical study of animal disguise in the British Isles* (Cambridge, 1978)

Cawte, E. C., Helm, Alex, and Peacock, N., *English ritual drama: A geographical index* (London, 1967)

Celander, Hilding, *Förkristen jul enligt norröna källor*, Göteborgs Universitets årsskrift, 61.3 (1955)

Celander, Hilding, 'Julbocken och hans historia', *Nordens kalender* (1933), 92–104

Celander, Hilding, *Nordisk jul*, 1 vol. printed (Stockholm, 1928)

Celander, Hilding, 'Oskoreien och besläktade föreställningar i äldre och nyäre nordisk tradition', *Saga och sed* (1943), 71–175

Celander, Hilding, 'Slakta julbocken', in *Nordiskt folkminne: Studier tillägnade C. W. von Sydow*, ed. Åke Campbell, Waldemar Liungman and Sigfrid Svensson (Stockholm, 1928), pp.25–36

Celander, Hilding, *Stjärngossarna, deras visor och julspel*, Nordiska Museets handlingar, 38 (Stockholm, 1950)

Celander, Hilding, 'Till Stefanslegendens og Staffansvisornas utveklingshistoria', *Arv*, 1 (1945), 134–164

Chadwick, H. Munro and N. Kershaw, *The growth of literature*, 3 vols (Cambridge, 1935–1940)

Chadwick, N. K., and Zhirmunsky, V., *Oral epics of Central Asia* (Cambridge, 1969)

Chambers, Sir Edmund K., *The English folk-play* (Oxford, 1933)

Chambers, E. K., *The mediaeval stage*, 2 vols (Oxford, 1903)

Chesnutt, Michael, 'The beguiling of Þórr', in *Úr Dölum til Dala*, ed. Rory McTurk and Andrew Wawn, Leeds texts and monographs, new series, 11 (Leeds, 1989), pp.35–63

Chesnutt, Michael, 'On the origin of Icelandic vikivaki', *Arv*, 34 (1978), 142–151

Christensen, Arne Emil, Ingstad, Anne Stine, and Myhre, Bjørn, *Osebergdronningens grav: Vår arkeologiske nasjonalskatt i nytt lys* (Oslo, 1992)

Cleasby, Richard and Guðbrandur Vigfússon, *An Icelandic-English dictionary*, 2nd ed. (Oxford, 1957)

Clover, Carol J., 'The Germanic context of the Unferþ episode', *Speculum*, 55 (1980), 444–468

Clover, Carol, 'Hárbarðsljóð as generic farce', *SS*, 51 (1979), 124–145

Clunies Ross, Margaret, *Skáldskaparmál. Snorri Sturluson's ars poetica and medieval theories of language*, The viking collection, 4 (Odense, 1987

The Codex Regius of the Elder Edda, MS no.2365 4to in the old Royal collection of the Royal Library of Copenhagen, introduced by Andreas Heusler, Corpus Codicum Islandicorum Medii Aevi, X (Copenhagen, 1937)

Il Codice di Terenzio Vaticano Latino 3226, ed. Sesto Prete, Studi e testi, 262 (Città del Vaticano, 1970)

Collinder, Björn, ed. and trans., *Den poetiska Eddan*, 2nd ed., rev. (Uddevalla, 1964)

La 'comédie latine' en France au XIIe siècle, ed. Gustave Cohen, 2 vols (Paris, 1931)

Commedie latine del XII e XIII secolo, ed. Ferrucio Bertini, 3 vols, Pubblicazioni dell' Instituto di filologia classica e medievale, 61 (Genova, 1980)

Constantin VII Porphyrogénète, *Le livre des cérémonies*, ed. and trans. Albert Vogt, 2 vols (Paris, 1935–1940)

Cornford, Francis, *The origins of Attic comedy*, with an introduction by Theodore H. Gaster (Cambridge, 1934)

Craigie, William A., ed. and trans., *Scandinavian folk-lore* (London, 1896)

Cronholm, Abraham, *Wäringarna* (Lund, 1832)

Crymogæa: See above, under Arngrímur Jónsson

Dalton, O. M., *Byzantine art and archæology* (Oxford, 1911)

Danielli, Mary, 'Initiation ceremonial from Norse literature', *Folklore*, 56 (1945), 229–245

Danmarks riges breve, I.5 (1211–1223), ed. Niels Skyum-Nielsen (København, 1957)

Davidson, Audrey Ekdahl, ed., *Holy week and Easter ceremonies from medieval Sweden*, Early drama, art and music monograph series, 13 (Kalamazoo, 1990)

Davidson, H. R. Ellis, *Gods and myths of Northern Europe* (Harmondsworth, 1964)

Bibliography

Davidson, H. R. Ellis, 'Hostile magic in the Icelandic sagas', in *The witch figure: Folklore essays by a group of scholars in England honouring the 75th birthday of Katherine M. Briggs*, ed. Venetia Newall (London, 1973), pp.20–41

Davidson, H. R. Ellis 'Insults and riddles in the Edda poems', in *Edda: A collection of essays*, ed. Robert J. Glendinning and Haraldur Bessason (Manitoba, 1983), pp.25–46

Davidson, Hilda Ellis, *The lost beliefs of Northern Europe* (London 1993)

Davidson, Hilda Ellis, *Pagan Scandinavia* (London, 1967)

Davidson, Hilda R. Ellis, *Scandinavian mythology* (London, 1969)

Davidson, Hilda Ellis, *The Viking road to Byzantium* (London, 1976)

Davidson, Hilda Ellis, and Gelling, Peter, *The chariot of the sun* (London, 1969)

Davíð Erlingsson, 'Eyjólfr has the last laugh: A note on Víga-Glúms saga, Chs I–III', in *Specvlvm Norroenvm: Norse studies in memory of Gabriel Turville-Petre*, ed. Ursula Dronke, Guðrún P. Helgadóttir, Gerd Wolfgang Weber, and Hans Bekker-Nielsen (Odense, 1981), pp.85–88

Davíð Erlingsson, 'Icelandic legendary fiction', *The heroic process: Form, function and fantasy in folk epic*, The proceedings of the International folk epic conference, University College, Dublin, 2–6 September 1985, ed. Bo Almqvist, Seamas Ó Catháin and Pádraig Ó Héalaí (Dublin, 1987), pp.370–393

Day, A. Grove, *The sky clears: Poetry of the American Indians* (New York, 1951)

Dean Smith, Margaret, 'The life cycle play or folk play', *Folklore*, 69 (1958), 237–253

Detter, F., and Heinzel, R., eds, *Sæmundar Edda mit einem anhang*, 2 vols (Leipzig, 1903)

Devlin, Diana, *Mask and scene: An introduction to a world view of theatre* (London, 1989)

The Digby plays: Facsimiles of the plays in Bodley MSS Digby 133 and e Museo 160, introduced by Donald C. Baker, and J. L. Murphy, Leeds texts and monographs, Medieval drama facsimiles, III (Leeds, 1976)

Diplomatarium Islandicum. Íslenzkt fornbréfasafn, ed. Jón Sigurðsson, Jón Þorkelsson, Páll Eggert Ólason, and Björn Þorsteinsson, 16 vols (Kaupmannahöfn, 1857–1972)

Diplomatarium Norvegicum, VIII, ed. C. R. Unger and H. J. Huidfeldt (Christiania, 1871)

Dínus saga dramblata, ed. Jónas Kristjánsson (Reykjavík, 1960)

Djurklou, G., 'Hvem var "Staffan Stalledräng"?', *Svenska fornminnesföreningstidskrift*, 11 (1902), 335–354

Drever, John, 'Papa Westray Games', *Proceedings of the Orkney Antiquarian Society*, 1 (1922–1923), 69–70

Dronke, Peter, *Latin and vernacular poets of the Middle Ages* (Aldershot, 1991)

Dronke, Peter, 'Narrative and dialogue in medieval secular drama', in *Literature in fourteenth-century England*, ed. Peiro Boitani and Anna Torti (Cambridge, 1983), pp.99–120; also published in Dronke, *Latin and vernacular poets of the Middle Ages*

Dronke, Peter, 'A note on Pamphilus', *The journal of the Warburg and Courthauld Institutes*, 42 (1979), 225–230; also published in Dronke, *Latin and vernacular poets of the Middle Ages*

Dronke, Peter, *Poetic individuality in the Middle Ages: New departures in poetry 1000–1150*, 2nd ed., rev., Westfield publications in medieval studies, I (London, 1986)

Dronke, Peter, *Women writers of the Middle Ages* (Cambridge, 1984)

Dronke, Ursula, 'Art and tradition in Skírnismál', in *English and medieval studies presented to J. R. R. Tolkien on the occasion of his 70th birthday*, ed. Norman Davis and C. L. Wrenn (London, 1962), pp.250–268

Droplaugarsona saga, in ÍF XI, ed. Jón Johannesson (Reykjavík, 1950), pp.135–180

Dumézil, Georges, *The stakes of the warrior*, trans. David Weeks, ed. Jaan Puhvel (Berkeley, 1983)

Durkheim, Emile, *The elementary forms of religious life*, trans. Joseph Ward Swain (London, 1964)

Early Middle English verse and prose, ed. J. A. W. Bennett and G. V. Smithers (Oxford, 1966)

Eckhoff, Emil, 'Hällristningar på Kinnekulle', *Svenska Fornminnesföreningens tidskrift*, 8 (1891–3), 102–126

Edda (1926): See Snorri Sturluson, *Edda*, ed. Finnur Jónsson (København, 1926)

Edda, trans. into German by Felix Genzmer, ed. Felix Neider, with notes by Andreas Heusler, 2 vols (Jena, 1914–1920)

Die Edda, trans. into German by Felix Genzmer, with notes by Kurt Schier (Köln, 1981)

Edda: Die lieder des codex regius nebst verwandten denkmälern, I: text, ed. Gustav Neckel, 4th ed., rev. Hans Kuhn (Heidelberg, 1962)

Eddadigte, ed. Jón Helgason, 3 vols, in Nordisk filologi, serie A: tekster: I: *Völuspá. Hávamál*, 2nd ed. (København, 1964), II: *Gudedigte*, 2nd ed. (København, 1971), III: *Heltedigte*, første del (København, 1961)

Eddica minora, ed. Andreas Heusler and Wilhelm Ranisch (Dortmund, 1903)

Edmonston, Arthur, *A view of the ancient and present state of the Zetland Islands*, 2 vols (Edinburgh, 1809)

Edmondston, Thomas, 'Notes on a straw masquerade dress still used in some parts of Shetland, and on certain woollen articles manufactured in "Fair Isle"; also of a supposed relic of the Spanish Armada', *Proceedings of the Society of Antiquaries of Scotland*, 8 (1869–70), 470–472

Eggert Ólafsson, and Bjarni Pálsson, *Ferðabók Eggerts Ólafssonar og Bjarna Pálssonar*, trans. into Icelandic by Steindór Steindórsson frá Hlöðum, 2 vols (Reykjavík, 1975)

Egils saga Skalla-Grímssonar, ÍF II, ed. Sigurður Nordal (Reykjavík, 1933)

Eike, Christine N. F., 'Oskoreia og ekstaseriter', *Norveg*, 23 (1980), 227–309

Einar Hafliðason, *Laurentius saga biskups*, ed. Árni Björnsson, Rit Handritastofnunar Íslands, III (Reykjavík, 1969)

Einar Hafliðason, *Saga Laurentius Hólabiskups*, in *Biskupa sögur* (1858–1878), I, pp.787–914

Einar Már Jónsson, 'Góður veðurviti' (Review of *Hávamál og Völuspá*, ed. Gísli Sigurðsson [Reykjavík, 1987]), *TMM*, 49 (1988), 381–388

Bibliography

Einar Már Jónsson, 'Heilsurækt fræðanna: Munnleg geymd og Eddukvæði', *TMM*, 51.1 (1990), 83–97

Einar Már Jónsson, 'Heilsurækt fræðanna: Munnleg geymd og Eddukvæði – Niðurlag', *TMM*, 51.2 (1990), 53–64

Einar Ólafur Sveinsson, 'Ágrip af andmælaræðu Einars Ól. Sveinssonar við doktorsvörn Halldórs Halldórssonar, 12. júní 1954', *Skírnir*, 128 (1954), 206–218

Einar Ólafur Sveinsson, *Íslenzkar bókmenntir í fornöld*, 1 vol. printed (Reykjavík, 1962)

Einar Ólafur Sveinsson, Review of Bertha Phillpotts, *The Elder Edda and ancient Scandinavian drama*, *Skírnir*, 45 (1921), 157–159

Eiríks saga rauða, in *ÍF* IV, ed. Einar Ólafur Sveinsson and Matthías Þórðarson (Reykjavík, 1935), pp.193–237

Ejder, Bertil, 'Eddadikten Vafþrúðnismál', *Vetenskaps Societeten i Lund. Årsbok* (1960), 5–20

Ekholm, Gunnar, 'De skandinaviska hällristningarna och deras betydelse', *Ymer*, 36 (1916), 275–308

Eliade, Mircea, *Cosmos and history: The myth of the eternal return*, trans. Willard B. Trask (New York, 1959)

Eliade, Mircea, *Myth and reality*, trans. Willard R. Trask (London, 1964)

Eliade, Mircea, *Patterns in comparative religion*, trans. Rosemary Sheed (London, 1958)

Eliade, Mircea, *Rites and symbols of initiation: The mysteries of birth and rebirth*, trans. Willard R. Trask (New York, 1965)

Eliade, Mircea, *Shamanism: Archaic techniques of ecstasy*, trans. Willard R. Trask, Bollingen series LXXVI (New York, 1964)

Elis saga. Strengleikar and other texts: Uppsala University Library Delagardieska Samlingen nos. 4–7 folio and AM 666b quarto, introduced by Mattias Tveitane, Corpus Codicum Norvegicorum Medii Aevi, quarto serie, IV (Oslo, 1972)

Ellekilde, Hans, *Vor danske jul gennem tiderne* (København, 1943)

Elucidarius, in *Þrjár þýðingar lærðar frá miðöldum*, ed. Gunnar Ágúst Harðarson (Reykjavík, 1989), pp.45–110

Elucidarius in Old Norse translation, ed. Evelyn Sherabon Firchow and Kaaren Grimstad (Reykjavík, 1989)

Eskeröd, Albert, *Årets fester* (Stockholm, 1965)

Esslin, Martin, *An anatomy of drama* (London, 1976)

Esslin, Martin, *The field of drama* (London, 1987)

Eyrbyggja saga, in *ÍF* IV, ed. Einar Ólafur Sveinsson and Matthías Þórðarson (Reykjavík, 1935), pp.1–184

Facsimile of British Museum MS. Harley 2253, introduced by N. R. Ker, Early English Text Society, 255 (London, 1965)

Fagrskinna, in *ÍF* XXIX, ed. Bjarni Einarsson (Reykjavík, 1984), pp.55–364

Faris, James C., 'Mumming in an outport fishing village: A description and suggestions on the cognitive complex', in *Christmas mumming in Newfoundland*, ed. Herbert Halpert and G. M. Story (Toronto, 1969), pp.128–144

Feilberg, H. F., *Bidrag til en ordbog over jyske almuesmål*, 4 vols (Kjøbenhavn, 1886–1914)

Feilberg, H. F., *Jul*, 2 vols (København, 1904)

Fenton, Alexander, *The Northern Isles: Orkney and Shetland* (Edinburgh, 1978)

Finnegan, Ruth, *Oral poetry: Its nature, significance and social context* (Cambridge, 1977)

Finnur Jónsson, *Historia ecclesiastica Islandiæ*, 4 vols (Havniæ, 1772–1778)

Finnur Jónsson, 'Eddadigtenes samling', *ANF*, 42 (1926), 215–233

Finnur Jónsson, ed. and trans. into Danish, *De gamle Eddadigte* (København, 1932)

Finnur Jónsson, ed., *Hauksbók* (København, 1892–1896)

Finnur Jónsson, 'Hárbarþsljóþ: En undersøgelse', *Aarbøger* (1888), 139–179

Finnur Jónsson, *Den oldnorske og oldislandske litteraturs historie*, 2nd ed., 3 vols (København, 1920–1924)

Finnur Jónsson, 'Sagnformen i heltedigtene i Codex Regius', *Aarbøger* (1921), 1–104

Finnur Jónsson, 'Sigurðarsaga og de prosaiske stykker i Codex Regius', *Aarbøger* (1917), 16–36

Finnur Jónsson, 'Tilnavne i den islandske oldlitteratur', *Aarbøger* (1907), 161–381

Finnur Magnússon (as Finn Magnusen), 'Forsög til Forklaring over nogle Steder af Ossian, mest vedkommende Scandinaviens Hedenhold', *Det Skandinaviske Litteraturselskabs skrifter*, 9 (1813), 143–386

Finnur Magnússon (as Finn Magnusen), *Veterum borealium mythologiæ lexicon* (Havniæ, 1828); published also in *Edda Saemundar hins froða*, ed. Finnur Magnússon and others, 3 vols (Havniæ, 1787–1828), III, pp.272–1142

Finnur Magnússon (as Finn Magnusen), *Den Ældre Edda*, 4 vols (Copenhagen, 1821–1823)

Flateyjarbok, ed. Guðbrandur Vigfússon and C. R. Unger, 3 vols, Det norske historiske kildeskriftfonds skrifter, 4 (Christiania, 1860–1868)

Fleck, Jere, 'The "knowledge criterion" in the Grímnismál: The case against "shamanism"', *ANF*, 86 (1971), 49–65

Flett, J. F., and T. M., 'Some Hebridean folk dances', in *The Journal of the English folk dance and song society*, 7,ii (1952), 112–127

Flóamanna saga, in *ÍF* XIII, ed. Þórhallur Vilmundarson and Bjarni Vilhjálmsson (Reykjavík, 1991), pp.229–327

FN: See *Fornaldarsögur Norðurlanda* below

Fontenrose, Joseph, *Python: A study of Delphic myth and its origins* (Berkeley, 1959)

Foote, Peter, 'Aachen, Lund, Hólar' in *Aurvandilstá*, ed. Michael Barnes, Hans Bekker-Nielsen and Gerd Wolfgang Weber (Odense, 1984), pp.101–120; originally published in *Les relations littéraires franco-scandinaves au Moyen Age*, Bibliothèque de la Faculté de Philosophie et Lettres de l'Université de Liège, CCVIII (1975), pp.53–73

Fornaldarsögur Norðurlanda, ed. Guðni Jónsson and Bjarni Vilhjálmsson, 3 vols (Reykjavík, 1943–1944)

Ett forn-svenskt legendarium, innehållande medeltids kloster-sagor om helgon, påfvar och kejsare ifrån det I:sta till det XII:de århundradet, ed. George Stephens, 2 vols (Stockholm, 1847–1858)

Fóstbræðra saga, in *ÍF* VI, ed. Björn K. Þórólfsson and Guðni Jónsson (Reykjavík, 1943), pp.119–276

Fragment RA.58 C. of Konongs skuggsja, ed. George T. Flom, The University of Illinois, The university studies, IV, no.2 (Urbana, 1911)

The Fragmentary classicising historians of the later Roman Empire. Eunapius, Olympiodorus, Priscus and Malcus, ed. and trans. R. C. Blockley, 2 vols, ARCA Classical and medieval texts, papers and monographs, 6 and 10 (Liverpool, 1981–1983)

Fragments of the Elder and the Younger Edda AM 748 I and II 4:o, introduced by Elias Wessén, Corpus Codicum Islandicorum Medii Aevi, XVII (Copenhagen, 1945)

Frank, Grace, *The medieval French drama* (Oxford, 1954)

Frank, Roberta, *Old Norse poetry: The dróttkvætt stanza*, Islandica, XLII (Ithaca, 1978)

Frazer, Sir James George, *The golden bough*, 3rd ed., 12 vols (London, 1936–1937)

Friedrich, Rainer, 'Drama and ritual', in *Themes in drama, 5: Drama and religion*, ed. James Redmond (Cambridge, 1983), pp.159–223

Fritzner, Johan, *Ordbog over det gamle norske sprog*, 2nd ed., 3 vols (Kristiania, 1886–1896)

Gade, Kari Ellen, 'Sigurðr – Göfuct dýr: A note on Fáfnismál st.2', *ANF*, 105 (1990), 56–68

Gailey, Alan, *Irish folk drama* (Cork, 1969)

Gamal norsk homiliebok, ed. Gustav Indrebø (Oslo, 1931)

Gammelnorsk homiliebok etter AM 619 QV, introduced by Trygve Knudsen, Corpus Codicum Norvegicorum Medii Aevi, quarto serie, I (Oslo, 1952)

Gaster, Theodore H., *Thespis: Myth, ritual and drama in the Near East* (New York, 1950)

Gautreks saga, in *FN* III, pp.3–41

Gelling, Peter and Davidson, Hilda Ellis, *The chariot of the sun* (London, 1969)

Gestorum Abbatum Trudonensium, ed. D. R. Koepke, in *Monumenta Germaniae historica*, ed. Georg Heinrich Pertz, Scriptores, X (1852), pp.213–448

Giraldus Cambrensis, *Descriptio Kambriæ*, in *Opera*, ed. James F. Dimock (London, 1868)

Giraldus Cambrensis, *The itinerary through Wales and The description of Wales*, trans. Sir Richard Colt Hoare, ed. W. Llewelyn Williams (London, 1908)

Gísla saga Súrssonar, in *ÍF* VI, ed. Björn K. Þórólfsson and Guðni Jónsson (Reykjavík, 1943), pp.1–118

Gísli Sigurðsson, 'Eddukvæði', in *Íslensk þjóðmenning, VI: Munnmenntir og bókmenning*, ed. Frosti F. Jóhansson (Reykjavík, 1989), pp.293–314

Gísli Sigurðsson, 'Fordómur fáfræðinnar', *TMM*, 49.4 (1988), 395–400

Gísli Sigurðsson, 'Munnmenntir og fornsögur', *Skáldskaparmál*, 1 (1990), 19–27

Gísli Sigurðsson, 'Munnmenntir og staða fræðanna', *TMM*, 51.2 (1990), 65–70

Gjerløw, Lilli, *Adoratio Crucis: The Regularis Concordia and the Delcrata Lanfranc* (Oslo, 1961)

Gjötterberg, Tore, 'Näbbefru och kuv i hatten', *Sörmlandsbygden* (1985), 13–28

Glob, P. V., *The bog people*, trans. Rupert Bruce-Mitford (London, 1977)
Glob, P. V., *The mound people*, trans. Joan Bulman (London, 1983)
Glosecki, Stephen O., *Shamanism and Old English poetry* (New York, 1989)
Gluckman, Mary and Max, 'On drama, and games and athletic contests', in *Secular ritual*, ed. Sally F. Moore and Barbara Myerhoff (Assen, 1977), pp.227–243
Die Gotische Bibel, ed. Vilhelm Steitberg, 6th ed. (Darmstadt, 1971)
Grambo, Ronald, *Norske trollformler og magiske ritualer* (Oslo, 1979)
Granlund, John, 'Barfotaspringning på Gregorius och i samband med Marie Bebådelsedag', *Saga och sed* (1960), 69–78
Granlund, John, 'Pingstbrud och lekbröllop i Sverige', *Saga och sed* (1970), 41–79
Granlund, John, 'Vinterns och Sommargrevens strid: Ett försök till källgranskning av Olaus Magnus' skildring', *Rig*, 31 (1948), 65–74
Grágás eftir det Arnamagnæanske haandskrift nr.334 fol., Staðarhólsbók, ed. Konráð Gíslason, P. G. Thoren, Vilhjálmur Finsen, Svend Grundtvig, and J. L. Ussing (Kjøbenhavn, 1879)
Grágás: Islændernes lovbog i fristatens tid (Konungsbók), ed. Vilhjálmur Finsen, 4 vols (København, 1850–1870)
Grettis saga Ásmundssonar, in ÍF VII, ed. Guðni Jónsson (Reykjavík, 1936), pp.1–290
Gríms saga loðinkinna, in FN I, pp.267–280
Grundtvig, Nikolai Fred. Sev., *Nordens mythologi, eller sindbilled-sprog*, 3rd ed. (Kiøbenhavn, 1870)
Grænlendinga þáttr, in *Flateyjarbok* (1860–1868), III, pp.443–454
Grönbech, Vilhelm, *The culture of the Teutons*, 3 vols in 2, trans. W. Worster (London, 1932)
Gräter, Friedrich David, *Nordische Blumen* (Leipzig, 1789)
Gudnitz, Fred, *Broncealderens monumentalkunst* (København, 1962)
Guðbrandur Vigfússon, and Powell, F. York, ed. and trans., *Corpus Poeticvm Boreale: the poetry of the Old Northern tongue from the earliest times to the thirteenth century*, 2 vols (Oxford, 1883)
Guðjónsson, Elsa E., *The national costume of women in Iceland* (Reykjavik 1970)
Guðmundar saga góða, in *Sturlunga saga* (1878), I, pp.57–125
Guðmundar sögur biskups, I: Ævi Guðmundar biskups. Guðmundar saga A, ed. Stefán Karlsson, Editiones Arnamagnæanæ, series B, vol.6 (Kaupmannahöfn, 1983)
Guðmundur Ólafsson, 'Jólakötturinn og uppruni hans', *Árbók hins íslenska fornleifafélags* (1989), 111–119
Gunnars saga keldugnúpsfífls, in ÍF XIV, ed. Jóhannes Halldórsson (Reykjavík, 1959), pp.341–379
Gunnell, Terence A., 'The concept of ancient Scandinavian drama: a recvaluation' (doctoral dissertation, University of Leeds, 1991)
Gunnell, Terry, 'Skírnisleikur og Freysmál', *Skírnir*, 167 (1993), 421–459
Gunnell, Terry, 'Spássíukrot? Mælendamerkingar í handritum eddukuæða og miðaldaleikrita', *Skáldskaparmál*, 3 (1994), 7–29
Gunnlaugs saga ormstungu, in ÍF III, ed. Sigurður Nordal and Guðni Jónsson (Reykjavík, 1938), pp.49–107

Bibliography

Gunnlaugur Leifsson, *Jóns saga helga*, in *Biskupa sögur*, ed. Jón Sigurðsson and Guðbrandur Vigfússon, 2 vols (1858–1878), I, pp.213–260

Gurevic, Elena A., 'The formulaic pair in Eddic poetry: An experimental analysis', trans. Mary P. Coote, in *Structure and meaning in Old Norse literature: New approaches to textual analysis and literary criticism*, ed. John Lindow, Lars Lönnroth, and Gerd Wolfgang Weber (Odense, 1986), pp.32–55

Gurevich, A. Ya., 'On the nature of the comic in the Elder Edda', *Mediaeval Scandinavia* (1976), 127–180

Göngu-Hrólfs saga, in *FN* II, pp.357–461

Haddon, Alfred C., 'A wedding dance-mask from Co. Mayo', *Folklore*, 4 (1893), 123–124

Hagen, Anders, 'Gjenklang fra en fjern fortid', a leaflet provided by the Bergen Historiske Museet dated 13 March 1982

Halldór Halldórsson, *Íslensk orðtök* (Reykjavík, 1954)

Halldór Halldórsson, *Íslenzkt orðtakasafn*, 2 vols, in *Íslenzk þjóðfræði* (Reykjavík, 1968–1969)

Halldórs þáttr Snorrasonar inn fyrri, in *ÍF* V, ed. Einar Ólafur Sveinsson (Reykjavík, 1934), pp.249–260

Hallström, Gunnar, ' "Halmstaffan". En julsed från Björkö, Adelsö socken, Upland. Meddelande och rekonstruktion', in *Etnologiska studier tillägnade Nils Edvard Hammarstedt* (Stockholm, 1921), pp.227–231

Halpert, Herbert, 'A typology of mumming', in *Christmas mumming in Newfoundland*, ed. Herbert Halpert and G. M. Story (Toronto, 1969), pp.34–61

Halpert, Herbert and Story, G. M., ed., *Christmas mumming in Newfoundland* (Toronto, 1969)

Hamilton, George Heard, *The art and architecture of Russia*, in the Penguin history of art (Harmondsworth, 1983)

Hammarstedt, N. E., 'Kvarlevor av en Frös-ritual i en svensk bröllopslek', in *Festskrift til H. F. Feilberg* (Stockholm, 1911), pp.489–517

Hammershaimb, V. U., 'Færøiske skikke og lege', *Antiquarisk tidsskrift* (1849–1851), 308–310

Hardison, O. B., *Christian rite and Christian drama in the Middle Ages* (Baltimore, 1965)

Hardy, Thomas, *The return of the native* (Oxford, 1990)

Harris, Joseph, 'Eddic poetry', in *Old Norse-Icelandic literature, a critical guide*, ed. Carol J. Clover and John Lindow, Islandica, XLV (Ithaca, 1985), pp.67–156

Harris, Joseph, 'Eddic poetry as oral poetry: The evidence of parallel passages in the Helgi poems for questions of composition and performance', in *Edda: A collection of essays*, ed. R. J. Glendinning and Haraldur Bessason (Manitoba, 1983), pp.210–235

Harris, Joseph, 'The senna: From description to literary theory', *Michigan Germanic studies*, 5.1 (1979), 65–74

Harris, Joseph, 'Ögmundar þáttr dytts ok Gunnars helmings. Unity and literary relations', *ANF*, 90 (1975), 156–182

Harris, Joseph, and Hill, Thomas D., 'Gestr's "prime sign": Source and signification in Norna-Gests þáttr', *ANF*, 104 (1989), 103–122

Harris, Richard L., 'A study of Grípisspá', *SS*, 43 (1971), 344–355

Harrison, Jane, *Ancient art and ritual* (London, 1913)

Harrison, Jane, *Themis: A study of the social origins of Greek religion*, 2nd ed. (London, 1963)

Harrsen, Meta, 'The manuscripts', in *Hroswitha of Gandersheim: Her life, times and works and a comprehensive bibliography*, ed. Anne Lyon Haight (New York, 1965), pp.42–46

Haugen, Einar, 'The Edda as ritual: Odin and his masks', in *Edda: A collection of essays*, ed. Robert J. Glendinning and Haraldur Bessason (Manitoba, 1983), pp.3–24

Hauksbók, ed. Finnur Jónsson (København, 1892–1896)

Hauksbók: The Arnamagnæan manuscripts 371,4to, 544,4to, and 675,4to, Manuscripta Islandica, V, ed. Jón Helgason (Copenhagen, 1960)

Havemeyer, Loomis, *Drama of savage peoples* (New York, 1966)

Hálfdanar saga Eysteinssonar, in *FN* III, pp.283–319

Heanley, Rev. R. M., 'The Vikings: Their folklore in Marshland', *Saga-Book*, 3 (1901–1903), 35–62

Hedeager, Lotte, *Danernes land: Danmarkshistorie*, II, ed. Olaf Olsen (Copenhagen, 1988)

Heilagra manna søgur. Fortællinger og legender om hellige mænd og kvinder. Efter gamle haandskrifter, ed. C. D. Unger, 2 vols (Christiania, 1877)

Heimskringla, ed. Bjarni Aðalbjarnarson, *ÍF* XXVI, 3 vols (Reykjavík, 1941–1951)

Heinesen, William, 'Grylen', in *Det fortryllede lys* (Copenhagen, 1970), pp.33–46; translated into English as 'The night of the Gryla', in Heinesen, *The wingéd darkness and other stories*, trans. Hedin Brønner (Paisley, 1983), pp.15–26

Helm, Alex, *The English Mummers' play* (Woodbridge, 1980)

Helm, Alex, 'The rushcart and the north-western Morris', *The journal of the English folk dance and song society*, 7, iii (1952), 172–179

Helskog, Knut, *Helleristningene i Alta* (Alta, 1988)

Hervarar saga ok Heiðreks, in *FN* I, pp.191–242

Heusler, Andreas, *Die altgermanische Dichtung*, 2nd ed., rev. (Potsdam, 1941)

Heusler, Andreas, 'Altnordische Dichtung und Prosa von Jung Sigurd', in *Kleine Schriften*, ed. Helga Reuschel and Stefan Sonderegger, 2 vols (Berlin, 1943–1969), I, pp.26–64; originally published in *Sitzungsberichte der Preussischen Akademie der Wissenschaften* phil.-hist. class (1919), 162–195

Heusler, Andreas, 'Anmälan: Bertha S. Phillpotts, The Elder Edda and ancient Scandinavian drama', *ANF*, 38 (1922), 347–353

Heusler, Andreas, 'Der Dialog in der Altgermanischen erzählenden Dichtung', in Heusler, *Kleine Schriften*, ed. Helga Reuschel and Stefan Sonderegger, 2 vols (Berlin, 1943–1969), II, pp.611–689; originally published in *Zeitschrift für deutsches Altertum*, 46 (1902), 189–284

Heusler, Andreas, introduction to *The Codex Regius of the Elder Edda, MS no.2365 4to in the old Royal collection of the Royal Library of Copenhagen*, Corpus Codicum Islandicorum Medii Aevi, X (Copenhagen, 1937)

Hibbert, Samuel, *A description of the Shetland Islands* (Lerwick, 1931)

Hirschfeld, M., *Untersuchungen zur Lokasenna* (Berlin, 1889)

Hjálmþés saga ok Ölvis, in *FN* III, pp.229–282

Hocart, A. M., *The progress of man* (London, 1933)

Hodne, Ørnulf, *Jørgen Moe og folkeeventyrene* (Oslo, 1979)

Hodne, Ørnulf, *The types of the Norwegian folktale* (Oslo, 1984)

Hoebel, E. Adamson, *The law of primitive man* (Cambridge, Massachusetts, 1954)
Holberg, Ludvig, *Julestue*, published in Holberg, *Comoedierne*, ed. Carl Roos (Kjøbenhavn, 1923), pp.381–401
Holberg, Ludvig, *The Christmas party*, trans. Henry Alexander, in *An anthology of Scandinavian literature from the Viking period to the twentieth century*, ed. Hallberg Hallmundsson (New York, 1965), pp.24–40
Hole, Christina, *A dictionary of British folk customs* (London, 1978)
Hollander, Lee M., 'Notes on the structure of ljóþaháttr', *Acta philologica Scandinavica*, 6 (1932), 39–54
Hollander, Lee M., trans. and ed., *The Poetic Edda*, 2nd ed., rev. (Austin, 1962)
Hollander, Lee M., 'Recent studies in the Helgi poems', *SS*, 13 (1924), 108–125
Holm, Gösta, *De nordiska anger-namnen*, Det Norske Videnskaps-Akademi, II. Hist.-filos. klasse, Skrifter, Ny serie no.18 (Lund, 1991)
Holm-Olsen, Ludvig, ed. and trans. into Norwegian, *Edda-dikt* (Oslo, 1975); 2nd ed., rev. (Oslo, 1985)
Holm-Olsen, Ludvig, ed., *Den gammelnorske oversettelsen av Pamphilus. Med en undersøkelse av paleografi og lydverk*, Avhandlinger, utgitt av Det Norske Videnskaps-Akademi i Oslo II. Hist.-fil. klasse, 1940, no.2 (Oslo, 1940)
Holmqvist, Wilhelm, 'The dancing gods', *Act.arch.*, 31, fasc.2–3 (1960), 101–127
Holmqvist, Wilhelm, 'Die Eisenzeitlichen Funde aus Lillön, Kirchspiel Ekerö, Uppland', *Act.arch.*, 25 (1954), 260–271
Holtsmark, Anne, 'Arbeidssanger', in *KLNM*, I (Reykjavík, 1956), pp.201–203
Holtsmark, Anne, 'Drama', in *KLNM*, III (Reykjavík, 1958), pp.293–295
Holtsmark, Anne, 'Leik og skjemt', in *Festskrift til Harald Grieg ved 25-års jubileet* (Oslo, 1950), pp.236–260
Holtsmark, Anne, 'Mannjevning', in *KLNM*, XI (Reykjavík, 1966), pp.325–326
Holtsmark, Anne, 'Myten om Idun og Tjatse i Tjoldovs Haustlong', *ANF*, 64 (1949), 1–73
Holtsmark, Anne, 'Senna', in *KLNM*, XV (Reykjavík, 1970), pp.149–152
Holtsmark, Anne, revision of Paasche, *Norges og Islands litteratur*: see below under Paasche
Holy week and Easter ceremonies from medieval Sweden, ed. Audrey Ekdahl Davidson, Early drama, art and music monograph series, 13 (Kalamazoo, 1990)
Honorius of Autun, *Gemma Animæ*, in *Patriologiæ cursus completus*, series latina, ed. J.-P. Migne, 219 vols (Paris, 1844–1862), CLXXII, pp.541–738
Hooke, S. H., ed., *Myth and ritual* (London, 1933)
Hougen, Bjørn, 'Osebergfunnets billedvev', *Viking*, 4 (1940), 85–124
Hrafnkels saga Freysgoða, in *ÍF* XI, ed. Jón Jóhannesson (Reykjavík, 1950), pp.95–133
Hreinn Benediktsson, *Early Icelandic script as illustrated by texts from the twelfth and thirteenth centuries*, Íslenzk handrit series in folio, II (Reykjavík, 1965)
Hreinn Benediktsson, ed., *The life of St Gregory and his dialogues* (Copenhagen, 1963)

Hrólfs saga kraka ok kappa hans, in *FN* II, pp.3–93

Hrómundar saga Gripssonar, in *FN* II, pp.273–286

Huizinga, Johan, *Homo ludens: A study of the play element in culture*, trans. R. F. C. Hull (London, 1949)

Hultkrantz, Åke, 'Hällristningsreligion', in Sverker Janson, Erik B. Lundberg and Ulf Bertilsson, eds., *Hällristningar och hällmålningar i Sverige* (Helsingborg, 1989), pp.43–58.

Hunningher, Benjamin, *The origin of the theatre* (Amsterdam, 1955)

Húngrvaka, in *Biskupa sögur*, ed. Jón Sigurðsson and Guðbrandur Vigfússon, 2 vols (1858–1878), I, pp.57–86

Håndskriftet nr.748, 4to, bl.1–6, i den Arna-magnæanske samling (Brudstykke af den Ældre Edda) i fototypiske og diplomatisk gengivelse, ed. Finnur Jónsson (København, 1896)

Håndskriftet nr.2365 4to gl.kgl.samling (Codex Regius af den Ældre Edda) i fototypisk og diplomatisk gengivelse, ed. Ludvig Wimmer, and Finnur Jónsson (København, 1891)

Hägg, Inga, *Die Textilfunde aus dem Hafen von Haithabu*, Berichte über die Ausgrabungen in Haithabu, ed. Kurt Schietzel, 20 (Neumünster, 1984)

Höfler, Otto, 'Das Opfer im Semnonenhain und die Edda', in *Edda, Skalden, Saga: Festschrift zum 70. geburtstag von Felix Genzmer*, ed. Hermann Schneider (Heidelberg, 1952), 1–67

Höfler, Otto, *Verwandlungskulte, Volksagen und Mythen*, Österreichische Akademie der Wissenschaften, philosophisch-historiche Klasse, Sitzungsberichte, 279. Band, 2. Abhandlung (Wien, 1973)

Indrebø, Gustav, ed., *Sverris saga etter Cod. AM 327 4°* (Kristiania, 1920)

Isidore of Seville, *Etymologiæ*, in *Patriologiæ cursus completus*, series latina, ed. J.-P. Migne, 219 vols (Paris, 1844–1862), LXXXII, pp.73–1060

ÍF: *Íslensk fornrit* (Reykjavík, 1933–); in progress

Íslendingabók, in *Íslendingabók. Landnámabók*, in *ÍF* I, ed. Jakob Benediktsson (Reykjavík, 1968), pp.1–28

Íslendingabók. Landnámabók, *ÍF* I, ed. Jakob Benediktsson (Reykjavík, 1968)

Íslendinga saga: see Sturla Þórðarson, *Íslendinga saga*

Jacobsen, M. A. and Matras, Chr., *Føroysk-Donsk orðabók*, 2nd ed. (Tórshavn, 1961)

Jacobsen, M. A., Matras, Chr., and Jóhan Hendrik W. Poulsen, *Føroysk-Donsk orðabók: Eykabind* (Tórshavn, 1974)

Jakobsen, Jakob, *An etymological dictionary of the Norn language in Shetland*, 2 vols (London, 1928–1932)

Jakobsen, Jakob, *Det norrøne sprog på Shetland* (København, 1897)

Jakobsen, Jakob, *Ordsamling og register*, in Jakob Jakobsen and V. U. Hammershaimb, *Færøsk anthologi*, 2 vols (København, 1891), II

Jakobsen, Jakob, 'Shetlandsøernes stedsnavne', *Aarbøger* (1901), 55–258

Janson, Sverker, Lundberg, Erik B., and Bertilsson, Ulf, eds, *Hällristningar och Hällmålningar i Sverige* (Helsingborg, 1989)

James, M. R., 'Two lives of St Ethelbert, king and martyr', *The English historical review*, 32 (1917), 214–245

Järlgren, Ulla, 'Julegoppan: En studie kring en försvunnen tradition', *Hembygden: Dalslands Fornminnes och hembygdsförbunds årsbok* (1978), 25–46

Jensen, Jørgen, *I begyndelsen: Danmarkshistorie*, I, ed. Olaf Olsen (Copenhagen, 1988)

Jensen, Stig, *Ribes vikinger* (Ribe, 1991)

Joensen, Jóan Pauli, *Fólk og mentan* (Tórshavn, 1987); a revision of Joensen, *Färöisk folkkultur* (Lund, 1980)

Jones, Gwyn, *A history of the Vikings*, 2nd ed. (Oxford, 1984)

Jones, W. Glyn, *William Heinesen* (New York, 1974)

Jón Hnefill Aðalsteinsson, 'Blót and þing: The function of the tenth century goði', *Themos*, 21 (1985), 23–38

Jón Hnefill Aðalsteinsson, 'Gátur', in *Íslensk þjóðmenning*, VI: *Munnmenntir og bókmenning*, ed. Frosti F. Jóhannesson (Reykjavík, 1989), pp.424–436

Jón Hnefill Aðalsteinsson, 'Norræn trú', in *Íslensk þjóðmenning*, V: *Trúarhættir*, ed. Frosti F. Jóhannsson (Reykjavík, 1988), pp.1–73

Jón Árnason, ed., *Íslenzkar þjóðsögur og æfintri*, 2 vols (Leipzig, 1862–1864)

Jón Árnason, *Úr förum Jóns Árnasónar*, 2 vols, ed. Finnur Sigmundsson (Reykjavík, 1950–1951)

Jón Helgason, ed., *Eddadigte*, 3 vols, in Nordisk filologi, serie A: tekster: I: *Völuspá Hávamál*, 2nd ed. (København, 1964), II: *Gudedigte*, 3rd ed. (Oslo, 1971), III: *Heltedigte, første del* (København, 1961)

Jón Helgason, ed., *Hauksbók*, Manuscripta Islandica, V (Copenhagen, 1960)

Jón Helgason, 'Norges og Islands digtning', in *Nordisk kultur*, VIII: *Litteraturhistorie*, ed. Sigurður Nordal, 2 vols (A and B) (Stockholm, 1942–1953), B, pp.3–179

Jón Helgason, *Norrøn litteraturhistorie* (København, 1934)

Jónas Jónasson frá Hrafnagili, *Íslenzkir þjóðhættir*, 3rd ed., ed. Einar Ólafur Sveinsson (Reykjavík, 1961)

Jónas Kristjánsson, *Eddas and sagas: Iceland's medieval literature*, trans. Peter Foote (Reykjavík, 1988)

Jónas Kristjánsson, 'Sigurðar saga and the prose passages in the Codex Regius', *Fourth international saga conference*, München, 1979 (München, 1979), pp.3–17

Jónas Kristjánsson, 'Stages in the composition of Eddic poetry', *Poetry in the Scandinavian Middle Ages: The seventh international saga conference: Spoleto 4–10 September 1988* (Spoleto, 1990), pp.201–218

Jónas Kristjánsson, ed., *Ögmundar þáttr dýtts*, in ÍF IX (Reykjavík, 1956), pp.LV–LXIV and pp.109–115

Jóns saga hins helga, in *Biskupa sögur*, ed. Jón Sigurðsson and Guðbrandur Vigfússon, 2 vols (1858–1878), I, pp.213–260

Jóns saga helga hin elzta in *Biskupa sögur*, ed. Jón Sigurðsson and Guðbrandur Vígfússon, 2 vols (Kaupmannahöfn, 1858–1878), I, pp.149–212

Jón Samsonarson, *Kvæði og dansleikir*, 2 vols, in Íslensk þjóðfræði (Reykjavík, 1964)

Jón Samsonarson, 'Marghala Grýla í görðum vesturnorrænna eyþjóða', in *Lygisögur sagðar Sverri Tómassyni fimmtugum, 5. apríl 1991* (Reykjavík, 1991), pp.48–54

Jón Samsonarson, 'Vaggvisor: Island', in *KLNM*, XIX (1975), pp.427–428

Jubinal, M. L. A., ed., *Nouveau recueil de contes, dits, fabliaux, et autres pièces inédites des XIIIe, XIVe et XVe siècles*, 2 vols (Paris, 1839–1842)

Jørgensen, Jon Gunnar, and Vésteinn Ólason, 'Fyrirlát mér jungfrúin hreina:

Et norsk religiøst dikt fra senmiddelalderen', in *Eyvindarbók: Festskrift til Eyvind Halvorsen*, ed. Finn Hødnebø (Oslo, 1992), pp.169–188
Kalkar, Otto, *Ordbog til det ældre danske sprog*, 6 vols (København, 1881–1918)
Ker, W. P., *Epic and romance* (London, 1908)
Ker, W. P., 'Review of The Elder Edda and ancient Scandinavian drama', *The modern language review*, 17 (1922), 201–202
Ketils saga hængs, in *FN* I, pp.243–266
Keyland, Nils, ed., *Julbröd, julbockar och Staffanssång* (Stockholm 1919)
Kirby, E. T., *Ur-drama: The origins of theatre* (New York, 1975)
Kirialax saga, ed. Kr.Kålund (København, 1917)
Kirk, G. S., *Myth: Its meaning and functions in ancient and other cultures* (Cambridge, 1970)
Kjalnesinga saga, in *ÍF* XIV, ed. Jóhannes Halldórsson (Reykjavík, 1959), pp.1–44
Kjellén, A., 'Några undersökningar rörande det liturgiska dramat i Sverige', *Samlaren* (1926), 1–32
Kjær, A., 'Zu Fáfnismál str 2', in *Festschrift für Eugen Mogk zum 70 Geburtstag 19. Juli 1924* (Halle an der Saale, 1924), pp.54–60
Klingenberg, Hans, *Edda – Sammlung und Dichtung* (Basel and Stuttgart, 1974)
Klintberg, Bengt af, ed., *Svenska folksägner* (Stockholm, 1972)
KLNM: See under *Kulturhistorisk leksikon for nordisk middelalder*
Kluckhohn, Clyde, 'Myths and rituals: A general theory', published in revised form in *Reader in comparative religion: An anthropological approach*, ed. William A. Lessa and Evon Z. Vogt, 3rd ed. (New York, 1958), pp.93–105; originally published in *Harvard theological review*, 35 (Jan 1942), 45–79
Knytlinga saga, in *ÍF* XXXV, ed. Bjarni Guðnason (Reykjavík, 1982), pp.91–321
Kolve, V. A., *The play called Corpus Christi* (London, 1966)
Kong Christian den femtes Norske Lov af 15de April 1687, ed. Otto Mejlænder (Christiania, 1883)
Konráðs saga keisarasonar, ed. Otto J. Zitzelberger, American university studies, series I: Germanic languages and literature, vol.63 (New York, 1987)
Konungs skuggsjá, Speculum regale: De norske håndskrifter i faksimile, introduced by Ludvig Holm-Olsen, Festgave fra Universitet i Oslo til H. M. Kong Haakon VII (Oslo, 1947)
Konungs skuggsjá, ed. Ludvig Holm-Olsen, Gammelnorske tekster utgitt av Norsk Kjeldeskrift-Institutt i samarbeid med gammelnorsk ordboksverk, nr.1 (Oslo, 1945)
Kormáks saga, in *ÍF* VIII, ed. Einar Ólafur Sveinsson (Reykjavík, 1939), pp.201–302
Krafft, Sophie, *Pictorial weavings from the Viking age: Drawings and patterns of textiles from the Oseberg finds* (Oslo, 1956)
Kragerud, Alv, 'De mytologiske spørsmål i Fåvnesmål', *ANF*, 96 (1981), 9–48
Krappe, Alexander Haggerty, 'Le legende de Gunnar Half', *Acta philologica Scandinavica*, 3 (1928–1929), 226–233
Kraus, Carl, 'Das gotische Weihnachtsspiel', *Beiträge zur Geschichte der deutschen Sprache und Literatur*, 20 (1895), 224–257

Bibliography

Kress, Helga, *Máttugar meyjar: Íslensk fornbókmenntasaga* (Reykjavík 1993)
Kristni saga, in *Biskupa sögur*, ed. Jón Sigurðsson and Guðbrandur Vigfússon, 2 vols (1858–1878), I, pp.3–32
Króka-Refs saga, in *ÍF* XIV, ed. Jóhannes Halldórsson (Reykjavík, 1959), pp.117–160
Kuhn, Hans, 'Philologisches zur Altgermanischen Religionsgeschichte', in *Kleine Schriften*, ed. Dietrich Hofmann, with Wolfgang Lange and Klaus von See, 4 vols (Berlin, 1969–1978), IV, pp.223–321
Kulturhistorisk leksikon for nordisk middelalder, ed. Magnús Már Lárusson, Jakob Benediktsson et al., 22 vols (Reykjavík, 1956–1978)
Kvideland, Reimund and Sehmsdorf, Henning K., ed. *Scandinavian folk belief and legend*, trans. Henning K. Schmsdorf and Patricia Conroy (Minneapolis, 1988)
La Fontaine, J. S., *Initiation: Ritual drama and secret knowledge across the world* (Harmondsworth, 1985)
La Piana, George, 'The Byzantine theatre', *Speculum*, 11 (1936), 171–211
La seinte resureccion from the Paris and Canterbury MSS, ed. T. A. Jenkins and J. M. Manly, completed by M. K. Pope and J. G. Wright, Anglo-Norman texts, IV, Anglo-Norman Text Society (Oxford, 1943)
Landnámabók, in *ÍF* I$^{1-2}$, ed. Jakob Benediktsson (Reykjavík, 1968), pp.29–397
Landnámabók: Melabók AM 106.112 fol., ed. Johannes Steenstrup, Finnur Jónsson, Sofus Larsen, Kr. Erslev, and Verner Dahlerup (København, 1921)
Laxdæla saga, in *ÍF* V, ed. Einar Ólafur Sveinsson (Reykjavík, 1934), pp.1–248
Laxdæla saga, ed. K. Kålund (København, 1889–1891)
Leabhar na H-Uidhri, lithograph facsimile by J. O'Longan, ed. J. J. Gilbert (Dublin, 1870)
Leach, Edmund R., *Political systems of highland Burma*, London School of Economics monographs on social anthropology, 44 (London, 1954)
Leach, Henry Goddard, *Angevin Britain and Scandinavia*, Harvard studies in comparative literature, VI (Cambridge, 1921)
Lebor na Huidre: The book of the dun cow, ed. R. I. Best and Osborn Bergin (Dublin, 1929)
Leifar fornra kristinna fræða íslenzkra, ed. Þorvaldur Bjarnason (Kaupmannahöfn, 1878)
Lid, Nils, 'Goa, Sporysj, Jumis og Cailleach', in *Nordiskt folkminne: Studier tillägnade C. W. von Sydow*, ed. Åke Campbell, Waldemar Liungman and Sigfrid Svensson (Stockholm, 1928), pp.199–206
Lid, Nils, 'Gudar og gudedyrking', in *Nordisk kultur*, XXVI: *Religionshistorie*, ed. Nils Lid (København, 1942), pp.80–153
Lid, Nils, *Joleband og vegetasjonsguddom*, Skrifter utgitt av det Norske Videnskaps-Akademi i Oslo II. Hist.-filos. klasse, 1928, no.4 (Oslo, 1928)
Lid, Nils, *Jolesveinar og grøderiksdomsguder*, Skrifter utgitt av det Norske Videnskaps-Akademi i Oslo II. Hist.-filos. klasse, 1932, no.5 (Oslo, 1933)
Lid, Nils, 'Julegeit og kveldskjøgle', *Ord og sed*, 8 (1941), 15–18
Lidén, Hans-Emil, 'From pagan sanctuary to Christian church: The excavation of Mære church in Trøndelag', *NAR*, 2 (1969), 3–32
Liestøl, Aslak, 'Runer frå Bryggen', *Viking* 27 (1963), 5–53
Liestøl, Knut, ed., *Norsk folkedikting*, III: *Segner* (Oslo 1963)

Liestøl, Knut, 'Til spørsmålet om dei eldste islendske dansekvæde', *Arv*, 1 (1945), 69–70
The life of St Gregory and his dialogues: Fragments of an Icelandic manuscript from the 13th century, ed. Hreinn Benediktsson, Editiones Arnamagnæanæ, series B,4. (Copenhagen, 1963)
Lindblad, Gustav, 'Centrala eddaproblem i 1970-talets forskningsläge', *Scripta Islandica: Isländska sällskapets årsbok*, 28 (1977), 3–26
Lindblad, Gustav, 'Snorre Sturlason och eddadiktningen', *Saga och sed* (1978), 17–34
Lindblad, Gustav, 'Poetiska Eddans förhistoria och skrivskicket i Codex regius', *ANF*, 95 (1980), 142–167
Lindblad, Gustav, *Studier i Codex Regius af Äldre Eddan* (Lund, 1954)
Lindow, John, *Scandinavian mythology: An annotated bibliography* (New York, 1988)
Lindow, John, 'The two skaldic stanzas in Gylfaginning', *ANF*, 92 (1977), 116–124
Lindquist, Ivar, 'Äringsriter i Bohuslän under bronsåldern', *Göteborgs och Bohusläns Fornminnesförenings tidskrift* (1923), 1–36
Lindqvist, Sune, *Gotlands bildsteine*, 2 vols (Stockholm, 1941–1942)
Lindqvist, Sune, 'Hednatemplet i Uppsala', in *Fornvännen*, 18 (1923), 85–118
Liungman, Waldemar, *Der Kampf zwischen Sommer und Winter*, FF communications Nr.130 (Helsinki, 1941)
Ljósvetninga saga, in ÍF X, ed. Björn Sigfússon (Reykjavík, 1940), pp.1–106
Ljunggren, Gustav, *Svenska dramat indtill slutet af sjuttonde århundradet* (Lund, 1864)
Lockhart, J. G., *Memoirs of Sir Walter Scott*, IV (Edinburgh, 1882)
Loomis, Roger, 'Some evidence for secular theatres in the twelfth and thirteenth centuries', *Theatre annual* (1945), 33–43
Loomis, Roger, and Cohen, Gustave, 'Were there theatres in the twelfth and thirteenth centuries?', *Speculum*, 20 (1945), 92–98
Lord, Albert B., *The singer of tales* (Cambridge, Mass, 1960)
Lowe, Pardee, Jr, 'Discourse analysis and the þáttr: Speaker tagging', in *Studies for Einar Haugen*, ed. Evelyn Scherabon Firchow, Kaaren Grimstad, Nils Hasselmo and Wayne A. O'Neil (The Hague, 1972), pp.339–348
Lund, Cajsa, 'Paa rangel 1974', *Stavanger Museum årbok* (1974), 45–120
Lunqvist, Lars, Rosengren, Erik, and Callmer, Johan, 'En fyndplats med guldgubbar vid Slöinge, Halland', *Fornvännen*, 88 (1993), 65–70
Lönnroth, Lars, 'The double scene of Arrow-Odd's drinking contest', in *Medieval narrative: A symposium*, ed. Hans Bekker-Nielsen, Peter Foote, Andreas Haarder, and Preben Meulengracht Sørensen (Odense, 1979), pp.94–109
Lönnroth, Lars, *Den dubbla scenen: Muntlig diktning från Eddan til Abba* (Stockholm, 1978)
Lönnroth, Lars, 'Hjálmar's death song and the delivery of Eddic poetry', *Speculum*, 46 (1971), 1–20
Lönnroth, Lars, 'Skírnismál och den fornisländska äktenskaps normen', in *Opuscula Septentrionalia: Festskrift til Ole Widding*, ed. Bent Chr. Jacobsen, Christian Lisse, Jonna Louis Jensen and Eva Rode (Hafniæ, 1977), pp.154–178

Läffler, L. Fr., 'Det evigt grönskande trädet vid Uppsala hedna-tämpel', in *Festskrift til H. F. Feilberg* (Stockholm, 1911), pp.617–696

Mac Cana, Proinsias, 'On the use of the term Retoiric', *Celtica*, 7 (1966), 65–90

Machan, Tim William, ed., *Vafþrúðnismál*, Durham medieval texts, 6 (Durham, 1988)

Mackeprang, Mogens B., 'Menschendarstellungen aus der Eisenzeit Dänemarks', *Act.arch.*, 6, fasc.3 (1935), 228–249

Maclagan, R. C., 'Notes on folklore objects collected in Argyleshire', *Folk-lore*, 6 (1895), 144–161

Macleod Banks, M., *British calendar customs: Orkney and Shetland*, Publications of the Folk-lore Society, CXII (London, 1946)

Macleod Banks, M., *British calendar customs: Scotland*, 3 vols., Publications of the Folk-lore Society, C, CIV and CVIII (London, 1937–1941)

Magerøy, Hallvard, ed., *Bandamanna saga* (Oslo, 1981)

Magnus, Olaus, *Historia de gentibus septentrionalibus* (Copenhagen, 1972)

Magnus, Olaus, *Historia om de nordiska folken*, trans. into Swedish by Robert Couto, Couta Thornell, Clemens Cavallin and others, commentary by John Granlund, 5 vols (Stockholm, 1909–1951)

Magnusson, Magnus, *Hammer of the North* (London, 1976)

The main manuscript of Konungs skuggsjá, in photographic reproduction with diplomatic text, ed. George T. Flom (Urbana, 1915)

Major, Albany F., A review of Bertha Phillpotts' *The Elder Edda and ancient Scandinavian drama*, in *Year book of the Viking society*, 6–16 (1914–1924), 70–72

Malmer, Mats P., 'Principles of a non-mythological explanation of North-European Bronze Age rock art', in *Bronze Age studies*, ed. Hans Åke Nordström and Anita Knape, The Museum of National Antiquities, Stockholm, studies 6 (Stockholm, 1989), pp.91–99

Malone, Kemp, 'Plurilinear units in Old English poetry', *Review of English studies*, 19 (1943), 201–204

Malone, Kemp, ed., *Widsith* (London, 1936)

Mannhardt, Wilhelm, *Wald- und Feldkulte*, 2 vols: I: *Der Baumkultus der Germanen und ihrer Nachbarstämme*; II: *Antike Wald- und Feldkulte aus nordeuropäischer Überlieferung erläutert*, 2nd ed., ed. W. Heuschkel (Berlin, 1904–1908)

Mariu saga. Legender om jomfru Maria og hendes jertegn efter gamle haandskrifter, ed. C. R. Unger, 2 vols (Christiania, 1871)

Marker, Frederick J., and Marker, Lise-Lone, *The Scandinavian theatre: A short history* (Oxford, 1975)

Marowitz, Charles, 'Notes on the Theatre of Cruelty', in David Williams, ed., *Peter Brook: A theatrical casebook* (London, 1988), pp.34–48; originally published in *Tulane drama review*, II,2 (1966)

Marshall, Mary, 'Theatre in the Middle Ages: Evidence from dictionaries and glosses', *Symposium*, 4 (1950), 1–39 and 366–389

Martin, John Stanley, *Ragnarök: An investigation into Old Norse concepts of the fate of the gods*, Melbourne monographs in Germanic studies, 3 (Assen, 1972)

Marwick, Ernest W., *The folklore of Orkney and Shetland* (London, 1975)

Marwick, Hugh, *The Orkney Norn* (London 1929)

Matras, Chr., 'Fornur hugsunarháttur. Gamlar siðir og gomul trúgv', *Varðin*, 4 (1924), 177–187

McCracken, Harold, *George Caitlin and the old frontier* (New York, 1959)

McKinnell, John, 'Motivation in Lokasenna', *Saga-Book*, 22 (1987–88), 234–262

McTurk, Rory, *Studies in Ragnars saga loðbrókar and its major Scandinavian analogues*, Medium Ævum monographs, 15 (Oxford, 1991)

Meletinsky, Eleazar M., 'Commonplaces and other elements of folkloric style in Eddic Poetry', trans. Mary P. Coote, in *Structure and meaning in Old Norse literature: New approaches to textual analysis and literary criticism*, ed. John Lindow, Lars Lönnroth, and Gerd Wolfgang Weber (Odense, 1986) pp.15–31

Meredith, Peter, and Kahrl, Stanley J., introduction, *The N-Town plays: A facsimile of British Library Cotton Vespasian DVIII*, Leeds texts and monographs, Medieval drama facsimiles, IV (Leeds, 1977)

The Middle English Harrowing of Hell and Gospel of Nicodemus, ed. William Henry Hulme, Early English Text Society, extra series 100 (London, 1907)

Mills, David, 'Drama and folk-ritual', in the *Revels history of drama in English*, I: *Medieval drama*, ed. A. C. Cawley, Marion Jones, Peter McDonald and David Mills (London, 1983), pp.122–151

Mjöll Snæsdóttir, 'Andlitsmynd frá Stóruborg undir Eyjafjöllum', in *Yrkja: Afmælisrit til Vigdísar Finnbogadóttur, 15. april, 1990*, ed. Heimir Pálsson, Jónas Kristjánsson, Njörður P. Njarðvík and Sigríður Th. Erlendsdóttir (Reykjavík, 1990), pp.169–171

Moffatt, William, *Shetland: The isles of nightless summer*, 2nd ed. (London, 1934)

Moisl, Hermann, 'Anglo-Saxon genealogies and Germanic oral tradition', *The journal of medieval history*, 7 (1981), 215–248

Montelius, Oscar, 'Solguden och hans dyrkan', *Nordisk tidskrift för vetenskap, konst och industri* (1911), 1–26 and 91–118

Moore, Bruce, 'The narrator within the performance: Problems with two medieval "plays" ', *Comparative drama*, 22 (1988), 21–36

Morkinskinna, ed. C. R. Unger (Christiania, 1867)

Motz, Lotte, 'Gerðr: A new interpretation of the Lay of Skírnir', *MM* (1981), 121–136

Motz, Lotte, 'Sister in the cave: The stature and function of the female figures in the Eddas', *ANF* (1980), 168–182

Muir, Lynette, 'Adam: A twelfth-century play translated from the Norman-French', *Proceedings of the Leeds Philosophical and Literary Society (Literary and philosophical section)*, 13 (1970), 149–204

Munch, Gerd Stamsø, 'Hus og hall. En høvdinggård på Borg i Lofoten', in *Nordisk hedendom: Et symposium*, ed. Gro Steinsland, Ulf Drobin, Juha Pentikäinen and Preben Meulengracht Sørensen (Odense 1991), pp.321–333

Murray, Gilbert, 'Excursus on "Ritual forms preserved in Greek tragedy" ', in Harrison, *Themis*, pp.341–363

Mustanoja, Tauno F., 'The presentation of ancient Germanic poetry: Looking for parallels', *NM*, 60 (1959), 1–11

Le mystère d'Adam, ed. Paul Aebischer, Textes littéraires francais (Genève, 1963)

Bibliography

Le mystère d'Adam: Édition diplomatique accompagnée d'une reproduction photographique du manuscrit de Tours et des leçons des éditions critiques, ed. Leif Sletsjöe (Paris, 1968)

Møller, J. S., 'Aarsfester fra Vaar til Høst i Danmark', in *Nordisk kultur*, XXII: *Aarets højtider*, ed. Martin P:n Nilsson (København, 1938), pp.113–142

Møller, J. S., 'Sommer i by i Danmark', *DS* (1930), 97–132

Müllenhoff, Karl, 'De alte Dichtung von den Nibelungen', *Zeitschrift für deutsches Alterthum und deutsche Litteratur*, 23 (1879), 113–155

Müllenhoff, Karl, *Deutsche Altertumskunde*, 5 vols (Berlin, 1870–1900)

Müller, Sophus, 'Billed- og fremstillingskunst i Bronzealderen', *Aarbøger* (1920), 125–161

The N-Town plays: A facsimile of British Library Cotton Vespasian DVIII, introduced by Peter Meredith and Stanley J. Kahrl, Leeds texts and monographs, Medieval drama facsimiles, IV (Leeds, 1977)

Neckel, Gustav, ed., and Kuhn, Hans, rev., *Edda: Die lieder des codex regius nebst verwandten denkmälern*, I: Text, 4th ed. (Heidelberg, 1962)

Needham, Joseph, 'The geographical distribution of English ceremonial dance traditions', *The journal of the English folk dance and song society*, 3,i (1936), 1–39 (and accompanying map)

Nerman, Birger, 'De äldsta Eddadikterna', *ANF*, 86 (1971), 19–37

Newall, Venetia, 'Up-Helly Aa: A Shetland winter festival', *Arv*, 34 (1978), 37–97

Nicolaysen, N., 'Den norske bukkevise', in *Historisk tidsskrift* (Kristiania, 1895), 212–215

Nicoll, Allardyce, *Masks, mimes and miracles* (London, 1931)

Nicoll, Allardyce, *The theory of drama* (New York, 1931)

Nielsen, H. Grüner, 'Danse på höj', *DS* (1918), 119–129

Nikolaus saga erkibyskups II, in *Heilagra manna sögur*, ed. C. R. Unger (Christiania, 1877), II, 49–158

Nilsson, Martin P:n, *Årets folkliga fester* (Stockholm, 1915)

Nilsson, Martin P:n, 'Julen', in *Nordisk kultur*, XXII: *Årets höjtider*, ed. Martin P:n Nilsson (København, 1938), pp.14–63

Nitida saga, in *Late medieval Icelandic romances*, V, ed. Agnete Loth, Editiones Arnmagnæanæ, series B, 24 (Copenhagen, 1965), pp.1–37

Non-cycle plays and fragments, ed. Norman Davis (London, 1970)

Non-cycle plays and the Winchester dialogues, ed. Norman Davis (Leeds, 1979)

Nordal, Guðrún, Sverrir Tómasson, and Vésteinn Ólason, *Íslensk bókmenntasaga*, I, ed. Vésteinn Ólason (Reykjavík, 1992)

Nordbladh, Jarl, 'Interpretation of South Scandinavian petroglyphs in the history of religion done by archeologists', in *Words and objects*, ed. Gro Steinsland (Oslo, 1986), pp.142–149

Nordén, Arthur, 'Hällristningarnas kronologi och betydelse', *Ymer*, 37 (1917), 57–83

Noreen, Erik, 'Eddastudier', *Uppsala universitets årsskrift, filosofi, språkvetenskap och historiska vetenskaper*, 5 (1921), 1–39

Noreen, Erik, 'Några anteckningar om ljóðaháttr och i detta versmått avfattade dikter', *Uppsala universitets årsskrift*, I (Uppsala, 1915), 1–50

Noreen, Erik, *Den norsk-isländska poesien* (Stockholm, 1926)

Noreen, Erik, 'Studier i fornvästnordisk diktning, III', *Uppsala universitets årsskrift, filosofi, språkvetenskap och historiska vetenskaper*, 3 (1923)

Norges gamle lov indtil 1387, ed. R. Keyser, P. A. Munch, Gustav Storm and Ebbe Hertzberg, 5 vols (Christiania, 1846–1895)

Norlind, Tobias, *Studier i svensk folklore*, Lund Universitets årsskrift N.F.AFD 1, Bd.7, Nr.5 (Lund, 1911)

Norlind, Tobias, 'Svärdsdans och bågdans', in *Festskrift til H. F. Feilberg* (Stockholm, 1911), pp.738–756

Norna-Gests þáttr, in *Flateyjarbok* (1860–1868), I, pp.346–359

Norske segner, ed. Olav Bø, Ronald Grambo, Bjarne Hodne and Ørnulf Hodne (Oslo, 1981)

Den norsk-islandske skjaldedigtning, ed. Finnur Jónsson, 4 vols (A.I–II, B.I–II) (København, 1912–1915)

North, Richard, 'How was Hávamál performed', in *The audience of the sagas: The eighth international saga conference, August 11–17, 1991: Preprints*, 2 vols (Göteborg, 1991), II, pp.153–162

De nuntio sagaci, ed. Gabriella Rossetti, in *Commedie latine del XII e XIII secolo*, II, ed. by Ferruccio Bertini (Genova, 1980), pp.11–125

Nylén, Erik, and Lamm, Jan Peder, *Stones, ships and symbols*, trans. Helen Clark (Stockholm, 1981)

Oddur Einarsson, *Íslandslýsing: Qualiscunque descriptio Islandæ*, trans. into Icelandic by Sveinn Pálsson (Reykjavík, 1971)

Oddverja annáll, in *Islandske annaler indtil 1578*, ed. Gustav Storm (Christiania, 1888), pp.427–491

OED, 2nd ed. (Oxford, 1989)

Oehlenschläger, Adam, *Nordiske Digte*, in Oehlenschlæger, *Poetiske Skrifter*, III, ed. H. Topsøe-Jensen (København, 1928)

O'Flaherty, Wendy Doniger, ed. and trans., *The Rig Veda* (London, 1981)

Ogilvy, J. D. A., 'Mimes, scurræ, histriones: entertainers of the early Middle Ages', *Speculum*, 38 (1963), 603–619

Ohlmarks, Åke, ed. and trans. into Swedish, *Eddans gudesånger* (Stockholm, 1948)

Olrik, Axel, *Danmarks heltedigtning*, 2 vols (København, 1903–1910)

Olrik, Axel, 'Episke lov i folkedigtningen', *DS* (1908), 69–89

Olrik, Axel, 'Gudefremstillinger på guldhornene', *DS* (1918), 1–35

Olrik, Axel, *Kilderne til Sakses oldhistorie*, 2 vols (København, 1892–1894)

Olrik, Axel, 'Middelalderens vandrende spillemænd in Norden og deres visesang', *Opuscula philologica*, utg. af Det Philol.-Hist. Samfund (1897), 74–84 and 265–266

Olrik, Axel, *Principles for oral narrative research*, trans. Kirsten Wolf and Jody Jensen (Bloomington, 1992)

Olrik, Axel and Jörgen, 'Kvindegilde i Middelalderen: En gråmunks vidnesburd fra 13de årh.', *DS* (1907), 175–176

Olrik, Axel and Ellekilde, Nils, *Nordens gudeverden*, 2 vols (København, 1926–1951)

Olsen, J., 'En Fastelavnsskik: At 'skyde Hjorten' (with a comment by Axel Olrik), *DS* (1912), 127

Olsen, Magnus, *Edda-og-skaldekvad*, 7 vols (Oslo, 1960–1964); published in Afhandlinger utgitt av Det Norske Videnskaps-Akademie i Oslo. Hist-filos. klasse

Olsen, Magnus, 'Fra gammelnorsk myte og kultus', *MM* (1909), 17–36
Olsen, Magnus, 'Göfugt dýr', *ANF*, 67 (1952), 30–34
Olsen, Magnus, *Hedenske kultminder i norske stedesnavne*, Videnskaps selskapets skrifter, II. Hist.-filos. klasse, 1914, no.4 (Kristiania, 1915)
Olsen, Magnus, 'Hild Rolvsdatters vise om Gange-Rolv og Harald Hårfagre', *MM* (1942), 1–70; also published in Magnus Olsen, *Fra norrøn filologi* (Oslo, 1949), pp.92–162
Olsen, Magnus, 'Kung Orre', *MM* (1912), 1–26
Olsen, Magnus, 'Til Haraldskvæði, strofe 23', *ANF*, 31 (1915), 381–382
Olsen, Magnus, 'Tjösnur og tjösnublót', *ANF*, 26 (1910), 342–346
Olsen, Magnus, 'Varðlokur', *MM* (1916), 1–21
Olsen, Olaf, 'Comments', *NAR*, 2 (1969), 25–27
Olsen, Olaf, *Hørg, hov og kirke*, Aarbøger (1965, published in 1966)
Olsen, Thorkil Damsgaard, 'Den høviske litteratur' in Hans Bekker-Nielsen, Thorkil Damsgaard Olsen, and Ole Widding, *Norrøn fortællekunst* (Copenhagen, 1965), pp.92–117
Omont, Henri, ed., *Fabliaux dits et contes en vers français du XIIIe siècle: fac-similé du manuscrit français 837 de la Bibliothèque Nationale publié sous les auspices de l'institut de France (Fondation Debrousse)* (Paris 1932)
Ong, Walter J., *Orality and literacy: The technologizing of the word* (London, 1982)
Opland, Jeff, *Anglo-Saxon oral poetry: A study of the traditions* (New Haven, 1980)
Ordish, T. Fairman, 'English folk-drama, I–II', *Folklore*, 2 and 4 (1891 and 1893), 2:314–335 and 4:149–175
Orkneyinga saga, in ÍF XXXIV, ed. Finnbogi Guðmundsson (Reykjavík, 1965), pp.1–300
Owen, Trefor M., *Welsh folk customs* (Cardiff, 1959)
Oxenstierna, Eric, *Järnålder, guldålder* (Stockholm, 1957)
Ó Suilleabháin, Seán, *Irish wake amusements* (Cork, 1967)
Óláfs saga Tryggvasonar en mesta, ed. Ólafur Halldórsson, 2 vols published so far, Editiones Arnamagnæanæ, series A, 1–2 (København, 1958–1961)
Ólafur Davíðsson, *Íslenzkar gátur, skemtanir, vikivakar og þulur*, II: *Skemtanir* (Kaupmannahöfn, 1888–1892)
Ólafur Davíðsson, *Íslenzkar gátur, skemtanir, vikivakar og þulur*, III: *Vikivakar og vikivakakvæði* (Kaupmannahöfn, 1894)
Ólafur Davíðsson, *Íslenzkar gátur, skemtanir, vikivakar og þulur*, IV: *Þulur og þjóðkvæði* (Kaupmannahöfn, 1898–1903)
Ólafur M. Ólafsson, 'Sigurðr duldi nafns síns', *Andvari*, 12 (1970), 182–189
Ólafr Þórðarson, *Málhljóða-og málskrúðsrit: Grammatisk-retorisk afhandling*, ed. Finnur Jónsson, Det Kgl. Danske Videnskabernes Selskab. Historisk-filologiske Meddelser, XIII, 2 (København, 1927)
Paasche, Fredrik, *Norges og Islands litteratur*, revised by Anne Holtsmark: Vol.1 of *Norsk litteratur historie*, ed. Francis Bull et al., 6 vols in 7 (Oslo, 1955–1963)
Palladius, Peder, *Visitatsbog*, ed. Lis Jacobsen, *Danmarks folkeminder*, 30 (København, 1925)
Páls saga biskups, in *Biskupa sögur*, ed. Jón Sigurðsson and Guðbrandur Vigfússon, 2 vols (1858–1878), I, pp.127–148
The Penguin book of oral poetry, ed. Ruth Finnegan (Harmondsworth, 1982)

Perkins, Richard, 'Rowing chants and the origins of dróttkvæðr háttr', *Saga-Book*, 21 (1984–85), 155–221

Petersen, Carl S., ed., *Breve fra Finn Magnusen til F. D. Gräter* (København, 1908)

Petersen, Jan, *Vikingetidens redskaper*, Skrifter utgitt av det Norske Videnskaps-Akademi i Oslo II. Hist.-filos. klasse, 1951, no.4 (Oslo, 1951)

Petrus Comestor, *Historia scholastica*, in *Patriologiæ cursus completus*, series latina, ed. J. P. Migne, 219 vols (Paris, 1844–1862), CXCVIII, pp.1054–1722

Pfister, Manfred, *The theory and analysis of drama*, trans. John Halliday (Cambridge, 1988)

Phillpotts, Bertha S., *The Elder Edda and ancient Scandinavian drama* (Cambridge, 1920)

Pio, Iørn, *Bogen om julen* (Viborg, 1990)

Planctus Mariæ, transcribed and translated by W. L. Smolden (London, 1965)

Polomé, Edgar, 'Etymology, myth and interpretation: On some problems of the use of Eddic materials in comparative religion. (Summary)', *The sixth annual saga conference, 28.7.– 2.8. 1985, Workshop papers*, 2 vols (København, 1985), II, pp. 033–011

Pontoppidan, Erik, *Fejekost til at udfeje den gamle Surdejg eller de i de danske Lande tiloversblevne og her for dagen bragte Levninger af saavel Hedenskab som Papisme*, ed. and trans. into Danish by Jørgen Olrik, Danmarks Folkeminder, 27 (København, 1923)

Propp, Vladimir, *Theory and history of folklore*, trans. Ariadna Y. Martin and Richard P. Martin and others, ed. Anatoly Liberman, *Theory and history of literature*, vol.5, ed. Wlad Godzich and Jochen Schulte-Sasse (Manchester, 1984); originally published in Vladimir Propp, *Istoriceskie korni volsebnoj skazki* (Historical roots of the wondertale) (Leningrad, 1946)

Quinn, Judy, 'Verseform and voice in eddic poems: The discourses of Fáfnismál', *ANF*, 107 (1992), 100–115

Raglan, Lord Fitzroy Richard Somerset, *The hero: A study in tradition, myth and drama* (London, 1936)

Ragnars saga loðbrókar ok sona hans, in *FN* I, pp.93–148

Randlev, Julie, 'Skírnismál: En tekst – og dens udsagn: Digtning og tradition', *MM* (1985), 132–158

Rasmussen, Rasmus, *Sær er siður á landi* (Tórshavn, 1985)

Revard, Carter, 'Gilote et Johane: An interlude in B.L.MS.Harley 2253', *Studies in philology*, 79 (1982), 122–146

Reykdæla saga ok Víga-Skútu, in *ÍF* X, ed. Björn Sigfússon (Reykjavík, 1940), pp.149–243

Rémundar saga keisarasonar, ed. Sven Grén Broberg (København, 1909–1912)

Robberstad, Knut, ed. and trans. into Norwegian, *Gulatingslovi*, 4th ed. (Oslo, 1981)

Rooth, Anna Birgitta, *Folklig diktning: Form och teknik* (Lund, 1976)

Rossetti, Gabriella, ed., *De nuntio et sagaci*, in *Commedie latine del XII e XIII secolo*, II, ed. Ferrucio Bertini (Genova, 1980), pp.11–125

Roy, Bruno, 'Arnulf of Orleans and the Latin "comedy"', *Speculum*, 49 (1974), 258–266

Rómverjasögur, ed. Rudolf Meissner (Berlin, 1910)

Rudwin, Maximilian J., *The origin of the German carnival comedy* (New York, 1920)
Ruodlieb: Faksimile-Ausgabe des Codex Latinus Monacensis 19486 der Bayerischen Staatsbibliothek München und der Fragmente von St Florian, 2 vols: Band I.i: Einleitung by Walter Haug; I.ii: Tafeln; II.i: Kritischer text, ed. Benedikt Konrad Vollmann (Wiesbaden, 1974–1986)
Rutherford, Ward, *Shamanism: The foundations of magic* (Wellingborough, 1986)
Rydquist, J. E., 'Nordens äldsta skådespel', *Skandia*, 7 (1836), 167–253
Rygh, O., *Norske gaardnavne*, 18 vols (Kristiania, 1897–1924)
Sacre rappresentazioni nel manoscritto zol della Bibliothèque Municipale di Orléans, ed. Giampiero Tintori, Instituta et monumenta serie I: monumenta n.2 (Cremona, 1958)
Saga Guðmundar Árnasonar Hóla-biskups hin elzta, in *Biskupa sögur*, ed. Jón Sigurðsson and Guðbrandur Vigfússon, 2 vols (1858–1878), I, pp.405–558
Sagan af Nikulási konungi leikara, ed. Helgi Árnason (Reykjavík, 1912)
Saga Þorláks biskups hin elzta, in *Biskupa sögur*, ed. Jón Sigurðsson and Guðbrandur Vigfússon, 2 vols (1858–1878), I, pp.89–124
Sahlgren, Jöran, *Eddica et Scaldica: Fornvästnordiska studier* (Lund, 1927)
Sahlgren, Jöran, 'Hednisk gudalära och nordiska ortnamn', *Namn och bygd*, 38 (1950), 1–37
Sahlgren, Jöran, 'Sagan om Frö och Gärd', *Namn och bygd*, 16 (1928), 1–19
Sallust, *Bella Iugurthinum*, in *Sallust*, ed. and trans. J. C. Rolfe, The Loeb classical library (London, 1965), pp.132–381
Samling af Sweriges gamla lagar (Corpus Iuris Sueo-Gotorum Antiqui), ed. D. H. S. Collin and D. C. J. Schlyter, 13 vols (Stockholm, 1827–1877)
Sawyer, Peter, *Da Denmark blev Danmark: Danmarkshistorie*, III, ed. Olaf Olsen (Copenhagen, 1988)
Saxby, Jessie M. E., *Shetland traditional lore* (Edinburgh, 1932)
Saxo Grammaticus, *The history of the Danes*, I: Text, trans. Peter Fisher, ed. Hilda Ellis Davidson (Cambridge, 1979)
Saxo Grammaticus, *Saxonis gesta Danorum*, ed. J. Olrik and H. Ræder, (Hauniæ, 1931)
Scardigli, Piergiuseppe and Raschellà, Fabrizio, 'A Latin-Icelandic glossary and some remarks on Latin in medieval Scandinavia', in *Idee. Gestalt. Geschichte: Festschrift Klaus Von See*, ed. Gerd Wolfgang Weber (Odense, 1988), pp.299–323
Schjødt, Jens Peter, 'The "meaning" of the rock carvings and the scope for religio-historical interpretation: Some thoughts on the limits of the phenomenology of religion', in *Words and objects*, ed. Gro Steinsland (Oslo, 1986), pp.180–196
Schlager, Karin, *Julbocken i folktro och jultradition* (Kristianstad, 1989)
Schmid, Toni, 'Mysteriespel', in *KLNM*, XII, p.103
Schmidt, August F., 'Helligtrekongersangere i Danmark', *Arv*, 4 (1948), 50–126
Schröder, Franz Rolf, Review of Bertha Phillpotts, The Elder Edda and ancient Scandinavian drama, *Anglia Beiblatt. Mitteilungen über englische Sprache und Literatur und über englsichen unterricht*, 32 (1921), 148–155

Schröder, Franz Rolf, 'Das Symposion der Lokasenna', *ANF*, 67 (1952), 1–29

Schutz, Herbert, *The prehistory of Germanic Europe* (New Haven, 1983)

Schück, Henrik, *Forntiden och den äldre medeltiden*, in *Svenska folkets historia*, ed. Henrik Schück, Helge Almquist, Arthur Stille, and Carl Hallendorff, Carl, 4 vols (Lund, 1914–1928), vol.I, parts 1–2

Schück, Henrik, *Studier i nordisk litteratur- och religions historia*, 2 vols (Stockholm, 1904)

Schück, Henrik, *Studier i Ynglingatal*, I–IV, *Upsala Universitets årsskrift* (1905–1907, 1910)

Schück, Henrik, and Warburg, Karl, *Illustrerad svensk litteraturhistoria*, 2nd ed., rev., 5 vols in 6 (Stockholm, 1911–1932); 3rd ed., re-revised, 8 vols (Stockholm, 1926–1949)

Scott, Sir Walter, *The pirate* (Edinburgh, 1886)

The Scottish national dictionary, ed. William Grant and David D. Murison (Edinburgh, 1934–1976)

Seip, Didrik Arup, 'Har nordmenn skrevet opp Edda-diktningen?', *MM* (1951), 3–33

Seip, Didrik Arup, introduction, *The Arna Magnæan manuscript 677, 4to* Corpus Codicum Islandicorum Medii Aevi, XVIII (Copenhagen, 1949)

Seip, Didrik Arup, 'Om et norsk skriftlig grunnlag for Edda-diktningen eller deler av den', *MM* (1957), 81–207

Seip, Didrik Arup, *Palæografi, B: Norge og Island*, in *Nordisk kultur*, XXVIII, *Palæografi*, ed. Johs. Brøndum-Nielsen, 2 vols (A and B) (Uppsala, 1954)

Seip, Didrik Arup and Wallén, Per-Edwin, 'Leikarar', in *KLNM*, X (Reykjavík, 1965), pp.462–467

Sharp, Cecil, *The sword dances of Northern England*, 3 vols published in one (East Ardsley, 1977; originally published 1911–1913)

Shetelig, Haakon, and Falk, Hjalmar, *Scandinavian archeology*, trans. E. V. Gordon (Oxford, 1937)

Shklovsky, I. W., *In far north east Siberia*, trans. L. Edwards and Z. Shklovsky (London, 1916)

Sievers, E., *Altgermanische Metrik*, Sammlung Kurzer Grammatiken germanischer Dialekte, Ergänzungsreihe, II (Halle, 1893)

Sigurðar saga þǫgla, in *Late medieval Icelandic romances*, II: *Saulus saga ok Nikanors; Sigurðar saga þǫgla*, ed. Agnete Loth (Copenhagen, 1963), pp.93–259

Sigurðar saga þǫgla: The shorter readaction, ed. M. J. Driscoll (Reykjavík, 1992)

Sijmons, Barend, ed., *Die Lieder der Edda*, 2 vols (Halle A.S., 1866–1906)

Sijmons, 'Einleitung': see Sijmons, Barend, *Die Lieder der Edda*, vol.II, ii

Simonsen, Poul, 'The magic picture: used once or more times?', in *Words and objects*, ed. Gro Steinsland (Oslo, 1986), pp.197–211

Simpson, Jacqueline, 'Some Scandinavian sacrifices', *Folklore*, 78 (1967), 190–202

Simpson, Jaqueline, ed. and trans., *Scandinavian folktales* (London, 1988)

Sjöberg, N., 'En germansk julfest i Konstantinopel på 900-talet', *Fataburen* (1907), 31–35

Skar, Johannes, *Gamalt or Sætesdal*, 3 vols (Oslo, 1961–1965)

Snorri Sturluson, *Edda*, ed. Finnur Jónsson, 2nd ed. (København, 1926)

Snorri Sturluson, *Heimskringla*: see under *Heimskringla*

Bibliography

Solheim, Svale, *Horse-fight and horse-race in Norse tradition* (Oslo, 1956)
Southern, Richard, *The seven ages of the theatre*, 2nd ed. (London, 1968)
Spiers, John, *Medieval English poetry: The non-Chaucerian tradition* (London, 1957)
Stefán Einarsson, 'Alternate recital by twos in Wídsíþ(?), Sturlunga and Kalevala', *Arv*, 7 (1951), 59–83
Stefán Einarsson, 'Dæmi um víxlkveðandi eða andsvarasöng á Íslandi og Finnlandi', *Skírnir*, 86 (1962), 107–129
Stefán Einarsson, 'Harp song, heroic poetry (Chadwicks) Greek and Germanic alternate singing: Mantic song in Lapp legend Eddas, sagas and Sturlunga', *Budkavlen*, 42 (1963), 13–28
Stefán Einarsson, 'Horse dance in the Sturlunga saga', in *Folkloristica: festskrift till Dag Strömbäck*, ed. Gustaf Adolf Bertil (Uppsala, 1960), pp.290–293
Stefán Einarsson, 'Víxlkveðandi í Wídsíþ(?), Sturlungu og á Finnlandi', *Skírnir*, 125 (1951), 109–151
Stefán Ólafsson, 'Grýlukvæði', in *Ljóðmæli*, ed. Andrés Björnsson (Reykjavík, 1948), pp.17–26
Steinsland, Gro, *Det hellige bryllup og norrøn kongeideologi: En analyse av hierogami-myten i Skírnismál, Ynglingatal, Háleygjatal og Hyndluljóð* (Oslo, 1991)
Stenberger, Martin, 'Ektorp's borg: A fortified village on Öland, Sweden', in *Act.arch.*, 37 (1966), 203–214
Stjórn, ed. C. R. Unger (Christiania, 1862)
Stumpfl, Robert, *Kultspiele der Germanen als Ursprung des mittelalterlichen Dramas* (Berlin, 1936)
Ström, Folke, 'Den döendes makt och Odin i trädet', *Göteborgs Högskolas årskrift*, 54.2 (1947)
Ström, Folke, *Nordisk hedendom*, 3rd ed., rev. (Göteborg, 1985), except where reference is made to an earlier edition
Strömbäck, Dag, 'Att helga land: Studier i Landnáma och det äldste rituella besittningstagandet', in Strömbäck, *Folklore och filologi* (Uppsala, 1970), pp.135–165; originally published in *Festskrift tillägnad Axel Hägerström* (1928), pp.198–220
Strömbäck, Dag, 'Cult remnants in Icelandic dramatic dances', *Arv*, 4 (1948), 132–145
Strömbäck, Dag, 'Icelandic dramatic dances and their West European background', *Universitet i Bergen årbok, Historisk-antikvarisk rekke* (1955), 92–99 (translation of 'Um íslenska vikivakaleiki')
Strömbäck, Dag, 'Isländska danslekar av kultiskt ursprung', in Strömbäck, *Den osynliga närvaron*, ed. Gerd Jonzon (Hedemora, 1989), pp.139–148 (Swedish translation of 'Cult remnants in Icelandic dramatic dances')
Strömbäck, Dag, 'Kölbigk och Hårga I', *Arv*, 17 (1961), 1–48
Strömbäck, Dag, 'Lytir: En fornsvensk gud?', in *Festskrift til Finnur Jónsson*, ed. Johs. Brøndum-Nielsen, Elof Hellquist, O. F. Hultman, Sigurður Nordal and Magnus Olsen (København, 1928), pp.283–293
Strömbäck, Dag, 'Några isländska folklekar från medeltiden', *Saga och sed* (1956), 43–51; republished in Strömbäck, *Folklore och filologi* (Uppsala, 1970), pp.229–237 (Swedish translation of 'Um íslenska vikivakaleiki')

Strömbäck, Dag, *Sejd*, Nordiska texter och undersökningar, 5 (Stockholm, 1935)
Strömbäck, Dag, 'Staffan, Herodes og "tuppundret" ', in Strömbäck, *Den osynliga närvaron*, ed. Gerd Jonzon (Hedemora, 1989), pp.185–197
Strömbäck, Dag, 'St Stephen in the ballads', *Arv*, 24 (1968), 133–147
Strömbäck, Dag, 'Um íslenska vikivakaleiki og uppruna þeirra', *Skírnir*, 127 (1953), 70–80
Strömbäck, Dag, 'Den underbara årsdansen', *ANF*, 59 (1944), 111–126; also published in Strömbäck, *Folklore och filologi* (Uppsala, 1970), pp.54–69
Studer, Paul, ed., *Le mystère d'Adam* (Manchester, 1928)
Sturla Þórðarson, *Íslendinga saga*, in *Sturlunga saga*, ed. Guðbrandur Vigfússon, 2 vols (Oxford, 1878), I, pp.189–409, II, 1–274
Sturla Þórðarson, *Magnús saga Hakonar sonar* (fragment), in *Icelandic sagas and other historical documents relating to the settlements and descents of the Northmen in the British Isles*, II, ed. Guðbrandur Vigfússon (London, 1887), pp.361–374
Sturlunga saga, ed. Guðbrandur Vigfússon, 2 vols (Oxford, 1878)
Sturlunga saga, ed. Jón Jóhannesson, Magnús Finnbogason, and Kristján Eldjárn, 2 vols (Reykjavík, 1946)
Støylen, Bernt, *Norske barnerim og leikar* (Kristiania, 1899)
Sundquist, Nils, *Östra Aros: Stadens uppkomst och dess utveckling intill år 1300, Uppsala stads historia*, ed. Herbert Lundh, vol.I (Stockholm, 1953)
Svabo, J. C., *Dictionarium Færoense (Færøsk-dansk-latinsk ordbog)*, I: *Ordbogen*, ed. Chr. Matras (København 1966)
Svarfdæla saga, in ÍF IX, ed. Jónas Kristjánsson (Reykjavík, 1956), pp.127–208
Svava Jakobsdóttir, 'Gunnlöð og hinn dýri mjöður', *Skírnir*, 162 (1988), 215–245
Sveinbjörn Egilsson, and Finnur Jónsson, *Lexicon poeticum*, 2nd ed. (København, 1931)
Sveinn Einarsson, 'Helgileikir og herranætur', *Skírnir*, 139 (1965), 103–126
Sveinn Einarsson, *Íslensk leiklist*, I: *Ræturnar* (Reykjavík, 1991)
Sveinn Einarsson, 'Theatre in Iceland', in *Theatre in Iceland*, ed. Aðalheiður Friðþjófsdóttir, Baldvin Halldórsson, Erlingur Gíslason, Óskar Ingimarsson, and Ævar R. Kvaran, trans. Christopher Sanders (Reykjavík, 1976), pp.3–16
Svensson, Sigfrid, 'Årsfester i Sverige och Svensk-Finland', in *Nordisk kultur*, XXII: *Aarets højtider*, ed. Martin P:n Nilsson (København, 1938), pp.64–88
Sveriges dramatiska litteratur til och med 1825, ed. G. E. Klemming, *Svenska fornskriftsällskapet. Samlingar*, hft.40,55,67,71,72 (Stockholm, 1863–1879)
Sverrir Tómasson, 'Erlendur vísdómur og forn fræði', in Guðrún Nordal, Sverrir Tómasson and Vésteinn Ólason, *Íslensk bókmenntasaga*, I, ed. Vésteinn Ólason (Reykjavík, 1992), pp.517–570
Sverrir Tómasson, *Formálar íslenskra sagnaritara á miðöldum* (Reykjavík, 1988)
Sverrir Tómasson, 'Veraldleg sagnaritun 1120–1400', in Guðrún Nordal, Sverrir Tómasson and Vésteinn Ólason, *Íslensk bókmenntasaga*, I, ed. Vésteinn Ólason (Reykjavík, 1992), pp.263–308, and pp.345–418
Sverris saga etter Cod. AM 327 4º, ed. Gustav Indrebø (Kristiania, 1920)
Szwed, John F., 'The mask of friendship: Mumming as a ritual of social relations', in *Christmas mumming in Newfoundland*, ed. Herbert Halpert and G. M. Story (Toronto, 1969), pp.104–118

Söderberg, Barbro, 'Formelgods och Eddakronologi', *ANF*, 101 (1986), 50–79
Söderberg, Barbro, 'Lokasenna: Egenheter och ålder', *ANF*, 102 (1987), 18–93
Sögubrot af fornkonungum í Dana- ok Svíaveldi, in *FN* II, pp.111–134
Sørensen, Preben Meulengracht, 'Loki's senna in Ægir's hall', in *Idee Gestalt Geschichte: Festschrift Klaus von See*, ed. Gerd Wolfgang Weber (Odense, 1988), pp.239–259
Sörla þáttr, eða Heðins saga ok Högna, in *FN* II, pp.95–110
Tacitus, Cornelius, *Germania*, trans. M. Hutton, rev. E. H. Warmington, in Tacitus, *Agricola, Germania, Dialogus*, ed. E. H. Warmington, The Loeb classical library (London, 1970), pp.127–215
Tacitus, Cornelius, *The histories. The annals*, 4 vols, trans. John Jackson (*The annals*) and Clifford H. Moore (*The histories*), The Loeb classical library (London, 1925–1937)
Tacitus, Cornelius, *On Britain and Germany*, trans. H. Mattingly (Harmondsworth, 1948)
Talbot, Annelisa, 'The withdrawal of the fertility god', *Folklore*, 93 (1982), 31–46
Táin Bó Cúailnge from the Book of Leinster, ed. Cecile O'Rahilly, Irish Texts Society, XLIX (Dublin, 1967)
Táin Bó Cúailnge, rescension I, ed. Cecile O'Rahilly (Dublin, 1976)
Táin Bó Cúailnge from the Yellow book of Lecan, ed. John Strachan and J. G. O'Keefe (Dublin, 1912)
Terence (P. Terentius Afer), *Comediae*, ed. Sextus Prete (Sesto Prete) (Heidelberg, 1954)
Terence, *The comedies of Terence*, ed. Sidney G. Ashmore, 2nd ed. (New York, 1908)
Thomassaga erkibiskops, ed. C. R. Unger (Christiania, 1869)
Thomson, Ian, 'Latin "elegiac comedy" of the twelfth century', in Paul G. Ruggiers, ed., *Versions of medieval comedy* (Oklahoma, 1977), pp.51–66
Thompson, Stith, *The folktale* (Berkeley, 1977)
Three Latin comedies, ed. Keith Bate, Toronto medieval studies (Toronto, 1976)
Thuren, Hjalmar, *Folkesangen paa Færøerne*, FF publications, Northern series, Nº 2 (København, 1908)
Tiddy, R. J. E., *The Mummers' play* (Oxford, 1923)
Tillhagen, Carl-Hermann, ed., *Taikon berättar* (Stockholm, 1946)
The Times literary supplement, Review of Bertha Phillpotts, The Elder Edda and ancient Scandinavian drama (Thursday, 16 December, 1920), 857
The Towneley cycle: A fascimile of Huntingdon MS HM1, introduced by A. C. Cawley and Martin Stevens, Leeds texts and monographs, Medieval drama facsimiles, II (Leeds, 1976)
Tranter, Stephen N., 'Marginal problems', in *Early Irish literature: Media and communication / Mündlichkeit und Schriftlichkeit in der frühen irischen Literatur*, ed. Stephen N. Tranter and Hildegard L. C. Tristram, ScriptOralia, 10 (Tübingen, 1989), pp.221–240
Tristrams saga og Ísoddar, in *Riddarasögur*, ed. Bjarni Vilhjálmsson, 6 vols (Reykjavík, 1949–1951), VI, pp.85–145
Troels-Lund, Troels Frederik, *Dagligt liv i Norden i det sekstende aarhundrede*, 4th ed., 14 vols (København, 1914)

Tulinius, Torfi H., 'Kynjasögur úr fortíð og framandi löndum', in Böðvar Guðmundsson, Sverrir Tómasson, Torfi Tulinius and Vésteinn Ólason, *Íslensk bókmenntasaga*, II, ed. Vésteinn Ólason (Reykjavík, 1993), pp.165–245

Turville-Petre, E. O. G., 'Fertility of beast and soil in Old Norse literature', in *Old Norse literature and mythology: A symposium*, ed. Edgar C. Polomé (Austin, 1969), pp.244–264

Turville-Petre, E. O. G., *Myth and religion of the North* (London, 1964)

Turville-Petre, E. O. G., *The origins of Icelandic literature* (Oxford, 1953)

Tydeman, William, *The theatre in the Middle Ages: Western European stage conditions, c.800–1576* (Cambridge, 1978)

Uldall, Kai, 'Dansehøj, Pinsebod og gildesvold', *Fortid og nutid*, 8 (1930), 131–151, and 169–192

Ussing, Henrik, *Om det inbyrdes forhold mellem heltekvadene i ældre Edda* (København, 1910)

Vafþrúðnismál, ed. Tim William Machan, Durham medieval texts, 6 (Durham, 1988)

van Hamel, A. G., 'The prose frame of Lokasenna', *Neophilologus*, 11 (1929), 204–214

Vatnsdæla saga, in ÍF VIII, ed. Einar Ólafur Sveinsson (Reykjavík, 1939), pp.1–131

Vatnsdæla saga, ed. Walther Heinrich Vogt (Halle A.S., 1921)

Verlaeckt, Koen, 'The Kivik petroglyphs: A reassessment of different opinions', *Germania*, 71.1 (1993), 1–29

Vestlund, Alfred, 'Åskgudens hammare förlorad: Ett bidrag till nordisk ritforskning', *Edda*, 11 (1919), 95–119

Vésteinn Ólason, 'Eddukvæði', in Guðrún Nordal, Sverrir Tómasson and Vésteinn Ólason, *Íslensk bókmenntasaga*, I, ed. Vésteinn Ólason (Reykjavík, 1992), pp.73–186

Vésteinn Ólason, 'Kveðskapur af fornum rótum: Eðli og einkenni', in Guðrún Nordal, Sverrir Tómasson and Vésteinn Ólason, *Íslensk bókmenntasaga*, I, ed. Vésteinn Ólason (Reykjavík, 1992), pp.45–72

Vésteinn Ólason, *The traditional ballads of Iceland* (Reykjavík, 1982)

Vídalín, Páll, *Skýringar yfir fornyrði lögbókar þeirrar, er Jónsbók kallast* (Reykjavík, 1854)

Víga-Glúms saga, ed. G. Turville-Petre (London, 1960)

Víga-Glúms saga, in ÍF IX, ed. Jónas Kristjánsson (Reykjavík, 1956), pp.1–98

Víglundar saga, in ÍF XIV, ed. Jóhannes Halldórsson (Reykjavík, 1959), pp.61–116

Vogt, Albert, *Commentaire* on Constantin VII Porphyrogénète, *Le livre des cérémonies*, 2 vols (Paris, 1935–1940)

von Hagen, Victor Wolfgang, *The ancient sun kings of the Americas* (St Albans, 1973)

von Massmann, 'Gothica minora', *Zeitschrift für deutsches Alterthum*, 1 (1841), 366–373

de Vries, Jan, *Altgermanische Religionsgeschichte*, 2nd ed., rev., 2 vols, in Grundriss der germanischen Philologie, ed. Hermann Paul, 12/I–II (Berlin, 1956–1957)

de Vries, Jan, *Altnordische Literaturgeschichte*, 2 vols, in Grundriss der germanischen Philologie, ed. Hermann Paul, 15–16 (Berlin, 1941–42); 2nd ed., rev. (Berlin, 1964–1967)

de Vries, Jan, *Altnordisches etymologisches Wörterbuch*, 2nd ed. (Leiden, 1962)

de Vries, Jan, *Contributions to the study of Othin especially in his relation to agricultural practices in modern popular lore*, FF communications Nr.94 (Helsinki, 1931)

de Vries, Jan, 'Die Helgilieder', *ANF*, 72 (1957), 123–154

de Vries, Jan, *Heroic song and heroic legend*, trans. B. J. Timmer (London, 1963)

de Vries, Jan, 'Om Eddaens visdomsdigtning', *ANF*, 50 (1934), 1–59

Vysotsky, S. A., *Svetskie freski Sofijskogo sobora v Kieve* (Kiev, 1989)

Vöðu-Brands þáttr, in *ÍF* X, ed. Björn Sigfússon (Reykjavík, 1940), pp.123–139

Völsunga saga, in *FN* I, pp.3–91

Watson, G. J., *Drama: An introduction* (London, 1983)

Watt, Margrethe, 'Guldgubberne fra Sorte Muld, Bornholm: Tanker omkring et muligt hedensk kultsentrum fra yngre jernalder', in *Nordisk hedendom: Et symposium*, ed. Gro Steinsland, Ulf Drobin, Juha Pentikäinen and Preben Meulengracht Sørensen (Odense 1991), pp.373–386

Weiser-Aall, Lucy, *Julenissen og julegeita i Norge*, in Småskrifter fra norsk etnologisk gransking (Oslo, 1954)

Welsford, Enid, *The fool* (London, 1935)

Wessén, Elias, 'Hästskede och lekslätte', *Namn og bygd* (1921), 103–131

Wessén, Elias, 'Hávamál: Några stilfrågor', *Filologiskt arkiv*, 8 (Stockholm, 1959)

Wessén, Elias, 'Den isländska eddadiktningen: Dess uppteckning och redigering', *Saga og sed* (1946), 1–31

Weston, Jessie, *From ritual to romance* (New York, 1957)

Whitaker, Ian, 'Traditional horse-races in Scotland', *Arv*, 14 (1958), 83–94

Wickham, Glynne, 'The beginnings of English drama: Stage and drama till 1660', in *English drama to 1710*, ed. Christopher Ricks, the Sphere history of literature, III, 2nd ed., rev. (London, 1988), pp.1–53

Wickham, Glynne, *The medieval theatre*, 3rd ed. (Cambridge, 1987)

Widding, Ole, and Bekker-Nielsen, Hans, 'A debate of the body and the soul in Old Norse literature', *Mediaeval studies*, XXI (1959), 272–289

Widdowson, J. D. A., and Halpert, Herbert, 'The disguises of the Newfoundland Mummers', in *Christmas mumming in Newfoundland*, ed. Herbert Halpert and G. M. Story (Toronto, 1969), pp.145–164

Widsith, ed. Kemp Malone (London, 1936)

Wieselgren, P., *Sveriges sköna litteratur*, 5 vols (Lund, 1834–1849)

Wiget, Andrew, *Native American literature* (Boston, 1985)

Williams, Arnold, *The drama of medieval England* (East Lansing, 1961)

Williamson, Kenneth, *The Atlantic islands* (London, 1948)

Woolf, Rosemary, *The English mystery plays* (London, 1972)

Worsaae, J. J. A., *Minder om de Danske og Nordmændene i England, Skotland og Irland* (Kjøbenhavn, 1851)

Wright, Edith Armstrong, *The dissemination of the liturgical drama in France* (Pennsylvania, 1936)

Wright, Stephen K., 'The oldest Swedish play: Sources, structure and staging of the De uno peccatore qui promeruit gratiam', *Journal of English and German philology*, 87 (1988), 49–72

Wyller, Torill, *Sankt Hans: Midsommerfeiring i Norge gjennom 150 år* (Oslo, 1987)

Ynglinga saga, in ÍF XXVI, ed. Bjarni Aðalbjarnarson (Reykjavík, 1941), I, pp.8–83

The York play: A facsimile of the British Library MS. Additional 35290, introduced by Richard Beadle and Peter Meredith, Leeds texts and monographs, Medieval drama facsimiles, VII (Leeds, 1983)

Young, Karl, *The drama of the medieval church*, 2 vols (Oxford, 1933)

Zeydel, Edwin H., 'Were Hrotsvitha's dramas performed in her lifetime?', *Speculum*, 20 (1945), 443–456

Ögmundar þáttr dytts, ed. Jónas Kristjánsson, in ÍF IX (Reykjavík, 1956), pp.107–115

Ölkofra þáttr, in ÍF XI, ed. Jón Jóhannesson (Reykjavík, 1950), pp.346–359

Örn Ólafsson, 'Finngálknað', *Lesbók Morgunblaðsins*, 13 February 1993, 10

Örvar-Odds saga, ed. R. C. Boer (Leiden, 1888)

Örvar-Odds saga, in FN I, pp.281–399

Þiðriks saga af Bern, ed. Henrik Bertelsen, 2 vols (København, 1905–1911)

Þorgils saga ok Hafliða, in *Sturlunga saga*, ed. Guðbrandur Vigfússon (Oxford, 1878), I, pp.7–39

Þorláks saga helga hin yngri, in *Biskupa sögur*, ed. Jón Sigurðsson and Guðbrandur Vigfússon, 2 vols (1858–1878), I, pp.263–404

Þorleifs þáttr jarlsskálds, ed. Jónas Kristjánsson, in ÍF IX (Reykjavík, 1956), pp.213–229

Þorsteins saga Víkingssonar, in FN II, pp.183–246

Þorsteins þáttr bæjarmagns, in FN III, pp.395–417

Þórðar saga hreðu, in ÍF XIV, ed. Jóhannes Halldórsson (Reykjavík, 1959), pp.161–226

INDEX

The entries in this index are ordered according to the Scandinavian alphabets, so that accented vowels follow simple vowels, and the letters Å, Ä, Ö/Ø, Þ and Æ follow on from those letters found in the English alphabet. Unless they use a family name, all Icelanders are listed under their Christian names.

Aalborg, 128, 132
Abingdon, 328
Abraham and Isaac (Brome), past tense stage directions in, 323
Adam de la Halle, speaker indications in manuscripts of works by, 298, 300 *n*
Adam of Bremen, *Gesta Hammaburgensis ecclesiæ pontificum*, on *pantomimi*, 360 *n*; on ritual at Uppsala, 61, 78–80, 83, 351
Adoratio Crucis, in Scandinavia, 328 *n*
Aestii, 61
Ailred of Rievaulx, on priests behaving like actors, 361 *n*
Alcuin, warnings about *histriones*, 359
Alexanders saga, 26 *n*, 324, 362 *n*
Alexandreis (Gautier de Châtillons), 362 *n*
Almgren, Oscar, on ritual drama, 6, 45–46
'alternate singing', 338–341
Alvíssmál, 5, 80, 86, 186, 188, 191, 195, 203 *n*, 206 *n*, 208, 212, 232 *n*, 235, 275, 281, 349, 352, 356
AM 748 manuscript of Eddic poems, marginal speaker notation in, 206–212, 217, 282, 318, 320, 322–323, 351–352, 357; general, 184–185, 202, 204, 222–223, 225, 230, 233, 235, 253, 329, 357
Ammianus Marcellinus, accounts of Germanic oral performance, 334–335
Andaðr, *leikari*, 362–363
annandagsskeið, 33, 100
anndasbrur, 134 *n*
anonymity of speakers in Eddic poems, 233, 239–241, 248–249, 251–252, 263, 267–268, 271–272, 279, 354
antiphony, 332–334, 361 *n*
Arboga, Sweden, 137
Aristophanes, 3–5, 205
Aristotle, The *Poetics*, 11, 19, 238–239
Arnaldus Jolahest, 82, 126, 157, 167
Arngrímur Jónsson: *see Crymogæa*

Arnhöfði, 63, 82
Arnórr Þórðarson, *Hrynhenda*, 87
Arnulf of Orléans, 304
Arras, 298, 300
arrow markings, use of in manuscript of drama to indicate movement, 304
Atlakviða in grænlenska, 189, 192, 196, 198–199
Atlamál in grænlensku, 186, 189, 192, 196, 198
Attila, and entertainers, 339, 359
autumn games, 35–36
Axton, Richard, definition of drama, 13
Aztec ball games, 33
álfablót, 340 *n*
Án trúðr, 364 *n*
Árna saga biskups, 144 *n*
Árni Magnússon, 145–146
Babio, marginal speaker indications in manuscripts of, 290–291, 311–312, 316, 318; manuscripts of, 308, 311–312; performance of, 308, 310; provenance of, 310, 320 *n*; general, 292, 324, 327
Baldrs draumar, manuscript of, 210, 215; performances of, 2; general, 189, 192, 196
Balestrand, Sogn, Norway, 117 *n*, 131, 139 *n*
Bandamanna saga, 341 *n*, 348
bark costumes: *see* 'Næframaðr'
Barking Easter play, speaker indications in manuscript of, 298
Basque tradition, 150, 155
basse, as a bear spirit, 121 *n*
basser as masked figures, 106
'Battle between Winter and Summer': *see* combat
Bárðar saga Snæfellsáss, 340 *n*
Beauvais, *Danielis ludus*, 323–324 *n*
Beauvais, tradition of liturgical drama, 327
bells and rattles, use of, 76–78, 102, 109, 146, 153, 163

Index

Benedictine monasteries, drama in, 327–328; monasteries in Iceland, 327
Bergen, Norway, 82, 96 *n*, 117–118, 119, 136 *n*, 324, 355
Bergmann, F. G., on Eddic poems as drama, 4, 8 *n*
Bergslagen, Sweden, 102 *n*, 109 *n*
berserkir, 64, 66, 68, 70, 81
Birka (Björkö) pendant, 64–65, 67
Bjarkarmál hin fornu, performance of, 235, 331
Björkö, Sweden, 103
'Black bear song' of Osage Indians, 20 *n*, 21 *n*
Blekinge, Sweden, 118
'blended' narrative-speech strophes, 187–190, 194–196, 207
blended prose-and-verse form, 184 *n*, 201–202, 212, 214, 216, 218, 234–235, 268
blomsterbrud, 135, 136 *n*
blót, 14, 356
blótnaut, 32
'Blåsa liv in den daude bukken', 119
boasting songs, 333 *n*, 342–343
Bodel, Jean, speaker indications in manuscript of *Le jeu de Saint Nicolas*, 298
Bohuslän, folk traditions, 98, 102, 118, 121–122; petroglyphs, 37–38, 40, 42, 44–47, 49–50, 82
bonfires in Scandinavian folk tradition, 136–137, 141, 355
Borgarþingslög, 98 *n*
Bornus Consort, 324 *n*
Bovi (also Bovmand), 55 *n*, 104–105, 161 *n*, 170–171, 353
Boy Bishop tradition, 134
Bósa saga ok Herrauðs, 89
Bragi, 245
Breakspeare, Nicholas, Cardinal, 327
Breiðabólstaðr, Iceland, 82
Brennu-Njáls saga: see Njáls saga
British folk customs, relationship to those of Scandinavia, 117 *n*, 132–133, 142–143, 150, 154, 156
Brook, Peter, 2, 11
Brot af Sigurðarkviðu, 189, 192, 196
Brot úr miðsögu Guðmundar biskups Arasonar, 27 *n*
'Buffalo dance' of Plains Indians, 20
Bury St Edmunds, 328 *n*
buse, flaying of, 122 *n*
Buskerud, Norway, 111
'Buslabæn', 89

Byggvir, as a possible straw-clad figure, 102, 246 *n*, 353; as a servant of Freyr, 245 *n*; named in full in *Codex Regius* manuscript, 208; not mentioned in *Prose Edda*, 226 *n*; not recognised by Loki in *Lokasenna*, 242
Bærings saga, 30 *n*
Caenby horned figure, 64, 67
Cailleach, 104 *n*, 174 *n*
Cambridge school of classical anthropology, 5 *n*, 7, 9, 15
candles, use of with costumes, 110 *n*, 145, 148–149, 151 *n*
Carmina Burana, longer Passion play, use of past tense stage directions in, 323
carols, relationship to Icelandic *vikivaki*, 156
'Carrying horse', 157, 168 *n*
Castle of perseverence, use of past tense stage directions in, 323 *n*
Celtic peoples, influences on Gallehus horns, 53; links with Dejbjerg wagons, 59 *n*; possibility of a Celtic origin for costumed traditions in Scandinavia, 122, 125
Charlemagne, capitulum regarding *mimi*, 364
Christkindlein, 123
church attacks on the performing arts, 124, 326, 358–359
church influence on folk traditions in Scandinavia, 93–97, 139, 158, 166, 179
circling land as a ritual, 142
classification of Eddic poems, 185–189, 191–192
Clovesho, canon of, 361 *n*
Codex Bembinus of plays of Terence, marginal speaker indications in, 295–296, 302, 310, 318, 320; general, 292 *n*
Codex Regius (Gml.kgl.saml.2365 4^(to)), of Eddic poems, editorial approach in, 182 *n*, 196–205, 218, 224–225, 229, 234; marginal speaker notation in, 206–213, 245, 252, 256–257 *n*, 259–260, 264 *n*, 282, 318, 322–323, 351–352, 357; general, 184–185, 196, 216, 219, 221–223, 227–228, 230, 233–235, 256, 281, 324 *n*, 329–330, 357
Codex Wormianus, 184
Colding, P. I., *Dictionarium Herlovianum*, 114
collection of Eddic poems, 184 *n*, 190 *n*, 200–201, 203–205, 218–219
combat in ritual and folk tradition, 41,

45, 51, 60, 76, 128–133, 141, 180; combat between *Staffan* and *julbock*, 119, 129; combat between Winter and Summer, 119, 128–130, 354; combat with a monster, 66–73, 80
comediæ, Latin, 288 *n*, 292, 304, 308, 322; *see also* Babio, *De nuntio sagaci* and *Pamphilus*
comes florialis, 128, 137
Constantin VII Porphyrogénète, *Book of ceremonies*: *see* gothikon
Constantinople, 3, 28, 32, 71–72, 74–76, 360
context markers, 237–238
'conversation poems', 333
Conversion of Scandinavia, 356–357
Copenhagen, 132
corn-grinding songs in Scandinavia, 337 *n*
Courtois d'Arras, manuscript of, 298 *n*
Crymogæa (Arngrímur Jónsson), 145 *n*, 149
Daaretønde, 114
Dalarna, Sweden, 99, 115, 120
Dalsland, Sweden, 98, 102–104, 109 *n*, 122
Dame Sirith, marginal speaker notation in manuscript of, 288 *n*, 304, 307, 318; narrator in, 304, 314, 323; performance of, 304, 306, 360; relationship to Latin *comediæ*, 304; general, 322, 324, 329
dance and dancing figures, 38–39, 42, 45, 49, 57–58, 60, 62, 65–68, 70–77, 79, 90, 91, 103–104, 112, 133 *n*, 155–156, 166 *n*, 336, 339 *n*, 346–347, 349, 364; particular references to dance in Old Icelandic sources, 30, 84, 144, 346–347; *see also* sword dance, and *vikivaki*
'danzleikar' and 'danza-gjörðir', 30, 84, 144
Darraðarljóð, 337–338, 340 *n*
dating of Eddic poems, 184–185, 191–192, 205 *n*, 216, 247 *n*, 260 *n*
Dejbjerg wagons, 59–60
Devil, and disguises, 99–100; 123–124, 127, 158, 160 *n*, 171–172; *see also* possessed images and straw figures
'dialogue poems', between Summer and Winter, 130; in Mongolia, 333; Eddic dialogues: *see* under individual poems; moral and theological dialogues in Scandinavia: *see Elucidarius*, Gregory the Great, *Konungs skuggsjá*, *Viðræða líkams ok sálar* (Norwegian), *Viðræða líkams ok sálar* (Icelandic), and *Æðru senna ok hugrekki*
Digby plays, speaker indications in manuscript of, 291 *n*, 300 *n*, 315 *n*
disguises in Old Norse literature, 80–84; *see also* masks and disguises
Dínus saga dramblátá, 362 *n*
dísablót, 34, 127 *n*
að draga jólasveina og jólameyjar, 156
dragon figures, lack of them in English folk tradition, 143
drama, conditions for development of, 23–24; definition of, 10–14, 25
drama and play, relationships between, 17–18
drama and ritual, similarities and differences, 12, 17–21
dramatic readings of texts in Middle Ages, 25 *n*
'Dráp Niflunga', 194, 196 *n*, 199
'dream verses', 338, 340
drinking the 'blood' of the 'bear', *julebukk*, *julegrisen*, and Stefan, 120 *n*
Droplaugarsona saga, 83 *n*, 364 *n*
drykkjebassann', 90
dux hyemalis, 128
Edgar, King, on *histriones* and *mimi*, 359, 360 *n*
Eggert Ólafsson and Bjarni Pálsson, on *vikivaki* games, 148 *n*, 178 *n*
Egils saga Skalla-Grímssonar, 26 *n*, 32 *n*, 33 *n*, 81 *n*
Einar Skúlason, on *leikarar*, 360, 363
Einar Ólafur Sveinsson, on Eddic poems as drama, 8 *n*, 9, 10 *n*
Eiríksmál, 5 *n*, 245 *n*, 270 *n*
Eiríks saga rauða, 31 *n*, 56 *n*, 82 *n*, 336, 349
Ekhammar amulet, 64–65, 67
Elucidarius (Honorius Augustodunesis), condemnation of *leikarar* in, 326; speaker indications in manuscripts of, 283–284, 286, 289, 292, 318
Erbsenbär, 122
eskimo: *see* Greenland Inuit
Estonia, 105, 112, 123, 159
Eymundar þáttr Hringssonar, 81 *n*
Eynsham, tradition of liturgical drama in, 327 *n*
Eyrbyggja saga, 26 *n*, 31 *n*, 33 *n*, 34, 83 *n*, 342
Eysteinn Erlendsson, Archbishop, 328 *n*
Eyvindr kelda, 337

Fagrskinna, 28 *n*, 362 *n*
Faroese traditions, dance, 133 *n*, 144, 166 *n*; disguises, *see grýla*, *jólahøna*, and *jólhestur*; games, 134; lack of bonfires in, 141 *n*
fastelavn: *see* Shrovetide
fastlagen: *see* Shrovetide
Fáfnismál, action in, 265–269; birds in, 82, 260, 264–265; characterisation in, 353; difficulties in solo performance of, 256–269, 281, 353; iconographic images depicting action of, 260, 266 *n*, 267, 269; links with ritual, 80, 269, 355–354, 356; marginal speaker indications in, 207–208, 256–257 *n*, 259–260, 264 *n*; prose in, 197, 199, 212, 223–225, 233–234, 256, 266–268; relationship to other Eddic poems, 203–206; relationship to *Reginsmál* and *Sigrdrífumál*, 256–260; Sigurðr Fáfnisbani as 'göfugt dýr', 81 *n*, 354–355; Snorri Sturluson's knowledge of, 219–225; general, 2, 5, 7, 26 *n*, 180, 186, 189–190, 192, 196, 200, 231, 239, 279, 306, 346; 354; *see also Hortlied*, 'Old play of the Wolsungs', and *Vaterrachelied*
female disguise, on Gallehus horn, 51–52; in *Þrymskviða*, 83; origins of, 122 *n*; general, 180, 337; *see also* Grýla, gyros, *Háu-Þóru leikur*, *kerlingarleikur*, and shield-maidens
Fetlar, Shetland, 168–169, 175 *n*
fiaðrhamr, 63, 82
'Fight of the guisers', 71–73, 75, 360
Fimafengr, 226
'Fingálpn': *see þingálp*
Finglesham buckle, 64–65, 67
Finland, 101, 104, 105, 132, 139 *n*, 339
finngálkn, 126 *n*, 144–145, 178 *n*; *see also þingálp*
Finnmark, Norway, 37–38
Finnur Magnússon ('Finn Magnusen'), on Eddic poems as drama, 3–4, 130 *n*, 353–354; on the *gothikon*, 74–75 *n*
Fjölsvinnsmál, 5 *n*, 186
Flatey, Breiðafjörður, Iceland, 345
Flateyjarbók, 55–57, 184
Fleury play-book, speaker indications in, 296–297
Flóamanna saga, 35 *n*
folk courts and folk justice, 88, 91, 127
foreign performers in Scandinavia, 362–363
fornaldarsögur, 212, 218, 268

Forn-svenskt legendarium, 161 *n*
fornyrðislag, characteristics of, and differences from *ljóðaháttr*, 192–194, 207, 339 *n*; general, 190–192, 203, 216, 218, 269, 352
Foula, Shetland, 173
Fountains Abbey, 324 *n*
Fóstbrœðra saga, 26 *n*, 27
'frantzensleikur', 149
Frazer, Sir James George, *The golden bough*, on idea of Scandinavian ritual drama, 5, 45
'Frá dauða Sigurðar', 197–199
'Frá dauða Sinfjötla', 185 *n*, 194 *n*, 197, 204 *n*
Frederikstad, Norway, 111
Freising *Nativity play*, speaker indications in manuscript of, 313 *n*; use of narrative passages in, 323
Freyja, 33 *n*, 60 *n*, 62–63, 78, 338
Freyr, 28, 32, 53 *n*, 78, 101–102, 143; *see also Gunnars þáttr helmings*, *Lokasenna*, and *Skírnismál*
'Freys leikr', 28, 35
Frigg, 63
Frostaþingslög, 86 *n*, 98 *n*
'Fyrirlát mér jungfrúin hreina', 119–120, 157
gadebasse, 90–92, 96, 134–136, 148, 156, 170
gadebassedrenge, 148
gaddebassesvende, 148
gadelamme, 90 *n*, 134–136
Gallehus horns, 32, 49–53, 60, 75, 79–80, 337, 355
Gamal norsk homiliebok, 284
games involving the killing and reviving of animal figures, 119; on the concept of 'game', *see leikr* and play
games leaders, 89–92; *see also gadebasse, leikgoði, skudler*, and *strawboys*
Gandersheim, 326 *n*
gardvord, 141
Gaster, Theodore, on ritual drama, 5 *n*, 7 *n*, 15–17, 19
Gautreks saga, 83 *n*
Gátur Gestumblinda, 275, 349
German influences on Scandinavian folk traditions, 128, 131 *n*, 132, 136–139, 154 *n*; *see also* under *julebukk*
Giftarleik, 134
Gilbert Islanders, 331 *n*
Gilote et Johane, marginal speaker notation in manuscript of, 306, 308–309,

318; narrator in, 306, 308, 314, 323; performance of, 308
Giraldus Cambrensis (*Descriptio Kambriæ*), on 'two part' singing by Scandinavians, 335
Gizurr Ísleifsson, Bishop, 326
Gísla saga Súrssonar, 34, 87 *n*; Gísli Súrsson as 'hermikráka', 84
glíma, 34
goat figures, 52–53, 59, 67 *n*, 76, 98–99, 102, 104 *n*, 116 *n*; possible associations with Óðinn, 83; *see further julebukk*, and *þingálp*
goat-skins and magic, 83 *n*
gold foils, 49, 57–58, 155
gothikon, 3, 71–72, 74–76, 79 *n*, 130 *n*, 131, 144
Gotland, picture stones, 51, 53, 67, 355; general, 75, 123
Góa, 97
grave mounds, as possible holy sites, 34, 139, 355; in vicinity of sites for mock-marriages, 139; offerings to, 18; worship of, 140 *n*
Grágás (*Staðarhólsbók*), on *trúðar*, 364
Greek drama, 7, 19, 23
Greenland Inuit, 'nith song', 333 *n*, 348–349; traditions of poetic duels, 332–333
Gregorius de Cresendio, Cardinal, 364
Gregory the Great, Pope, speaker indications in manuscripts of *The Dialogues*, 283–284, 286–287, 318, 322; on pagan ritual custom, 94
Grettis saga Ásmundssonar, 26 *n*, 66 *n*, 83 *n*, 86
Grevensvænge figurines, 41, 43–44, 67 *n*
gríma ('mask'), concept of, 81, 83, 86
Gríma, 87 *n*
Grímnir, 83, 87 *n*, 127, 354
Grímnismál, 5 *n*, 70, 83, 186, 188, 191, 194–195, 200, 203 *n*, 204, 214 *n*, 219, 232 *n*, 268, 279, 352, 354–356
Grímr, 83, 87 *n*, 127, 354
Gríms saga loðinkinna, 341 *n*
Grípispá, 182 *n*, 184*n*, 188, 191, 195, 199, 204 *n*, 206
group singing and poetic performance, 331–332, 334–337
Grottasöngr, 189, 192, 196, 337, 340 *n*
Grógaldr, 5 *n*, 186
Grýla/ grýla (-*ur*), 82; in Faroes, 112 *n*, 124 *n*, 162–167, 169 *n*, 174–175, 178–179, 351, 354; in Iceland, 160–162, 165, 172–179, 351; in Old Icelandic sources, 161–162, 165, 173, 175–178; *see also skeklers* and *grøleks*, and *gyros*
Grýla verses, 161, 165, 173, 176, 179
Grýlu-Brandr, 82 *n*, 161, 177
grýlukvøld, 162
'grýlumaður', 176–177
Gräter, Friedrich David, on Eddic poems as drama, 3, 5
grøkle, 175
grølek (*grøli*, *grölik*, *grulek*, *gruli*, *grulick*, *grulja*, *grülik*, *grillock*): see *skeklers* and *grøleks*
Grönbech, Vilhelm, on Eddic poems as drama, 6, 19
Grænlendinga þáttr, 342 *n*
Gudbrandsdal, Norway, 118
guddursbassen, 90
Guðbrandur Vigfússon and F. York Powell, on Eddic poems as drama, 4–5, 205
Guðmundar saga góða: see *Guðmundar sögur biskups*
Guðmundar sögur biskups, 30, 144 *n*, 338
Guðrúnarhvöt, 189, 192, 196
Guðrúnarkviða I (in fyrsta), 189, 192, 196–197
Guðrúnarkviða II (önnur; in forna), 86–87, 186, 189, 192, 194, 196, 199
Guðrúnarkviða III (in þriðja), 189, 192, 196, 199
guessing games, 117 *n*, 354
Guillaume de Conches, 284
Gulaþingslög, 86 *n*, 98 *n*, 140 *n*
Gummersmark brooch, 57–58
Gunnars saga keldugnúpsfífls, 30 *n*
Gunnars þáttr helmings, 54–60, 83, 85, 101, 337, 353
Gunnlaugs saga ormstungu, *háð* in, 29–30, 84, 144; general, 26 *n*, 32 *n*
Guro Rysserova, 160–161 *n*, 174–175
Gutenstein bracteate, 66–67, 70
Gylfaginning: see Snorri Sturluson, *Prose Edda*
Gymir, as threat in *Skírnismál*, 251–253
gyre-karl and *gyre-karline*, 174 *n*
Gyro night, 174
gyros, 102 *n*, 174–175
Göngu-Hrólfs saga, 26 *n*, 30 *n*
Habergeiss, 122
Hagendrup horned headdress, 43–44
Hagia Sophia Cathedral, Kiev, frescos in, 28 *n*, 71–73, 75, 360
Halland, Sweden, 138 *n*

Halldórs þáttr Snorrasonar inn fyrri, 86 *n*
Hallingdal, Norway, 110 *n*, 159 *n*
halmgubbar, 102
Halm-Staffan, 33, 101–105, 109 *n*, 137, 148, 168, 171, 180, 351, 353
Halton Cross, 260, 267
Hamðismál, 185–186, 189, 192, 196, 203 *n*
Haraldr hárfagri, 28, 34, 337, 362
Haraldskvæði, or *Hrafnsmál* (Þorbjörn hornklofi), 28, 66, 341 *n*, 362–363
Hardanger, Norway, 98, 139
Hardy, Thomas, 85 *n*
Harley 2253 manuscript, 306, 308–309, 314, 316–317
Harrison, Jane, on ritual drama, 5 *n*
Harrowing of Hell, marginal speaker indications in manuscripts of, 290–291, 300, 311, 316–318, 322, performance of, 316; use of past tense narrative in one manuscript of, 323; general, 329
Hauksbók, 283–284
Hauks þáttr hábrókar, 34, 54
Haustlöng (Þjóðólfr úr Hvini), 10 *n*, 82
Hákonarmál, 5 *n*, 245 *n*, 270 *n*
Hákon the Old (Hákon gamli Hákonarson), 284
Hálfdanar saga Eysteinssonar, 27 *n*, 34
Hárbarðsljóð, action in, 274; characterisation in, 353; demand for use of costumes in, 271–272; difficulties in solo performance of, 269–274, 281; prose in, 200, 212, 232–233; relationship to other Eddic poems, 203–205, 206 *n*; setting of, 271, 274, 343; speaker indications in, 207–210, 213, 215, 313, 318; structure of, 270–271; general, 2–4, 10, 81 *n*, 130, 180, 186, 188, 191, 195, 219, 231, 265, 279, 306, 322, 341 *n*, 349–350, 352–353, 356 *n*
Háu-Þóru leikur, 112 *n*, 149, 150–153, 155–156, 158–160, 163–164, 171, 178
Hávamál, 5, 80, 83 *n*, 186, 188, 191, 195, 206, 212 *n*, 241 *n*, 268 *n*, 279, 344, 352, 354, 356
Hedeby (Heiðabær), animal masks from, 73, 76
Heimskringla (Snorri Sturluson), 27 *n*, 28 *n*, 337, 340, 342
Heinesen, William, 'Grylen', 112 *n*, 163–165, 179 *n*
Helgakviða Hjörvarðssonar, marginal speaker notation in, 207, 208 *n*, 259; prose in, 197, 203 *n*, 212, 214, 216 *n*;

general, 7–8, 17, 82, 184 *n*, 185 *n*, 188, 190–191, 195, 200–202, 204–205, 231, 270, 272 *n*, 304, 341 *n*, 343, 352, 354
Helgakviða Hundingsbana I, 7–8, 17, 188, 190–191, 195, 198–200–202, 203 *n*, 212, 214, 272 *n*, 341 *n*, 343, 348, 354
Helgakviða Hundingsbana II, prose in, 197, 203 *n*, 212, 214, 216 *n*; general, 7–8, 17, 184 *n*, 188, 190–191, 194–196, 200–202, 204, 206, 231, 272 *n*, 341 *n*, 343, 352, 354
Helligtrekongerspill, 95, 171 *n*; *see also* Three Kings plays
helmet-masks, possible, 61, 81, 83, 87, 266–267, 269, 355
Helreið Brynhildar, 189, 192, 196–197, 200 *n*, 206, 234, 330, 345–346
Herford, 326 *n*
Hervarar saga ok Heiðreks, 86, 189 *n*, 273, 349 *n*
hestaþing, 35
hestleikur (*hestreiðarleikur*), 149–151, 153–155, 157–158, 160, 167
Heusler, Andreas, on Eddic poems as drama, 8, 351
Hibbert, Samuel, on Shetland sword dance, 132–133; on *skeklers*, 169
hieros gamos, 45–46, 49, 57, 76, 80, 98, 133, 138, 140, 353; *see also* mock-marriages
Hilarius, speaker indications in manuscript of *Ludus super iconia Sancti Nicolai*, 298; speaker indications in *The raising of Lazarus* and *The play of Daniel*, 313 *n*
Hildesheim, 326 *n*
hindarleikur, 149, 156, 158 *n*
Hindeleik, 134
Hippodrome, Constantinople, 28, 32, 71, 74
histriones: *see leikarar* and *loddarar*; *mimi* and *histriones*; and *trúðar*
hjartarleikur (*hjörtleik, hjartleikur*), 110 *n*, 112 *n*, 149–151, 154, 158, 172
'Hjálmar's death song', 186
Hjálmþés saga ok Ölvis, 34, 145 *n*
Hliðskjálf, 229–230
Hlöðskviða, 186, 189, 192, 196
Hobby Horse, 14, 114
Hoffinsleikur, 154, 156
hofgoði, 89
Holberg, Ludvig, *Julestue*, 110, 179 *n*
Holtsmark, Anne, on idea of Scandinavian ritual drama, 10

Index

Honorius of Autun, *Gemma animæ*, relation of Mass to a tragedy, 325; in early Icelandic libraries, 325
hoop dance, 130–131
Hordaland, Norway, 110 *n*, 159 *n*
horned figures, in archaeological finds, 37–38, 41–46, 51–53, 58, 60–68, 70–71, 76; in folk tradition, 98–99, 102, 114, 163, 171, 179–180; *see also hjartarleikur, julebukk, julegeit* and *þingálp*
horned helmets, 43–44, 61–62, 64–68, 70–71
horse-fights, 31, 35–36
horse-figures in folk tradition, 143 *n*, 157 *n*; *see also* Arnaldus Jolahest, 'Carrying horse', *hestleikur*, Hobby Horse, *Hvegehors*, *jólhestur*, and Padstowe horse
horse-races, 31, 33, 35–36, 91, 96, 100–102, 174
Hortlied, 220–221, 224, 257–258
hólmganga, 32
Hrafnkels saga Freysgoða, 31 *n*
'hringbrot', 149
Hrotsvitha of Gandersheim, speaker indications in manuscripts of her works, 292, 294; general, 326 *n*
Hróðolfr, Bishop, 328
Hrólfs saga kraka ok kappa hans, 66 *n*, 81
Hrómundar saga Gripssonar, 81, 82 *n*
Huggetønde, 114
Huginn and Muninn, Óðinn's ravens, 70
Hugleikr (Huglecus), King, 360 *n*
Hugo of St Victor, *Soliloquium de arrha animæ*, 284
Huizinga, Johan, definition of 'play', 17
Hungrvaka, 326 *n*, 328
Hvegehors, 110 *n*, 114, 156
Hvidebjørn, 114
Hylestad portal, 260, 266 *n*, 267
Hymiskviða, 185 *n*, 188, 191, 195, 199, 204, 209, 219, 225
Hyndluljóð, 7, 63, 189, 192, 196, 200 *n*, 232 *n*
håmenn, 105, 148
Härjedalen, Sweden, 113
Höfler, Otto, on idea of Scandinavian ritual drama, 10
Höfuðlausn, performance of, 235
images of gods that seem to be alive (Þórr and Freyr), 54–55, 255, 353
incremental repetition in dialogic Eddic poems, 6

initiation rituals, 66 *n*, 71, 80, 127, 180, 280, 349 *n*, 356
Interludium de clerico et puella, marginal speaker indications in manuscript of, 291; relationship to *Dame Sirith*, 304, 306; relationship to Latin *comediæ*, 304 *n*; general, 322, 360
Inuit: *see* Greenland Inuit
ioculatores, 24, 326, 358, 360; *see also leikarar* and *loddarar*; *mimi* and *histriones*; and *trúðar*
Irish folk customs, relationship to those of Scandinavia, 142–143, 170–172
Isidore of Seville, *Etymologiæ*, definitions relating to dramatic activities, 325; in early Icelandic libraries, 325
Isungr, *leikari*, 29, 363–364
Ísleifr Gizurarson, Bishop, 326
Íslendingabók, 326 *n*, 328
Íslendinga saga (Sturla Þórðarson), 82, 84, 144, 145 *n*, 161, 177, 338, 340–341
íþróttir, 25–26, 27 *n*; *see also leikr*
Jarlmaðr, *leikari*, 363
Jaroslav the Wise, 71
Jensøn, C., *Norsk dictionarium*, 116
Jespersen, Bishop Niels, 114
Le jeu d'Adam: *see Le mystère d'Adam*
Le jeu de la feuillée (Adam de la Halle), speaker indications in manuscripts of, 298, 300 *n*
Le jeu de Robin et Marion (Adam de la Halle), speaker indications in manuscripts of, 298, 300 *n*
Le jeu de Saint Nicolas (Jean Bodel), speaker indications in manuscript of, 298
joculatores: *see ioculatores*
John of Salisbury, *Polycraticus*, 359 *n*
'jolebassann'', 90 *n*
joleskjekel, 172, 175
'jolesvein', 99, 107; *see also julesveinar*
Jonsok, 131, 136–138
Jordanes, accounts of Germanic oral performance, 334
Josef, in *Stjärnspel*, 118
jól, references to games and ritual at *jól* in Viking Age, 34–35, 57; *see also* 'Freys leikr'
jólahøna, 166–167, 171
jólakötturinn, 160; *að fara í jólaköttinn*, 160, 175, 177
jólasveinar, 156, 160, 177; *see also julesveinar*
jóleskekil, 172
jólhestur, 82, 157, 166–167, 180 *n*, 351

Index

Jón Árnason, 344–345
Jón lærði Guðmundsson, 144–145, 147
Jón Helgason, on performance of *Hárbarðsljóð*, 10, 270, 274
Jón Ólafsson frá Grunnavík, on *vikivaki* games, 148, 150, 178 n
Jóns saga (hins) helga (Gunnlaugr Leifsson), 85–86, 144 n, 326 n, 346–347
Jóns saga helga hin elzta, 26 n, 144 n, 326 n
Jón Ögmundarson, attack on remnants of old ritual, 85–86, 140; disapproval of works of Ovid, 325; on *mansöngsvísur*, 346–347
Judas, in *Stjärnspel* and Three Kings plays, 107, 171–172
'jul-Anders', 106
julbockar: see julebukk
julbrudar, 134 n
julebisp, 91, 110 n, 114, 134, 148, 156
julebukk/ julbock, Norwegian distribution map, 106; as a spirit, 106–107, 110, 112, 126, 145, 177–178; costume and general behaviour, 107–113, 115, 117, 159 n; in straw costume, 102, 109, 126, 170; in Denmark, 107, 109 n, 110, 116, 124; earliest accounts of, 114, 116; as name for bread or a cake, 121; killing of the *julebukk*, 117–121; drinking the blood of 120 n; laws against, 116; origin of, 122–128; similarities with, and relationship to German and Austrian figures, 109–110, 122–125; general, 3, 33, 51 n, 76 n, 90 n, 95, 96 n, 98–99, 100–101, 129, 134, 143 n, 144–145, 154, 164, 174–175, 351, 354–355; *see also* Faroese *grýla, hestleikur, hjartarleikur, jólhestur,* and *þingálp*
julebukk song, 117–119, 148; use of coloured cloaks in, 118, 121
julegeit, Norwegian distribution map, 108; as name for bread or a cake, 121; as a spirit, 108; general, 76 n, 95, 112, 134; *see also julebukk*
julegoppa, 102, 103 n, 122, 137, 166, 171
julenisse, 112
Juleskreia: see Oskoreia
julestuer, 91
julesveinar, 99, 110, 160–161 n
juletyppa, 122 n
julevætten, 148
julgubbe, 103, 109 n
julgås, 122

Julian calender, influence of, 97
julkråka, 122
julkyppa, 122
jultomte, 112
Jylland, 53, 90, 109 n, 139 n, 148
Kallsängen petroglyphs, 47, 50
Karlskrona, 116
kerlingarleikur, 153, 156, 159–160, 178
Ketils saga hængs, 341 n
Kiev, 28 n, 71–73, 75, 360
'King of Morieland' in Three Kings plays and *Stjärnspel*, 120, 157 n
Kinken, 123
Kink Nissen, 123
Kirialax saga, 362 n
Kivik stones, 47–49, 82
Kjalnesinga saga, 33 n
Klapperbock, 122
Klængr Þorsteinsson, 325
knattleikr, 26, 30 n, 34–35
knowledge contests, 349, 356; *see also Alvíssmál*, and *Vafþrúðnismál*
Knut, 95–97, 107, 171, 175
Knutsgubbe, 88, 102–103
Knytlinga saga, 360 n
'Kongeleg', 114, 134 n; *see also* 'Kóngsleikur'
Kong Haakon Magnussöns retterbod om klædedragten, 362 n
Konráðs saga keisarasonar, 362 n
Konung Christoffers landslag, 362 n
Konung Magnus Eirikssons landslag, 362 n
Konungs skuggsjá, speaker indications in manuscripts of, 284–286, 298, 313, 322
Kormáks saga, 32, 81, 84
Kóngsleikur, 89; *see also* 'Kongeleg'
kransdräng, 135
kranspiga, 135
Kristni saga, 326 n
Króka-Refs saga, 26 n, 34
Kungälv, 116
að kveðast á, 344–345
Kveldsjøgl, 122 n, 159 n, 172; *see also kveldskiøglar*
kveldskiøglar, 108, 110 n, 172; *see also Kveldsjøgl*
Kölbigk, dance at, 104, 161 n
'lame goat', 104 n
Landnámabók, 31 n, 81 n, 88 n
Langefaste (*langeføsta, Lengeføsta*), 162–163
lange gjente, 159
Laon, 327

lappbrud, 134 *n*
Lapp ritual practice and poetic performance, 338–340
Latin schools, 96, 134, 320
Laurentius saga biskups (Einar Hafliðason), 144 *n*, 335 *n*, 361 *n*
laws, ban on theatre in Denmark, 124; bans on weddings at Yuletide, 98 *n*, 134; ban on worship of grave mounds, 140; church bans on mock-marriage traditions, 138 *n*; church ban on plays and dances in churchyard, 364; laws against *julebukk*, 114, 116; laws regarding *leikarar*, 362 *n*; law regarding *trúðar*, 364
Laxdæla saga, 27–28, 33 *n*, 34, 336–337
Leach, Edmund, on myth and ritual, 15–16
leaf-clad figures, 14, 137
Lebor na Huidre, marginal speaker notation in, 288 *n*
Legenda aurea, 98
Leikanger, Sogn, 30 *n*; see also *leikvangr*
'leikara læti' and 'leikaraskapr', 361 *n*
leikarar and *loddarar*, as secondary motifs in sagas, 361–362; as translations for *histriones* and *mimi*, 29, 360; in Iceland, 364; general, 84, 358–364; see also *ioculatores*, *mimi* and *histriones*, and *trúðar*
leikgoði, 87–91, 170
leikmót, 33–34, 85
leikr, concept and various meanings of, 14, 23–36, 76, 85; in sense of a ritual, 27–28; *leikr* and *íþróttir*, similarities and difference between, 25–26, 27 *n*; *leikr* and ritual, 32–36, 356; *leikar* and *vetrnætur*, 34; in translations from Latin, 26
leikskáli in placenames, 31, 34
leikvangr in placenames, meaning of, 30–31, 36, 76
leikvin in placenames, meaning of, 30–31, 36, 76
leikvöllr in placenames, meaning of, 30–31, 36, 76
Lent: see Shrovetide
Lincoln, 326, 327
Lindisfarne, 359
Linköping, liturgical drama in, 329
liturgical drama, evidence for in Scandinavia, 328–329; origin of, 334; speaker indications in manuscripts of, 296–298, 300, 302, 323, 329 *n*
að ljóða á, 343–346, 349

ljóðaháttr, characteristics of, and differences from *fornyrðislag*, 192–194, 207, 214, 216, 268, 277 *n*, 353; on age of, 216; general, 190–192, 199, 203 *n*, 204 *n*, 218, 234 *n*, 269, 281, 344, 346, 351–354, 357
Ljóðatal (*Hávamál*, sts 146–163), 344
Ljósvetninga saga, 27 *n*, 35 *n*
Ljunggren, Gustav, on Eddic poems as drama, 4
loddarar: see *leikarar* and *loddarar*
Loddfáfnismál (*Hávamál*, sts 111–137), 5, 188, 191, 195, 352
Loftr Pálsson, 84, 144, 161, 165–166, 173, 176–177
Lokasenna, action in, 238–239, 246; characterisation in, 353; difficulties in solo performance of, 238–247, 281; marginal speaker indications in, 207–208, 245; performances of, 2, 246 *n*; prose in, 199–200, 212, 225–229, 233–234; published as a play, 3, 5; relationship to other Eddic poems, 203, 205–206, 355; Snorri Sturluson's knowledge of, 219–223, 247; structure of, 239; general, 1–5, 102, 186, 188, 191, 195, 233, 248, 254, 262, 263 *n*, 279, 306, 322, 341 *n*, 346, 349–350, 353–354, 356
Lucia, 95, 97–100; see also Lussi
Lucian, 3, 205
Lund, Sweden, 138 *n*
Lusse, see Lussi
Lussebock, 98–99, 107
Lussebrud, 98, 133; as straw doll in a dance, 103–104
Lusse dance, 102
Lussegubbe, 97–98, 102
Lussegummar, 97
Lusse långenatt, 97, see also Lussi
Lussi, 97–99, 159–161, 174 *n*, 175
'Lussia', 98–99, 107; see also Lussi
Lussiferd, 98
Lussiner, 99, 102
Lýtir, 54
løvgubbe, 137
Lübeck sword dance, 132 *n*
Magnus, Olaus, *Historia de gentibus septentrionalibus*, Combat between Winter and Summer, 128–130, 137; horse-races on ice, 33, 35; Shrovetide celebrations, 114; sword and hoop dances, 129, 130–133
Magnús Andrésson, on *vikivaki* games, 145 *n*, 146–148

Magnús saga Hakonarsonar (Sturla Þórðarson), 36
Magnússona saga, 342, 343 *n*
maibrud, 135
Mainland, Shetland, 167
majdronning, 135–136
majgreve, 91, 135–136, 137 *n*, 138
majgrevinna, 135–136, 137 *n*
majinde, 91 *n*, 135, 138
majkonge, 135–136
make-up, possible use of by *leikarar*, 363
Malew cross, 266–267 *n*
Malmö, 114, 116, 124 *n*
Maltegården cremation urn lid, 49
Man, Isle of, 129–130, 266–267 *n*
Mannhardt, Wilhelm, *Wald- und Feldkulte*, 5, 45
mannjafnaðr, 130, 180, 186, 270–271, 273–274, 280, 341–343, 348–350, 352
mansöngsvísur, 346–348, 349
marginal speaker notation in manuscripts, 206–213, 217, 245, 257, 282, 295, 298, 300–324, 329; provenance and origin of, 320, 322; speech verbs in, 322–323
Marie de France, *lais* of, 324
Maríu jartegnir, 360 *n*, 362 *n*
masks and disguises in Scandinavia; animal disguise, general, 51–52, 60–62, 66–76, 81; bird disguises, 37–38, 43–44, 47–50, 60–61, 63–64, 71–72, 76, 82, 122, 166–167 *n*; bear disguises, 76, 121, 364; boar masks, 61–63, 87 *n*; bull masks, 76, 121; goat disguises, 43, 76, 83 (*see also julebukk*, and *þingálp*); horse disguises, 121 (*see also* Arnaldus Jolahest, *jólhestur*, and *hestleikur*); sheep masks, 76; stag disguises, 44, 121 (*see also hindarleikur* and *hjartarleikur*); wolf masks, 66, 70–71, 76; origins of Scandinavian disguises, 122–128; general, 13, 57; *see also gríma*
Mass, Catholic, as drama, 13, 17–18, 325
málaháttr, 192, 203, 269–270
Máni, on *leikarar*, 363
Melabók, 87 *n*
memorization of poetic texts, 184 *n*, 354 *n*
Michaels saga, 162 *n*
Midsummer traditions, Midsummer weddings, 131, 136–140, 351; general, 124 *n*, 136
Miðvágur, Faroes, 163

Le miracle de Théophile, Rutebeuf, speaker indications in manuscript of, 298–299
mimes: *see mimi*
mimi and *histriones*, at Uppsala, 76–79; in Constantinople and Kiev, 28 *n*, 360; in Scandinavia, 84, 358–364; general, 29, 334, 353, 358–364; *see also ioculatores*; *leikarar* and *loddarar*; *scurræ*; and *trúðar*
mixed verse-and-prose form: *see* blended prose-and-verse form
mock-kings: *see* 'Kongeleg', and *Kóngsleikur*
mock-marriages and pairing games, at spring and midsummer, 135–140; at Yuletide, 57, 98, 133–135, 156; general, 91, 180, 351, 353
Mongolian oral tradition, 202, 333, 334
monster figures, 66–72, 80, 180, 269; *see also* masks and disguises
Morkinskinna, 26 *n*, 28 *n*, 32, 342 *n*, 363 *n*
Mummers' plays, 14, 85 *n*, 141
Murray, Gilbert, on ritual drama, 5 *n*, 7
music, use of by performers, 362–363
Le mystère d'Adam (*Le jeu d'Adam*, *Ordo repræsentationis Adæ*), marginal speaker indications in manuscript of, 290–291, 316, 318–321; performance of, 316, 318; provenance of, 316 *n*; general, 326, 329
myth and ritual, relationships between, 15–21
Møre og Romsdal, Norway, 110 *n*
Müllenhoff, Karl, on idea of Scandinavian ritual drama, 3–4, 8
N-Town plays, speaker indications in manuscript of, 291 *n*, 300 *n*
Naharvali, 51
narrator, use of in dramatic works, 314, 323
Native American ball games, 33
Native American ritual songs and myths, 15, 16 *n*, 19–21, 332 *n*, 333 *n*
Navajo, sacred chants of, 16 *n*, 184 *n*
Nerthus cult and procession, 49 *n*, 53–60, 143
Niðurraðan, 145, 148 *n*, 151, 153
'Niklas': *see* St Nicholas
Nikolaus saga erkibyskups, 361 *n*, 362 *n*
Nikulás saga leikara, 362 *n*
Nilsson, Martin P:n, *Årets folkliga fester*, 5
Nitida saga, 26 *n*

Index

Njáls saga, Gunnar as Kaupa-Heðinn, 85; general, 29, 35 *n*, 83 *n*, 337, 342 *n*, 364
Njörðr, 60; *see also Lokasenna*
Nordland, Norway, 37
Noreen, Erik, on Eddic poems as drama, 8
Norna-Gests þáttr, 200 *n*, 203 *n*, 212, 234–235, 259, 330, 345–346
De nuntio sagaci, marginal speaker notation in manuscripts of, 302, 304–305; performance of, 304; provenance of, 320 *n*; use of narrative in, 302–304, 323; general, 308, 310, 322, 324, 329
Nyland, Finland, 101, 104, 105
Nyårsbokk, 107
Nyårsgeit, 107
nyårsgås, 122
'Næframaðr', 56 *n*, 80, 85, 101, 109 *n*
Obrigheim bracteate, 66–67, 70–71
Ockelbo stone, 260, 267
Oddrúnargrátr, 185–186, 189, 192, 196, 199
Oddverja annáll, 326 *n*
Oehlenschläger, Adam, on Eddic poems as drama, 3 *n*
'Old play of the Wolsungs', 5, 205–206, 214, 256–260
Old Tup, 117 *n*, 143
Olrik, Axel, 'Law of two to a scene' ('totalslov'), 237, 241, 243, 247 *n*, 249 *n*, 252, 261, 306
Olsen, Magnus, on idea of Scandinavian ritual drama, 5–6
oral performance, amongst Germanic tribes, 187, 333–335, 348; of the Eddic poems, 183–184, 236–281; in Scandinavia, 330–331, 335–350; general, 183, 202, 270, 331–334
oral presentation of dialogue, rules for, 236–238, 270
oral storytellers in Scandinavia, 3 *n*, 183
oral tradition, 16, 165–166, 236–238; and Eddic poems, 182–184, 270
Ordish, T. Fairman, 133 *n*
Orkney, Christmas football games, 33; other traditions, 102 *n*, 157, 174–175; in *Old Swedish legendarium*, 161 *n*
Orkneyinga saga, 26 *n*, 27 *n*
Orre, King, 97
Oseberg tapestry, 58–67, 70, 75, 79–80, 82–83, 112, 155, 166, 351, 356
Oseberg wagon, 59–60
Oskoreia, 100, 110, 127, 160–161 *n*, 174, 177

Oskoreien: *see Oskoreia*
'oversigtsprincip' in *Codex Regius*, 182 *n*, 199
Ovidius de arte amandi, 325
Ovidius puellarum: *see De nuntio sagaci*
Óðinn, connection with *seiðr*, 338; possible connection with goat figures, 83, 127; general, 60, 63, 70, 81 *n*, 133 *n*, 354; *see also* Arnhöfði, Grímnir, Grímr, *Hárbarðsljóð*, *Lokasenna*, and *Vafþrúðnismál*
Ólafr Tryggvason, renaming of pagan festivals, 94, 136
Ólafs saga Tryggvasonar en mesta, 54, 55 *n*, 59
paðreimsleikr, 28, 32, 35
Padstowe horse, 14, 150–151
pairing games: *see* mock-marriages and pairing games
paleography, probable influence of English and Anglo-Norman paleography on Scandinavian scribes, 324, 328–329
Palladius, Peder, *Visitatsbog*, 114
Pamphilus, Norwegian manuscript of, 324–325; performance of, 304; general, 308
pantomimi, 360; *see also mimi* and *histriones*
Papa Stour sword dance: *see* under Shetland
Papa Westray, Orkney, 174
paragraph markers, use of in manuscripts to indicate beginnings of new speeches, 302 *n*, 306, 308–309, 310 *n*, 313–315
parasiti, 358, 361 *n*
Paris, 326–327
Paris, Matthew, 328
partial context marking, 236–237
Páll Jónsson, Bishop, 327
Páls saga biskups, 327 *n*
Pedersen, Christiern, *Jærtegnspostil*, 114
Peko, fights for, 130 *n*; processions with, 101; relationship to *Staffan*, 105
performances of Eddic poems in dramatic fashion, 2 *n*
petroglyphs, Stone Age, 37–38, 47; Bronze Age, 37–50, 60, 63, 155; images: acrobats, 38–39; bird figures, 43–44, 47, 49–50; dancers, 38–39, 42, 45; giant figures, 40–41, 159; horned figures, 41–43, 46; horn (*lurer*) players, 38, 39, 41–42, 45; ship processions, 37–41, 45, 54; sun symbols, 37, 39–41, 45; pictures of ritual

drama, 6, 45–46, 351; purpose of, 37, 39; role in later folk tradition, 138 n
Petrus, Danish monk in Dublin, 104
Petrus Comestor, *Historia scholastica*, 26
phallic figures, 57 n, 105, 112, 159, 163–164, 362–363
Phillpotts, Bertha S., *The Elder Edda and ancient Scandinavian drama*, 1–2, 6–8, 21–22, 351; critical reactions to, 1–2, 8–9, 351; on ljóðaháttr, 214–216 n; on prose in Eddic poems, 203 n, 232, 323
Þingsebrud, 135
Þingsebrudgom, 135
Þingstbrud, 135, 138
Planctus Mariæ (Cividale), marginal speaker notation in manuscript of, 300–301
Plautus, plays of, 292 n
play, definitions of, 17–19, 25–36; see also *leikr*
play and ritual, relationships between, 17–18, 32–36
Pleizhausen bracteate, 66
plough processions, 96 n
poetic duels, 332, 341–342, 348–350, 354; role in legal disputes, 342, 348–349
poetry competitions, 332–333, 339 n
Poland, oral disputes at weddings, 332 n
Pontoppidan, Erik, *Everriculum fermenti veteris*, 124 n
possessed images and straw figures, 55 n, 104–105
Priscus, accounts of Germanic oral performance, 334–335, 339
Prose Edda: see Snorri Sturluson, *The Prose Edda*
prose in Eddic poems, 7, 187–190, 194, 196–203, 212, 214, 216, 218, 221, 223–235, 266–268; as 'stage directions', 234, 323
Qualiscunque descriptio Islandæ (Oddur Einarsson), 150 n
Querolus, speaker indications in manuscript of, 292, 314 n
'raddlið' in *seiðr*, 336–337, 341 n
Raglan, Lord Fitzroy Richard Somerset, on Eddic poems as drama, 9 n
Ragnars saga loðbrókar ok sona hans, 28
Ralph of Coggeshall: see *Thurkill's vision of Hell*
Ramsey cross, 266–267 n
Ramsundsberg petroglyph, 260, 267

rangle: see under bells and rattles
Rauðúlfs þáttr, 26 n
readings of dramatic and semi-dramatic texts in the Middle Ages, 334
recording of Eddic poems, 184–185 n, 281, 353
red ink, use of for speaker indications, 208, 284 n, 286
reed cart procession, 143
Reginsmál, relationship to *Fáfnismál*, 256–260; speaker indications in, 207, 259; general, 5, 184 n, 189–190, 192, 194, 196, 200, 204, 206, 234, 272 n, 330; see also 'Old play of the Wolsungs'
Regularis Concordia (Æthelwold), in Scandinavia, 328, 334 n
reverse speech, use of by disguised characters, 117, 164–165, 169
Reykdæla saga ok Víga-Skútu, 83 n
Reykhólar wedding, 332, 342–343, 348
Rémundar saga keisarasonar, 27 n
Rhineland, 326, 328
Ribe buckles, 64
Rig Veda, and ritual drama, 20; antiphonal recital of, 332; relationship to riddle poetry in Scandinavia, 349 n
Rísuleikur, 89
ritual and drama, similarities and differences, 12, 17–21
ritual and myth, relationships between, 15–21
ritual and play, relationships between, 17–18, 32–36
ritual drama, 4–8, 14–21, 45–46
Rígsþula, 27 n, 186, 189, 192, 196, 198
rímur, 347
rock carvings: see petroglyphs
Rogaland, Norway, 37, 49, 58, 98–99, 109 n
Roman *Corpus Iuris Civilis*, regarding *mimi*, 364
Roman theatre, dissolution of, 358–359
Rome Council on English affairs, 359
Rouen, possible connection with Iceland, 328; tradition of liturgical drama, 327
Rouen, *Play of the Prophets*, speaker indications in manuscript of, 298
Rouen, *Play of the shepherds*, speaker indications in manuscript of, 296 n
rowing chants, 340
Rómverjasögur, 29 n, 361 n
runes, magical, the use of, 355, 357
'runo chants', 339

Index

Ruodlieb, marginal speaker notation in manuscript of, 288, 290
Rutebeuf, speaker indications in manuscript of *Le miracle de Théophile*, 298–299
Rydquist, J. E., on Eddic poems as drama, 3, 7 *n*
Rögnvaldr réttilbeini, 337
Rögnvalds þáttr ok Rauðs, 54, 55 *n*, 59
'sacred time', 18 *n*, 20, 350
'sagaprincip' in *Codex Regius*, 199, 202
Saga Þorláks biskups hin elzta, 327 *n*
Salisbury *Visitatio sepulchrum*, speaker indications in manuscript of, 296 *n*
Sallust, *Bella Iugurthinum*, 29 *n*
satire, 363
Saxo Grammaticus, *Gesta Danorum*, disguises in, 80; on Icelanders as historians, 219 *n*; on *mimi, histriones* and related performers, 358, 360–361 *n*; on Uppsala festival, 76–80, 83, 351, 358; *sennur* and *mannjafnaðir* in, 341 *n*; general, 66, 78 *n*, 83, 228, 331 *n*
Saxony, 326, 328
Schleswig (Slesvig), 49, 70
Schück, Henrik, on idea of the Scandinavian ritual drama, 5–6
Scott, Sir Walter, *The pirate*, on Papa Stour sword dance, 85 *n*, 132–133; other traditions in, 169–170 *n*; general, 179 *n*
scurræ, 358, 360
seaweed, use of in costumes, 163
seiðr, as *leikr*, 27; general, 56 *n*, 335–341, 347, 349–350
La seinte resureccion, Canterbury manuscript of, 313; marginal speaker indications in Paris manuscript of, 290–291, 313–316, 320; performance of, 313; provenance of, 313; use of past tense in stage directions of, 314, 323; general, 327, 329
semiotics of drama, 12
Semiramis, marginal speaker notation in manuscript of, 302–303, 318, 320; performance of, 302; general, 322
Semnones, 61
senna, 186, 239, 270–271, 273–274, 280, 341–343, 348–350, 352
Setesdal, Norway, 90, 98 *n*, 104, 111, 174 *n*
shamanism, and dramatic performance, 27 *n*, 37–38, 43–45 *n*, 81 *n*, 350; and poetic performance, 338–340, 349; general, 355

shape-changing, in Eddic poems, 83; in sagas, 64, 81
Shetland, connections with Iceland, 179; sword dance in, 132–133, 169–170; weddings in, 135, 168, 170–171, 172 *n*; other traditions, 33, 148, 157; *see also skeklers* and *grøleks*
'shield-maidens', 105 *n*, 148, 151, 155, 158–159; *see also valkyrjur*
ship procession from Aachen to Loos, 54
'shooting the bear', 120
'shooting the stag', 121
'Shoupeltins', 170 *n*
'Shrewsbury fragments', 300 *n*, 302 *n*
Shrovetide, 91 *n*, 96, 114, 116, 120, 124 *n*, 128, 130, 138, 159, 162, 166–167, 169 *n*
Sighvatr Þórðarson, 340
Sigrdrífumál, 5, 186, 189, 192, 196, 199–200, 204 *n*, 256, 258 *n*, 259–260, 269, 352, 354–355; *see also* 'Old play of the Wolsungs'
Sigurðarkviða in skamma, 186, 189, 192, 196
'Sigurðar saga', 196, 200, 204, 218, 221, 224, 234
Sigurðar saga þögla, 362 *n*
Sigurðr Jórsalafari, 28, 342, 343 *n*
Sigurður Guðmundsson, on *vikivaki* games, 145 *n*, 151 *n*, 154, 158
Sjælland, 41, 43, 57, 121, 124
skalds, threatened by *leikarar*, 360, 363
skeið in placenames, 31
Skekla, 173
skeklers (*skekels, skakelers*) and *grøleks*, 70 *n*, 124 *n*, 137 *n*, 167–175, 351, 353; *see also skudler*
Skessuleikur, 89
'Skinnpilsa', 345
Skírnismál, action in, 248, 250–251, 253–255; characterisation in, 353; difficulties in solo performance of, 247–255, 281; dramatic performance of 2, 254–255; marginal speaker indications in, 207–208, 210, 217, 252; prose in, 200, 214, 229–234, 254; relationship to other Eddic poems, 203–205, 206 *n*; ritualistic associations, 80, 253, 353–355; Snorri Sturluson's knowledge of, 219–223, 250; general, 1–7, 57, 180, 185, 186, 188, 190–191, 193, 195, 216, 236–237, 239, 245, 261–263, 265–266, 268–269, 279–280, 306, 322, 340–341, 346, 349, 353

411

skjaldmeyjar: see 'shield-maidens'; *see also valkyrjur*
'Å skjuta björnen', 120
Skollaleikur, 172 n
skråbuker, 102 n, 107
skudler (*scuddler, skuddler, skudlar*) 91, 168–170, 172
'at skyde hjorten', 121
Skåne, Sweden, 42, 47–48, 91 n, 102, 118, 138 n
'Slakta bocken', 119
'Slakta juloxen', 119
Smiss stone ('the snake charmer'), 67, 69
Småland, Sweden, 97, 109 n, 329 n
Snorri Sturluson, *Háttatal*, 87 n
Snorri Sturluson, *The Prose Edda*, as inspiration for collection of Eddic poems, 219, 233; relationship to Eddic poems, 194 n, 218–225, 226–230, 233–235, 247, 250, 269; use of words *leikr* and *íþróttir* in *Gylfaginning*, 25 n, 27 n; general, 202
Sogndal, Sogn, Norway, 138 n
solo performances of oral works, 23–24, 236–238, 330–331; difficulties in solo performances of dialogic works, 236–281
Southern, Richard, *The seven stages of drama*, 13–14
speaker indications in medieval manuscripts, 206–213, 215, 217, 282–324, 329
speech in Eddic poems, 187–192, 191–192, 194
Sponsus, speaker indications in manuscript of, 298
'spook verses', 338, 340
Staffan, 95–96, 97 n, 100–105, 115, 119, 123, 129; *see also Halm-Staffan* and St Stephen
staffansbock, 102, 107
Staffansdrängar, 100, 159
staffansgossar, 102
Staffansmanden, 102–103
Staffans reid, 33, 95, 100–101, 174
Staffansritt, 100–101
Staffans skeid, 95, 100–101
Staffansvisa, 100–101
stage directions in past tense in medieval plays, 323
St Albans, 328
Stallo, 105, 112, 156, 160–161 n, 164
Starkaðr (Starcatherus), as figure in sword dance, 132; encounters with theatrical entertainers, 358, 360–361 n

St Ethelbert, 339
Steinarr Önundarson, 81, 84
Steingrímr Skinngrýluson, 82, 161, 177, 179
Stjórn, 26, 360 n
stjärngossar, 33, 97 n, 159
Stjärnspel, 95–96, 100, 107, 116, 118, 120, 123–124, 171–172
St Knut: *see* under Knut
St Lucia: *see* under Lucia
St Nicholas, as disguised figure, 100 n, 122–125, 160 n; plays of, 123, 298, 326 n
Stockholm area, liturgical drama in, 329
Stóraborg mask, 146–147, 160, 164
Strassburg *Play of the Magi*, speaker indications in manuscript of, 296, 298, 313 n
strawboys, 170–172
straw-figures, 56 n, 102–105, 108–109, 122 n, 180, 353; as figures of public rebuke, 102–103; as figures of reverence, 103–104, 126; their rarity in English folk tradition, 143 n; *see also Halm-Staffan; skeklers* and *grøleks; strawboys;* and *strawmen*
strawmen, 170
Strengleikar, 324
Strömbäck, Dag, on idea of Scandinavian ritual drama, 10
St Stephen, 95, 100, 119, 157
Stumpfl, Robert, on Eddic poems as drama, 9 n
Sturlu saga, 144 n
Sunnfjord, Fjordane, Norway, 16, 118
Sutton Hoo helmet, 61, 87; helmet plates of, 64–67, 70–71, 155
Svabo, J. C., on Faroese *grýlur*, 162–163
Svarfdæla saga, 35 n
'sveinaleikar', 32
Sverris saga, 177–178, 363
Svinoy, Faroes, 164
sword dances, 18, 51 n, 71, 129, 130–133; *see also* combat
'Syrpuvers', 89
Syrpuþingslög, 87–89, 91–92
Södermanland, Sweden, 101
Sögubrot af fornkonungum í Dana- ok Svíaveldi, 26 n
Sörla þattr, eða Heðins saga ok Högna, 228
Sæmundr Sigfússon, 326
Tacitus, Cornelius, accounts of Germanic oral performance, 334–335, 348; *Germania*, 49, 51, 53–54, 59, 61

tagging, 236
Tartuffe, 4
Táin Bó Cúailnge, marginal speaker indications in manuscripts of, 288
Telemark, Norway, superstitions regarding horse-fights in, 35; general, 104, 109 *n*, 174–175
Terence (Publius Terentius Afer), performance of his plays, 292; popularity of in Middle Ages, 291–292, 320; speaker indications in manuscripts containing his plays, 291–293, 295–296, 300, 310, 318, 326
theatre, as opposed to drama, definition, 11
theatrum, use of the word by Adam of Bremen, 79–80
Thomas de Cabham, *Penitential*, 359
Thomassaga erkibiskops, 29 *n*, 361 *n*
'Thor og Urebø-Urden', 59
Three Kings plays, 95–96, 119–120; *see also* Stjärnspel, and *Helligtrekongerspill*
Thurkill's vision of Hell (Ralph of Coggeshall), 359–360
Thursdays, as holy days, 140
tjugondagsbrud, 134 *n*
'tjösnublót', 32
Toda poetry, 332
torfleikr, 26
Torslunda helmet matrices, 66–71, 75, 79–80, 83, 110, 112, 155, 166, 180, 356
Townley cycle, speaker indications in manuscripts of, 291
transportation of folk customs, 141–142, 180
trettenbekren, 107
trettondagsbrud, 134 *n*
Trettondagsspel, 95
'að tripla', 335 *n*
Tristrams saga og Ísoddar, 26 *n*, 30 *n*, 324
Trondheim, 327
trope-singing, 335 *n*
Trundholm sun chariot, 41
trúðar, in Iceland, 364; general, 360–361
Trøndelag, Norway, 59, 78, 104, 112, 134 *n*
Trønninge figure, 63 *n*
'tvísöngr', 335
twin dancers, 65, 67
ulfheðnar, 66, 70, 81; *see also berserkir*
De uno peccatore qui promeruit gratium, use of past tense stage directions in, 323

Unst, Shetland, 167, 175 *n*
Up-Helly Aa, 168 *n*
Uppland, Sweden, 40, 64–65, 101–102, 109 *n*, 113
Uppsala festival, games at, 32, 89; general, 61, 76–80, 358
Uppsala horned figure, 64, 67, 70
Vafþrúðnismál, action in, 280, 275; characterisation in, 353; difficulties in solo performance of, 275–281; marginal speaker indications in, 207–208, 210–211; narrative strophe in, 277; relationship to other Eddic poems, 203–204, 206; setting of, 274–275, 279–280; structure of, 275–276, 278; general, 5 *n*, 7, 80, 180, 185 *n*, 186, 188, 190–191, 195, 216, 219, 232–233, 237, 238–239, 242 *n*, 258, 263 *n*, 266–267, 271, 283, 349, 354, 356
Valdres, Norway, 110, 112 *n*
valkyrjur, 47, 61–64, 82, 148, 201 *n*, 269; *see also* shield-maidens
Valsgärde helmet plates, 64, 66–67, 70
Vangsnes, Sogn, Norway, 137
Varangian Guard, 72, 74–75, 360
Varðlokur, 336, 338, 349
Vaterrachelied, 220–221, 257
Vatnsdæla saga, 34 *n*, 83 *n*, 87–89, 91
Vegusdal portal, 260, 266 *n*, 267
Vendel helmet, 87; helmet plates of, 66–67
Versås church door, 260
Vest-Agder, Norway, 111–112, 122 *n*, 159 *n*
Vestfyn, Denmark, 91 *n*
Vestlund, Alfred, on Eddic poems as drama, 6
vetrnætur, games and weddings during, 34; cf. 135, 167
Viðræða líkams ok sálar (*Soliloquium de arrha animæ*; Icelandic), speaker indications in manuscript of, 284, 286 *n*, 322
Viðræða líkams ok sálar einn laugardag að kveldi (*Un samedi par nuit*; Norwegian), speaker indications in manuscript of, 284, 286, 322
Vigersted, Denmark, 123
vikivaki games, 144–160; origin of, 154–160; origin of *vikivaki* songs and dances, 149 *n*, 156 *n*, 347, 349
Viksø helmet, 43–44, 67 *n*
Vitalis, *Geta* and *Aurularia*, 308
Vitalis, *mimi*, 358–359
Vídalín, Páll, 154 *n*

Víga-Glúms saga, 34, 35 *n*, 66 *n*
Víglundar saga, 27 *n*
Voss, Hordaland, Norway, 34, 110 *n*, 118
de Vries, Jan, on Eddic poems as drama, 9
Vulgata, 26, 360 *n*
Värmland, Sweden, 102–104, 107, 110 *n*, 115, 118, 122, 134 *n*, 135, 329 *n*
Västergötland, Sweden, 33, 58, 75, 97, 99
Västmanland, Sweden, 137
Vöðu-Brands þáttr, 88–89
vökunætur, 91, 105 *n*, 149–150, 177 *n*
Völsunga saga, 81, 196 *n*, 200, 202, 216 *n*, 218, 225 *n*, 234–235, 258, 265 *n*
Völundarkviða, 47, 82 *n*, 186, 188, 191, 195, 198, 200, 206–207, 216–218 *n*, 225
Völuspá, 2, 6, 17, 185–186, 188, 191–192, 195, 203 *n*, 204, 212 *n*, 219, 350
wagons, sacred, 53–60, 78
wakes: see *vökunætur*
weapon dances, 65–68, 70–75; see also sword dances
weaving songs in Scandinavia, 337 *n*
weddings, at Christmas, 134–135; at *vetrnætur*, 34; oral conflicts at, 332–333; 341 *n*, 342–343; 348; poetic performances at, 345
Whitsun mock-marriage traditions, 135–140
Widsith, 339–340
Wieselgren, P., on Eddic poems as drama, 4
Wildman, Bavarian, 14
'Wild Ride': see under *Oskoreia*
Worsaae, J. J. A., on origin of sword dances, 132
Yell, Shetland, 168, 175 *n*
Yellow book of Lecan, marginal speaker notation in, 288 *n*
Ynglinga saga, 27 *n*, 32 *n*, 78 *n*, 81 *n*, 360 *n*, 361
York cycle, speaker indications in manuscripts of, 291
Young, Karl, definition of drama, 13
Yuletide: see *jól*
Zuñi, sacred chants of, 16 *n*, 184 *n*
Zürich, 71
Ålleberg collar, 57–58, 77 *n*
Århus, 90 *n*

Äldre Västgötalagen, 362 *n*
Ögmundar þáttr dytts, 54–55; see also *Gunnars þáttr helmings*
Öland, 117–118
Ölkofra þáttr, 341 *n*, 348
Örebro, Sweden, 116
Örvar-Odds saga, 27, 80, 85, 145 *n*, 336–337, 341 *n*, 343
Österbotten, 134 *n*
Östergötland, Sweden, 33, 37, 40, 75, 98, 101–102, 109 *n*, 136 *n*, 138 *n*, 159 *n*
Østfold, Norway, 37
Östgotalagen, 362
Þiðriks saga af Bern, 26 *n*, 29, 219, 363–364
þing meetings, as venues for performances and games, 24, 35, 348, 356, 364
þingálp(n) (*fingálf; fingálpn*), 57 *n*, 110 *n*, 112 *n*, 116, 117 *n*, 144–151, 153, 155–160, 166, 176, 178, 351, 354; see also *finngálkn*
Þorgils saga ok Hafliða, 30, 144 *n*, 341 *n*, 342–343
Þorgils saga skarða, 161–162
Þorlákr Þórhallsson, Bishop, 326
Þorláks saga helga hin yngri, 327 *n*
Þorleifs þáttr jarlsskálds, 81, 85, 125–126, 337
Þormóðr Bersason, 331
Þorri, 'að bjóða Þorra í garð', 97
Þorsteinn Pétursson, *Manducus eður leikafæla*, 124, 154 *n*, 176–178
Þorsteins saga Víkingssonar, 30 *n*
Þorsteins þáttr bæjarmagns, 27 *n*
Þórðar saga hreðu, 162 *n*
Þórhildarleikur, 149, 156, 159 *n*
Þórólfr leikgoði, 87–89
Þórr, images of in *Ólafs saga Tryggvasonar hin mesta*, and *Rögnvalds þáttr ok Rauðs*, 54, 55 *n*, 59; and *julebukk*, 126–127; general, 97 *n*; see also *Hárbarðsljóð*, and *Lokasenna*
Þriðja málfræðiritgerðin, 145 *n*
Þrymskviða, 2, 6–7, 16–17, 63, 82–83, 188, 191, 195, 219, 352, 354
Æðru senna ok hugrekki, speaker indications in manuscripts of, 284, 322
ægishiálmr, 224, 262, 265 *n*, 266, 269, 354–355
Æthelwold: see *Regularis Concordia*